A Short History of the Movies

ABRIDGED NINTH EDITION

Gerald Mast

Late, of the University of Chicago

Bruce F. Kawin

University of Colorado at Boulder

Abridged by

William Costanzo

Westchester Community College

PEARSON
Longman

New York   Boston   San Francisco
London Toronto Sydney Tokyo Singapore Madrid
Mexico City Munich Paris Cape Town Hong Kong Montreal

Publisher: Joseph Opiela
Marketing Manager: Suzan Czajkowski
Production Manager: Ellen MacElree
Project Coordination, Text Design, and Electronic Page Makeup: Nesbitt Graphics, Inc.
Cover Design/Manager: John Callahan
Cover Image: Universal Pictures/Courtesy: Everett Collection
Manufacturing Buyer: Roy Pickering
Printer and Binder: Courier Corporation
Cover Printer: Courier

For permission to use copyrighted material, grateful acknowledgment is made to the copyright holders on pp. 503–505, which are hereby made part of this copyright page.

Library of Congress Cataloging-in-Publication Data

Mast, Gerald, 1940–
  A short history of the movies / Gerald Mast, Bruce F. Kawin;
abridged by William Costanzo.—Abridged 9th ed.
      p. cm.
  Includes bibliographical references and index.
  ISBN 0-321-41821-2 (alk. paper)
  1. Motion pictures—History.   I. Kawin, Bruce F., 1945–   II. Costanzo, William V.   III. Title.
PN1993.4.A1M39 2006b
791.4309—dc22

                                        2006000909

Please visit our website at http://www.ablongman.com/mast9e

ISBN 0-321-41821-2

1 2 3 4 5 6 7 8 9 10—CRS—09 08 07 06

Contents

Chapter 13 Neorealism and the New Wave   258

Chapter 14 National Cinemas 1: 1945–   296

Preface to the Abridged Edition

From its first edition, Gerald Mast's *A Short History of the Movies* helped to focus the field of film studies; it has its own role in film history. Comprehensively conceived, evocatively illustrated, and readable, drawing useful generalizations and analyzing key works in depth, it became the foundation for the modern film history course as well as an ideal book for anyone who wants to know more about movies. And as the field developed, so did the book. With each edition it grew longer and more comprehensive, responding vigorously to new movies and new conceptions of film history.

Although the *Short History* remains shorter than most books of similar scope, it is still more than twice as long as it once was. The title itself called out for an abridgment. Working in consultation wih me and drawing on his years of using the *Short History* in class and finding what students most needed to know, William Costanzo, Professor of English and Film at Westchester Community College, has prepared this abridged version of the ninth edition. It should please teachers and students in search of a shorter but still comprehensive textbook and should prove useful for the growing number of one-semester courses in film history. Where, in the original version, a point might have been made or a development traced with three or four examples, there are now one or two. Most of the long analyses and readings have been removed or judiciously condensed. There are fewer illustrations, and the chapters have filmographies and DVD lists but not bibliographies. The essential facts and works are still here, and they stand out even better thanks to the absence of digressions and the pruning of details.

What follows applies to both versions of the ninth edition.

When Gerald Mast died in 1988, I took over the responsibility of revising and updating the *Short History*, beginning with the fifth edition. Like the previous editions, this ninth edition has been completely updated, scrupulously corrected, and comprehensively expanded. Playing the role of a respectful but aggressive editor, I have tightened and cut the text to make room for discussions of new or previously undiscussed films, filmmakers, and national cinemas, as well as scientific, technical, and business developments.

No vital material has been taken out; instead, a great deal has been added. Many of the discussions have been revised to make their essential points more clear, to provide more detailed examples, and to fix the mistakes. Hundreds of names, dates, titles, and shot descriptions have been corrected, based on such primary resources as original signatures and complete prints.

Readers of previous editions should be alerted: This edition, which marks the fifth time I have rewritten the book, is significantly different from earlier editions, especially in Chapters 2, 3, 18, and 19. In Chapter 2, in addition to a new section called "Frames per Second," the section on the persistence of vision has been completely redone. This is the first time, to my knowledge, that a film history textbook has acknowledged that persistence of vision has nothing to do with the perception of apparent motion, and the alternative explanation presented here is based on solid research. This new material is followed by a thorough revision of the early history of film itself, cameras, projectors, and the narrative film.

The second fundamental change is a new chapter on digital cinema—Chapter 19—which is preceded by a completely rewritten history of audiotape and videotape that includes digital video. The history and the explanations of digital filmmaking given in the last two chapters are comprehensive and technically detailed, but they should be clear to readers whose knowledge of computers is advanced or just beginning. Not only are the sections on video and digital cinema up to date—to the end of 2004—but Chapter 19 also covers a completely new generation of equipment, including Sony's unreleased 4K digital projector and Panavision's new Super 35mm digital camera system, called "Genesis"—a phenomenal revision of the 24p digital camera that had been used to shoot *Attack of the Clones* and other pictures. These are the most important developments since the digital soundtrack, and no book currently in print reveals any knowledge of them.

Some sections of chapters now bear different titles. For example, "Up from Down Under, Down from Up Above" now is "Other English-Language Cinemas." The Appendix has been broken up to follow each chapter and includes annotated lists of DVDs.

Many filmmakers are new to this edition, but the most important may be William Heise, who worked with Dickson at Edison, shooting many of their films and collaborating with him in the invention of the Edison film cameras and viewer. There are many new films and films not previously discussed, including *Kill Bill, Time Code, Russian Ark, Whale Rider*, and Ingmar Bergman's final picture, *Saraband*. Box-office figures and business history have been updated through 2004, covering the birth of NBC Universal and Sony's bid to purchase MGM. Some names have been corrected, notably those of the founders of American Biograph, as have numerous dates. The aspect ratio of anamorphic Panavision is correctly given as 2.4:1. Even the names of some films have been corrected (*Greeting by George Bernard Shaw, 1928*). These changes run throughout the book, as do 16 new photographs. Speaking just of the photos, this edition includes Lillian Gish on the set of *Way Down East*, Paul Robeson in Micheaux's original *Body and Soul*, Laurel and Hardy and the Marx Brothers for the first time, and a close-up of three digital soundtracks and a Dolby analog track from a 35mm print. While some of the information in this book may contradict that in other books, I have done my best to make sure that all of it is accurate.

In the 16 years I have been working on the *Short History*, I have revised more than half of it and added the rest. But this is still Gerald Mast's book—in its solid, efficient structure; in its *auteurist* emphasis on the directors of narrative films; in its engaged and engaging tone; in its interdisciplinary approach and humanistic spirit; and in many of its analyses, arguments, and conclusions. But it has been exhaustively researched, corrected, expanded, and brought up to date—tasks made easier by how well the *Short History* was thought out and put together in the first place.

In his prefaces Gerald always warmly thanked those who contributed to this book through its many editions. There are those who helped him in preparing and revising the manuscripts: Joe Adamson, Richard Meran Barsam, Madeline Cook, Jeanne Eichenseer, Tag Gallagher, Steven Jack, Bruce Kawin, Antonín J. Liehm, Richard Dyer MacCann, John Matthew, Ned McLeroy, Leonard Quart, William Reiter,

Burnell Y. Sitterly, and Tom Wittenberg. There are those who helped him see films or collect stills: Mary Corliss (of the Museum of Modern Art/Film Stills Archive), Walter J. Dauler (of Audio-Brandon Films), Darrell Flugg, Bill Franz, Murray Glass (of EmGee Films), Steven Harvey, Peter Meyer (of Janus Films), Adam Reilly, Emily Sieger, and Charles Silver (of the Museum of Modern Art).

For their help in obtaining the new stills for the fifth through eighth editions, I am especially grateful to Mary Corliss and Terry Geesken (of the Museum of Modern Art/Film Stills Archive), Bruce Elder, Robert A. Harris (of Biograph Entertainment and the restorer of *Lawrence of Arabia*), the staff of the Margaret Herrick Library, Barbara Kowalczuk, Helen LaVarre (of Columbia Pictures), Rick McBride (of the Korean Cultural Center), Howie Movshovitz, Herbert Nusbaum and Joan Pierce (of MGM/UA), Martin Scorsese, Phil Solomon, the staff of the Telluride Film Festival, and William Van Wert.

The fifth, sixth, seventh, and eighth editions could not have been completed without the help, advice, and support of Stan Brakhage, Ann R. Cacoullos, Ray Carney, Tony English, Dan Greenberg, Andrew Horton, David James, Lori Janssen, Paul Jarrico, Marian Keane, Marsha Kinder, Pablo Kjolseth, Barbara Kowalczuk, Fred Link, Susan Linville, Frank McConnell, Brock DeShane McDaniel, Bill McLeod, Charles Middleton, Howie Movshovitz, Charles Nilon, Herbert Nusbaum, Jim Palmer, Stan Reubenstein, Donald Richie, David Shepard, Hershel Toomim, William Van Wert, Donald Yannacito, and Maurice H. Zouary.

I would also like to thank the reviewers for the ninth edition: Gary Copeland, University of Alabama; Charles H. Harpole, University of Central Florida; Ken Nolley, Willamette University; and James B. Steerman, Vassar College.

Finally, let me thank those who lent their expertise and encouragement to the immense project of researching, illustrating, and writing the ninth edition: Jack Anderson; Kristina Baumli; William Costanzo; Dan Greenberg; Alan Hardy; the staff of the Margaret Herrick Library; David James; Victor Jendras; Lisa Kennedy of the *Denver Post*; Pablo Kjolseth; Barbara Kowalczuk; Mike Mashon at the Library of Congress; Howie Movshovitz; Peter Becker and David Phillips at The Criterion Collection; Scott Poston; Harold Schechter; David Shepard; Hershel and Marjorie Toomim; Forrest Walker; and my editorial assistants, Theresa Kawin and Charles Wilcox. All of these people helped to make this book the best it has ever been.

Bruce F. Kawin

1

Introductory Assumptions

An audience first watched a motion picture flicker on a screen in 1895. Since then, the movies have developed from a simple recording device—the first films merely captured a scenic or not-so-scenic view—to a complex art and business. The important question for the first film audiences was, "Is the image discernible?" rather than, "Is the image meaningful?" From the simple beginning of cranking a camera to record a scene, filmmakers have learned that their art depends on the way the camera shapes the scene they are recording. Analogous to the novel, the completed narrative film is not just a story, but a story told in a certain way, and it is impossible to separate what is told from how it is told.

The history of the movies is, first of all, the history of a new art. Though it has affinities with fiction, poetry, drama, dance, painting, photography, and music, like each of these kindred arts it has a "poetics" of its own. When the early films turned from scenic views to stories, directors assumed that the poetics of the film were similar to those of the stage. Stage acting, stage movement, stage stories, stage players, and stage perspectives dominated early story films. The camera was assumed to be a passive spectator in a theatre audience, and just as the spectator has only one seat, the camera had only one position from which to shoot a scene.

Time and experimentation revealed that the camera was anchored by analogy alone—and that the analogy was false. The scene—the locale—is the basic unit of the stage because space in the theatre is so concrete. The audience sits here, the characters play there, the scenery is fixed in

space behind the action. But space in the film is completely elastic; only the screen is fixed, not the action on it. Filmmakers discovered that the unit of a film is the shot, not the scene, that shots can be joined together in any number of combinations to produce whole scenes, and that scenes can be varied and juxtaposed and paralleled in any number of ways. Unity of place, a basic and practical principle of the stage, does not apply to the movie. More applicable is what the earliest film theorist, Hugo Münsterberg, adapting another stage term, called the "unity of action," a succession of images that produces the desired narrative continuity, the intended meaning, and the appropriate emotional tension of the film as a whole. By the end of the Silent Era, this principle had been superbly demonstrated.

The discovery of sound raised doubts about the discoveries of the preceding 30 years. Once again the analogy with the stage was pursued; once again stage actors, stage writers, stage directors, and stage techniques flooded the movies. And once again, the analogy was found to be false. Just as the stage is anchored visually in space, so too is it anchored by sound. Words come from the speaker's mouth; you listen to them and watch the mouth. But movies were free to show any kind of picture while the words came from the speaker's mouth. Synchronization of picture and sound also allowed for the disjunction of picture and sound. Further, the freedom of the movies from spatial confinement allowed a greater freedom in the kinds of sounds they could use: natural sounds, musical underscoring, distortion effects, private thoughts, and

1

more. To appreciate the importance of the *integration* of picture and sound, consider a *Gone With the Wind* without Max Steiner's music or Vivien Leigh's and Clark Gable's voices, the creaking wagons and the rustling skirts.

Just as the history of the novel is, to some extent, a catalogue of important novels, the history of film as an art centers on important films. In film history, a discussion of the significant movies is especially relevant, for the individual films are not only milestones on a historical path, but also significant artistic discoveries that almost immediately influenced other filmmakers. Although Shakespeare drew from Seneca and Brecht from Shakespeare, even more immediate was the influence of Griffith on Ford or Hitchcock on De Palma. Without years of stage tradition to draw on, film artists have drawn on the exciting discoveries of their contemporaries. The internationalism of film distribution has always guaranteed the rapid dispersal of any significant discovery.

To keep track of this dispersal of discoveries, it is necessary to know when a particular film was released—that is, when it was first shown to a public audience—for that is usually the earliest that it could have influenced audiences and other filmmakers. This is much like learning the publication date of a novel, rather than its completion date or the number of years it took to complete. In this book, the date that follows a film's title is, in almost all cases, the year the film was *released in its country of origin*. If a film was released long after it was completed, both the completion and release dates are given. If it has become customary to refer to a particular film by the year in which most of it was shot (*Caligari*, 1919), but it came out the following year, both dates are given. And both dates are given if the release date is so early in the year as to be misleading; a film released on January 8, 1929, like Dziga Vertov's *The Man with a Movie Camera*, is a 1928 work as well as a 1929 release. If it matters when a foreign film opened in the United States and affected American audiences, the U.S. release date is also provided; Fellini's *La dolce vita* won a 1961 Oscar, but it came out in Italy in 1960. In any case, most films open the year they are completed and need only one date.

The title of *La dolce vita* is given in Italian, following Italian conventions for capitalization, because the film is known worldwide by its original name and was never released in English-speaking countries as *The Sweet Life*. The most reliable way to establish the actual title of a movie is to watch the movie: The original posters and most books may call Capra's picture *It's a Wonderful Life*, but the movie calls itself *It's A Wonderful Life*. Aside from cases where the Art Department has been allowed to spell the title any way it wants (*tHE tHING*), the onscreen title has an authority like that of the title page of a novel. The use of italics for the title of a film of any length is a literary convention that has been widely adopted.

When there is a conflict over the choice or spelling of a name, professional names take precedence over birth names. Cary Grant, born Archibald Leach, is Cary Grant in film books, as Marion Michael Morrison is John Wayne; the pre-studio name is a footnote. Early in the 21st century, Wong Kar-wai began spelling his name "Wong Kar Wai" in the credits; that is respected as the name under which he has chosen to work. When there is a dispute over the spelling of a name and no conflict between birth and industry names, an original legal signature has authority, and after that a tombstone. There is no consistency in this, but most Western books and film distributors put the family name first for a Chinese person (as it is done in China: Zhang Yimou) but last for a Japanese person (as it is not done in Japan: Akira Kurosawa was Kurosawa Akira).

Many film historians subscribe to a basic, if far from absolute, assumption: The very best films have generally resulted from the clear vision and unifying intelligence of a single, controlling mind with primary responsibility for the whole film. Just as there is only one conductor per orchestra, they argue, there can be only one dominant creator of a movie. The "*auteur* theory," as defined by François Truffaut in France and Andrew Sarris in America, identifies the director (whose personal artistic signature is evident in the work) as a film's "author" or dominant creator. Whether the *auteur* improvises the whole film as it goes along or works according to a preconceived and scripted plan, a single mind shapes and guides the work of film art.

But if many of the best movies are dominated by an *auteur*, it is also true that any movie represents an immensely collaborative venture. There are examples of very good movies with two co-directors (Gene Kelly and Stanley Donen, Ján Kadár and Elmar Klos). Many of the best directors have worked in frequent partnership with the same scriptwriter (Frank Capra with Robert Riskin, John Ford with Dudley Nichols), or the same cinematographer (Sergei Eisenstein with Eduard Tisse, D. W. Griffith with Billy Bitzer), or assistant director (Truffaut with Suzanne Schiffman), or composer (Alfred Hitchcock with Bernard Herrmann, Federico Fellini with Nino Rota).

Strictly speaking, however, an *auteur* is a director who also writes the script and edits the film (for example, Japan's Takeshi Kitano); in practice, she or he may just work closely with the writer and the editor. But no commercial filmmaker works alone. And although any director has the authority and duty to make creative decisions that ensure the quality and coherence of the work, the *auteur* is a director whose work expresses a vision that develops in the course of what may appropriately be discussed as an artistic career. Not every director is an *auteur*, and some *auteurs*—like producer Val Lewton—are guiding artists in every sense of the term but are not directors.

Even if very many movies are made outside or in opposition to the film industry, any history that intends to reveal the genesis of today's film world must acknowledge the dominant role of the industry as well as address a wealth of social and technical matters. In addition to discussing the film as art, it must deal with three related problems that have always influenced the artistic product and continue to influence it today: the cinema as business, the cinema as cultural product and commodity, and the cinema as technology.

Movies today are a multibillion-dollar business. The choice of directors, stars, and scripts is in the hands of businesspeople, not of artists. The company that invests $50 million in a picture ought to be able to ensure the safety of its investment. When push comes to shove, commercial priorities outweigh artistic ones.

The awesome financial pressures of Hollywood are partly responsible for the growing number of independent films and digital videos. Young filmmakers often prefer to work alone, their sole expenses equipment and film or tape. These filmmakers are, in a sense, returning to the earliest period of film history.

Why do movies cost so much to make? Put the question this way: How much would you expect to pay if you employed an army of the most specialized artisans at their trade for a period of, say, three months? Making a film is such a massive and complex task it is a wonder that an artistically whole movie can be made at all. The huge sums of money required to finance a movie merely reflect the hugeness of the task of taking a movie from story idea to final print. Shooting is painfully slow. It takes time to perfect each setup: Lights must be carefully focused and toned, the shot's composition must be determined, the set must be found—or built—and dressed, background actors (extras) must be coordinated with the action of the principals, actors must have rehearsed their movements and mastered their interpretations of lines so that a single shot fits into the dramatic fabric of the whole film, makeup must be correct, costumes must be coordinated, and so forth.

Because it takes so much time to set up a shot, producers economize by shooting all scenes together that require the same location, set, or setup, regardless of their position in the film's continuity. In other words, the film is shot "out of sequence." But even with such economies, to get three minutes of screen time "in the can" is a hard, well-organized day's work.

The only way to retrieve production expenses is with sales—selling tickets, renting prints, leasing television rights to networks or cable franchises, selling videocassettes and DVDs outright, and licensing tie-ins from toys and computer games to novelizations.

The history of the movies as a business is inextricably linked with the history of the movies as a mass entertainment medium. To get the public to spend its money at the box office, the producer must give the public what it wants or make the public want what it gets.

Film art has changed radically in the course of its history, and so have film audiences. The first movie patrons in America were also patrons of vaudeville houses and variety shows. When those audiences tired of the same kinds of film programs, the movies found a home with lower- and working-class patrons. Small theatres sprang

Fig. 1-1

The movies as mirror of American social history. Fig. 1-1: Social institutions responsive to human needs and challenges (Jean Arthur in the U.S. Senate of Mr. Smith Goes to Washington, *1939). Fig. 1-2: Three returning servicemen view the land they fought to save (from left, Dana Andrews, Fredric March, and Harold Russell in* The Best Years of Our Lives, *1946).*

Fig. 1-2

up in the poor sections and commercial districts of cities; admission was a nickel or a dime. The rich and educated saw movies only as an afternoon or evening of slumming. As film art and craft improved, larger and more expensive movie theatres opened in the respectable entertainment centers of the cities. Films tried to appeal to a wide range of tastes and interests, much as television does today. In this period there was little consciousness of movies as an art; they were mass entertainment. H. L. Mencken sardonically lauded the movies as the appropriate artistic attainment of the American "booboisie." Similes linking movies with tastelessness and movie patrons with morons continually popped up in fiction and articles of the 1920s and 1930s. Sixty years later, people like Mencken were writing film criticism, a movie actor had served as president of the United States, and going to the movies had become both intellectually respectable and socially necessary.

This discussion of the evolving audiences for movies indicates the close connection between the movies as cultural artifacts and conditions in the culture as a whole. Particular cultural conditions influence, if not dictate, the particular qualities and quantities of films in any given era. For a specific movie to become a major hit at a specific time indicates, at least partially, the cultural fact that a sufficient number of people wanted, needed, demanded, or responded to just that film then. To compare *Mr. Smith Goes to Washington* of 1939, with *The Best Years of Our Lives* of 1946, with *Rebel Without a Cause* of 1955, with *The Graduate* of 1967 is to write a history of three decades of American culture. Any history of the movies must both take account of and account for these cultural shifts and conditions.

But if movies convey an overt and explicit cultural content—a war-torn society attempting to heal its wounds in *The Best Years of Our Lives* or a working-class woman attempting to express and distinguish herself in *Flashdance*—they can also convey covert and "invisible" ideological messages. For example, happiness in an American film is so equated with a synthesis of material comfort (home, job, car, stereo) and spiritual contentment (usually a monogamous romantic relationship) that any alternative idea of happiness, or even a critique of the idea of happiness itself, is almost unthinkable.

This ideological analysis has been especially useful to feminist critics and theorists who seek the underlying sources of sexist thinking in our cultural history. Women in films seem banished to the kitchen, the bedroom, or the pedestal. And whether they are cast in the cliché roles of virgin, whore, mother, wife, assistant, or boss, they are usually presented in terms of their relation to men. Feminist films define women as selves, not as objects.

Another radical approach to film theory suggests that our very way of looking at the world, of seeing nature, reality, and all the persons and things within it, is itself a cultural construct. The principles of Renaissance perspective—of a deep, receding space presented for the eye of the single, privileged viewer—have been ground into the lenses of cameras. Others have argued that bourgeois culture privileges a single sense—sight—over all others. The apparently innocent act of "seeing the world"—whether through our eyes or through a lens—is not at all innocent because both the seeing and the seen are cultural constructs.

Appropriately enough, our technological period has produced an art that depends on technology. The first filmmakers were not artists but tinkerers. The same spirit that produced a light bulb and a telephone produced a movie camera and projector. The invention of the first cameras and projectors was first exploited as a novelty in itself and only later integrated as one tool in making the whole film. The first movie camera merely exploited its ability to capture images of moving things. The first synchronized sound films exploited the audience's excitement at hearing the words that the actor's lips were mouthing. Most of the first color films were merely colorful, many of the first wide-screen films merely wide.

No other art is so tied to machines. Some of the most striking artistic effects are the products of expanding film technology. Research has converted the camera from an erratic, hand-cranked film grinder to a smooth, precise clockwork. Research has developed faster and sturdier film stocks, enabling greater flexibility in lighting, composition, and shooting conditions. Research has developed the computer, digital effects, and digital videotape. Film equipment is so sophisticated that no film artist can master all of it; yet despite the difficulties of money and machine—and the many achievements in the other arts—movies became the dominant art of the 20th century and remain essential to life in the 21st.

This short history will follow the road the movies have traveled to get here. To keep a history even this "short" has required several decisions. First, this history aims at revealing significant trends and turns along the road rather than detailing exhaustive lists of titles, directors, and dates.

Second, because the history of the American film is most relevant to American readers, this short history allots more space to a discussion of American movie practices than to international films. Those countries and cultures that have produced the most sigificant films are treated in as much depth as a "short history" allows.

Third, there is no room here to explain more than the most essential technical terms, equipment, standards, and procedures. A Glossary at the end of the book defines key terms for easy reference.

Fourth, this history concentrates heavily on the fiction film, also called the narrative film. Nevertheless, the documentary *is* discussed in this book, particularly in the context of such filmmakers as Robert Flaherty, Dziga Vertov, Leni Riefenstahl, and Marcel Ophuls. Animators from Émile Cohl and Walt Disney to computer-graphics artists make their appearance, and in addition to discussions of the silent avant-garde film in Europe, a significant portion of a chapter is devoted to the American avant-garde. These discussions are essential to giving a sense of the whole of film art, but they are necessarily brief and suggestive.

Finally, the reader must realize precisely what this book of history (and any book of history) really is—not a collection of all the facts that must be accepted as absolute truth but a selection of facts that have been fitted into a pattern. No matter how much it aspires to be an accurate record of change over time, a history is inevitably an interpretive narrative, a telling, a story; after all, five-sevenths of the word *history* is *story*. This story is perpetually revised and rethought: New data are selected, old data are rejected or reinterpreted, and new ways of viewing are found. Like plays, novels, and movies, histories are stories told to a particular audience at a particular time, embodying the values, hopes, ideals, and commitments of those times. Histories of movies, no less than the movies themselves, construct a view of the world and of human experience.

For Further Viewing

NOTE: The films and DVDs in these lists, found at the end of each chapter, present a range of the materials available for further research and enjoyment. The lists are suggestive but not exhaustive. Each filmography contains a representative sample of the major films of each director and period. The date after each film is the year it was released in its country of origin; within a given year, films are listed in release order if the exact release dates are known. English, alternate, and untranslated titles are given if the films are widely known by or distributed under those titles. Most of these films are available for rental in 16mm, but many are also worth studying on DVD. In almost all cases, the DVDs listed here have useful supplements (not all of which are listed) and contain good, complete prints—in the case of silents, at the correct speed. Only Region 1 and region-free discs are listed.

FILMS

Introductory Miscellany

Shorts

Un Chien andalou (1929, Luis Buñuel and Salvador Dalí). Surrealism, structure.

Duck Amuck (1951, rel. 1953; Chuck Jones). Editing, sound, reflexivity.

The Fatal Glass of Beer (1933, Clyde Bruckman), starring W. C. Fields. Language, repetition, parody, artificiality.

La Jetée (1962, rel. 1964; Chris Marker). Time, memory, stills and motion, editing.

Ménilmontant (1925, Dimitri Kirsanov). Silence without intertitles.

Meshes of the Afternoon (1943, Maya Deren). Avant-garde, structure, identity.

Mothlight (1963, Stan Brakhage). Avant-garde, filmmaking without a camera.

October: Raising of the Bridges Sequence (1928, Sergei Eisenstein). Montage, time.

Olympia: Diving Sequence (1938, Leni Riefenstahl). Editing, music.

One Week (1920, Eddie Cline and Buster Keaton). Silent comedy.

FEATURES

The Apple (1998, Samira Makhmalbaf). Realism, national cinema.

Before The Rain (1994, Milcho Manchevski). Narrative structure, national cinema.

Gabbeh (1996, Mohsen Makhmalbaf). Fantasy, realism, color, structure, national cinema.

Greed (1924, Erich von Stroheim). Realism, adaptation, mise-en-scène.

Lawrence of Arabia (1962, David Lean). Widescreen color cinematography.

The Love of Jeanne Ney (1927, G. W. Pabst). Melodrama, camerawork, editing.

The Magnificent Ambersons (1942, Orson Welles). Black-and-white cinematography.

The Man with a Movie Camera (1928, rel. 1929, Dziga Vertov). Editing, camerawork, reflexivity.

Medea (1969, Pier Paolo Pasolini). Compare von Trier/Dreyer adaptation.

Medea (1988, Lars von Trier; script by Dreyer). Authorship, adaptation.

Microcosmos (1996, Claude Nuridsany and Marie Pérennou). Extreme close-ups.

Moolaadé (2004, Ousmane Sembene). Feminism, Third World cinema.

The Passion of Joan of Arc (1928, Carl Theodor Dreyer). Faces, camerawork, editing.

Seven Samurai (1954, Akira Kurosawa). Pace, editing, national cinema.

Singin' In The Rain (1952, Stanley Donen and Gene Kelly). Early sound, studio credits, genre.

2 or 3 Things I Know About Her (1967, Jean-Luc Godard). Analyzed realism, reflexivity, language, people and objects, analysis of systems (social, economic, semiotic, cinematic), influence of Brecht, thinking with film, voice-over, *auteur* theory.

Weekend (1967, Jean-Luc Godard). Long takes.

DVDs

by Brakhage—an anthology. Criterion Collection. Includes 26 films, a documentary, and many interviews with **Stan Brakhage.** Excellent for detailed study of one filmmaker and his evolving thoughts on his work. Optimized for single-frame as well as full-speed viewing.

The Five Obstructions (2003, **Lars von Trier** and **Jørgen Leth**). Koch Lober. Von Trier tells Leth five different ways to remake his 1967 short, *The Perfect Human*—e.g., with no shot longer than 12 frames. Includes *The Perfect Human* and commentary by Leth.

John Cassavetes: Five Films. Criterion Collection. Includes *Faces* and its alternate opening, *The Killing of a Chinese Bookie* in two versions, *Shadows* with related drama workshop footage and a **restoration** demonstration, *A Woman Under the Influence*, *Opening Night*, documentaries on **John Cassavetes,** many interviews and commentaries, and a booklet. Excellent for detailed study of one filmmaker and his working methods.

Night and Fog (1955, **Alain Resnais**). Criterion Collection. Includes interviews with Resnais and articles by film historian Peter Cowie, music historian Russell Lack, and essayist Phillip Lopate.

Peeping Tom (1960, **Michael Powell**). Criterion Collection. Includes commentary by theorist Laura Mulvey and documentary on screenwriter **Leo Marks**.

Treasures from American Film Archives: 50 Preserved Films. Image Entertainment/ National Film Preservation Foundation. A great variety of silent and sound films, from home movies and cartoons to rare features and shorts, including *Blacksmithing Scene* (**Edison–Dickson–Heise**), *The Fall of the House of Usher* (**Webber** and **Watson**), *Hell's Hinges* (with **William S. Hart**), *The Lonedale Operator* (**Griffith**), *Rose Hobart* (**Joseph Cornell**), and *The Toll of the Sea* (in 2-strip Technicolor), with information on each archive and a detailed book.

2

Birth

Some film historians trace the origin of movies to cave paintings, to Balinese shadow puppets, or to Plato's mythic Cave of the Shadows in Book VII of the *Republic*. Many theorists find a valid conceptual model in Plato's mass of spectators, entranced by the flickering shadows of objects on the cave wall that are merely projections of the light behind them, diverted from the real objects they would see if they could only ascend from the shadow-show to examine them in the light itself. The nonmetaphoric history of the movies, however, begins with the steps leading to the invention of the movie camera and projector.

The 19th-century mind created machines for travel, machines for work, machines for the home, and machines for entertainment—and the light bulb. By the end of the century, three developments had combined to create the motion picture: research into persistence of vision (wrongly thought to be the reason movies appear to move), the invention of still photography, and increasing public interest in glass-slide shows and mechanized entertainments.

Frames per Second

Movies are an optical illusion. We believe we are watching a completely continuous, fluid motion on the screen, while all we really watch are short, discontinuous bits of the motion, mere 24ths of a second of action.

To create the cinematic illusion of motion, a series of stills must be presented rapidly to the eye, which sends the information to the brain. Each picture in a movie, whether photographed or drawn, is perceived as a clear, stable, unmoving image, as individual as a page in a flip book. But the brain does something with the information received from the eye, something that will not be fully understood until more research has been done into the neural and cognitive aspects of the perception of cinematic movement. Given certain conditions, we see the elements of one picture appear to move to their positions in the next picture. To discuss how that phenomenon has been explained, we need to understand a number of concepts and terms.

When images that present tiny changes in the photographed or drawn subject succeed each other at a rate of more than 11 or 12 per second, the viewer imagines seeing the subject move. That is, to be sure, a jerky movement. At 16 pictures per second, the apparent movement begins to seem fluid and normal, so that was the speed at which most of the first movies were photographed and projected. What we see in a movie is called *apparent movement* because no *real movement* is shown; there are only stills. Creating apparent movement from still pictures is the *cinematic illusion*.

Pictures on Film

Because each picture in a movie is an individual, rectangular image, or *frame*, on a strip of film—we'll address the digital cinema later in this book and refer until then to movies shot and printed on celluloid—the rate at which film images succeed each other is expressed in *frames per second* (*fps*) or in feet per minute (*fpm*). Most sound movies run at 24 fps, or 90 feet of 35mm film per minute, though many run at 25 fps to work with the PAL video format. The professional, theatrical standard around the world, *35mm film* is 35 millimeters wide (its *gauge*) and holds 16 frames per foot.

Film stock—unprocessed or *raw* film—consists of a base coated with an emulsion. The *base* is made of celluloid: originally cellulose nitrate (*nitrate film*), which was extremely flammable and deteriorated (shrank, dissolved, and worse) within a few decades, and then cellulose tri-acetate (*safety-base film*, also called *acetate film*), introduced in 1949, which burned slowly and would not deteriorate for a few hundred years. Nitrate film gave a better image but was kin to nitroglycerin. Since 1951 every film has been shot on safety-base stock. The exact formula has been continually improved.

One side of the base is coated with the *emulsion*, a layer of photosensitive chemicals. When film is processed, it is the emulsion that is developed. The most important chemical in a black-and-white emulsion is silver nitrate, which turns black when it is exposed to light, creating a *negative* (film that has black where the photographed subject was white, dark gray where the subject was light gray, and so on). The black-and-white values of a negative are reversed to *positive* values when it is copied onto blank film to make a projectable print. Because the printer's light shines through the negative onto raw stock that also turns black when it is exposed to light, what is white in the negative becomes black in the print. Some color emulsions —whose negatives are in the complements of the colors on the print—consist of several layers and include microscopic globules of dye. While most professionals shoot negative film and then strike positive prints, *reversal* film, whether black and white or color, can be processed to yield a positive image.

All movie film has a line of rectangular *perforations* (informally, perfs) or *sprocket holes*, which are rectangular with slightly rounded corners, running just inside one or both of its edges. The holes are engaged by the teeth of *sprocket wheels* (or *sprockets*), which hold the film as the wheels advance and stop it.

The frame itself, which appears once the film has been processed, consists of microscopic bits of silver and dye that are sometimes described as minimal picture elements (*pixels*). In most sound films, an optical soundtrack runs between the frame and one line of sprocket holes. In 1931, to make room for the soundtrack, the size of the frame on most 35mm prints was officially reduced to the *Academy aperture* of .868 x .631 inches. All along, the proportions of a full frame have been, or been very close to, 4 units wide by 3 units high—which can be expressed, as a TV engineer would put it, as 4:3 or 4x3; with the height reduced to a constant, it is properly expressed, in film terms, as an aspect ratio of 1.33:1. Wider frames can be created by anamorphic squeezing and unsqueezing, as in CinemaScope, or by the equivalent of letterboxing, as in flat widescreen. For these terms and many related ones, please see the Glossary.

Speed

Sound speed is usually 24 fps, but there are exceptions: Todd-AO, for example, ran at 30 fps in the 1950s. *Silent speed* was approximately 16 fps—conveniently, 1 foot/sec—from 1895 to the late 1910s, but it often passed 20 fps in the 1920s. Many silents ran at 20.5 or 22 fps, and Edison's early films were shot at an average of between 30 and 40 fps. Because the first cameras were hand-cranked rather than run at a regular speed by a motor—and because there was no soundtrack running at a fixed rate that the film had to match—silent speed was always flexible. Today's most advanced variable-speed projectors can adjust to a film's original speed so that the filmed movements seem natural.

For the illusion of normal motion, then, the projector has to show the pictures at the same rate as the camera photographed them. The camera can shoot *slow motion* by exposing more than the normal number of frames per second; when the frames are projected at normal speed, the movement takes longer on screen than it did in the real world. For *fast motion*, the camera exposes fewer frames per second than normal.

By opening and closing a *shutter*—so called because it can shut out the light and also because window shutters open and close only to admit or block light completely—a movie camera exposes one frame at a time. Each frame is a still photograph, blurred a bit if the subject or the camera has moved. To take each picture, the camera stops the film and opens the shutter for about

1/50th of a second. To record a second of action at sound speed, it exposes and advances 24 frames during that second. The shutter on a conventional movie camera—or a very simple projector—resembles a hemisphere joined halfway down its base to the end of a rod; like all movie shutters it revolves once for every frame, letting the light in when the film has stopped moving and shutting the light out while the film is being advanced. It is called a *single-bladed shutter* because it uses a single flat piece of metal (the blade) to block the light. The one open area might be 180° (hemispheric), but the *variable shutter* found on the best movie cameras can be set, for example, to a 140° or 120° wedge of light for a sharper exposure.

Flicker and the Continuous Signal

The shutter comes between the lens and the *film gate*, the windowed metal sandwich where film is exposed or displayed. While a camera's shutter is closed, no light reaches the film. While a projector's shutter is closed, none of the projector's light passes through the frame onto the screen. The alternation of light and dark caused by the opening and closing of the projector's shutter causes an unpleasant distraction, termed *flicker*. If it takes about 12 fps for us to perceive motion and 16 fps for the motion to begin to look smooth, it takes 48 fps or more (the human eye's CFF or *critical flicker frequency*, the point at which the stuttering light fuses) to get rid of the flicker that produced one of the cinema's early names, the flicks. *Flicker fusion* occurs when one perceives interrupted light as an uninterrupted or *continuous signal*. Below the CFF, flicker is very noticeable, and it plagued early films.

The solution to flicker, arrived at during the silent period (by Biograph in 1903), was to shoot at 16 fps and show each of the 16 frames three times, using a *three-bladed shutter* that had three blades to block the light and three open areas. That gave a flicker rate of 48/sec at a projection rate of 16 fps, with still less flicker at 18 or 20 fps. For a 24-fps sound film, which also has a normal flicker rate of 48/sec, a *two-bladed shutter*, resembling a bow tie, flashes 48 images per second, 24 of which are different.

The periodic starting and stopping of the film in the gate of a camera, printer, or projector is called *intermittent movement*, and it is responsible for the sharpness of the immobilized image as well as for the shutter's alternating instants of light and black in a dark theatre. Although we see no flicker at 48 images per second, the dark periods between images are still there. There is an interrupted, off-and-on, discontinuous signal, which may be represented graphically as ----------. But our minds fill in or ignore the blanks, linking the fragments, and we perceive a continuous signal, which may be represented as _____. Ironically, about half of the time we spend watching a movie, the screen is literally blank, devoid of any image at all.

Persistence of Vision and Other Phenomena

When darkness follows a bright image, the light receptors in the eye (whose action diminishes rapidly but does not instantly shut off) retain the image for a fraction of a second, so that the retina briefly continues to send the last visual information it received to the brain.

This optical phenomenon is known as *persistence of vision* or *retinal retention*. It accounts for the way that a flashlight—or a glowing orange coal at the end of a stick—when swung around rapidly in the dark appears to produce a circle of light. In the darkness, the retina retains the individual points of light long enough to make a circle.

For many years it was assumed that persistence of vision accounted for the way we perceive apparent movement when a series of slightly different, successive images is shown to us at a certain rate. It was assumed that each image that was flashed in the dark left its imprint on the retina long enough for it to be combined with the next image. It was also assumed—before the discovery of flicker fusion—that retinally retained images were necessary to keep us from too distinctly noticing the darkness between the bright images, when the shutter is closed.

However, research begun as early as 1910 and continuing to the present has made it clear that the illusion of motion is created at a higher level of processing in the brain. Even if the retina retains an image under certain circumstances, that is not why we see movies move.

Seeing with the Brain

After the retina has delivered its information to the optic nerve, visual data are processed at a number of way stations (visual nuclei) in the brain. As the information travels, every aspect of it is interpreted by highly specialized nerve cells. It can take milliseconds, even hundreds of them, for us to become conscious of what we are seeing.

Visual Masking and Retinal Retention

Images are interrelated in the brain. Successive fragments of movement, like those shown in a series of movie frames, can be read by the brain as continuous action well after the pictures have entered the visual system. Images don't wait on the retina to be compared or combined. If they did, we would see a blurry mess of overlapping stills—not just two combined stills but many, because a retinal afterimage can last much longer than 1/20th of a second, even several seconds in the case of a very bright image. Far from accomplishing it, persistence of vision gets in the way of the cinematic illusion. The brain needs to stop perceiving one image to perceive the next. Only then can it notice and process any differences between the images. Late 20th-century research found that when a frame is followed by a fraction of a second of visual noise—a period of no information or random information—the brain stops processing the frame and clears the mental slate. This crucial phenomenon, called *visual masking*, defeats any image-confusing effects that might be caused by persistence of vision.

Although retinal retention is responsible for some images—for example, the afterimage produced by staring at a candle at night—it generally produces *unmoving* ones, like that circle made by the spun flashlight or like the apparently curved, frozen spokes of a turning wheel if it is viewed through the upright bars of a fence—the phenomenon addressed by Peter Mark Roget, the English physician best known for his thesaurus, in an 1824 paper that influenced most later discussions. (Roget's paper, "Explanation of an optical deception in the appearance of the spokes of a wheel seen through vertical apertures," responded to a query posed in 1821, probably by John Murray.)

Persistence of vision has been a persistent explanation of the cinematic illusion, and that is why it remains part of film history: because generations of scientists, camera makers, and film historians thought the explanation was accurate. It is part of the history of thinking about the cinema. Furthermore, early research into persistence of vision and the invention of devices designed to exploit it were inseparable from the invention of movie cameras and projectors. The machines based on the incorrect assumption that persistence of vision was responsible for the cinematic illusion turned out to be movie machines.

Scientific Toys

In 1829, the French inventor Joseph Antoine Ferdinand Plateau published his investigations on persistence of vision, and in 1832 he created his own toy to demonstrate his theoretical research. Painted on a flat, circular piece of board were individual designs in slightly varying positions. When the board was grasped by a handle, held up in front of a mirror, and then spun, the individual designs became a continuous, animated sequence. To see the designs moving (rather than as a blur), the viewer looked into the mirror through little slits cut into the circular board. Sales of Plateau's toy began in 1833 under various names chosen by the manufacturers. Although Plateau preferred "Phenakisticope," the name that stuck was Phenakistiscope (from the Greek "deceptive viewer"). Plateau's research was important, for in the course of it he discovered that 16 images per second was the optimal rate for producing continuous movement. In addition, the Phenakistiscope required instants of darkness, without an image (when one saw the dark or blank side of the turning card instead of the view, through a slit, of the mirror and its reflected drawings), to make the images appear to move. Perhaps the eye needed resting time to soak in the images. A successful projector would not be invented until an analogy to Plateau's slits was discovered.

In 1834, William George Horner created a stroboscopic machine that used a circular drum rather than a flat circular board. Exchangeable paper strips fit inside the circular drum. When the viewer looked through the slits in the spinning

Early persistence of vision toys: the Thaumatrope, a Zoetrope wheel with paper strip, and (left rear) a primitive version of what would become a Mutoscope.

Fig. 2-1

drum, which allowed instants of darkness, the pictures on the paper strips appeared in delightfully sequential motion. Horner called his toy the Zoötrope (or Zoetrope, from the Greek "life turning" or "wheel of life").

Émile Reynaud

The Praxinoscope was invented by Émile Reynaud in 1877. It resembled the Zoetrope, but the drum had no slits. Instead, the viewer looked over the edge of the drum at an inner, central wheel on which mirrors were set at angles to one another. The mirrors reflected the images Reynaud had drawn on Zoetrope-like paper strips and set inside the drum, and in the instant that each mirror directly faced the viewer, it reflected that image into the eye. Between images, nothing was seen but the angled edge of a turning mirror. Reynaud soon created the Projection Praxinoscope (1880), which added the magic lantern to his mirrors, and the image-combining Praxinoscope-Théâtre (1887), in which the reflected moving image was combined with the reflection of a miniature set or a painted or printed background. These inventions finally led him to design the Théâtre Optique, a complex device,

patented in 1888 and first exhibited in 1892, that showed long animated tales. Reynaud's image sequences were not limited to short repeated actions—because they were painted not on turning cards or paper loops but on long transparent strips, some of them over 100 feet long and wound on a reel.

With Reynaud, the theatrical, projected, perforated, and (even if he painted his frames) photographed cinema had been envisioned. Reynaud should also be recognized as the maker of the first animated movies. He didn't use a camera to put his paintings on film, but neither do many 21st-century digital animators.

By the end of the 19th century, hundreds of variations on these toys and shows abounded. All these heirs of the Thaumatrope were designed to exploit persistence of vision. Most were stroboscopic in the sense that they presented bright images and darkness in rapid alternation. There was a striking simultaneity of discoveries in different countries, primarily in France, England, Germany, and the United States. Even today these four countries each claim to have invented the motion picture.

Photography

Before there could be motion pictures, there had to be pictures. A moving picture was born from the union of the stroboscopic toys and the still photograph. The principle of photography dates back at least to the Renaissance and Leonardo da Vinci's drawing of a *camera obscura*. This device—literally translated as "dark room" or "chamber"—was a completely dark enclosure that admitted light only through a small hole. The *camera obscura* projected an inverted reproduction of the scene facing it on the wall opposite. After a lens was put in the hole to brighten and sharpen the image, all the *camera obscura* needed to become a camera was a photographic plate to replace the back wall. Inventors and scientists set out in pursuit of this plate that could fix the inverted image permanently.

As early as 1816, Joseph Nicéphore Niépce, a Frenchman, used metal plates to capture rather fuzzy images—the first photographs. He called them Heliographs, because they were drawn by the sun. (Photography, also from the Greek, means "light writing.") But it was another Frenchman, Louis Jacques Mandé Daguerre, the late Niépce's partner, who in 1839 determined the future of photography by making clear, sharp, permanent images on silvered copperplate. It was also in the 1830s that the English inventor William Henry Fox Talbot began his research in paper printing—the principle of the photographic negative, and with it, the reproducible photograph.

Muybridge and Marey

The first attempts at motion photography were posed stills that simulated continuous action. But a real motion picture required a continuous live action to be first analyzed into its component units and then resynthesized, rather than a simple synthesis of static, posed bits of action.

The first person to break a continuous action into discrete photographic units was an Englishman transplanted to California, Eadweard Muybridge. Muybridge was a vagabond photographer and inventor. In 1872, he was hired by the governor of California, Leland Stanford, to help win a $25,000 bet. Stanford, an avid horse breeder and racer, bet a friend that at some point in the racehorse's stride all four hooves left the ground. In 1877, after faster exposures became possible,

Muybridge set up 24 cameras in a row along the racing track. He attached a string to each camera shutter and stretched the string across the track. He chalked numerals and lines on a board behind the track to measure the horse's progress. The horse then galloped down the track, tripping the wires, and Mr. Stanford won the $25,000 that had cost him only $40,000 to win.

For the next 20 years, Muybridge perfected his multiple-camera technique. He shot—and published—motion sequences of horses and elephants and tigers, of nude women and wrestling men and dancing couples. He mounted his pictures on a Phenakistiscope wheel and combined the wheel with the magic lantern for public projections of his work in 1879. Unfortunately, what he mounted and projected were not his photographs but drawings made from them. He called his invention—a variation on the Projecting Phenakistiscope—the Zoöpraxiscope (from the Greek "life-constructing viewer"). Muybridge traveled to Europe, where he gave special showings of the Zoöpraxiscope to admiring scientists and photographers. Years later, in February 1888, Muybridge suggested to Edison that they combine the phonograph with the Zoöpraxiscope—or a newer apparatus on which he said he was working. Edison rejected the idea but soon began making notes for another way of integrating moving pictures and sound.

Muybridge's pictures were serial photographs—not fully achieved motion-picture photography but on the verge of it—and they were of very brief actions, as short as anything in a Zoetrope loop. Continuous motion had been divided into distinct frames, but it had not yet been photographed by a single camera.

One of Muybridge's hosts in Paris in 1881 was another student of movement, the physiologist Étienne-Jules Marey, who also was experimenting with serial photography. In 1882, Marey was the first to shoot multiple pictures with a single camera. "Shoot" applies quite literally to Marey's experiment, for his camera looked like a shotgun. The photographic gun ("fusil") used a long barrel for its lens and a circular chamber containing a single glass photographic plate. The circular plate rotated 12 times in the chamber per second of shooting, leaving all 12 exposures arranged in a ring around the glass plate. Whereas Muybridge had

Fig. 2-2
Muybridge's leaping horse.

gone from one camera to another, each loaded with a glass plate that had been coated with a light-sensitive emulsion, Marey moved one plate through one camera and maintained a single point of reference; Muybridge's point of view had moved horizontally, from camera to camera. Like Muybridge, Marey photographed people and animals: runners, fencers, trotting horses, falling cats, gorgeous flying birds. But Marey's Chronophotographs produced a much more fluid analysis of motion, the finished print resembling a surreal multiple exposure. He shot most of these sequential exposures not with the Photographic Gun of March 1882 but with a very heavy camera, shaped like a box, which produced a better image and which he

patented only a few months after the gun. Marey introduced this new camera, the Photochronograph, in July 1882; it revolved a glass plate 10 times per second and exposed one picture with each revolution. In 1888, Marey redesigned the camera to use coated paper film; this new, lighter camera was called the Photochronograph until 1889, when Marey changed its name to the Chronophotographe or Chronophotographic Camera. It exposed 20 fps, though it could also run as slowly as 10 fps and—to catch the movement of flying birds—as rapidly as 40 fps. Marey called the medium Chronophotography, emphasizing its ability to photograph time (or to "write light" as time progressed). Paper film could hold many more frames than a glass disc. Photography had reached the threshold of cinematography.

Because the photosensitive paper strip, wound on a spool, could be any length, Marey's 1888 camera, demonstrated to the Academy of Sciences in Paris in October, was free of the problems of the repeating loop and of the short unrepeated action. That same year, Reynaud had begun painting his extremely long strips for the Théâtre Optique. The crucial element of Reynaud's apparatus that Marey's Chronophotograph lacked was the line of perforations to help control the strip's movement. What Reynaud's perforated strip lacked was what Muybridge had brought to the project of inventing cinema: photographs.

The first paper-film movie camera was invented not by Marey in October 1888, however, but by Louis Aimé Augustin Le Prince in January 1888. Operating on unique principles, using six lenses and multiple strips of paper film, it was part of an integrated camera–projector that survives. Between January and October, Le Prince invented a single-lens camera for paper film, but it has not survived. In October 1888, the same month that Marey unveiled his own paper-film camera, Le Prince made two paper films with his single-lens camera, and they do survive on paper rolls. Le Prince also invented a three-lens projector that used perforated celluloid (March 1890)— the first celluloid-film projector. But late in 1890, Le Prince disappeared from a train between Dijon and Paris, and nothing ever came of his work.

In 1890, Marey made the first known movie camera designed to use celluloid film instead of paper film. It was his fourth camera—after the 1882 glass-disc gun, the 1882 glass-disc box, and the 1888 paper-film box—and he called it the "complete" version of the Chronophotographic Camera. He went on to make over 600 films. In 1892, Marey completed his Chronophotographic Projector, which threw images from a strip of celluloid onto a screen; even with his unperforated film, Marey became the inventor most responsible for the use of intermittent movement in film cameras and projectors.

Edison, still thinking about what he had learned from Muybridge, met Marey while attending the Paris Exposition in 1889, and from Marey—whose lab the trusting scientist invited

Edison to visit—he got the idea to use a single camera loaded with celluloid that would stop in front of the lens long enough to be exposed. Edison described this idea for an invention in November 1889, 13 months after he wrote his first notes about motion pictures. (These notes were called *caveats*.) Because the post-cylinder cameras invented in the Edison Laboratory between 1890 and 1892 used perforated film, it is possible that Edison saw the Théâtre Optique in Paris too.

To produce a movie that was more than a snippet of activity, a material had to be developed that could hold thousands of images and pass through machines without tearing. Coated-paper film was an option only until celluloid—which produced sharper, richer pictures and was much stronger and more flexible—was perfected.

In 1884, George Eastman began his own experiments with celluloid and with paper-roll film, the latter for use in his Kodak still camera. (Eastman perforated the still paper film, not to advance it but to mark the positions of the frames.) By 1888, photography, which had been the sole property of professionals, had become any person's hobby (Kodak's slogan was "You push the button, we do the rest"). Eastman's 1889 celluloid film became the natural material for further experiments in motion photography. The American discovery of celluloid film shifts the history of the movies back across the Atlantic from France.

Thomas Edison

It was in February 1889 that Edison assigned employees and laboratory space to the project of inventing motion pictures, but he did not personally invent them. He did, of course, invent the incandescent lamp (1879), without which most of the cinema would be impossible, and the phonograph (1877), which led to the soundtrack.

By 1889 George Eastman began to produce and market his version of celluloid film. The film was transparent, thin, strong, and of the same width and quality from one batch to another, thanks to Eastman's great skill at designing efficient, effective means of manufacturing. In 1892, the Eastman Dry Plate and Film Company (founded 1881) took the name by which it is still known, the Eastman Kodak Company.

W. K–L. Dickson and William Heise

Edison's director of the motion picture project was William Kennedy–Laurie Dickson. He was the primary inventor of the Edison cameras and viewers, and with his associate, William Heise, he made the first American films.

From early 1889 to late 1890, Dickson worked on the pinpoint-photo project with his first associate, Charles A. Brown. In October 1889, when Edison returned from the European tour during which he had met Marey, he saw the cylinder movies and agreed that they looked bad. After writing the fourth caveat, Edison told Dickson to invent a camera that used a strip of film. Dickson soon began experimenting with celluloid, but he also kept working on cylinders.

At first, Dickson bought sheets of celluloid film from inventor John Carbutt and cut them to size. (For several years, film was sliced and sometimes perforated by the purchaser.) Late in 1889, Dickson placed his first order with Eastman. He also bought 35mm film from other manufacturers—in 1893, for example, from the Blair Camera Company—but Eastman eventually became Edison's sole supplier.

Edison assigned William Heise to work with Dickson in October 1890. Dickson and Heise began wrapping sheets of coated celluloid around the cylinders instead of coating them directly, and they took bigger pictures. The first of these sheet-films survives in its entirety; called *Monkeyshines, no. 1*, it was shot in November 1890. Two other Monkeyshines survive only in part. After that, Dickson and Heise stopped working with cylinders but kept working with film.

Early Cameras and Films

By May 1891 Dickson and Heise had built a camera that used perforated celluloid (a single row of perfs) that was 3/4 inch wide; the film ran horizontally through the camera. Only a fragment of the first film shot with this camera—the first American movie shot on a strip of film—survives. Called *Dickson Greeting*, it starred Dickson and was shot by Heise sometime before May 20, 1891, for it was on that date that Edison showed this film to members of the Federation of Women's Clubs when they visited his lab. Looking in the eyepiece of a boxy viewer, each woman saw a man who bowed, smiled, waved his hands to demonstrate natural motion, and gracefully took off his hat. When he showed that film to reporters a few days later, Edison described his plan for "a compound machine consisting of a phonograph and a kinetograph" that could reproduce an opera in one's parlor.

Edison decided the apparatus had a commercial future and applied for his first camera and viewer patents in 1891. In mid-1892, Dickson and Heise built a camera that used film that was $1\frac{1}{2}$ inches wide and ran it vertically. By October they had perfected the vertical-feed camera, which now used film that was 1 9/16 inches wide (a bit wider than 35mm) and had two lines of sprocket holes, with four perfs to the left and right of each frame. Film moved evenly and reliably through the October 1892 version of the huge, heavy camera, the completed Kinetograph. The next major improvement to an Edison camera, portability, would come in May 1896.

In April 1893, Dickson and Heise began using this camera to make 35mm films that could be shown to the public. These first pictures were shot on film made by the Blair Camera Company. The first of these—called *Blacksmithing Scene* or *Blacksmiths*—was the 16th Edison film (a count that includes the first three sheet-films); it showed a blacksmith and two assistants passing around a bottle, then forging a piece of iron, and like most of the first commercial Edison films it was 50 feet long and lasted less than half a minute. The 17th, in which one man shod a horse while another heated iron in a forge, was *Horse Shoeing*. These were the two films shown in the vertical-feed 35mm "peephole" or eyepiece viewer, the Kinetoscope, at its first public exhibition—on May 9, 1893, at the Brooklyn Institute of Arts and Sciences. The last of the known 1893 films, made in August or September, was *The Barber Shop*, a comedy in which a man gets the fast shave the barber has advertised and customers laugh at a joke. Unlike the previous two, it was more than a picture of a job being done—on a set made to resemble a workplace; *The Barber Shop* made up a little story about a job and became the first narrative film (or the first American one, if Reynaud's unphotographed strips, shown in 1892, are considered films). The next major narrative film was made by the Lumières in 1895: *The Gardener and the Little Scamp*, discussed later.

Fig. 2-3
Fred Ott's Sneeze, *one of the earliest surviving, complete films.*

After *The Barber Shop* came *Fred Ott's Sneeze*, also known as *Edison Kinetoscopic Record of a Sneeze, January 7, 1894*. This two-second picture was the first movie ever copy-righted. According to legend, one of Edison's mechanics, Fred Ott, was a comical fellow who could sneeze on cue. Dickson decided to film him, and Heise ran the camera. During the next 12 months, Dickson and Heise made about 100 more 50-foot films for commercial use.

Worried about the poor quality of projected images, Edison decided on direct viewing. Rather than seeing an image projected for large groups, the customer would look through an eyepiece into a machine and view the single filmstrip inside it. Edison's decision was based on his integrity as an inventor as well as his greed. He saw the greater clarity of reproduction in the peephole machine, and he was sure he would make more money from the novelty if it were dis-played to one person at a time rather than to a hall full of people. Although he was wrong about the commercial potential of projection, he made up for it a few years later by marketing an Edison projector. But another decision, made at the same time, was impossible to reverse. Perhaps because he was aware of similar work in Europe, especially Marey's patented machines, Edison de-cided not to spend $150 to extend his American patent rights overseas. This "oversight" (if it was a mistake rather than a legitimate decision—no one knows) meant that outside America, the Kinetoscope could legally be cloned: broken down to discover its secret, then manufactured and sold under another name, perhaps with an improved design and perhaps with a camera to make films for it.

The Kinetoscope

When he applied for their patents in 1891, Edison called the camera the Kinetograph (from the Greek "motion writer") and the viewer the Kinetoscope ("motion viewer"). Previously he had been calling both machines the Kinetograph, to complement his phonograph. When the patents were finally granted in 1893, Edison al-lowed the Kinetoscope to be demonstrated in public—and soon after that was charging the public a nickel apiece.

By 1894, Edison was marketing his own ma-chines through a firm fronted by Norman Raff and

Fig. 2-4
The Kinetoscope mechanism.

Frank Gammon. The first Kinetoscope Parlor opened in New York City on April 14, 1894; soon many more sprang up across the country. The Kinetoscope also debuted in Europe in 1894. Ancestors of the late 20th century's video arcades, the parlors offered not only phonographs, but also rows of handsomely made, nickel-in-the-slot Kinetoscopes, beckoning the customer to look at the new marvel of mechanically recorded life.

The design of the Kinetoscope strongly influ-enced the films Dickson and Heise shot for it. Wound around spools inside the Kinetoscope, the film's ending led continuously into its beginning, exactly as the Phenakistiscopic wheels or Zoetrope strips had done. The difference was that although the film itself had its head spliced to its tail, the *movie* could begin and end with very dif-ferent images. Electronically powered, the Kinetoscope ran the loop of film only once per nickel, rather than over and over, so it was free to develop a record or narrative that moved from A to B to C . . . rather than from A to B to A. The average film lasted only 20 seconds. The most popular filmstrips were views of famous people, like Sandow or Annie Oakley (who were the movies' first stars and human spectacles, attractive and accomplished people seen up close); other spectacles and attractions interesting to watch in themselves; animal acts; bits of dancing or clowning; and even some staged historical and news events.

A Sound Film and a Studio

One of the later movies Dickson made for Edison—before resigning in April 1895 to pursue his own career—was a picture of two male employees dancing while Dickson played a violin into a funnel that gathered sound into a recording phonograph. That picture, which survives as *Dickson Experimental Sound Film* (Edison #125), was synchronized with the music the camera shows being recorded. We know that because in 1964, the long-lost recording was found: a broken wax cylinder labeled *Violin by W.K.L. Dickson with Kineto*. That 40-foot, 16-second movie, played in sync with a phonograph cylinder, was the first sound *film* (earlier experiments had synchronized a sound cylinder with a picture cylinder), and it was made sometime between September 1894 and April 1895. The cylinder was started before the camera; about two minutes in, one can hear Dickson saying, "Are the rest of you ready? Go ahead." Then Heise started the camera at 40 fps, and the rest of the sound is in sync with the picture. Dickson called his apparatus the Kineto-phonograph (from the Greek "motion-sound writer"); in 1889, he had shown an early version to Edison, apparently with a recorded greeting, but there is no surviving evidence of this. For reasons unknown, Edison decided not to pursue the Kineto-phonograph.

Despite his mistake about projection, Edison certainly left his mark on the future of film. Most influential were Edison's artificial illumination and sound recording—as well as his later cut-throat behavior as a leader of the film business—and Dickson and Heise's decision to puncture the sides of movie film with sprocket holes.

The Edison–Dickson–Heise perforations quickly became the standard throughout the world and were known as the American Perforation. By the time Dickson left Edison, the experiments of Muybridge, Reynaud, Marey, and others had been integrated into a sturdy, reliable camera; motion pictures had become a viable entertainment business even without an Edison projector; and "8-perf" celluloid (that is, with four sprocket holes on the left and right sides of each frame) approximately 35mm wide had become what most people meant by movie film. Beyond all that, Edison and Dickson also created the movie studio.

In December 1892, at Dickson's request, Edison authorized construction of a small building that was designed for the exclusive purpose of making motion pictures. Built on the grounds of the Edison Laboratory in West Orange, New Jersey, it was finished in February 1893. A few months later, Dickson and Heise made the first films ever shot in a studio, *Blacksmithing Scene* and *Horse Shoeing*.

Because the outside of the studio was protected with black tar paper (to exclude unwanted light), the room became known as the Black Maria, at that time slang for paddy wagon. Dickson mounted the camera on a trolley inside the Black Maria so that it could move closer or farther away, depending on the subject of the picture. The camera never changed position during the shooting. To light the action, the roof opened to catch the sunlight. The whole one-room studio—actually a shooting stage—could be rotated to catch the sun, so that the scene would always be sufficiently lit.

The disadvantages of the Black Maria are obvious. The room was really a small sunlit theatre with the camera as single spectator. There was even a specified stage area for the performer. Mobility was further curtailed by the bulky heaviness of the camera—the result of Edison's insistence on using electricity rather than a hand crank to run it, so that the machine remained perpetually indoors and inert.

To free the camera from its cage and the filmstrip from its viewing box were the next essential steps in the evolution of the movie machine. For these steps the history of film travels back across the Atlantic.

Projection

The problem of projecting motion pictures was surprisingly difficult to solve. After the principles of motion photography had been discovered and a camera developed to demonstrate the principles,

The first movie studio: Edison's Black Maria (1893). The first studio with glass walls and roof was built by Méliès in 1897.

Fig. 2-5

one would have thought that projecting the images would come easily. In fact, early projection attempts produced blurry images, ripped film, fires, and a great deal of noise. Edison's initial decision to shelve projection was as much a realization of practical difficulties as a business error. But it was clear to other inventors that a projected motion picture was the next step. For hundreds of years audiences had delighted in projected-light shows. Even before photography, audiences had sat in darkened rooms and watched puppets' shadows or projected images on a screen.

The Magic Lantern

The invention of the magic lantern is attributed to Father Athanasius Kircher who, in 1646, made drawings of a box that could reproduce images by means of a light passing through a lens. It is likely that the first working model was invented by Christiaan Huygens in 1659. That box was similar to today's slide projector and the ancestor of all projectors.

In the 18th century, showmen trooped across Europe giving magic lantern shows, projecting glass slides with drawings, paintings, and, much later, photographs for paying customers. From the beginning, the magic lanternists sought to make their static images move. They developed lantern slides with moving parts and moving patterns. They used multiple lanterns to give the impression of depth and sequence. The most famous of these multiple-lantern shows was the Phantasmagoria (or, in French, the Fantasmagorie), in which ghosts and spirits were made to move, appear, and disappear with the aid of moving lanterns and mirrors. All the projection equipment was behind the screen, not in front of it. The showman who, overstating his role, claimed to have invented the Phantasmagoria in 1798 was Étienne-Gaspard Robert, a Frenchman who called himself Robertson. (The original inventor is unknown, but similar shows first appeared in the 1770s.) Around 1770, a "nebulous lantern" projected images of ghosts on smoke. The stroboscopic toys of the 19th century further enlarged the lanternist's bag of motion tricks.

One of the most significant of the pre-movie projection entertainments was the Photo Play. In the late 19th century, an American author and lecturer named Alexander Black combined the magic lantern slide, photography, and narration to produce a complete play with live narrator, live actors, and pictorial slides. The goal of the Photo Play was not to reproduce motion, nor to weave moving lights, but to realize the same stories and dramas that drew audiences to the live theatre. One of Black's plays lasted a full two hours and contained as many as four slides a minute, based on the same kind of melodramatic plot and suffering characters that the early movies (which were often called "photoplays") would themselves use.

By the late 19th century, several other audience entertainments combined visual images, the play of light, and the telling of a story. The Panorama, invented by the English painter Robert Barker, was first exhibited in London in 1792 and remained popular for a century; it presented a huge painted mural that turned around the audience and that evolved from day to dusk to night to dawn to day again, while the action—the history of a great battle, for instance—moved across the variously illuminated surfaces of the picture. The Diorama, invented by Daguerre, debuted in Paris in 1822. Like the Panorama, it varied the light on and behind an immense painting—but the Diorama had more than one painting, and it was the audience that did the turning. As we have seen, Reynaud combined a Praxinoscope with a magic lantern in 1880, and in 1892 he exhibited his Théâtre Optique, which reflected as well as projected images and whose moving pictures were painted on a celluloid-like strip that had one perforation per frame.

The Loop and Other Solutions

Such predecessors clearly indicated the potential popularity of projected movie shows. The problem was to develop a machine that could project the filmstrips.

One of the first successful projections was made by a Virginia family of adventurer–inventors, the Lathams. Major Woodville Latham, former officer in the Confederate Army and former chemistry instructor, together with his two dashing sons, Gray and Otway, invented a camera and a projecting machine in 1895. The Lathams were helped significantly by their friend W. K–L. Dickson and his friend Eugène Lauste. Dickson was unhappy at Edison but had not yet left the company. In an attempt to dodge Edison's patents, Dickson and Lauste doubled the size of the film—producing a brighter, sharper image—and devised a nonintermittent way to move film through a projector. (The movement in the camera they built to go with it was intermittent.) The Lathams showed the press their projector, the Panoptikon, on April 21, 1895, and a month later they showed movies for money. By 1896 their projector was called the Eidoloscope. The most important element of the Latham projector was, as we shall see, a slack point, a curl of film called a *loop*, that Dickson and Lauste introduced into the film path (after they had put two loops in their camera, one on either side of the gate). Although the Lathams' exhibitions in New York and the urban south were very important and rewarding, the tempting life of the big cities converted the younger Lathams from scientists to playboys. The Lathams and their invention ended in the obscurity of financial disaster.

A successful projector had to do more than just enlarge the image. It had to feed and take up film on reels rather than run the film as a necessarily short, continuous circle, and it required a totally new principle of moving the film past the gate. The new principle, discovered and developed in Europe rather than America, was to move film intermittently through the projector: to stop each frame in front of the lamp. Thanks to Dickson and Heise's perforations, the Kinetograph had used intermittent movement to stop the film during exposure, but the Kinetoscope had moved the film continuously—behind a rotating, slotted shutter that allowed a glimpse of each frame as the film rolled by. Intermittent movement in the projector allowed a clear, sharp image, for the stationary frame used the available light more economically.

The intermittent movement of film past the shutter was, in principle, precisely the same as the slits in the Phenakistiscope; rather than a continuous succession of whirring images, each image was separated from the others into an individual piece of the whole. Although the intermittent movement of frames through the projection gate solved the problem of insufficient illumination, it could not cure the disease of ripping film without a tiny adjustment to take the tension off the jerkily speeding filmstrip. That adjustment was to create a small loop of excess film just before the gate, easing the tension from the feeding reel. Because the initial loop was first used—and patented—by the Lathams (although it was invented for them by Dickson and Lauste), it became known around the world as the *Latham loop*, a version of which all movie-film cameras and projectors still use, in most cases both before and after the gate. The loop also provided a key legal loophole that allowed Edison—once he bought the rights—to drag his competitors into court for almost a decade.

The Lumière Brothers

Auguste Marie Louis Nicolas Lumière, the elder, and Louis Jean Lumière, the younger and more important of the brothers, started dabbling with Edison's Kinetoscope and Kinetograph in 1894. They also were familiar with the work of Marey. Their father, an avid photographer, had founded a factory in Lyon for manufacturing photographic plates and, later, celluloid film. Interested in the new motion photography, the brothers—who were excellent mechanics as well as budding industrialists, scientifically curious and brilliantly creative—had developed their own machine within a year. They called it the Cinématographe (from the Greek "motion recorder" or "kinetic writer," but more directly from Kinetograph, which it simply translated into French). It ran perforated 35mm film at 16 fps, and it used a unique claw mechanism to engage and advance the film. Louis always made sure his brother shared full credit, but Louis was the primary inventor of the Cinématographe—the final design came to him in a dream—and he shot the early films. Unlike Edison's bulky indoor camera, the Lumière camera was portable; it could be carried to any location. The operator turned a hand crank rather than pushed an electric button. Most significantly, the same machine that shot the pictures also printed and projected them. While the machine admitted light through its lens during filming, it projected light through its lens during projection. It printed by running raw and processed film through at once; they were in contact in the gate when light exposed the blank film. (This was later called bi-pack printing.) Intermittent movement and steady alignment were guaranteed for movie photography, printing, and projection.

Early in 1895, the Lumière brothers shot their first film, *Workers Leaving the Lumière Factory*. Beginning in March of the same year, the Lumières projected this film and several others to private, specially invited audiences of scientists and friends throughout Europe. The first movie theatre opened to the paying public on December 28, 1895, in the basement room of the Grand Café in Paris. This date marks the generally accepted birthday of the movies. The choice of birthdate reflects the importance of the theatre—where the Lumière pictures continued to play for months and where money could be earned on a regular basis—but it also honors the first release to the public of what turned out to be the most comprehensive and influential solution to the problems of exposing and projecting movie film. The date they first presented their work—March 22, 1895—was as significant as December 28, the date their theatrical exhibition defined the business.

The Lumières projected several films, among them a later version of *Workers Leaving the Lumière Factory*, a Lumière baby's meal (*Le Repas de bébé*, the first home movie), a comical incident about a gardener's getting his face doused through a boy's prank (*Le Jardinier et le petit espiègle*, the first well-known narrative film, happily a comedy), and a train rushing into a railway station (*L'Arrivée d'un train en gare*). The last film (or one called *The Sea*) provoked the most reaction; the audience is said to have shrieked and ducked when it saw the train or the water moving toward them.

The Lumière discovery of 1895—especially its elegant technical simplicity and public success—established the brothers as the most influential and important men in motion pictures in the world, eclipsing the power and prestige of Edison's Kinetograph and Kinetoscope. The Lumières sent the first camera crews all over the globe, recording the most interesting scenes and cities of the earth for the delight and instruction of a public who would never be able to travel to such places on their own. Theirs were the first films to be shown in India, Japan, and other countries, inspiring film industries and filmgoing around the world.

The Lumière brothers adopted and established conventions and practices that have remained standard throughout the history of film. The Lumières stabilized film width at precisely 35mm, still the standard gauge today. (Dickson's had been about 39mm.) They also established the exposure rate of 16 fps, a functional silent speed

Fig. 2-6

The Lumières' first film:
Workers Leaving the Lumière Factory.

until the invention of sound required a faster one for better sound reproduction. The slower exposure rate used less film—thus saving money—and allowed their machine to run more quietly and dependably, whether it was shooting, projecting, or printing—for all of which it used intermittent movement. Another Lumière contribution was the fancy name of their invention—the Cinématographe. In many countries today, the movies are the cinema, and shooting is cinematography.

R. W. Paul

Almost simultaneously with the Lumières, other Europeans were making progress on their own machines. At the Berlin Wintergarten on November 1, 1895, Max and Emil Skladanowsky offered the first commercial presentation of projected films in Europe. In the years since 1892, Max had been improving his invention, a camera and double projector called the Bioskop or Bioscop ("life viewer," from the Greek for "life," *bios*, and "to see," *skopein*), working on completely independent principles.

In England in 1894, R. W. Paul, a maker of scientific instruments, was asked by two shady characters to build Kinetoscopes for them. Paul refused, but when he subsequently discovered that Edison's machine had not been patented in England, he bought a Kinetoscope, took it apart

to study it, and built a new one. With photographer Birt Acres, he invented a portable camera in March 1895. The Paul–Acres Camera was the first movie camera made in England. Paul and Acres soon dissolved their partnership, however, and invented competing projectors. Acres presented his projector, England's first, on January 14, 1896. Paul presented his, the more influential Theatrograph, less than a month later, on February 20—the very day the Lumières' films were first projected in London.

Paul's projector was the first to control intermittent movement by means of a device in the shape of a Maltese cross (a variant of which became the world standard). Converting rotary movement into intermittent movement by means of a pin that rides its curved and slotted rim, the original Maltese-cross apparatus was created for the Swiss watch, though it was adapted for the sewing machine and other devices. In cinema, it moves film through the gate: advancing it, holding it steady, then releasing it.

Paul sold cameras and projectors to others, in part so that he would have more American-perforation movies to show. His Cinematograph Camera No. 1 (built in April 1896) was the first that could be cranked in reverse, allowing the same footage to be exposed several times; thus it is of great significance that the first camera Georges Méliès used was built by R. W. Paul.

Although he left the business in 1909, R. W. Paul—an exhibitor, filmmaker, and father figure, known to his movie friends as "Daddy" Paul—was the founder of the British film industry.

The Vitascope

In America, a young real-estate salesman named Thomas Armat and his partner, C. Francis Jenkins—the more significant inventor of the two—developed a projector whose drive movement was intermittent. Called the Phantoscope, it was completed in August 1895 and commercially exhibited a month later. Jenkins and Armat had discovered—on their own, so they said—the equivalent of the Latham loop as well as the Lumière principle that *all* film movement should be intermittent. Soon, however, they dissolved their partnership. Early in 1896, Armat and Edison came to a business arrangement, one that Jenkins fruitlessly opposed. Edison would sell Armat's projector—the Phantoscope, with a few modifications made by Armat—as his own invention, enhancing the prestige and sales potential of the machine. Armat would silently receive a percentage of the sales. The Edison Company promptly announced the Wizard's latest invention, the projector it called the Vitascope ("life viewer"—from the Latin "life" and the Greek "to see," a linguistic mix that Armat disliked).

The Lathams projected a boxing film to a paying audience in May 1895—a world first as well as a national one, to be sure, but the machine's non-intermittent drive reduced its influence. The first commercial exhibition of an intermittent-drive projector in the United States was the premiere of the Phantoscope in September 1895, months before Armat sold the machine. But the debut that attracted the most notice was the first Edison projection for a paying audience, on April 23, 1896, at Koster & Bial's Music Hall on 34th Street and Broadway in New York City—the present site of Macy's. Edison was now popularly believed to have invented the American movie camera and projector. The "amazing Vitascope" was only one act in a vaudeville bill; movies soon became a typical part of vaudeville shows.

For the first Vitascope program, Edison converted several of his Kinetoscope strips for the projector; he also pirated a few of the R. W. Paul films from England. As with the first Lumière showings, the most exciting films were those with action that threatened to invade the space of the audience. During the showing of Paul's *Rough Sea at Dover* (1896, shot by Birt Acres), patrons in the front rows were said to have run screaming from their seats, afraid they were about to be drenched. Those cynics who were unimpressed were sure that the film had been shot in New Jersey.

The First Films

The movies were very much a part of the process that has produced what today seems a global culture—our ability to view and to travel to any place on earth. Newspapers (which rose to cultural prominence in the mid-18th century), the train (a development of the early 19th century), the photograph (in the mid-19th century), the automobile, airplane, telephone, radio, computer, TV—these are the media of transportation and communication that have shrunk the world and practically erased the distances between its inhabitants. At the center of this communication–transportation process are the movies. The Lumière catalogue is the ancestor of the newsreel, the global telecast, and the Internet.

The first films understandably exploited their visual wonder. A movie lasted between 15 and 90 seconds. The camera was stationed in a single spot, turned on to record the action, and turned off when the action had finished. These films were really "home movies"—unedited scenery, family activity, or posed action—that depended for their effect on the same source as today's home movies: the wonder of seeing something familiar and transitory reproduced in a permanent way. Nowhere is the home-movie quality of the first films more obvious than in the Lumières' *Le Repas de bébé* (*Feeding Baby*, or *Baby's Breakfast*, 1895), which has been duplicated uncounted times by later generations of parents with their own 8mm or video equipment.

A major difference between the first Edison films and the first Lumière films is that the Lumières have more of this home-movie quality of merely turning the camera on to record the events that happened to occur around it. The Edison films, despite their initial lack of editing and plot, were gropings toward a fictional, the-atrical film, many of them shot indoors. The Lumière films, with a nose for the news, roamed around outdoors: They were freer, less stilted, better composed, more active.

One of the most celebrated Lumière films is the comic jest *Le Jardinier et le petit espiègle* (*The Gardener and the Little Scamp*, 1895), re-made in 1896 as *Arroseur et arrosé* (*The Sprinkler Sprinkled*, or *Watering the Gardener*). This incident—staged, but shot outdoors—con-tains the seeds of what was to blossom into one of the most important contributions of the silent film: physical comedy. While a man waters a gar-den, a boy sneaks behind him and steps on the hose. The flow of water stops, the gardener looks into the nozzle to see what's wrong, and the boy steps off the hose. Water gushes into the gar-dener's face; the boy laughs. The gardener catches the boy, drags him back into camera range (since the camera did not pan to follow the action), spanks him, and—in a hurry, because the film was running out—resumes his watering.

This little movie contains many elements of a comic art that would soon mature: The gag is completely physical; despite the improbability of the result, the causes are clear and credible; the butt of the joke is the victim of circumstances of which he is unaware; despite the victim's igno-rance and innocence, the audience participates in the joke with the boy, laughing when the gar-dener gets drenched; the comic punishment (the spanking) is a blow to the ego more than to the body; the comic participants have obvious one-dimensional traits and roles so that complexity of character cannot interfere with the force of the jest; and the original situation is restored after the comic disruption. Above all, the comic incident is fictitious, even though the Lumières are correctly considered the fathers of the non-fiction film (the *actualité*, or direct, unbiased look at reality—as well as its successor, the *doc-umentary*, which is organized to express a con-viction or make a point about the factual material it presents).

For all their appearance of recording un-staged, spontaneous, real events, the Lumière films subtly incorporate the conventions of two artistic traditions that would powerfully influ-ence the movies to follow. First, the Lumière films are very carefully composed, with symmet-rical balancing of the left and right areas of the frame and interplay between the foreground and the deep space of the background (especially for those actions that move toward or away from the camera).

Second, the Lumières organized their filmed events as little stories according to the most

A "home movie": the Lumières' Feeding Baby; Mr. and Mrs. Auguste Lumière with their daughter.

Fig. 2-7

basic narrative pattern of beginning, middle, and end. The very first Lumière film, *Workers Leaving the Lumière Factory*, establishes this pattern. As the film begins, the large double doors of the factory are closed. They swing open for the camera, almost like the curtain rising in the theatre, and the workers pour out. Some move off frame to the right and some to the left (for compositional balance and to avoid hitting the camera), some manipulate "props" (a bicycle), and some are accompanied by a companion (a dog). In one of the very earliest examples, the movies showed their affinity for machines and animals as well as people. Only after the workers have all left the factory do the double doors begin to swing shut, concluding the film with the suggestion of the event's ending and the curtain's falling. However innocent and lifelike such a film might seem, it is not at all unstaged, unplanned, or unstructured.

The early Edison films lack the outdoor freshness and freedom of those produced by the Lumières. Edison's fail to understand and exploit the wonder and beauty of watching the world at work and at play, at rest and in motion. Typical is the staged heaviness of the first special-effects film, *The Execution of Mary, Queen of Scots* (August 1895, Edison #142), shot by Heise for the Kinetoscope and directed by Alfred Clark, one of Dickson's successors. In less than half a minute of film, guards lead Mary to the block, push her on it, and cut off her head.

Despite its primitive quality, several elements of this originally terrifying film are worth special attention. As in many early movies, the camera clearly thinks of itself as a spectator in the theatre. It watches from a fixed angle, a good seat. The characters move left and right in a single plane, rather than using the full depth that the movies were later to discover. Further, the film has a strong sense of entrance and exit, two more stage devices the mature film would discard. This stage mentality would continue to influence the movies for over 15 years. Beyond that, however, the film shows one clear, historically momentous realization of the potential of the film medium. After Mary (a male actor) sets her head on the block, the camera stops to allow a dummy to be substituted for Mary and be decapitated. The ability to stop the action and start it again without any apparent break is one of the advantages that the camera enjoys over the stage. Within a very few years, a French magician, Georges Méliès, would make much of this camera advantage.

But there is more going on here than using the camera to effect a magical substitution. *The Execution of Mary, Queen of Scots* is the first film to consist of more than one shot. It was made to look like one shot and had only one scene, so it would remain for others to invent the conventional multi-shot film, where the setups change. Nevertheless, the fact remains that long after the camera had been stopped and restarted—important in itself as the first special-effects shot—Clark *edited the film*. He trimmed a few frames from the end of the actor footage and a few more from the start of the dummy footage, and made a splice.

Edison developed a portable camera in 1896 and began sending cameramen outdoors, enabling the company not only to compete in the actualities market, but also to stage their made-up scenes outside the confines of the studio. It was the ability to mix dramatic studio and location footage that eventually led to the Edison Company's 1903 masterpiece, *The Great Train Robbery*, and beyond that to the conventional narrative film itself.

For their part, after seeing Edison's success with historical scenes, the Lumières staged some of their own, such as *The Death of Robespierre* and *The Death of Marat* (both 1897).

In addition to borrowing successful formulas—a practice that would continue throughout movie history—the two companies literally stole each other's films, made up duplicate prints (*dupes*) or reshot them without significant changes, and sold them as their own. In addition to competing with and stealing from each other, Edison and the Lumières faced competition and thievery from rivals who were springing up in England, America, and France. The next ten years of film history would be a period of commercial lawlessness as well as aesthetic discovery.

For Further Viewing

FILMS

THOMAS ALVA EDISON (1847–1931)
Monkeyshines, no. 1 (1890)
Blacksmithing Scene or *Blacksmiths* (1893)

The Barber Shop (1893)
Fred Ott's Sneeze (1894)
Dickson Experimental Sound Film (ca. 1894)
The Execution of Mary, Queen of Scots (1895)
May Irwin Kiss or *Kiss* or *The Kiss* (1896)
Uncle Josh at the Moving-Picture Show (1902)

LOUIS (1864–1948) AND **AUGUSTE (1862–1954) LUMIÈRE**

Workers Leaving the Lumière Factory or *Leaving the Factory* (1895)
Le Jardinier et le petit espiègle (*The Gardener and the Little Scamp*, 1895). Remade 1896 as *Arroseur et arrosé* (*The Sprinkler Sprinkled* or *Watering the Gardener*)
Le Repas de bébé (*Baby's Breakfast* or *Feeding Baby*, 1895)
Boat Leaving the Port (1895)
L'Arrivée d'un train en gare (*Arrival of a Train at the Station*, 1895)
Demolition of a Wall (1896)
Flood at Lyons (1896)

DVDs

Blacksmithing Scene is in *Treasures from American Film Archives* (see Chap. 1 list).
Lumière & Company. Fox Lorber. Lumière-like films made in 1995 by 40 directors.
*The **Lumière Brothers**' First Films.* Image Entertainment. Numerous films, 1895–97; narrated by Bertrand Tavernier.
***Dickson** Experimental Sound Film*—with the original sound and a very useful commentary—is in *More Treasures from American Film Archives* (see Chap. 3 list).

The Movies Begin: A Treasury of Early Cinema, 1894–1913. Kino Video. An absolutely essential set of 133 films, many not available elsewhere, in archival prints with very informative commentaries (unfortunately, not on a separate track) and notes. Also on VHS. Includes *Homage to Eadweard Muybridge*, 8 **Edison–Dickson–Heise** films (*The Barber Shop, Sandow, Serpentine Dances, Feeding the Doves, The Kiss*); 27 **Lumière** films (*Leaving the Factory, The Sprinkler Sprinkled, Baby's Breakfast, Arrival of a Train at the Station, Demolition of a Wall, Leaving Jerusalem by Railway*); 16 **Méliès** films (*Long Distance Wireless Photography, A Trip to the Moon*); 4 **Porter** films (*The Gay Shoe Clerk, The Great Train Robbery, The Whole Dam Family and the Dam Dog, Dream of a Rarebit Fiend*); **British** films starting with *Rough Sea at Dover*, with 5 by **Hepworth** (*How It Feels To Be Run Over, Rescued by Rover*), 7 by **Paul** (*The Countryman and the Cinematograph*), 7 by **Smith** (*Let Me Dream Again, Grandma's Reading Glass, Sick Kitten, Mary Jane's Mishap*), 5 by **Williamson** (*The Big Swallow*); also films by **Alice Guy Blaché** (*Making an American Citizen*), **Durand** (*Onésime horloger*), **Linder** (*Troubles of a Grass Widower*), **McCay** (*Winsor Mc Cay The Famous Cartoonist of the N.Y. Herald and His Moving Comics*), **Sennett** (*Bangville Police*), and **Zecca** (*The Golden Beetle*); and many other short narrative films, actualities, and documentaries.

3

Film Narrative, Commercial Expansion

The two film rulers of 1896, Lumière and Edison, would encounter crafty and powerful competitors within the year. In France, the Lumière superiority was attacked by an artist on one side and by industrialists on the other. Georges Méliès, owner–prestidigitator of the Théâtre Robert-Houdin, saw the movies as a means of inflating his bag of magical tricks. He immediately recognized the cinematic possibilities for fantasy and illusion. In 1896 he asked the Lumières to sell him a camera and projector. When the Lumières, who insisted on licensing their own franchises to shoot and show their own kinds of actualities, refused to sell a Cinématographe, he bought a camera from R. W. Paul in London. Méliès shot his first film, *A Game of Cards*, in the spring of 1896. By 1902, Méliès was supplying the world with films and the Lumières had almost ceased production.

Early Companies

About the same time as Méliès, two other Frenchmen, Charles Pathé and Léon Gaumont, also began building film empires.

In 1894, Charles Pathé and his three brothers formed Pathé Frères; the company started to make films in 1899. They began by imitating the familiar Lumière views and actualities. Soon they were copying ideas and techniques from Méliès and from the British—but the Pathé films had much better production values. Pathé's ultimate goal was not simply to produce the slickest entertainments, but to conquer all branches of the French film industry. Within a few years, although it had not been able to wipe out the

competition, Pathé embraced everything to do with motion pictures. It built cameras and projectors, manufactured raw film stock (after acquiring Eastman's European patent rights), produced films, and owned a chain of theatres in which to show them. This method of controlling everything from the top, from production to distribution, is called *vertical integration*, and the American film industry would grope hesitatingly toward this monolithic structure that the Pathés quickly realized.

Léon Gaumont's business perceptions were similar. In 1895, he founded a film empire whose activities ultimately ranged from manufacturing machine parts to collecting receipts at the theatre door. After seeing an early demonstration of the Cinématographe, he dedicated his photographic equipment company—eventually known simply as Gaumont—to developing a new projector, which the company began selling in 1896. It was also in 1896 that Léon Gaumont approved the suggestion of his secretary, Alice Guy, that she begin making films based on her own scripts. At 24, she became the world's first woman director as well as the first woman to head the production arm of a studio, and by 1897 Gaumont found himself at the head of the first working model of the *studio system*—in which projects are supervised by studio executives and created by writers, designers, cinematographers, directors, performers, and other artists employed by the studio, using studio equipment and facilities. Alice Guy made her first film, *The Cabbage Fairy* (*La Fée aux choux*), on 60mm stock in August and September of 1896— three months after Méliès shot his simple game of cards—and remade it on 35mm stock in 1899. By the time she left Gaumont, in 1907, Guy had produced more than 370 films, many of which she wrote and directed; among those that survive are *The Life of Christ* and *On the Barricades* (both 1906). She left for America with her husband, Herbert Blaché (an Englishman, also employed by Gaumont), where she founded her own film company, Solax (1910–13), and made films as Alice Guy Blaché (*Making an American Citizen*, 1912; *Matrimony's Speed Limit*, 1913; *A House Divided*, 1913). Back at Gaumont, Louis Feuillade—a scriptwriter who had been Guy's assistant—took over her job, selecting the scripts, directors, and performers for all Gaumont pictures; while directing 642 films of his own, he remained head of production until his death in 1925.

The English film between 1900 and 1906 was perhaps the most innovative in the world. R. W. Paul, who had been displaying the products of his Theatrograph for almost a year, began attracting other inventor–photographers to experiment with moving pictures. G. A. Smith, James Williamson—the key members of the "Brighton School"—and Cecil Hepworth made significant and rapid progress with the principles of editing and composition. Until the emergence of D. W. Griffith, the films of these British directors were the most visually imaginative on the screen, precisely because they had discovered the importance of systematic camerawork and editing in building their stories and driving their rhythms. They discovered the close-up, the cross-cut, the traveling or track shot, the POV shot, and the pan or panoramic shot. It is not clear whether the Brighton school or Méliès first discovered superimposition.

An American, Charles Urban, journeyed to London and founded the Warwick Trading Company. He built it into the major distributor of early British films between 1898 and 1903, then left Warwick to found the Charles Urban Trading Company. The new company, which became the largest in the prewar British film industry, also pioneered in its production of scientific films using microcinematography and in its development of the first successful color process, which Urban called Kinemacolor (1908, based largely on the discoveries of G. A. Smith).

In the United States, the two companies that would share the power with Edison—Biograph and Vitagraph—had begun making and showing films by 1897. The American Mutoscope and Biograph Company (American Biograph for short) manufactured both a peepshow machine and a projecting machine that outperformed Edison's. The primary inventive intelligence behind "Biograph" ("life recorder"), as the company was to be called, was Edison's own film pioneer, W. K–L. Dickson. Having left Edison and having found the social life of the Lathams too "fast" (according to his own legal testimony), Dickson officially became the "D" of the K.M.C.D. Syndicate late in 1895. The early film companies often took their names from the initials of their owners; Dickson's initial joined Elias Koopman's, Harry Marvin's, and Herman Casler's. They had enjoyed working together before: In 1893, they had invented a miniature camera for detectives that looked like a watch.

The K.M.C.D.'s first project was the Mutoscope, their peephole machine, whose effectiveness put the Kinetoscope out of business. Like the Kinetoscope, the Mutoscope offered a series of moving photographs to the eyes of a single viewer. Unlike the Kinetoscope's celluloid frames, however, the Mutoscope pictures were large photographs mounted on individual cards. When the viewer flipped the series of cards with a hand crank, they were held still for an instant by a hook, allowing a good steady view of each frame and producing the same appearance of movement as a motion picture. (In principle it was similar to the flip book, which had been invented in England in 1868 by John Barnes Linnett.) The large picture cards made the Mutoscope pictures clearer, more detailed, and more lifelike than the Kinetoscope's. The hand crank added to the viewer's pleasure by allowing the motion to go slower, go faster, or stop. The ultimate testimony to the Mutoscope is that of all the archaic and outdated machines of the invention era, it survives most prominently today—in penny arcades and amusement parks—delighting children with some of the same moving drawings and photographs that their great-great-grandparents flicked through so long ago.

The K.M.C.D. motion-picture apparatus also bested its Edison opponent. Working with Herman Casler, Dickson invented the Mutograph—a camera that used unperforated 70mm film—in 1894 and adapted it for projection in 1895. Dickson adopted this large-format film not merely to improve photographic clarity, but also to circumvent Edison's patents on all methods of transporting perforated and small-gauge film. Dickson, in effect, invented the motion picture several times: for Edison, for the Lathams, and for Biograph.

Edison's second major competitor was the Vitagraph Company, which had a less spectacular career than Biograph but a longer one. Vitagraph's founder and director of production was J. Stuart Blackton. Though his first films were partly distributed by Edison, Blackton soon set up his own company. Realizing the appeal of the Edison company, Blackton and his partners, William "Pop" Rock and Albert E. Smith, chose a name for their company that was as close to Edison's as the law would allow. One of Vitagraph's first films, *Burglar on the Roof* (1898), was filmed on the roof of their office building in Chelsea. For several years Manhattan rooftops doubled as film studios. Another early Vitagraph film was *Tearing Down the Spanish Flag* (1898), an attempt to capitalize on the Spanish-American War. Although the film claimed to have been shot in the heat of battle, Blackton actually staged it in the heat of Manhattan on his friendly rooftop.

Blackton was also a pioneer in the field of animation. He developed a camera that would expose only one frame with each turn of the crank, which made it possible to shoot one drawing after another. The first commercial film in which a drawn figure moved was Blackton's *Humorous Phases of Funny Faces* (1906).

It was also in 1911 that Blackton convinced cartoonist Winsor McCay—whose comics *Little Nemo in Slumberland* and *Dreams of the Rarebit Fiend* were the most inventive of their day, full of wild metamorphoses and ambitious graphics—to make animated films. Their first film, for which Blackton did the live-action sequences and McCay the animation, was *Winsor Mc Cay The Famous Cartoonist of the N.Y. Herald and His Moving Comics* (1911), familiarly known as *Little Nemo*. McCay went on to make some of the best silent American cartoons, notably the endearing *Gertie the Dinosaur* (1914).

Others all over the country were catching the movie craze, assembling machines, and capturing images. Movie projectionists trooped across the country with their filmstrips much as the magic lanternists had trooped across Europe with their slides a century earlier. One of these projectionists toured the Caribbean, drawing audiences and applause with the unauthorized adopted name of Thomas Edison, Jr.; his real name was Edwin S. Porter.

Narrative

Despite the frenzy of movie activity in the United States, the films did not change much until 1902 or 1903. New films imitated the successes of earlier ones; like TV and film producers today, the earliest film producers copied successful formulas. The motion picture, formerly the highlight of a vaudeville bill, became the "chaser," the part of the program that was so dull that it chased the old audience out so that the new one could file in. By 1900, the movies were suffering the first of a series of business crises.

The rope that pulled the movies from the abyss was the development—to the point of industry dominance—of a new kind of screen entertainment. The rope-abyss image is an apt one, for the new kind of movie, the story film, was to use this and similar heart-stopping devices to weave its spell. The movies were born into the age of theatrical producer David Belasco; they have never quite outgrown that heritage. The Belasco theatre era traded on extreme emotional effects—violent tears, violent suspense, violent laughter. The two dominant theatre genres were melodrama and farce; they were to become the two dominant film genres as well. Melodrama was a world of pathos, not of tragedy, of fears and tears, not of ideas. No action was irreversible; no matter what mistake the good-hearted character made, it would eventually be erased by his or her essential goodness. The era's farce was just as extroverted: A series of comic mistakes would arise, entangle, and explode until the denouement put all the pieces of the puzzle together. There was no reason a film could not tell the same kinds of stories.

The problem was to translate these dramatic stories into film terms. Many of the early narrative films merely pieced together the same kinds of static, unedited scenes that were shot for the first Kinetoscope—expanding the 50-foot strip to a whole reel. (A *reel* of film—up to 1,000 feet of 35mm—lasted about 15 minutes at silent speed.) A good example of one of these films is *Pullman*

Honeymoon (1898). This Edison product (shot in the large multiset studio that replaced the Black Maria) records a series of events that might take place in one of George Pullman's sleeping cars between porters and passengers, lovers, comics, bandits, and the police. The film is strikingly inert. The movie set is merely a stage set, the film uses only one setup, and the effect is ploddingly static; the passive camera never manipulates space either, never works with size and distance, never picks out any details. No action, character, or object is made to be more important than anything else.

The French fantasist, Georges Méliès, was a much better film storyteller, precisely because he exploited the very difference between time in nature and in the cinema that *Pullman Honeymoon* tried to cover up.

Georges Méliès

The Méliès films owe their superiority to the wild imagination and subtle debunking humor of their master. Méliès was by trade a magician; just as earlier magicians had adopted the magic lantern, Méliès adopted moving pictures. He saw that the camera's ability to stop and start again (*stop-motion photography*, an effect achieved in the camera rather than through cutting) brought to perfection the magician's two greatest arts—disappearance and conversion. Anything could be converted into anything else; anything could vanish.

One of Méliès's most enjoyable films, *The Conjuror* (1899), is nothing but one fast minute of disappearances and transformations. The magician (played by Méliès himself) vanishes, his female assistant vanishes, she turns into snow, he turns into her, and she turns into him. Pure cinema—as pure in its own way as its opposite, the realism of Lumière. For if Louis Lumière documented the world, Méliès transformed it. If Lumière established that the camera could create a factual record of an event, Méliès proved that the camera could create an event that never happened. Lumière set the pattern for realism; Méliès opened the door to the impossible. Méliès gave the cinema the tools of fantasy, illusion, and distortion, allowing the new art to address new subject matter—notably the interior world of psychology, imagination, and dreams; the theatrical world of magic, spectacle, and set design; and

the narrative world of genres and long, developing stories. In 1898, Méliès made the first or second narrative film to consist of more than one scene. Because it had three distinct scenes—an astromomer falls asleep in an observatory (1), the moon comes down and eats him (2), and his dream ends when he meets a moon goddess (3)—*The Moon at One Meter* had more than one shot and let the audience know it. In 1899 he made more multi-scene films, notably *Cinderella* and *The Dreyfus Affair*. Although R.W. Paul is often given credit for the first multi-shot film (*Come Along Do!* 1898), Méliès used many shots in his earliest films. Always the magician, Méliès repeatedly stopped and started the camera to make things disappear. These in-camera cuts were hidden because the rest of the shot didn't change.

It was much earlier, however, that the first true multi-shot film was made: one in which the camera positions, locations, and subjects changed. Whether it was filmmaker Birt Acres or distributor R. W. Paul who joined them, *Rough Sea at Dover* cut from a shot of water rushing forward to a shot of water rushing sideways in a different location. This crucial achievement went unnoticed.

Having more than one shot in a film amounted not just to giving the cinema the theatre's ability to proceed from one scene to another, but even more significantly, to joining two elements that had previously been considered necessarily complete, self-sufficient visual worlds. It must have seemed as rash as putting two novels together to tell one story. On the other hand, it might have seemed as familiar as moving from one "view" to another in a magic lantern show. *The Dreyfus Affair* had 10 scenes, each one—like every scene Méliès ever photographed—a single shot, usually incorporating stop-motion and multiple-exposure effects, taken by an unmoving camera. We may be tempted to take them for granted, but Méliès's joined scenes and Paul's are the beginning of *montage*, the art of editing. And the sets and costumes and props he designed, the effects he engineered—in short, the "look" he wanted each film to have—make him the first master of the cinema's other great tool, *mise-en-scène*: the art of designing and staging a scene for the camera.

Between 1896, when he founded the Star Film Company, and 1913, he made at least 500 movies, of which fewer than 140 survive. He may well have been the first filmmaker ever to use super-imposition (multiple exposure), hand-painting (a dab of red on the photographed dress, orange on the fire, blue on the curtain, every single frame), the dissolve, and time-lapse photography. The position of Méliès as the father of the special-effects film—and every cinematic use of the fantastic—is beyond challenge, and the narrative film itself belongs on the list of his credits.

Griffith said "I owe everything to him."

Méliès's most famous work is the 30-scene *A Trip to the Moon* (1902), which successfully combines his fantasy and his humor into a charming film full of trick effects. Méliès parodies the intellectual doings of academics in the opening scene as a professor (played by Méliès) earnestly demonstrates his points and makes his opponents disappear. Méliès's parody of the intelligentsia continues in his later *The Doctor's Secret* (1909) and *The Conquest of the Pole* (1912). Delightfully whimsical in *A Trip to the Moon* are the rocket ship's landing with a splat in the eye of the man in the moon, the lines of chorus girls who wave goodbye to the moonship and lend their faces to the seven stars of the Pleiades, and the jumpy gymnastics of the moon creatures who go up in puffs of smoke when the scientists whack them with their umbrellas. In *A Trip to the Moon*, stars and planets twirl about the heads of the sleeping scientists, and the explorers gesticulate with delight when they see the earth rise.

For all his cinematic inventiveness, Méliès was still very much a stage creator, shaping effects for a passive camera, delighting in the play of plaster, pulleys, and paint. The earth's rising was contrived by pulling up the earth and pulling down the rear part of the moon's crust. The ship's approaching the moon was contrived by moving the moon closer to the camera, not by moving the camera closer to the moon. Méliès clearly saw the film as parallel to a stageplay, and he referred to his technique as making "artificially arranged scenes." The structure of *A Trip to the Moon* reveals his thinking: Though the film shifts locations, each scene is presented in a single, unedited shot.

Theatricality aside, however, Méliès's camera tricks relied completely on his realization of the essential difference between natural time, which is perfectly continuous, and cinematic time, which seems continuous in projection even if it was not so in filming.

Méliès's A Trip to the Moon: *A chorus line of gunners waves after loading the spaceship.*

Fig. 3-1

Méliès had an immense influence on other directors in France and all over the world. To take only one example, Porter's *Dream of a Rarebit Fiend* (1906) is as indebted to Méliès as it is to the hallucinatory comic strip (*Dreams of the Rarebit Fiend*) by Winsor McCay.

Film theorists of a later generation—particularly Siegfried Kracauer and André Bazin—observed that Méliès and Louis Lumière established the two potential directions of the cinema in the very infancy of the art: Lumière's realism (the rendering of the world as it is) and Méliès's fantasy (the re-creation of the world—or the creation of any world—through the filmmaker's imagination). Interestingly, these theorists found Lumière's realism the more legitimate path. But the Méliès films reveal a wit behind the camera's lens still capable of delighting an audience that has seen decades of later films. The Méliès films abound in surreal surprises and audacious sight gags, clearly demonstrating that a movie can result from the human acts of creation and imagination, do far more than record physical reality, and even lie.

After 1899, Méliès's peak year as a creative artist and as a businessman was 1902. By 1914 he had lost his audience, made his last film, turned his studio into a theatre where he went back to performing magic tricks, and disappeared from the screen like a moon creature hit with an umbrella. Fourteen years later a journalist discovered him selling toys and candy at a kiosk in the Gare Montparnasse. After receiving the Legion of Honor as well as a small pension from his admirers, he died in 1938.

Cohl and Others

Blackton may have been the first to move a character composed of photographed drawings, but the first genius of the animated film was Émile Cohl. Like Méliès, he was a supremely imaginative Frenchman who delighted in the irrational surprises of a world of tricks. Cohl applied the tricks that Méliès played with the natural world—and more—to animated drawings. The surreal illogic of the Cohl cartoons is much closer in spirit to the wild transformations of characters and objects in the early Disney cartoons, in Warners' Looney Tunes, or in the trippy *Yellow Submarine* (1968) than to the realism of the later Disney cartoons. Like his American contemporary,

McCay, Cohl delighted in converting one kind of drawn figure into another: a stick that becomes a man that becomes a window, an angry woman whose head rolls off and turns into a parrot, a pool cue that becomes a straw. One of the best of Cohl's transformation films is *Un Drame chez les fantoches* (*Puppet Drama* or *A Love Affair in Toyland*, 1908), in which the constant metamorphosis of the white-on-black line drawings and figures takes farce to a whole new level—and that was only his third movie. In another witty Cohl film, *The Neo-Impressionist Painter* (1910), an artist tries to sell his very arty abstract canvasses, each of which consists only of a single color, to a buyer. As he describes each painting (explaining, for example, that the red canvas actually shows "a cardinal eating lobster with tomatoes by the banks of the Red Sea"), the events and qualities he discusses come alive in line drawings on the canvas of the tinted screen.

One of the most influential French filmmakers in the first decade of the 20th century was more famous for his performing than for his directing of the films in which he starred. Max Linder was the first internationally famous star of motion pictures. Like the American John Bunny, who died in 1915, Linder was one of the first great film clowns. *A Skater's Debut* in 1906, in which a clumsy man meets a pair of ice skates for the first time, was also the debut of a comic character, Max, who was to become the leading figure of hundreds of comic one- and two-reel films over the next decade. By 1910, Linder's yearly salary had jumped to over 1 million francs and his face had become one of the most familiar in Europe. Linder, like Chaplin, Keaton, Lloyd, and Langdon who followed him, was a tiny man, and he used his smallness and his screwy wit to contrast with the bigger opponents and baffling obstacles he frequently faced. Linder's dancing moustache and dandyish mannerisms with hat and cane also set a pattern that Chaplin would follow and expand. He enjoyed debunking the intellectual, pretentious, and arty, as in *Max Plays at Drama* (c. 1912), which parodies classical tragedy and romantic melodrama, primarily by means of delightful anachronisms.

While Pathé had Linder, Gaumont had Cohl, Feuillade, and Jean Durand. Durand made a series of comedies that influenced the French avant-garde of the 1920s; it starred Ernest

Bourbon as Onésime, a character whose bizarre logic and anarchic spirit were reflected in the aesthetics of the movies themselves. In *Onésime horloger* (1912), when Onésime decides to speed up time so that he can collect an inheritance sooner, Durand switches to fast-motion photography, and all the events of the world rush by. *Onésime horloger* announces one of the great subjects of the French cinema: the nature of time. The New Wave filmmakers of the 1960s would learn much from Durand.

Edwin S. Porter

In most of the early French, German, and American films, one shot equaled one scene; the finished film was a series of scenes—only incidentally a series of shots. Each scene progressed chronologically, following the central character

Fig. 3-2

Porter's **Life of an American Fireman:** *the interior and exterior views of the rescue process.*

Fig. 3-3

about. There were no leaps in time, no ellipses in the sequence of events. The camera was usually distant enough from the playing to include the full bodies of all the players. It remained for filmmakers to learn to move the camera, to build scenes out of several shots, and to combine scenes and individual shots into sequences, the work of filmmakers from G. A. Smith in England to D. W. Griffith in America.

One of those crucial filmmakers was Edwin S. Porter. After Porter returned from the Caribbean, he paid a visit to his "father" and asked for a job. Edison hired him as a cameraman in 1900; within a year or two, Porter had become director of production for Edison's film company.

Porter's two most important films were released in 1903. *Life of an American Fireman* (shot late in 1902) begins with the fireman-hero falling asleep, the subject of his reveries appearing in a superimposed white space near his head (a vignette, or "dream balloon"). This was the first time any American film had attempted to present a character's thoughts, converting part of the movie screen into a "mindscreen."

As the fireman dreams of a mother and child, then wakes—worried about those who may be in danger from fire at the moment—there is a cut to a close-up of a fire alarm box and a hand setting off the alarm. The scene changes again to the fire station as the men tumble out of their beds—obviously in response to the alarm, which implies causal continuity from shot to shot. The cause-and-effect relationship between these shots is as important in the history of film continuity, in the very logic of film editing, as the cut to the close-up of the faraway alarm box. Before, there had been virtually no way to move a story from one shot or location to another without having the same character in both of them. Now the cut could be seen as the agency of a force exerted by one shot on another, a cinematic act that went beyond juxtaposition into the realm of asserted meaning and effective relationship. Like the British, Porter found that editing *had* a logic, one that would be explored by filmmakers from Griffith and Eisenstein to Hitchcock and Resnais. That close-up itself was not the first ever made, by the way, but it was the first Porter had cut into an ongoing narrative.

Having leapt out of bed, the firemen slide down the pole in one shot and reach the ground floor in the next shot. Two sets, two shots, apparently one pole, and a cut in the right place, establishing the continuity of action and location from shot to shot—and all at once Porter's audience understood the relative location of both sets, the layout not just of the two-story firehouse but of the cinematically defined landscape.

Then the firemen rush out on their horse-drawn fire engines. The exterior shots of the fire brigade charging out of the station and down the street were bits of stock footage Porter found and cut into the narrative; that was an economical move, saving the cost of shooting a new scene, but it was also a demonstration that the actors and the real firemen would be read by the audience as the same firemen. At the site of the fire, Porter cut from the stock footage to a new shot—and achieved yet another breakthrough, for as the fire engines rush up, the camera *pans* (that is, it pivots horizontally or turns sideways) to follow the engines and reveal a burning house. This was not a simple matter of panning to cover a wide subject, like a city skyline; what it did was discover the logic for the pan, making a camera movement part of the film's dramatic strategy—because it followed a moving object and because it kept the burning house *out* of the frame until Porter chose to reveal it.

There are two surviving versions of the film, referred to as "the copyright version" and "the cross-cut version"; each does the rescue scene differently.

In the copyright version, the audience sees the entire rescue and the putting out of the fire first from inside the house, then repeated in its entirety from outside the house.

The cross-cut version is more comprehensible and daring. It cuts back and forth between the interior and the exterior of the house—that is, intercuts the two takes into a 13-shot sequence—turning the two place-bound setups into the coherent narration of a single temporal process. The fireman climbs up the ladder (outside), steps into the room and saves the woman (inside), climbs down the ladder with her and then up again when the woman tells him about the baby (outside), gets the baby (inside), and so on. Porter was thought to have realized and shown here that the basis of film construction was not the scene but the shot.

The question is, did he edit the film that way? Which of these copies represents the film as it was originally released? The answer, established by film historian Charles Musser, is that the copyright version corresponds to the release version. The cross-cut version was re-edited (not by Porter) in the Griffith era. The fact that to cut back and forth between the interior and exterior views would have been logical does not mean that Porter thought of it in 1902.

Porter seems to have intuited that the cinema's narrative logic creates a unity of place where none exists in nature. As later theorists have demonstrated, we make sense of a narrative, a story, not merely on the basis of the action as presented but on the interplay between those events and our mental ability to connect them into a meaningful sequence. Porter's constructing the rescue process from two distinct views demanded that we mentally connect them into a single process—one event happening at one time—and the interior and exterior shots into views of a single building.

Porter's later film of 1903, *The Great Train Robbery*, makes even greater use of this interplay between filmed event and mental connection, and probably owes to that its terrific success as the single most popular film in America before 1912. The first series of shots in the film shows the same kind of step-by-step, one-shot–one-scene

editing of the Méliès films. The outlaws enter the telegraph office and tie up the operator, board the train as it stops for water, rob the mail car and shoot the railroad man, seize the locomotive, unhook it from the rest of the train, rob all the passengers and shoot one who tries to escape, run to the locomotive and chug off, get off the locomotive and run to their horses in the woods. Up to this point in the film any director might have made it, except for the flow and careful detail of the narrative sequences and the beauty and vitality of the outdoor shots. But the cut to the last scene of this sequence reveals a new editing idea. It is clearly an elliptical jump in time (from when the outlaws started their escape in the train to when they stopped the train and got off to find and mount their horses), and it contains a pan shot that follows the outlaws through the woods.

But the next shot identifies the director's cinematic imagination more clearly. He *cuts back* to the opening scene, the telegraph office, and shows the discovery of the assaulted operator. Although the cut may be a backward leap in time and certainly deserts the spatial focus of the film (the outlaws and their getaway, which we understand to be an action that continues, unshown, while we watch the operator be revived), it makes perfect sense in the story's continuity. Making the mental connection, linking the film's events with our thinking about them, it *answers*

The Great Train Robbery: *the murder of a fleeing passenger, composed in depth along a diagonal.*

Fig. 3-4

the question the audience naturally asks: How will the outlaws be caught?

In the film's final shoot-out, three of the four bandits meet overacted, hands-in-the-air, pirouette-and-fall deaths. Apart from these stagey deaths, the film's cinematic showmanship is evident in the final shot—a close shot of a bandit firing at the audience—which was intentionally unrelated to the whole film and could, according to the Edison catalogue, be shown before or after the rest of the movie. Like 3-D of later years, the shot thrilled customers with a direct assault. For the next five years, it became almost obligatory to end a film with a close shot of its major figure.

For all the understandable later attention to the editing of this landmark film, several other sources of its power and popularity cannot be overlooked: its violence, its careful production design, its fluid mixing of scenes shot in the studio and on location, and its detailed demonstration of how to rob a train.

From Brighton to Biograph

While Porter was developing the tools of continuity and ellipsis in America, the "school of Brighton" was making similar and even more rapid progress in England. Porter and Griffith were among those who studied the early British films with care.

The group of filmmakers who clustered around the resort town of Brighton, especially George Albert Smith and James Williamson, built on the achievements of R. W. Paul, experimenting with ways to carry an action from one scene to the next, to break scenes into shots, and to use the camera and editing to define the landscape cinematically rather than theatrically. Paul had made the first multi-shot films in England (the very first, with Acres), and his ideas and techniques had been imitated around the world.

In 1900, G. A. Smith made what may well be the first mindscreen film: *Let Me Dream Again.* In the first shot, a man romances an attractive woman; the image goes out of focus, there is a cut, and the second shot comes into focus, revealing the man in bed with his unattractive wife, whom he had begun to embrace while still asleep. The rude awakening in the second shot indicates that the first shot was a dream.

Smith appears to have invented the point-of-view (POV) shot, in which a shot is defined—through editing, camera position, and narrative context—as what a particular character sees. If a *mindscreen* shows what is seen by the mind's eye, the *POV shot*—also called *subjective camera*—shows what is seen by the physical eye. In his vignetted POV shots, Smith put a mask over part of the frame—an iris, for instance, so that

The Great Train Robbery: *the freedom of the outdoors and the visual assertion of the frame's depth.*

Fig. 3-5

the image became a circle surrounded by black and appeared to be seen through a telescope (*As Seen Through the Telescope*, 1900). When Pathé imitated this technique in *Peeping Tom* (1901), the mask was in the shape of a keyhole. The most important of Smith's masked-POV-shot films, *Grandma's Reading Glass* (1900), intercuts medium shots of a boy and his grandmother—as he borrows the magnifying glass with which she has been reading the paper, and looks through it—with close-ups and extreme close-ups, shot through a circular mask, that show what he sees: the newspaper, the workings of a pocket watch, his grandmother's eye. Linking long with close views and breaking a scene into sharp, fascinating shots, it is a landmark in the history of editing.

James Williamson also achieved major advances in continuity editing. *The Big Swallow* (1901) had two shots that were edited into three—but made to look like a continuous view of one scene: (1) a man walks toward the camera—from a medium view to extreme close-up—and opens his mouth until it surrounds the lens and the screen goes black; (2) the camera and the cameraman fall into the maw—a backdrop of black velvet; (3) the black screen yields an image as the mouth pulls away and the man walks back to a medium view, chewing in triumph. All the cuts were from one completely black frame to another (similar to a technique Hitchcock would use to hide cuts in *Rope*), to create the impression that shot 2 is a view from inside the mouth seen at the end of shot 1 and at the start of shot 3. Shots 1 and 3 had, of course, originally been a single shot.

In another 1901 Williamson movie, *Stop Thief*, a thief is chased out of the frame (that is, the field of view) in shot 1, runs into and out of shot 2, and runs into shot 3, where he tries to hide and is caught. Widely imitated, *Stop Thief* set the pattern for the chase film, from *The Great Train Robbery* to Alfred Hitchcock's *The 39 Steps* (1935).

Apart from Brighton, important work was being done elsewhere in England.

Cecil Hepworth's *Rescued by Rover* (1904, remade 1905) is one of the most energetically edited pre-Griffith films, a decided advance over Porter in narrative construction and rhythm. In the first expositional shot, a nurse wheeling a baby carriage insults a gypsy woman, who vows revenge. In the second shot, a carefully blocked

sequence with a camera pan—a general strategy that would later be described as *plan-séquence*, the complicated blocking of a lengthy shot—the gypsy steals the baby as the nurse chats with a beau. Then Hepworth makes a huge elliptical jump. Rather than sticking with nurse, watching her discover the loss and run home to tell baby's parents, the film's third shot begins with nurse bursting into the family living room to tell her news. As she recites her tale, Rover, the family collie, listens intently; he jumps out the window in search of the stolen baby.

Then begins the most remarkable sequence in the film: a series of individual shots documenting Rover's finding baby, returning to tell his master, and leading master back to baby. The sequence, most of which is shown in Fig. 3-6, ends with baby, master, mistress, and Rover happily united in their living room; Hepworth has elliptically omitted the process of returning home, knowing that the sequence was not necessary and would weaken the emotional tension of the film. This is a crucial early instance of leaving out what the audience can figure out for itself, a basic lesson of filmmaking.

Hepworth's careful editing of *Rescued by Rover* produced two effects that had not been achieved before, which communicated themselves to the audience by completely cinematic means. His systematic use of the same setups (or camera positions) to mark Rover's progress both toward and away from the baby firmly implanted in the audience's mind exactly where Rover was in relation to the object of the rescue (the gypsy hovel) and the agent of the rescue (the master's house). Without any titles or explanations, the audience had a complete understanding of the rescue process. Second, this documentation produced not only awareness, but also suspense. Because the audience knew where Rover's path was leading, it could participate in the excitement of Rover's finally reaching the end of it. Hepworth increased this excitement with the dynamic fluidity of cuts from one setup to the next.

Despite the slower pace of visual and narrative discovery in the American films of the period, the years from 1903 to 1908 laid the foundation on which Griffith built.

Even before Griffith, the Biograph company had been producing the most interesting American films on the market. There were

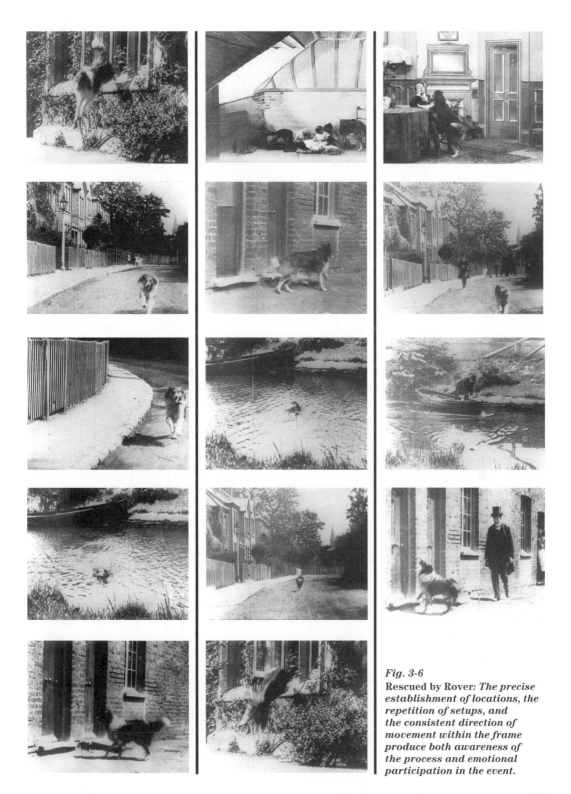

Fig. 3-6
Rescued by Rover: *The precise establishment of locations, the repetition of setups, and the consistent direction of movement within the frame produce both awareness of the process and emotional participation in the event.*

frantic seriocomic chases, clearly modeled on Zecca's, like *Personal* (1904), *The Lost Child* (1904), and *Tom, Tom, the Piper's Son* (1905). Within a half decade, two directors at this same studio would refine these chases into their purer but opposite types—D. W. Griffith's last-minute rescues and Mack Sennett's physical farces. Biograph also made films of ingenious thefts, like *The Great Jewel Mystery* (1905), in which the thief hides in a coffin on a train, and *The Silver Wedding* (1906), which concludes with a chase through the city sewers.

Also in this period at Biograph, G. W. ("Billy") Bitzer, the man who was to shoot all of Griffith's most inventive and important films, had begun to master the art of cinematography, notably in *Tom, Tom, the Piper's Son.* Biograph's *The Paymaster* (1906) may well use available light more creatively and beautifully than any other American film before 1908; especially effective are Bitzer's capturing the reflections of light on the river and his shots inside an old mill, lit entirely by oblique streams of light pouring through its window.

Although film theorists and historians may not agree on the underlying reasons, the fact is that between 1895 and 1908 movies changed from one-shot "views" to increasingly fluid sequences of visually effective shots that produced a continuous—if not necessarily complex or evocative—narrative. The next evolution of narrative would require a master with a firmer and bolder sense, not so much of the individual cinematic elements but of the means to synthesize them into clearer, more credible, and more powerful narrative wholes. It would require a filmmaker not only with a strong visual sense, inherited from observing the accomplishments of Western painting, but also with a strong feeling for the plays and novels of the previous century. D. W. Griffith proved to be that artist before the end of 1909.

Business Wars

While moviemakers gradually discovered the elements of film construction, American movie exhibitors gradually converted commercial chaos into order. In the last five years of the 19th century, the American picture business enjoyed the protection of neither law nor professional ethics. Cameramen and exhibitors blatantly ignored

machine patents, pirating and duplicating any instrument that could make them money. Even more vulnerable were the filmstrips themselves, which were not yet protected *as films* by copyright laws. The French and English films were the most vulnerable; although many Méliès films were shown legitimately in the United States, his Star Film Company made no money from the prints that had been smuggled out of France and duped. Piracy had become so pervasive that film companies hung or painted their identifying logo on the sets themselves. The Edison trademark can be clearly seen on a burning wall in *Life of an American Fireman,* and the American Biograph monogram—the letters AB in a circle:

—was even pasted on the street organ of *Her First Adventure* and is easy to spot throughout *The Lonely Villa.* A war entangled all producers and exhibitors of motion pictures.

In December 1897, Thomas Edison served his first legal writ, announcing his intention to eliminate all competitors in motion pictures. For the next 11 years, Edison would bring suit against any company that used a loop of film in either a projection machine or a camera, claiming he owned the rights to all loops because of the Armat patent on the Latham loop, the generic name for all loops in all film machines. Edison's private detectives roamed the country searching for shooting companies, serving any they discovered with legal writs or extralegal wreckage. Edison steadily coerced the smaller companies into accepting his terms, eventually bringing suit against the big ones like Biograph.

Then Thomas Armat, dissatisfied with Edison's taking full credit for the Vitascope, took to the courts. Edison had double-crossed Armat commercially by manufacturing his own projecting machine, the Projecting Kinetoscope, just two years after marketing Armat's. Armat, like Edison, brought suit against everyone who used his loop projector; he also sued Edison. Biograph, meanwhile, was preparing its own legal dossiers. With some careful bargaining it bought both the Armat patents and the Latham patents, arming itself with plenty of ammunition to use against

Edison. For ten years the motion picture companies busied themselves with suits and countersuits. Some 500 legal actions were taken, over 200 of them making their way into court.

While the company lawyers were busy at each other's legal throats, the movie companies continued making and selling an ever-increasing number of films. Originally, when movies were part of vaudeville bills or amusement arcades, the film company sold the finished picture directly to the exhibitor at between 5 and 25 cents per foot, depending on the expenses of the film, its potential popularity, whether it was hand colored, and so forth. The exhibitor then owned the film and could show it until the print wore out, then buy a new one.

But a new exhibiting development, just after the turn of the century, produced a new distributing practice. In 1902, an enterprising Los Angeles showman opened a small theatre in a store specifically for the purpose of showing motion pictures. Thomas L. Tally's Electric Theatre was the first permanent movie theatre in the United States. More and more of these store theatres sprang up until, in June 1905, a Pittsburgh store theatre opened that was a bit plusher, accompanied its showings with a piano, and charged its customers a nickel. It was the first *nickelodeon*, or "nickel theatre." Within three or four years there were over 5,000 nickelodeons in the United States. So popular were they that in 1908 it was estimated that they drew 80 million admissions every week—at a time when the entire population of the United States was about 100 million.

The permanent movie theatre forced a fundamental change in the relationship of the movie exhibitor and the movie producer. The nickelodeon required a large number of films each week; about six films of one or one-half reel (a *reel* is up to 1,000 feet of 35mm film, about 15 minutes of silent projection time) each made up a single hour-long program.

To keep the customers coming, programs had to change several times a week. The theatre owner had no use for owning a film outright; after several showings, the regular patrons would not want to see it again. Between the film producer and the film exhibitor stepped a middleman who either bought the film or leased it from the producer and then rented it to the many exhibitors. The exhibitor paid less money for a larger supply of films; the producer was certain of selling films. The three-part structure of the American film industry—the producer who makes the film, the distributor who arranges for its most effective circulation, and the exhibitor who shows it in the theatre—worked out well for all parties. That structure, with some wrinkles, survives today.

Edison tried to use this three-level structure to control the chaotic American film world. It was particularly important to work out a treaty between the two top competitors, Edison and Biograph, along with the key people and companies allied with each of them. Pressure, threats, bankruptcy, and collusion led to a combining of the nine leading film companies of 1908—Edison, Biograph, Vitagraph, Essanay, Lubin, Selig, Kalem, Méliès, and Pathé (the latter two had both begun producing in America)—along with inventor Thomas Armat and distributor George Kleine (the importer of Gaumont and Urban productions). The combine, called the Motion Picture Patents Company, was incorporated on September 9, 1908, and activated on December 18, 1908; Méliès was added to the group on July 20, 1909. The members of the combine agreed to share the legal rights to their various machine and film patents (including the Latham loop, which was part of virtually every movie camera), to buttress each other's business procedures, and to keep all other parties and machine parts out of the film business permanently. The Motion Picture Patents Company could make its rules stick because it also agreed not to sell or lease to any distributor who bought a film from any other company. The exchange (distributor) that wanted to handle Patent Company films—the best pictures then on the market—could not handle any other company's films. Further, the Patent Company made an exclusive contract (on January 1, 1909) with George Eastman's factory: Eastman would sell perforated raw film stock to the Patent Company and only to the Patent Company. The Patent Company was such a big account that Eastman could not afford to sell to interlopers. After ten years of piracy and bickering, the "War of the Patents" was over. American film production was the exclusive property of nine companies: They leased their films only to those distributors who would accept their terms and pay their fees; and these "licensed" film exchanges, soon to become amalgamated as the powerful General Film Company, rented only to exhibitors who paid a weekly licensing fee ($2) and agreed to show Patent Company pictures exclusively. From first shot to final showing, law and order had come to motion pictures.

Having temporarily ended the warfare within the industry, the Motion Picture Patents Company sought to silence the increasing moral clamor outside it. The staggering success of the nickelodeons, the huge numbers of Americans who had caught the "nickel madness," troubled the moral principles of both amateur advocates and professional politicians. As early as 1907, states and cities began to establish censorship boards to ensure the cleanliness of movie content and licensing boards to ensure the cleanliness and safety of movie theatres. These boards became commercially troublesome for an increasingly national industry. What if a film were acceptable in Pennsylvania but not in Philadelphia? To silence its critics and to ensure the commercial health of its product, the infant motion picture industry took the first step of the kind it would take throughout its history when faced with a moral attack that endangered its financial welfare: It established its own censorship board to control film content. The National Board of Censorship, founded in 1908 (in 1915 it changed its name to the more tolerant-sounding National Board of Review), did not put an end to state and local censorship actions, but it greatly reduced their inconsistencies by establishing standards and principles that most of them could (and did) accept.

Less fortunate for the Motion Picture Patents Company and its General Film Company was the rebellion of some distributors and exhibitors within the industry itself against this monopolistic control. It eliminated bargaining, it eliminated profits from duping, and it raised prices. Within months after the peace had been signed in 1908, two distributors, William Swanson of Chicago and Carl Laemmle of New York, decided to "go independent." The two pacesetters urged other film exchanges to follow their example. The Patent War had ended; the Trust War had begun.

The independent distributor faced one problem: obtaining films to distribute that were not made by a Patent Company studio. One of the obvious solutions was for a distributor to turn producer. Carl Laemmle, film exchangeman, became Carl Laemmle, film producer, and gave birth to the organization that would eventually become Universal Pictures. William Fox, distributor and theatre owner, became William Fox, producer, and the organization that would eventually become 20th Century–Fox was born. Fox also retaliated against the Patent Company by suing them and their General Film Company as an illegal trust. The lawyers were back in the movie business—to stay.

Until 1915, movie companies fought in the courts and in the streets. Jeremiah J. Kennedy, a major executive of the Patent Company, sent gangs of gentlemen to visit unlicensed studios, shooting holes in cameras and leaving bits of wreckage about for calling cards. To escape this, some companies set up shop in faraway Hollywood. Some Patent companies set up studios there, too. Despite the strong-arm tactics of the Trust, the Independents prospered. Adam Kessel and Charles Bauman, two former bookies, formed the New York Motion Picture Company, which eventually founded the film careers of Thomas Ince, Mack Sennett, and Charles Chaplin. When Edison had the gall to demote him in 1907, Porter left Edison to go independent, making films for his own Rex Company; it would one day be swallowed by Paramount. Most successful of all the Independents was Laemmle's Independent Motion Picture Company, known as IMP.

When the smoke of this second film war had cleared, by late 1915, the Motion Picture Patents Company had been busted in court as an illegal trust (it disbanded in 1917, when the case was finally settled), and the individual companies that formed the Trust were dying or dead. The Independent, for reasons that we will see, propelled the movies into their next era. Three of the Independent companies (Fox, Universal, and Paramount) survive today. The last of the original Trust companies, Vitagraph, was swallowed by Warner Bros. in 1925.

The Film d'Art

An important influence made itself felt toward the end of the decade. In 1907, a French company announced the intention of creating a serious, artistic cinema, of bringing together on film the most important playwrights, directors, actors, composers, and painters of the period. The company, which called itself the Société Film d'Art, produced its first film in 1908—*The Assassination of the Duc de Guise.* Featuring actors from the Comédie Française and incidental music by Saint-Saëns, the movie was hailed as introducing the nobility and seriousness of the stage to the film (always a bad sign). Ironically, the Film d'Art ran the movies headlong back into the theatre: theatrical staging, unedited scenes, theatrical acting. It was the first in a series of attempts to produce "canned theatre," the most successful of which was the American Film Theater of the mid-1970s with its filmed productions of plays like *The Iceman Cometh* and *A Delicate Balance.*

The first of these Films d'Art to be seen in the United States was *Queen Elizabeth* (1912), featuring Sarah Bernhardt and members of the Comédie Française, directed by Louis Mercanton. This bombastic film version of Elizabeth's love for Essex, whom she must eventually send to the block, reveals all the plodding staginess of the Film d'Art technique. Characters enter and exit from right and left; groups of soldiers, ladies in waiting, or courtiers stand immobile in the background; the actors, Bernhardt included, indulge in a grotesque series of facial grimaces, arm swingings, fist clenchings, and breast thumpings (once even raising dust from the costume). And yet these were among the most skillful stage actors in the world!

One clear lesson of the Film d'Art was that stage acting and film acting were incompatible. The stage, which puts small performers in a large hall, requires larger, more demonstrative movements.

The way to improve film acting was not just to make the actors underplay but to let cinematic technique help the actors act. A camera can move in so close to an actor's face that the blinking of an eye or the flicker of a smile can become a significant and sufficient gesture. Or the field of view can cut from the actor to the subject of the actor's thoughts or attention, thereby revealing the emotion without requiring a thump on the chest. Film acting before Griffith—and before his greatest star, Lillian Gish—not only in the Film d'Art but in Méliès and Porter as well, had been so bad precisely because the camera had not yet learned to help the actors.

Sarah Bernhardt in **Queen Elizabeth:** *stage composition and stage acting, with no help from the camera. As Elizabeth watches, Essex is led to his trial.*

Fig. 3-7

Although the Film d'Art had nothing to do with film art, the company had a lot to do with the direction that film art would take. *Queen Elizabeth* was a huge success. That success launched the career of its American distributor, Adolph Zukor, who decided to form an American Film d'Art called Famous Players in Famous Plays, which would eventually become Paramount Pictures. Its success also proved that highbrow pictures and, more important, *long* pictures could make money. It was to the advantage of the Motion Picture Patents Company to maintain that audiences would not sit through a single picture of over 15 minutes, for the whole film business they had solidified was built on programs of one-reelers. The General Film Company could not distribute any film longer than two reels; it served the nickelodeons exclusively. *Queen Elizabeth*, a 44-minute three-reeler, squashed the Trust myths. Feature films were on the way.

For Further Viewing

FILMS

GEORGES MÉLIÈS (1861–1938)
A Game of Cards (1896)
The Moon at One Meter (1898)
The Conjuror (1899)
The Dreyfus Affair (1899)
A Trip to the Moon (1902)
The Palace of the Arabian Nights (1905)
The Conquest of the Pole (1912)

EDWIN S. PORTER (1869–1941)
Life of an American Fireman (1903). Completed 1902
Uncle Tom's Cabin (1903)
The Great Train Robbery (1903)
The Whole Dam Family and the Dam Dog (1905)
Dream of a Rarebit Fiend (1906)

OTHER FILMS OF THE ERA
Rough Sea at Dover (1896, R. W. Paul and Birt Acres)
The Cabbage Fairy (1896, Alice Guy)
Tearing Down the Spanish Flag (1898, J. Stuart Blackton)
Come Along Do! (1898, R. W. Paul)
The Kiss in the Tunnel (1899, G. A. Smith)
The Big Swallow and *Stop Thief* and *Fire!* (1901, James Williamson)

The Funeral of Queen Victoria and *The Countryman and the Cinematograph* (1901, R. W. Paul)
Dream and Reality (1901, Ferdinand Zecca)
Rescued by Rover (1904, Cecil Hepworth). 1905 version co-directed by Lewis Fitzhamon
Tom, Tom, the Piper's Son and *A Kentucky Feud* (1905; Biograph)
On the Barricades (1906, Alice Guy)
The Black Hand and *The Paymaster* (1906; Biograph)
A Skater's Debut (1906, Max Linder)
Rescued from an Eagle's Nest or *The Eagle's Nest* (1908, J. Searle Dawley). Completed 1907
The Assassination of the Duc de Guise (1908, Charles Le Bargy and André Calmettes; Film d'Art)
Fantasmagorie and *Un Drame chez les fantoches* or *A Love Affair in Toyland* (1908, Émile Cohl)
Une Dame vraiment bien! (*A Truly Fine Lady!*, 1908, Louis Feuillade)
Meeting of the Motion Picture Patents Company (1909; Biograph)
Princess Nicotine (1909, J. Stuart Blackton)
The Vampire (1910; Selig)
Little Nemo (1911, Winsor McCay and J. Stuart Blackton)
Onésime horloger (1912, Jean Durand)
Queen Elizabeth (1912, Louis Mercanton; Film d'Art)
Matrimony's Speed Limit and *A House Divided* (1913, Alice Guy Blaché)
Fantômas (1913–14, Louis Feuillade)
Gertie the Dinosaur (1914, Winsor McCay)
Les Vampires (1915–16, Louis Feuillade)

DVDs

Judex (1917, **Louis Feuillade**). Flicker Alley. Complete serial, tinted.
More Treasures from American Film Archives, 1894–1931: 50 Films Image Entertainment/ National Film Preservation Foundation. Important silent and early sound films, most not available elsewhere, with expert commentaries. Includes ***Dickson*** *Experimental Sound Film* with the original sound, Dickson's *Rip Van Winkle* (shot by **Bitzer** for American Mutoscope), **Porter**'s *Life of an American Fireman*, **Griffith**'s *Country Doctor*, a **Pearl White** serial episode, several early color films,

a 1910 adaptation of *The Wizard of Oz*, a 1912 film about child labor, the original **Rin-Tin-Tin**, a film with Sioux actors, the feature *Lady Windermere's Fan* (**Lubitsch**, 1925), *Greeting by George Bernard Shaw*, two Phonofilms by **de Forest** (Eddie Cantor in 1923, President Coolidge in 1924), fieldwork footage shot in 1928 by **Zora Neale Hurston**, many actualities and documentaries, a detailed book, and of course *Gus Visser and His Singing Duck* (1925).

16 **Méliès** films, including *Long Distance Wireless Photography* and *A Trip to the Moon;* most of the early **British** films discussed in the text, including *Rough Sea at Dover, Let Me Dream Again, Grandma's Reading Glass, The Big Swallow, Sick Kitten, Desperate Poaching Affray, An Interesting Story,* and *Rescued by Rover;* 4 **Porter** films, including *The Great Train Robbery* and *Dream of a Rarebit Fiend;* **McCay**'s *Little Nemo;* and **Durand**'s *Onésime horloger* are in *The Movies Begin* (see Chap. 2 list).

Rescued from an Eagle's Nest (1908, **J. Searle Dawley**) is in *Griffith Masterworks* (see Chap. 4 list).

Les Vampires (1915–16, **Louis Feuillade**). Image Entertainment. Complete serial, tinted.

4

Griffith

David Wark Griffith never intended to make movies. The accidental path that eventually led him to films stretched from his rural Kentucky home to selling books, picking hops in California, reporting for a Louisville newspaper, and finally writing and acting for the legitimate stage. The young Griffith had decided he was a playwright. One of his plays, *The Fool and the Girl*, even played two tepid weeks in Washington and Baltimore. Like the movies themselves, Griffith's dramatic apprenticeship was rooted in the world of Belasco. It would be Griffith who would most successfully translate the Belasco effects for the screen—melodrama, suspense, pathos, purity. Griffith began with the same dramatic structures, the same sentimental characters, and the same moral assumptions of the Belasco stage, and he never deserted them, even when his audiences did.

Griffith's playwriting ultimately brought him to the movies. Like all stage actors, Griffith regarded the moving pictures as an artistic slum. But he had written an adaptation of *Tosca*, which he failed to peddle as a stageplay. He then decided to try to sell it to the pictures. In 1907, over 30 and out of work, he took his manuscript up to the new Edison studios in the Bronx. The film companies had deserted city rooftops for more spacious and secretive quarters in the Bronx and Brooklyn. Edwin S. Porter, by then head of production at Edison, thought Griffith's *Tosca*, with its many scenes and lengthy plot, too heady for the movies (this was five years before the Film d'Art's *Queen Elizabeth*). Instead of buying Griffith's script, Porter offered him an acting job

at $5 a day. Griffith, recently married to Linda Arvidson, needed the money and took the job. But he insisted on playing under the assumed name of Lawrence Griffith, thinking he would save his real name for the day when one of his plays opened on Broadway. Things would work out differently.

Apprenticeship

In Griffith's first role for Porter he played a lumberjack (a very thin lumberjack!) and father in *The Eagle's Nest* (1907, released 1908; also known as *Rescued from an Eagle's Nest*), produced by Porter and directed by J. Searle Dawley. When his wife informs him that baby has been swooped away by a huge bird, Griffith climbs down a cliff to the bird's mountain lair, fights the puppet eagle to the death, and brings back baby. This melodramatic film was not without significance for Griffith's later career. First, Porter provided Griffith's introduction to film technique. Porter was the American director before Griffith who best understood the power and logic of editing in building a story. Second, the melodramatic plot was to find its reincarnations in Griffith's movies throughout his career, from the early short films to the epics and later features. Whether Griffith acquired the taste for the last-minute rescue from the Belasco stage or the Porter screen, by the time he started to direct his own films, that taste had become his own.

By 1908, the devouring nickelodeon's demand for films was so great that Biograph needed to step up production to several reels per week and

Fig. 4-1

D. W. Griffith: a portrait of the artist as a film director.

therefore needed another director. Griffith was offered the job. He was not sure he wanted it. He was content with the daily $5 wage; failure as a director might cost him the steady income from acting. Biograph promised him that he could go back to acting if he failed as a director. The sincerity of the promise was never tested. Griffith directed his first film, *The Adventures of Dollie*, in June 1908.

Biograph: The One-Reelers

The Adventures of Dollie displays Griffith's thorough knowledge of the successful formulas of the past. Dollie's one-reel adventures are terribly familiar. An insulted gypsy takes vengeance on a family by kidnapping baby Dollie and hiding her in a water cask. As the gypsies ride away, the cask falls off the wagon and into a stream, where it moves steadily toward the vicious rapids. Dollie eventually escapes a watery death when her cries attract the attention of a nearby boy who is fishing; the picture ends with the inevitable happy family reunion.

Although Griffith's film sticks to extremely conventional narrative material, he handles those conventions with a narrative fluidity and symmetry uncommon in films of the period. Griffith establishes the agent of Dollie's rescue, the boy fisherman, in the first shot. He walks along the river bank and away from the camera at the same time that Dollie and her family walk toward the camera. This narrative linking in the film's opening shot makes the action's resolution more probable and logical. The final sequence with the floating cask also flows more continuously and rhythmically (using the consistent direction of motion across the frame and cutting on movement) than is usual for films of 1908. And the film's most interestingly planned shot is a long shot that shows a farmer cutting grain as the gypsy runs through the field with Dollie in his grasp. Because the farmer is occupied with his task and submerged in the tall stalks, he does not see the mischief that passes so near him. The shot gives the convincing feeling that these episodes of movie fiction have been plucked out of the random and continuous flow of life itself.

It was this paradox of film narrative—that films look so spontaneously real and natural and yet are so fictional and patterned—that Griffith would develop and master in the five years that followed. His general method would be to push each of these paradoxical qualities to its extreme—to make filmed life look as natural and random as real life and yet to make filmed stories as carefully structured and patterned as any well-constructed fictions.

Griffith, shouldering the production demand of directing several one-reel pictures every week, had been given an ideal laboratory for experimentation and development. Between 1908 and 1913, clearly Griffith's apprenticeship period, he directed over 450 movies for Biograph; this gave him the opportunity to test a new idea immediately. He could test each method day by day in front of and with the camera, rejecting what failed, refining what worked.

Griffith realized that the content of the shot should determine the camera's relationship to it. The accepted shot in the film world of 1908 was what is called the *full shot* or far shot today. This shot necessarily included the full figures of all the characters in the scene, plus enough of the scenery to show the audience exactly where the characters were and how carefully the set had been painted.

In his apprentice years, Griffith developed a full series of different shooting perspectives. Beginning with the standard full shot, he moved the camera closer to the players to produce the *medium shot*—including, say, two actors from the knees up (a shot later christened the

"American shot"). And then the camera moved still closer to produce the *close shot*, including only the head and shoulders of a single actor; the *close-up*, revealing only a hand or face; and the *extreme close-up*, showing perhaps just an eye. (Most of the "close-ups" in Porter's films were actually close shots.) Griffith also saw that he could move the camera in the other direction, farther away from the actors. He produced the *long shot*—a much more distant view of one or more players—which emphasized more of the scenic environment than the far shot. And then he moved the camera still farther from the players, producing the *extreme long shot* that would emphasize huge vistas and panoramas.

Griffith was not, of course, the first to use these shots, but he made them standard and combined them into sequential wholes. One could cut freely between long and medium, close and medium, close and long to produce a whole scene. Griffith broke the theatrical scene into the cinematic unit of the shot.

Griffith discovered, at the same time, the power of two moving-camera shots: the pan and the traveling shot. Again, both of these shots had been used before. But Griffith realized that these special shots were just two more potential units in creating the whole. The panoramic shot, or *pan*, with its horizontal sweeps from left to right or right to left, not only is functional for following a moving action, but also transfers its feeling of sweeping movement to the viewer. The *traveling shot* (also called a *track shot* or *tracking shot* because the camera's platform often rolled along, railroad style, on tracks) produces an even more magnified sensation of physical movement: the perfect tool for communicating the emotions of people riding rushing trains or walking alongside a river.

Griffith also realized that, just as the camera was not the servant of space, neither was the final editing of a film the servant of space or time. Most of the early films had followed a focal character slavishly from place to place, unable to leap to other places and other people regardless of the needs of the narrative. Griffith discovered that two places vastly separate in space or time could be brought together in the audience's mind. This back-and-forth editing technique, called the *cross-cut* (or parallel cut, switchback, or several other synonyms), which produced closeness out of distance, became a standard Griffith tool, fulfilling several primary functions. The cut could be a leap in space (from the victims of an attack to their potential rescuers), a leap in time (from a crisis to the earlier scene that caused it, or from modern to ancient customs), or a leap controlled by a character's mind (from the face of a sad woman to a shot of her husband lying dead on the battlefield). A fourth kind of Griffith cross-cut served a more symbolic and intellectual purpose. In *A Corner in Wheat* (1909, released as *Corner in Wheat*), Griffith cross-cut between a lavish and lively banquet for the rich and a frozen portrait of the poor, waiting in line for a meager loaf of

Fig. 4-2

Fig. 4-3

A Corner in Wheat: *Griffith's cross-cut from the banquet table of the rich to the bread line of the poor.*

bread. The cross-cut clearly and effectively underlined the injustice of these simultaneous social conditions. When the Biograph management wondered whether audiences would be able to understand these shifts, Griffith's answer revealed both his insight and his influences: "Doesn't Dickens write that way?"

Griffith had learned, by trial and experience, what the earliest film theorist, Hugo Münsterberg, discovered by watching movies at almost the same time: Films were capable of mirroring not only physical activities, but also mental processes. Films could re-create the activities of the mind: the focusing of attention on one object or another (by means of a close-up), the recalling of memories or projecting of imaginings (by means of a flashback, flash forward, or mindscreen), the division of interest (by means of the cross-cut). Griffith's "discovery" was far more than a mere technique or assortment of devices; it was the way to make film narrative, storytelling with moving images, *consistently coherent.*

While Griffith's narratives learned to leap from space to space, they also began to deepen the texture of life within each of those spaces. Not content with the two-dimensional settings that dominated the interior scenes of most films of the era (so flat that many painted their furniture and props onto the backdrop), Griffith insisted on making his interior scenes appear as three dimensional as his outdoor ones. He thrust desks and tables into the shooting area, perpendicular to the walls of the set and to the frame line, rather than lining them up parallel to the walls, as they might be on the stage. He pushed pieces of furniture out at oblique angles to the set, the camera, and each other, and he shoved chairs, tables, and vases close to the camera itself, further increasing the sense of depth in the cramped quarters where the early Biograph films were shot. By mid-1909, he was also taking his cast and crew out of New York City to shoot on location, first in upstate New York and later (1910) in California.

Griffith's innovations went beyond the camera and the editing table. Almost simultaneous with Griffith's debut in films came the debut of the electric light in the studios. Artificial lighting gradually replaced the sun's harsh and inconstant performances. When film companies left Manhattan rooftops for the Bronx and New Jersey, they also

left behind the sun and the muslin sheets that diffused its glare. But the first directors merely used the new arc lights as though they were the sun—to produce bright, even, untuned light with no regard to the tonal and narrative requirements of the scene. Does the scene take place indoors or out? During night or day? Should it feel harsh or gentle, cool or warm? Griffith—and G. W. ("Billy") Bitzer, the cameraman who experimented along with Griffith and taught him the ropes much as cinematographer Gregg Toland later taught director Orson Welles—realized the importance of such questions and the ways lighting could be effective in answering them. But neither the flat, even sunlight nor all the arcs on full blast could duplicate the texture and atmosphere of indoor life, let alone create a mood or explore a character. And so—though they were not the first to do this (Porter did it in *The Seven Ages,* 1905, and Griffith had seen a similar effect while acting in Biograph's 1908 *The Music Master*)—Griffith and Bitzer lit *The Dunkard's Reformation* with a dim, flickering, low-angle light that convincingly imitated a fire's glow, giving the scene the look of real life and creating a hearth that was tonally and metaphorically related to the film's plot: the drunkard's returning from the theatre to the warmth and comfort of home and family.

Griffith was as innovative with people as with machines. First, he demanded underacting: no more huge gestures and demonstrative poses. Because he had developed the expressive power of the camera and editing, he had the tools to allow a player to underact and still be understood. Second, he showed a much greater attention to selecting actors to play the roles, realizing that in a photographic medium, which depicts only visible surfaces, the actor's physical type was as crucial as acting style in the conveying of internal emotional and mental states.

Third, he developed a lexicon of gesture and movement, stylized enough to be clear and evocative, yet subtle enough to seem real and unaffected. As early as *A Corner in Wheat,* there is a basic stylistic difference in the movement and gesture of the poor and rich folks. While the poor farm people and customers at the bakery move slowly, with open, fluid hand gestures, the rich Wheat King and his cronies move briskly, with sharp, pointed, grasping hand gestures. This contrast between their styles of movement culminates in the awesome *tableau vivant* (resembling what today would be called a freeze-frame), when the movement of the poor becomes so slow that it stops altogether.

Fourth, Griffith shocked his employers with what they considered an obvious waste of time—rehearsals. The actors rehearsed the scenes before Griffith shot them. In an era when directors could scream their instructions during the shooting, Griffith's method seemed extravagant and unnecessary. It was crucial.

Finally, Griffith realized the applicability of one of the key artistic principles of the stage: A whole production requires an ensemble, not a collection of individual players. Griffith began building the

Fig. 4-4

Fig. 4-5

The Lonely Villa: *Griffith's cross-cutting—the husband gallops to the rescue . . . of the family under attack at home.*

Biograph stock company as a cohesive group of talented, attuned performers. His success is reflected in the number of important actors that Griffith's stock company produced, either for his own films or for the films of others. Mary Pickford, Lionel Barrymore, Lillian and Dorothy Gish, Mae Marsh, Blanche Sweet, Harry Carey, Henry B. Walthall, Robert Harron, and Donald Crisp all had worked for Griffith by 1913.

A close look at three Griffith one-reelers reveals his growing mastery of the film form. In *The Lonely Villa* (1909; onscreen title, *Lonely Villa*), his skill in cutting adds excitement to a melodrama about a mother and children who are attacked in their home by intruders. Early in the film, the fluid and rhythmic cutting adds pace to an exposition that establishes the husband's leaving home while the assailants hide outside in the bushes. The opening sequence is full of match cuts—shots from different angles and distances that have been assembled to give the impression of fluid, continuous movement—as the husband walks through the house and out the front door. These match cuts also establish—as systematically as the repeated locations in *Rescued by Rover*—the various domains of the house: the hallways and rooms that will play significant roles in the film's climactic sequence as the family retreats room by room from the intruders (the steady retreat into

the protective depths of the home would become a consistent Griffith motif).

That climactic sequence reveals the power of Griffith's cross-cutting. As the intruders begin their assault, Griffith cuts to the husband, many miles distant and ignorant of the danger to his family. Luckily, his car breaks down and he calls home. The wife retreats to the telephone to tell her husband what's going on, and Griffith cuts to the husband as he listens to the phone and reacts; like the telephone line, the cut firmly links the two distant locations in the narrative flow despite the separation in space. Griffith then cuts back and forth between the besieged wife's trying to hold out against the attackers and the husband's getting help and rushing home to the rescue. Griffith tightens the screws by cutting each shot shorter and shorter, increasing the excitement and suspense until the husband arrives home just in time.

The Lonedale Operator (1911) drives to its climax both more forcefully and more personally. The whole film shows a surer and more fluid technique than *The Lonely Villa*. The exposition, establishing the relationship of the woman (Blanche Sweet) and her beau, and that he is a railroad engineer and she a telegraph operator, is much clearer and more detailed than the exposition in the earlier film. The acting is much

The Lonedale Operator: *The close-up reveals that the "gun" was a wrench.*

Fig. 4-6

quieter, much more natural; the scene in which he courts her is credible and touching. Griffith captures the woman's spirit and her joy as she unexpectedly leaps on one of the railroad tracks and walks, tightrope-style, on the track while she talks to her beau. As soon as she and the beau separate, he to his engine and she to her office in the depot, Griffith builds toward the climax with a series of fluid match cuts showing her entering the office—door by door, as in *Villa*—and setting to work. In her office is a strongbox full of money; two tramps see it.

Once the attack begins on her and her office, Griffith begins his relentless and rhythmic cross-cutting, which alternates among three clearly established locales: the attackers on the outside trying to get further and further into the depot, the operator in the inner office trying to protect herself from the assault, and the speeding train on its way to answer the distress signal that the operator intelligently wired to the next station. Griffith cuts with increasing rapidity from outside to inside to train, outside, inside, train, until the beau arrives just in time to find his sweetheart holding the culprits at bay with a "pistol" that is revealed in close-up to be a wrench—a definitive use of the close-up to show something important that cannot be seen or fully appreciated from a distance. The woman has brains as well as energy. She also has a sense of humor; she cheerfully acknowledges

the comic, mock-gallant bow that the two vanquished but admiring tramps extend to her at the film's conclusion. Griffith was beginning to make his women not merely frail victims but forceful, clever, and able human beings who could take care of themselves when they had to.

Five years of one-reel films show Griffith laying the foundation not only for his technical achievements but also for the themes and motifs that would dominate his later films. He had made films about periods of American history (such as *1776 or The Hessian Renegades*, 1909), films about the contemporary social problems of poverty and of vice (such as *What Shall We Do With Our Old?*, 1910, released 1911, and *The Musketeers of Pig Alley*, 1912, the first gangster picture), films that were stylistically careful adaptations of literary classics (Shakespeare, Poe) and contemporary fiction (Frank Norris, Helen Hunt Jackson). Griffith had also begun making moral–religious allegories (*The Devil*, 1908; *The Way of the World*, 1910). Griffith particularly excelled at the close and affectionate study of American rural life—either the gently comic, tender study of rural customs and courtship, as in *A Country Cupid* (1911), or the compassionate view of the difficulty of rural living and survival, as in *A Corner in Wheat*. The latter film also provided a very early conscious reference to a specific painting—Jean-François

Fig. 4-7

A Corner in Wheat: *an image of the natural unity of humans, animals, and field, based on Millet's painting* **The Sowers.** *The rest of the movie is based on Frank Norris's story "A Deal in Wheat."*

Millet's *The Sowers*. Griffith was obviously bringing his entire 19th-century background into the movies—the paintings he had seen, the novels he had read, the plays he had performed, the Bible his mother and father had taught him.

Now that Griffith had discovered how to say things with cinema, he found he had things he wanted to say.

Two Reels and Up

Although no member of the audience yet knew Griffith's name (no Patent Company director or actor received screen credit until after 1912), they all knew that Biograph pictures were the best on the market. So did Griffith. By 1913, he wanted to break loose from the one-reel limit on his thoughts. He had earlier made two-reel films, but the General Film Company insisted on releasing them in two parts, one reel at a time. By popular demand, however, Griffith's 1911 two-reeler, *Enoch Arden*, based on the poem by Tennyson, had been shown as a single film shortly after it had been released as two.

Griffith's longer films used the earlier innovations to assimilate and communicate more complex material. And that material was, as he saw it, simply the Truth. He wanted the images on the screen to illuminate his personal vision of good and evil. Griffith was not the cinema's first technician, nor even its first *auteur* (that would be Méliès); he was its first moralist, poet, and master storyteller. A cliché in the criticism of Griffith is that his moral system is essentially that of the Victorian patriarchal sentimentalist. The positive values are social order, peace, intellectual freedom, loyalty, the home and family, womanhood/motherhood, children who are happy and safe, and marital fidelity. The negative values are, correspondingly, social change, war, censorship, treachery, the high life, sexual license, and the broken or abusive home. But these specific values are really consequences of Griffith's central vision rather than the vision itself.

The poles of Griffith's moral world are gentleness and violence. From gentleness come all the virtues of peace and the home, usually depicted by images of women. The figures of oppression and violence are almost always male, though his men can also be dedicated, honorable, valiant, and even gentle.

Griffith's difficulty was integrating his vision into his melodramatic, plotty films. All too often Griffith fell back on two artificial devices that seemed superimposed on the films rather than integral to them. One of them was literally superimposed. He often thrust allegorical meanings on the films by superimposing angels and visions up in the heavens to comment on the earthly action. His allegory also extended to giving characters allegorical names—the Dear One, the Friendless One, Evil Eye. A second Griffith device was to soup up the film's meaning with purple, rhetorical titles that told the audience what moral conclusions it should draw from the actions it was about to witness. The titles constantly tell us that war's slaughter is *bitter* and *useless* (italics Griffith's), that women turn to social reform when they can no longer turn a man's fancy, that "the loom of fate weaves death." Griffith's titles (also called *intertitles* or *title cards*) were far more florid and didactic than the titles in other films of the era. Some of them even had footnotes. Griffith's last-minute rescues were so exciting partly because they required few or no titles.

By late 1913, Griffith's innovativeness and the growing length and cost of his films had irked Biograph into kicking him upstairs, making him director of studio production and relieving him of the opportunity to direct movies personally. But Griffith wanted to make feature films—and the irony was, so did Biograph, which had noted the commercial success of *Queen Elizabeth*; they just didn't want to make long Griffith films.

Thoroughly angry, Griffith left Biograph for an independent company, Mutual/Reliance– Majestic, signing a contract with producer Harry Aitken that gave him the freedom to make one picture of his own each year in addition to several program pictures of the company's choosing. It was a new beginning for Griffith; it was the end for Biograph, which folded in 1915. When Griffith left for Mutual and California, he took Bitzer with him as well as nearly the entire Griffith stock company of actors. He also took out a full-page ad in the *New York Dramatic Mirror* in which he identified himself as the director of "all great Biograph successes," of which he listed 151 (out of the 455 movies he made at Biograph

Fig. 4-8
Griffith's framing in The Musketeers of Pig Alley. *The tension of the oversized close-up* **(Elmer Booth and Harry Carey).**

from 1908 to 1913). Griffith plainly asserted the right of the director to be called a film's creator, and his personal right to be credited with "revolutionizing Motion Picture drama and founding the modern technique of the art."

The Birth of a Nation

For his own independent project for 1914, Griffith chose a novel by Thomas Dixon, *The Clansman*. The book appealed to Griffith for several reasons. It was a vast story with a strong hero, covering the final years in the graceful life of the old South before the Civil War; the turbulent, violent years of war; and the painful, political years of Reconstruction, during which the Ku Klux Klan arose to defend the rights of the whites. (The prewar and war scenes were Griffith's, not Dixon's.) In addition to this novel, Griffith also used material from Dixon's stage version of *The Clansman* and from another Dixon novel, *The Leopard's Spots*, all of which were extremely racist. Griffith, a Southerner whose father served in the

Confederate Army, was attracted by Dixon's slant. Dixon, also a Southerner, saw the Reconstruction era as a period of chaos in which the "civilized" white South, presented as the gallant underdog, struggled but survived. It was this film, with its inflammatory messages and dangerous social and political implications, that Griffith set out to make. Shooting began on the Fourth of July, 1914.

The project was vast: It took six weeks to rehearse and nine weeks to shoot, an incredible amount of time in an era when most films were cranked out in a week. It required thousands of people and animals and many huge and detailed indoor sets. Its cost, $110,000, was the most ever invested in a motion picture. At the film's official premiere in Clune's Auditorium in Los Angeles on February 8, 1915, audiences finally saw how huge Griffith's plan and project were. The 13-reel film was still called *The Clansman* at that opening. When the author of the novel finally saw the film, however, Dixon told Griffith, in his enthusiasm, that the original title was too tame. Griffith should call his film *The Birth of a Nation*.

Dixon's point was that the nation was truly born only when the whites of the North and South united "in defense of their Aryan birthright." For Griffith, however, the "real nation" began when North and South united to heal the wounds of the Civil War and Reconstruction; in a 1915 interview he said that "there can exist no union without sympathy and oneness of sentiment." While he did not acknowledge the racism that was part of that shared sentiment, he credited the KKK with beginning "the birth." Dixon's and Griffith's interpretations of the title were not all that different.

The retitled version opened in New York on March 3, 1915, still 13 reels long. But in response to social protests, Griffith deleted about nine minutes from the film (footage that has never been recovered), leaving it just over 12 reels long. The most complete surviving version lasts three hours.

The Birth of a Nation is as much a document of American social history as of film history. Though President Wilson, a former historian at Princeton, described the film as "like history written with lightning," its action openly praises the Ku Klux Klan. Wilson may well have offered the simile to help his old school chum, Dixon. The film, which contributed significantly to the resurgence of the Klan in the 20th century, is a very difficult morsel for today's liberal or social

activist to swallow. It was just as difficult for the liberals of 1915. The NAACP, the president of Harvard, social activist Jane Addams, and liberal politicians all damned the work for its bigoted, racist portrayal of the Negro. The film was suppressed in some cities for fear of race riots; politicians spoke for or against it according to their dependence on the black vote. At a revival of the film some ten years after its original opening, mobs poured into Chicago to see it as well as to attend a Ku Klux Klan convention. With all of the controversy over the film, it might be wise to look at Griffith's handling of the black man and woman before moving on to other aspects of the picture.

Two of the three villains—Lynch (the false reformer) and Sarah (Stoneman's mistress)—are not pure Negroes but mulattoes. Both possess qualities that Griffith had already damned in whites—hypocrisy, selfishness, social reforming, and sexual license. That they were mulattoes may indicate that Griffith's main target was not the blacks but miscegenation—an objective of the third villain, a black soldier named Gus, when he forces his attentions on a Southern white girl. (His marriage proposal—a rape in the novel—causes Flora, the "little pet sister," to throw herself off a cliff to her death; in the novel, and reportedly in the censored footage, Gus is

The Birth of a Nation:
Griffith's "historical facsimile" of Ford's Theater.

Fig. 4-9

castrated by the KKK when they kill him.) The miscegenation theme flows through the movie like a poisonous river—in the scenes of the lecherous black legislature, in signs at the black-dominated polling place, in Lynch's attraction to Elsie (Lillian Gish) and Gus's to Flora (Mae Marsh), and in the outrages that drive the hero, Ben Cameron (Henry B. Walthall), to dream up the KKK. The mixing of bloods is one of the principal sources of "evil" in this picture. Griffith's stance against miscegenation stems from an assumption about blacks and whites that is perhaps more central to the film's offensiveness. For Griffith, whites are whites and blacks blacks; the white race is naturally superior; each race has "its own place." If Griffith's view seems outrageous—well, it is. Not every masterpiece is "politically correct," and part of dealing with *The Birth of a Nation* lies in examining, rather than explaining away, how offensive it is. Although Griffith recognized that slavery was the root of America's racial problems, his solution (proposed in part of the censored footage, an ending originally meant to balance the all-white harmony of the surviving conclusion) was to send the blacks back to Africa.

There are "good" blacks and "bad" blacks in Griffith's film. The good ones are the "faithful souls" who "know their place" and stay with their white family after the war. Perhaps Griffith's most offensive scene is the one in which the empty state legislature suddenly (with the aid of a dissolve) springs to life, full of black lawmakers with bare feet on desks, swilling booze and eating fried chicken while they eye the white women in the gallery. But Griffith's treatment of these blacks is not an isolated expression of racial prejudice; it is a part of his lifelong distrust of the "evils" of social change and disruption. (To be consistent, of course, he should also have denounced the KKK as a disruptive social movement—but he evidently saw its actions as restorative.)

The key to *The Birth of a Nation* is that it is both strikingly complex and tightly whole. It is a film of brilliant parts carefully tied together by the driving line of the film's narrative. Its hugeness of conception, its acting, its sets, its cinematic devices had not been equaled by any film before it and would not be surpassed by many that followed it. Yet surprisingly, for such an obviously big picture, it is also a highly personal and intimate one. Its small moments are as impressive as its big ones. Though Griffith summarizes an entire historical era in the evolution of the nation in general and the South in particular, his summary adopts an intimate, personal focus: two families, one from the North (the Stonemans), one from the South (the Camerons), who, despite the years of death and suffering, survive the Civil War and Reconstruction. The eventual marriage between the two white families becomes a symbol or emblem for Griffith's view of the united nation. Love, courage, racism, sincerity, and natural affection triumph over progressive movements and selfish reformers. The close observation of people and their most intimate feelings, the techniques of which Griffith had been developing for five years, propels the film, not its huge battle scenes, its huge dances and political meetings, or its detailed "historical facsimiles" of Ford's Theater and the Appomattox courthouse. The big scenes serve as the violent social realities with which the central characters must contend.

Even in the mammoth battle sequences Griffith never deserts his human focus. His rhythmic and energetic editing constantly alternates between distant, extreme long shots of the battles and close concentration on the individual men who are fighting. Griffith takes the time for such touches as his cut from the living, fighting soldiers to a shot of the motionless dead ones who have found "War's peace," or his cuts from the valiant effort on the Union side to shots of a similar effort on the Confederate, including Ben Cameron's heroic charge of the Union lines, ramming the Southern flag down the barrel of a Union cannon. Griffith increases the power, the violence, the energy of these battle sequences by cutting on contrary movement across the frame, by cutting in rhythm with the action, and by cutting to different distances and angles that mirror the points of view of the different participants. But in the midst of such violence, Griffith takes time for quiet moments: the moment when the two boys, one Cameron and one Stoneman, die in each other's arms; the moment in which a mother on a hilltop views the invading army in the valley.

This shot, one of the most celebrated in the film, shows Griffith's control of the masking or irising effect, another of the techniques he and Bitzer had explored at Biograph. The *iris shot* masks a certain percentage of the frame, concentrating the viewer's attention completely on a circle of light within the blackened screen rectangle. In *The Birth of a Nation*'s most famous iris shot, Griffith begins tightly on the weeping mother's face and then irises out to reveal the awesome army below her, the cause of her sorrow. Of the many masking shots that reveal cause and effect, or event and context, in the picture, this is the one that most brilliantly uses the iris to work with near and far views in a single but redefined visual field.

Another of Griffith's artistic devices is his use of the main street in the town of Piedmont as a barometer of the film's emotional and social tensions. At the film's opening the street is full of people and carriages: active, sociable, friendly. As the Confederate soldiers first march off to war, the street becomes a carnival: fireworks, cheering townspeople, rhythmic columns of men on horses. When "the little Colonel" (Ben Cameron) returns home after the war, the street is desolate, ruined, dusty. And finally, when the town is overrun with carpetbaggers and reconstruction-

ists, drunken gangs of blacks rove the street; the street has become a very unfriendly, ungentle place. By capturing emotion in concrete images Griffith successfully renders feeling—rather than a parody of feeling, as in *Queen Elizabeth*.

Griffith never deserts the principles of his early melodramatic one-reelers as the means to keep his story moving. The suspense and excitement of Griffith's cross-cutting create the dramatic tension of many of the sequences: the attack of a band of black renegades (significantly their captain is white) on the defenseless town and the Cameron home; the assassination of Lincoln in Ford's Theater; the rapacious Gus chasing the youngest Cameron sister through the woods until she jumps to her death. The most thrilling and upsetting sequence of all is the climax, in which Griffith gives us not one but two last-minute rescues. Griffith cross-cuts between two sets of victims and their common rescuers—the Ku Klux Klan—furiously galloping forth to eradicate the forces of rapine and death and social change. Not only is this rescue sequence Griffith's most complex up to this point, it is also his most sensitive to the kinetic excitement of editing rhythms and the moving camera.

Ben Cameron (Henry B. Walthall) rams the Confederate flag down the throat of the Union cannon.

Fig. 4-10

Fig. 4-11

The street as emotional barometer: the total emptiness and loneliness of the "little Colonel's" return from the war.

But after the dust from the galloping climax has settled, Griffith makes fun of the blacks who retreat from the ballot box in fear of the Klan—and then, moving from the infuriating to the ridiculous, he celebrates the peaceful union of Elsie Stoneman and Ben Cameron with a superimposed allegorical pageant in the heavens. Elsie and Ben see Christ replacing the military general; Christ cuts the Gordian knot, and all humanity rejoices as the City of God replaces the Kingdoms of the Earth. There are several remarkable things about this closing vision: its audacity, its irrelevance, and the passion and sincerity of Griffith's commitment to it. But exactly how is this City of God to become a reality? Certainly not by the efforts of the Ku Klux Klan alone. It is the evil in the human soul that must be exorcised. And once again Griffith reveals his nearsightedness in probing what he considers evil.

The evil in the film is instigated by three people. They are evil (1) because they are evil or (2) because they have mixed blood. They succeed in doing evil because they entice the easily tempted Congressman Stoneman to the abolitionist cause. In the misguided Stoneman, Griffith takes another potshot at social reformers. Stoneman's temptation stems from his vanity despite his physical deformity (Griffith uses a club foot, parallel to the classic deformity of Shakespeare's Richard III, and an ill-fitting wig to define these traits) and from the "fatal weakness" of being sexually attracted to his mulatto housekeeper. According to the film's action, the chaos of the Civil War was the direct result of the nation's Stonemans, who became entangled in an evil of which they were totally ignorant or that they unwisely thought they could control. Even granting Griffith this preposterous premise, how is one to be sure the future contains no Stonemans? And how can one abolish slavery without abolition? *The Birth of a Nation's* final vision is an innocent and mystical wish rather than the intellectual consequence of what preceded it. The film remains solid and engaging as a big, complex narrative and a formal cinematic achievement, flimsy and repulsive as social theory.

Right after *The Birth of a Nation*, Griffith made *The Mother and the Law* (1915, released

Ben (Walthall) and Elsie (Lillian Gish) see the City of God replacing the strife of the world—a matte shot made in the camera by masking the top left of the frame when shooting the lovers, then masking the bottom right when shooting the model of the heavenly city on the same footage.

Fig. 4-12

1919), a tightly constructed melodrama starring Mae Marsh (the Dear One), Bobby Harron (the Boy), and Miriam Cooper (the Friendless One); it indicted reformers and big business while telling a powerful story of love, loss, and endurance.

Griffith's treatment of blacks provoked public condemnation, even riots. The criticism stung Griffith deeply, since he felt he had gone to some trouble to present good and bad blacks *and* whites, as he had watered down or cut out the novel's most inflammatory, racist passages. What he kept of Dixon's prose included "the opal gates of death"; what he left out sounded like this: "For a thick-lipped, flat-nosed, spindle-shanked negro, exuding his nauseating animal odour, to shout in derision over the hearths and homes of white men and women is an atrocity too monstrous for belief." The KKK had permanently disbanded in 1869, and Dixon nostalgically dedicated his 1905 "historical romance," *The Clansman,* to the memory of his "Scotch-Irish" uncle, a "Grand Titan Of The Invisible Empire"; unfortunately, *The Birth of a Nation* used the medium so powerfully that Griffith's film unexpectedly but indisputably inspired the birth of the 20th-century Klan in late 1915.

Griffith began defending himself against the charges of bigotry and hatred; he angrily protested the film's suppression in several cities and wrote

The Rise and Fall of Free Speech in America, a pamphlet that championed the "Freedom of the Screen." *Intolerance* (1916) was to be his cinematic defense, his pamphlet in film form against intellectual censorship. Fortunately for Griffith, *The Birth of a Nation* became the first authentic blockbuster in film history, earning untold millions of dollars; he would need his entire share of that money for *Intolerance.*

Intolerance

Intolerance was Griffith's longest, greatest, and most narratively complex film. It cost $1.9 million to produce—over 15 times more than *The Birth of a Nation.* It was 14 reels long, though only about 12 reels survive.

Intolerance told not one story but four. In Belshazzar's Babylon (6th century B.C.), the evil high priest conspires against the wise and just ruler, betraying the city to the Persian conqueror, Cyrus; by the end of this story, every "good" character is dead. In Judea, the close-minded Pharisees intrigue against Jesus; ultimately, the gentle savior is sent to the cross. In Reformation France (16th century A.D.), ambitious courtiers persuade the Catholic king to slaughter all the Protestant Huguenots on St. Bartholomew's Day, a massacre that includes the rape and murder of a young Protestant and the killing of her fiancé.

Fig. 4-13
Intolerance: *the full-scale walls of Babylon.*

In 20th-century America (the "Modern Story," which used to be *The Mother and the Law*), strikers are gunned down, a Boy is falsely convicted of murder, and his wife loses her baby thanks to the meddling of a group of reformers; the facts eventually surface to save the Boy from the gallows. (In *The Mother and the Law*, they do not get the baby back; in the most complete prints of *Intolerance*, they do.)

Instead of telling one story after the other, Griffith tells these stories all at once, interweaving them—and 2,500 years of history—into an intellectual and emotional argument, a demonstration that love, diversity, and the little guy have always had to struggle against the overwhelming forces of hypocrisy, intolerance, and oppression. Because the colliding, streaming, *juxtaposed fragments* of these stories implied an *idea* that went beyond the "moral" of each individual story, making the whole greater than and different from the sum of its parts, *Intolerance* is recognized as the cinema's

first great Modernist experiment in what Sergei Eisenstein would later call intellectual (or dialectical) montage. Indeed, Griffith's editing influenced the Soviets as much as his psychological lighting and control of *mise-en-scène* influenced the Germans. If *The Birth of a Nation* set the course for the American cinema, *Intolerance* did so for the Soviet cinema and *Broken Blossoms* for the German. The next American film to be organized this complexly would be *Citizen Kane* (1941); the next to be structured as a dialectical montage would be *The Godfather Part II* (1974).

The four stories are linked across time and space by the bold editing and by their consistent theme: the machinations of the selfish, the frustrated, and the inferior; the divisiveness of religious and political beliefs; the triumph of injustice over justice; the pervasiveness of violence and viciousness through the centuries. Also tying the stories together is Griffith's brilliant control of editing, which keeps all the parallels in the

Fig. 4-14   *Fig. 4-15*

Intolerance: *the faces of women. Fig. 4-14: the Mountain Girl (Constance Talmadge); Fig. 4-15: the little Dear One (Mae Marsh).*

stories quite clear and which creates an even more spectacular climax than that of *The Birth of a Nation*. In *Intolerance*, there are four frenzied climaxes, including one successful and two *failed* last-minute rescues. The excitement in each of the narrative lines reinforces the others, all of them driving furiously to their breathtaking conclusions. Griffith's last-minute rescues cross-cut through the centuries.

And finally, tying the four stories together, is a symbolic mother-woman, rocking a cradle, bathed in a shaft of light, representing the eternal evolution of humanity through time and fate (the three Fates sit behind her), fulfilling the purpose of the creator. The cradle, inspired by Whitman's lines, "Endlessly rocks the cradle, Uniter of Here and Hereafter," is a transitional device, an emblem of unity, and a symbol of history, out of which all the epochs and stories flow, and in which they are united. The woman is a figure of peace, of light, of fertility (sometimes flowers

bloom in her cradle), of ultimate goodness that will eventually triumph. She is played by Lillian Gish, who assisted Griffith in the editing of *Intolerance*.

The film's bigness is obvious: the high walls of Babylon, the hugeness of the palace (and the immense moving camera shot that Griffith uses to span it), the battles, the care with each of the film's periods and styles. The costumes, the lighting, the acting styles, the decor, and even the intertitles are so distinct in each of the four epochs that viewers know exactly whether they are: in the squalid, drab poverty of a contemporary slum, the elegant tastefulness of the French court, or the garishness of ancient Babylon. But as with *The Birth of a Nation*, *Intolerance* is a big film that works because of its little, intimate moments. The film revolves around the faces of women—from the bubbling, jaunty, comically vital face of the Mountain Girl in the Babylonian Story to the luminous, tear-stained, soulful faces of Brown Eyes in the French Story and the little Dear One in the Modern Story. *Intolerance* makes it perfectly clear that social chaos takes its toll on the women.

The film is also rich in the same kind of metaphoric detail found in *The Birth of a Nation*. The Dear One shows her humanity and tenderness as she lovingly throws grain to her chickens; when she moves to the oppressive city, she keeps a single flower in her flat, a metaphor for all that is simple and natural and struggling to live.

Griffith's technique is as effective at conveying hatred as it is at evoking tenderness. A deeply felt film, *Intolerance* makes it clear what Griffith detests: those who meddle and destroy, those who take advantage of the poor, schemers, hypocrites, and monsters of lust and power. One of Griffith's devices of caricature is the cross-cut—particularly effective in the sequence in which he captures the cold inhumanity of the factory owner. Griffith cuts from the shots of the workers being mowed down by military or hired gunfire (violent, quick cutting, frenetic) to a shot of the owner of the factory sitting alone in his vast office (a long shot, perfectly still, that emphasizes the size of the office and the moral smallness and isolation of the big businessman). The contrast clearly defines the man's responsibility and his unsympathetic inhumanity.

The audience of 1916 found the film confusing and unpleasant. Unlike *The Birth of a Nation*, *Intolerance* aroused no social protest; worse, it aroused little audience interest of any kind. Whatever the reason, *Intolerance* was a financial disaster, costing Griffith all his profits from *The Birth of a Nation*. The failure of *Intolerance* began Griffith's financial dependence on other producers and businessmen, from which he would never recover.

1917–31

The cliché of Griffith criticism is that with *Intolerance* the director reached a peak from which the only direction was down. The final years of Griffith's career are often dismissed as years of repetition, a retreat into sentimentality, and a lack of attention to audience tastes. No matter how good some of the later pictures are, there is some truth in the truism. In the final period of his career, Griffith was less of an inno-

vator; the cinematic advances of his youth had solidified into a stable, controlled mastery of the film form beyond which he rarely went. Some of his major pictures are more striking in their parts than in their wholes: *Hearts of the World* (1918), *America* (1924). After the fiasco of *Intolerance*, Griffith also had to look to his wallet, a concern that led to uninspired program pictures to fulfill contracts: *The Idol Dancer* (1920), *One Exciting Night* (1922, dull).

In 1917 Griffith went to Europe with Billy Bitzer, Robert Harron, Lillian and Dorothy Gish, and other members of his brilliant ensemble—who had, under his guidance, refined the arts of cinematography and film acting to an extent unparalleled in film history. Their object in Europe was to film the First World War (1914–18) for Artcraft, a production company headed by Adolph Zukor, whose films were released by Famous Players–Lasky, soon to be reorganized as Paramount. Designed as a propaganda film for the British war effort and to show Americans what the suffering and valor of the war were all about, the 12-reel *Hearts of the World* deserted the labyrinth of *Intolerance* for the relatively linear narrative style Griffith was to use till the end of his career. This decidedly unpacifist film, one of whose aims was to urge America to join the war, aroused and manipulated emotion in the manner of *The Birth of a Nation*—but without causing riots (by the time the film came out, America was in the war anyway). There is no significant change in the propagandistic narrative formula when the KKK, charging to the rescue, becomes the cavalry or anyone or anything the movie has made the audience like.

In 1920, at the studio he had set up in Mamaroneck, New York, he made two awful films (*The Idol Dancer* and *The Love Flower*) and the classic melodrama *Way Down East*. He followed that with *Dream Street* (1921, a lyrical allegory with haunting, intriguing moments), *Orphans of the Storm* (1921, released 1922, a 12-reel melodrama set in the French Revolution, his last film with either of the Gish sisters), *The White Rose* (1923, a deeply moving film starring Mae Marsh), the clunker *America*, the superb *Isn't Life Wonderful* (1924, starring Carol Dempster; significantly, the last film for which he wrote the script), five more duds, and his last silent, *Lady of the Pavements* (1929),

Fig. 4-16
Broken Blossoms: *Cheng Huan (Richard Barthelmess) and Lucy (Lillian Gish).*

a great-looking love story starring Lupe Velez and photographed by Karl Struss, *assisted* by Bitzer.

Broken Blossoms and *Way Down East*

Despite Griffith's troubles, at least two of the late films rank in power and interest just behind the two great epics. In fact, *Broken Blossoms* (1919) and *Way Down East* (1920) are more entertaining and easier for today's audiences to sit through than either *The Birth* or *Intolerance*.

Broken Blossoms is Griffith's most polished, most finished gem, a tight triangle story of one woman between two men. Out of this triangle come the film's values, rather than from Griffith's subtitles and allegorical visions. If the film is less weighty than the epics, it is also less pretentious. Like so many Griffith films, *Broken Blossoms* is an adaptation of a work of fiction—Thomas Burke's

"The Chink and the Child," from his collection *Limehouse Nights.* As with *The Clansman*, Griffith took another man's work and made it his own.

The film is Griffith's most explicit and poetic hymn to gentleness. It is also a film of grime and failure, terrible violence and absolute horror. Even so, an aura of tenderness and idealism suffuses the film. The gentle man in the film comes from China to bring the message of the gentle Buddha to the vicious, violent West. Once he arrives in London's dockside slum, Limehouse, Cheng Huan (Richard Barthelmess) runs into the "sordid realities of life"—gambling, whoring, opium smoking—that constitute life in the West. He virtually gives up.

Then Griffith switches to the female figure of gentleness, Lucy (Lillian Gish). Raised by a prize fighter, Battling Burrows (Donald Crisp), Lucy is

Fig 4-17

Lillian Gish in Broken Blossoms: *the smile. The sides of her mouth pushed up by her fingers, the eyes wide with fear, Gish creates an unforgettable image of terror and submission.*

an unloved child who spends her time wandering around the Limehouse district, trying to scrape up enough tin foil to buy herself a flower. Flowers are the primary visual metaphor for gentleness in the film, as the title indicates. Lucy's gentleness, however, like Cheng Huan's, runs into sordid realities. Her reality is her father, Burrows, a brutal alcoholic who uses Lucy as both slavish servant and defenseless punching bag. One of the most poignant touches in the film is Burrows's insistence that Lucy smile for him, regardless of her real feelings. Since she is unable to summon a genuine smile, she uses two fingers to force one. Gish improvised that gesture in a rehearsal, and Griffith decided to use it throughout the film.

Cheng Huan is attracted by Lucy's gentle purity, which he instantly perceives. They first meet, appropriately, over the purchase of a flower. She later collapses in his shop after a terrific beating by her father. Cheng Huan enthrones her in his room as a Princess of Flowers, and the two celebrate a brief but beautiful time apart from the world. Lucy even smiles without the aid of her fingers for the first time, and Cheng Huan's one weak moment of animal lust (brilliantly communicated by a painfully tight close-up) is soon conquered by his realization of the ideal perfection of his guest and their relationship.

But the world breaks in on the paradise. Burrows finds her at Cheng Huan's, trashes the place, drags her back to their slum room, and begins his inevitable attack. She retreats to a closet; he smashes it open with a hatchet. Gish creates one of the most accurate renditions of human frenzy in screen history as Lucy turns helplessly in a circle inside the closet—trapped, frantic, terrified. Cheng Huan, rushing to the rescue, arrives too late, and Burrows beats Lucy to death. Her final gesture is to use two fingers to raise her mouth into a smile. Cheng Huan shoots Burrows, takes Lucy's body back to his room, then stabs himself. Blossoms, despite their loveliness, cannot survive for long in a violent, unkind world. A perfectly nuanced and deeply moving tragedy, *Broken Blossoms* broke new narrative ground by proving that a movie could have an unhappy ending and still please an audience. And its perfect control of *mise-en-scène*, from its sets and costumes to its lighting, enhanced the control of tone and mood beyond anything Griffith or anyone else had yet achieved.

Broken Blossoms remains one of the most beautifully lit films in screen history, supported by the evocative color tinting and toning of its original 35mm prints. The lighting of scenes in Cheng Huan's shop and room is an atmospheric blend of beams of light and pools of shadow. Lillian Gish, as the Princess, becomes luminous, surrounded by the gray and black regions of her flowery kingdom. Griffith uses low-key lighting exclusively for these scenes. The lighting is not only atmospheric,

The river scenes for **Way Down East** *were shot in White River Junction, Vermont; Lillian Gish on location.*

Fig. 4-18

but also a precise visual translation of the film's metaphoric contrast between gentleness and violence. While Lucy is enthroned in Cheng Huan's room, Battling Burrows fights his title match. Griffith cross-cuts between the place of love—the room—and the place of violence—the ring. The boxing ring is harshly lit with bright, even, white light; the room is suffused with shafts and shadows. *Broken Blossoms* asks less of its audience than the epics do, but it keeps its promises.

Way Down East, although more uneven than *Broken Blossoms*, contains sections that are as fine as anything Griffith ever did. The most famous sequence in the film is the climax, the last-minute rescue of Anna Moore (Lillian Gish), floating steadily toward the deadly falls. The river was in Vermont; the falls were Niagara Falls; Griffith merely spliced in bits of stock footage. Here was the ultimate proof of the logic of cross-cutting: Although the actress was really nowhere near any falls (especially Niagara), the audience felt her nearness because of the cuts and narrative links that bound the locations. Soviet filmmakers would soon seize on this editing principle, naming it "creative geography."

The Struggle
There are several theories that attempt to explain Griffith's creative decay in the final years

of his career, years in which he struggled to find work, to move the audience as he had before, and to control his drinking. Perhaps he ran out of ideas, both technically and intellectually. The solidifying of his cinematic technique may have contributed to the congealing of his ability to make exciting, moving, powerful films. Or he may not have found the right challenge. There might never have been an *Intolerance* to surpass *The Birth of a Nation* if the controversy over the first epic hadn't fired Griffith's anger and imagination. He may well have been unable to do his best work in regimented studios. Indeed, *Isn't Life Wonderful* (1924) is so fine partly because it was shot outside any studio, on location in Germany during its disastrous postwar hyperinflation (where a bushel of banknotes *might* buy a loaf of bread; the exchange rate in 1923 rose to 4.2 trillion marks per dollar). Shot on the streets, with many non-professionals in the cast, *Isn't Life Wonderful* (1924) was the first precursor of Italian Neorealism. It was also his last independent production until *The Struggle*.

Another popular theory is that Griffith's ideas had become outmoded in the 1920s. The flapper morality of the Jazz Age rejected the sentimentality of Griffith's Victorianism. Belasco's melodrama had been supplanted by urbane, domestic comedy-dramas of sexual innuendo and visual

Fig. 4-19

Fig. 4-20

Waiting in line for food during a period of disastrous inflation. Fig. 4-19: Isn't Life Wonderful (1924), shot on location in Germany by Griffith, anticipated many of the techniques and values of the Neorealists; here Carol Dempster (fourth from the left, in wide-brimmed hat) checks to see how much the price of pork has gone up since she first got in line. Fig. 4-20: The Joyless Street (1925), set in Vienna during the same economic disaster, shot on a set by G. W. Pabst. Note the differences between street and studio realism.

wit. The high life of dancing while holding a cocktail, which Griffith depicted so blackly and so clumsily, was exactly what audiences vicariously wanted to experience. Griffith no longer gave the public what it wanted.

The truth probably lies somewhere among the various theories. Griffith certainly seemed to be running out of creative gas. As his pictures became more and more formulaic, he was more and more dependent on public acceptance of his formulas—but his formulas, as formulas, were 10 to 20 years out of date. The Griffith mastery when he was working at the top of his powers could make Victorian formulas exciting; *Broken Blossoms*, *Way Down East*, and *Orphans of the Storm*, all of which were heavily Victorian and released during the Jazz Age, were huge box-office successes—as big as Griffith ever had. When the mastery flagged, however, audiences saw the bare bones of sentimentality and took themselves to other pictures.

The final years of Griffith's career were scarred by his disastrous fling with the sound picture. In *Abraham Lincoln* (1930), a film that won high praise at the time, he returned to American history—but in spite of a moving and natural performance by Walter Huston as Lincoln, the result was stylistically inept and narratively inert. *The Struggle* (1931) was a fervent, sentimental, sociological study of alcoholism and one man's struggle to overcome it—a struggle about which Griffith knew firsthand. The script was by John Emerson and Anita Loos, who had gotten her start with *The New York Hat*; the sound recording was of high quality. The budget was low, so the film was shot on the streets of New York and looks it: *The Struggle* has, in its best moments, a tough flavor of suffering and authenticity. It also, in typical Griffith fashion, blames alcoholism on Prohibition (1919–33), which converted a beer- and wine-drinking nation to whiskey. Audiences laughed it off the screen in a week.

The Hollywood brass was convinced that Griffith—without whom none of them would have had a job—was old fashioned, that his day was done. He spent his final 17 years barred from an art that he had practically fashioned by himself. He received an honorary Oscar in 1935, but public praise for his achievements could not ease the bitterness of his rejection by the business. He died alone in Hollywood in 1948.

For Further Viewing

FILMS

Griffith's Biograph films, including: *The Adventures of Dollie* (1908); *Those Awful Hats, The Drunkard's Reformation, The Lonely Villa* (or *Lonely Villa*), *Pippa Passes*, and *A Corner in Wheat* (or *Corner in Wheat*) (1909); *The Way of the World, The Unchanging Sea, Ramona*, and *The Sorrows of the Unfaithful* (1910); *The Two Paths, The Lonedale Operator*, and *Enoch Arden* (1911); *The Musketeers of Pig Alley* and *The New York Hat* (1912); *The Mothering Heart* (1913); *Judith of Bethulia* (1914)

The Avenging Conscience (1914)
The Birth of a Nation (1915)
Intolerance (1916)
Hearts of the World (1918)
A Romance of Happy Valley (1919). Completed 1918
Broken Blossoms (1919)
True Heart Susie (1919)
The Mother and the Law (1919)
The Greatest Question (1919)
Way Down East (1920)
Orphans of the Storm (1922). Completed 1921
The White Rose (1923)
Isn't Life Wonderful (1924)
Abraham Lincoln (1930)
The Struggle (1931)

DVDs

Cabiria (1914, **Giovanni Pastrone**). Kino Video. One of the Italian spectacles that influenced Griffith.

Country Doctor (1909, **D. W. Griffith**) is in *More Treasures from American Film Archives* (see Chap. 3 list).

Griffith Masterworks. Kino Video. A mixed bag. *Intolerance* looks fine but runs too slowly, taking up an extra half hour with no additional footage; it is emphatically not recommended for a first viewing, even if the print is clean and there is no other *Intolerance* on

DVD as of this writing. *Broken Blossoms* has the wrong tints, no toning, and a new score instead of the original (for a better experience, see the Connoisseur Video VHS). However, *The Birth of a Nation*, *Orphans of the Storm*, and the Biographs are fine. The 23 Biographs include *The Adventures of Dollie*, *Those Awful Hats*, *Corner in Wheat*, *His Trust*, *His Trust Fulfilled*, *Enoch Arden*, *An Unseen Enemy*, *The Painted Lady*, *The Musketeers of Pig Alley*, *The New York Hat*, and *The Battle at Elderbush Gulch*. Extras include *Rescued from an Eagle's Nest*, the happy ending of *The Fall of Babylon*, the song "Broken Blossoms," documents and clips concerning the 1992 re-release of *The Birth of a Nation*, the prologue (with **Griffith** and **Walter Huston**) to the sound re-issue of *The Birth of a Nation*, footage of Griffith's funeral, a radio eulogy by **Erich von Stroheim**, short talks by **Orson Welles** and **Lillian Gish**, several documentaries, and galleries of stills.

Way Down East (1920, **D. W. Griffith**). Image Entertainment.

5

Mack Sennett
and the Chaplin Shorts

In 1907, the year that Griffith took his ride on the "El" up to the Edison studios in the Bronx, Mack Sennett (born Mikall Sinnott in Canada) took the same ride for the same purpose. Like Griffith, Sennett then wandered from Edison to Biograph to take up a longer residence there. Like Griffith, he admired Belasco. Like Griffith, Sennett later moved from his apprenticeship at Biograph to maturity as an independent producer and director. Sennett even worked for Griffith at Biograph, as director, actor, and writer. In his years with Griffith, Sennett absorbed many lessons on cutting, shooting, and construction. Sennett would later repay his teacher both by adopting his cutting methods and by parodying Griffith's plots and last-minute rescues. Sennett always wanted to make comic films. He began directing for Biograph in 1910, and for years he tried to get them to let him make a comedy about cops. He finally got his chance with his own independent company, Keystone, in 1912.

Krazy Keystones

The marriage that Sennett effected between physical comedy and the silent film was one of those happy, inevitable unions. The purely visual film medium was perfectly suited to the purely visual comic gags that Sennett concocted. Although there were comic films before Sennett—particularly the comic surprises of the trick films and the energy of the chase films—no one before him so forcefully revealed the comic effects of motion, of human bodies and machines and inanimate objects hurtling across the screen and colliding.

It may not be coincidence that one of the most famous essays on comedy—Henri Bergson's *Le Rire* (*Laughter*, 1900)—was contemporary with the early films. Sennett—and later Chaplin, Keaton, Lloyd, and Laurel and Hardy—would unknowingly apply the Bergson theories. No theoretical aesthetic ever had the advantage of such concrete data. The Bergsonian principle that Sennett best demonstrated was that the source of the comic was the conversion of a human being into a machine. We laugh at the mechanical, inelastic motions of a man who fails to alter his responses to suit some change in the environment: the man who slips on a banana peel but continues walking as if no peel were under him until he inevitably falls. Further, we cannot laugh if we have any real fears for the man's safety; we must view him externally as a kind of imperishable object rather than as a man who can suffer pain and broken bones and lasting bruises. It is significant that, with the exception of Oliver Hardy's nosebleeds, there is virtually no blood in silent and early sound physical comedy.

At the center of Sennett's comic technique is the conversion of people into moving objects, a principle explored quite independently by Henri Bergson in his theoretical essay *Le Rire* (*Laughter*, 1900). Sennet's characters zip across the screen like mechanical toys, tossing bricks and pies and crashing into walls, furniture, and one another. Sennett furthers the impression of human machines by undercranking the camera. He saw that by recording the action at only 8 to 12 fps and then projecting it at 16 or 24 fps, the action became so speeded up that the effect

Barney Oldfield's Race for a Life. *Ford Sterling has Mabel Normand tied to the tracks in an exaggerated parody of melodramatic gesture and acting.*

Fig. 5-1

became even more artificial, more frantic, and, hence, more comical. In one Sennett film, *A Clever Dummy* (1917), Ben Turpin actually plays a robot. Sennett's characters rarely experience deep emotion; they scheme rather than think, react rather than reflect; and they are individuated strictly by physical type—fat, thin, short, tall, dark, fair, male, female.

The use of people as objects makes them perfectly suited to run into trouble with the other objects and machines in their universe. Whatever terrific collisions they suffer, we know that the injury will be no more serious than a dent in a fender. Although many Sennett characters brandish guns, the audience knows that a bullet is no more lethal than a kick in the pants or a pie in the face. If we thought these characters were feeling real pain, we couldn't laugh at them. A variant of this principle is at work in the contemporary action genre, where the spectacle would be painful instead of exciting, unbearable rather than fun, if the picture urged us to care about the people who are blown up, mowed down, or in the way of a car chase.

Like a jazz musician, Sennett depended heavily on improvisation. A rough plot outline was the basis for staff meetings each week when Sennett, the cast, and the crew would get together to see what zany bits they could inject into the story line. Sennett adhered to only one principle of construction: A gag had to begin, develop, and finish itself off within 100 seconds. (He said there were two kinds of gags, "the fall of dignity and the mistaken identity.") Because Sennett cared so little about whole plots, the stories seldom go anywhere; they end when the series of gags has been played out.

Sennett's first feature—and the first American feature-length comedy—*Tillie's Punctured Romance* (1914, six reels), is a good example of the formulaic plot that strings gags together, much as a martial arts picture advances from one fight sequence to another. The completely conventional story concerns a farm girl who falls prey to the false advances of a city slicker; he wants her only for her money.

Tillie, the farm girl, is played by the enormous Marie Dressler in her first film role; her city-slicker boyfriend is the small and skinny Chaplin (before he adopted the tramp character exclusively). Sennett plays with the disproportion in their sizes, showing Tillie besting her beau in all sorts of contests in which Charlie winds up with a brick or a stone or a boot hitting him in the head or the seat of the pants. The "other woman" in the film is played by Mabel Normand, a coy and subtle comedienne of genius who became Sennett's creative ally. Sennett draws on the incompetent Keystone Kops for the final chase, and he throws all the main characters off the Santa Monica pier and into the Pacific Ocean to end the film. The best things in the film are the gratuitous gags, the surprises that Sennett throws in. The gratuitous becomes the essential.

Each of the Sennett "riffing" films is structured as a pure series of gags, held together only by pace and by the general locale or situation (the same could be said of an avalanche). Several of the films Chaplin made for Sennett use the riffing structure—a structure that encourages, as the name suggests, a jazz of comedy. In *The Masquerader* (1914), Sennett and Chaplin pull as many gags as they can on the premise that a disruptive actor on a movie set can wreak havoc in a studio. Chaplin plays the actor; the director boots him out; Charlie sneaks back in as a seductive woman; chaos follows until Charlie winds up soaked in a well and the riffing stops. *The Rounders* (1914) riffs on the troubles that two drunks (Chaplin and Roscoe "Fatty" Arbuckle, two obviously contrasting physical types) can get into and on the reactions of their two shrewish wives.

The Sennett parody films are less zany but more whole. *Barney Oldfield's Race for a Life* (1913) features a villain (Ford Sterling) who ties the young damsel (Mabel Normand) to the railroad tracks and then steals a train for the express purpose of running over her. Her boyfriend, played by Sennett, races to the rescue in an automobile. The cops pump to the rescue on a handcar. Sennett, in the best Griffith tradition, cuts among four locales: Mabel on the tracks, anxious; Ford in the train, gleefully looking forward to squashing Mabel; Mack and Barney in the auto; the cops on the handcar. Sennett draws out this rescue to an impossible length; the train, which we know is not very far from Mabel's bound body, takes forever to get to it, just long enough for Mack and the cops to get there in time.

The Sennett farces set a comic standard for zaniness, non sequitur, and physical activity that has served as a model ever since—for, among others, René Clair, Richard Lester, Mel Brooks, Chuck Jones, and the Monty Python troupe. Not as technical a cinematic innovator as Griffith, Sennett still realized that the tricks the camera could play with motion were highly suited to physical comedy.

By 1915, Sennett had moved on to fulltime producing. His films became more expensive and polished, losing much of the improvisational, slaphappy quality of the earlier Keystones for which he is best known. The particular qualities of that Sennett style become most obvious when compared with the completely different methods and emphases of his most distinguished disciple.

Charlie

In 1913, the English stage comedian Charles Chaplin was touring American vaudeville stages with a music-hall act, Fred Karno's English Pantomime Troupe, a troope that included Stan Laurel. Keystone offered Chaplin a job, believing Chaplin's gymnastic talents were perfectly suited to Sennett's athletic menagerie. Chaplin wasn't sure he wanted to work in that zoo; he shared the prejudice of many stage performers against working in films, suspecting, with his typical hardheadedness, the impermanence of a novelty that seemed more monkey business than show business. After Chaplin drove Kessel's offer up from $75 to $150 a week, including a one-year guarantee, he decided the risk was worth it. He appeared on the Sennett lot in December 1913. His first Sennett film was *Making A Living* (1914, directed by Henry Lehrman); Chaplin hated it.

Sennett tried to use Chaplin as one more cog in his factory of human gears and puppets. Sennett capitalized on Chaplin's gymnastic abilities: his ability to fall and stagger and roll and bounce off both people and the floor. Chaplin's smallness was the perfect foil for the bigness of Arbuckle or Dressler. In *The Knockout* (1914, like all Chaplin's Keystone films), he plays a referee in a boxing match, ducking, sliding, squirming, and falling between the fighters and the ropes. This was Chaplin as pure physical comic.

But tension soon developed between Chaplin and Sennett. Sennett's rapid, pure-motion principle bothered Chaplin, who wanted to add character and individuality to his gymnastics. As early as his second and third Keystone films, *Mabel's Strange Predicament* and *Kid Auto Races at Venice* (the latter shot after *Mabel* but released before it), Chaplin began to evolve the tramp character, borrowing the idea of using a cane and hat from the earlier French comic, Max Linder, borrowing an old pair of Ford Sterling's shoes (too big for Charlie's feet) and an old pair of Fatty Arbuckle's oversized pants. He also used a small derby that belonged to Arbuckle's father-in-law, Charles Avery's small jacket, and Mack Swain's false moustache (which he shortened considerably)—all found in

Fig. 5-2

Fig. 5-3

Chaplin's appearance in his first Keystone releases. Fig. 5-2: as an English type with an animatedly dancing cane in Making A Living; *Fig. 5-3: in his tramp costume for* Kid Auto Races at Venice.

the Keystone dressing room. Such individuation was unwanted and unneeded in Sennett's world. Sennett neither took the time nor placed the camera close enough to make such characterization count. Even so, after only one year with Sennett, the little clown with the bowler hat, baggy pants, reedy cane, and floppy shoes had become one of the most familiar figures and faces in the country. He had also, in April 1914, become a director. Chaplin directed 19 of the 35 films he acted in at Keystone; in most cases he wrote what he directed. From 1915 on, he wrote and directed and usually edited every one of his films.

As he moved from contract to contract, from company to company, Chaplin rose to fame, fortune, power, and artistic maturity. Over the four years between 1913 and 1917, his salary jumped from $150 a week as a Sennett pawn to $10,000 per week (plus a $150,000 bonus) with the Mutual Corporation. By 1917, he had a million-dollar contract with First National. Each deal brought Chaplin more money and more creative independence—to write, direct, produce, and even own the rights to his films (as he did, beginning in 1918).

Such awesome numbers indicate not only the general expansion of the movie industry, but also the personal accomplishment of a man who became history's first truly international superstar and the first maker of movies (and comic movies at that) acknowledged as a genius and primary influence by an entire generation of 20th-century artists and intellectuals.

Temperamentally, Chaplin never could see comedy as Sennett saw it. For Sennett, the comic world was a realm of silly surfaces; for Chaplin, the comic world provided the means to examine the serious world of human needs and societal structures. For Sennett, comedy was an end; for Chaplin, it was a means. Chaplin revealed another dimension of Bergson's theory of comedy in *Le Rire*—a moral force to correct the mechanical and inelastic constrictions of social norms.

Chaplin's own experience played a tremendous role in shaping his outlook. With his father and mother separated and his mother battling ill health and insanity, Chaplin spent almost two years of his Dickensian childhood in a workhouse for the poor. The boy in the workhouse quickly perceived the power of wealth and social status. The young Chaplin was an outsider, beyond the embrace of social and material comforts. The nameless screen character he created—whom we are calling Charlie (the French call him Charlot)—is also an outsider. He is a tramp, a criminal, an immigrant, a worker—someone excluded from the beautiful life. And yet Charlie yearns for that life. He longs for money, for love, for legitimacy, for social station, for etiquette, for recognition. Ironically, Charlie as outsider serves to show both the gleaming attractiveness of the beautiful life for those who don't have it and the false emptiness of the beautiful life for those who do. Chaplin was mature enough as an artist to show the ambivalence of power and wealth, its attractiveness and its emptiness—an ambivalence that Chaplin the man felt when he became rich and powerful.

The critical cliché is that Chaplin slowed down Sennett's dizzy pace. He did slow it down, but he did so to put something else in. The structures of the films reveal a key shift. If Sennett's films are strings of gags, Chaplin's films are structured as three or four beads on a string. His classic Essanay film *The Tramp* (1915), in which Chaplin first demonstrates a complete consciousness of his clown persona, breaks into four clear sections: Charlie the tramp protecting the pretty girl from other, meaner tramps; Charlie as farmhand on the girl's farm; Charlie foiling the other tramps' plot to rob the farm; and Charlie losing the girl when her wealthy boyfriend arrives.

The shift in film structure from the gag to the scene demands that each of the sequences be more detailed, richer, fuller. The gags actually define the characters. When Charlie twirls his cane at a fancy party (in *The Count*, 1916) and then accidentally stabs the turkey, which he inadvertently swings above his head, he defines his sociable attempts to be suave and his frustrating lack of success at it. Charlie's sly and jaunty crap shooting and card shuffling when surrounded by big, mean opponents (*The Immigrant*, 1917) show he has guts as well as style. Despite the size of his opponents and the social obstacles, Charlie insists on enjoying the last laugh or the last kick in the pants. His attempts to enjoy the last boot are not only ingenious and funny; they also define his pluck.

Another dimension of the mature Chaplin tramp is that despite the toughness, opportunism, and dishonesty that help him survive, he has a kind and generous heart. He demonstrates this trait repeatedly by using a Griffith-like woman who evokes Charlie's milder qualities: tender and kind, instantly perceiving the redeeming characteristics in the unworldly tramp. From 1915 to 1922, Chaplin used the same actress, Edna Purviance, to portray her.

For Chaplin, the woman was not just a sentimental character—although she certainly was that; she was also a metaphor for natural human beauty uncorrupted by social definitions and unburied by material possessions.

Chaplin's characters also comment on the assumed values of the society that produces them. Like Sennett, Chaplin uses physical types for comic effect. Unlike Sennett, the physical type also implies moral, social, economic, political, romantic, and psychological values. Eric Campbell, the heavy, is invariably a member of the film's social in-group; he naturally hates Charlie because Charlie is not a member of that group. Eric is the giant in *Easy Street* (1917); Charlie is the runt. If the social "ins" are as brutal, as coarse, as empty, as vicious as Eric, then there is value in being "out," like Charlie.

Consistent with his social view, Chaplin's cops are very different from Sennett's incompetent and cockeyed loons. From *Easy Street* to *Modern Times* (1936), they're a rough bunch and they often do the wrong thing. The cops in *The Adventurer* shoot rifles at the escaping Charlie, and their bullets, unlike those in Sennett comedies, look as though they might hurt somebody.

The short Chaplin films—like the later features—contain ironic and pointed social commentary in the action as well as in the characters. The comedies treat several controversial themes that we might think the exclusive property of our own generation: drug addiction, poverty, hunger, crime on the streets, homosexuality, religious hypocrisy. In *The Immigrant*, Chaplin juxtaposes the Statue of Liberty with a cattle boat full of immigrants. As soon as a title announces, "The land of liberty," government officials rope all the immigrants together and start checking their identification tags. Men in uniform are inevitably damned in the Chaplin shorts, whether the uniform is a policeman's, a

Easy Street: *the runt and the giant (Charlie and Eric Campbell).*

Fig. 5-4

fireman's, a government official's, or a banker's. This is just one sense in which Chaplin can be seen, like Griffith, as one of the major 20th-century heirs of Charles Dickens.

Aside from *The Immigrant, Easy Street* may be the most socially conscious of the early two-reelers. In the opening sequence, Charlie gets uplifted in the Hope Mission, singing hymns and feasting on Edna's pure face. He is so uplifted that he gives back the collection box he has stolen. The inspired Charlie goes off into the world only to find that it is a vicious place, full of hunger, poverty, thieves, drug addicts, bullies, and rapists; Easy Street is not so easy, a jungle world of animals striving to survive. As a cop in the slums (now an outcast *because of* the uniform), Charlie subdues all the foes of goodness, ironically inspired to perform his heroic deeds by a shot of dope. In the final sequence, the den of thieves has been miraculously transformed into the New Hope Mission; all the thugs, including the ominous Eric Campbell, have dressed in their Sunday suits and Sunday smiles, all of them marching meekly and politely into the mission for their own uplifting.

Though the social and moral implications of the Chaplin shorts are striking, Chaplin never deserts the objective tool of comedy for making his points. One of the most brilliant examples is the beginning of *The Bank*. Charlie strides into the bank, goes directly to the safe, twirls the dials of the huge safe, checking his cuff to make sure that he remembers the combination, finally opens the door of the safe, steps in, and brings out his mop and pail. Not only does Charlie demonstrate the difference between capital and labor, but he does it in a stunning surprise that plays on our expectations. At the beginning of *The Immigrant*, people are lying about the boat, seasick. The camera cuts to Charlie, leaning over the side of the pitching ship. We expect he is sick like all his fellow passengers. Then he turns around, displaying the fish he has just caught. In *The Tramp*, he enters walking down a dusty road; a car rushes by, spraying him with dust—another contrast of rich and poor. Charlie takes out a brush, whisks himself off, buffs his fingernails, and continues on his way. The spunky tramp is a fastidious gentleman—in himself, a perfect comic contrast. As an integrator of contrasts, of the good–bad, sneaky–brave, poor–rich, lucky and out of luck in all of us, Chaplin's tramp crossed worlds and,

through laughter and pathos, brought people and worlds together.

An essential element of Chaplin's comic technique—and that of every other silent comedian—was the ingenious use of objects. Unlike Sennett, Chaplin did not use objects simply as comic weapons (the pie in the face); the object could be either weapon or tool, could define the character using it, could be used in a surprising way, could foul Charlie up or help him out. If Chaplin's favorite structure was to exhaust a situation of some length before moving on to the next, one way to exhaust a situation was to exhaust all the objects in it. And in exhausting an object, Chaplin frequently transformed it into a completely different thing—not by stopping the camera, as Méliès had, but by manipulating the object in a witty and unexpected way. Chaplin, like Méliès, was a kind of magician, but his was a magic without camera tricks.

Chaplin's most famous short film with objects is *One A.M.* (1916). With the exception of a cab driver in the first sequence, Charlie is the only character in the film—except for a roomful of objects. In this film Charlie returns to one of his favorite incarnations, the drunk; the play with objects begins in the first section when the drunken Charlie, returning from a night on the town, gets tangled with the taxi door and then with the taxi meter. Charlie can't find the key to his front door, so he climbs in the window, stepping in a goldfish bowl as he does so. Inside the house he finds the key in his vest pocket. Back out the window he goes (foot in the goldfish bowl again) so that he can enter properly through the door.

In the second section—Charlie in the living room—Chaplin uses every piece of inanimate matter with which the set has been decorated. He feels he is being attacked by the tiger rug on the floor. He tries to walk on a circular table toward a bottle of booze and seltzer; the table spins, and Charlie walks a treadmill, unable to reach the booze. He tries to walk up the stairs only to discover himself at the bottom again. He finally gets upstairs by climbing a coatrack.

Then, in the third section—Charlie and the bed—the game with objects culminates in a 5-minute duel between the drunk and a Murphy bed. The bed flips down, flips up, reverses itself, loses its frame, bounces, rises, falls as it pleases.

Fig. 5-5
One A.M.: *Charlie and the tiger rug.*

Charlie finally beds down in the bathtub. With the bed, Chaplin has succeeded in bringing an inanimate object to life. Though he excludes living people to play against in *One A.M.*, Chaplin has not excluded living opponents, who draw their breath of life from the power of cinema to record an event over and over again, until the choreographed interaction is perfect. (Chaplin's films were expensive to make because he called for so many retakes.) Chaplin virtually refuses to cut during the final duel with the bed; except for a brief close shot, the climax consists of two long takes from a single setup. The lack of cutting rivets our attention on the two combatants. All consciousness of the cinematic medium disappears.

As opposed to D. W. Griffith's sharp contrast of idealized goodness and idealized evil, Chaplin examined the inherent contradictions within the definitions of good and evil in bourgeois industrial society. The comic tramp was himself a walking contradiction, a figure who loathed (and feared) the falsity of the established order and who yearned toward the purity of the ideal, but also envied the comforts and rewards of the es-tablished society and realized that he had better administer a kick unto others before they kicked unto him. This tension between naïveté and instinctive, tough pragmatism in the tramp produces the moral ambivalence of the mature Chaplin films: the contrast between societal definitions of paternity and more human ones in *The Kid* (1921, his first feature), the ambivalent contrasts between rich and poor in *City Lights*, and the choice between civilization and nature in *Modern Times*. In his first four years, Chaplin created and developed the character whom he would use to explore the cultural landscape of civilization itself.

Chaplin's early films demonstrated the appeal of the performer on the minds of his public. Millions of fans rushed to the novelty shops that sold mechanical dolls and plaster statuettes in the tramp's image, much as later generations of children bought Mouseketeer and *Star Wars* paraphernalia. Chaplin was the very first national and international craze generated by the motion-picture industry. Chaplin hobnobbed with the most famous figures of his generation—Albert Einstein, Winston Churchill, H. G. Wells,

The Pawn Shop: *the clock as patient.*

Fig. 5-6

Mahatma Gandhi. George Bernard Shaw proclaimed him the only authentic genius the cinema ever produced.

If there was a single quality that most struck this generation of admirers, it was Chaplin's tremendous range, his paradoxical combinations of diametrically opposed human sentiments and reactions. Charlie was a terrific cynic and a romantic, selfish and generous, combative and cowardly, crude and delicate, vain and unself-conscious, pathetic and heroic. He was a total outsider to bourgeois middle-class propriety and its institutions, both above it in his gentlemanly disdain and below it in his destitute station. But Charlie understood the comforts and bases of those institutions as well as their constrictions. They simply weren't for the likes of him, who belonged everywhere and nowhere at all on earth.

By 1918, the time of his million-dollar contract with First National, a firm that only distributed and exhibited films, Chaplin had become a totally independent producer and the owner of his own film studio.

With First National, the later phases of his career began—with silent and sound feature films. Although the long films were among his best,

Chaplin never exerted a greater cultural influence, both in America and abroad, than in those first four years between 1914 and 1918.

For Further Viewing

FILMS

MACK SENNETT (1880–1960)
Mabel's Dramatic Career (1913)
Tillie's Punctured Romance (1914)
Teddy at the Throttle (1917)
The Fatal Glass of Beer (1933)

CHARLES CHAPLIN (1889–1977)
Chaplin's Keystone films, including: *Mabel's Strange Predicament, Twenty Minutes of Love, Caught in the Rain, The Knockout, Laughing Gas, The Property Man, The Masquerader, The Rounders, His Musical Career, Getting Acquainted,* and *His Prehistoric Past* (all 1914)
Chaplin's Essanay films, including: *His New Job, A Night Out, The Tramp, The Bank,* and *A Night in the Show* (1915); and *Police* (1916)
Chaplin's Mutual films: *The Floorwalker, The Vagabond, One A.M., The Count, The Pawn*

Shop, and *The Rink* (1916); *Easy Street, The Cure, The Immigrant*, and *The Adventurer* (1917)
A Dog's Life (1918)
Shoulder Arms (1918)
The Kid (1921)
The Idle Class (1921)
A Woman of Paris (1923)
The Gold Rush (1925)
The Circus (1928)
City Lights (1931)
Modern Times (1936)
The Great Dictator (1940)
Monsieur Verdoux (1947)
Limelight (1952)
A King in New York (1957)

DVDs

Bangville Police (1913, **Henry Lehrman**, produced by **Mack Sennett**), a parody of Griffith featuring the Keystone Kops, is in *The Movies Begin* (see Chap. 2 list).

*The **Chaplin** Collection, Vol. 1.* Warner Home Video. Includes *The Gold Rush, Modern Times, The Great Dictator, Limelight,* and many extras.
*The **Chaplin** Collection, Vol. 2.* Warner Home Video. Includes *A Dog's Life, Shoulder Arms, Sunnyside, A Day's Pleasure, The Kid, The Idle Class, Pay Day, The Pilgrim, A Woman of Paris, The Circus, City Lights, Monsieur Verdoux, A King in New York,* a documentary, and many extras.
***Charlie Chaplin** Short Comedy Classics: The Complete Restored Essanay & Mutual Collection.* Image Entertainment. Includes a documentary on **Eric Campbell**.
The Fatal Glass of Beer (1933, **Clyde Buckman**, produced by **Mack Sennett**) is in ***W. C. Fields**: Six Short Films* (see Chap. 11 list).
Slapstick Encyclopedia. Image Entertainment. Over 15 hours of well-selected shorts, including many by **Sennett**.

6

Movie Czars
and Movie Stars

Griffith, Sennett, and Chaplin were three of the most important figures of the moving picture's second major period, 1908–19. The first, 1894–1907, was dominated by Edison (and Dickson and Porter), Lumière, and Méliès. The year 1908, when Griffith started making pictures, marks one boundary; the start of the 1920s marks the other, beginning a third period that would end with the coming of sound. The 1920s would see Keaton, Gance, Murnau, Dreyer, Eisenstein, and von Stroheim—and, of course, new work by Griffith, Chaplin, and Sennett.

After trailing the art and industries of England and France in the first years of commercial film-making, the American film asserted its dominance in the years just preceding World War I and, with the help of that war (and the films of Griffith, Sennett, and Chaplin; the star system; and the beginnings of the studio system), established a commercial supremacy that has never been challenged.

World War I came at an opportune time for the American film industry. In 1914, just as the American film imagination had begun to swell, the war came along to cripple the European film industry. By the time the war ended in 1918, the American film had become, as it has remained, the dominant cinema force in the world.

Wealth began pouring into the American film business with the appearance of the nickelodeons in 1905, converting that business into a powerful industry and pushing it to untangle the legal and commercial chaos of its infancy. In 1910, the war against the Trust was raging as the impish Independents valiantly kept fighting and produc-

ing pictures. Ten years later, all but one of the original Trust companies had folded, and the leaders of the opposition had themselves become more autocratic and powerful than their earlier adversaries. Carl Laemmle, William Fox, Adolph Zukor, Jesse Lasky, Marcus Loew, Samuel Goldfish, Lewis J. Selznick, and Louis B. Mayer were all lucky enough to be in the right place at the right time. They were fortunate to be running a studio or buying up theatres at the moment when everyone in America started going to the movies and when everyone abroad went to American movies because there were few others. These men, who became the first movie moguls, had outlasted their Trust competitors—the Motion Picture Patents Company—simply because they rode the crest of the new wave of film merchandising rather than trying to stop it.

The business of the Trust's distributor was to market one-hour programs of short films for the nickelodeons; the new feature films, lasting up to two hours, were for larger, more comfortable theatres devoted to and equipped for a full evening's entertainment. To produce 52 features a year (the equivalent of one film program per week) required a huge permanent staff of actors, writers, directors, and technicians; a major investment in equipment; a complex administrative office for scheduling the shooting and selling the films; and big theatres. Zukor, Goldfish, Laemmle, Fox, and some others made the investment; many of the Trust companies could not or did not, certain that the new feature craze was a passing fancy. The fancy never passed; the Trust companies did, succumbing to the courts in 1917.

Stars over Hollywood

The years between 1910 and 1920 determined the direction the American film industry would take. By 1915, the film program consisted of a single feature film supplemented by a short or two. A second practice was born at the same time—the star system. In the healthy days of the Trust, no Biograph actor ever received screen credit. Performers were known either by the names of the characters they played—"Little Mary"—or by the studio—the Biograph Girl. There even seems to have been some doubt in the minds of the earliest patrons about whether they were watching a dramatization or real life.

The First Stars

Biograph opposed giving screen credit for the same short-sighted commercial reasons that it opposed the feature film: Star actors would cost more than anonymous faces on a screen. The reasoning was correct. But the Independents reasoned that although a star would cost more, a film with a star would earn more. The Independents had the stronger argument: To make more, it was necessary to spend more. The Independents launched their career when Carl Laemmle hired the Biograph Girl in 1910 and featured her in IMP pictures under her real name, Florence Lawrence. Laemmle and other Independents did the same with "Little Mary" Pickford, King Baggott, Arthur Johnson, and many other formerly anonymous players. The power of the star system, begun by the Independents, was such that in 1917—only a few years after its inception—two stars, Chaplin and Pickford, were vying with producers and with each other to become the highest paid performers in the business, both of them signing contracts for over $1 million. And every major producer in the industry was trying to sign them and pay them that million.

The movie star, no longer an anonymous character in a film but a human being in his or her own right, seized the imagination of the public. In 1912, just after audiences started learning their favorites' names, America's first motion picture fan magazine, *Photoplay*, appeared. It and subsequent fan magazines featured pictures, stories, and interviews that made the figure on the screen an even more intimate and personal being for each member of the audience. Producing companies needed publicity departments to sell the stars as well as the pictures to the public.

Later film theorists have speculated about the appeal, value, and utility of movie stars. For some critics, movie stars are a commodity of industrial production, another means for the film industry to package and market its products to the public. For others, movie stars are symptomatic of a superficial culture—they are beautiful but shallow, powerful visual presences and may be uncritically accepted even if their range and skills are limited. Still other critics see this unity and consistency of star personality as the most interesting and powerful accomplishment of movie stars: Movie stars do not so much play characters (as stage actors do); they *are* the characters. The movie star capitalizes on an essential paradox of movies—that they are fictional truths. A movie star is also a fictional truth, a fictional character in a fictional narrative, and yet a real human being whose face and actions have been documented by the camera and who has a powerful and familiar persona. And the character resonates with this persona; together they create the complete portrayal. As commodity, actor, and persona, the movie star had become a powerful component of American cultural experience by 1915.

The greatest stars of the silent films created their own images and types; the lesser stars merely filled the patterns that the great stars had already sketched. There were imitations of Mary Pickford's spunky, good-hearted, pranksterish little girl with the golden curls. There were sultry sirens in the Theda Bara image, many of them imported from Europe. There were gentle, soulful juveniles—Richard Barthelmess, Charles Ray. There were exotic Latin leading men—Rudolph Valentino, Ramon Novarro. There were lecherous, jaded roués, often from decadent foreign shores—Erich von Stroheim, Owen Moore, Adolphe Menjou. There was the basically pure woman who rose to the demands of experience (Lillian Gish); there was the stubborn, sophisticated, and often tragic lady (Gloria Swanson); there was the strong, competent, virile male (Thomas Meighan); there was the serious, tough cowboy with the sad eyes (William S. Hart); there was the fat man (John Bunny, Fatty Arbuckle), and the little man (Chaplin, Harold Lloyd, Buster

Fig. 6-1

Fig. 6-2

Early archetypes. Fig. 6-1: the vamp, Theda Bara; Fig. 6-2: the rough good–bad man of the frontier, William S. Hart.

Keaton), and the everyman (Lon Chaney). And as the stars flourished, so did the character actors, who specialized in playing nonromantic roles and types.

California, Here We Come

As significant as the birth of the star system in this decade was the move west. As early as 1907, production companies—perhaps evading the law or the Patents Company wrecking crews—discovered southern California. The vast, open plains, the dependability of the sun, the nearby mountains and deserts and ocean, all attracted the eyes of people whose art depended on the power of the visual.

By 1915, most of the film companies had settled down to business in Los Angeles and its suburbs—known colloquially and generically as Hollywood. Real estate speculators, who suddenly discovered that miles of apparently useless land were of great use to the movie men, sold it to them by the tens of thousands of acres, at absurdly reasonable prices. Vast studios, like Thomas Ince's Inceville (1911; in 1915, he built a

new lot in Culver City) and Carl Laemmle's Universal City (which opened in 1915), with rows of shooting studios, office buildings, back lots (for the outdoor sets), and even ranches completely stocked with cattle and horses and other beasts of the field, sprang up in and near Los Angeles. Enjoying the harvests of chance, the emperors of the new film world now ruled vast, tangible empires.

The Emperors and Their Rule

The most significant accident in the history of the American film is that this first generation of influential movie producers, those gentlemen who made the concrete decisions about the artistic and moral values worthy of inclusion in films, were themselves deficient in formal education and aesthetic judgment. Most of them were either Jewish immigrants from Germany or Russia or Poland, or the sons of Jewish immigrants. Most came to the movies by accident. They sold herring or furs or gloves or secondhand clothes. They jumped from these businesses into running

Fig. 6-3

Fig. 6-4

*A gallery of stars. Fig. 6-3: "Little Mary" Pickford
(note how the huge sets and furniture make her
seem truly little); Fig. 6-4: a cool Gloria Swanson.*

amusement parks and penny arcades just when Edison's Kinetoscope and Biograph's Mutoscope were bringing new life to the novelty business.

There were two reasons Jewish immigrants could thrive in this business, and they were the same reasons that Jews thrived in another contemporary entertainment business—the writing, publishing, and selling of popular music on New York's 28th Street, known colloquially as Tin Pan Alley. First, these were new businesses that had not evolved their structures of corporate control that always tend to keep newcomers out. Second, they were the kinds of risky, "illegitimate" businesses that respectable businessmen and social prejudice always allowed the Jews to run—like the lending of money in medieval and Renaissance Europe.

When movies left the peepshow box for the screen, these arcade owners converted their stores into nickelodeons. They built more and more of these theatres, which became bigger and plusher. Soon they began producing films for their theatres, what with the pressures of the Trust and its licensing fees. Such was the series of small steps by which a Goldfish (later Goldwyn) or Zukor or Mayer climbed out of the ghetto and into a multimillion-dollar throne of power over national artistic tastes. It is the same route that later generations of disadvantaged Americans have traveled; for many, the quickest and most glamorous road to the American Dream of fame and fortune is show business (sports, music, television, and movies).

By 1915—even as early as 1908—there were three types of movie executives, and the differences among them reveal the structure of the American film industry as a whole. Out in Hollywood, the most famous of the movie moguls were those who controlled the actual production of films; they were the film producers and studio heads whose private lives and personal salaries made the headlines. Back in New York, on the East Coast, were the parent companies, whose executives supervised and budgeted the entire operation of the studio, marketing its products, reinvesting its revenues, and managing its assets as profitably as possible. Then, scattered throughout the country were the owners of theatres and theatre chains who needed films from the studios and returned to them the revenues that the film companies needed to make more films. The three-tiered structure of the American film industry—production, distribution, and exhibition—evolved in the middle years of the century's second decade.

Major Studios

The most powerful film company of the silent era was Paramount Pictures. Paramount was the child of Adolph Zukor, the final stage in the evolution of his Famous Players in Famous Plays. Zukor, who began by distributing *Queen Elizabeth* in 1912, jumped aboard the feature-film wagon at the very beginning—one of the chief reasons for his success. Zukor bested his competition by buying it out. The huge company then had the power and the money to hire the most popular stars and demand the highest fees from exhibitors who wanted the films of its stars.

Zukor had been working in a steady, octopal manner, snatching up theatres as well as studios and exchanges. One of Zukor's commercial innovations was the system of block booking. The theatre owner had to agree to buy all of Zukor's products to get any of them. If he wanted Mary Pickford or William S. Hart, he had to buy all 52 weekly programs from Paramount. But even block booking, tyrannical as it was, was less efficient than owning the theatres. The studio owner not only had to produce films, but also had to guarantee that each of them would be shown. What better guarantee than to own the theatres to show them?

Another powerful studio emerged in the mid-1920s: Metro–Goldwyn–Mayer. The monolith was assembled by theatre owner Marcus Loew, who wanted to control the profit from the pictures that he showed in his national chain of theatres. In 1924, Loew bought the Metro Picture Company and merged with the Goldwyn Picture Company. Loew then put Louis B. Mayer, another theatre owner recently turned producer, in charge of production at MGM. Mayer brought with him a young assistant, Irving Thalberg, who had been at Universal, to supervise the shooting of the pictures. (In other words, Mayer was the executive in charge of the production—as opposed to the distribution—arm of the studio, and Thalberg was in charge of the actual activity of film production: planning, approving, and supervising the making of all MGM films.) From these parts, Loew assembled the most solid film factory in America. Anchored by his chain of classy and genteel theatres, Loew's MGM studio began to manufacture the kind of classy and genteel films that would perfectly mesh the ambiance of the environment to the tone of the entertainment within it. Loew, like Zukor, had succeeded in creating the kind of vertically integrated empire that Gaumont and Pathé had established 20 years earlier; he controlled all three branches of the theatrical film business: production, distribution, and exhibition.

Understandably, the theatre owner did not enjoy the strong-arm pressures of block booking or the unavailability of those popular films that had been made by the studios for their own theatres. In 1917, a group of theatre owners joined together specifically as an antidote to Zukor's commercial poison, calling themselves the First National Exhibitors Circuit. First National contracted with individual stars (Chaplin, for example, and Harry Langdon) to make pictures for their theatres. The star gained independence and financial backing; the theatre owner gained the lucrative products of popular, established stars. The idea was so felicitous that First National was among the three great powers of the 1920s film world.

Yet another new wrinkle was the emergence of the artist as producer. If film producers could turn theatre owners and if theatre owners could turn producers, then artists could also turn producers and work for themselves. In 1919, D. W. Griffith, Charles Chaplin, Mary Pickford, and Douglas Fairbanks joined together to form the United Artists Corporation. Each would produce his or her own films, which would then be distributed by the common company, United Artists. United Artists owned neither studio nor theatre; it was exclusively a distributing organization for pictures made elsewhere. However flimsy such an organization seemed compared with the giants like Paramount and First National, the company survived, eventually merging with MGM (in 1981). The idea for United Artists was years ahead of its time. Today, the major studios themselves are often merely distributors for pictures that have been made by independent producers.

Carl Laemmle went into the nickelodeon business in 1906, then into film distribution, then into film production. He formed the Independent Motion Picture Company in 1909, merged IMP with some smaller companies to create the Universal Film Company in 1912, and opened Universal City in 1915. Universal's major silent hits ranged from *Traffic in Souls* (1913) to *The Phantom of the Opera* (1925, revised 1929).

William Fox began distributing films in 1904 and producing them in 1913; in 1915, he changed the name of his company from Box Office Attractions to the Fox Film Corporation, and in 1916, he set up a studio in Los Angeles. Fox was known for its quality productions—Fox himself received

The four United Artists after the signing (from a contemporary newsreel)— from left: Fairbanks, Griffith, Pickford, and Chaplin.

Fig. 6-5

the first and only Academy Award for "artistic quality of production" for *Sunrise* (1927)—and for its early sound films and newsreels. The company merged with Darryl F. Zanuck's 20th Century Productions to become 20th Century–Fox in 1935.

The four Warner brothers—Albert, Harry, Sam, and Jack—opened their first nickelodeon in 1904, produced a feature in 1917, moved their independent operation from New York to Hollywood in 1919, and formed Warner Bros. Pictures in 1923. In 1925, they bought Vitagraph and began experimenting with sound. Warner Bros. was a minor studio until *The Jazz Singer* (1927) made it a giant; in 1928, it even took over First National.

Another major company that got a late start was founded by Harry and Jack Cohn and Joe Brandt in 1920; it took the name Columbia Pictures Corporation in 1924. What contributed to Columbia's rise was not a technology like sound but an immensely popular and gifted director: Frank Capra began working for Columbia in 1927. Later in the Studio Era, Columbia and Warner Bros. were very much counted among the major studios, a list that included Fox, MGM, Paramount, United Artists, Universal, and RKO. The last of these, the Radio–Keith–Orpheum Corporation, was not founded until 1928. Walt Disney Productions, a major studio today but not in the 1920s or 1930s, grew out of companies founded as early as 1922 and was incorporated in 1929.

The Hollywood film studios of the 1920s had traveled a long way from Edison's Black Maria— and even from the glass-walled studio of Méliès; now they made their own light. Vast expanses of land and a complex maze of buildings had replaced the single little tar-paper shack that pirouetted with the sun. The Hollywood studio had become an entertainment factory, mass producing movies on an assembly line much as Henry Ford manufactured cars. There was a specific section for writers in the studio—those who conceived the original story ideas, those who wrote the final scenarios, and even those who created the film's intertitles, a separate and highly developed art of its own. There was a specific section for costuming, one for the construction of sets, and another for the care and maintenance of the increasingly complicated equipment, still another for the shooting of the films, and one for publicizing, marketing, and financing the finished product. The arts of the writer, the costumer, the cinematographer, the art director, the electrician, and the editor had become as significant as the contributions of the producer, director, and actor.

Movie Palaces

As the film studio evolved, so did the movie theatre. Almost simultaneous with the birth of the feature film came the huge, plush theatre to glorify the longer films and show them in comfort.

The interior of the Roxy, from the ceiling to the orchestra.

Fig. 6-6

Fig. 6-7

Fig. 6-8

Fig. 6-9

Fig. 6-10

Fig. 6-11

Grauman's Chinese Theatre. Fig. 6-7: the newly constructed theatre on Hollywood Blvd. Fig. 6-8: a few weeks before the 1927 opening, Mary Pickford and Douglas Fairbanks made their marks in the cement outside the theatre; left, Sid Grauman. It turned out that they needed two cement blocks for their names (Figs. 6-9, 6-10). Fig. 6-11: in 1949, cowboy star Roy Rogers left the imprints of his gun and horse along with his hands and boots.

The same feature phenomenon that enriched the studios enriched the theatres. The earlier nickelodeons were small and often dirty; in New York, the feature-length movies left these little stores for huge theatres on Broadway. The first of the new palaces was the Strand, constructed on Broadway in 1914, followed immediately by the Vitagraph. The new theatres could accommodate over 2,000 patrons, who trod on carpeted floors and relaxed in plush, padded chairs. The manager of the Strand Theatre, Samuel L. Rothafel (born Rothapfel), soon went on to buy, build, and conceive huge movie palaces of his own. Roxy (his nickname) opened or salvaged a string of mammoth New York houses: the Rialto, Rivoli, Capitol, Roxy, and the Radio City Music Hall, his finale and *chef d'oeuvre*. Roxy brought the same tone of quasigentility to the movie theatre that his colleagues, like Zukor and Mayer, brought to the films themselves. Roxy supplemented the film showing with symphony orchestras, corps de ballets, live variety acts, and, at Radio City, the last survivor of the Roxy era, the legendary Rockettes. Whereas vaudeville had supported the movies in their first years in America, the movies had now begun to support vaudeville.

The Roxy of the West Coast, Sid Grauman, paid as much attention to the outsides of his theatres as Roxy paid to the inside. His Chinese Theatre welcomed the patron with a complex system of pagoda roofs and Oriental carvings—and the cement footprints of the stars; his Egyptian Theatre offered patrons a waterfall and a wishing well as they walked in the door. The Roxies of the Midwest, Balaban and Katz, gave the same grand treatment to the many theatres in their chain, pulling out all the stops for their glorious flagship, The Chicago. Even the smaller neighborhood theatre imitated the attractions of the movie palaces—electric stars twinkled in their stucco heavens as plaster copies of Greek gods and goddesses stared down from an Olympus decorated as a Spanish hacienda.

Even though some of them may strike us as tacky in their splendor, the movie palaces were carefully designed, luxurious fantasy worlds of their own, dedicated to the democracy of high-class entertainment. They were open to everyone, for the American movie theatre had always been, from the time of nickelodeons, a place where workers and vagabonds mingled with the middle and upper classes. They were warm in the winter, "refrigerated" in the summer. If you were a kid or out of work—particularly after 1929, as the Great Depression spread out from Wall Street to engulf the world—you could stay in that rich space all day long and dream.

Morality

The movies have waged a perpetual cold war with the forces of religion and righteousness. In 1896, the moralists denounced the improprieties of *The Kiss*. *Fatima* (1897), which depicted the bumps and grinds of a noted hoochy-coochy dancer of the day, so offended some members of certain communities that exhibitors superimposed broad white stripes across the screen to cover the areas where Fatima displayed her most lascivious wares.

Throughout the Nickelodeon Era the movies had been criticized as cultivators of iniquity; the theatres had been attacked as unsavory or unsafe.

In the early 1920s, several national scandals involving movie stars brought the film business to the attention of the U.S. Congress and to the edge of federal censorship—the last thing any producer wanted. The industry decided once again to clean its own house, to serve as its own censorship body. In 1922, it found Will H. Hays, President Harding's campaign manager, Postmaster General of the United States, Presbyterian elder, and Republican.

Hays became president of the Motion Picture Producers and Distributors of America (MPPDA), an organization supported and financed by all the major film companies in America. It became known colloquially as the Hays Office, and he headed it for 23 years. In 1945, the MPPDA became the MPAA (Motion Picture Association of America), and Hays was succeeded by Eric Johnston, who headed the MPAA until 1966, when Jack Valenti became its president.

Rather than taking concrete censorship actions, the Hays Office sought to counter bad publicity with good, to keep the press from magnifying its tales of Hollywood debauches, to regularize business procedures, and to encourage producers to submit their films voluntarily for prerelease examination. The loose, informal advising of the Hays Office in the 1920s was another in a series of successful Hollywood attempts to keep films out of the hands of

Fig. 6-12

Early film censorship: the 1897 hoochy-coochy dancer Fatima, without and with her censorship stripes.

Fig. 6-13

government censors, a strategy that would be duplicated by the enforcement of the much stricter and more formal Hollywood Production Code of the 1930s and the MPAA Rating System that was set up in 1968 and is still in force.

Films and Filmmakers, 1910–28

The ever-increasing problem of the American director was how to make an individualized, special film in a factory system geared toward standardization and mass production. The Griffith era of anarchy and improvisation was rapidly passing. Rather than being the artistic creator of his own films, the director was more and more expected to be the mechanic who hammered together the machine that others, the producer and writer, had earlier designed. Griffith himself noted with dismay the widening gap between producer and director, between the business of making a film and the art of making a film. Each movie, rather than being an important work in itself, became only one unit of the studio's yearly output. This industrialization of the film business is most relevant to the career of Thomas H. Ince, Griffith's contemporary and one of the most interesting American producers and directors of noncomic films before 1919.

Thomas Ince

Ince's films are almost the paradigmatic opposites of Griffith's. Whereas Griffith's technique aimed at developing the characters, their emotions, and the metaphoric implications of the action, Ince concentrated ruthlessly on the narrative flow. Ince was as avid a film editor as Griffith, but whereas Griffith cut to develop rhythm, emotion, and ideas, Ince—like Howard Hawks after him— cut to keep the story moving. Griffith's interest was in why the characters did something and what that implied symbolically; Ince's focused on what they did. Ince's symbolic antiwar epic, *Civilization* (1916), is an exception. More typical of Ince, however, is a film like *The Coward* (1915), a Civil War story that avoids all the symbolic freight of a *Birth of a Nation* to concentrate on one young man's earning his "red badge of courage." The titles of the films (the specificity of Ince's, abstractness of Griffith's) are indicative.

In an Ince film, one of the most common and beautiful images is smoke—the swirling, enveloping movement of gunpowder or dust, shot through refractive beams of light. The producer Ince's most able director of these early westerns was Francis Ford, whose crisp, deep-focus shots established the photographic conventions of the western. Ince's productions also popularized one of the western's most enduring character types, the good–bad man—embodied by William S. Hart. A little too tough, stubborn and ornery, sometimes even on the wrong side of the law, he could always be depended on to do the right thing in a crunch.

Ince, Ford, and Hart would later pass on these legacies—the power of movement within vast western vistas and the dignity of the good–bad men who inhabit these spaces—to their successors: Ford's younger brother, John, as well as Howard Hawks, Sam Peckinpah, and many others.

As a supervisor of production, Ince could keep his finger on several projects at the same time. And as producer of his own films, he had complete control. Many current directors (Steven Spielberg, for example) have both directed and produced. Ince insisted on a detailed shooting script, which he eventually approved and stamped "Shoot as is." The Ince director then went about the business of constructing from the producer's blueprint. Ince supplemented the shooting script with a detailed production breakdown and schedule, making sure that all people and animals and equipment went to the right place at the right time for the fewest number of hours. If Griffith was the American cinema's first real director, Ince was its first important producer, instituting the system that divided the artistic responsibility for a film between two people—or camps. Ince showed the future studio heads how to run a studio.

Ironically, Ince's career waned in the Studio Era itself. He was the hardest hit by the failure of the Triangle Film Corporation, which depended on his films and his Culver City studio. The company collapsed in 1919. Ince, the movie man of system and efficiency, died mysteriously (after having been shot on William Randolph Hearst's yacht—apparently by Hearst, who mistook him for someone else) in 1924, just when the era of system and efficiency had officially arrived with the Mayer–Thalberg rule at MGM, which stood on Ince's old lot.

Douglas Fairbanks

The films of Douglas Fairbanks also reveal the changing values of Hollywood. Fairbanks broke into films with Griffith at Triangle; the young actor was so athletic, so bouncy, so perpetually in motion that Griffith gave up on him and suggested he go see Mr. Sennett. Triangle eventually let Fairbanks go his own way, pairing him with writer Anita Loos, her director–husband John Emerson, and cameraman Victor Fleming. Between 1915 and 1920, the group produced a series of breezy, parodic, energetic comedies that combined the star's athleticism, energy, and sincerity with the writer's and director's wit and style. The early Fairbanks films—like the utterly outrageous *The Mystery of the Leaping Fish* (1916)—are refreshing surprises. They are parodies that make fun of a personality trait (American snobbishness, the fascination with royalty, the hunger for publicity, the ambition to achieve the impossible) or a genre of films (the western, the mystery, the melodrama). Fairbanks is the center of the parody, the magnified version of whatever the film is satirizing. But Fairbanks, because of his naïveté and enthusiasm, because of his obvious love of life and people, always succeeds in engaging our sympathies at the same time that we may be laughing at him.

One of the key contrasts in his early films is between the dull, routine, banal life Fairbanks must live in conventional society and the imaginative, free, vigorous life he wants to live. Fairbanks was the foe of the dull and regimented; the row upon row of similar desks in the button factory of *Reaching for the Moon* (1917) was an image of everything he hated.

The later Fairbanks films of the 1920s—*The Mark of Zorro* (1920, where he leads a real, not imaginary, double life as the movies' original caped crusader), *Robin Hood* (1922), *The Thief of Bagdad* (1924), and *The Black Pirate* (1926, shot in two-strip Technicolor)—make quite a contrast with the earlier, breezy ones. Fairbanks is still a great athlete; he still has his smile and energy. But he is no longer a contemporary American trying to strike a blend between his own imaginative impulses and the conventions of society. Fairbanks has been transported to faraway, romantic lands of long ago.

DeMille and von Stroheim

No two directors more clearly show the problems of the filmmaker in the 1920s than Cecil B. DeMille and Erich von Stroheim (he added the "von" himself and may be referred to as Stroheim or von Stroheim). As were Griffith and Ince a few years earlier, the two are almost paradigms for the whole industry. Von Stroheim gave the public what he wanted; DeMille gave it what he thought it wanted. Von Stroheim was a ruthless realist committed to his art and his vision; DeMille was willing to throw in any faddish or striking hokum. Von Stroheim's greatest tools were close observation and detail; DeMille's were size and splash. DeMille was a big producer; von Stroheim's tragedy was that he had to depend on producers. Von Stroheim's films, despite their adult themes, were controlled by the director's taste and intelligence; most of DeMille's films had everything but taste and intelligence.

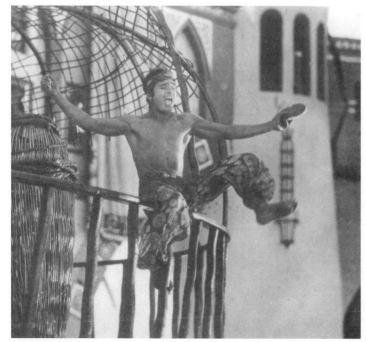

Fig. 6-14

The Americano gone exotic—
Douglas Fairbanks in **The Thief of Bagdad.**

The two films that most clearly reveal the differences in the two men are DeMille's *Male and Female* and von Stroheim's *Blind Husbands.* Both were released in 1919; both capitalized on the new audience interest in sexual amours and the doings of the rich. Both suggested the importance of sex in human relationships. There the similarities stop. *Male and Female* is a lavish, pretentious, and inconsistent examination of the class question, which seems to suggest both that masters may marry their servants and that masters may not marry their servants. Although some of the film's confusion stems from the J. M. Barrie play DeMille was adapting, *The Admirable Crichton*, the most dazzling stupidities are DeMille's "additions." For example, the film begins with an irrelevant sequence that does not exist in the original play, a series of shots of oceans and the Grand Canyon, followed by a biblical quote, "God created man in his own image." Much of DeMille's later work also uses the Bible to dignify its distinctly lay interests.

After spending a lot of time in Gloria Swanson's elegant bathroom (she plays the wealthy Mary), the film takes her whole household—including the butler and the maid—on a yachting trip. When the yacht runs aground, the butler (his name is Crichton) becomes the natural leader while the upper crust becomes the soggy bottom. After Mary and Crichton vow their love for one another, there is an instantaneous and unmotivated cut to Babylon (the scene does not exist, of course, in Barrie's play). The motivation for the shift is the line of poetry that Crichton and Mary have read in the film (Barrie uses the line just once, but DeMille repeats it several times so we don't miss it), "If I were a king of Babylon. . . ." DeMille is not one to leave his ifs iffy. In this sequence, Crichton is indeed king, and Mary is a Christian slave. The fact that the Babylonian empire had evaporated hundreds of years before the coming of Christ does not offend DeMille's sense of history.

This film is clearly one of the bastard progeny of *Intolerance* in its combination of different epochs in a single film. But in *Male and Female*, the diversity is pointless and pretentious, and the moralizing is hypocritical, as DeMille's often was.

His racy films (like *Why Change Your Wife?*, 1920, and *Forbidden Fruit*, 1922) flirt with naughtiness and sell conventionality; his religious films—including both the 1923 and 1956 versions of *The Ten Commandments*—magnify both righteousness and lewdness.

Nevertheless, DeMille's importance is extreme. *The Squaw Man* (1919)—Hollywood's first feature–length western—put Hollywood on the map, and for decades DeMille remained, in many minds, the ultimate Hollywood director and producer. In *Sunset Boulevard* (1950) Billy Wilder cast him as an exemplary professional. His pictures were always big, good-looking, and entertaining, a guaranteed good time. His westerns (*The Virginian*, 1914; *The Plainsman*, 1936, released 1937) and some of his melodramas were gripping. The very best of his silents, *The Cheat* (1915, starring Sessue Hayakawa as a Japanese collector—changed to Burmese in the 1918 reissue—who brands a woman who reneges on a sexual deal), is so darkly and richly lit that it could be mistaken for a post-Expressionist *film noir.*

Von Stroheim's *Blind Husbands* is a far less complicated story than *Male and Female*. A doctor and his wife travel to the Alps; he pays her insufficient sexual attention. A German military officer named von Steuben (played by von Stroheim) seduces the young wife. The husband's blindness finally clears up; on a climactic hiking trip, the two males confront each other on the pinnacle, and the rival perishes, more a victim of the mountains and of cowardice than of the husband. The power of the film lies in von Stroheim's reduction of the quantity of incidents (quantity was DeMille's credo) to develop the quality, the feeling, the texture of the incidents he includes. Von Stroheim was such a master of *mise-en-scène* that his films remain powerful even if they were recut (actually, massacred) by lesser talents after having been taken out of his hands; we can still see what's *in the shot* and respond to that. Details develop the film's emotional dynamics: the calm husband's pipe; the wife's provocative ankles and shoes; the officer's handling of his monocle and his careful primping with brush, comb, and vaporizer of cologne to make himself sexually attractive.

Von Stroheim's technique owes its greatest debt to his first master, Griffith. As Griffith had, von Stroheim realized that the filmmaker's principal tools are editing (montage) and staging and design (*mise-en-scène*). Von Stroheim's care with sets, lighting, costumes, and decor is so meticulous in creating his seamy world that you can almost smell it.

As an editor, von Stroheim further developed Griffith's devices of the cross-cut (to show parallel events in different places at the same time) and the subjective cut (to show the mental projection of a character: what is in his or her mind's eye at a particular moment). In *Blind Husbands*, von Stroheim's cross-cutting develops both tension and irony. For example, he shows the doctor delivering a baby at the same time that von Steuben courts his wife, obviously trying to perform the act that produces babies.

André Bazin described von Stroheim's "one simple rule for direction": "Take a close look at the world, keep on doing so, and in the end it will lay bare for you all its cruelty and ugliness." Von Stroheim's films are populated with physical cripples and mental defectives, but even beneath the surfaces of his more elegant characters—their polished manners, white gloves, and spray perfume—lurk animal rapacity, vicious cruelty, obsessive desire, and the brutal will to power.

Foolish Wives made von Stroheim world famous. When Jean Renoir saw it, he decided to make movies instead of ceramics. Like *Blind Husbands* and *The Devil's Pass-Key* (1920, now lost), and even his later *The Merry Widow* (1925), *Foolish Wives* was extremely popular with audiences who appreciated its careful examination of bedroom tensions. The haughty independence of its director was less popular with the heads of studios. The greatest realist of the Silent Era, von Stroheim, in his refusal to compromise, made stunning films and lasting enemies.

Erich von Stroheim was a completist, a perfectionist, an idealist who took film and its possibilities absolutely seriously. He was forced to work with executives (much like those who run Hollywood today) who maintained that they had an instinct for show business and knew better than anyone else what made a good picture—or had experience with budgets and could recognize an advisable investment. Most of them regarded von Stroheim as an egomaniac whose projects always needed to be brought under control.

Irving Thalberg, who was to become MGM's most creative production executive before his early death, hated von Stroheim and his work. When Thalberg was Carl Laemmle's assistant at Universal, he removed von Stroheim from *Merry-Go-Round* (1922) in the middle of

Fig. 6-15

Foolish Wives: *Erich von Stroheim (as Karamzin, the bogus Russian Count) defines his murderousness on a seaside pistol range.*

On location: Gibson Gowland and ZaSu Pitts in Greed.

Fig. 6-16

shooting, firing him for his "inefficient" (that is, perfectionistic and uncompromising) production methods, his wasteful expenditures on "invisible" details (which were actually quite visible in the convincing realism and texture of the film), and his insubordination (von Stroheim said they often "crossed swords"). At MGM, Thalberg would get the chance to fire von Stroheim again—and beyond that, to destroy his greatest work, in one of film history's true horror stories, the re-editing of *Greed* (1924).

Greed

Von Stroheim had long wanted to film a complete novel, and the one he chose—by Frank Norris, a writer he knew Griffith admired—was *McTeague, A Story of San Francisco* (1899). In 1922, he interested Samuel Goldwyn in backing the project and was hired by the Goldwyn Company, whose slogan was "the author and the play are the thing."

Von Stroheim did not, as it is often said, set out to film *McTeague* page by page; his script includes most of the novel but changes and adds a great deal, and where the novel was strictly realistic, the film was that and more. Shot almost entirely on location in an era of studio shooting, it was also an experiment in Expressionism; it observed behavior from the outside, as tightly and scrupulously as the job

has ever been done, but it also dipped into the mind and displayed its disturbing contents.

In the leading roles, he cast Gibson Gowland as McTeague, ZaSu Pitts as Trina (one of the silent screen's greatest performances), and Jean Hersholt as Marcus. In addition to Ben Reynolds, the cinematographers were William H. Daniels and Ernest B. Schoedsack. With cast and crew, von Stroheim went to San Francisco to shoot on the very streets named in the novel, and even to Death Valley (in the summer!) to obtain absolutely authentic details. Jean Hersholt had to be hospitalized after the grueling takes in Death Valley. The film took seven months to shoot and cost $470,000; then von Stroheim edited it for months.

The original version of *Greed*—previewed to two journalists, who wrote about what they saw, and one director—ran 42 reels, a mere 9 hours at 20 fps. That first audience felt they had seen the greatest movie ever made or likely to be made. Von Stroheim himself shortened the film to 24 reels (just over 5 hours, considered the "director's version"), to be shown in two parts, with a dinner break after the wedding sequence. His friend at Metro, Rex Ingram (who had been the director in that first audience), cut the film to 18 reels and forbade von Stroheim to let anyone take another foot out of it. By this time the Maria/Zerkow and Baker/Grannis stories, to be discussed below, had been trimmed drastically but not deleted, and the film was still in two parts.

Meanwhile, as mentioned earlier, the Goldwyn Company merged in 1924 with Metro Pictures and with Louis B. Mayer Productions, forming Metro–Goldwyn–Mayer. Mayer hired Thalberg away from Universal and put him directly in charge of production. All this made *Greed* an MGM property and put von Stroheim at Thalberg's mercy, which was not a good place to be. Fully backed up by Mayer, Thalberg turned the film over to the MGM story and editing departments; under the loose supervision of June Mathis, a hack cutter and title writer named Joseph W. Farnham—who had not read the book or the script—completed the hatchet job. What was left of a long, tight masterpiece was a mess; von Stroheim said the cutter had nothing on his mind but a hat.

The final version of *Greed* began with a very bad poem about gold. The lengthy prologue was cut to less than 5 minutes. Mathis and Farnham wrote idiotic intertitles to patch up some of the holes they had created in the story's continuity and in the characters' motivations. In addition, many scenes were shuffled out of order, and three Expressionist shots—out of all those sequences, many of which had presented the dreams and hallucinations of a crazy junkman, obsessed with discovering a 100-plate service of solid gold, but some of which had used grotesque shadows and figures to convey the violence and madness of the waking world—were randomly cut into the realistic footage as "symbolic" commentary on the greed of the characters. *Greed* was released at 10 reels (2¼ hours with no intermission), no copies of the earlier versions were made, and except for the 10 reels used in *Greed*, the negative was destroyed along with all the outtakes so that the silver might be retrieved from the celluloid.

The *Greed* that exists (the release version) must be watched as a series of parts rather than as a whole. It's all that's left. For one who hasn't read Norris's novel, the film's narrative is almost incomprehensible. The concrete process of the dissolution of the relationship between the dentist, John McTeague (Mac), and his wife, Trina Sieppe, makes no sense in the film, for in the novel Norris carefully charts it by moving the

couple to shabbier and shabbier living quarters— a practice followed in von Stroheim's script (which was faithful to the novel but not afraid to add a feature-length prologue, a funeral at a wedding, or a second pet bird). Each degradation in their physical surroundings implies or contributes to their bodily, emotional, moral, and psychological degradation. But in *Greed*, although we may notice that the walls of the McTeague household change as the film progresses, we never know exactly when, why, and where the couple has moved, or how the delicate Trina became so rough and sloppy. Although in one shot we may notice that Trina's bandaged hand is missing several fingers, the film only hints that she lost them because they became infected after her husband bit them. The dissolution from happy marriage to vicious, insane combat—which is, both psychologically and economically, the meticulously observed subject of at least half of the novel (and of the screenplay)—barely exists in the film.

Another reason this sense of gradual, inevitable dissolution is lost is that the 10-reel version had to do without two other "love" relationships in the novel that undoubtedly seemed superfluous to a hack writer and cutter but that are really essential. The relationship between Trina and Mac is bounded, on the one hand, by old Grannis and Miss Baker, a couple of timid old folks who carry on a genteel, unphysical love affair, and, on the other, by Zerkow (the crazy junkman) and Maria Macapa, two obsessed, slovenly human beasts whose "love" is based on Zerkow's almost sexual pleasure in listening to the equally insane Maria's story of her hoard of gold. Maria remains in the released film barely long enough to sell Trina the fateful lottery ticket; Zerkow is deleted entirely. All that remains of their love story are a few shots of skeletal, photographically distorted arms playing with distorted treasures; taken out of the Maria–Zerkow context and applied to Trina, these shots seem irrelevant and pretentious. In the novel, we understand the original love of Mac and Trina, together with their originally rational view of money, as a median between the sexual repression and parsimony of the old folks and the crazed passion of the gold lovers. Trina begins as Miss Baker's close friend, somewhat repulsed by Maria's crudeness, and gradually drifts into becoming Maria's confidante. Mac and Trina even move into the squalid hovel where Zerkow and

Maria lived (which became vacant when Zerkow cut Maria's throat). Without the two poles of these other couples, *Greed* has no moral scale on which to measure the direction and degree of decay in the central couple; it is a triptych missing its outer panels.

Despite the incoherence of *Greed* as a whole, the *mise-en-scène* survives within the surviving shots. The wedding ceremony is a mixture of the comic and the somber: a parody of wedding customs that is overshadowed by the sight of a funeral cortege through an open window (a great use of deep focus and an omen of the direction the marriage will take). The scene in which Trina realizes that she is alone—with no one to protect her except the stranger who is her husband—is a rich examination of her feelings. The mad scene that climaxes her perverse confusion of money and sex, where she lies naked in bed with her gold, is daring, terrifying, and cinematically unprecedented. Mac's murder of Trina is a study in shadow—indoors, at night, as dark as any *noir*—while the showdown between Mac and Marcus in Death Valley is all pitiless light.

Because his production methods seemed extravagant, because he seemed mean and tyrannical, unwholesome and unpleasant, Erich von Stroheim was very easy to fire, even if his films made money. *The Merry Widow* (1925), a cynical adaptation of the Viennese operetta, was his last film for MGM and MGM's first big hit. He went to work for Zukor and had as little success with him as with Thalberg. After two very interesting projects of 1926–29, *The Wedding March* (released in 1928) and *Queen Kelly* (released 1932; produced by Gloria Swanson, who fired him, too), Erich von Stroheim directed only one other film, *Walking Down Broadway* (1932, released 1933 as *Hello, Sister!* after much tampering and reshooting by others). For the next 25 years von Stroheim continued acting in films, most memorably as von Rauffenstein in *Grand Illusion* (1937; directed by Renoir, whose entire career and aesthetic he had decisively influenced) and as Max, the chauffeur and former movie director, in *Sunset Boulevard*. The irony of this late film was not only that von Stroheim played a character whose career echoed his own (the clips Norma Desmond screens in the movie are from his own *Queen Kelly*), but also that he played the devoted servant of Gloria Swanson, who was with him at the stormy end of his Hollywood road.

Henry King

Despite his long career, Henry King may always be remembered as the director of *Tol'able David* (1921), a powerful film in which King, the student

The wedding scene of Greed, *composed in depth, with the funeral procession outside on the street below.*

Fig. 6-17

of Griffith and the employee of Ince, combines the best of both masters. King's world in *Tol'able David* is similar to Griffith's Kentucky: rural, homey, gently comic, touching, pastoral. Into the peaceful world come the violent figures from outside, three fugitives from justice, who are as vicious, as nasty, as psychotically mean as Battling Burrows. Like Griffith, King defines the characters by their responses to animals: David lovingly plays with his dog, Rocket; the invaders kill Rocket out of pure meanness. And the worst thing anyone can do in a Hollywood movie is kill a dog.

King directed Lillian Gish in two very successful silents, *The White Sister* (1923) and *Romola* (1924). His later works include *Alexander's Ragtime Band* (1938), *Twelve O'Clock High* (1949), *The Gunfighter* (1950), *Carousel* (1956), and *Tender is the Night* (1962).

Oscar Micheaux and the Race Movie

Oscar Micheaux, born in Metropolis, Illinois, in 1884, was one of the earliest black filmmakers. After a brief, unsuccessful effort to direct films in Hollywood, he started his own one-man studio, based primarily in Manhattan but active in the Midwest and elsewhere. Between 1918 and 1948,

Micheaux singlehandedly wrote, produced, directed, edited, and distributed more than 30 features for the Micheaux Film Corporation.

His first picture, *The Homesteader* (1918), was based on his own novel—the book that Lincoln Pictures had wanted someone else to direct. In 1919, he made *Within Our Gates* (released 1920), the first picture to present a lynching from an African-American point of view. In 1920, he showed blacks fighting back against the KKK in *The Symbol of the Unconquered*, whose title played cleverly on a line from *The Birth of a Nation*, where the burning cross is called the "symbol of an unconquered race"; the unconquered here are brave, honest, hardworking blacks. During the 1920s, his most popular film was *Body and Soul* (1924, remade 1925), which starred the great singer Paul Robeson in the double role of a nice young man and an evil phony preacher.

After starring in *The Emperor Jones* on stage and screen, Robeson left for England, where the industry was more open to giving serious roles to blacks. There he starred in such films as *Song of Freedom* (1936), *King Solomon's Mines* (1937), and *The Proud Valley* (1940), though he also dropped back to the U.S. to sing "Ol' Man River"

Paul Robeson in the 1924 version of Micheaux's Body and Soul.

Fig. 6-18

in *Show Boat* (1936), a song whose lyrics he would ironically revise in his peace concerts and leftist rallies.

Never as political as Robeson, but just as determined to make the world listen to a black voice, Micheaux set the pattern and created the market for the "race movie." Race movies were made with black casts for black audiences and played in segregated theatres (or in special after-hours showings at other theatres), and they lasted about as long as segregated theatres did, falling to the civil rights movement as much as to such all-black-cast Hollywood pictures as *Carmen Jones* (1954). Although few filmmakers followed Micheaux in building their plots around mixed-blood romances, they did follow him in ditching Hollywood stereotypes of black characters and in tackling a broad range of genres, including the gangster picture (*Dark Manhattan*, 1937), the "woman's picture" (*The Scar of Shame*, 1926), and the western (*Two-Gun Man from Harlem*, 1938).

Whether it was set in a strict religious context or in a nightclub, the battle between good and evil became a dominant theme of the race movie, without any urging from the Hays Office. From the troubling image of the duplicitous "man of God" in *Body and Soul* to the dripping holy blood that saves a soul in Spencer Williams's devout afterlife folk drama, *The Blood of Jesus* (1941), sin is a serious matter in these pictures, not something to flirt with, and choices are made at genuine moral crossroads, by real characters.

Resenting the way Hollywood portrayed blacks (whether they were cast as servants, in comic roles, or picking cotton—as they usually were—he found the actors "ugly"), Micheaux filled his films with beautiful women, decent and handsome men, and children who were as attractive and perceptive as Hollywood's white kids. Though his films did good business around the country, and great business in Latin America, Micheaux was particularly aware that his films were needed in the South, where black audiences had no other opportunity to see blacks who (like many rich blacks in the big cities of the North) lived in penthouses, had servants, and went out to the best nightclubs; only in Micheaux's films could they see African-American actors playing leading roles and, as Micheaux actress Bee Freeman put it, "really dressed up, really living, and talking like people talk."

The majority of his films were made in big cities, on tight, precise budgets and with smart showmanship. He was the first African American to make a talkie: *The Exile* (1931), based on his first novel, *The Conquest.* As he had once sold that and his other novels (*The Homesteader, The Forged Note*) from door to door, he drove from town to town with his sound pictures, bringing the Cotton Club to Georgia and (since it went unrepresented in other pictures) Harlem to Harlem—in his own way, of course, with melodramatic plots that often turned on issues of racial identity. Many of Micheaux's films climax with the characters' finding out who they are—that is, who their parents are (*Within Our Gates*) and whether they have black or white blood. *The Exile* concerns a black man from Chicago who goes to South Dakota and falls in love with a white woman, who fortunately turns out to be partly black. *God's Step Children* (1938)—a film that combined and went beyond *Imitation of Life* and *These Three*, as its trailer pointed out—told the unhappy story of a light-skinned girl described by a schoolmate as "stuck up, and she don't want to be colored."

Micheaux's pictures looked and sounded rough. Even if his camera might be in the right place, the microphone never was. He shot no retakes. His cutting was ham handed, and sometimes he even had problems with screen direction—as when characters in separate shots run away from each other into each other. But even when the stories were corny and the acting was awful, the films were exciting because they showed blacks living lives far more genuine than anything Hollywood had even thought of offering. A diversely talented man, Micheaux got the films made, and he got them shown. He was the first black filmmaker anywhere in the world to become widely known, and not coincidentally the most persistent.

Webber and Watson

One of the challenges the narrative film has regularly set itself is that of adapting a literary work for the screen. From *Greed* to *The Maltese Falcon* (1941), the problem—and the solution—has been to discover cinematic ways of conveying the essence as well as the characters, style, plot, and point of the purely verbal original.

In 1928, one of the greatest of all avant-garde teams—in effect, the American rivals of the Surrealists Luis Buñuel and Salvador Dalí in France—independently shot and released their masterpiece, *The Fall of the House of Usher*, based on the story by Edgar Allan Poe; they were James Sibley Watson (director and cinematographer) and Melville Webber (writer and art director). This one-reel Expressionist film—a silent whose music track was added later—uses torn and multiplied images, ominous shadows, stylized figures and sets, superimposed graphics, extreme shooting angles, every possible special effect, and jagged, dizzying movement to conjure a mood—entirely true to Poe—of intermingled beauty and horror. (The same year, in France, Jean Epstein directed a four-reel Impressionist version, *La Chute de la maison Usher.*) Webber and Watson's only other film was *Lot in Sodom* (1933), a biblical adaptation whose sexual content proved too strong for audiences of the day.

Weber and Women

As a producer reporting to Thalberg at MGM, but given a free hand by him, Lillian Gish took on the challenge of adapting Nathaniel Hawthorne's *The Scarlet Letter*, a project that had been opposed by every women's club in the country because its plot concerns adultery with a capital A, not to mention with a clergyman. When MGM told her "it wasn't allowed," she said, "What do you mean it's not allowed? It's an American classic, and I'm an American—why can't I make it?" When Gish contacted the women's clubs and told them she would be in charge of the project, their respect for her good taste and judgment led them to drop all opposition. To direct *The Scarlet Letter* (1926), she brought Victor Sjøstrøm (who signed his American pictures Seastrom) to Hollywood from Sweden. The picture was a great success—as were Gish's other productions, including the 1926 *La Bohème*, adapted from the novel and play on which Puccini's opera was based. But her greatest production, and the second film Sjøstrøm directed for her, was *The Wind* (1928), based closely on the 1925 novel by Dorothy Scarborough and shot in the Mojave Desert. In this film Gish gives one of her very finest performances—her best since *Way Down East*—as a woman driven mad by the relentless, demonic,

almost sexually charged wind that drives the sand across the Texas plains and through every crack in the shack she shares with her husband.

Other women worked in Hollywood, and not just in front of the camera. A great many were script supervisors, screenwriters, film editors, and negative cutters. As a producer of narrative films, Mary Pickford was one of the most important figures in the industry. Margaret Winkler Mintz was the first woman to produce and distribute cartoons; in 1922, when she was 25, she founded M. J. Winkler & Co. in New York, and within a year it became the world's largest distributor of shorts.

In the 1910s and early 1920s, at least 30 women directors were active in Hollywood, many of them—like Ida May Park and Ruth Ann Baldwin—at Universal Pictures, where Carl Laemmle was in favor of hiring women. The greatest of them all was Lois Weber, who was born in Pennsylvania in 1882. Weber became a street evangelist and then an actress. In 1908, she began making films at Gaumont in New Jersey, under the supervision of Herbert Blaché—whose wife, Alice Guy Blaché, had been the first woman to make a film. Weber joined Universal as a contract director in 1912. Between then and the end of the Silent Era, she was the best known American woman director and the most highly paid female director in the world.

In 1917, Weber set up her own Los Angeles studio, Lois Weber Productions. Her husband, Phillips Smalley, was her "advisory director" and co-author, but she was by far the dominant creative figure. Between 1912 and 1927 she wrote, directed, and in most cases produced 45 films, many of which starred either herself or the woman she made a star, Claire Windsor. Weber was deeply concerned with social and spiritual issues and saw the cinema as a way to spread moral messages to a vast audience. Like Griffith (*What Shall We Do With Our Old?*), she was a pioneer in what would later be called the "problem picture," and the issues addressed in her timely, insightful, compassionate, superbly crafted films remain relevant. Her works include *Hypocrites* (1914), *Where Are My Children?* (1916, about birth control), and *The Blot* (1921, about underpaid professors). She lost her studio in 1923 when she and Smalley divorced. In the late 1920s, she made a few pictures for Universal and her last silent (*The Angel of Broadway*, 1927, about a

Alice Guy's **The Tigress** *played to packed houses in 1914.*

Fig. 6-19

Salvation Army worker) for DeMille. She directed one talkie (*White Heat*—not the one with Cagney) in 1934.

Dorothy Arzner, who was to become the best known American woman director of the 1930s (as Ida Lupino was in the early 1950s), was born in San Francisco in 1900. She worked as a waitress in her father's Hollywood café before becoming an ambulance driver in World War I. At Paramount she went from secretary to script clerk to negative cutter to film editor. Her brilliant editing of the bullfight scenes in the Valentino hit *Blood and Sand* (1922) won her the chance to edit *The Covered Wagon*. For the next few years she was a highly respected editor and screenwriter. To keep her from leaving, Paramount made her a director in 1927. That first year, she directed what Paramount considered appropriate projects for a woman: *Fashions for Women, Ten Modern Commandments*, and *Get Your Man*. But soon she was making the films that would make her famous: *The Wild Party* (1929), *Honor Among Lovers* (1931), *Working Girls* (1931), *Merrily We Go to Hell* (1932), *Christopher Strong* (1933), *Nana* (1934), *Craig's Wife* (1936), and *Dance, Girl, Dance* (1940).

As the big studios flourished, many of the Independents folded. Pickford had been the only woman involved in the founding of a Hollywood

major (United Artists), but some of these smaller companies had been founded by women, notably Alice Guy, Lois Weber, and Nell Shipman.

Alice Guy, now Mme. Blaché in the American press, which found the existence of a woman director newsworthy in itself—and for over 15 years, she *was* the only one in the world—founded the Solax Company in 1910. She hung signs all around her New Jersey studio that reminded the actors, "Be Natural." In the next three years she produced, supervised, and in many cases directed over 320 shorts and eight features for Solax, while Blaché handled the business affairs and directed some of the pictures. "A husband easily doubts the talent of a wife," she wrote in her autobiography. In 1913 her husband founded Blaché Pictures, which, with Guy's consent, absorbed Solax. The new company survived under various names—after 1917, without Guy—till the end of the decade, when Blaché finished it off by leaving his wife and children and debts to head for Hollywood with his leading actress. Like Weber, Guy was brought down by her husband and junior collaborator.

Nell Shipman worked outside Hollywood too, but not in New Jersey. She preferred wild, open country; the company of animals, her co-stars; and a small company of professionals, like her cameraman, the great Joseph B. Walker.

A Canadian, she was responsible for Canada's first extant feature, *Back To God's Country* (1919, directed by David M. Hartford), starring in the film and co-producing it after having made the initial decision to adapt the novel. Revolted by the cruel ways animals were treated and the unnatural ways women were dressed and groomed—breasts strapped flat, hair in little curls—she rejected Hollywood's acting contracts and founded Nell Shipman Productions (1921–25). Her co-producer and occasional co-director was her second husband, Bert Van Tuyle.

Entirely outside Hollywood, in France, the most important woman director of the 1920s was Germaine Dulac. Her avant-garde films—particularly *The Seashell and the Clergyman* (1928)—broke the barriers of reason and perception along with those of gender. There were still a few years to go before the best known woman director, in Europe or anywhere else, would be Leni Riefenstahl.

King Vidor

King Vidor effectively mixed wartime humor, anti-war propaganda, and a touching love story in *The Big Parade* (1925), the fifth or sixth top-grossing film of the decade (at the box office, it did as well as *The Jazz Singer*), then followed it with his masterpiece, *The Crowd* (1928), a brilliantly composed film full of powerful and daring camera movements, made deliberately without stars, that tells the story of an ordinary man—and his long-suffering wife—who can't stand the thought that he's not marked out for some special destiny, that he's not better than everyone else. In the extraordinary final shot, when the man and wife and their surviving child are shown having a good time in a theatre, reconciled to each other, to their little triumphs, and to being ordinary, the camera rapidly pulls back to reveal row after row of patrons, leaving the momentary hero behind in the crowd—a crowd of theatre patrons facing, in the real movie theatre, a crowd of moviegoers.

Among Vidor's many subsequent films, the one that most complements and opposes *The Crowd* is his superb adaptation of Ayn Rand's *The Fountainhead* (1949), which takes for its hero a man who *is* presented as morally and intellectually superior to most of those around him and who is last seen atop a skyscraper, well above any crowd. The hero of *The Fountainhead* is an uncompromising architect who makes his own dreams come true, and perhaps that is the key to Vidor's idealistic puzzle: that some of his characters are practical dreamers, like the heroes who bring water to their commune in *Our Daily Bread* (1934) or the architect who creates his skyscraper; and that some, whose ambitions are frustrated or self-contradictory from the start, or who *just* dream, are destroyed by their dreams, like the heroine of *Duel in the Sun* (1947), if they do not learn to find joy in what they have, like the hero of *The Crowd*—but that all of them are compelling in their idealism, however misguided or on target it may be, and in the emotion and the sense of being that they pour into their obsessions. Only King Vidor, working with Barbara Stanwyck, could make the self-denying/self-fulfilling obsessive project of *Stella Dallas* (1937) so credible and involving.

Lubitsch and Others

Among the most important of the newcomers was a German director, Ernst Lubitsch. Hollywood had begun importing many of the leading directors of Europe: Mauritz Stiller, Victor Sjøstrøm, Fritz Lang, F. W. Murnau, E. A. Dupont. But none found Hollywood so comfortable and so amicable a home as Lubitsch. Mary Pickford imported him specifically to direct a costume spectacle, *Rosita*, for her. Pickford, like her husband, sought to change her adolescent image: to grow up, cut her curls, and show she was a woman. Lubitsch, who had directed a string of costume pageants in Germany (*Gypsy Blood, Passion, Deception*) that had become popular in America for their comic "humanizing" (i.e., eroticizing) of history, was Pickford's choice. *Rosita* (1923) proved the beginning of the end of Pickford's career and the beginning of Lubitsch's. He immediately turned to polite, witty, understated drawing-room comedies: *The Marriage Circle* (1924), *Lady Windermere's Fan* (1925), *So This Is Paris* (1926).

Lubitsch's comedy derived from one essential theme: the limits and defects of human vision. Characters see either too little or too much in Lubitsch's silent comedies. They see too little because their views are blocked—by their own willful blindness, the prejudices of their society, or the simple physical fact that they can see only part of the whole picture, framed by some window or door that obscures as much as it reveals. When Mary Pickford quarreled with Lubitsch, she called him a director of doors, not of people. Lubitsch would use these doors (and windows) to reveal something about people: that human vision is always limited—by assumption, attitude, and prejudice.

If Lubitsch's people see too little, they also see too much when they make some inference about another character based on the mere sight of a physical object—the straw hats, canes, and fans that play such a large role in Lubitsch's comedies of manners—because they imply where and *with whom* a character has been. To make movies about the fallibility of human vision is a highly appropriate piece of cinematic irony and self-reference, since cinema itself depends on structuring human vision, framing visual limitations, and encouraging us to draw inferences from sights of material objects. Lubitsch's clever ability to manipulate the cinema frame and to imply so much with seemingly trivial details would soon allow him to make some of the very best early American sound films.

Flaherty and the Silent Documentary

Many directors of the 1920s worked outside the fences of the Hollywood formulas. One of them was Robert Flaherty, the father of the documentary feature, who had been taking his camera to Hudson Bay since 1913; the eventual result was *Nanook of the North* (1922).

The first films had been nonfiction: records of actual human activity, snapshots in which things moved. There were *actualités* of trains rushing by, of life in foreign lands, and of newsworthy events (on-the-spot footage of the 1906 San Francisco earthquake). There were also faked reconstructions of events, from *Tearing Down the Spanish Flag* (1898) to the *Eruption of Mount Vesuvius* (1905).

Beginning in 1918, Dziga Vertov made newsreels by assembling the bits of film sent to him by traveling cameramen, in which the people and activities of the new Soviet Union were recorded. In 1922, the year of *Nanook*, Vertov began shooting film and expanding his experiments both in montage and in ways to capture unstaged reality ("life unawares"); he named the new series *Kinó-Pravda*, as if it were the film version of the newspaper *Pravda* ("truth"). Vertov's work led

him to the genres of the "compilation film," in which a movie is created out of found footage; the "candid camera," in which people are photographed without being asked and without at first being aware of any camera, so that they have no opportunity to pose or to behave in an unnatural manner; *cinéma vérité* ("film truth"; French for *kinó-pravda*) or "direct cinema," in which the camera is an acknowledged element of the scene it records; and the newsreel itself. He was also a pioneer in the feature-length avant-garde documentary, a genre that included not only his *The Man with a Movie Camera* (1928, released 1929), but also such poetic "city films" as Walter Ruttmann's *Berlin: The Symphony of a Great City* (1927).

So *Nanook* was not the first nonfiction film, even if it did set the pattern for what would later be called the documentary (the term was coined in 1926 by John Grierson—the prime mover of the British documentary film movement of the late 1920s and 1930s—in a review of Flaherty's *Moana*). But it was the first feature-length documentary to become a huge commercial hit.

It was important to the young Flaherty not to impose a story on his materials, but to live long enough with the people whose lives he was recording, and to shoot enough film, that the material would tell its own story, that the truth would reveal itself. Once that inner story, the key to organizing the material, had become clear to him, Flaherty could edit the footage into a nonfiction narrative that would convey that truth—the essence of the subject and the point he wanted to make about it. That was the theory, and it is one that has inspired nonfiction filmmakers ever since—but in practice Flaherty was a bit heavy handed in conveying what was inevitably his interpretation of the material, the story he thought it told. Like many early ethnographic filmmakers, he brought back crucial records of distant cultures but was also willing to make up a fiction that would encapsulate what he wanted to convey about the actual; he did this in several films, including *Moana* (1926) and *Louisiana Story* (1948).

Flaherty's *Nanook* is significant for the beauty of its photography of the white, frozen plains of ice and for its care in revealing the life of the man—and the family—who lived there. Flaherty's greatest asset was Nanook's lack of

Nanook.

Fig. 6-20

inhibition before the camera. Although he was clearly conscious of being watched, suggested many of the scenes, and knew he was performing, he did not quite know what a camera and movie were. Nanook was carefully directed to perform his specific business—hunting, building an igloo with his family, feeding the dogs—while Flaherty's camera recorded and, inevitably, commented. From *Nanook* on, the documentary has been defined as a nonfiction film that organizes factual materials in order to make a point—as distinguished from the *actualité*, which simply records an event. (A newsreel might be either one.)

Nanook was released by Pathé (which had, along with Revillon Frères, produced it) after Paramount and three other studios refused it. After *Nanook* proved itself at the box office, Hollywood asked Flaherty to make pictures for commercial release. For Paramount he made *Moana: A Romance of the Golden Age*—an idyllic study of life on a South Seas island. Hollywood, which expected a movie full of hula dancers, was disappointed and teamed Flaherty with other directors, W. S. Van Dyke and F. W. Murnau, for his later silents, of which the greatest was his and Murnau's exquisite, troubling *Tabu* (1931). To preserve his independence, Flaherty left for England, where a whole group of filmmakers applying his

principles had begun to produce films, and where he made *Man of Aran* (1934).

In America, the success of Flaherty's first documentary stimulated his contemporaries, Merian C. Cooper and Ernest B. Schoedsack. Their silent documentaries, *Grass: A Nation's Battle for Life* (1925) and *Chang: A Drama of the Wilderness* (1927), were also close and sensitive studies of people whose existence was totally dependent on the earth, the cycles of nature, and their own skills at adapting to them. For *Chang*, shot in the jungles of Siam (now Thailand), Cooper and Schoedsack made up a story; many find it the most entertaining of all the silent documentaries embellished by fiction. But *Grass* was the real thing. To shoot it, they and journalist Marguerite Harrison went to Persia (now Iran), where they joined a tribe of nomads on their incredibly difficult biannual journey across the Zardeh Kuh mountain range to find grass for their sheep and cattle. After the 46-day trek, they had 80 feet of film left to shoot an ending. With screenwriter Ruth Rose and stop-motion animator Willis O'Brien, Cooper and Schoedsack would later make the most famous and effective mixture of Hollywood fiction, documentary anthropology, and parody of documentary anthropology—*King Kong* (1933).

The Comics

One other group of 1920s films maintained an inventiveness and individuality that remain fresh today. The silent film, which had already proved itself the ideal medium for physical comedy, continued to nurture its most legitimate children. Several new comic imaginations joined the established Sennett, who still supervised films, and Chaplin, who had begun to make features: most significantly, Harold Lloyd, Buster Keaton, Harry Langdon, and Laurel and Hardy.

Laurel and Hardy and Hal Roach

Stan Laurel and Oliver Hardy perfected their material late in the silent period, then became the most popular comic team of the Sound Era. Laurel and Hardy had been put together in 1926 by Hal Roach, Sennett's major rival as a producer of comedies, who reasoned that one of his fat players and one of his thin ones might go well together. The premise was entirely Sennett-like, and indeed Laurel and Hardy's method was a return to the solid, physical world of Sennett gags.

But Laurel and Hardy films were more tightly structured than the Sennett romps. Their films demonstrate the classic structure of farce—from Plautus to Feydeau: to begin with a single prob-

lem and then multiply that problem to infinity, catastrophe. If an auto gets dented in a traffic jam at the start of the film, every car on the highway gets stripped by the end of it.

As does every great silent-film comedy, a Laurel and Hardy picture depends on physical objects. Most of their films are built around breaking things and getting hurt. Always trying to get away with something, get out of a jam, or get even, the "adults" of this world are overgrown, spiteful children squashing each other's mud pies. Stan is the weepy, sneaky, why-blame-me kid, while Ollie is the pompous, bullying, know-it-all, incompetent kid. The best loved of their sound features are *Sons of the Desert* (1933), *Our Relations* (1936), and the great *Way Out West* (1937).

When Hal Roach was a boy, he knew Mark Twain; when he died in 1992 at the age of 100, he was buried near Twain. One of the great American humorists in his own right, Roach was an actor, a writer, a director, and a producer with a genius for identifying and developing talent. He was responsible not only for developing Laurel and Hardy (who made all their films with him until 1940, after which their work became mediocre), but also for giving Harold Lloyd his start and urging him to develop his own comic persona rather than imitate Chaplin. Roach put

Stan Laurel (left) and Oliver Hardy.

Fig. 6-21

Fig. 6-22
High and Dizzy: *Harold Lloyd with a*
sleepwalking Mildred Davis on a scary ledge.

Harold Lloyd

Except for a brief tour at Keystone, Harold Lloyd worked with Roach from 1914 to 1923, then became his own producer. In many ways, Lloyd was a combination of Chaplin and Fairbanks. Like Chaplin, he was a little guy, slightly inept, trying to succeed. Like Fairbanks, he was energetic, athletic, and engagingly charming, with a smile calculated to snare us as well as the heroine. Like Chaplin, he had trouble with objects and with the world while trying to achieve his desires. But unlike Chaplin—and like Fairbanks—he invariably achieved those desires.

Rather than developing character or social commentary, Lloyd generates pure comedy from the situation, from topical satire, from his own limber body, and from daring stunts. In *High and Dizzy* (1920), the first of his high-rise comedies of thrills, Lloyd plays a doctor who falls madly in love with a patient who walks in her sleep.

She starts sleepwalking out on the hotel ledge, many frightening stories above the hard pavement below. Lloyd goes out on the ledge to save her and, predictably, gets locked out there when she decides to stroll inside. Lloyd tightropes, trips, and stumbles on the ledge, playing on many emotions in us at the same time. We laugh at his fright and perplexity; we admire his underlying competence and control. This same synthesis of cliff-hanging serial and burlesque

black and white children together (a first) in an integrated assault on the adult world; he created the Our Gang series in 1922 and produced it until 1938, when he sold the rights to MGM. Roach won Academy Awards for Laurel and Hardy's *The Music Box* (1932) and Our Gang's *Bored of Education* (1936). "The best comedy comes from children," said Roach; "Laurel and Hardy acted like children. 'Our Gang' was children acting like adults."

Harold Lloyd rushes through
New York in **Speedy.**

Fig. 6-23

comedy created the excitement and success of his feature *Safety Last* (1923). The greatest of his chase films, *Speedy* (1928) tore through New York rather than dangled above it.

Unlike the comedy of Chaplin and Keaton, Lloyd's remains content with emotional and psychological surfaces, never cutting very deeply, never going beyond comic sensations to confront us with ironies and paradoxes. Lloyd's films effectively distill the urges and values of American society as a whole in the 1920s—the success ethic of get up and get. Further, the Lloyd comedies reveal an extremely cunning and complex sense of comic construction, setting up a comic problem and driving it to such dizzying heights that an audience becomes helplessly hysterical in the presence of Lloyd's comic ingenuity (as opposed to Chaplin's comic genius).

Harry Langdon

Harry Langdon was Lloyd's opposite: His comic style was constructed almost exclusively of personal sensations and emotional reactions with almost no dependence on external business and physical gags. His career was also the shortest of any of the comic stars of the silents. He broke into films at Mack Sennett's studio in 1924, reached stardom with a series of features written or directed by Frank Capra in 1926 and 1927, and fell from popularity just as suddenly in 1928 when Langdon went off to direct his own films and when sound invaded Hollywood.

The union of Capra and Langdon was significant for both men, for like Capra's later heroes, Langdon was a figure of innocence trapped in a mean, brutal world where foolish angels should indeed fear to tread. Langdon was like Mr. Deeds or Mr. Smith, distilled into an essential and pure naïveté. He was like an overgrown baby. The Langdon–Capra films put this innocent hero into harrowing situations from which the child–man could escape only by a miracle, for only a miracle could save an infant in a lion's den.

In *The Strong Man* (1926), Harry is a weightlifter's assistant who is unexpectedly forced to substitute for his boss. He manages to subdue a whole gang of bootleggers in the course of his act, ridding a small town of the mobsters who have usurped it. Harry's girlfriend in this film is blind, a figure as pure as little Harry himself. At the end of *The Strong Man* the couple of

meeklings inherit the earth. But in *Long Pants* (1927), Harry is unhappy with the purity and innocence of small-town life. He deserts the small-town gal and runs off to the "Big City" in pursuit of an exotic "Bad Woman." Harry discovers, however, that the lady of his dreams is no lady, and he scampers back to his small-town family and sweetheart, a sadder and wiser child.

Although Langdon lacked the comic range and physical gifts of the other silent clowns, his comic style revealed how restrained, how subtle, how slow, how unphysical a silent, physical comedian could be. His films were constructed so that a tiny smile, a blink of the eyes, the wave of a hand, or even, as James Agee observed, a twitch of the muscles at the back of the neck was as significant as a whole sequence of Lloyd's spectacular slips and falls.

Buster Keaton

Of the new comics, only Buster Keaton could rival Chaplin in his insight into human relationships, into the conflict between the individual and society; only Keaton could rival Chaplin in making his insight both funny and serious at the same time. The character Keaton fashioned— with his deadpan, understated reactions to the chaos that blooms around him—lacks the pathos of Chaplin's tramp, but Keaton compensates for this apparent lack of emotion with the terrific range of his resourcefulness and imagination.

A vaudevillian from childhood, Keaton was far more a classic American type than the more European working-class tramp. Born in Kansas in 1895, Keaton's dour face and dry personality are reminiscent of Grant Wood's farmers in *American Gothic.* Beneath this "Great Stone Face," Keaton's brain conceived one outrageously inventive gag after another, many of them based on bizarre machines and gadgets. The idol of Keaton's generation was Thomas Alva Edison, the supreme inventor as tinkerer, and Keaton loved to tinker with machines (especially trains). One of those machines was the camera, and, very unlike Chaplin, Keaton loved to find new ways to manipulate cinematic gadgetry and cinematic space. He was by far the most cinematically innovative comedian in film history, but he never saw himself as a genius; he just thought he was good at gags.

Fig. 6-24

Fig. 6-25

The montage sequence from Sherlock Jr.: Keaton dives into the sea (Fig. 6-24) but lands in a snowy forest (Fig. 6-25).

On the road to the success he achieves (like growing up in *The Navigator*, 1924) or the goals he is forced to redefine (the house in *One Week*, 1920, will never be perfect and is wrecked by the end of the film, but the honeymooners are happy with each other), the environment throws staggeringly huge obstacles into Buster's path: an avalanche, a locomotive, a steamboat, a spinning house, a waterfall, a cyclone, a herd of cattle. Like Chaplin, Keaton has his troubles with cops, but not just with one or two; in *Cops* (1922),

Keaton runs into the entire police force. Given the size and complexity of his problems, Keaton can take no reliable action, despite his most sensible, practical efforts. The perfect metaphor for the Keaton man is in the three-reel *Daydreams* (1922) in which Keaton, to avoid the police force, takes refuge in the paddle wheel of a ferryboat. The wheel begins turning; Keaton begins walking. And walking. He behaves as sensibly as a man can on a treadmill that he cannot control, but how sensible can life on a treadmill ever be?

Keaton's most magnificent contrast between sensible human behavior and an absurd universe is *Sherlock Jr.* (1924), one of the greatest movies about the movies themselves. Keaton plays a projectionist in a small town (similar to the town in which Keaton was born) who falls asleep and dreams himself into the movie he is projecting. The film-within-a-film that follows permits Keaton to demonstrate spectacular physical skills; he was one of the greatest performer–athletes in film history, and his chase sequences are superb. As opposed to Sennett's miscellaneous chases of frantic puppets and Chaplin's chases as choreographed ballets, Keaton's chases are breathtaking exercises by a single racing body—running faster, leaping higher, falling more gracefully than any other body ever could, or maneuvering a vehicle at top speed through an impossible situation.

In the most celebrated sequence of *Sherlock Jr.*, Keaton is practically at rest. It is the world itself that moves, thanks to the cinema's ability to shift spaces instantaneously by means of editing. Keaton, a mortal being, has been trapped in the universe of cinema, which operates according to spatial and temporal laws unknown to physical reality. He simply stands, sits, or jumps, occupying the identical space within the frame, while the physical universe surrounding him switches from desert to ocean to mountain to city street. It is the ultimate comic gag created by and commenting upon the cinematic apparatus itself.

Chaplin and Keaton are the two poles of silent comics. Chaplin is sentimental; his gentle smiling women become idols to be revered. Keaton is not sentimental; he stuffs his females into bags and hauls them around like sacks of potatoes; he satirizes their finicky incompetence and praises their competence. It was especially appropriate and touching to see the two opposites, Chaplin and Keaton, united in *Limelight* (1952). Chaplin's direction of that sequence—in which they attempt to play a tune on piano and violin—shows how well he understood both Keaton and himself, for while Chaplin has trouble with his body (his leg gets shorter) and plays the romantic violin, Keaton plays the kinetic piano and has trouble with gravity (the music sheets won't stay put) and with the mechanism of the piano.

The Gold Rush and The General

No two films more clearly reveal the contrasting strengths and interests of the two clowns than *The Gold Rush* (Chaplin, 1925) and *The General* (Keaton and Clyde Bruckman, 1926, released

The Gold Rush: *Charlie's forks dance the "Oceana Roll."*

Fig. 6-26

1927). Like Chaplin's short comedies, *The Gold Rush* is an episodic series of highly developed, individual situations. *The Gold Rush* uses one of Chaplin's favorite figures, the circle, to structure the sequence of episodes: Prologue (arriving in Alaska), the Cabin, the Dance Hall, the Cabin, Epilogue (leaving Alaska for home).

The individual sequences of *The Gold Rush* are rich both in Chaplin's comic ingenuity and in his ability to render pathos. Several of the comic sequences have become justifiably famous. In the cabin, a hungry Charlie cooks his shoe, carves it, and then eats it like a gourmet, twirling the shoelaces around his fork like spaghetti, sucking the nails like chicken bones, offering his disgruntled partner (who has been chewing the upper half of the shoe as if it were just a shoe) a bent nail as a wishbone. This is the Chaplin who treats one object (a shoe) as if it were another kind of object (a feast), the same minute observation he used in dissecting the clock in *The Pawn Shop*; it is also the definitive example of the tramp as a gentleman—that is, of comic contrast. And unlike the Sennett world where bullets can't kill, the funny business here has permanent consequences: Characters really die in *The Gold Rush*, and once his boot has been boiled, Charlie spends the rest of the picture with his foot wrapped in rags.

But the comic business is matched by the pathos that Charlie can generate, often growing out of the comic business itself. Charlie's saddest moment is when Georgia (played by Georgia Hale), the woman he loves, callously stands him up on New Year's Eve. When Charlie realizes that it is midnight and she is not coming, he opens his door and listens to the happy townspeople singing "Auld Lang Syne." The film cuts back and forth between Charlie, the outsider, standing silently and alone in a doorway, and the throng of revelers in the dance hall, clasping hands in a circle and singing together. But this pathetic moment would have been impossible without the previous comic one in which Charlie falls asleep and dreams he is entertaining Georgia and her girlfriends with his "Oceana Roll." Charlie's joy, his naïve sincerity, his charm, his gentleness, all show on his face as he gracefully makes the two rolls kick, step, and twirl over the table on the ends of two forks. The happiness of the comic dream sequence sets up the pathos of the painful reality.

The Gold Rush consistently indicts what the pursuit of gold, power, and even food does to the human animal; as in *Greed*, it makes them inhuman animals. Charlie has come to the most materialistic of places—a place where life is hard, dangerous, brutal, uncomfortable, and unkind. The quest for gold creates a Black Larsen who casually murders lawmen and purposely fails to help his starving fellows. It creates a Jack, Georgia's handsome boyfriend, who treats people like furniture. Just as Charlie's genuine passion reveals the emptiness of Jack's protestations of love, Chaplin's film technique makes an unsympathetic bully out of the conventional Hollywood leading man.

The rush toward gold perverts both love and friendship. Georgia herself, though Charlie perceives her inner beauty, has become hardened and callous from her strictly cash relationships with people in the dance hall. And Charlie's partner, Big Jim McKay (Mack Swain), is one of those fair-weather friends whose feelings are the functions of expediency. When Big Jim gets hungry, he literally tries to eat Charlie; although Jim's seeing his buddy as a big chicken is comic, the implied cannibalism is not. Later, Big Jim needs Charlie to direct him to his claim; once again Charlie becomes a friend because he is needed. In the end, Big Jim shares the claim with Charlie, as he promised, and the two millionaires head for home on a steamship—the same one Georgia has taken. Charlie dresses in his tramp outfit for a news photographer, and Georgia, thinking he is a stowaway, offers to pay for his passage—an *un*materialistic gesture that shows her moral growth and leads properly to her and Charlie's romantic union.

Whereas *The Gold Rush* combines a thematic unity with the episodic structure that exhausts individual situations, the thematic coherence of *The General* is itself the product of the film's tight narrative unity. *The General* is the first, probably the greatest comic epic in film form. Like every comic epic, *The General* is the story of a journey, of the road (albeit a railroad). As in every comic epic (think of the *Odyssey*), the protagonist suffers a series of hardships and dangerous adventures before achieving the rewards and comforts of home. As in every comic epic (think of *Don Quixote*), there is a comic insufficiency in the protagonist

Fig. 6-27
The pragmatist turns obstacles into tools.

and a disparity between his powers and the task he sets out to accomplish—but Buster triumphs despite his insufficiencies. Everything in the Chaplin film, every gag, every piece of business, every thematic contrast, is subordinate to the delineation of the tramp's character and the qualities that make him both lonely and superior to the men who have betrayed their humanity to keep from being lonely. Everything in *The General*—every gag, every piece of business— is subordinate to the film's driving narrative, its story of Johnny Gray's race to save his three loves: his sweetheart, his country, and, most important of all, his locomotive (whose name is "The General").

The great question posed by *The General* is how to perform heroic action in a crazy universe, where the easy and the impossible are reversed, as are the heroic and the mundane. Buster tries to go about his business while the world around him goes mad. At one point, Johnny/Buster is so

busy chopping wood to feed his engine that he fails to notice that the train is racing past row after row of blue uniforms marching in the opposite direction; he has inadvertently crossed behind the enemy's lines. Johnny Gray simply wants to run his train; unfortunately, Union spies have stolen the train and want to use it to destroy the Confederate railroad (a real incident in the Civil War). In the course of trying to save "The General," chasing it with another train, Johnny rescues his lady love and accidentally wins a terrific victory for the South.

That heroism occurs as a series of frantic yet graceful accidents in *The General* is at the center of its moral thrust. It is a lucky accident and a triumph of geometry, the core of Keaton's visual comedy, that a cannon, aimed squarely at Johnny, does not go off until the train rounds a curve, discharging its huge ball at the enemy instead. It is another accident, also a matter of trajectory and line (much as the chases in *Sherlock Jr.* play with vacuum and volume), that Johnny's train comes to a rail switch just in time to detour the pursuing train. How less heroic, how less pretentious, how less grand can a man be than the pragmatic and unassuming Buster?

The denigration, or redefinition, of the heroic is as constant an element in *The General* as the denigration of gold (the redefinition of wealth) is in *The Gold Rush.* The plot is triggered by Johnny Gray's rejection by the Confederate Army. He fears he has been found wanting, but the Confederacy vitally needs him at home, running his locomotive. Nevertheless, his girlfriend and her family ostracize Johnny as an unheroic coward, a shirker, and the rest of the film demonstrates what heroism really is and what it is worth. Hardheadedness and improvisation, not ego and gallantry, win the day.

What distinguishes *The General* is the clarity of its journey, laid out on a maze of rails but aiming and arriving at fulfillment. Johnny Gray's sweetheart (played by Marion Mack), a typical figure of sentiment and romance (her name is Annabelle

Lee!), is an incompetent twit—until she learns the ropes. In the course of the film, Johnny becomes an actual officer and Miss Lee grows up.

The ultimate proof of the power of *The Gold Rush* and *The General* is that they need not be referred to as great silent films; they are merely great films. For both, silence was not a limitation but a virtue. It is inconceivable that they could have been any better with talk; by removing our complete concentration on the visual, they could only have been worse. With such control of physical business, thematic consistency, narrative structure, camera placement, and functional editing, neither *The Gold Rush* nor *The General* requires speech to speak.

Hollywood and the Jazz Age

American movies of 1915–27 are important collectively as a social barometer, indicating the evolving spirit, values, and attitudes of American society during that period. It was a period of

Fig. 6-28
Before the feature, some theatres offered a live stage prologue.

Fig. 6-29

Fig. 6-30
*Jazz Age portraying of the Veddy Veddy Rich in MGM's **This Modern Age** (1931)—with Joan Crawford and Neil Hamilton (Fig. 29); Fig. 30: Clara Bow, the "It" Girl.*

creative excitement and invention—the profuse flowering of an artistic tradition over the full spectrum of arts and letters. Later critics would find a name—Modernism—for this international explosion of artistic activity that rebelled against the forms and norms of a previous generation. And somewhere in the middle of it were the movies. They may not have been as consistently committed to experimental innovation as some of the other arts, but all the artists went to the movies, and so did everyone who read their novels, saw their plays, discussed their poems, and hummed their tunes. James Joyce and Sergei Eisenstein knew of each other's work, Eisenstein found the seeds of montage in Dickens (although they were also evident in Whitman's 1855 *Leaves of Grass* and earlier work by others), and Beckett studied the films of Pudovkin. The great montage experiments of the 1920s were not confined to the cinema but included such poems as Eliot's "The Waste Land" (1922) and Pound's *The Cantos* (which began appearing in 1919) as well as such novels as Joyce's *Ulysses* (1922) and Faulkner's *The Sound and the Fury* (1929). Fragmentation and synthesis, essential concerns of Modernism from Cubist painting to 12-tone music, had been recognized as the essence of montage since *Intolerance*, but the cinematic apparatus itself had long posed exciting phenomenological questions about the continuous and intermittent recording of reality. Both the montage novelist John Dos Passos and the definer of the "continuous present," Gertrude Stein, readily admitted that they were doing what the cinema was doing.

Jazz, Booze, and It

The postwar years of the late 1910s and 1920s saw many important changes in American life. It is all too easy to mystify history by selecting a single image to stand for a whole period, but there is something inevitable about the image of a flapper, a "jazz baby," in a short beaded dress and bobbed hair, wearing a jeweled headband, holding a glass of champagne, dancing the Charleston.

The word *jazz* entered mainstream American language at the same time. For those who loved it, jazz was rhythm and riffs, the music you danced to and made love to, music that could go

anywhere, whether by black composers and musicians like Bessie Smith, and Duke Ellington or white composers and musicians like George Gershwin and Helen Kane. Jazz meant about the same thing that rock did a half-century later—the exuberant, liberating music to which young Americans danced.

At the center of these changes and contradictions was the new American woman—or, rather, women. At one extreme there was Mary Pickford, "America's Sweetheart," who personified the woman as child—sweet, innocent, virgin (for sure), but perky, bright, and charming, too. At the opposite pole there were several alternatives to Pickford. One was the woman of adventure and daring, personified by Pearl White, the Queen of American serials, beginning with *The Perils of Pauline* in 1914. Another alternative was the more dignified, controlled woman of grace and manners, represented by such stars as Gloria Swanson and Pauline Frederick.

The rebellious alternative to Pickford's adolescent spunk was Clara Bow, the "It" Girl, and *It*, like jazz, was another of the important if vague words that indicated the values of the decade. *It* was a vague euphemism for sex and implied

Fig. 6-31
European It: Greta Garbo.

a wide range of suggestions: sex appeal, sexual drive, the sex act itself, or a more general attitude toward that sexual activity. The girl, like Clara Bow, who had It exuded sexual energy and appeared as if she might welcome a sexual invitation (even if she coyly never accepted It). One could have It, want It, show It, or think about It, but not *do* It.

American It was somewhat different from European It. While American-born stars with It (Clara Bow, Joan Crawford, Mae McAvoy) were bouncy flappers with get-up-and-go, European-born stars with It were deep, intriguing Circes (Greta Garbo, Pola Negri) with lie-back-and-wait. Louise Brooks was the rare American It girl who flowered in German soil (*Pandora's Box* and *Diary of a Lost Girl*, both directed by G. W. Pabst and released in 1929). Brooks and Garbo (who did her best work in such MGM films as *Flesh and the Devil*, 1926, and *Queen Christina*, 1933) were more than international stars: They were essential mysteries, icons of the cinema.

When Hollywood reflected on its own cultural history, with the writing of those explicit moral instructions that became the Production Code of 1930, it confessed that its films of the 1920s were more lascivious and suggestive than they ought to have been. The writers of the Code then blamed that permissiveness on the mores of the period itself, whose "roaring" hedonism and "wonderful nonsense" came tumbling down with the Wall Street crash of October 1929. This recantation of Jazz Age values indicated not only the differences in American social attitudes just one decade later, but also the changes in an industry seeking not to lose the patronage of its most dependable middle-class customers.

The powerful images of female stars are among the most enduring and revealing traces of this era's films. There were exceptional male figures, but relatively few male faces from the 1920s have survived in our cultural memory. Of course, many of the films themselves have been lost, so little did anyone think of preserving them. The faces of the era's women suggest a portrait of American life as a whole. As Norma Desmond (played by Gloria Swanson) put it in *Sunset Boulevard*: "We had faces then." For most of us, those faces are the Jazz Age.

For Further Viewing

FILMS

MERIAN C. COOPER (1893–1973) AND ERNEST B. SCHOEDSACK (1893–1979)
Grass (1925)
The Four Feathers (1929)
The Most Dangerous Game (1932)
King Kong (1933)

CECIL B. DeMILLE (1881–1959)
The Squaw Man (1914). Co-director, Oscar Apfel
The Virginian (1914)
The Cheat (1915)
Don't Change Your Husband (1919)
Male and Female (1919)
Why Change Your Wife? (1920)
The Ten Commandments (1923)
Cleopatra (1934)
The Plainsman (1937). Completed 1936
Union Pacific (1939)
The Ten Commandments (1956)

DOUGLAS FAIRBANKS (1883–1939)
Flirting With Fate (1916)
The Mystery of the Leaping Fish (1916)
The Americano (1916)
Reaching for the Moon (1917)
The Mark of Zorro (1920)
The Three Musketeers (1921)
Robin Hood (1922)
The Thief of Bagdad (1924)
The Black Pirate (1926)
The Iron Mask (1929)

ROBERT FLAHERTY (1884–1951)
Nanook of the North (1922)
Moana: A Romance of the Golden Age (1926)
Man of Aran (1934)
Louisiana Story (1948)

THOMAS H. INCE (1882–1924)
The Taking of Luke McVane (1915). With W. S. Hart
The Coward (1915). With Charles Ray
Civilization (1916)

BUSTER KEATON (1895–1966)
Shorts, including: *One Week, The Scarecrow,* and *Neighbors* (1920); *The Haunted House, The*

Playhouse, and *The Paleface* (1921); *Cops, The Blacksmith, The Frozen North, Daydreams,* and *The Electric House* (1922)
Our Hospitality (1923)
Sherlock Jr. (1924)
The Navigator (1924)
Go West (1925)
The General (1927). Completed 1926
College (1927)
Steamboat Bill, Jr. (1928)
The Cameraman (1928)

HARRY LANGDON (1884–1944)

Shorts, including: *Picking Peaches, Smile Please,* and *Feet of Mud* (1924); *Boobs in the Woods,* and *Lucky Stars* (1925); and *Saturday Afternoon* (1926)
The Strong Man (1926)
Long Pants (1927)

STAN LAUREL (1890–1965) AND OLIVER HARDY (1892–1957)

Shorts, including: *The Call of the Cuckoo* (1927); *Leave 'Em Laughing* (1928); *Liberty* and *Bacon Grabbers* (1929); *Brats* and *Another Fine Mess* (1930); *Beau Hunks* (1931); *The Music Box* (1932); and *Thicker Than Water* (1935)
Sons of the Desert (1933)
Our Relations (1936)
Way Out West (1937)

HAROLD LLOYD (1893–1971)

Early shorts, including: *Lonesome Luke* (1915); *Birds of a Feather* (1917); *Nothing But Trouble* (1918); *Just Neighbors, Chop Suey & Co.,* and *Going, Going, Gone* (1919)
High and Dizzy (1920)
Never Weaken (1921)
Dr. Jack (1922)
Safety Last (1923)
The Freshman (1925)
Speedy (1928)

OSCAR MICHEAUX (1884–1951)

The Homesteader (1918). First New York showing, 1920
Within Our Gates (1920). Completed 1919
Body and Soul (1925). First version, 1924
Spider's Web (1926)
Wages of Sin (1928)
The Exile (1931)

Harlem After Midnight (1934)
God's Step Children (1938)

ERICH VON STROHEIM (1885–1957)

Blind Husbands (1919)
Foolish Wives (1922). Completed 1921
Greed (1924)
The Merry Widow (1925)
The Wedding March (1928)
Queen Kelly (1932). Shot 1928–29

LOIS WEBER (1882–1939)

Suspense (1913)
Hypocrites (1914)
Where Are My Children? (1916)
The Blot (1921)
The Angel of Broadway (1927)

REPRESENTATIVE FILMS

Vitagraph Comedies: *Stenographer Wanted* (1912), *Goodness Gracious, or, Movies As They Shouldn't Be* (1914)
Broncho Billy's Capture (1913, Gilbert M. Anderson)
Traffic in Souls (1913, George Loane Tucker)
The Perils of Pauline (1914 serial). With Pearl White (Louis J. Gasnier)
The Tigress (1914). With Olga Petrova (Alice Guy Blaché)
A Fool There Was (1915). With Theda Bara (Frank Powell)
Alias Jimmy Valentine (1915, Maurice Tourneur)
Regeneration (1915, Raoul Walsh)
Tol'able David (1921). With Richard Barthelmess (Henry King)
The Four Horsemen of the Apocalypse (1921). With Rudolf Valentino (Rex Ingram)
Blood and Sand (1922). With Rudolf Valentino (Fred Niblo)
Salomé (1922, rel. 1923). With Alla Nazimova (Charles Bryant)
The Hunchback of Notre Dame (1923). With Lon Chaney (Wallace Worsley)
The Covered Wagon and *Hollywood* (1923, James Cruze)
The White Sister (1923). With Lillian Gish (Henry King)
The Phantom of the Opera (1925, revised 1929). With Lon Chaney (Rupert Julian)
The Big Parade (1925, King Vidor)

The Unholy Three (1925). With Lon Chaney (Tod Browning)

Tumbleweeds (1925). With W. S. Hart (King Baggot)

Sparrows (1926). With Mary Pickford (William Beaudine)

The Scarlet Letter (1926). With Lillian Gish (Victor Sjøstrøm)

Ben-Hur (1926, Fred Niblo)

Son of the Sheik (1926). With Rudolf Valentino (George Fitzmaurice)

What Price Glory (1926, Raoul Walsh)

Wings (1927, William Wellman)

It or *"it"* (1927). With Clara Bow (Clarence Badger)

The Wind (1928). With Lillian Gish (Victor Sjøstrøm)

Lonesome (1928, Paul Fejos)

The Crowd (1928, King Vidor)

The Fall of the House of Usher (1928, James Sibley Watson and Melville Webber)

DVDs

Arbuckle, Chaplin, Keaton, Langdon, Lloyd, Sennett, and others are in *Slapstick Encyclopedia* (see Chap. 5 list).

The Art of Buster Keaton. Kino Video. The only **Buster Keaton** set to consider. Includes 10 features and 19 shorts—every film he made from *One Week* (1920) to *Steamboat Bill, Jr.* (1928)—and over 3 hours of rare footage, including home movies. The best prints of *The General, The Navigator, Our Hospitality,* etc.

The Best Arbuckle Keaton Collection. Image Entertainment. **Roscoe "Fatty" Arbuckle** and **Buster Keaton** in their 12 surviving shorts, from *The Butcher Boy* (1917, Keaton's first appearance on film) to *The Garage* (1919, rel. 1920; their last collaboration, Keaton's favorite).

The Black Pirate (1926, Albert Parker). Kino International. Starring **Douglas Fairbanks.** **Restored**; 2-strip color.

Blind Husbands (1919, **Erich von Stroheim**) and *The Great Gabbo* (1929, **James Cruze,** starring Stroheim). Kino International. An excellent tinted print of *Blind Husbands* (from the Museum of Modern Art) with many extras, including a radio play and excerpts from the pressbook. *Gabbo* was **restored** by the Library of Congress.

The Blot (1921, **Lois Weber**). Image Entertainment/Milestone. **Restored.** Commentary by film historian Shelley Stamp concentrates on Weber's career.

Cecil B. DeMille's Manslaughter and The Cheat. Kino International. *Manslaughter* (1922, **DeMille**) is tinted and has music by the Alloy Orchestra. The print of *The Cheat* (1915, **DeMille**) is superb but is the 1918 re-issue.

The Charley Chase Collection. Kino International. **Charley Chase** in 6 Hal Roach shorts.

The Douglas Fairbanks Collection. Image Entertainment. **Fairbanks** in *The Mark of Zorro, The Three Musketeers, Robin Hood, The Thief of Bagdad, Don Q Son of Zorro,* and *The Black Pirate,* with extras. (A better version of *The Black Pirate* is listed separately.)

The Fall of the House of Usher is in *Treasures from American Film Archives* (see Chap. 1 list).

Foolish Wives (1922, **Erich von Stroheim**) and *The Man You Loved To Hate* (a 1979 documentary on Stroheim). This excellent print of *Foolish Wives* was carefully **restored** by the American Film Institute to 143 minutes and has the original score. Commentary by biographer Richard Koszarski, censorship information, a note by Stroheim, and more.

Grass (1925, **Merian C. Cooper** and **Ernest B. Schoedsack**). Image Entertainment. Includes an audio interview with Cooper.

It or *"it"* (1927, Clarence Badger). Image Entertainment. Starring Clara Bow. Commentary by film historian Jeanine Basinger.

The Harold Lloyd Collection. Kino International. **Harold Lloyd** in *Grandma's Boy* and 7 shorts.

Harry Langdon . . . the forgotten clown. Image Entertainment. **Harry Langdon** in *Tramp, Tramp, Tramp; The Strong Man;* and *Long Pants.*

Laurel & Hardy. Lions Gate/Fox. **Laurel** and **Hardy** in the feature *Sons of the Desert* and the shorts *Another Fine Mess, Busy Bodies, County Hospital,* and *The Music Box.*

The Lon Chaney Collection. Warner Home Video. Contains *The Ace of Hearts; The Unknown* (the crucial film in this group, directed by **Tod Browning**); *Laugh, Clown, Laugh;* commentary by **Lon Chaney** biographer Michael Blake; stills from *London After Midnight* (offered as a reconstruction); and a documentary.

The Lost Films of Stan Laurel and Oliver Hardy: The Complete Collection. Image Entertainment.

The best available prints; each volume about 2 hours of **Laurel** and **Hardy,** separate or together. Volume One includes *Big Business.* Volume Three includes *Liberty.* Volume Eight includes *Two Tars* and *From Soup to Nuts.*

Male and Female (1919, **Cecil B. DeMille**). Image Entertainment. Also in a DeMille set.

The Man Who Laughs (1928, **Paul Leni**). Kino Video/Universal. Excellent **restoration** with the original Movietone soundtrack, home movies, many stills, an excerpt from the Italian release version, an informative essay by **Conrad Veidt** biographer John Soister, a documentary, etc.

Nanook of the North (1922, **Robert Flaherty**). Criterion Collection. Director's cut at 21.5 fps: 79 min.

The Origins of Film: 1900–1926. Image Entertainment. The Library of Congress Video Collection; previously issued on VHS and laserdisc. Includes *Alias Jimmy Valentine, Within Our Gates, Too Wise Wives, The Scar of Shame,* other features, and many shorts.

The Phantom of the Opera: The Ultimate Edition (1925 and 1929, Rupert Julian and others). Image Entertainment. Starring **Lon Chaney.** New score by Carl Davis (the best composer in the field) and an original Vitaphone soundtrack, color sequences, stills including deleted scenes, original and re-issue trailers, and both versions of the film.

Salomé (1922, rel. 1923, Charles Bryant), starring **Alla Nazimova,** and *Lot in Sodom* (1933, **Melville Webber** and **James Sibley Watson**). Image Entertainment. *Lot in Sodom* has the original music by Alec Wilder.

The Stan Laurel Collection. Kino International. **Stan Laurel** in 17 shorts.

Tabu (1931, **Robert Flaherty** and **F. W. Murnau**). Image Entertainment. Commentary by film scholar Janet Bergstrom.

Without Lying Down: Frances Marion and the Power of Women in Hollywood (2001, Bridget Terry). Image Entertainment. Informative documentary. DVD includes a 1917 film written by **Frances Marion:** *A Little Princess,* starring **Mary Pickford** and **ZaSu Pitts.**

7

The German Golden Age

In the final year of World War I, the German government wondered whether preferring bullets to pictures had been a tactical error. Whatever the results of the battles at the front, the German nation and German character were losing terribly on the screens of the world. In a number of very popular films made in America during and after the war, the enemy was portrayed as a villainous, vicious Hun; the evil, sinister, outwardly polished and inwardly corrupt Erich von Stroheim was the perfect stereotype of this newest movie bad guy. There was no screen antidote to this single stereotypic portrait, so the German government decided to produce one.

In November 1917, the government set up a private company that soon began to buy and merge many studios into a single, large filmmaking unit, Universum-Film AG, known subsequently to the world as Ufa. Ufa's job was to make movies that would boost the German spirit at home and sell the German character and position abroad. The war ended before Ufa could accomplish either goal—but the huge movie company was still in business after the armistice had been signed. In 1920, Ufa moved into a huge new studio at Neubabelsberg, near Berlin, and it was there that the great era of German films was born.

Expressionism, Realism, and the Studio Film

The German Golden Age of film was a very short one, from the shooting of *The Cabinet of Dr. Caligari* in 1919 to Hitler's absorption of the German film industry in 1933. The great burst of

artistic activity that followed the fall of the Kaiser and the founding of the Weimar Republic, the new spirit of intellectual and creative freedom in Germany, made itself felt in all the arts, but especially in the cinema.

If Griffith's two great accomplishments were his realization of the power of atmosphere, decor, and texture within a shot and the power of editing to join shots, it was the genius of the German film to refine and develop the former; the Soviet film developed the latter. The German film, in an era of silence, made the aura, the mood, the tone of the shot's visual qualities speak—so well that the best German films of the era contain the barest minimum of intertitles, or none at all. As the Soviet films emphasized montage and politics, the German films emphasized *mise-en-scène* and psychology. In general, the Soviets shot on location and rarely moved the camera, while the Germans shot in studios and moved the camera freely. If Griffith's *Intolerance* was the decisive influence on Soviet filmmaking in the 1920s, many German films of the 1920s can be seen as an extension of *Broken Blossoms*—which looked realistic but was shot in a studio; conveyed its psychological insights through lighting, gesture, and costume and set design; and told the intense, tragic story of a small number of characters.

In addition to liberating the camera, the Germans realized that it could function as a window into the mind. The camera, rather than taking the stance of an impartial observer, could itself mirror the perceptions, thoughts, and feelings of a character experiencing an event. To use an analogy with the novel, the German filmmaker realized that the camera, like the pen, could narrate a story in the first person as well as the third. Griffith used an occasional flight into subjectivity—his cutaways to reveal a character's thoughts, even the long dream in *The Avenging Conscience*—but Griffith's subjective moments were always in brackets. He used specific conventions to inform the audience that it was entering the personal experience of a character. Subjectivity in the German film is rarely set off in brackets; instead, the boundary between subjective and objective perceptions becomes indefinite: The world might look crazy because someone sees it that way or because it *is* that way, burdened with wordless meaning. To this idea—that the look or style of the visible, external universe can take its shape, color, and texture from the artist's intuition of its essential inner being or from internal human sensations—critics assigned a single term: Expressionism. The principle dominated the early 20th-century painting and drama of Germany as well as the often theatrical, always moving, graphic art of German cinema.

The harsh, bold graphics and revelatory distortions of German Expressionist drawing and painting inspired an attempt, in *The Cabinet of Dr. Caligari*, to film a completely Expressionist universe—one so unnatural that it had to be created in a studio. If an Expressionist painter might distort the look of an object to express its nature, to reveal the energy of an inner essence bursting to reveal itself—in effect, to show the skin of the nightmare or the scream of a lake—the Expressionist filmmaker had to design and construct an artificial landscape that was graphic in inspiration and boldly disturbing, on and beneath the surface.

But having made one world from scratch, the German filmmakers realized that they could create *any* kind of artificial world, including a realistic one. Whereas the Soviets' "artificial landscape" (or "creative geography") was assembled by cutting together shots taken in different locations, the Germans built and lit their artificial landscapes in studios, determining and controlling their every detail, often in the service not of Expressionism but of realism. The controlled, artificial realism of the studio film—as practiced, for example, by Wyler or Hitchcock—began not in the Black Maria but at Ufa.

The dependence of the German film on the evocations of its *mise-en-scène* led to its becoming completely a studio product. The only way to make sure that the lighting, the decor, the architectural shapes, the relationships of blacks, whites, and grays were perfect was to film in a completely controlled environment. Even some outdoor scenes were shot inside the four walls and ceiling of a studio. The vastness, the freedom of the outdoors that had become one of the sources of power of both the American and the Swedish film, was rejected by most of the Germans. The totally studio-produced films emphasized the importance of the designer, whose job was to conceive and decorate everything from one-room sets to enormous indoor cities (often "built" or realized with the aid of special effects). These designers—later called art directors or in some cases production designers—came to films from painting, theatre, and architecture, having absorbed the styles of many of the new artistic movements of postwar Europe: Expressionism, Cubism, Constructivism, and other forms of abstraction and analysis. The German film could never have exerted its influence without its talented painter-architect designers, the most notable of whom were Hermann Warm, Walter Röhrig, Walter Reimann, Robert Herlth, Albin Grau, and Ernö Metzner.

Unlike the competing factories of Hollywood, the German studio was far more a combination of artists working with each other rather than trying to outguess each other. Although there were competitors with Ufa in the 1920s, many of them worked so closely with the major producer that merger was inevitable (Decla-Bioscop, for example). Ufa's great producer, Erich Pommer, was a man of artistic judgment and business acumen who stimulated mediocre directors to do their best work (E. A. Dupont's *Variety*, 1925, for example). Instead of building a star system, the German studio developed a repertory company, emphasizing the play and not the player, the character and not the personality. The German film actor needed variety and range, not a single trait to be milked over and over again. Among the best of the German repertory actors were Emil Jannings, Werner Krauss, Conrad Veidt, Fritz Körtner, Lil Dagover, Brigitte Helm, Asta Nielsen, Lya de Putti, and Pola Negri.

Many of these actors had been trained by the greatest German stage director of the period, Max Reinhardt, who had conceived a style of theatre that depended as much on decor as on the actor and playwright. Among the directors who studied with Reinhardt were F. W. Murnau (later his assistant) and Lotte Reiniger, whose animated films, inspired by the German shadow-play and by the Greek and Balinese shadow puppets, featured detailed paper figures in silhouette. In 1926, Reiniger made the world's first full-length animated feature, *The Adventures of Prince Achmed.*

Reinhardt was influential on the German cinema of the Weimar Republic not only for his actors, pupils, and Expressionist visual conceptions, but also for the style and genre he pioneered in his theatre, the *Kammerspiele*, a "chamber theatre" for small audiences, with small casts, intimately psychological portraits, and dim lighting (with spotlights to isolate part of the stage or action and with extensive use of *chiaroscuro*). Some of the greatest German films of the 1920s would be intimate "chamber" dramas, a genre called the *Kammerspielfilm*.

Weimar cinema went through three major stages: (1) Expressionism, the best examples of which are *Caligari* and Karl-Heinz Martin's *Von Morgens bis Mitternacht* (*From Morning to Midnight*, 1920); (2) the *Kammerspielfilm*, which had few or no intertitles in order to intensify and deepen what the actors, lighting, and set design conveyed, and which featured psychological studies of a few characters in ordinary middle- and lower-class environments; examples include Lupu Pick's *Sylvester* (1923) and Murnau's *The Last Laugh* (1924); and (3) *die neue Sachlichkeit*, or the "New Objectivity," whose often fatalistic and grimy lower-class realism found a home in the studio (Pabst's *The Joyless Street*, 1925) and in the streets (Metzner's *Überfall*, which would more accurately be translated *Police*, 1929).

The German films of this great era fell generally into two types: either fantastic and mystical or realistic and psychological. One was steeped in the traditional German Romanticism of love and death; the other revealed the new German intellectual currents of Freud and Weber. In the films of fantasy and horror, the action revolves around the occult, the mysterious, the metaphys-ical. These are films of fantastic monsters in human dress, of what lives beyond the grave, of dream kingdoms of the past and future. The architect–painters could turn these eerie, abstract, intangible regions into concrete, visual domains. In the psychological film, the action revolves around the thoughts and feelings of the characters, their needs, their lusts, their jobs, their frustrations. Unlike the fantasy films, which usually are set in some romantic time and place, the psychological films are set in the urban present. The architect–painters could turn the tawdry, dirty, depressing rooms and streets into complex, detailed, realistic studio slums.

Fantasy

Caligari

The film that signaled the start of the new era, *The Cabinet of Dr. Caligari* (released in February 1920), is a tale of fantasy and horror with a psychological twist. It was produced by Erich Pommer for Decla-Bioscop before that company was absorbed by Ufa. The camerawork is wretched and the direction is uneven, but the mood of this definitively antirealist film is unshakably disturbing.

Its central plot is a story of horror, murder, and almost mystical power. An enigmatic and menacing yet oddly seductive hypnotist, who calls himself Dr. Caligari (Werner Krauss), opens a stall at a fair in the town of Holstenwall; his act demonstrates his mastery over a sleepwalker he has apparently hypnotized, Cesare (Conrad Veidt). A rash of murders breaks out in the town. The police have no clues. The film's narrator–protagonist, Francis (or Franz, played by Friedrich Feher), suspects Caligari, shadows him, and eventually discovers that he forces his slave, Cesare, to murder the victims while the hypnotist substitutes a life-sized dummy resembling Cesare in the coffin-like box (the cabinet) to fool the police. Francis continues to follow the master who, it turns out, is also the director of the state insane asylum. The keeper of the insane is himself insane, a monster who has discovered the medieval formula of Caligari for controlling men's minds and who has set out to "become Caligari." Francis exposes the monster; the monster goes mad. The orderlies stuff Caligari into a straitjacket and lock him in a cell. This is as far

Fig. 7-1

The Cabinet of Dr. Caligari:
*a madman's vision of the
world—impossibly shaped
windows, exaggeratedly
high furniture, and
geometric shadows.*

as the central plot of *Caligari* goes. It is also as far as its writers, Carl Mayer and Hans Janowitz, wanted it to go.

But *Caligari* goes further. The entire central plot is bracketed by a frame, conceived by Fritz Lang. The film begins with Francis informing a listener (and us) that he has a dreadful story to tell. To set a horrific, supernatural tale within a frame is, of course, a traditional literary device (as in Mary Shelley's *Frankenstein* or Henry James's *The Turn of the Screw*), the means to anchor a fantastic story in reality (as well as isolate it, fence it in) and thereby increase our credulity. The setting of this opening, framing sequence seems like a park—there are trees, vines, a wall, benches. But it is too bare, too cold; the woman (Lil Dagover) who walks past seems somnambulistic, ethereal. Only at the end of the film do we discover that the opening and closing framing sequences are set not in a park but on the grounds of an asylum, that Francis himself is a patient, that many of the characters in his tale (like the gentle Cesare—who had died in the inner narrative but is now quite alive) are also patients, and that the so-called Caligari is the director of the asylum. And it is not Caligari who winds up in a cell with a straitjacket but Francis. The surprise

at the end of the film is our discovery that the tale we assumed to be true is a paranoid's fantasy.

Our discovery of the disease in the narrator's brain suddenly illuminates the principle of the film's unnatural decor. Throughout the film the Expressionist world of the horror tale has been striking: the grotesque painted shadows on streets and stairs; the irregular, nonperpendicular chimneys, doors, and windows; the exaggerated heights of the furniture; the boldly painted make-up. This grotesque world is not simply a decorative stunt; it is, thanks to Lang's psychological "twist," the way Francis sees the world. That was how Lang, the original director assigned to the project, saw it; how Robert Wiene did direct it; and why the writers objected. Rather than exposing an insane world (that could tyrannically send an innocent—or soldier—like Cesare to kill against his will), their story now implied that the world is fine, Francis is nuts, and Caligari knows best.

Caligari is interesting not just for how it looks but for the ambiguities generated by the tension between its inner and framing narratives. The central story is no simple tale told by an idiot. If the kindly doctor is really not the demented Caligari, why does it feel so creepy when he says, at the very end, that he now knows "how

Fig. 7-2

Fig. 7-3

Caligari's *faces of paint*. Fig. 7-2: Dr. Caligari (Werner Krauss); Fig. 7-3: Cesare (Conrad Veidt).

to cure" Francis? And why does the asylum look no more natural in the closing framing sequence (supposedly an objective point of view) than it did in Francis's narration? Are we crazy, or is it the government? Is this the world of Franz Kafka come true?

Perhaps the film's ambiguities and internal contradictions stem from the conflict between the writers, who conceived one kind of story, and the director, who accepted another. Whatever the underlying reason, the ambiguities and ambivalences of *Caligari* enrich it.

Although it started the Expressionist film movement, decisively influenced the horror film (which had flourished in Germany since 1913), and set the pattern for a film with an "unreliable narrator"—one of the key devices of modern fiction—*Caligari* has been attacked since it came out. Theorists André Bazin, Erwin Panofsky, and Siegfried Kracauer are unanimous in believing that the film is a cinematic mistake, that it "prestylizes reality," that it violates the inherent photographic realism of the medium, that it substitutes a world of painted artifice for the rich resources of nature. Despite these later arguments, the film had an immense influence not only in Germany but in France, where "Caligarism," though detested by some, inspired many of the early avant-garde experiments in abstract cinema, in film as "painting-in-motion" rather than as realistic narrative of natural events in natural

settings. If it was the first "art film" and the first feature that *had* to be shot in a studio, *The Cabinet of Dr. Caligari* has also been capable of scaring and fascinating audiences, of weaving its horrific, hypnotic spell, for scores of years.

Metropolis

A later film, Fritz Lang's *Metropolis* (1926, released 1927), was the most important science fiction film since *A Trip to the Moon*. *Metropolis* is a fantasy of the future and technology uses its fantastic setting to demonstrate an abstract theme. Unfortunately, *Metropolis* is all eyes and no brain, all visual with no convincing vision. The film depicts a socially engineered world of the future where the rich and intelligent live on the earth's surface with their airplanes and trams and skyscrapers, and the workers—who make the society go—live beneath the surface in a drab, utilitarian "city," below which are dark, labyrinthine caverns. The hero (Freder, played by Gustav Fröhlich), a young rebel, rejects the sheltered lifestyle of the rich—his father, who dresses and behaves like a modern executive, runs Metropolis—and goes to live and struggle with the workers of the underworld. There he meets the spirit of the workers—Maria (played by Brigitte Helm), a proletarian version of the Virgin Mary and Christ all in one—who urges peaceful change and nonviolent progress. Maria is a Christian Democrat–Humanist (literally Christian since she delivers her political sermons in a candlelit cave full of crosses) who formulates the film's political argument: The heart must mediate between head and hands.

The young hero's father, the Master of Metropolis, will have none of this. He hires the evil scientist–magician, Rotwang (played by Rudolf Klein-Rogge: the direct ancestor of Dr. Strangelove, even to the black glove), to manufacture a sexy, vicious robot (Brigitte Helm) who looks exactly like Maria and who will incite the workers to riot; the father's troops can then use the riot to enslave the workers. The workers riot, flood their underground city, and almost destroy the whole society, until the kidnapped Maria escapes and the hero kills Rotwang. The Master learns his lesson, and his enlightened son, who has lived in both worlds, is designated the society's official "heart" to mediate between head (administration—his dad) and hands (labor— he shakes hands with the foreman of the workers).

The film demonstrates the dangers of the purely architectural–pictorial premise of many of the German studio films. Shot by Karl Freund and Günther Rittau, *Metropolis* is a series of stunning images, sequences, and effects, held together by a silly and oppressive fable.

Fig. 7-4

Fig. 7-5

Metropolis: *human beings reduced to dispirited masses of architecture.*

Science as magic: bringing the robot to life in Metropolis.

Fig. 7-6

Part of the emptiness of the film lies in the way it reduces people to patterns—to units of geometrical architecture. What is most fascistic about *Metropolis* is its portrayal of the general lot of human beings as a mass of plodding slaves or wild rioters—in either case, indistinguishable ciphers. Unable to take care of themselves, swayed just as easily by the robot as they are by Maria, the workers are utterly dependent on the beneficence of the ruler above.

The implications of *Metropolis* did not pass unnoticed in its time. It was one of Hitler's favorite films; another was Lang's *Die Nibelungen* (1924), which was based on the same medieval epic poem that inspired *The Ring of the Nibelungs*, the four-opera cycle—containing the story of Siegfried, with whom Hitler identified—by Hitler's favorite composer, Richard Wagner. (No one knows what Hitler thought about Lang's 1922 *Dr. Mabuse, the Gambler*, in which a mesmerizing, power-mad criminal exercises his irresistible will to control the people and world around him, until he is destroyed by his own demons.) After Hitler had seized control of the government, he invited Lang—a leftist and half Jew—to make films for the Nazis. That Lang diminished people into puppets, crowds into patterns, and political problems into romantic abstractions exactly suited Hitler's

purposes. Lang, however, fled the country; his wife, Thea von Harbou, stayed, joined the Nazis, and took the job, which she held until she was displaced by Leni Riefenstahl.

Much as *Caligari* influenced the horror film in Germany and abroad, *Metropolis* foreshadowed many developments in the science fiction film (as did Lang's *Woman in the Moon*, 1928 [released 1929], which introduced the countdown), particularly in its vision of the futuristic upper city, in its use of telescreens for spying and communication (seen in Universal's Flash Gordon serials as well as in Chaplin's *Modern Times*), and in the design of Rotwang's laboratory, where scientific apparatus, Expressionistic magic, and pure light bring the robot to life (much as in the labs designed at Universal to conduct the juices of life into Frankenstein's monster). The film's most impressive special-effects shots were achieved through the "Schüfftan process," which was invented by Eugen Schüfftan specifically for *Metropolis*. The Schüfftan process allowed actors and miniature or model sets to be photographed together. Between the actors, who might be on a full-scale but partial set, and the camera, a mirror was placed at a 45° angle; the model set, which was off to the side, was reflected in the mirror. One or more holes were made in this reflected image by scraping the silver off the back of the mirror, and through those areas of clear glass the actors could be seen and photographed; the partial set behind them would match and line up with the miniature, creating the impression of a complete full-scale set with actors in it. In Fig. 7-4, for example, the buildings in the background are a miniature set, and the actors and gong are full size.

Nosferatu

The most noteworthy and effective of the purely horrific descendants of *Caligari* was F. W. Murnau's *Nosferatu, a Symphony of Horror* (1922), an unauthorized adaptation—with a script by Henrik Galeen—of Bram Stoker's *Dracula. Nosferatu*, Murnau's first major success, was distinguished in the aura of horror and gloom with which it surrounded the vampire's activities. Unlike later incarnations of Dracula—Bela Lugosi, Christopher Lee, and many others—Murnau's vampire (Max Schreck) was no sexy, suave, intriguing gentleman. Murnau's vampire was hideous—a shriveled, ashen man with rat teeth, not long canines. He is pestilential, and his visits are mistaken for a rat-borne plague. *Nosferatu* creates a feeling of mystical parasitism, of the way that death perpetually feeds off the living. Also memorable are the shots that evoke the deadly emanations of the vampire: the rats in the streets; the phantom ship sailing by itself; the use of negative film and single-frame exposure to depict the gulf between the natural

Fig. 7-7
Nosferatu: *The vampire (Max Schreck) brings the demons of hell into the regions of nature.*

world and the supernatural world of the vampire's castle; the bare, stony walls of the castle itself. Murnau had Fritz Arno Wagner shoot these sequences outdoors, in nature; rather than "prestylize" reality as *Caligari* had, Murnau and Wagner and art director Albin Grau found ways to make reality creepy—in many respects, the most crucial and impressive of *Nosferatu's* achievements.

Psychology

The Last Laugh

F. W. Murnau's *The Last Laugh* (*Der letzte Mann*, 1924) is the most influential of the films that concentrated on psychology and realism rather than fantasy and the unnatural. Although it contains an Expressionist dream sequence, for the most part the film is a good example of the *Kammerspiel* movement. *The Last Laugh* teamed the greatest of Ufa's talents: director, Murnau; producer, Pommer; writer, Carl Mayer; cinematographer, Karl Freund; designers, Röhrig and Herlth; and central figure, Emil Jannings. The plot is as simple as the plots of the mystical–fantasy films were complex; its emotions are as personal and as carefully motivated as the concepts of the metaphysical films were abstract.

A porter–doorman at a posh hotel (Jannings) bases his self-respect on his belief in the importance of his job, which is symbolized by his passionate devotion to his ornate uniform. The almost military uniform (he salutes when he wears it) both defines his existence and impresses his status-conscious, less fortunate neighbors. Because he is old and beginning to slow down, the doorman is stripped of this uniform and given a new one: the plain linen jacket of the lavatory attendant. The film then details the impact of this loss of dignity on his emotions—his ego collapses—and on his family and acquaintances, who reject and taunt him. Rather than leaving the old man stooped in abject despair, the film "takes pity on him" (apparently at Erich Pommer's insistence) and gives him a happy ending: a sudden inheritance of money that turns him into a kindly but gluttonous gobbler of caviar. The effect of this deliberately contrived ending will be discussed in a moment. Worthy of the fullest and most immediate attention in the film is the rendering of the steady de-

terioration of the old man's soul once he has lost the uniform that covers his body.

One of the film's great virtues is the performance of Jannings, his clear yet subtle portrayal of the two states of the unnamed doorman's mind. Wearing his uniform, Jannings walks quickly and erect; his gestures are smart and precise; his whole body exudes pride and self-esteem, as well as smugness and vanity. Without the gaudy coat he ages 25 years—his body stoops; his gestures are vague and languid; he becomes a hunched, shuffling, broken man.

The director and cameraman give Jannings a new and useful ally—the camera itself. Freund's camera tracks and swings and tilts and twirls at key moments in the film. The key principle is not just that the camera moves for the sake of visual variety, but that it has been freed from its stationary tripod in order to illuminate narrative and psychological content. The camera becomes, in effect, the other major character with whom Jannings plays his scenes, and they work so well together that verbal explanations (titles) become almost unnecessary. *The Last Laugh* has no intertitles for dialogue, but it does have one narrative intertitle—to introduce the unrealistic ending—and several shots of objects that we read: a newspaper article about the legacy, a wedding cake. For export prints, shots were taken of cakes decorated and newspapers printed in French, English, and other languages, just as the one intertitle was translated.

The power of the moving camera—which, more than anything else, made *The Last Laugh* internationally famous—strikes the viewer in the very opening of the film. In the first shot, the camera (mounted on a bicycle) rides down the elevator of the Hotel Atlantic; after a cut, it tracks through the bustling lobby, as if it were a guest who had walked out of the elevator, and over to the constantly revolving door, where it stops to look through the door at the rainy night and the doorman, with his big umbrella, ushering patrons to and from cabs. In the next shots, the camera joins the old man in the rain. This fast, busy sequence imparts excitement with its movement, but also establishes every crucial expository detail the film's action requires: the size and importance of the hotel, the old man's conscientious devotion to his job, the difficulty and triumph of his managing a heavy trunk in the rain

Fig. 7-8 *Fig. 7-9*

The Last Laugh: *the old man (Emil Jannings) in the treasured, prestigious uniform of a hotel doorman (Fig. 7-8) and in the humble uniform of a hotel lavatory attendant (Fig. 7-9).*

(which leads him to take a rest, which leads the manager to decide he's too old for the job, which precipitates the catastrophe and motivates the rest of the story), and the indifference of that symbol of the inhuman, continuous efficiency of business, the revolving door.

When the old man receives his notice of demotion from the manager, the subjective camera (a POV shot) shows us the letter and then blurs; the doorman can no longer read the piece of paper. When he gets drunk at his daughter's wedding party, the room whirls; the spinning camera mirrors his spinning head and makes the audience a bit dizzy, so that we share some of how he feels.

In spite of its oddly "Hollywood" ending, *The Last Laugh* differed markedly from the Hollywood films of the 1920s, both in its emphasis on psychology rather than action and in its depiction of a world of moral grays rather than blacks and whites. On one hand, the film condemns the callous social process that values the man's function rather than the man himself. On the other hand, our particular hotel doorman is portrayed as foppish, vain, class-conscious, and image-conscious. For a man to define his essence by a uniform and by what others think of him is false and foolish.

But the other members of the doorman's own working lower-middle-class world are themselves callous and petty, unsympathetic and inhumane, and prone to define a man by his uniform. He was his neighbors' connection to the military and economic ruling classes, and they honored him only until he fell, when they could take their revenge on him (now that he had become ordinary, one of them, or even lower) and on the oppressive social system he once incarnated. As social analysis— precisely focused on the uniforms of doorman and lavatory attendant and on the individual who wears them both, before he ends up in the "uniform" of a rich gentleman—this is a far more insightful reading of the class structure than anything in *Metropolis*. The complexity of the film's moral system contributes to the feeling that it mirrors life rather than forms some simplistic paradigm for it. In its rendering of character and its relativity of values, *The Last Laugh* was not only a mature contrast with the escapist Hollywood

Subjective vision in **The Last Laugh:** *the hungover porter's view of a woman (Emilie Kurz) bringing his morning coffee (Fig. 7-10); the distorted face of a neighbor (Fig. 7-11).*

Fig. 7-10

Fig. 7-11

product; it also set a kind of pattern that has, with exceptions of course, continued through the years: The Hollywood film has traditionally been the film of action and clear-cut values, the European film of character and moral ambiguities.

The one odd note in the film is the old man's sudden good luck. In a way like *Caligari*, whose revised ending was also approved by Pommer,

The Last Laugh has an ending that doesn't "fit," dividing the film against itself in an act of self-contradiction, in this case in the service of irony. Before our eyes, a tragedy switches to a comedy. It even uses an American character to motivate the happy ending, which is a parody of a Hollywood happy ending, seen from a Brechtian distance.

Wrenching us out of the story and announcing that the rest of the film is chimera, Carl Mayer's title card reads: "Here the story should really end for, in real life, the forlorn old man would have little to look forward to but death. The author took pity on him, however, and has provided a quite improbable epilogue." Whereas the film had not previously required a single title to clarify the thoughts or feelings of its characters, it suddenly uses one to show that the writer is sticking something on with narrative paste. Then, after shots of people laughing in the hotel as they read the paper, an insert shot of the article allows us to read with them that an American millionaire had left his fortune to the man who would be by his side when he died. We gather immediately that the rich man died in the washroom of the Atlantic Hotel. The German title of the film, *Der letzte Mann*, translates as *The Last Man* but also connotes "the least of men"—our martyred hero, when he is at his lowest ebb, as well as our restored hero, the "last man" of the will. But he does, in any case, have the last laugh.

Pabst and *die neue Sachlichkeit*

If one kind of German realist film was the close examination of a single psyche (usually a man's), the other examined the whole political or social milieu. Some of these movies, later known as "Street films," consistently use "street" in their titles: Karl Grune's *The Street* (1923), Bruno Rahn's *Tragedy of the Street* (1927). They use the unifying locale of the street as a means of tying together diverse kinds and classes of people—often to force a sheltered or repressed middle-class man to confront the seamy dangers of the real world. The street becomes a microcosm of society as a whole. And it's rough out there.

Among the most interesting of the Street films is *The Joyless Street* (1925), the first important film of the Austrian G. W. Pabst. Pabst's street runs through postwar Vienna, a city of striking contrasts: of feast and starvation, of family traditions and whoring. On Pabst's street the poor wait in line in front of a butcher's shop, hoping that the brutal man (Werner Krauss, who played Dr. Caligari) will give them a shred of meat. In the same building as the butcher's shop is Mrs. Greifer's nightclub, a frivolous, orgiastic late-night gathering spot for the rich, which also serves as a brothel. The film examines several lives on that street of contrasts where the women must choose between the poverty of standing in the slow line for the butcher's meat or the fast line to riches at Mrs. Greifer's (where the butcher is a

Fig. 7-12
The realistic mise-en-scène *of Pabst's* **The Love of Jeanne Ney;** *Fritz Rasp as the seedy villain.*

steady customer). Two women take opposite paths. One (Asta Nielsen) sells her body and eventually commits murder; the other (Greta Garbo) holds out as long as she can and is rescued at the last minute. *The Joyless Street* was so realistic and controversial that it was banned in England and recut for distribution in many countries, including Italy, France, and even Austria.

Pabst typically combines a social theme with melodramatic action. The unity of this film lies in Pabst's consistent condemnation of the society that allows such poverty and opulence to exist at the same time, that gives no choice to the poor except starvation or capitulation to the perverted values of the rich. But while we are thinking about these social and moral issues, we are also rooting for Garbo; we are still in the world of melodrama, where goodness confronts evil and emotions are extreme.

Pabst belonged to the third major movement in German film (after the Expressionist and *Kammerspiel* movements), the "New Objectivity" (*die neue Sachlichkeit*); this "new realism," which included but went beyond the Street films, took a close look at the surfaces and circumstances of reality without "prestylizing" it or pouring on the symbolism. So although he dabbled in Expressionism, Pabst was better at looking at people from the outside. From that vantage point, his psychological insight was flawless. Although some of his villains are as hissable as the butcher in *The Joyless Street* or the con artist in *The Love of Jeanne Ney* (1927), and some of his heroes are as true-hearted as Jeanne Ney and her Bolshevik lover, there are also characters who are scrutinized profoundly and yet remain impossible to label or sum up, like Lulu (Louise Brooks) in *Pandora's Box*. Both in the terms of melodrama and in those of social and moral consciousness, everything in a Pabst film is examined for its value, to see what values it possesses or reflects. And the answers are not always simple.

In keeping with his psychological objectivity, in his greatest films Pabst strives for a realistic *mise-en-scène*—whether in the studio-made worlds of Ufa (*The Joyless Street*, like *The Last Laugh*, was shot entirely in the studio) or on the actual streets of Paris (*Jeanne Ney* combines location and studio footage). He defines characters through their possessions and surroundings as well as their behavior, using *mise-en-scène* in a way that is both relentless and subtle, telling but not overstated. *The Love of Jeanne Ney* opens not with an establishing long shot but with a close-up of the worn-out shoes on the villain's feet (with one foot nervously twitching), which goes exactly against narrative convention, puts extreme emphasis on a realistic detail, and does establish a great deal about this cheap character (the despicable con artist Khalibiev, played by Fritz Rasp).

But what Pabst is most known for is the fluidity of his camerawork and editing. He might well be thought of as the director who perfected classical film continuity. His camera tracks so readily, pauses or turns so appropriately, that we accept it as an element of the film's world and as the transparent vehicle of our attention. But if he wants us to notice the camera, we *do*—as in the shot in *Jeanne Ney* when an old woman screams and the camera moves in so close and so fast that the cracks in her tongue almost fill the screen. His lighting can appear natural but can just as easily plunge us into a world of shadows, madness, and evil (as in the murder of Jeanne's greedy uncle). His editing is so rapid and smooth that we can watch sequences in *Jeanne Ney* that contain more than ten shots per minute (like the one in which Khalibiev meets Jeanne and her father) and hardly be conscious of a cut. At its most extreme, this is called "invisible editing," the exact opposite of the Soviet practice of calling attention to montage. But Pabst did not hide every cut; his skillful combination of cross-cutting and the moving camera often produces vividly effective cuts that are meant to be noticed. Between *The Joyless Street* and *The Love of Jeanne Ney*, Pabst saw Eisenstein's *Battleship Potemkin* and Pudovkin's *Mother* (which were great hits in Germany, as *The Last Laugh* was in Russia), and that is why *Jeanne Ney* is so much more intricately edited than any previous German film, why it was based on a novel in which the heroine's true love is a Bolshevik, and why it implies socialist solutions that had not been available to the characters of *The Joyless Street*.

The smoothness of Pabst's cuts depends on the absolute coordination and integration of camerawork and editing, which themselves work in concert with the movements of the actors and even the movements of the audience's eyes. Pabst discovered that one could charge a scene with invisible energy by cutting in the middle of a character's motion. The moving hand or leg, the rising body, the opening door all hide the camera's shift in distance and angle while propelling the eye into the next shot. Pabst also cut on *eye* movement—as when we watch one thing or person move from the left side of the screen ("screen left") to the center, and then something totally different move at the same pace from the center to screen right, and the trajectory of our eye movement is neither changed nor interrupted, so that it feels as if we're watching one motion even if the moving subject changes. Having mastered this, Pabst could direct a movie so that it became a dance for the eye.

The End of an Era

The key question about the death of the German film is whether it ended with a bang or a whimper—with Hitler's tyranny over the individual artist and the state's tightening control of Ufa, with the gradual decay that had been afflicting the German film mind even before Hitler came to power, or with its export to Hollywood. There is evidence that the claustrophobia of the studio production, the dependence on architecture and paint, which had liberated the visual imagination in 1919, began to inhibit it by 1926. The weakest parts of *Metropolis* employed decoration for the sake of pure decorativeness. It was time to take to the streets—the real ones.

Beyond the Studio

In 1927, the great writer of studio films, Carl Mayer, and the great photographer of studio films, Karl Freund, broke out of the studio completely to shoot a candid documentary of Berlin life. Directed, edited, and co-written (with Freund; Mayer, who disliked the director's purely pictorial approach, left the picture and was credited with having had the idea for *Berlin*, much as he had the idea for *The Street*) by the abstract artist and architect Walter Ruttmann, *Berlin: The Symphony of a Great City* (1927) was the antithesis of the traditional German film. It used no story; it was merely a chronological progression of some 18 hours in the city's life, from the arrival of an early morning train to the late-night activities of the Berliners. The film had no protagonist but the city itself.

The power of *Berlin* lies in its candid photography and its rhythmic cutting. To guarantee the authenticity of revealing the city at work and play, Freund hid the camera in a truck.

Berlin: The Symphony of a Great City—*the geometry and visual music of everyday life.*

Fig. 7-13

Though the shooting of the film was haphazard, Ruttmann's editing of it was not. His two controlled editing principles were form and rhythm (this was, after all, two years after *Battleship Potemkin*, and Ruttmann had also read Vertov's theoretical manifestos). As he cut from shot to shot, constructing the film, Ruttmann capitalized on either parallels or contrasts in form (circles, verticals, heavy masses). To combine whole sections of shots he used principles of music composition, endowing the sequence with a rhythm and tone appropriate to its content (an idea Vertov published in 1922). The opening movement of this "symphony," the train approaching the sleeping city, is *allegro moderato*—alive with expectation but a bit cautious, sleepy, hesitant. The next sequence, of the city's waking, is a *largo*—slow, peaceful. As the city wakes and goes to work, the tempo changes to *allegro vivace*—vibrant, active. There is an *andante* at the lunch hour when work stops, another *allegro* when it begins again, and another *andante* in

the quiet, gear-changing hours of the evening between work and play. The film ends with a *presto finale*, a fast, frenzied sequence of neon lights, night life, dancing, movies. With its use of pure visual form, musical rhythms, and real life, *Berlin* is clearly an attempt to exceed the limits of studio production.

Exodus to Hollywood

If the limitations of the studio film had begun to cramp the German imagination, it was also possible that the exodus of so much film talent to Hollywood had not left enough imaginations in Germany to get cramped. Murnau had gone to Hollywood to work for William Fox. After making his formal masterpiece—the lyrical study of a married couple's antagonism and reunion, *Sunrise: A Song of Two Humans* (1927, written by Carl Mayer, starring George O'Brien and Janet Gaynor, and photographed by Charles Rosher and Karl Struss), which won the first Oscar for Cinematography as well as a special Oscar for

Fig. 7-14
German filmmakers and film practice come to Hollywood: **The Mummy** *(1932), directed by Karl Freund at Universal; Boris Karloff, as the reanimated Imhotep, takes the Scroll of Thoth from an unbeliever in a scene strongly influenced by German Expressionist horror.*

"Artistic Quality of Production" and was one of the pictures that won Gaynor the first Oscar for Best Actress—Murnau died in California in 1931, the victim of an automobile crash. Lubitsch had left Ufa for Hollywood in 1922, never to return. Mayer went to Hollywood with Murnau but settled in England, where he adapted plays for the screen and worked with Paul Rotha on documentaries. Between 1927 and 1933, actors such as Marlene Dietrich and Peter Lorre; the Reinhardt-trained directors William Dieterle, Otto Preminger, and Edgar G. Ulmer; other important directors including Paul Leni, Robert Siodmak, Billy Wilder, and Fred Zinnemann; as well as Reinhardt, Brecht, Freund, and Lang all headed for Hollywood.

If the export of German talent to Hollywood bled the native film industry as steadily as a Dracula kiss, it would inject its powerful juices into the American film for the next three decades. Many of the best directors of American films between 1933 and 1960 had either worked in the German industry or had been trained there: Alfred Hitchcock, Max Ophüls, Douglas Sirk, Michael Curtiz, and others already mentioned. The great American horror films of the 1930s and 1940s at Universal (the dark tales of Frankenstein, Dracula, the Mummy, and the Wolf Man) descended either directly or indirectly from the German horror films. Karl Freund shot *Dracula* (1931) for Tod Browning and *Murders in the Rue Morgue* (1932) for Robert Florey, both at Universal, before directing his own horror classics, *The Mummy* (1932, Universal) and *Mad Love* (1935, MGM). One of the cinematographers on *Mad Love*, Gregg Toland, was decisively influenced by Freund—an influence that is clear in the film Toland shot six years later, *Citizen Kane*. Freund's contributions to the American industry would extend to the three-camera shooting technique that he developed for Desi Arnaz at Desilu for the *I Love Lucy* and *Our Miss Brooks* television series in the 1950s.

Moody Expressionist lighting and claustrophobic decor dominate American crime films of the 1940s and 1950s, the *films noirs;* despite the name given them by postwar French film critics, the disturbing themes and moods of these films came directly from the German cinema. Like Lang's *M*, these are paranoid nightmares in which there is little difference between the aims and methods of cops and crooks. It is difficult to imagine the history of American cinema without this infusion of both visual imagery and thematic commentary from Weimar Germany.

Using Sound

It is also possible that Hitler's political victory in 1933 killed a thriving film culture with terrible suddenness. The early German sound films were as good as anyone's, or better. *The Blue Angel* (1930), despite its American director (von Sternberg), was a completely German film. Its heritage is evident in its careful studio-controlled atmospheres (the smoky chaos of the nightclub hung with nets) and even in its close examination of a Jannings character (Professor Immanuel Rath's steady degeneration into a humiliated clown). The film was as careful with sound as with pictures: the contrast of the singing of Lola Lola (Marlene Dietrich) and the traditional tune chimed by the town clock, the contrast between the noisy chaos in Rath's classroom before he enters and the deadly silence when he does.

Pabst's use of sound was also developing: the wheeze and crash of exploding shells in his antiwar war film, *Westfront 1918* (1930), the effective contrast of singing soldiers and dying ones, the use of musical leitmotifs in *The Threepenny Opera* (1931).

Lang's use of sound was equally astute. In *M*, his first talkie (1931), a mother's calls—for the daughter she does not know has been abducted and murdered—are heard offscreen while the camera reveals the empty spaces where no living being stirs. The murderer (played by Peter Lorre, whose first American film was Freund's *Mad Love*) is identified by the Grieg tune he repeatedly whistles, and Lang effectively depicts the moment when a blind man, who is totally dependent on sound, recognizes the murderer.

M is also a significant example of Lang's interest in the trial as a dramatic opportunity for a society to investigate itself, or for a movie to investigate a society. In *M* the child-murderer is tried by criminals, and the insanity defense is explored. In Lang's first American film, *Fury* (1936), the apparent burning alive of an innocent man (Spencer Tracy) is explored in an equally complex trial in which movies (newsreel close-ups) provide crucial evidence against the members of the often

Fig. 7-15

Fig. 7-16

Fig. 7-17
Sound and image in M. As her mother calls for "Elsie," Lang shows her absence.

architecturally arranged lynch mob, and the victim's showing up alive in court proves a triumph for conscience without dismissing the moral culpability of the violent mob.

As for the man who played Cesare, the somnambulist conscripted by Dr. Caligari, Conrad Veidt left Nazi Germany for America, where—with a vengeance—he played the Nazi villain in

Michael Curtiz's *Casablanca* (1942). Werner Krauss—Caligari—stayed and was honored as an Actor of the State.

Leni Riefenstahl

Rather than dying slowly, the German age may well have been translated abruptly from one of gold into one of iron. As of 1933 the Nazis were in, Jewish filmmakers were out, and there was a new agenda. The German sense of architecture and composition, the rhythms of cutting and movement, found a new use in the masterful propaganda films of Leni Riefenstahl. The heroic architectural configurations of her documentary on the 1934 Nazi Party Convention at Nuremberg, *Triumph of the Will* (1935), are descendants of *Metropolis*; the stirring integration of musical motifs, the control of camera angle, the incorporation of mythic elements all aim at presenting the Führer as a combination of Pagan god of strength and charismatic savior.

An athlete, dancer, and actress, Riefenstahl appeared in mountain films—notably *The White Hell of Piz Palü* (1929), directed by Arnold Fanck and G. W. Pabst—before directing her own beautiful, mystical, and powerful mountain film, *The Blue Light* (1932). She liked Hitler and thought he could lead Germany out of its economic troubles, but after the war she maintained that she had known nothing about the genocidal campaigns and had never joined the Nazi Party. In the autobiography she published at age 90, she strained credulity by insisting that even the Nazi convention she documented in *Triumph of the Will* was merely an artistic opportunity. She also said she went out of her way to arrange private rather than government funding for *Olympia* (1938), one of the reasons that Hitler's minister of propaganda, Joseph Goebbels—as she put it—hated her guts. When she made *Tiefland* (shot 1945, edited 1954), she borrowed gypsies from a concentration camp to act as extras. After the war she devoted herself primarily to still photography—working first with African tribes and then underwater—and to defending her reputation, which rests not only on the films whose propaganda content and function she attempted to deny, but also on the most physical and metaphysical of all documentaries, *Olympia*. In that grand, two-part masterpiece, a record of the 1936 Berlin Olympic Games—which she edited for 18 months and which ranks her

Fig. 7-18   **Fig. 7-19**
The triumph of Metropolis: *Human beings become architecture again in Leni Riefenstahl's 1935 Nazi celebration film,* Triumph of the Will.

among the very greatest of all filmmakers—the techniques used to consecrate and glorify the body, the athlete, a physicality so pure that it becomes transcendent, build on the achievements in purely rhythmic editing of Ruttmann (who assisted her) and Pabst but take them to an entirely new level of power, notably in the diving sequence that climaxes the film.

Obeying the dictates of Goebbels, the German industry turned out musicals, comedies, period pieces, and dramas of military life that were calculated to entertain—with none of that annoying, depressing, psychological rot, let alone the decadence of Expressionism—and to convince the public that it was a sensitive, well-meaning bunch whose values and valuables needed to be defended against a host of deceitful enemies. Some of these enemies, particularly Jews, were portrayed as subhuman, whereas the Aryan characters had real feelings and suffered real losses (the propagandistic method of *The Birth of a Nation*). Other films simply took the dominant ideology for granted and set out to deliver romantic comedy (the as-if-apolitical method of bourgeois cinema in general). In 1939–40, when the campaign against the Jews had intensified, several features (notably Veit Harlan's *Jew Süss*, 1940) and documentaries (Fritz Hippler's *The Eternal Jew*, 1940) were devoted to portraying Jews as worthy only of expulsion or extermination; in contrast to the majority of Nazi films, which may have contained a few scenes or

subplots directed against the Jews and other designated "enemies," such as the British and the Bolsheviks, these were full-length efforts in support of the Final Solution.

Architecturally grandiose, glossily lit, and intensely serious when they were not viciously comic, such stirring, manipulative melodramas as *Jew Süss* and *Hitler Youth Quex* (Hans Steinhoff, 1933) were about as subtle as the Nazis. If the German cinema began with horror films, it ended with films that were horrors.

For Further Viewing

FILMS

FRITZ LANG (1890–1976)
Destiny (Der müde Tod, 1921)
Dr. Mabuse, the Gambler (2 parts, 1922)
Die Nibelungen (2 parts, 1924)
Metropolis (1927). Completed 1926
M (1931)
The Testament of Dr. Mabuse (1933)
Fury (1936)

F. W. MURNAU (1888–1931)
Nosferatu, a Symphony of Horror (1922)
The Last Laugh or *The Last Man (Der letzte Mann,* 1924)
Faust (1926)
Sunrise: A Song of Two Humans (1927)
Tabu (1931). Co-director, Robert Flaherty

G. W. PABST (1885–1967)

The Joyless Street (1925)
Secrets of a Soul (1926)
The Love of Jeanne Ney (1927)
Pandora's Box (1929)
Westfront 1918 (1930)
The Threepenny Opera (1931)
Kameradschaft (1931)

LENI RIEFENSTAHL (1902–2003)

The Blue Light (1932)
Triumph of the Will (1935)
Olympia (2 parts, 1938)

REPRESENTATIVE GERMAN FILMS

The Student of Prague (1913, Stellan Rye)
The Golem (1914, Paul Wegener and Henrik Galeen)
The Cabinet of Dr. Caligari (1920, Robert Wiene). Shot 1919
The Golem: How He Came into the World (1920). Script by Paul Wegener and Henrik Galeen (Paul Wegener and Carl Boese)
The Street (1923, Karl Grune)
Waxworks (1924, Paul Leni)
Variety (1925, E. A. Dupont)
The Student of Prague (1926, Henrik Galeen)
Berlin: The Symphony of a Great City (1927, Walter Ruttmann)
Überfall (*Accident* or *Police Report: Surprise Assault*, 1929, Ernö Metzner)
Mädchen in Uniform (1931, Leontine Sagan)
Kuhle Wampe (1932, Slatan Dudow and Bertolt Brecht)
Hitlerjunge Quex (1933, Hans Steinhoff)

DVDs

Berlin: The Symphony of a Great City (1927, **Walter Ruttmann**). Image Entertainment. Includes Ruttmann short, *Opus II*.

The Blue Angel (1930, **Josef von Sternberg**). Kino Video. Includes both versions of the film—the German original, **restored**, and the "English" version—plus **Marlene Dietrich**'s screen test, and more.

The Cabinet of Dr. Caligari (1920, **Robert Wiene**). Kino International. **Restored** authorized edition. Despite some print damage near the beginning, a superb archival restoration. The intertitles match the original in style and wording (there's a sequence in German for comparison) and divide the film into its original 6 acts; tinted, toned, and with the Decla logo.

Dr. Mabuse the Gambler (1922, **Fritz Lang**). Image Entertainment. Correct speeds throughout. Commentary by Lang scholar David Kalat.

The Love of Jeanne Ney (1927, **G. W. Pabst**). Kino Video. An Ufa print.

M (1931, **Fritz Lang**). Criterion Collection. **Digitally restored**. Includes commentary by film scholars Eric Rentschler and Anton Kaes, interviews with Lang, a **Chabrol** film inspired by *M*, production sketches, and more.

Metropolis (1921, **Fritz Lang**). Kino International. Excellent **digital restoration** with full restoration information and demonstrations, documentaries, commentary, script and novel excerpts, etc. Edited into a far more coherent story. Recommended over unrestored 16mm prints.

Nosferatu: A Symphony of Horror (1922, **F. W. Murnau**). Kino Video. **Restored** authorized edition. This version has well-designed and -translated intertitles, includes the original act breaks, is more convincingly edited than earlier restoration attempts, and was mastered from an archivally restored negative with the original tints. At the correct projection speed and with some previously missing shots, it runs 12 minutes longer than most versions; it also shows more of the frame.

Triumph of the Will (1935, **Leni Riefenstahl**). Synapse. Includes Riefenstahl short, *Tag der Freiheit*, and commentary by historian Anthony R. Santro.

8

Soviet Montage

The Soviet film was born with the Russian Revolution. Before 1917 the Russian film industry was a colony of Europe—of Pathé or Lumière or Scandinavia's Nordisk. No film was shot in Russia by a Russian company until 1908. However distinguished the features of Evgenii Bauer (*A Child of the Big City*, 1914; *Daydreams*, 1915) and the stop-motion animations of Ladislas Starewicz (*Revenge of a Kinetograph Cameraman*, 1912), the majority of czarist films followed the narrative patterns set by other industries, and very few of them were exported. Costume films, horror films, and melodramas—the typical formulas of Europe and America—were the staples of the pre-1917 Russian film diet. The revolution changed all that.

Lenin considered the cinema the most influential of all the arts. Movies not only entertained but, in the process, molded and reinforced values. The film was a great teacher; with portable power supplies it could be shown to huge groups of people in every remote corner of the new Soviet Union. While the flickering images held their audiences captive, the events on the screen emphasized the virtues of the new government and encouraged the people to develop those traits that would best further it. Whereas the American film began as an amusing novelty, the Soviet film was created explicitly as teacher, not as clown. In 1919, after a chaotic year in which the Soviets had let the film industry go its own commercial way, the Russian industry passed under government control.

Whereas the German innovators concentrated on the look, the feel, the psychological and pictor-

ial values of the individual shot, the Soviet innovators concentrated on the effects of joining the shots together. Like so many of the earlier innovations in film technique, the Soviet discoveries were the products of experience and experimentation; they did not grow out of abstract theorizing. But as early as 1919, the Soviets began developing a bold new literature of film theory; many of the writings of Vertov, Eisenstein, and Pudovkin proved as influential as their films and grew out of the experiments undertaken in those films—as well as the Russians' legendary fondness for debate.

The Kuleshov Workshop

Two significant accidents determined the paths Soviet experimentation would take. The first was the shortage of raw (unexposed) film stock. As in the rest of Europe, film stock was scarce in Russia during and just after the war years. The Russian film famine was even more severe, for the still-fighting Red and White armies erected blockades against each other to keep supplies from getting through. Lacking quantities of stock, the Soviet filmmakers had to make the most of what they had.

The raw stock that was available consisted mostly of the tail ends of reels left in the czarist studios and labs; it was not the material with which to develop an aesthetic of the long take. Shots had to be planned carefully and were necessarily brief; the art grew out of joining these rigorously composed fragments into wholes. And with so little stock available, regardless of the

137

length of the individual celluloid strips, it was more important to use film for newsreels rather than features. One of the first major newsreels, *Kinó-Nedelia* (*Cinema Weekly*), was supervised by Lev Kuleshov and employed the services of a young editor who called himself Dziga Vertov. The editing of these newsreels—and the full-length compilation films that began to appear in 1919—was exceptionally brisk and dynamic, largely because the cameramen had to shoot on mere scraps of film.

The scarcity of film stock also created the Kuleshov workshop (1919–25). Lev Kuleshov, who taught a workshop class at the newly established Moscow Film School, led his students in a series of editing experiments. Pudovkin was to become the most famous of those students (Vertov was not in the workshop), but even those filmmakers who did not study with Kuleshov (for example, Eisenstein) could not escape his influence. Lacking the raw stock to shoot films of their own, the Kuleshov workshop experimented in drafting scenarios, in editing and re-editing the pieces of film they already had on hand, and in re-editing sequences of feature films imported from the West.

The second of the influential accidents directly affected the Kuleshov group. In 1919, a print of Griffith's *Intolerance* successfully wriggled through the anti-Soviet blockade. *Intolerance*, which Lenin greatly admired, became a Kuleshov primer. His students examined its boldness in cutting—cuts to drive the narrative, to integrate tremendously diverse and disjointed material, to imply concepts and draw conclusions, to intensify emotion with its rhythms, to mirror private thoughts and sensations. The Kuleshov workshop screened *Intolerance* incessantly, even re-editing its sequences to examine the resulting effects on the film's power and to discover the reasons for Griffith's particular choices. With such a thorough mastery of the principles of Griffith's cutting (and of the 1922 Abel Gance film, *La Roue*, as important for its rapid cutting as *Intolerance* was for its dialectical "drama of comparisons"), the Soviet directors would extend those principles to their limits—when they got the money and the film.

Until then they experimented. Each of the experiments furthered their control of the effects of editing and their conviction that editing was the basis of film art. In the "Mozhukhin Experiment,"

conducted in or before 1923, Kuleshov used some old footage of a prerevolutionary actor, Ivan Mozhukhin. Kuleshov cut the shot of Mozhukhin's face into three pieces. He juxtaposed one of the strips with a shot of a plate of hot soup; he juxtaposed the second with a shot of a child (in some accounts, an old woman) in a coffin; he juxtaposed the third with a shot of a little girl playing with a toy bear. When viewers, who had not been let in on the joke, saw the finished sequence, they praised Mozhukhin's acting: his hunger when confronted with a bowl of soup, his sorrow for "his dead child" or "his dead mother"(their interpretation), his joy when watching "his daughter" playing. Mozhukhin's neutral expression was identical in all three pieces of film. The juxtaposed material (face + soup = hunger) evoked the concept or emotion in the audience, which then projected it into the actor. Editing alone had created the scenes, their emotional content and meaning, and even a brilliantly understated performance!

The Kuleshov student learned that editing served three primary purposes in building a film. First, a cut could serve a *narrative* function. For example, a man walks toward the camera; something to his right catches his attention and he turns his head. The audience's natural question is: What does he see? The editor then cuts to an old tramp who pulls a pistol on the man. The audience's next question is: How will the man react to this attack? The editor cuts back to the man to show his fear or his courage. And so forth. The narrative cut allows the director–editor to analyze an action into its most interesting psychological elements and then to resynthesize these elements of the event into a powerful sequential action. Another kind of narrative cut is the flashback or flash forward—a cut to a past or future event. Yet a third kind of narrative cut is the cross-cut. While the tramp attacks the man with a pistol, the police, aware of the attack, charge to the rescue. All this had been learned from Griffith.

But the Soviet film students realized that a cut could do more than narrate: It could generate an *intellectual* response. One kind of intellectual cut was the metaphorical or associational cut. From a group of workers running from soldiers, the director could cut to the slaughter of a bull in a stockyard (as Eisenstein did in *Strike*). The image of the dying animal comments on the killing of the workers; the two shots at the end of the sequence (the bleeding bull, then the dead workers) also generate a metaphor of "slaughter." A second intellectual effect could be produced by the contrast cut. The filmmaker cuts from the dinner table of a poor man, who eats only a few pieces of bread, to the table of a rich man laden with meats, candles, and wine. The contrast comments on the injustice of the fact that two such tables can exist at the same time. Such cuts can also be traced back to Griffith. The parallel cut produces a third kind of intellectual response. From the condemned man sentenced to die at five o'clock, the filmmaker cuts to a thief who murders a victim at precisely five o'clock. The parallel acts of violence at the same time reinforce each other. Significantly, the intellectual cut—metaphoric, contrast, or parallel—also has an emotional dimension. The cut not only comments on the injustice of the rich man's dinner, but also makes us hate the rich man for his gluttony and pity the poor man for his need.

The third kind of cut that the Kuleshov students discovered is a purely *emotional* one: The very method of joining the strips of celluloid together, rather than their content, produces an almost subliminal kinetic response in an audience that the director—working with or as the editor—can unobtrusively control. A single cut can function on all three levels—narrative, intellectual, emotional—at once. In fact, the Soviet directors discovered that most cuts *must* function on all three levels at once.

To this set of discoveries they gave the name "montage." In French, *montage* simply means editing; for the Soviet directors and theorists, the word signified dynamic editing and the ways it could control a film's structure, meaning, and effect. By 1924, the Kuleshov students had acquired the stock, the equipment, and the budgets to turn their lessons into films. They went out to develop their personal notions of montage. The surprise was that despite the similarities in theory, the individual filmmakers produced strikingly individual and personal films.

Sergei M. Eisenstein

Eisenstein was the greatest master of montage. Eisenstein's sense of cutting transformed his didactic lessons on the virtues of brotherhood and Marxism into dynamic, moving works of art—even for the non-Marxist. The Eisenstein silents break all the rules of "good" narrative construction. They lack central protagonists, and they move from action to commentary to analysis at Eisenstein's whim. Although they lack a conventional plot, they lack neither compelling action nor a unified structure.

The Eisenstein film holds together by means of its theme rather than its story: the experience of the workers who learn what it means to strike and to take collective action against a wicked state, the ability of a single revolutionary action on a battleship to unite a whole people, the replacement of a false revolutionary government by a true one, the superiority of the new agricultural and social methods to the old ones. The theme gets its flesh from Eisenstein's depiction of the people who embody it. Although the central character is the mass, the people as a whole, Eisenstein never forgets that the mass is made up of individuals. Although the Eisenstein film is full of magnificent shots of streaming rivers of people, he invariably shows the faces of the men and women in that river. A consistent difference between right- and left-wing films is their opposite ways of depicting the worker—as a mass of indistinguishable faces (as in Lang's *Metropolis*) or as strongly individuated human types (as in the Soviet silents).

Eisenstein's geometric compositions, as careful and as visually attractive as they are, are never static. The individual shots are full of dynamic movement. And Eisenstein's montage increases the sense of movement and tension as the individual shots collide, crash, explode into each other.

Eisenstein defined his principle of montage as one of collision, of conflict, of contrast. He does not simply build shots with particular meanings into a whole, but sees each shot, even each frame, as a unit with a dynamic visual charge of a particular kind. His goal is to bring the dynamic charge of one shot into conflict with the visual charge of the next. For example, the shots can conflict directionally—a ship sailing from right to left, followed by a wave breaking from left to right. The shots can conflict in rhythm—a group of people running chaotically, followed by a group of soldiers marching steadily, slowly, inexorably. The shots can conflict in bulk—from a mass of

Fig. 8-1

Fig. 8-2

Fig. 8-3

Battleship Potemkin: *from the mass to individual detail, from geometry to people.*

workers to a single worker's face. The shots can conflict in camera angle, lighting, emotional intensity, and so forth. Eisenstein's great films are the products of his combining many and diverse gifts—his visual sense of composition, his feeling for rhythm and tempo, his ability to understand and manipulate emotion, and his perceptive intellect, which could create meaning by joining two or more apparently unrelated images.

Eisenstein formally studied engineering and architecture. During the Civil War of 1918–20, he organized an impromptu theatre troupe in the Red Army. Attracted to the theatre, he started directing plays in Moscow after the war, where he was heavily influenced by the innovative, anti-Naturalist director, Vsevolod E. Meyerhold. A committed formalist and Constructivist, Meyerhold later became one of the first to oppose Socialist Realism. Eisenstein staged his last play, *Gas Masks* (1924), in the Moscow Gas Works. He could go no further with stage reality; the leap into films was inevitable. His first feature film, *Strike* (1924, released 1925, made when he was 27), revealed the bold, broad strokes of a new master.

Strike contains many of the traits that make an Eisenstein film pure Eisenstein. There is the director's control and alternation of moods: from the peaceful, idyllic sequences of the striking workers at rest and play to the violent, vicious slaughter of the workers in their tenements. There is the satirical treatment of the rich and the informers for the rich: The company finks are depicted as sneaky animals; the rich factory owners sip cocktails while the workers starve and die (Griffith cross-cutting, of course). There is the director's sense of visual composition: the geometrical patterns and shapes of the factory and of the workers' tenements where the Cossacks attack. There is Eisenstein's construction of a metaphor out of two images, to comment on the action: The shot of the dying bull, juxtaposed with the shot of the dead workers, as said before, generates the metaphoric statement that the workers were "slaughtered." And uniting the film is the Eisenstein vision: that the capitalistic, czarist system is fundamentally inhumane, an obstacle not only to physical survival, but also to human fellowship, family, and brotherhood. *Strike* was co-shot by cinematographer Eduard Tisse, who would shoot or co-shoot all of Eisenstein's major films through the first part of

Ivan the Terrible (1944). Indeed, Eisenstein and Tisse are regarded as one of the greatest director–cinematographer teams in film history, along with Griffith and Bitzer, and Chaplin and Totheroh.

Battleship Potemkin

Battleship Potemkin (1925) was Eisenstein's next film. Originally titled *1905*, the work was intended to depict the general workers' revolt in Russia of that year. Instead, Eisenstein pared down his conception to linking two events in that revolt—the rebellion on the battleship *Potemkin* and the Odessa reprisals by the Czar's troops and Cossacks—to serve as a microcosm for the 1905 revolution. The five-reel film's five parts, deliberately mirroring the five-act structure of classical drama, form a taut structural whole: from the unity the sailors build on the ship, to the unity between ship and shore, to the unity of the entire fleet.

Eisenstein's uniquely powerful editing brings the film to life. At the end of Part 1, Eisenstein wants to emphasize that the men have had it, that the last straw has been laid on the camel's back. A sailor washing the dishes sees a plate inscribed, "Give us this day our daily bread." The biblical platitude infuriates him since they have no decent daily bread. He smashes the plate. To emphasize this act of smashing, Eisenstein divides this physical action, which takes only a few seconds, into 11 different shots (see Fig. 8-4). Dividing an action into such a process analyzes the event *and* makes it more violent, more purposeful, more dynamic and more memorable as a pivotal point in the film. The edited version of the action (six seconds without the fade-out) takes longer than the physical act itself if one could perform it.

No better example of tonal montage exists than in the opening passage of "An Appeal from the Dead." The entire sequence is saturated in the lyric calm of the sailor's death. Eisenstein cuts slowly from shot to shot, each of them growing lighter, revealing the rising of the sun through the fog. In the languid cuts, the sea is calm as glass, ships glide through the mist, gulls hover in the air. The editing of the mourning Odessans in the final section of "An Appeal from the Dead" adds a note of strength and determination to the moody silence. Eisenstein cuts from far shots of

Fig. 8-4
The plate-smashing sequence in Battleship Potemkin: *a brief action broken into a dramatic and dialectical process.*

the immense mass of people to medium shots of three or four faces, to close-ups of single faces and clenched fists. Having expressed their solidarity with the mutineers, the people of Odessa become targets.

The most dazzling editorial sequence in all of *Battleship Potemkin* is the massacre of the citizens of Odessa on that city's great outdoor staircase: the second half of the "Odessa Steps" section. Eisenstein constructs this horrifying, brutal sequence from many different kinds of shots: far shots from the bottom of the steps showing the citizens running chaotically; traveling shots along the side of the steps that flee with the workers; shots from the top of the steps showing the relentless, metric pace of the marching soldiers, only their boots, their bayonets, and their awesome shadows in the frame; close-ups of faces in shock, pain, horror, fear, confusion, anger. Eisenstein intercuts all these different shots, alternating them according to different principles of his montage of collisions.

But *Battleship Potemkin* is more than montage. For a film with a mass protagonist, the faces of individuals are strikingly memorable. Out of the geometric organization of sailors' hammocks emerge the faces of the young sailor who gets beaten and Vakulinchuk, the sailor who leads his comrades in revolt. The sharp-featured, beady-eyed faces of the sneaky ship's doctor, the cunning ship's mate with the moustache of a melodrama villain, and the egomaniacal captain convey Eisenstein's condemnation of the vicious ruling class. But the most memorable faces are those in the most active and violent sequence of all—the Odessa Steps. Eisenstein creates the horror of the slaughter not just with mass murder, chaotic movement, fast cutting, and conflicting compositions, but also with the individual reactions and sensations of the victims: the elderly lady with the pince-nez, the mother with her shot and trampled son, the student with the glasses, the dark-clad mother with the baby carriage. As the soldiers attack, Eisenstein follows the fortunes and reactions of each of these individuals, using their emotional responses to evoke ours.

So much of the viewer's experience of *Battleship Potemkin* proceeds not from the eyes to the brain (the film's ideological statements) but from the eyes to the nerves. Like music, one *feels* the film as rhythm, mood, tone, and texture in addition to perceiving its concrete images.

October

Eisenstein's next film, properly titled *October* (1928, co-directed by Grigori Alexandrov), was released in a shortened and oversimplified version in the United States and England as *Ten Days that Shook the World* (for no reason other than to exploit the interest in John Reed's book). *October*, a loose historical survey of the months between the February Revolution of 1917 and the Bolshevik Revolution of October, is more intellec-

tual, more satirical, and more specifically political than *Battleship Potemkin*. It is also, unfortunately, less unified dramatically, less consistent thematically, and less effective emotionally. Unlike *Battleship Potemkin*, its parts are far more striking than its whole.

Eisenstein's consistent method in this film is to use inanimate objects to comment, often sarcastically, on the activities of the living. Although he used the method rarely in *Battleship Potemkin*, *October* is full of "stone lions" that come to life.

A series of objects comments on the values of Kerensky, leader of the Provisional Government after the February Revolution. As Kerensky poses, Eisenstein cuts to a statuette of Napoleon. Eisenstein further debunks Kerensky's imperial ambitions by showing all the possessions in his quarters, formerly occupied by the Czar and his family—gleaming china plates, goblets of cut glass, chalices of silver, an army of toy soldiers, the king he plays with from a chess set—or by showing him repeatedly ascending the same staircase every time he gets promoted. Most damning of Kerensky is the series of shots that shows him fleeing in his Rolls Royce, a little American flag planted firmly on the radiator.

Eisenstein uses other objects satirically. To burlesque the glories of war, he shows a collection of gaudy medals; to burlesque the emptiness of religion (a consistent Eisenstein theme, since the church supported the czar as well as the Provisional Government), he shows an explosive series of icons: crosses, statues of Buddha, wooden figures of primitive gods. All of the statues emphasize the artificiality of turning the abstraction of a deity into a tangible object. To burlesque the idealism of the Mensheviks, a group that advocated peaceful change rather than revolution, Eisenstein cuts sarcastically from one of their speakers to a group of harps plucked languidly by graceful hands. The parodic yet urgent tone of *October*, and the rigor of its montage experiments, hold together its sprawling, semihistorical structure.

Eisenstein's next film, his last silent, was *Old and New* (1929). Often called *The General Line* and also directed with the assistance of Alexandrov, *Old and New* demonstrates the difficulties and the virtues for the peasant of discarding the old ways of farming and thinking.

Fig. 8-5
Nine shots from the Odessa Steps sequence. Note the graphic conflicts between long and close shots, symmetrical and asymmetrical compositions, a human face and the inexorable march of an armed machine.

Fig. 8-6

Fig. 8-7

Fig. 8-8
October: Eisenstein "explodes" religion with a satiric montage of religious objects.

The film represents some departures for Eisenstein. In the manner of Pudovkin, he uses natural rather than inanimate imagery—fields, soil, animals, and crops—and he also uses a central figure—a peasant woman who supports collective farming—rather than the masses to embody the film's social progress.

But Eisenstein was beginning to run into trouble with the Soviet line and leaders. Stalin was dissatisfied with the ending of *Old and New*, finding it untrue to the spirit of the new nation and the people. Eisenstein—a half-Jewish, bisexual iconoclast, a devoted artist, an avid reader of everything from T. S. Eliot and Proust to Joyce and Kafka, from Dickens to Japanese poetry—began to feel the pinch of tightening state control. He did not complete another feature for nearly ten years.

Sound and Color

Both political problems and aesthetic challenges frustrated and motivated Eisenstein during this hiatus. Sound had suddenly overtaken the world's industries, and in 1929 Eisenstein, Alexandrov, and Tisse were sent abroad to study foreign studio methods and sound techniques. Eisenstein lectured all over Europe and met, among others, George Grosz and Luigi Pirandello in 1929 and Abel Gance, James Joyce, and Jean Cocteau in 1930.

Eisenstein spent much of 1930 in America, where he met Chaplin, Disney, and Theodore Dreiser. For several months he was under contract at Paramount, trying to get them to accept any of the projects he had developed (notably Dreiser's *An American Tragedy* and a biopic called *Sutter's Gold*). Paramount decided otherwise. In 1931, Eisenstein, Tisse, and Alexandrov were in Mexico, filming an epic of the Mexican people, *¡Qué viva México!*, financed by Upton Sinclair. Eisenstein fought with Sinclair, and the film was canceled. Eisenstein never got the chance to edit the finished footage, much of which he never saw.

Returning to the Soviet Union, Eisenstein submitted several projects that were rejected by the state film committee. Eisenstein was accused of formalism—to Stalin, a pedestrian realist, the great sin of Soviet art—of paying too much attention to the formal beauty and structure of the work and not enough to its narrative content and political clarity. His methods were wasteful and time-consuming. His perfectionism was demanding and inconsiderate of budgets and schedules. He seemed to be a director without a country, too political for 1930s Hollywood, too aesthetic for 1930s Moscow, and too intellectual for both of them. *Bezhin Meadow*, the project he cared the most about during the 1930s and had begun to shoot in 1935, was canceled by official order in 1937. Finally, in 1938, he made his first sound feature, *Alexander Nevsky*.

Eisenstein's theory of the sound film—expressed in a 1928 "Statement" co-signed but probably not co-written by Pudovkin and Alexandrov—was that the "talkie" was a fundamental error in the use of the medium. There was no artistic purpose in showing an actor's lips move while the audience hears the words pour out. "Satisfying simple curiosity," he wrote, "increases the inertia of each shot as a montage element." For Eisenstein, sound was to be used asynchronously and contrapuntally: to become one more element of a film's montage. The visuals and sound should play *against* one another, not plod in unison. Although Eisenstein's theory of the sound film was contrary to the practice of his contemporaries—except for Vertov, who wrote in 1929 that sounds could be edited as easily as pictures, "in harmony or not" with the visuals—years of experience with the sound film have since proved the solidity of his theory.

Eisenstein, whose use of images had always been musical, was especially interested in the precise synchronization of visual images with musical passages and motifs. One of the best demonstrations of his musical theory is in "The Battle on the Ice" sequence in *Alexander Nevsky*, as the invading Teutonic hordes (symbolic of the Nazi threat) encounter the valiant Russians who have gathered to defend themselves. Aided by the power and complexity of Prokofiev's score, Eisenstein turns "The Battle on the Ice" into a cinematic symphony. The successive tones and rhythms of the music—slowly expectant, playfully fast, steadily victorious—play both with and against the content of Eisenstein's images of battle and the rhythms and shapes that control the editing of the images.

Eisenstein's only other completed works before his death in 1948 were two of the three intended parts of *Ivan the Terrible* (Part I released 1944, Part II [1946] released 1958, Part III

Fig. 8-9
Ivan the Terrible, Part I: *A master of editing, Eisenstein was also a master of composition.*

[1946] unfinished). In Part II, he experimented with Expressionist color in two sequences. As with sound, Eisenstein believed that color should not be exploited for its novelty, its colorfulness, but that color should play a functional role in controlling the film's tone and effects. Again, the years would prove his sensitivity to one potential of a cinematic device. But the most striking fact of Eisenstein's career is that he completed four full-length pictures in his first five years and three in his next twenty. Eisenstein became a teacher and theoretician; he taught at the State Film School; he wrote lengthily and convincingly on the powers and effects of montage, although Stalin suppressed the publication of many of Eisenstein's books. But his greatest achievements in filmmaking had been accomplished before the end of the silent era.

To some extent his career mirrors the artistic vitality of the Soviet film as a whole. The Russian film made the transition into the Sound Era with great difficulty, partly because the Soviet cinematic method was so visual, partly because the great Soviet directors became politically suspect, and partly because the Soviet industry had difficulty acquiring reliable machines to shoot and project sound pictures.

Vsevolod I. Pudovkin

Pudovkin and Eisenstein were friendly opponents. Whereas Eisenstein's theory of montage was one of *collision*, Pudovkin's was one of *linkage*. For Pudovkin, the shots of the film combine to build the whole work, as bricks combine to make a wall, rather than conflict with one another in dynamic suspension. Pudovkin, a trained scientist, sometimes considered film viewers to be a bit like the dogs in the experiments of his contemporary, Pavlov: The proper cinematic stimulus could elicit the desired intellectual, physical, or emotional response. Eisenstein, however, following the theories of Hegel, Marx, and Engels, believed that the method of argument itself must be rigorously *dialectical:* Shot A collides with shot B to create concept (or metaphor) C. Eisenstein's goal was to convert cinematic practice into a means of dialectical reasoning. The pictorial *thesis* in conflict with its *antithesis* would produce a new abstract *synthesis*. The synthesis, often a metaphor or a concept, is generated not on the screen but in the mind of the viewer, because an idea is notoriously hard to photograph. If Eisenstein's primary method was *dialectical montage*, Pudovkin's was *constructive editing*.

Whereas the tone and pace of an Eisenstein film are generally nervous and tense, exciting and jostling, the tone and pace of Pudovkin's are more intimate and relaxed. He reserves the shocking, violent montage effects for sequences of fighting and rebellion—or exuberance. Whereas Eisenstein's usual human focus is the mass, Pudovkin's is the individual, a single person's revolutionary decision rather than the revolutionary action of a whole group. Whereas Eisenstein's montage is rich in intellectual commentary, Pudovkin's assembles the scene or sequence out of *relatively* complementary shots to construct the action and advance its metaphoric and emotional complexity.

Pudovkin believed that the "plastic material"—visually expressive objects and images—could communicate emotions and ideas more effectively than any other cinematic tool. The writer or director must, he wrote, "know how to find and to use plastic (visually expressive) material: that is to say, he must know how to discover and how to select, from the limitless mass of material provided by life and its observation, those forms and movements that shall most clearly and vividly express in images the *whole content* of his idea." The fact that he followed this principle throughout his career gives his work a deeply rewarding degree of richness, power, and precision.

In 1920, Pudovkin began his studies at the State Film School, entering Kuleshov's workshop two years later. His scientific training ably suited him for his first major project, *Mechanics of the Brain* (1926), a cinematic investigation of Pavlovian research on conditioned reflexes in animals and children. He took time off from the Pavlov picture to shoot his first fiction film, *Chess Fever* (1925), an ingenious and charming short comedy that paid homage to his teacher, Kuleshov.

Mother

Pudovkin's unique style emerged in his later fiction films. In *Mother* (1926), he reveals his ability to combine sensitive treatment of a human story, fluid narrative editing that uses the shock cutting of montage for isolated, showcase effects, and natural images that comment on the action and reinforce the film's values. Produced, like *Battleship Potemkin*, for the 20th anniversary of the ill-fated 1905 revolution, *Mother* is a loose adaptation of Gorky's novel about a woman (Vera Baranovskaya) who learns that radical action is the only protection against a wicked state. In 1905, her abusive, drunken husband (who isn't in the novel) is lured into helping a group of strikebreakers; he is shot and killed in a scuffle. The mother then betrays her own son, Pavel (Nikolai Batalov), revealing to the police, whose promises she naïvely trusts, that the youth was in collusion with the strikers. The judges are more interested in dozing or breeding race horses than in administering justice; the unsympathetic gallery has come to the trial for a good sadistic show. The unjust social process turns the old woman into a radical. She helps her son escape from prison, and together they march in the forefront of a workers' demonstration. Although both she and Pavel die, cut down by the bullets of the Cossacks and the hooves of their horses, the story of her education serves as a model for all the workers of

Fig. 8-10
**Mother: *Pudovkin's use of the "plastic material." Defining a
bureaucratic policeman by his gloved hands.***

Russia and a metaphor for the results of their education that would eventually surface in 1917.

Pudovkin's handling of actors and shaping of scenes are exceptional. His principle of acting—that the film's context, its decor, its business, its use of objects work with the actor to create a performance—is demonstrated throughout *Mother*. A most effective example is the scene of mourning in which the mother sits by the corpse of her husband. Pudovkin alternates among several setups: a far shot of the mother sitting beside the bier, the walls gray and bare behind her; a close shot of water dripping in a bucket; a close shot of the mother's face, motionless. The mother's face needs no motion. Her still, quiet face—expressive plastic material, as much as the pan—mirrors all the sorrow that has been built around her.

The camera angle Pudovkin uses to shoot a scene is always significant. The far shot of the mourning mother beside the corpse is a downward shot from a high camera position (a high-angle shot). Pudovkin discovered that the downward angle emphasizes the characters' smallness, their feeling of being alone, their insignificance. Conversely, the extreme upward angle (a low-angle shot) can magnify the self-importance of characters, their smugness and petty self-esteem—or can make them appear more formidable, like the guard outside the courthouse. Pudovkin mirrors the state of the mother's mind and the progress of her education with his choice of camera positions. He often shoots her from above before her conversion; he shoots her from below to ennoble her after it.

Pudovkin relies primarily on the narrative cut, breaking down, analyzing, and constructing scenes in a manner that builds on Griffith's. Like Griffith, he works for fluidity in building a scene, constructing it "brick by brick" out of shots that work together; the montage is evident but not disruptive.

Like Eisenstein, Pudovkin knew how to analyze a quick action into its component movements to add emphasis, shock, and drama to the event. For example, in the climactic demonstration sequence, Pudovkin emphasizes the brutality of the slaughter by breaking the moment of the soldiers' initial attack into 13 shots (see Fig. 8-11). Out of the sudden loss and violence of this moment the mother learns her last political lesson; courageously, she picks up the fallen flag and walks

Fig. 8-11
*The beginning of the slaughter
in* Mother.

Fig. 8-12

Fig. 8-13

Fig. 8-14

Fig. 8-15

The End of St. Petersburg: *the deflation of war—soldiers without heads, flying flags, a fancy orator (note the upward angle to burlesque him), as men die in the smoke and carnage on the battlefield.*

toward the charging troops (an excellent series of cuts with contrasting directions and rhythms). Though they kill her, she dies a rebel, the metaphorical mother of the nation that is born with her death.

Later Works

Like *Mother, The End of St. Petersburg* (1927) is a story of political education, of a character who betrays the revolutionists early in the film only to join them before the end of it. A young peasant from the country must leave for the city to survive; there is neither enough land nor enough food on the farm to support him.

Pudovkin draws a visual contrast between city and country with the opening shots of animals, fields, rivers, and trees, and the later shots of factories and buildings and statues. The youth feels dwarfed in the city of St. Petersburg. Pudovkin shoots from high angles down at the boy, making him seem small and worthless in comparison with the huge statues, high buildings, and vast public squares.

The youth, ignorant of political realities, becomes a strikebreaker and betrays the leaders of the strike, one of whom is his own cousin. It takes the rest of the movie for him to redeem himself.

Although *The End of St. Petersburg* was intended to commemorate the tenth anniversary of
the final, Bolshevik Revolution, it goes beyond
that to become an epic of the people and the
land, embracing all the country in its tale of farm
and factory, class and change.

The film makes a relentless visual contrast
between the idealistic glories and the realities of
war. When war is declared, Pudovkin shows the
military leaders only from the neck down—their
uniforms, their medals, their gold braid, their
boots. Not their heads. They obviously have no
heads. As the parade of soldiers marches off to
war, Pudovkin cuts the sequence rhythmically to
look and feel like a gaudy carnival. From the
rhythmic shots of celebration, Pudovkin cuts to a
quiet shot of the sky; a shell explodes, splattering
the earth in the foreground. The glory of war has
been replaced by the reality. Later he cuts back
and forth between the violent war at the front
and violent men haggling at the stock exchange,
in a sequence clearly inspired by *A Corner in
Wheat.* While men die in the military war, others
get rich in the financial war.

Pudovkin's next film, *The Heir to Genghis
Khan,* also called *Storm Over Asia* (1928), is yet
another story of revolutionary education, of potential betrayal converted into political camaraderie.

Like Eisenstein, Pudovkin believed that the
value of the sound film would be its asynchro-
nous, tonal use of sound rather than a synchronized dialogue and picture. In discussing the way
he would have used sound in *Mother*, Pudovkin
said he would have evoked the sorrow of the
mourning scene not with the synchronized sound
of the mother's weeping but with the steady,
hollow sound of water dripping into a bucket. Like
Eisenstein, Pudovkin had difficulty putting his
stheories into practice. *The Story of a Simple
Case* (1932), planned and apparently shot as a
sound picture, was released silent. His next picture, *Deserter* (1933), is his most respected sound
film: the story of a young German worker who,
like the protagonists of Pudovkin's silent films,
receives an education in political radicalism.

Pudovkin continued to direct and act in films
until his death in 1953; during those last 20 years
he directed only about a half-dozen interesting
films. Like Eisenstein, he was castigated for his
formalism and spent much of his later life teaching and writing.

Other Major Figures

Alexander Dovzhenko

Alexander Dovzhenko was the third of the great
Soviet directors. Though he shared both the political philosophy of Marx and the montage
methods of Kuleshov with Eisenstein and Pudovkin, Dovzhenko's style was completely original.
Unlike Eisenstein and Pudovkin, Dovzhenko came
from the provinces, not the capital, from Ukraine,
not Moscow or St. Petersburg. As early as his first
major work, *Zvenigora* (1928), Dovzhenko's films
are saturated in Ukrainian life and customs as
well as in the folk-legend spirit and poetry of the
country. His is a world where horses talk, where
paintings of heroes in picture frames roll their
eyes at the bastardization of their principles,
where animals sniff the revolutionary spirit in the
air. The Dovzhenko film is structured not as narrative but as lyric, a visual poetry that develops
a theme and allows immense elliptical jumps in
time, space, and continuity.

Arsenal (1929) is the first of his mature film
poems. Its subject is, roughly, the birth and
growth of the revolutionary spirit in Ukraine.
Whereas Pudovkin might develop such a theme
by showing a single Ukrainian's radicalization,
Dovzhenko seems to spread all the events of the
revolutionary years before him and then to select
those images and vignettes that appeal to him.

Dovzhenko uses a central figure—a soldier
who deserts the czar to serve the revolution—as a
loose peg on which to hang the film's action.
Scenes with the soldier flow through *Arsenal*'s
many vignettes. In the final sequence, the White
army captures the soldier, leads him in front of a
firing squad, and shoots him. The Ukrainian soldier does not die; the bullets do not strike him.
He stands there defiantly. Although the forces of
tyranny can capture a single arsenal, although
they can shoot a single rebel, they cannot murder
the spirit of rebellion and freedom in the hearts of
the people. The Ukrainian becomes an image of
that spirit. His presence throughout the film has
been as metaphor, not as traditional protagonist.
Dovzhenko's films are not narratives of events
but metaphors for the feeling and the significance
of the events.

Dovzhenko's striking compositions in light
and space reveal the eye of the painter he once
was. Though his montage sequences are vivid

and powerful, even more effective are the relatively long takes in which he allows a great image all the time it needs. And his painter's eye sees the power and tension of shooting with the tilted camera, on an angle to rather than parallel with the world he is filming.

Dovzhenko's greatest silent film poem, *Earth* (1930), is another series of images and vignettes, this one revolving around the earth, the harvests, the relationships of people, machines, and the cycles of life. His sound films, *Ivan* (1932), *Aerogard* (1935), and *Shchors* (1939), also were daring, episodic, and imagistic. Not surprisingly, Dovzhenko ran into stiff Soviet criticism; he was the most elliptical director of them all. How could his films be socially useful if the audiences could not follow them? Dovzhenko made only two films in his last 15 years and died in 1956, another great innovative mind stifled by the state's ever-narrowing definitions of artistic utility.

Dziga Vertov

Dziga Vertov, one of the Soviet Union's pioneers in combining documentary footage with political commitment, experimental cinema with ideological statement, suffered similar artistic strangulation as Stalinism took hold—partly because he was a Jew, partly because his aesthetic stood for the truth, and partly because he didn't praise Stalin enough in the last film he was allowed to make, *Three Songs About Lenin* (1934). His brother, cameraman Boris Kaufman, left Russia to shoot all the films of Jean Vigo in France before going to Hollywood, where he shot such pictures as *On the Waterfront* (1954) and *The Pawnbroker* (1965). His other brother, cameraman Mikhail Kaufman, stayed to direct documentaries and shoot Vertov's *The Man with a Movie Camera* (literally, *Man with Movie Camera*; 1928, released 1929), one of the most distinctive and adventurous films of any era.

Dziga Vertov's intense energy was evident not only in his documentaries and manifestos, but also in the name he chose for himself, which translates roughly as "fidgety spinning top" (*Dziga* is Ukrainian for "spinning top" or "restless person"; *Vertov* is derived from the Russian verb "to rotate" or "to fidget"); he was born in Poland as Denis Kaufman. As mentioned in Chapter 6, Vertov began by compiling footage into weekly newsreels in 1918–19, went on to edit full-length compilation films and shoot some of his own footage in 1920–22 (he called the camera his "Kino Eye"), then invented a documentary form that went beyond the reportage of the newsreel into creative journalism: a series of shorts that were called newsreels but each focused on specific topics and themes. That series, which ran from 1922 to 1925, was *Kinó-Pravda* ("film truth"; the French term, in homage to Vertov, is *cinéma vérité*), and its powerful emotional and didactic effects were created by the ways Vertov and his wife, editor Elizoveta Svilova, assembled the absolutely unstaged footage that was sent in from all over Russia. Beginning in 1919, he also published manifestos that were as brilliant and playful as they were radical; no film theorist is more fun to read. He attacked not only the narrative feature, but also the ordinary ways of looking at things, explored the cinema's relation to radio and television, and argued that montage—of pictures as well as sounds—was an art not of the sequence but of a film's concept from start to finish.

In many of his films, Vertov brings to life the ordinary, laborious tasks of building a nation (laying an airstrip, planting crops, finishing a tram line) by examining the progress of the task from many stirring and awesome angles, endowing the ordinary with wonder and exploring, as would many later Soviet films, the vitality of machines and the powerful potential of the union of people and machines.

Like Ruttmann's *Berlin*, *The Man with a Movie Camera* is organized as an examination of life in a major city—its work and play from morning to night. Unlike Ruttmann, however, Vertov depicts the ways that the cinema itself has become an intrinsic part of modern life and a marvelous aid to seeing and understanding that life. Early in the film, we see an empty movie theatre. When the patrons arrive, the seats fold down by themselves to greet them. Thus the film begins itself. The film they see is the film we see—for *The Man with a Movie Camera* is a film-within-a-film about filmmaking. Vertov compares the lens of the movie camera and its operations to the human eye and its operations—declaring the cinema an extension of human vision. He demonstrates the processes of editing (the movie "stops" while the editor decides which shot to use next) and the relationship of still frames to moving shots. He also draws parallels

Fig. 8-16   **Fig. 8-17**
Two consecutive frames from **The Man with a Movie Camera.**

between the processes of cinema and other societal occupations that depend on machines that
spin, wheel, or cycle repeatedly—the pumping of
pistons, the winding of threads, the packing of
cigarette boxes. If Vertov takes the "magic" out of
cinema by exposing how it does its tricks, he also
endows it with another form of magic—the magic
of all processes of modern mechanical life that,
like the movie camera, do their work in the
service of human beings and the world they
are building together.

Despite this inspired synthesis of radical
form and radical ideology, Vertov made few films
after 1930, the most important of which were
Enthusiasm (1931), which had a loud, complex,
contrapuntal soundtrack, exploding with the energy of sound/picture montage, and *Three Songs
About Lenin,* which combined documentary
footage with lyrical passages in honor of the
founding father. He died in 1954 after 20 years
of reduced influence and enforced idleness.

Socialist Realism

Stalin's pet aesthetic, Socialist Realism, demanded
that art serve the interests of the state—not by
stimulating and challenging people but by entertaining them with obvious, inspiring tales that had
to be clear to anyone. To concentrate on the form
of a work was to be arty and confusing, and to deviate from the Stalinist line was to fail to communicate plain reality. By the mid-1930s, this was the
only permissible way to make a film.

In the early years of sound, the more realistic
and less elliptical directors triumphed. Behind
the struggle between realism and abstraction in
the cinema lay a more general battle that was
being waged between two conflicting forces in
all the Soviet arts: the struggle between Socialist
Realism and Constructivist abstraction for control of the "true path" of the People's Revolutionary Art.

The central arena for the struggle was the
theatre, where the principles of Stanislavski's
Moscow Art Theatre (detailed, realistic characters; lucid stories of human interaction in a
clear social setting) triumphed over those of
Vsevolod Meyerhold's brand of Constructivism
(more abstract and symbolic settings; epic
stories of vast social forces and movements).
The official canonization of the Stanislavski
method (despite the Moscow Art Theatre's
czarist and elitist origins) led to the vilification
and ostracizing of Meyerhold. This conflict of
values in the theatre necessarily spilled over
into the cinema, where several film directors
(Eisenstein, for example) had been extremely
influenced by Meyerhold.

Nikolai Ekk, whose *Road to Life* (1931) was
the first commercially successful Soviet sound
film, found the assumptions of Socialist
Realism quite congenial. His film is a close,
warm study of human feelings and exertion as
well as a social lesson on how the "wild boys"
of Russia—the homeless juvenile delinquents
roaming the streets—found a purpose in life

through collective labor. The Vasiliev Brothers' *Chapayev* (1934) became the model for the study of revolutionary heroes, the intimate portrayal of a military leader whose great strengths are his energy, passion, humor, and love for the people, and who overcomes his great weaknesses—excessive individuality, a stubborn refusal to study the new ways—to unite his heroic band of guerrillas with the spirit of the entire Red Army.

Yakov Protazanov was another of the successful realist directors of the first decade of sound, one of the few film directors of the czarist era to return to Soviet Russia. Grigori Kozintsev and Leonid Trauberg founded the actor-oriented "FEX" group (Society for Eccentric Actors) in the silent period in answer to the montage-oriented Kuleshov group; they continued to make films into the 1960s. Mark Donskoy made the careful, literate biographical trilogy of Maxim Gorky's growth from youth to maturity (*Childhood of Gorky*, 1938; *In the World*, 1939; *My Universities*, 1940).

But for almost 25 years the imagination and creativity of the Soviet film were tightly reined by a government policy and aesthetic that forced artists into prescribed channels of expression.

For the critical years from 1929 to 1937—the transitional years between silence and sound—Stalin replaced Lenin's sympathetic commissar for information, Anatoly Lunacharsky, who encouraged artistic innovation, with a flunky, Boris Shumyatsky, a business-minded bureaucrat who viewed his job as bringing the eccentric, "formalistic" artists in line. Shumyatsky's "bringing the artists in line" was as responsible for the silence of Eisenstein in those key years as the triumph of Socialist Realism. Stalin dismissed Shumyatsky in 1937 for failing to produce enough films and enough significant films; the Soviet filmmakers then enjoyed a few years of freedom. But the war against Germany in 1941 (ending a nonaggression pact that had lasted two years) imposed restrictions again; certain kinds of films were needed to boost morale. After the war, Stalin clamped down on the directors and the people yet again. Only with his death in 1953 did the Soviet film begin to regain prestige on the international screen.

For Further Viewing

FILMS

ALEXANDER DOVZHENKO (1894–1956)
Arsenal (1929)
Earth (1930)
Aerogard (1935)
Shchors (1939). Asst. director, Yulia Solntseva

SERGEI M. EISENSTEIN (1898–1948)
Strike (1925). Completed 1924
Battleship Potemkin (1925)
October (1928). Co-director, Grigori Alexandrov
Old and New or *The General Line* (1929). Co-director, Grigori Alexandrov
¡Qué viva México! (1930–32). Unfinished. Co-director, Grigori Alexandrov. Portions of the footage assembled and released as *Thunder Over Mexico* (1933, Sol Lesser), *Time in the Sun* (1939, Marie Seton), and *Que Viva Mexico!* (1979, Grigori Alexandrov)
Alexander Nevsky (1938). Co-director, Dmitri Vasiliev
Ivan the Terrible (1944). *Part II*, 1946, released 1958; *Part III*, unfinished, shot 1946

VSEVOLOD I. PUDOVKIN (1893–1953)
Mechanics of the Brain (1926)
Mother (1926)
The End of St. Petersburg (1927)
The Heir to Genghis Khan or *Storm Over Asia* (1928)
Deserter (1933)

DZIGA VERTOV (1896–1954)
Kinó-Pravda (1922–25)
The Man with a Movie Camera or *Man with Movie Camera* (1929). Completed 1928
Enthusiasm (1931)
Three Songs About Lenin (1934)

PRE-SOVIET AND SOVIET MISCELLANY
A Child of the Big City (1914, Evgenii Bauer)
Father Sergius (1918, Yakov Protazanov)
Extraordinary Adventures of Mr. West in the Land of the Bolsheviks (1924, Lev Kuleshov)
Moscow (1927, Mikhail Kaufman)
Bed and Sofa (1927, Abram Room)
Girl with the Hatbox (1927, Boris Barnet)

Road to Life (1931, Nikolai Ekk)
Chapayev (1934, Sergei and Georgy Vasiliev)

DVDs

The Cameraman's Revenge & Other Fantastic Tales (1913 and later, **Ladislas Starewicz**). Image Entertainment. Contains *Revenge of a Kinetograph Cameraman, The Insects' Christmas, The Frogs Who Wanted a King, Voice of the Nightingale, The Mascot,* and *Winter Carousel.*

Eisenstein: The Sound Years. Criterion Collection. Restored prints of *Alexander Nevsky* and *Ivan the Terrible, Parts I and II,* a reconstruction of *Bezhin Meadow,* an audio essay by film historian David Bordwell, deleted scenes from *Ivan,* drawings and production stills, a **restoration** demonstration, as well as multimedia essays on **Eisenstein**'s collaboration with **Prokofiev,** Eisenstein's visual vocabulary, etc.

Kinó-Eye and Three Songs About Lenin (1924 and 1934, **Dziga Vertov**). Image Entertainment. The last reel of *Kinó-Eye* has been reconstructed from outtakes; this feature version was rarely shown outside the Soviet Union. *Three Songs* is a sound film.

The Man with a Movie Camera (1928, rel. 1929, **Dziga Vertov**). Image Entertainment. Commentary by film historian Yuri Tsivian. Music by the Alloy Orchestra.

Mother (1926, **V. I. Pudovkin**). Image Entertainment. The only available DVD but not a great print. Similar problems with **Eisenstein**'s *October* (the only version is missing over an hour), **Dovzhenko**'s films, etc.

Qué viva México! (1930–32, **Sergei Eisenstein**). Kino Video. Another attempt to restore Eisenstein's unfinished film. Also includes *Romance sentimentale,* an excerpt from *Misery and Fortune of Woman,* and representative documents concerning production and release.

9

Sound

According to legend, sound unexpectedly descended on the film industry from the skies, like an ancient god out of a machine, when *The Jazz Singer* opened on Broadway on October 6, 1927. Although the success of *The Jazz Singer* overthrew the film industry of 1927 with incredible speed, preparation for the entrance of sound had been building for over 30 years. The idea for the sound film was born with the film itself. W. K–L. Dickson even claimed to have produced a rough synchronization of word and picture in 1899, and he did use the Kineto-phonograph to synchronize music and picture in 1894 or 1895 for the first surviving sound film.

Imaginative inventors in France, Germany, and America experimented with various processes for synchronizing moving pictures with sounds using discs, cylinders, and film. Aside from these early picture–sound novelties, live sounds were extremely common in the nickelodeons of 1905–12. Not only was there the piano, the organ, or a trio of musicians, but live actors sometimes stood behind or beside the screen to speak the lines accompanying the pictures—or a narrator (called the *benshi* in Japan, where this practice flourished throughout the Silent Era) might comment on the action as well as deliver the dialogue. It seemed inevitable that movies would make their own noise.

Processes

The first practical, dependable synthesis of picture and sound came just after World War I. Two primary problems confronted the inventor of a sound-film process. The first was synchronization. How were the film and the sound to be kept permanently and constantly "in sync"? (*Sync* is short for synchronization.) The problem with using one machine was that the picture had to stop and start for every frame but the sound had to roll evenly, like a tape. The problem with two machines was that they *were* two machines. The method of coupling a projected film with a recorded disc was risky; it was terribly easy for the two to slip "out of sync." The film could break; the stylus could skip. *Singin' In The Rain* (1952), a marvelous parody of the transitional era from silent to sound films, revealed the unintentionally comic results when the cavalier's voice issued from the damsel's moving lips. Although the first commercially successful American sound-film process, the Vitaphone, synchronized a record player with the film projector, a more stable method had been developed as early as 1919. Three German inventors had discovered the means of recording the soundtrack directly on the film itself (optical sound) and crucially smoothing, with a simple flywheel, the movement of film through a sound projector; they were Josef Engl, Joseph Massole, and Hans Vogt. Using the principle of the oscilloscope, the Germans used a photocell to convert the sound into light beams, recorded the beams on one side of the strip of film, and then built a reader on the projector that could retranslate the light beams into sound. This German discovery, known as the Tri-Ergon Process, later became the ruling sound-film patent of Europe. Successfully demonstrated in 1922, the Tri-Ergon Process was very similar to the optical-sound process on which the American inventor Lee de Forest had begun working in 1913 and which he perfected in 1920: the Phonofilm.

An earlier de Forest invention solved the second problem of the sound film—amplification. The sound not only had to be synchronized, it had to be audible. A film had to make enough noise to reach all the patrons who filled the movie palaces. The earliest phonographs and radios, lacking the means of amplification, could entertain only one listener, who wore a listening tube. In 1906, de Forest invented the audion tube, which magnified the sound so that an entire audience could hear it. De Forest patented an early version of the audion tube in 1906 and the perfected version in January 1907. It used three electrodes: a cathode to produce electrons, a plate to attract them, and—the crucial innovation—a grid to control them, so that a signal could be reduced or increased without distortion. The tube's amplifying power was increased in 1913 by Edwin Howard Armstrong.

It was in 1913 that de Forest experimented with the photographing of sound; his first subject was an acrobatic barking dog. The phonograph, he said, was "a triumph over a bad principle" because it relied on a needle that could scratch the record; his solution—similar to that employed in today's compact disc—was to use light, not a metal shaft, as the vehicle for writing and reading the sound. From 1919 to 1921, he invented and improved the Phonofilm, whose optical soundtrack ran between the picture area and one row of sprockets. He began shooting sound films in 1921, making hundreds of shorts between then and 1927. In 1924 he invented the sound newsreel; his first subject was President Calvin Coolidge.

The optical soundtrack in use today is a direct outgrowth of de Forest's Phonofilm—as the Academy of Motion Picture Arts and Sciences acknowledged when it awarded him a special Oscar in 1959. But de Forest made little money, and for decades received little credit, for bringing sound to the motion picture. And the optical-sound processes demonstrated in 1922 in Europe (the Tri-Ergon Process) and America (the Phonofilm) were not the first to succeed commercially.

A competing process that recorded the soundtrack on 78 RPM records (sound on disc), with each record large enough to hold ten minutes of sound so that there could be one disc for each reel of film, yielded inferior sound quality but was used on the right movie: *The Jazz Singer.* Both sound-on-film and sound-on-disc processes, as well as all subsequent sound filming, required that the speed with which film was exposed and projected be standardized. A speed of 24 fps was established as an industry standard, the normal duration of a reel became ten minutes, and film length began to be given in minutes rather than feet or meters.

The sound-on-disc process—a "double system" that relied on two interlocked machines, the projector and the turntable, as opposed to the "single system" of sound-on-film projection—was developed by Bell Telephone's research lab, Western Electric. In 1925 they began trying to market the invention, which they named the Vitaphone.

Rejected by the most powerful producers, Western Electric offered Vitaphone in 1926 to Warner Bros., a family of four producing brothers, whose small company had recently embarked on a costly program of major expansion. Having bought the remains of the Vitagraph Company (the last of the original Trust Companies) in 1925 and made it their distribution chain, the Warners wished to expand their small network of theatres, to achieve full vertical integration, and to take on the big boys—Loew, Zukor, First National—who controlled enough theatre and distribution chains to choke the market for Warners' films. The Warner brothers bought the Vitaphone. Within three years they had swallowed First National and digested most of the theatres in that chain.

The Warner sound films started cautiously enough. On August 6, 1926, the Warners presented a program of short sound films; the first was an address by Will Hays praising the possibilities of the sound film, followed by the New York Philharmonic Orchestra and by leading artists of the opera, the concert, and the music hall. The Vitaphone shorts were similar to de Forest's Phonofilms. But on the same program, the Warners presented a feature film, *Don Juan* (directed, like *The Jazz Singer,* by Alan Crosland), with a synchronized musical score. A canned orchestra had replaced the live one in the pit. This put many musicians out of work, but it allowed filmmakers to decide *exactly* what music

Fig. 9-1

Shaw Talks for Movietone News: *the playwright scowls his "Mussolini look."*

would accompany their images, a significant advance in artistic control.

Like the Warners, another lesser producer, William Fox, was a film businessman who gazed enviously at the Zukors and Loews on the heights. Fox decided to use sound the same way as the Warners did. Early in 1927 Fox began presenting mechanically scored films, the greatest of which was Murnau's *Sunrise* (planned and shot as a silent), whose music and sound effects were post-synchronized. The effects on these soundtracks were recorded in a studio rather than created on the spot with musical instruments, an advance in realism that proved as important to the sound film as audible dialogue. Like the Warners, Fox presented a series of short novelty films— performances by famous variety artists and conversations with famous people. In addition, Fox started his own sound newsreel, the Fox Movietone News. Unlike Vitaphone, the Fox system, called Movietone, was a sound-on-film process, exactly like the Phonofilm.

Fox exploited the novelty of coupling the sound of the human voice with the picture of moving lips. In the Movietone short referred to as *Shaw Talks for Movietone News* (1928) and as *Greeting by George Bernard Shaw, 1928*, the

audience is amused by seeing the image of the crusty playwright, hearing his voice, enjoying his garrulous, improvised pleasantries, and recognizing the mechanical reproduction of other natural sounds like birds chirping and gravel crackling on the garden path. The moving pictures had become a simple recording device once again. The camera stopped speaking as the movies learned to talk.

The Jazz Singer was neither the first sound film nor the first film to synchronize picture with speech and song. It was, however, the first full-length feature to use synchronized sound as a means of telling a story. Most of the film was shot silent, with intertitles and a post-synchronized score. In this respect Warners' *Jazz Singer* went no further than their *Don Juan.* But at least five sequences used synchronized speech.

In one, the jazz singer (Al Jolson) returns to his Orthodox Jewish home to visit his parents. His mother (Eugenie Besserer) enjoys seeing him and listening to his "jazzy" singing of "Blue Skies." His father (Warner Oland), a cantor, orders an end to all profane jazz in his house. The father's command to stop the music is the cue for the film to revert to silence. That brilliant strategy made the sound film modern and the silent film old-fashioned.

Fig. 9-2
The Jazz Singer: *Jolson sings "Blue Skies" for his mother (Eugenie Besserer) and a frozen camera.*

The divided nature of *The Jazz Singer*—part silent, part talkie—revealed both the disadvantages and the advantages of the new medium. Whereas the silent sections of the film used rather flowing camera work and terse narrative cutting, the synchronized sections were visually inert. For Jolson's third song, "Blue Skies," the camera was restricted to two setups: a medium shot of Jolson at the piano, and a close shot of Besserer responding (intercut sparingly). Most visually inert of all is the dialogue shot: a rambling, improvised series of Jewish jokes between choruses of the song—a full shot of Jolson and mama, one long take. When the film starts making synchronized noises, the camera stops doing everything but exposing film.

On the other hand, this moment of informal patter at the piano is the most exciting and vital part of the entire movie. In the silent sequences Jolson is a poor mime, with hammy, overstated gestures and expressions. But when Jolson acquires a voice, the warmth, the excitement, the vibrations of it, the way its rambling spontaneity lays bare the imagination of the mind that is making up the sounds, convert the overgesturing hands and the overactive eyes into a performance that seems effortlessly natural. "Wait a minute," Jolson tells an applauding audience in his first song-and-dialogue scene, "You ain't heard nothin' yet! Wait a minute, I tell ya, you ain't heard nothin'. You want to hear 'Toot Toot Tootsie'? All right, hold on . . ." The addition of a Vitaphone voice revealed the particular qualities of Al Jolson that made him a star. Not only the eyes are a window on the soul.

Problems

The Jazz Singer was a huge hit; it put new zip in a film business that had begun to sag in 1927. Warner Bros.' next Jolson vehicle, *The Singing Fool* (1928), was the top-grossing film of the 1920s and the top-grossing sound film until Disney's *Snow White and the Seven Dwarfs* (1937). The movie czars who resisted sound because it would disrupt their stable business now had to convert to sound to stay in business. Americans no longer wanted to see silent films. Silent films had taught them to see; the new invention of radio had taught them to hear, and its programs were free, like broadcast TV today. They would not leave their homes and spend their money if they could not both see and hear at the same time. By 1929, the silent film was virtually dead in America. Only Chaplin resisted sound for aesthetic reasons, releasing *City Lights* with synchronized music but no dialogue—a silent that did tremendous business in 1931.

The new sound film caused filmmakers and film critics three primary problems: artistic, technical, and commercial. The camera, which had spent the previous 32 years learning to take an active part in filmed fiction, suddenly became motionless and inexpressive, unless the scene was shot silent and then post-synchronized. Cuts were rare. Although the silent film had declared its independence from the stage, the early sound film became the vassal of the theatre once again—and rushed to hire its actors for their voices. The moving picture stopped moving and stopped using pictures. Critics and theorists sang a requiem for the film art and said amen.

Many of the aesthetic shortcomings of the first sound films were less the result of theoretical problems than of the practical and technical problems of mastering the new machines. The stasis, the inertia of the early sound films resulted partly from the difficulty of silencing the whirring camera and partly from the difficulty of recording with a single, fixed microphone. To baffle the camera's clatter, the machine and its operator were imprisoned in a soundproof, windowed booth. The camera could neither tilt nor travel. The most it could manage was a slight pan. Scenes soon were shot from several booths at once; footage from the secondary setups could be cut into the synchronized footage from the primary camera, as long as the new footage was exactly the length of the footage it replaced. That helped. But in the era before sound mixing and the boom microphone, a single mike had to be buried in a pivotal, stationary spot on the set; the easiest scenes to shoot were those in which an actor spoke into a telephone. Of necessity, the microphone nailed the action to a tiny circle. The comic attempts to hide the mike in *Singin' In The Rain*—in a bush, in the star's bosom—are exaggerated but accurate.

Yet another problem of the new sound equipment was its cost. Studios invested huge sums in the new machines and new soundproof buildings (sound stages) in which to use them. The theatre owner also faced enormous expenses, forced to buy new sound projectors, new speakers, and new wiring to link the two. Both studios and theatres borrowed from the banks to convert to sound. The movies, big business though they were, became subsidiaries of the banks. The interrelationship of movies and high finance has continued ever since. By acquiring this large debt, the movie industry became dependent on Wall Street brokerage houses and banks to underwrite the costs of production. For many later historians and Marxist critics, this dependence on conservative American capital necessarily pushed the movies that the industry produced toward more conservative themes, socially and politically.

The new invention caused commercial problems with people as well as with paper. Studios suddenly discovered that popular stars and directors of the silent films were liabilities in the era of speech. The incoming tide of foreign talent—the Negris and Janningses and Stillers—reversed and started flowing back to native shores. The actor or director with faulty English had no place in the Hollywood world of dialogue film. American-born stars also had troubles with dialogue; their voices had to harmonize—as Keaton's, for example, did not—with the visual images they had projected in the Silent Era. The beautiful actress with a nasal rasp, the handsome Latin with a squeaky twang might as well have been unable to speak at all. Diction coaches opened offices in the studios to polish the pronunciation of those voices that did not irreparably offend the microphone. Along with the diction coaches came dialogue writers, many of them novelists or playwrights, whom the studios also needed. Old stars and old jobs died; new ones were born.

Eisenstein predicted that the sound film would try to solve its problems by taking the path of least resistance: by drifting into dialogue films and merely exploiting the audience's interest in seeing and hearing a person or event at the same time. Hollywood did just that, grandly advertising its films as "all-talking" and even as "100% all-talking, all-singing, and all-dancing." Gunshots, ringing telephones, and banging doors were everywhere. Musical numbers became obligatory—and soon the previously impossible genre of the film musical was born. Hollywood imported Broadway directors, players, and plays. At least the talk in a play had already been tested, and its actors (for example, Bela Lugosi in the stage version of *Dracula*) had demonstrated their ability to speak it. Moving pictures were in danger of becoming hand-servants of the theatre once again, oblivious to the years of development that had created a unique narrative art.

Solutions

While film aesthetes sang the blues, a few creative film artists worked to turn talkies into moving pictures with sound, certain that the movies could absorb sound rather than the other way round. Hollywood began to solve some of the technical problems. Although the noisy camera had to be encased, it could be released from its glass-windowed prison for those shots that did not require synchronized dialogue. In *Hallelujah* (1929), King Vidor let the camera roam silently over the fields, through a forest, aboard a train, and then dubbed in the singing of spirituals. Music in *Hallelujah*, its rhythms precisely synchronized with the visual action and emotional "beats," carried much of the film's meaning and effect. In *All Quiet on the Western Front* (1930), Lewis Milestone shot battle scenes with silent, sweeping tracking shots of the lines of attacking armies and post-synchronized the sounds of machine guns and grenades during the editing.

Soon even the dialogue scenes gained mobility with the invention of the camera blimp, a device that slipped over the camera to muffle its noise without banishing it to a soundproof booth;

one blimp was invented by Lee de Forest. By 1929, Victor Fleming (in *The Virginian*) could shoot dialogue sequences outdoors, including tracking shots in which men on horseback spoke to passengers on a moving train.

Hollywood solved the microphone problem, too. Rouben Mamoulian, one of the theatre directors imported from New York, suggested using two microphones to shoot a single scene, balancing and regulating the relative volumes of the two with a sound mixer. In Mamoulian's *Applause* (1929), two characters could speak to each other from opposite ends of the room without trotting together to speak into the same flowerpot.

An even more flexible method of capturing the voice was the invention in 1929 of the boom, a rod or mechanical arm that kept the microphone hovering above the speaker's head, just out of the camera's frame. Whenever the actor moved, the microphone could silently follow.

Just as technicians began to conquer the mechanical problems of sound filming, directors began to discover the means of using sound artistically in a primarily visual medium.

Ernst Lubitsch's first sound films, *The Love Parade* and *Monte Carlo*, show a creative film mind wrestling with the problems of integrating sound and picture in 1929–30. The film contains subtle effects that would have been impossible without synchronized sound: the coordination of the valet's physical business with the precise rhythms of his opening song, an adieu to Paris sung by a dog, the booming sound of cannon (a typical Lubitsch use of a comic Freudian symbol), which both implies and interrupts the couple's wedding night amours.

In *Monte Carlo*, another Jeanette MacDonald musical, Lubitsch's most famous device was to set the song "Beyond the Blue Horizon" as a duet between the soprano and a speeding train. As MacDonald sings the song, the sounds of the train (chugging wheels, tooting whistle, puffing smoke) become her percussion accompaniment, underscored by the equally percussive rhythms of the editing. Lubitsch's original idea had been an innovative and ingenious combination of picture, sound, and cutting —a synthesis of Soviet montage and American musical comedy.

The most innovative early sound films, however, were the animated cartoons of Walt

Fig. 9-3
Monte Carlo: *This rhythmic montage of eight shots of a speeding train serves as the introduction to "Beyond the Blue Horizon"—joining the Soviet adoration of machines with the exuberance of American song.*

Disney. Disney began as a commercial artist and cartoonist in Kansas City; he made his film debut with animated ads and satiric, short cartoons—*Fred Newman's Laugh-O-Grams*. He migrated to Hollywood in 1923 and produced a series of short films that integrated cartoons and a living girl (each cartoon in the series was "An ALICE Comedy"; hence, the *Alice Comedies*); Disney would again mix people and drawings in *Song of the South* (1946) and *Mary Poppins* (1964), and his studio would continue the tradition after his death with *Who Framed Roger Rabbit* (1988). By

Fig. 9-4

Fig. 9-5

Disney's clever wedding of sound and image. Two xylophones: a cow's teeth in Steamboat Willie (Fig. 9-4), a human skeleton in The Skeleton Dance (Fig. 9-5).

the end of the Silent Era, he and his animator, Ub Iwerks, had mastered the methods and art of animation.

But it was sound that turned Disney into one of the most influential producers in the film industry. Adding sound to a cartoon was considered commercially insane and an artistic mistake—until Disney pulled it off. He also pioneered the Technicolor cartoon (*Flowers and Trees*, 1932) and the American animated feature (in 1937 *Snow White* was billed as the first full-length animation, in ignorance of Reiniger's work). Disney's cartoons, which were not compelled to photograph the real world, escaped the tyrannies of sound recording that enslaved the directors of theatrical features. Disney's drawn worlds were shot and edited with all the fluidity of the silents, as if by a real camera moving through an artificial landscape to a perfectly synchronized soundtrack; because the animation camera shot no live action and required no soundproof booth or blimp or microphone, the Disney films moved like movies. The cartoon—which is free from all natural laws, from all human and spatial realities—also granted its creator complete freedom in playing with sound. The Disney sound cartoon united three of the great traditions of silent filmmaking and carried them into the Sound Era: the wacky, speedy physical comedy of Mack Sennett; the fantasy world of Méliès in which what cannot happen happens; and the genius of Chaplin, Winsor McCay, and especially Émile Cohl for transforming one kind of object into a totally different one.

Iwerks and Disney's first sound film, *Steamboat Willie* (1928, the first Mickey Mouse cartoon to be released), used optical sound and shows complete mastery of the counterpoint of picture and sound. The most imaginative sequence is the "Turkey in the Straw" number. A billy goat has eaten a guitar and a copy of the tune "Turkey in the Straw." Mickey Mouse (voice by Disney) twists and starts to crank the goat's tail; the notes pour out of the animal's mouth; the music on the soundtrack accompanies the visual notes. Then Mickey (or "Willie") uses whatever he can find as an accompanying percussive instrument. He rattles on a garbage pail and a series of different-sized pots; he scratches a washboard; he swings a cat around by its tail to produce syncopated wails; he squeezes a duck's throat to produce rhythmic quacks; he pulls the tails of nursing

piglets to produce a scale of squeaks; he bangs on a cow's teeth to produce the tones of a xylophone. (The subtle sadism of Disney's work is already evident here.) Whereas silent montage created meaning by juxtaposing dissimilar images, Disney perceived the similarity of apparently dissimilar sounds and images. An Eisenstein simile that the workers (visual) are like a bull (visual) contrasts with Disney's that a cow's teeth (visual) are like a xylophone (sound).

The Skeleton Dance (1929), the first of the Silly Symphonies, is an even more skillful weaving of motion, music, and rhythm. Its opening sequence —an atmospheric painting of the mood of midnight and goblins—combines the eerie, tense whine of violins with percussive effects produced by an owl hooting, bats' wings flapping, wind whistling, and cats screeching. Then the skeletons creep out of their graves. The surprising activities of the bones are carefully coordinated with the beats of the music. Disney's sensitivity to musical tones and rhythms became the outstanding feature of every Silly Symphony, eventually culminating in the cinematic tone-poem *Fantasia* (1940). Though his studio's greatest achievements were the animated features *Snow White and the Seven Dwarfs* and *Pinocchio* (1940), Disney's synthesis of image, music, and rhythm had begun with his first sound cartoons. The means of turning sound into a resource for film rather than a liability were being found.

For Further Viewing

FILMS

WALT DISNEY (1901–66)
Alice Comedies Series (1923–27)
Steamboat Willie (1928)
The Skeleton Dance (1929)
The Three Little Pigs (1933)
Thru the Mirror (1936)
Snow White and the Seven Dwarfs (1937)
Pinocchio (1940)
Fantasia (1940)
Dumbo (1941)
Bambi (1942)
Song of the South (1946)
Cinderella (1950)
Alice in Wonderland (1951)
Peter Pan (1953)
The Living Desert (1953)

Lady and the Tramp (1955)
Sleeping Beauty (1959)
Mary Poppins (1964)

ERNST LUBITSCH (1892–1947)
Gypsy Blood or *Carmen* (1918)
Lady Windermere's Fan (1925)
The Love Parade (1929)
Monte Carlo (1930)
Trouble in Paradise (1932)
The Merry Widow (1934)
Ninotchka (1939)
The Shop Around the Corner (1940)
To Be or Not To Be (1942)

ROUBEN MAMOULIAN (1898–1987)
Applause (1929)
City Streets (1931)
Dr. Jekyll and Mr. Hyde (1932). Completed 1931
Queen Christina (1933)
Becky Sharp (1935)
The Mark of Zorro (1940)
Blood and Sand (1941)

KING VIDOR (1894–1982)
The Big Parade (1925)
The Crowd (1928)
Hallelujah (1929)
Our Daily Bread (1934)
Stella Dallas (1937)
Duel in the Sun (1947)
The Fountainhead (1949)

ILLUSTRATIVE TRANSITIONAL FILMS
Love's Old Sweet Song (1924, Lee de Forest)
Sunrise: A Song of Two Humans (1927, F. W. Murnau)
The Jazz Singer (1927, Alan Crosland)
Greeting by George Bernard Shaw, 1928 or *Shaw Talks for Movietone News* (1928; Fox)
Lights of New York (1928, Bryan Foy)
The Singing Fool (1928, Lloyd Bacon)
Broadway Melody (1929, Harry Beaumont)
The Virginian (1929, Victor Fleming)
King of Jazz (1930, John Murray Anderson)
Whoopee! (1930, Thornton Freeland)
L'Age d'or (1930, Luis Buñuel and Salvador Dalí)
All Quiet on the Western Front (1930, Lewis Milestone)
Scarface (1932, Howard Hawks). Uncensored version completed 1930

Vampyr (1932, Carl Theodor Dreyer)
Minnie the Moocher (1932). With Betty Boop and Cab Calloway (Max and Dave Fleischer)
Duck Soup (1933, Leo McCarey)
Modern Times (1936, Charles Chaplin)

DVDs

L'Age d'or and Un Chien andalou (**Luis Buñuel** and **Salvador Dalí**). British Film Institute. Includes commentary by art historian Robert Short.
Betty Boop Cartoons. Platinum Disc Corp. Betty in *Minnie the Moocher* and 22 other black-and-white cartoons by **Dave and Max Fleischer**.
The Cocoanuts (1929, Joseph Santley and Robert Florey), starring the Four **Marx Brothers**, is in *The Marx Brothers Silver Screen Collection* (see Chap. 11 list).
Greeting by **George Bernard Shaw** and 2 Phonofilms by **Lee de Forest** are in *More Treasures from American Film Archives* (see Chap. 3 list).
Modern Times (1936, **Chaplin**) is in *The Chaplin Collection, Vol. 1* (see Chap. 5 list).
Pinocchio (1940, **Disney**). Disney Studios/Disney Gold Classic Collection. Other Disney features were released in this out-of-print series and others.
Snow White and the Seven Dwarfs (1937, **Disney**). Disney Studios/Disney Special Platinum Edition. Includes many documentaries, storyboard-to-film comparisons, live-action test footage, **restoration** information, and other extras.
Walt Disney *Treasures: Mickey Mouse in Black and White*. Walt Disney Home Video. Includes *Steamboat Willie, Plane Crazy, Mickey's Service Station*, and 31 other black-and-white Mickey Mouse cartoons.
Walt Disney *Treasures: Mickey Mouse in Living Color*. Walt Disney Home Video. Includes *The Band Concert, Thru the Mirror, Moving Day*, and 25 other color Mickey Mouse cartoons.
Walt Disney *Treasures: Silly Symphonies*. Walt Disney Home Video. Includes *The Skeleton Dance, The Three Little Pigs* (censored), *The Old Mill*, and 38 other cartoons.

10

France between the Wars

The French film in the first decade of sound may have been the most stimulating of its generation: a subtle blend of effective, often poetic dialogue; evocative visual imagery; perceptive social analysis; complex fictional structures; rich philosophical implications; wit and charm. The maturity of the French film in the 1930s was partially the result of the growth of the French film in the 1920s. The final ten years of silent films laid the foundations for the great sound structures that would follow in the next ten. Abel Gance, René Clair, Jean Renoir, Jacques Feyder, Julien Duvivier, and Jean Epstein all conquered purely visual expression before they began combining picture and sound.

Surrealism and Other Movements

Paris of the 1920s was the avant-garde capital of the world in art, literature, music, and drama. It was the city of Picasso and Dalí, of Stravinsky, Milhaud, Poulenc, and Satie, of Proust and Cocteau, and the home away from home of Joyce and the American expatriate writers. Modernism—the urge to experiment, to create new forms, to challenge the established artistic norms in music, painting, sculpture, poetry, fiction, and drama—also dominated the new machine art of the motion picture, which had, after all, begun with Marey, Lumière, Guy, and Méliès as much as with Muybridge, Edison, and Dickson, and which depended on the French invention of photography. Paris was the city of many movements: Surrealism, Cubism, Dadaism. Painters exulted in manipulating pure shapes and colors—often

"ugly" ones, difficult and stimulating, as dissonant as modern music. The painting did not need to reproduce external reality—photography could handle that—or honor Renaissance codes of perspective; it could mirror life's moods, tones, hidden structures, and dreams, or depart from "reality" altogether. Time and consciousness were investigated to the point of reinvention, notably by Gertrude Stein, Marcel Proust, and James Joyce. If the world was irrational, art could mirror that irrationality or dispense with the whole job of mirroring and description. All bets were off: Practically anything could be done in a new, modern way. In fact, given the fragmentation of the postwar world—whose ideal aesthetic was montage—the history and resources of art had to be *made* new to become viable and useful.

It was the age when a premiere—like that of Igor Stravinsky's *The Rite of Spring*—could spark a riot or start a movement. Colonies of artists would gather at parties or salons to show each other works they had sculpted, painted, or written—works devoted to form and sensation as well as to unconventional logic and new ways of creating meaning. At these parties some of the artists would show little movies, created on the same formal principles, to their gathered friends. They discovered that of all the arts, the moving picture was capable of the most bizarre tricks with form and time: a series of purely visual images, of shapes, of lights, of double exposures, of dissolves; a series of worlds out of focus, moving too fast or too slow, making their own chronology with cuts that defied ordinary sequence and development.

Ironically, the great experimental leap forward of the French film in the 1920s was also a step into the past, analogous to Ezra Pound's lifelong effort "to gather from the air a live tradition." In 1919, at the dawn of this avant-garde decade, Louis Delluc and Ricciotto Canudo, two zealous film buffs, founded the first of many subsequent French societies for the presentation and preservation of great films of the past. Delluc and Canudo canonized the movies as the Seventh Art and urged attention to the directors of an earlier era: to Méliès, Zecca, Cohl, Linder, Durand, Feuillade. They ignored the theatrical, stagey, Comédie-Françaiseish, Film d'Arty pictures of the decade of the war. This first generation of *cinéastes* urged a return to the wild fantasies of Méliès, to the motion-filled chases of Zecca and Sennett, to the tricks with camera speed and motion of Jean Durand's *Onésime horloger* (1912), in which a magical clock makes the world speed up so that Onésime can collect his inheritance "sooner." Like the French *cinéastes* of the 1960s—Godard, Truffaut, Malle—those of the 1920s used film history not only to pack movies with historical echoes and allusions, but also to embellish earlier film ideas with the filmmakers' own distinct and personal extensions of them. The Parisian avant-garde filmmaker of the 1920s used one hand to rip up accepted film conventions and assumptions and the other to pull the traditions of the film past into the movies of the present.

The experimental French films of the 1920s were of three approximate types: (1) films of pure visual form; (2) Surrealistic fantasies in which tricks with time, juxtaposition, transition, and form create a symbolic-dreamlike-irrational universe; (3) Naturalistic studies of passion and sensation in which symbols and surreal touches help to render elusive human feelings. The three types were far from distinct. A movie could begin as an essay in pure form and then change into a surreal dream-fantasy (René Clair's *Entr'acte*, 1924). Sometimes the film would begin as a surreal journey and change into a study of form (Man Ray's *Mysteries of the Chateau Dé*, 1929). Or the film could begin as an impressionistic study of emotions and relationships only to end as a dream (Jean Renoir's *The Little Match Girl*, 1928). Dadaism, Surrealism, and Poetic Naturalism—sometimes called Poetic Realism, especially when it brought out the beauty of the unglamorized world—flowed into one another to create new compounds in the movies.

The films of Man Ray, a photographer and painter born in America, are the purest examples of movie Dada—of a collage of visual shapes and patterns with no meaning other than the chaos of forms themselves. Ray's films began quite literally as collages: In *Return to Reason* (1923)—an ironic title, since the film rejects reason—he randomly scattered springs, nails, tacks, salt and pepper, and other items over strips of film and then exposed the littered film to light, leaving shadows of the objects imprinted on the celluloid. Ray gradually abandoned such random methods for more controlled essays in form, such as *Emak-Bakia* (1927), in which

Fig. 10-1

Fig. 10-2
Man Ray's Return to Reason: *exposing the celluloid to nails (Fig. 10-1) and thumbtacks (Fig. 10-2) directly, without a camera.*

visual similarities and differences of form control Ray's choice of images.

The most famous of the Surrealist films is the Salvador Dalí–Luis Buñuel fantasy, *Un Chien andalou* (1929). Like the title (*An Andalusian Dog*), the film is a series of non sequiturs, a series of daring vignettes juxtaposed irrationally, as in the leaps of a dream, to amuse, shake up, and even attack the viewer. From the opening sequence in which Buñuel slits an eyeball with a razor in gruesome close-up to the final one in which a man and woman are inexplicably buried in the wasteland/sand of a rocky beach, the film's goal is to excite, to shock, to surprise, to make us "see" differently rather than to preach or explain.

On the other hand, Jean Epstein's *The Fall of the House of Usher* (1928) uses gentler dream effects to create the atmosphere for his relatively lucid Poe plot. Epstein uses the tools of cinematic Impressionism—slow-motion effects; out-of-focus lenses; multiple exposure; contrasts of light and shadow; distortion; cavernous, dreamworld sets—as a means of turning the House of Usher into a house of mirrors and visual music.

Even the Naturalistic psychological studies of human interaction try to probe beneath familiar surfaces to reveal irrational, chaotic passions. Alberto Calvalcanti's *Rien que les heures* (1926), on the surface a documentary study of 24 hours of Paris life, relies on avant-garde juxtapositions and special effects to paint the city's moody picture, including freeze frames, double exposures, split-screen effects, matte shots, and obtrusive wipes.

Fig. 10-3

Fig. 10-4

Fig. 10-5

Fig. 10-6

The dream-space of Un Chien andalou. ***Four consecutive shots: the man falls, indoors (Fig. 10-3), to slither against the torso of an outdoor nude (Figs. 10-4, 10-5), who evaporates (Fig. 10-6).***

Fig. 10-7
Nadia Sibirskaïa in **Ménilmontant.**

Dimitri Kirsanov's *Ménilmontant* (1925), a half-hour narrative film without any intertitles, uses quick cutting, unique images that visualize thought and feeling, and the sordid atmosphere of Paris slums to tell its story of two sisters from the country whose parents are killed by an ax murderer in the opening montage; later, as adults in the city, they are sexually betrayed by the same man. As rapid and violent as *Ménilmontant* often is, it slows down to present the monotony of ordinary life; its control of the pace of scenes and the passage of time is complete. *Ménilmontant* is as complex, stirring, and beautiful as the French cinema gets, and a good introduction in itself to the art of silent film.

Gance and Dreyer

Abel Gance was French; Carl Dreyer, who made films all over Europe, was Danish. They were among the greatest filmmakers of any country or period, and they suffered rejection, unemployment, and incomprehension throughout their careers. The more they awakened the cinema to a new day, the more the film business hit the snooze button.

Abel Gance

The most important commercial director of the decade, whose Promethean ambitions led many a bureaucrat to feast on his liver and whose vast energy pushed his films beyond the limits of commerce and convention, Abel Gance applied an experimental, almost avant-garde concern with visual forms, tricks, and devices to the narrative feature. This should not be surprising, since his 1915 short, *The Folly of Dr. Tube,* used distorting mirrors to convey distorted perception and may well have been the first "experimental" film. His *J'accuse* (*I Accuse,* 1919) and *La Roue* (*The Wheel,* 1922) explored tragedy and social injustice in the context of intimate, melodramatic studies of passion and vision. *J'accuse,* which took its title from Émile Zola's 1898 article in defense of Alfred Dreyfus, let the ghosts of the soldiers of World War I ("the war to end all wars") return to discover whether their sacrifice had been effective and worthwhile. Shot in 1918 with soldiers on temporary

Speaking with their bodies, soldiers of the First World War spell out "J'accuse," the title of Gance's 1919 film and an accusation against the masters of war.

Fig. 10-8

leave from the front, who expected—in most cases, correctly—to be killed within the month, so that they knew they were playing their own ghosts and trusted Gance to carry their message into a future they would not see but urgently demanded to affect, *J'accuse* was the greatest antiwar film yet made. In 1937 Gance remade the film, hoping to stop the Second World War by re-evoking the horrors and lessons of the First. An overpowering masterpiece, the second *J'accuse* did not halt the coming conflict but remains a gesture of immense belief in the power of the cinema and a heartbreaking, almost infuriating act of faith in the good sense of humanity.

Of *La Roue*, an eight-hour movie released in 1922, Jean Cocteau observed that "There is the cinema before and after *La Roue* as there is painting before and after Picasso." A tragic story of the wheel of fate (a crushing wheel that

doubles as a rack), told with the romantic energy of a Victor Hugo and the melodramatic impact of a Euripides, this compelling picture brought its first audience to a standing ovation—no matter how long it was, they refused to leave until the final reel had been shown again—and decisively influenced the Soviets, who studied *La Roue* and *Intolerance* with equal care. Its rapid cutting—some of its shots only one frame long—came to be called "Russian cutting" once *La Roue* had, like Gance, been forgotten. Gance resembled Griffith in many ways, not the least of which is that neither could find work in the conservative Studio Era, though each had, through his vision of what the cinema could be, brought the art to the peak of its powers. When they met in 1921 (immediately after the editing of *La Roue*), Gance and Griffith congratulated each other for having independently discovered the possibilities of the

Fig. 10-9
La Roue: *Séverin-Mars as Sisif, the tragic "Man of the Wheel."*

close-up, the dolly shot, and rhythmic editing. Each made films that were inseparably melodramatic and political, and each put much of himself into his typical romantic hero: for Griffith, the caring man who finds himself in right action, and for Gance, the inventor–genius who wants to change the world.

Like *The Birth of a Nation*, the 1927 *Napoleon* (which originally ran 9 hours—42 reels at 20 fps, polished by Gance to 29 reels—about 6 1/2 hours—and premiered at 17 reels in a special short version) used individuals to explore the history of an entire nation in a period of political instability and crisis. Unlike Griffith's concentration on a group of ordinary citizens, Gance's is on Napoleon, the idealized leader, the mythic man of destiny who pulls a divided nation out of the ideological chaos of the French Revolution. Some critics have found *Napoleon* either naïvely worshipful of a heroic leader or implicitly fascist. But one must note the stern warning delivered near the end of the film by ghosts of the leaders of the Reign of Terror (a key to Gance's plans), that Napoleon will fall if he betrays the original goals of the Revolution. Because of a lack of funding Gance was prevented from showing Napoleon's tragic development and fall in subsequent films (*Napoleon* closes with the Italian campaign, well before the general became the emperor). The energy of *Napoleon* is, like that of *La Roue*, the energy of an idealized cinema: a grand, vaulting belief in what unhindered genius can accomplish. The hero of *Napoleon* is Gance.

Among the many breakthroughs of *Napoleon* was its use of multiple imagery, for which Gance's general term was polyvision. Polyvision referred to superimposition (as many as 16 images laid on top of one another), the split screen (as many as 9 distinct images in a frame), and the multiple screen (the triptych—used three times in *Napoleon*, although two of them have been lost—whereby three cameras and projectors and screens could create a single wide-screen image with an aspect ratio of 4:1, or three separate, side-by-side images that reinforced, reversed, or played against each other in counterpoint). With polyvision and rapid cutting, Gance became the unchallenged master of montage in France.

The Passion of Joan of Arc

The "isms" of 20th-century French painting also captured its cinema. The culmination of this decade of film painting was a feature that seemed to synthesize and incorporate the history of painting, from Renaissance religious iconography to the modern abstract concern with texture and line: Carl Theodor Dreyer's *The Passion of Joan of Arc* (1928; shot 1927). Despite its Danish director and German art director (Hermann Warm, the principal designer of *The Cabinet of Dr. Caligari*), the film's aesthetics and effects are also consistent with the French. Narratively, the film condenses Joan's long trial and eventual execution into a single day, but the trial feels both endless and, in the transcendental sense, timeless. For emotional continuity, it was shot in sequence.

The details of Joan's trial are precise and intense; the enormity of her suffering, her sorrow, her spiritual fire are clear. The film examines Joan the immense emotional being rather than Joan the militant, or even Joan the religious iconoclast. The sainthood of Dreyer's Joan (played by Renée Falconetti) can be seen on her face and exists within her; it is in her faith and her intense ability to feel and suffer and glow. In Shaw's play, Joan's comments are witty, intelligent, and shrewd; Dreyer's Joan, with her glowing face and visionary eyes, keeps her answers short and operates primarily on a level beyond verbal expression. Dreyer's film presents and transcends the tale of the trial and death of Joan in the same way that Bach's *The Passion According to St. Matthew* relates, dramatizes, and goes beyond Matthew's account of the martyrdom of Christ.

To create a feature film of almost musical sensations and ritual power, Dreyer fills the frame with faces and seeks out each one's essence. Rudolf Maté's camera travels ceaselessly over the faces of the judges and Joan—or holds on one. The bare white walls of the set make the richly textured human features and make-up–free skin leap out at the viewer. Warm's decor gives the film the flavor of medieval starkness *and* the texture of modern design and abstract painting with its sharp, clean lines.

For many critics, *The Passion of Joan of Arc* was the ultimate silent film, the ultimate example of the power of purely visual expression. In fact, it was planned as a talkie but shot silent because of the lack of equipment; that turned out to be

Fig. 10-10

Fig. 10-11

Fig. 10-12

The Passion of Joan of Arc: *a film of faces without makeup—Joan (Renée Falconetti, Fig. 10-10), her one compassionate accuser (Antonin Artaud, Fig. 10-11 right), and the wrinkled imperfections of the faces of her accusers (Fig. 10-12).*

a good thing. In its silence, *Joan* is one of the most expressive pictures ever made.

Dreyer went on to make four of the greatest and most demanding of all sound films, in which people still didn't talk very much, and which continued his examination of the conflict between the earthly, mortal, and material, and the mystical, spiritual, and eternal: *Vampyr* (1932), *Day of Wrath* (1943), *Ordet* (1954, released 1955), and *Gertrud* (1964).

René Clair

René Clair mastered the purely visual cinema, the painting-in-motion of the 1920s, before he began to address both eye and ear in the 1930s. Clair looked back admiringly at the zany, frenetic worlds of Sennett, Zecca, and Durand, and that looking backward allowed his own kind of zany frenzy to move forward. Despite Clair's historical influences, despite his maturing as an artist, despite the new adjustments that the talking machines forced him to make, a René Clair movie—silent or sound—is unmistakably his own. The clearest Clair traits are his delight in physical movement and his comic fancy, which converts two things that are obviously different into things that are surprisingly the same: a funeral becomes a wedding party; a prison is a factory, and a factory is a prison. Clair's dissolving of differences into similarities is designed as much for imaginative fun as for social commentary. Clair's best silent films, *Entr'acte* (1924) and *The Italian Straw Hat* (1927), and his best sound films, *Le Million* (1931) and *A nous la liberté* (1931), are those in which his flights of visual fancy drop the most explosive intellectual bombs on the director's two favorite targets—social convention and money.

Entr'acte was made specifically as the intermission piece, the *entr'acte*, for a performance of the Ballets Suedois in Paris. The film is pure romp, the whimsical, choreographic Clair who does not stop at satirizing the social order but brings down order itself. The film begins with a series of Dadaist non sequiturs: two men playing checkers on a high building, two others hunting birds on skyscrapers, a ball dancing on jets of water, a ballerina (shot from underneath) whose billowing skirt spreads and shuts like the petals of a flower. Then the two checker players see the Place de la Concorde materialize on their checkerboard; the dancing ball dangles inexplicably in midair, defying gravity, after the water jets have been turned off; the ballerina turns out to be a bearded man.

In the second half of the film, society gathers for a funeral. But the mourners dress in white and they throw rice at the hearse. When the hearse starts running away by itself; the mourners rush after it. Clair uses fast motion, slow motion, traveling shots, freeze frames, interpo-lated cuts of racing cars and roller coasters to energize the chase. Eventually the coffin falls off the hearse, and the corpse rises from the box and blithely makes everyone disappear. A man leaps through the screen that dares to say "The End."

Clair's silent feature *The Italian Straw Hat*, set in 1895, takes its visual style from the era of the pre-Griffith French "primitives," from the decor of the Zecca and Linder films. A young bridegroom's horse eats a young lady's straw hat as the groom drives to meet his bride. Since the young lady lost her hat while enjoying an extra-marital afternoon with a beau, she must replace the rare hat to allay her husband's suspicions. The young groom, who looks suspiciously like Max Linder, must juggle his wedding party with his comically frantic attempts to replace the hat.

Le Million revolves about two favorite Clair motifs—money and the chase. A poor artist discovers that he has won a million francs in the lottery; unfortunately, the lottery ticket is in the pocket of a coat that has been stolen by a fleeing thief. The film becomes a furious chase for the elusive jacket. When the artist finally finds his coat at the Opera, he grabs it, only to find that the tenor insists on using the old coat as part of his pauper's costume. The artist, the tenor, and the police engage in a mock-heroic struggle for the jacket. Clair adds crowd noises, officials' whistles, and cheering to the soundtrack while the men play keepaway in the Opera's corridor. The coat has become a football, the struggle a game.

Clair's next film, *A nous la liberté* (*Liberty For Us*), was to be his last masterpiece. Clair again combines his comic and musical inventiveness with the thematic wholeness and seriousness that make a great film. Two convicts escape from prison. One of them, using stolen money, builds a huge factory to manufacture phonograph records and machines; the other, his friend in prison, becomes a worker in that factory. The tycoon eventually discovers that the life of a "respectable" factory owner, with its rules, its social obligations, its emotional infidelities, its devotion to money and machines, is no different from the life of a prisoner. Neither plutocrat nor prisoner is truly free. The film ends as the capitalist and the worker turn their backs on the factory and on money to stroll off down the road, two tramps, finally free of restraint and convention.

Fig. 10-13

A nous la liberté: *Clair's
visual parallels—the prison
as assembly line (Fig. 10-13),
the assembly line as prison
(Fig. 10-14).*

Fig. 10-14

Uniting the film is its consistent examination of the term *liberty*. For Clair, society and freedom are incompatible. Everyone attached to the factory—Clair's microcosm for society—is a prisoner of his or her role in the system: owner, member of the board, worker, foreman, secretary. The film's brilliance lies in the translation of this Marxist–humanist cliché into imaginative images. The two central characters, one tall and fat, the other short and skinny, are spirits from the world of silent comedy, reminiscent of Fatty and Charlie,

of Laurel and Hardy. Their ultimate choice of vocation—tramp—also echoes the asocial yet human choice that Charlie so often makes. If Clair's tramps seem indebted to Charlot, Chaplin later collected the debt by borrowing one of *A nous la liberté*'s assembly-line scenes for *Modern Times* (1936).

Clair's consistent technique for illuminating the lack of liberty is to set up visual parallels. The film opens with shots of men in prison, manufacturing little toy horses as they sit in rows on the prison's assembly line; they eat their meals as they sit in rows in the prison's dining room. Later, Clair shows the factory workers sitting in the same rows as the men in prison, eating in the same formations as the men in the prison mess hall. Factory and prison are visually identical. Prison uniforms have become factory uniforms; prison guards have become factory foremen.

The film hits its visual and thematic climax in the wild scene in which the social elite gather to honor the great factory owner (former crook) who has created this phonographic empire. The ceremony begins with perfect formality: the guests wearing top hats and tails, the orators sitting stiffly on the rostrum, the workers standing in formation listening to the boring, droning speeches. Suddenly a wind sweeps through the factory courtyard. It drowns out the speech of the old rhetorician; it blows the top hats all over the courtyard; it scatters the factory's profits—paper money— all over the ground. The liberating wind turns the factory into a swarming mass of chaotic free activity. In the most Sennett-like manner, the dignitaries abandon their dignity to chase their hats and the blowing bills all over the courtyard in frenzied, choreographed patterns.

After this climax, a peaceful coda shows the effect of this whistling wind of freedom. The two prisoners, pals again, become tramps; the factory's workers sit by the river dreamily fishing; the now totally automated factory continues producing phonographs by itself. In Clair's idyll, the people are free to be human, leaving the machines to tend the machines.

Jean Renoir

Like René Clair, Jean Renoir—son of the Impressionist painter Pierre Auguste Renoir—started making films in the 1920s and reached the peak of his powers in the 1930s. Like Clair, Renoir was a social satirist. But there the similarities stop. Renoir's satire was bitter and melancholy, whereas Clair's was ebullient and whimsical. Clair's satire condemned institutions and praised the human spirit; Renoir's satire declared hollow institutions to be the inevitable products of flawed, erroneous humans. If Clair let his films go crazy once in a while, Renoir kept his tightly

structured even when they lightened up. Like Clair, Renoir saw that the claims of nature and civilization were antithetical; unlike Clair, Renoir never resolved the dilemma by simplistically espousing one of the two alternatives because Renoir realized both the attractiveness of nature that seems so innocent and the need for civilization that seems so complicated.

Renoir emphasizes the inseparable connection of civilization and nature with a favorite setup, shooting from indoors through windows and doorways that frame the outdoors with their architectural presence. His visual signature, composition in depth, allows the *mise-en-scène* to make its own statements; foreground and background figures, civilization and nature, upper and lower classes, winners and losers—all are included in Renoir's complex comedies of manners. If Clair's roots were in ballet and in song, Renoir's were in painting and ceramics, in the sensitivity to light and shadow, form and texture.

Throughout the 1930s Renoir's films threw a cold, hard light on the crumbling social and political structures of Europe. An effete aristocracy was gradually sinking under the weight of its own artificial conventions, and the new rising classes were barrenly following in the steps of their former masters. The 1930s, in France as well as in America, had become the age of the scenarist, and Renoir's screenplays (which he wrote in collaboration with other writers) novelistically emphasized parallel structures, parallel characters, parallel details. The attention to visual and intellectual parallels gave the Renoir film the rich complexity of the novel. But the literary structures of the films were enhanced by Renoir's sensitivity to the visual: Shots of nature, of faces, of social groupings in deep space visually generate the film's meaning and control its tone. *La Chienne* (1931), a comedy of betrayal and survival that in Fritz Lang's hands became the fatalistic *Scarlet Street* (1945); *Boudu Saved from Drowning* (1932), an exuberantly comic clash between a tramp, a rough man of nature, and the stifling conventions of polite, bourgeois society; *Toni* (1935), a sensitively tragic clash between the passions of love and restrictive societal codes—and a crucial precursor of Neorealism; *The Crime of Monsieur Lange* (1936), a comedy about a publishing house that becomes a successful co-op, almost a communist utopia, after the boss leaves; *La Marseillaise* (1938), a historical study of the French Revolution, made for the French Popular Front, which reveals its leftist sympathies by its focus on the common foot soldiers; and an adaptation of Gorky's *The Lower Depths* (1936), which attracted Renoir with its bitter microcosmic study of society—all show the director warming up for his greatest films at the end of the decade.

Grand Illusion

Grand Illusion (1937) is also a microcosmic study. Its superficial action is the story of two French soldiers who eventually escape from a German prisoner-of-war camp during World War I—and one who does not. Its real action is metaphor: the death of the old ruling class of the European aristocracy and the growth of the new ruling classes of the workers and bourgeoisie. The prisoner-of-war camp is a microcosm of European society. The prison contains French and Russian and English, professors and actors and mechanics and bankers, Christians and Jews, nobility and capital and labor.

At the top of the social hierarchy are the German commander, Rauffenstein (played by Erich von Stroheim, the director whose films most influenced Renoir's), and the French captain, Boeldieu (played by Pierre Fresnay). Though the two men fight on opposite sides, they are ideologically identical: They both use a monocle; they both wear white gloves; they both share the same prejudices and snobberies, the same educated tastes in wine, food, and horses. They are united by class more than they are divided by country. The supreme irony of the film is that the German commander must kill this man to whom he feels most closely allied because the rules of the war game demand that the commanding officer of the prison shoot men trying to escape, just as they demand that the prisoner (gentleman or not) attempt to escape. The two men are inflexibly, tragically responsible to their codes, their rules, and their duties. United as members of the cultured international elite, divided as prisoner and warden, they both transcend boundaries and acknowledge them in a paradox of roles whose only constant is honor. They are part of a dying breed that, like the old Europe, would not survive the war.

The two tougher, hardier prisoners do escape, while Boeldieu, attired in his white gloves, smartly covers for them and gives up his life in gentlemanly sacrifice. Maréchal (played by Jean Gabin), a mechanic, and Rosenthal (played by Marcel Dalio), a Rothschildean Jew whose family owns banks, land, and several chateaux, escape together from the German prison. The animosities, the tensions, the prejudices of the two men surface as the going gets rough, but the two finally make it to Switzerland—and they make it together. Overcoming their own set of social boundaries, they are the new Europe.

Grand Illusion opens on a gramophone horn: The machine plays "Frou-Frou," a popular French song; we are in the French camp. A few minutes later, the camera captures a second gramophone horn; the machine plays a Strauss waltz; we are in the German camp. The songs have changed; the camps are the same. Most indicative of the film's tone and statement is the drag-show sequence in which the prisoners entertain each other by putting on a show, a French revue that includes a number performed by British prisoners dressed and made up as cancan girls. Just before the show, the French prisoners receive word that the German army has captured the French town of Douaumont. Despite their sadness, the show must go on—to show their *esprit.* In the middle of the drag show, the French receive word that the Allies have recaptured Douaumont. Maréchal makes the announcement; the cancan boys stop dancing and remove their wigs. Led by one of the British dancers, everyone sings the "Marseillaise." Renoir's shots of these rouged, lipsticked men singing the patriotic anthem are simultaneously stirring and tawdry, transcendent and transvestite.

Music is used to create leitmotifs. The trifle "Frou-Frou" recurs several times. When the captured French prisoners first hear a German military band, united by the rhythmic tramping of marching feet and the soaring descant of piping fifes, Boeldieu remarks, "I hate fifes."

Consistent visual imagery is another source of the film's unity. Renoir's camera contrasts things that are hard, cold, and dead with things that are soft, warm, and vital. The final sequences take place during the winter; the consistent pictures of snow and frozen ground throw their cold, damp shadow over the entire film. The

Grand Illusion: *the coldness of stone and metal; Rauffenstein (von Stroheim), Boeldieu (Pierre Fresnay), and Maréchal (Jean Gabin) in the German fortress.*

Fig. 10-15

two escaped prisoners must struggle across an immense meadow of snow to reach safety in Switzerland. But the Swiss border is invisible. It is impossible to distinguish different nations beneath a common blanket of snow. Only the German officer's announcement that the two have made it—to freedom, in one of Renoir's characteristically open endings—informs us where the snow of Germany ends and the snow of Switzerland begins. That one can make such nationalistic distinctions is one of the film's grand illusions—as a breeder of war, perhaps the most destructive and coldly heartless.

Equally cold is the bare, stony castle that keeps the prisoners captive. And unforgettable is the piece of iron that replaces Rauffenstein's chin; it supports his face since his real chin has been shot away. The rigid, inflexible Rauffenstein himself is literally held together by metal—in the chin, the back, the knee—the embodiment of the film's contrast of the vital and the dead. The one soft thing in the prison castle is Rauffenstein's little geranium, which he carefully nurtures. When Boeldieu dies, Rauffenstein lops off the single blossom; he knows that his world is dead. Emphatically warm and vital are the woman and child, Elsa and Lotte, that Maréchal and Rosenthal encounter on their flight. Elsa's warmth touches Maréchal, as does her daughter, Lotte, with her sparkling blue eyes. Maréchal vows to return to Elsa after the war is over. But he tells her in French, a language she cannot understand.

Grand Illusion shows how, with the Great War, the aristocracy of Europe committed elegant suicide. To turn life into a cold, murderous game with a series of artificial rules is ultimately to turn life into death. But how can a class that has lived according to certain codes and manners for centuries suddenly change to fit the new bourgeois and proletarian times? Rauffenstein and Boeldieu are admirable for their taste, their elegance, their integrity, and their honor. Is it their fault that they have been condemned by history to live in a century that barely understands those virtues? As Renoir would put the problem in his last film of the decade, "Everyone has his reasons."

The Rules of the Game

These ironies and paradoxes become the central issues of that last 1930s film, perhaps Renoir's greatest, *The Rules of the Game* (*La Règle du jeu*; shot, released, censored, and banned in 1939; restored in 1956). The film uses sex rather than war to provoke a crisis of values in a dying society—two mutually dependent societies, in fact: the society of wealthy masters and the society of genteel servants. Both masters and servants value good form over sincerity and the open expression of emotion; both are equally aware of class distinctions. The rabbit hunt is one of the key sequences that shows how death is the price—paid by nature, innocence, and the innocent—for the masters' dying way of life. But as in *Grand Illusion*, the dancers in this dance

Fig. 10-16
The Rules of the Game: *the perfect orderliness of conventionalized murder—the aristocrats at the hunt.*

of death try to balance the demands of social form with the demands of human spontaneity. Like the aristocrats of *Grand Illusion*, they find that the conflicting demands are ultimately, and unfortunately, mutually exclusive and unbalanceable.

Renoir's complex structural parallels play several love stories against each other. In the main plot, a romantic aviator, André Jurieux, petulantly confesses his love for a stylish upper-class married lady, Christine de la Chesnaye. Although the rules of the game do not prohibit adultery, they do condemn such frank, impulsive, sincere expressions of it. In the subplot, the lady's maid begins her own adulterous dabbling with a new servant, Marceau: a poacher, an outsider (like André), not a genteel (if excitable) servant like her own husband, Schumacher. The servants, who ostracize Marceau, are just as snobbish and conventional as their masters, who ostracize André because he is romantic and Christine because she is foreign. Other subplots

concern Christine's husband's attempts to break off a boring love affair and André's best friend's discovery that he, Octave (played by Renoir), loves Christine. The love plots cross paths, as in a dance with changing partners or a wildly complicated bedroom farce. The maid's jealous husband, who also has problems observing the rules of the game, mistakenly shoots the aviator, thinking that André is really Octave, that Octave has become his wife's new lover (he has not), and that the woman wearing his wife's coat is his wife (it is Christine). The romantic aviator dies, and the game of lies goes on, but both represent codes that are dying out. The Marquis de la Chesnaye, Christine's husband (played by Marcel Dalio), formally announces to his guests that André has met with a "regrettable accident"; the group admires and accepts the baron's lie as a gentlemanly display of good form.

Renoir's sense of style and imagery again sustain the film. Its most memorable visual sequence is the rabbit hunt, a metaphor for the society's murderous conventionality and insensitivity. The wealthy masters go off to shoot rabbits; this hunt, like the lives of the rich, has its etiquette, its rules, its gentility. It is a civilized form of killing. The servants also serve as accomplices in the murder, for their job is to beat the trees and bushes, driving the pheasants and rabbits out of cover and into the open where they can be gunned down. Servants and masters are partners in this murderous game.

One of the film's key visual metaphors is the marquis's collection of mechanical toys—ornate clockwork birds and music boxes. The marquis collects people—his wife and mistress—the way he collects toys, and he prefers winding up intricate predictable machines to manipulating unpredictable people. But even the machines break down—chaotically but momentarily, like the supposedly inviolable rules of correct behavior. All those, the marquis can restore—but what dies cannot be fixed.

And yet Renoir's method is not so naïve as to condemn artifice and praise the simplicities of spontaneity. For one thing, the Marquis de la Chesnaye—Renoir's representative of polite civilization—is a compassionate, considerate man who is trying not to hurt anyone, whereas the aviator—Renoir's representative of spontaneity—is a selfish, blundering fool. Although the music

boxes are indeed mechanical, they also represent a degree of orderly and delicate perfection. De la Chesnaye's problem is that he would like to achieve an impossible ideal: a world in which the demands of love (which can be notoriously disruptive) and order are harmonious rather than mutually exclusive—or at least are pursued with restraint and good manners, with "class." As he tells his gamekeeper, he wants no fences around his property and he also wants no rabbits.

Renoir's comedies of manners are dark, bitter, and very ironic. If *Grand Illusion* is a tragedy with a comic ending, *The Rules of the Game* is a comedy full of failure and death. Even such comedies of survival as *Boudu* and *La Chienne* have an almost Chaplinesque sense of loss, along with a delight in reversed expectations.

During the Second World War, Renoir, like Clair, made excellent films in the United States: *Swamp Water* (1941), *This Land Is Mine* (1943), *The Southerner* (1945), *Diary of a Chambermaid* (1946). After the war, he, like Clair, returned to France. But he took a while to get there. In India, where he inspired Satyajit Ray, Renoir made his first color film, *The River* (1951). By way of Italy and another movie, he was back in the Paris studios by 1954 for *French Cancan*, which starred Jean Gabin. His eye, his sense of style, his perception of social structures and human relationships

Fig. 10-17
The marquis (Marcel Dalio, left) with one of his mechanical pets and Octave, the sponger (played by Renoir).

were still keen. Renoir would serve as a historical bridge, uniting the tradition of French "literary" filmmaking with the emerging cinematic breeziness of the New Wave.

Vigo and Others

Not all French films were successful at combining literary values with the visual powers of moving pictures. As in America, the early sound years in France produced a curious and inert hybrid, the filmed play. "Canned theatre" became one obvious but clumsy way to solve the dialogue problem in French as well as American films. The success of the French playwright, Marcel Pagnol, as a producer and director of dialogue films (*Marius*, 1931; *Fanny*, 1932; *César*, 1936) was symptomatic. But in translating his own plays and novels for the camera, Pagnol showed more cinematic sense than did many theatre-inspired French or Hollywood directors. He often preferred shooting outdoors to shooting on the sound stage, a very untheatrical choice. He also had the vision to ask cinematically minded directors to work for him, like Jean Renoir (*Toni*).

Jean Vigo

The young iconoclast Jean Vigo, however, was totally unfettered by the theatrical and literary biases of the early 1930s. Vigo made only four films—two shorts, one picture of medium length, one feature—before his death in 1934 at the age of 29. That Vigo should be free of theatrical and even cinematic conventions was appropriate, for freedom was his primary theme. His characters struggle to create temporary pockets of freedom in the midst of the society that confines them.

Zéro de conduite contrasts the energetic freedom of boyhood with the prison-like school that the children must attend. The boys eventually rebel against the institution, staging a demonstration on alumni day in front of all the wooden guests. They lower the flag of France and raise the skull and crossbones. They stand against the sky as the film ends. The freedom of Vigo's surprising images reveals the spirit of this film about freedom, which strongly influenced both Truffaut's *The 400 Blows* (1959) and Lindsay Anderson's *If . . .* (1969).

Vigo's primary visual choice is to subvert realistic, three-dimensional space and replace it with an imaginative, metaphoric sense of space that takes its spatial coordinates from the emotions and sensations of his characters. In the opening sequence, two boys, in a moment of youthful communion, transform the cramped space of a train compartment into an imaginative realm of play and joy, almost a mental universe. There are surprising shots from varied angles and perspectives in the tiny train compartment, brilliantly photographed by Boris Kaufman, the émigré brother of Dziga Vertov. The spatial magic of the opening sequence is matched by that of the final shot, as four young rebels, apparently climbing to the peak of a tiled roof, seem to ascend into the sky itself, since Vigo has deliberately stripped the shot of all familiar spatial coordinates.

Surprisingly beautiful is the slow-motion pillow fight in the bare, sterile dormitory. This scene is a metaphor for the whole film: In the midst of the confining, regularized room the children leap and bound, swing pillows, spill feathers in slow motion, the feathers falling about their bodies and laughing faces like snow. This wild, iconoclastic film was itself given a zero for bad behavior: It was banned by the French government in 1933 because it ridiculed authority. The film was not shown in France until after the war in 1946, when all forms of repression became understandably unpopular.

If *Zéro de conduite* was the young director's anarchistic, sarcastic swipe at authority and the system, his next film and only full-length feature, *L'Atalante*, is a mature, romantic look at two young adults as they discover what is important. Recently married and deeply in love, they discover each other's flaws, then drift apart and separate, and then find each other again, now knowing how empty their lives are without each other. It is a movie in which unsentimentalized reality and romantic dreams are equally vivid. Tying the film together is the river barge, L'Atalante, where the newlyweds must live. The man (Jean, played by Jean Dasté) owns the barge, and running the boat is his life. Juliette (the bride, played by Dita Parlo) longs for life on the shore. The barge becomes the rival that drives the couple apart. Although Juliette does not know it, the open space of the shore, which seems so attractive, is really more confining, less

Fig. 10-18
Jean Dasté (Jean) and Dita Parlo (Juliette) in L'Atalante.

free than the apparently cramped space on the barge. As in *Zéro de conduite*, Vigo set himself the problem of translating emotion into spatial coordinates. Jean surrenders to love by diving underwater in search of love's image, where the world has no form or limit—a triumph of romantic space. Juliette learns that the cramped, cluttered, but at times unforgettably lyrical space on the barge is spiritually and emotionally richer than the deep space on shore, where excitement and "fun" turn out to be loveless, painful, costly, and unfulfilling. The barge, adrift on the river, gliding on the water, in the sunlight, through the fog, becomes, like the community established by the boys in *Zéro de conduite*, an ideal community— man, wife, old crew member, young apprentice— because it is not contaminated by contact with "official" society at all.

Whatever romantic heights the film reaches, Vigo's approach remains unglamorous and tight.

By turns ecstatic at the beauty that shines through reality and cluttered with reality's debris, *L'Atalante* is one of the greatest achievements of Poetic Realism.

Carné and Prévert

The films of Jacques Feyder and Marcel Carné took their literary qualities from the novel rather than the stage. In this age of the scenarist, both directors enlisted talented writers. Charles Spaak (who also wrote *Grand Illusion* for Renoir) wrote for Feyder the scripts of *Le Grand jeu* (1934), *Pension Mimosas* (1935), and *Carnival in Flanders* (1935). Even more fruitful was the collaboration of Carné and the novelist–poet Jacques Prévert. Prévert, whose poetic obsessions with fatalism and death dominated both romantic melodramas (like *Le Jour se lève* or *Daybreak*, 1939) and light comedies (*Drôle de drame* or *Bizarre Bizarre*, 1937), wrote Carné a series of scripts in which admirable men die (for no reason other than that men die), in which people are dragged against their wills into complicated webs of human interactions from which there is no escape, in which people lose what they want and achieve what they do not want, in which symbolic figures of death weave pointedly through the realistic action, in which images of fog and gloom and chaos are pervasive.

Like Renoir, Clair, and Vigo, Carné and Prévert explore what is clearly the key theme of the 1930s, freedom. But for Carné and Prévert the limit to human freedom is human life itself: its fallibility, its mortality, its futility, its existence in an indifferent universe. Prévert's existential void is the precursor of Camus's or Beckett's, but charged with a romantic sense of doom. The seriocomic irony of Renoir contrasts with the profoundly vivid despair of Carné.

The richest of the Carné–Prévert films is *The Children of Paradise* (shot under the Nazi occupation in 1943–44, released 1945). Like the reader of Hugo, Tolstoy, or Dickens, the viewer of *Les Enfants du paradis* lives through a novelistically complicated series of interlocking events with many interesting figures over a long period of time. There are six central characters: two actors, two women (the possessive Nathalie and the unpossessable Garance), an aristocrat, and a murderous thief. All have difficulty deciding what they really want; each achieves material success only to discover that it is meaningless.

Central to the film is the contrast between the two actors: One, Frédérick Lemaître (Pierre Brasseur), is the man of words; the other, Baptiste Deburau (Jean-Louis Barrault), is the mime. Frédérick is the man of surfaces, of words, of fine talk and phrases; he becomes a success in cheap, hack dramas that he saves with his own imaginative theatrics. Baptiste is the man of deep feeling and the real artist, moonstruck and vulnerable; he transforms his emotions into theatre. Although Frédérick is the matinee idol of Paris, Baptiste is the delight of artists and the common people.

Between the two actors stands a woman named Garance (played by Arletty), after the flower. She casually becomes Frédérick's mistress, although Baptiste is the shy man who really loves her. Only years later, after she has found wealth and glamor as the mistress of

a fastidious count (Louis Salou), does she realize the power of Baptiste's passion, the power that makes him a great mime. But when she returns, Garance sees that Baptiste is saddled with a possessive wife he does not love and a child. At that point the film's vast, intricate plot falls into place, and fate and chance work their will on the characters in the carnival of passion and loss.

Carné and Prévert use the theatre as the film's central metaphor. Both the first and second parts of the film open on a theatre curtain, which rises to reveal the movie world of *Les Enfants*. Both parts of the three-hour film end with the curtain's coming down. Carné and Prévert sustain the theatre metaphor by paralleling the dramatic, fictional roles of the actors on stage with their actual longings and choices off the stage. The theatre is life, and life is the theatre.

The "Paradise" of the title is not a heavenly, metaphysical one but an earthly one: It is the slang name for the second balcony (in English theatre, "the gods"), the highest, cheapest seats in the theatre, the seats where sit the masses, those who love the theatre and mix intimately in all its passions. The chaotic, energetic masses (the "gods" who watch, who are to be pleased, and without whom the entertainers would not exist) in "Paradise" parallel the masses just outside the theatre on the teeming, vital, packed Boulevard du Temple, the "Street of Crime."

Weaving through the film is a dirty, vulgar old-clothes man called Jericho (Pierre Renoir). Baptiste hates Jericho, for the old tramp tauntingly reminds him of the ethereal unreality of the sentiments on which he bases his life and his art.

At the end of the film, Baptiste loses Garance once more, perhaps never to see her again. He follows her through the "Street of Crime," vainly calling her name. But Garance, on her way to meet a man she does not know is dead, cannot hear him; the masses of humanity—carnivalesque revelers on the theatre of the street—slow Baptiste's pursuit, keeping him from reaching his love. At his side we glimpse Jericho, a symbol of broken dreams and human failure. Surrounded by all this activity, so alive and yet so senseless, Baptiste is swallowed by the crowd, and the curtain falls.

For the first 15 years after the war, the best French films—those of Ophüls, Bresson, Tati, and Renoir—very clearly looked backward to the

Fig. 10-19

Fig. 10-20
Les Enfants du paradis: *the theatre as life and life as the theatre. Fig. 10-19: the seething activity in "the gods." Fig. 10-20: Frédérick (Pierre Brasseur, left) as Harlequin, Garance (Arletty) as the Moon Lady, and Baptiste (Jean-Louis Barrault) as Pierrot, acting out a version of their offstage love triangle in a pantomime scripted by Baptiste.*

literary-scenario films of the prewar era, a "tradition of quality" whose major wartime expression was *Les Enfants du paradis* itself. Not until 1959—when the New Wave (*la nouvelle vague*), which had been building since the mid-1950s, crested and broke on the shores of the film world it was to transform—would the French cinema strike off in a new direction.

For Further Viewing

FILMS

MARCEL CARNÉ (1906–96)
Quai des brumes (*Port of Shadows*, 1938)
Le Jour se lève (*Daybreak*, 1939)
The Children of Paradise (1945). Shot 1943–44

RENÉ CLAIR (1898–1981)
Paris qui dort (*The Crazy Ray*, 1923)
Entr'acte (1924)
The Italian Straw Hat (1927)
Sous les toits de Paris (1930)
Le Million (1931)
A nous la liberté (1931)
The Ghost Goes West (1935)

ABEL GANCE (1889–1981)
J'accuse (*I Accuse*, 1919)
La Roue (*The Wheel*, 1922)
Napoléon vu par Abel Gance (*Napoleon*, 1927)
Napoléon Bonaparte vu et entendu par Abel Gance (1935)
Un Grand amour de Beethoven (1936)
J'accuse (1937)

MARCEL PAGNOL (1895–1974)
Marius (1931, Alexander Korda)
Fanny (1932, Marc Allégret)
César (1936)

MAN RAY (1890–1976)
Return to Reason (1923)
Les Mystères du Château du Dé (1929)

JEAN RENOIR (1894–1979)
The Little Match Girl (1928)
La Chienne (1931)
Boudu Saved from Drowning (1932)
The Crime of Monsieur Lange (1936)
The Lower Depths (1936)
A Day in the Country (1936). Unfinished; first shown, 1946

Grand Illusion (1937)
La Bête humaine (1938)
La Marseillaise (1938)
The Rules of the Game (1939)
The Southerner (1945)
The River (1951)
The Golden Coach (1952)
French Cancan (1954)

JEAN VIGO (1905–34)
A propos de Nice (1930)
Zéro de conduite (1933)
L'Atalante (1934)

REPRESENTATIVE FILMS
Fièvre (1921, Louis Delluc)
Ballet mécanique (1924, Fernand Léger)
Ménilmontant (1925, Dimitri Kirsanov)
Anémic cinéma (1926, Marcel Duchamp)
Rien que les heures (1926, Alberto Cavalcanti)
The Seashell and the Clergyman (1928, Germaine Dulac)
The Fall of the House of Usher (1928, Jean Epstein)
The Passion of Joan of Arc (1928, Carl Theodor Dreyer). Shot 1927
Un Chien andalou (1929, Luis Buñuel and Salvador Dalí)
The Blood of a Poet (1930, Jean Cocteau)
Carnival in Flanders (1935, Jacques Feyder)

DVDs

A nous la liberté (1930, **René Clair**). Criterion Collection. Includes deleted scenes, *Entr'acte*, and a BBC interview with Clair.
Abel Gance's Beethoven (1936, **Abel Gance**). Image Entertainment. Contains *Un Grand amour de Beethoven*.
L'Atalante (1934, **Jean Vigo**). New Yorker Video. **Restored** version.
The Children of Paradise (1945, **Marcel Carné**). Criterion Collection. Includes an introduction by Terry Gilliam, commentaries by film scholars Charles Affron and Brain Stonehill, a digital **restoration** demonstration, and **Prévert**'s original treatment.
The Fanny Trilogy (1931–36, **Marcel Pagnol**). Kino International. Contains *Marius*, *Fanny*, *César*, a prerecorded audio commentary by Pagnol, and a documentary.

Grand Illusion (1937, **Jean Renoir**). Criterion Collection. Digital transfer from the recently discovered camera negative, with a commentary by film historian Peter Cowie, a trailer with Renoir, Renoir and Stroheim on the radio, and a **restoration** demonstration.

The Passion of Joan of Arc (1928, **Carl Theodor Dreyer**). Criterion Collection. **Restored** from newly found original materials. Includes history of Dreyer's versions, with clips; interview with Falconetti's daughter; production designs; audio essay by Dreyer scholar Casper Tybjerg; and several soundtracks, but take the silent option.

The Rules of the Game (1939, **Jean Renoir**). Criterion Collection. **Digitally restored** image and sound, an introduction by Renoir, side-by-side comparisons of both endings of the film, unique information on the release version, Jean Gaborit and Jacques Durand on their restoration and re-release of the film, an excerpt from a TV program on Renoir by **Rivette**, other documentaries and interviews, essays by Truffaut and others, and a commentary by film scholar Alexander Sesonske.

Under the Roofs of Paris (1930, **René Clair**). Criterion Collection. Includes *Paris qui dort.*

11

The American Studio Years: 1930–45

In the 1930s, Americans went to the movies; in the 1990s, they went to a movie. The difference is not merely semantic. In 1938, there were some 80 million movie admissions every week, a figure representing 65 percent of the population of the United States. In 1994, there were some 25 million movie admissions every week, less than 10 percent of the population of the United States. Over 500 feature films were produced by the major studios in the United States in 1937, but fewer than 100 in 1983. In the relatively active year 1987, the major studios released 135 features and the independents another 380. The film industry of the 1930s thrived on a felicitous circle of economic dependence on attendance, exhibition, and production. The huge number of movie admissions necessitated a huge number of theatres, which necessitated a huge number of films to be shown in the theatres, which necessitated large, busy studios that could produce enough films to keep the theatres filled. Only after World War II did the circle of dependence reverse itself and turn vicious.

The need for enormous quantities of films guaranteed the survival of the studio system, which was geared for production in quantity. The huge studios of the 1920s converted to sound by adding new departments to their already complex organizations; specialization and division of labor, two pillars of the silent-film factories, became even more essential to the sound-film factory. New departments of music, of sound mixing and dubbing, of sound technicians and machinery joined the older, established departments on the lot. The writing department became even more specialized; some writers roughed out general treatments, others converted and expanded the treatments into screenplays, and still others polished the dialogue.

The film property traveled through the studio, from department to department, from story idea to finished script, until it finally landed in the hands of its director, sometimes just before shooting began. After 15 to 30 shooting days (for a typical "program picture"), the director relinquished the negative to the cutting department, which edited the picture and sound into final form, as instructed by the film's producer. Only the most important directors of the most special films enjoyed the opportunity to shape the script before shooting and to cut the footage afterward. From the cutting department the film went to distribution offices, and from there to the waiting chains of theatres that the company itself owned. The film product rolled down the assembly line from the original idea to final showing, all stages controlled by the studio factory. The film industry had evolved its structure for the next 16 rich years, from 1930 to 1946.

The years of wealth were not without their moments of worry. At first, the Wall Street crash of 1929 had little effect on the film business. Although America was officially broke, Americans kept scraping up dimes, quarters, and dollars to see movies. The economic sag first hit the movie industry in 1933; admissions declined, theatres closed, production dropped. But prudent studio economy measures and a new moralistic path of righteousness helped to nurse the movie business back to health.

Film Cycles and Cinematic Conventions

The Studio Era was dominated not only by big filmmaking companies, but also by a number of assumptions about how movies should be produced, who should star in which kinds of films, and the need to acknowledge the ordinary conventions of society.

The Production Code

In 1930, Martin Quigley, a Roman Catholic layman, and Daniel Lord, S.J., drafted the Hollywood Production Code, another in a series of the motion picture industry's official statements on the proper moral content of films. But the Code might never have been enforced if the Catholic Legion of Decency had not threatened an economic boycott in 1933, the same year that movie revenues first began to feel the effects of the Depression. In July 1934, Joseph I. Breen, another Roman Catholic layman, went to work for the "Hays Office" (see Chapter 6) as the head of its new Production Code Administration (PCA), an agency that would award the industry's seal of approval only to those films that observed the Code's moral restrictions. Any producer or distributor who released a film without the industry's seal would be fined $25,000. Because every major producer and distributor was a member of the Motion Picture Producers and Distributors of America (MPPDA, later the MPAA), they all subscribed to the PCA's rulings and, as of 1934, submitted all their scripts to the Hays Office for approval before shooting.

The Code declared that movies were to avoid brutality (by gangsters and especially by the police), they were to avoid depicting any kind of sexual promiscuity (unwedded, extramarital, or "unnatural"), and they were to avoid making any illegal or immoral life seem either possible or pleasant (goodbye to the gangsters who lived well until the law gunned them down). The Production Code viewed marriage as more a sacred institution than a sexual one; even the

sophisticated Nick and Nora Charles of *The Thin Man* (1934) slept separately in twin beds—which became known as "Hollywood beds." Even more restrictive were the new Code's specific prohibitions against certain words. Not only were "sex," "God," "hell," and "damn" forbidden, but so were such flavorful and healthy Americanisms as "guts," "nuts," and "louse," which were considered deficient in gentility and "tone." Ironically, the Code, which Hollywood adopted for business reasons in 1934, perished 34 years later for the same reasons. The very words and deeds that crimped sales in the 1930s spurred them in the 1960s.

Some historians see the Code as the era's institutional means for eliminating political dissent and narrowing discussion of the important social issues. The large banks, whose investment capital allowed the movie industry to function, could dictate the conservative content of films through the Code, constricting political change and cultural consciousness. Within the film industry at the time, the Code was a particularly useful instrument for studios to keep writers in their place. A producer could always settle a dispute with a writer by claiming that the Code said "No."

But its administrators claimed that the purpose of the Code was not to keep films from being made, but to allow them to be made—without damaging the commercial health of the film, the studio that made it, and the industry as a whole. Americans inside and outside the film industry knew that adultery, crime, and injustice were not only a part of life but the elementary materials of playacting and storytelling from their beginnings. It's hardly a joke to say that the Greek tragedies would have been sent back for rewrite. The Code was a unique historical document that attempted to formulate, concretely and precisely, the publicly admissible mores of an entire culture—the kinds of deeds suitable for public depiction and, especially, the kinds of words (now that movies could talk) suitable for public utterance.

In addition to soothing its audiences' moral sensitivities, Hollywood pulled itself out of the Depression by offering a bargain. Double features—two pictures for the price of one—became standard in all but the poshest of first-run theatres. Hollywood added a third attraction to the two movies (plus trailers, cartoons, shorts, and a newsreel): Audiences could play exciting games between the films—Keno, Bingo, Screeno—that sent the winner home with cash or a set of dishes. The studios survived the financial crisis of 1933, and profits shot up in 1935; they survived the crisis of 1938, and profits shot up in 1939. The boom years of the war eliminated all money crises for several more years. The Second World War lasted from 1939 (1941 in America) to 1945. The film industry enjoyed its biggest business year in 1946.

Cycles

The studio system controlled both the subjects of film narrative and the styles in which they were shot. Formulas for story construction, characterization, casting, decor, music, and photography dominated Hollywood's films. A key principle in the selection of story material was—and remains—simply that an idea that had worked before would probably work again. Films were not seen as special, individual conceptions but tended to bunch together as types, in cycles.

The new sound equipment introduced audiences to the hard-bitten street slang of mobsters; Hollywood produced a cycle of pictures that made the tough talk of gangsters as familiar as polite conversation around the family dinner table. The first gangster cycle condemned and glorified the brutality of the underworld: *Little Caesar, Scarface, The Public Enemy.* Later

gangster cycles, purified by the antiviolence, antiillegality sections of the Breen Code, merely put the tough-talking guys on the right side of the law—that is, on the other side of the badge: *The Public Enemy*'s James Cagney in *"G" Men.* A cycle of films about prison, the "big house," spun off from the mobster films; the big house also had its slang, its underworld morality, its tough guys behind bars and behind the warden's desk: *The Big House, San Quentin, The Criminal Code.* Yet another close relative of the mobster cycle was the journalism cycle. The newspaper reporters often seemed like gangsters who had accidentally ended up behind a typewriter rather than a tommy gun; they talked and acted as rough as the crooks their assignments forced them to cover: *The Front Page, Big News, The Power of the Press.*

A succession of musical cycles accompanied the cops-and-robbers cycles. Just as synchronized sound brought the pungent, brittle crackle of thug talk to American audiences, synchronization also brought the possibility of complex rhythmic and musical effects. Singing and dancing could be synchronized to the exact beat; picture and sound could be wed in their own kind of audiovisual montage. Musical sequences were almost obligatory in early talkies, just as most 1940s films included at least one song—whether integral and relevant, as in *Casablanca*, or unnecessary, as in *The Big Sleep.* Among the first "100 percent" talkies released by every major studio in 1929 was

Fig. 11-1

Fig. 11-2

The assault of gangsters on American life. Fig. 11-1: Paul Muni as the hero/villain of the 1932 Scarface; Fig. 11-2: George Raft as his coin-flipping friend.

a musical—MGM's *Broadway Melody*, Fox's *Sunny Side Up*, and *Paramount on Parade*.

The first musicals were either filmed versions of Broadway shows or suave, continental musical–comic pictures à la Lubitsch. The second cycle of musicals was a series of "backstage" stories—the struggling young composer, the young hopeful in the chorus (who is catapulted to stardom when the leading lady falls ill), the down-and-out director who needs one last hit—epitomized at Warner Bros. by *42nd Street* and other films with musical numbers directed by Busby Berkeley.

The Berkeley musicals were contradictory mixtures of the blandest, most formulaic dramatic sections (which Berkeley did not usually direct) and the most dazzling kaleidoscopic visual style for the musical sections. Berkeley's accomplishment was not merely that space itself became a "dancer" in these numbers but that his radical shifts of camera position stripped the frame of any clear geographical or theatrical referents. His numbers may begin or end on a stage, but most could never be performed on one; they happen in cinematic space and are addressed to the camera, which may be on the ceiling. Berkeley's numbers invite us into a visual labyrinth; the viewer's eye absorbs a kind of visual "music," scored solely by abstract contrasts of black and white, circle and line, camera angles and editing rhythms.

But for all this dazzling dancing geometry, one never forgets that Berkeley's evolving abstract forms are based on smiling female faces and shapely female limbs, presented for the delight of the male viewers, just like Florenz Ziegfeld's seminude showgirls on the Broadway stage (and Berkeley had worked for Ziegfeld). The keepers of the Production Code had similar suspicions about the Warners' backstage musicals. Although less than six months separate *42nd Street* from *Gold Diggers of 1933*, there is a clear contrast between the suggestive sleaziness and sexuality of *42nd Street* and the innocent showgirls of the later film, unjustly accused of illicit and mercenary intentions.

A cycle of smoother, more integrated comedies-of-romance-with-music starred Fred Astaire and Ginger Rogers at RKO. For Astaire and Rogers, dancing was not merely a generic inevitability of backstage musicals but a means of human interaction and connection. The characters embodied by Astaire and Rogers discovered one another's feelings through the dances they performed together, discovered that, no matter what social obstacles confronted them, they belonged together because they danced so perfectly together.

America's greatest composers for the musical theatre wrote original songs and scores for Hollywood films: the Gershwins (*Shall We Dance?* and *A Damsel in Distress* for Astaire at RKO in 1937); Jerome Kern (*Swing Time*, 1936, and *You Were Never Lovelier*, 1943, also for Astaire); Irving Berlin (*Top Hat*, 1935, *Follow the Fleet*, 1936, and *Carefree*, 1938, for Astaire; *Alexander's Ragtime Band*, 1938, for Fox); Rodgers and Hart (*Love Me Tonight*, 1932, for Maurice Chevalier and Jeanette MacDonald at Paramount); Cole Porter (*Born to Dance*, 1936, and *Broadway Melody of 1940* for MGM's Eleanor Powell).

Any successful Hollywood film spawned many imitations, just as one successful television show begets half a dozen progeny on all the major networks. Like television, the Hollywood of the 1930s faced the weekly pressure of entertaining a huge percentage of the national population; as in television, fear of a dollar disaster was a constant spur to produce safe mediocrities. The parallels with TV programming are even more obvious with those successful films that spawned not only imitations but sequels. The film series was the ancestor of the TV series: the Andy Hardy pictures, the Maisie series, the Charlie Chan films, Mr. Moto, and—the closest possible parallel with network TV—the series of films springing from MGM's *Young Doctor Kildare*. Yet another studio formula was to patch together a film with what seemed like all the stars they had under contract: MGM's *Broadway Melodies* (of 1936, 1938, and 1940). The studios made the same films over and over again, with similar titles or different ones. And they put their stars into roles they felt would suit them so that audiences could enjoy their favorite actors doing what was expected of them. Even today, the right star in the right genre (Harrison Ford in an adventure film) is the key to big profits.

Studios and Style

Formulas for style were as binding as formulas for plotting. Hollywood films of the decade, with surprisingly few exceptions, looked strikingly

Fig. 11-3
The monochrome musical. Busby Berkeley's kaleidoscopic white pianos on a black floor (**Gold Diggers of 1935**).

alike. Many directors' impulses toward personal style were suppressed before shooting began by the studio's general policies of lighting, design, cinematography, and cutting.

The key characteristic of film style in the Studio Era was that sound films were talking films. The talk was better now that writers of screen dialogue knew how to write screen dialogue. The scenes of talk were smoother now that the speakers could move from place to place and both camera and microphone could follow them. The careful decor added insightful nuances and contrapuntal resonances to the scenes of talk. But talk still propelled the talkies. Camerawork, cutting, and lighting supported this emphasis on dialogue, highlighting the stars and what they said on screen. Yet for all their apparent standardness, the movies never demonstrated a higher degree of craftsmanship and artisanship—neither in America nor elsewhere—than in these 15 years of Hollywood studio style.

Despite their common assumptions and conventions, each of the studios displayed a unique personality in applying them. The two giants—MGM and Paramount—were the most distinctive and the most different from one another. MGM was the studio with almost dictatorial central control—exerted by Louis B. Mayer and Irving Thalberg. Paramount, under B. P. Schulberg, was a much looser organization, granting more freedom to individual producers, directors, and writers. MGM was a studio of stars: Greta Garbo, Katharine Hepburn, Mickey Rooney, Clark Gable, Spencer Tracy. Paramount was a studio of writers and directors: Ernst Lubitsch, Josef von Sternberg, Cecil B. DeMille, Billy Wilder. In the early 1930s, Paramount was the iconoclast's haven: the home of Mae West, W. C. Fields, and the Marx Brothers. Unless it was making a horror film like *Mad Love*, MGM flattened all excesses into a shiny, respectable, beautifully lit wholesomeness. When the Marx Brothers left

Fig. 11-4
RKO's **I Walked with a Zombie,** *produced by Val Lewton and directed by Jacques Tourneur.*

Paramount for MGM, they lost much of their lunacy and spark. Ironically, in the 1930s the MGM policy seemed the wiser of the two, for Louis B. Mayer's devotion to family entertainment made MGM the most respected and successful film factory in Hollywood—a studio that could release *The Wizard of Oz* and *Gone With the Wind* in the same year (1939)—while B. P. Schulberg's chaotic individuality ran Paramount into severe financial difficulties, resulting in the studio's loss of many of its stars and Schulberg's loss of his job.

Warner Bros., which invested less money in production values (sets, costumes, crowds), was more dependent on good talk. The studio specialized in gangster films, biographies, and musicals. Warner Bros. was also the studio most committed to the depiction of contemporary social problems—whether in its musicals (the "Forgotten Man" and "Shanghai Lil" numbers of Berkeley musicals), its gangster pictures (like *Little Caesar* and *The Public Enemy*), its problem pictures (like *I Am a Fugitive From a Chain Gang*), its socially conscious "biopics," as *Variety* called them (the biographies of Zola, Pasteur, and Curie), or its "woman's pictures"—the choices and conflicts of women in contemporary American society (often embodied by Bette Davis). Warners was also the most pro-Roosevelt of the studios and, like FDR, openly critical of the Nazi menace abroad. And Warners had the best cartoons. In contrast, the Disney cartoons were bourgeois, reverent, and tame. On the level of sheer visual inventiveness, Warners' only competitors were Max and Dave Fleischer, who first brought Ko-Ko out of an inkwell, then created the Betty Boop, Popeye, and Superman cartoons.

Universal's **Frankenstein,** *directed by James Whale, was influenced more by German Expressionism than by Mary Shelley's novel; sets by Charles D. Hall.*

Fig. 11-5

Twentieth Century–Fox excelled in historical and adventure films directed by John Ford and Henry King, in show business musicals with Don Ameche and Alice Faye, and in the folksy comedies of Will Rogers and Shirley Temple. If Warners was committed to general social problems, Fox was committed to the problems of American family life. Even Fox musicals confront a woman with the difficult choice between career and family.

RKO, the least financially stable of the major studios, was most memorable for the smooth musicals of Fred Astaire and Ginger Rogers, the suave comedies with Cary Grant, the literate horror B pictures produced by Val Lewton, and the occasional film by Howard Hawks (*Bringing Up Baby*), Orson Welles (*Citizen Kane, The Magnificent Ambersons*), and John Ford (*The Informer*)—not to mention *King Kong.*

Universal excelled in the horror films—*Frankenstein, Dracula,* and *The Wolf Man*—directed by James Whale, Tod Browning, and others; in the later comedies of W. C. Fields; and in the saccharine singing pictures of Deanna Durbin and Gloria Jean.

Columbia was the creation of a single producer, Harry Cohn, who hitched his "minor" studio to director Frank Capra in 1927 and rode to respectability on the coattails of Capra's many

successes (especially *It Happened One Night* in 1934).

The most aesthetically and commercially successful of the independent production companies were Samuel Goldwyn, Inc., Selznick International Pictures, and Walt Disney Productions; at some point, each distributed its films through United Artists, which remained the independents' releasing company of choice but also had begun to produce films on its own.

The two "Poverty Row" studios, Republic and Monogram, specialized in cheap westerns, cheap hoodlum pictures, and—like Universal—serials.

The studios forced their directors to be eclectic. A director jumped from jungle adventure to backstage musical to historical pageant to contemporary comedy. The director's sole qualification for handling so many styles and settings was the ability to get any job done well.

Typical of the competent impersonality of the Studio Era was the career of Warner Bros.' Mervyn LeRoy. Within a three-year period, he directed *Little Caesar*, the tough story of a mobster's rise and fall; *I Am a Fugitive From a Chain Gang*, a true story of brutality in a southern prison; and the "dramatic" sections of the backstage musical *Gold Diggers of 1933*. In those same three years, 1930–33, LeRoy directed 20 other films,

Clark Gable and Vivien Leigh in Gone With the Wind.

Fig. 11-6

including journalism pictures, homespun comedies, and show-business musicals.

In addition to asking their directors to select from the smorgasbord, the studios found that some directors did a better job with a single dish. Some directed comedies, primarily Gregory LaCava (*She Married Her Boss, My Man Godfrey*). Other directors specialized in adventure, horror, or mystery: Tod Browning (*The Unholy Three, Dracula, Freaks*), William Wellman (*The Public Enemy, The Ox-Bow Incident*).

If the most conventional studio films displayed any personality, it often reflected the general moral assumptions and values of the era as a whole. Almost all the films took the view that the sincere, the sensitive, the human would inevitably triumph over the hypocritical, the callous, the oppressive. From the screwball comedies to the horror films, wit and resourcefulness saved the day. If the optimism of Hollywood films provided the audiences with the tranquilizer they needed, it also strengthened the audience's belief that eventually good people would make bad times better.

The American film offered not only escape but also subtle propaganda. Whereas many Americans lacked the money to buy warm clothing, American movie characters wore fashionable gowns and well-tailored suits. Whereas many Americans lacked the money to pay the rent, American movie characters lived in elegant apart-

ments filled with expensive furniture. The tasteful richness of the studio films, supported by the inexorable workings of poetic justice in their plots, answered a very deep need in a people working hard to achieve the kind of comfort, plenty, and fairness that it saw in the films every week. Just as the cynical materialism of the 1920s succeeded the innocence and honor of the Griffith era, the optimism and wholesomeness of the 1930s succeeded the values of the Jazz Age.

The Comics

Some of the most distinctive American films of the 1930s, like those of the previous two decades, were comedies. It was the great period of screwball comedy. Sophisticated romantic comedies flourished along with low-budget spoofs. There were also films that took a dark look at some of the roughest and most disappointing aspects of life, using comedy to set the world as right as it could be.

Late Chaplin

Chaplin survived the transition to sound by making no apparent transition at all. His first two sound films, *City Lights* and *Modern Times*, used a synchronized score and clever sound effects but little synchronized speech (none at all in *City Lights*). Chaplin was certain that Charlie, the little tramp, was a man of mime, a character not made for a world of words.

Fig. 11-7
Along with Music for Millions *(1944), the Capitol Theatre in Manhattan offered a stage show with Tommy Dorsey; it was World War II, and war bonds were sold "day and night."*

In *City Lights* (1931), Charlie's pantomime takes him into the society of the rich, where he makes friends with a suicidal millionaire who is friendly and generous when drunk, cold and callous when sober—and forgetful of whatever had happened while he was drunk. Charlie's intermittent closeness to the world of the rich, as the millionaire remembers or forgets him, allows him to help a poor blind girl (Virginia Cherrill) who, significant in the Chaplin symbolism, sells flowers to keep herself alive.

In *City Lights*, Chaplin raises the question of whether the tramp is capable of finding a romantic partner; in *Modern Times* (1936), Chaplin asks whether the tramp is capable of achieving marriage, for marriages require homes, and homes require payments, and payments require jobs. And this is the Depression. So in *Modern Times*, the little tramp, as always, is at the mercy of the social order, especially of the immense industrial machinery of our increasingly technological society. At the end of *Modern Times*, the tramp and his "wife"

(Paulette Goddard, soon to become Chaplin's actual wife) walk away from the camera and from society, literally heading for the hills, for their kind of marriage cannot survive in such a society.

In his next picture, the talkie *The Great Dictator* (1940), Chaplin played two roles: a Jewish barber, closely akin to his underdog tramp, and the villainous top-dog Führer, whom Chaplin—with his short, toothbrush moustache—resembled. The comic action of the film pleads eloquently and ironically for the rights of individual human expression against the stifling, murderous power of the tyrant. Unfortunately, Chaplin discovered that the dialogue film could plead with speeches as well as with comic action. The didacticism of the film's final speech, a fervent but overlong and sentimental appeal for world peace, is a dramatic letdown.

The same overt moralizing and sentimentality cloud Chaplin's last two masterpieces, *Monsieur Verdoux* and *Limelight. Monsieur Verdoux* (1947), like *The Great Dictator*, begins with a brilliant

Fig. 11-8   **Fig. 11-9**
Modern Times: *A televised Boss spies on Charlie in the washroom, then feeds him by machine.*

seriocomic premise (suggested to Chaplin by Orson Welles): A delightful, witty, urbane gentleman marries a series of rich women specifically to bump them off, using their legacies to support his crippled wife and child on an idyllic country estate. The film necessarily questions the relationship of the means of an action to its end, whether murder is justifiable if its ultimate purpose is virtuous.

But as in *The Great Dictator*, Chaplin deserts comic objectivity at the end of *Monsieur Verdoux* to spell out the film's implications in a bald and unnecessary speech.

Comic insight and uncomfortable sentimentality pull *Limelight* (1952) in two directions. The flashback scenes that re-create the music-hall routines of the old vaudevillian, Calvero (Chaplin), are funny and touching, the former music-hall clown's ultimate tribute to the world that fostered his mime and art. The scenes in the present—of the clown's love for a ballerina (played by Claire Bloom) whom he saves from suicide and despair—suffer from overstatement. Even so, *Limelight* is profoundly moving, and the climactic routine with Keaton is a revelation.

It was only in his last two pictures that Chaplin really faltered. *A King in New York* (1957), which takes on everything from McCarthyism to the wide screen, is interesting but rarely engaging, and *A Countess from Hong Kong* (1967) has a severe, classic style that interferes with the film's painful attempts to be funny.

Chaplin maintained his power and individuality in the Studio Era because he needed to make

no concessions to Hollywood's commercial structure. Chaplin produced and owned his own pictures, ran his own studio, and released through United Artists; the popularity of his films earned him the profits to make more pictures just as he wanted to make them. At the opposite extreme, the career of Buster Keaton, who in the Sound Era was "just an actor," turned into a disaster.

Disney's World

Walt Disney, like Chaplin, made the transition into the Studio Era by maintaining his commercial and, consequently, artistic independence. Disney, whose fantasies of drawing and music, movement and rhythm had evolved in the first years of sound, found one further ally in the 1930s. The same advantage that Disney enjoyed over realistic films in the free use of sound also gave him the freedom to manipulate color—surrealistically, as in the "pink elephants" sequence of *Dumbo* (1941), or realistically, as in most of *Bambi* (1942). Disney brought Technicolor to his Silly Symphonies, to his animal characters (Mickey, Donald, and Pluto), and eventually to his first feature, *Snow White and the Seven Dwarfs* (1937), one of the biggest hits of the decade and of all time.

The Disney fantasies of color and motion were perfectly suited to the audience's craving for happiness, wholesomeness, and optimism in films—even if they often terrified children. His "Who's Afraid of the Big, Bad Wolf?" from *The Three Little Pigs* (1933) became not only a popular song but also a metaphor for the whole country's cheerful defiance of the big, bad "wolf at the door," the Depression. The film itself was a socially acceptable Protestant-ethic lecture: to build with bricks, not straw. (Less acceptable anti-Semitic elements have been deleted from most prints still in circulation.) But Disney's happy cleanliness began taking its toll on his visual imagination. Disney gradually deserted the short for the feature, the fantasy–abstract film of color, music, and movement for the sentimental story film that attempted to blend fantasy and realism. After the climactic *Fantasia* (1940), his films took fewer chances. Everything became too controlled and perfect—an aesthetic he extended in the 1950s to Disneyland.

Lubitsch and Sound

Ernst Lubitsch, whose camera had learned to comment on a character or situation by shooting an apparently insignificant detail that was loaded with implications, discovered that sound, as well as pictures, could make such touches. In his first sound films, the continental musicals, he mastered the new machines and learned to make the sound film as fluid and effortless as the silent one. But his greatest sound films were dialogue pictures, slick comedies of manners, translated by his cinematic imagination (often from the stage) into his unique film terms: *Design for Living* (1933), *Angel* (1937), *Ninotchka* (1939, with Garbo), *To Be or Not To Be* (1942, with Jack Benny and Carole Lombard), and, especially, *Trouble in Paradise* (1932).

Trouble in Paradise is the story of an urbane, elegant crook whose charm and social graces allow him to work his way into the hotels and hearts of the very rich where he performs his high-stakes thievery. Eventually the master crook, Gaston Monescu (Herbert Marshall), finds himself caught between his love for two women, Mariette Colet (Kay Francis), the rich perfume heiress he is swindling, and Lily (Miriam Hopkins), his clever accomplice. Because he is a thief, because he is merely a pretender to propriety in the gleaming world of the rich and proper, because his past has determined his future, Monescu eventually leaves Mariette for Lily.

Lubitsch handles Monescu's sexual relationships with his two ladies with the greatest wryness and subtlety. In the first sequence, Lily and Monescu fall in love by discovering each other's crooked cleverness. The two dine in Monescu's elegant hotel suite. Like the opening's garbage gondola, the scene plays the elegant surfaces off against the corruption beneath: The two are not Baron and Countess enjoying a slyly seductive supper but two crooks trying to fleece one another. As the two trade polished banalities, they steal each other's watches, wallets, jewelry. After they discover and sort out each other's goods, Monescu bends over to kiss Lily as she sits on a sofa. Lubitsch dissolves to an empty sofa. Then he cuts to a male arm, its white sleeve implying a discarded dinner jacket, hanging a "Do Not Disturb" sign on the door of his hotel room. Later, Lubitsch implies the direction of Madame Colet's and Monescu's intentions by throwing

Fig. 11-10

Fig. 11-11

Lubitsch's sexual wit in Trouble in Paradise—*from a reflection of the embracing lovers in the mirror (Fig. 11-10) to the shadows of their bodies on the bed (Fig. 11-11).*

the shadows of their embracing bodies on the coverlet of her bed. The implications of such juxtapositions are obvious, clearly a sign of the screen's pre-Breen sexual suggestiveness.

Add to Lubitsch's subtle images and clever music his satiric handling of the minor characters (Edward Everett Horton, Charles Ruggles, C. Aubrey Smith), and Samson Raphaelson's sparkling dialogue, which consistently pins a new tail on an old cliché: "If you behave like a gentleman, I'll break your neck"; "a member of the *nouveau* poor." The combined ingredients make *Trouble in Paradise* one of the most polished comedies of manners in the history of film.

Frank Capra

Frank Capra also turned to comedies of manners in 1934. But instead of the suave manners of Lubitsch's shiny Europe, Capra, born in Sicily, focused on the ingenuous, homespun manners of the most American America—and, in an insightful part-talkie, *The Younger Generation* (1929), on the conflicts that assimilation raises in a family of immigrants. Although Capra's career in films stems from silent comedy when he was a gag man and staff director at both the Sennett and the Hal Roach studios, Capra became an important director in the era of the talkies after he signed with Columbia Pictures, where producer Harry Cohn guaranteed him creative freedom. At Columbia, he met Robert Riskin, who was to write most of his important scripts. The Capra–Riskin film was generally a witty contemporary morality play that pitted a good man—usually a "little guy" who is naïve, sincere, folksy, unaffected, unintellectual, apolitical—against evil social forces: money, politics, affectation, social status, human insensitivity. The "little guy" emerges from the struggle not only victorious but also wiser about the ways of the world.

It Happened One Night (1934), the first movie to "sweep" the Oscars—winning Academy Awards for best picture, director, actor, actress, and adapted screenplay—examines the clash of a snooping newspaper reporter (Clark Gable) and a rich society woman (Claudette Colbert) fleeing her wealthy father to marry a worthless boyfriend. The two travel cross-country by bus, discovering the hazards as well as the charms of rural, uncitified America—motels, bad roads, hitchhiking, and

people. Among the people they discover are themselves and one another—what makes them alike and makes them like others despite the gulf between their material and intellectual backgrounds.

In *Mr. Deeds Goes to Town* (1936), a man from the country (Gary Cooper) inherits a pile of money and comes to the city to discover how to spend it. The city folk belittle the country ways of the hero "hick," and leading the laughter is the snobbish reporter (Jean Arthur) with whom Deeds has fallen in love. Deeds eventually converts the woman, discovers that he must use his money to help the poor and starving, and vanquishes the rich who try to prove him insane so they can control his fortune. In *Mr. Smith Goes to Washington* (1939), Mr. Deeds has changed to Mr. Smith, Gary Cooper has changed to James Stewart, and his problem has changed from money to politics. The woman is still Jean Arthur. Although Capra's vision may seem corny and populistic, the consistency of Capra's material, the solid scripts, the sharp cinematography, the unforced acting in his films and their crisp comic timing make them sincere, intelligent statements of the era's optimism and humanism—as well as batty celebrations of comic anarchy.

But there is a dark side to the Capra films as well. In *Meet John Doe* (1941) Capra demonstrates that the folksy slogans of an ordinary John Doe (Gary Cooper again) are uncomfortably close to the fascistic slogans of an Adolf Hitler (personified by the American millionaire D. B. Norton and played by Edward Arnold). In *It's A Wonderful Life* (1946), made one year after World War II and widespread knowledge of the Nazi death camps, George Bailey (James Stewart, who co-produced the film) has become so frustrated by his drab middle-American existence that only a heavenly miracle can rescue him from suicide and restore his faith in his own accomplishments. The legions of God and the Devil struggle mightily in these allegorical Capra comedies, and it takes a terrifyingly long time for justice, truth, and salvation to triumph.

Preston Sturges

Preston Sturges wrote and directed witty moral comedies on American subjects, but he was an ironist and satirist who stood many of the era's

It's A Wonderful Life: *"Little guy" George Bailey (James Stewart, right) refuses to abandon his values and sell out to the heartless big capitalist, Potter (Lionel Barrymore, seated).*

Fig. 11-12

wholesome and optimistic conventions on their ear. He was also the first major writer–director of the Sound Era—and in Hollywood, the first writer allowed to direct his own scripts. *The Great McGinty* (1940), the first film Sturges directed after a distinguished career as a screenwriter, ridicules American democratic politics and the naïve notion that the voter really controls the government. *Christmas in July* (1940) satirizes the American dream of getting rich quick without hard work. *The Lady Eve* (1941) is a burlesque of American sexual—romantic conventions. *Sullivan's Travels* (1941) is the story of a Hollywood director (Joel McCrea) who is weary of making entertaining fluff and aspires to make films laden with Serious Moral and Social Significance; he decides that in order to make such films, he must learn firsthand what it feels like to be poor. In the course of his travels, the director discovers true love (Veronica Lake) as well as the value of "merely" making people laugh.

During the war years, Sturges courageously extended his satire to American perceptions of the war, our confused sexual standards in wartime (*The Miracle of Morgan's Creek*, 1943 [released 1944]), and our superficial definitions of heroism and patriotism (*Hail the Conquering Hero*, 1944). Sturges could get away with his

audacious iconoclasm because of the unmatched verbal richness of his scripts, the spirited wit of his acting ensemble, and the ingenuity of his physical slapstick comedy.

George Cukor

George Cukor was another comic ironist, but of a very different sort. Like Lubitsch, Cukor also made comedies of sexual manners; but unlike Lubitsch, these were the manners of monogamous America. And as in Sturges's films, these were American manners filtered through the lens of Hollywood convention.

Cukor was known best as a "woman's director." From Hepburn to Harlow to Garbo (*Camille*, 1936, released 1937) to Holliday to Judy Garland (*A Star Is Born*, 1954) to another Hepburn (Audrey in *My Fair Lady*, 1964), Cukor elicited superb performances from female stars.

The reason was Cukor's consciousness that the sharp distinctions between male and female sexual identity were not as simple as they seemed in American movies. Cukor was the one major director of Hollywood's Studio Era who was gay—or, at least, was willing to admit it in the 1970s, when it was safe to come out. He disguised his alternative sexual taste behind heterosexual comic arguments that stood the prevailing assumptions of male domination on their heads. For example:

Fig. 11-13

Sullivan's Travels: *Aided by his valet (Eric Blore, left), millionaire director John L. Sullivan (Joel McCrea) tries on his hobo outfit.*

Why shouldn't the male lawyer, Adam (Spencer Tracy), and the female lawyer, his wife Amanda (Katharine Hepburn, defending Judy Holliday), adopt fundamentally different strategies of law in *Adam's Rib* (1949), since these laws have been written by men for men?

Cukor's films never answer such questions; instead, the director presents his carefully balanced and amusingly paradoxical evidence. He is very much an outside observer looking in, refusing to take a side in the battle of the sexes. In Cukor's carefully balanced frames, conflicting decor and symmetrical composition often indicate the moral and social paradoxes of the film. Though less idiosyncratic than the social comedies of his contemporaries, Cukor's films have worn wonderfully well, for social and sexual consciousness have finally caught up with his subtle ironies.

The Marx Brothers

As with the silent comedies, many of the sound comedies wore the personalities of their comics rather than their directors. Because Langdon and Keaton and numerous other clowns who were schooled in the silent tradition never successfully combined talk and movement, Hollywood imported clowns from Broadway who had already effected the combination. The Marx

Brothers even shot their first films in New York. In 1929 they re-created their current stage hit, *The Cocoanuts*, for the screen. The Marx Brothers combined the great traditions of American physical comedy with a verbal humor that perfectly suited their physical types. The plots of the Marx Brothers' films were irrelevant, providing occasions for gags and irreverent parodies of conventional behavior: self-important worlds into which the zany comics dropped.

The Marx Brothers made some of the funniest movies in history. People are still arguing about whether *Duck Soup* (1933) and the Paramount films are better than *A Night at the Opera* (1935) and the MGM films. Starting with the eldest, the five brothers were Chico (Leonard), Harpo (Adolph, called Arthur), Groucho (Julius Henry), Gummo (Milton), and Zeppo (Herbert). In vaudeville, Milton was part of the team; on Broadway and in the first films, he was replaced by Zeppo. When Zeppo left after *Duck Soup*, the Four Marx Brothers became three: Groucho, Chico, and Harpo. In a number of the best pictures, Margaret Dumont played a conventional woman trying to manage the chaos but also attracted to it. Almost all of their movies featured musical sequences in which Chico plays the piano or Harpo plays the harp; they were part of the act as much

Fig. 11-14
The Four Marx Brothers in Duck Soup. *From left, Chico, Zeppo, Groucho, and Harpo.*

as Groucho's cigar and painted mustache—or the verbal and visual puns.

The Marx Brothers pictures were brilliantly written and directed at a screwball pace that could slow down to watch in wonder as an almost infinite joke became more funny the more it went on. They were masters of timing, both visual and verbal, and they were planted in the silent and the sound comedy by Harpo's miming and Groucho and Chico's dialogue. In themselves they were figures as fundamental as Chaplin's tramp. The films abound with physical comedy and mad visuals: the football sequence in *Horse Feathers* (1932), the mirror scene in *Duck Soup*, the stateroom packed with human sardines or the split-second timing of the bed-shifting sequence in *A Night at the Opera*. And for brilliant verbal doubletalk there is the "Why-a-duck?" sequence in *The Cocoanuts* in which Groucho tries

to sell Chico a piece of island property with a viaduct. Like their puns, their gags built and built until audiences were weak with laughter. From Harpo's horn to Groucho's walk, the Marx Brothers films revealed the key elements of sound comedy—comic physical types suited to their comic personalities, to the physical-comedy situations, and to the verbal wit. Comic talkies had to move as well as talk.

Mae West

And sometimes the talk was dirty. Mae West, another Broadway import, had her own comic personality, a parody of the amoral, sensual female hedonist who frankly enjoyed nice clothes, nice food, and a nice tumble in the hay. She physically suited that personality. No petite, lithe, virginal ingénue was Mae, but a buxom, hefty broad. Her rolling eyes, her gyrating hips, her falling, throaty

Mae West: The caricature of female sensuality poses beside a caricature of her own sensuality in a 1932 publicity photo.

Fig. 11-15

voice consciously tried to unmask an opponent or undress a friend. And her comic lines fit the eyes, the voice, and the body: "Beulah, peel me a grape"; "Are you packin' a rod or are you just glad to see me?" Even her croaking "Oh" said much more than oh. Like the Marx Brothers' plots, Mae West's film stories, which she wrote herself, were slender lines on which to hang her own personal business: her gyrations, her comments, her songs. The films' action inevitably ran Mae up against the forces of respectability and legality.

Ironically, only one of her films, *She Done Him Wrong* (1933), is, because of its pre-Code date, fully a Mae West film. Despite the financial success of *She Done Him Wrong*, Mae West's film career was cut up and cut short by the Breen sanctions against overt sexuality and the glamorous portrayal of vice. In her later films—*Goin' to Town* (1935), *Klondike Annie* (1936), and even *My Little Chickadee* (1940) with W. C. Fields—Mae West becomes a clean-scrubbed caricature of her own sexuality, which was, in its original frankness, a caricature of sexuality in the first place.

W. C. Fields

W. C. Fields was another great comedian of the sound stage. Like Mae West and the Marx Brothers, Fields's comedy stemmed from himself rather than from the stories in which he found himself. Like Mae West and the Marxes, Fields combined a comic personality, a comic physical type, and a style of verbal wit that fitted both his mind and his body.

The Fields character is a mixture of external polish and inner nastiness. Fields is the great spinner of words—of melodious euphemisms, euphonious malapropisms, florid rhetoric. Some of his greatest comic routines—as in *The Fatal Glass of Beer* (1933)—push repetition to the limit. At once obnoxious and charming, his affectation of polite speech is like all his other pretensions to politeness—pure sham. Beneath the fancy waistcoats and purple prose beats the heart of a dirty old man who drinks, smokes, swears, and gambles, who hates women (especially sweet old ones), children (especially cute little ones), animals, sobriety, and all

W. C. Fields caught in the trap of respectable American life in **The Bank Dick.**

Fig. 11-16

respectable social institutions (especially marriage, work, honest business dealings, and the law). In *Never Give a Sucker an Even Break* (1941), he tells the audience that the soda-shop scene he is in was supposed to have been set in a bar, but the censors changed it. (Other great reflexive films of that year were *Sullivan's Travels* and Ole Olsen and Chic Johnson's *Hellzapoppin'*, which was directed by H. C. Potter.) In films like *Tillie and Gus* (1933), *It's a Gift* (1934), and especially *The Bank Dick* (1940), Fields—like the Marx Brothers and Mae West—was the foe of everything sentimental and nice. In an era of glamorized sentimentality and niceness, their essential vulgarity and comic crudeness were especially refreshing. They provided the era's comic snore to puncture the Hays Office's American Dream.

Masters of Mood and Action

A number of noncomic directors made individualistic films that were powerful exceptions to the studio rule. The most significant of these *auteurs* were Josef von Sternberg, John Ford, Howard Hawks, Alfred Hitchcock, and Orson Welles.

Josef von Sternberg

By turns brooding and extravagant, the *mise-en-scène* of von Sternberg's films was obsessive and intricate; at times it was more impressive than the movies themselves. Visually the von Sternberg films were gleaming gems, rich in atmospheric detail, shimmering pools of light and contrasting shadow, the excitement of a perpetually moving, prowling camera, the luminous face of Marlene Dietrich—in shadow, in blazing light, veiled, feathered, powdered, hazed. But beneath von Sternberg's gleaming surfaces—the exotic locales, the symbolic details, the smoke, the shafts of light, the audacious sexual innuendoes that could have gotten past the censors only because they didn't understand visual symbols—his films reveal certain problems of plotting and characterization.

The Blue Angel (1930), von Sternberg's second sound film, was shot in Germany for Ufa. In the early sound years, Hollywood discovered a new problem: the language barrier. The silent cinema—a genuinely international language— simply substituted new titles in new languages as a film leaped from country to country. But with sound, before film distributors discovered dubbing and subtitling, it was common in Hollywood and Europe to shoot the same film in different languages and sometimes with different casts.

Fig. 11-17

The Blue Angel: *the chaotic clutter of the nightclub; Marlene Dietrich on stage.*

Fig. 11-18

The Blue Angel: *the antiseptic order and clarity of Emil Jannings's classroom, invaded by the influence of Lola Lola.*

Von Sternberg, an American born in Vienna, went to Germany to take part in this cinematic internationalism and direct, in German and English versions, Ufa's first talkie.

The Blue Angel is a Circe story. A bewitching woman, the nightclub singer Lola Lola (Marlene Dietrich) steadily turns a compulsively orderly school teacher (Emil Jannings) into a beast; he even crows like a cock to show his transformation. If the film is among von Sternberg's best, that is because it is based on a strong novel, Heinrich Mann's *Professor Unrat*, and because the director renders every step in Professor Rath's demise with the greatest intimacy and clarity. Atmosphere and visual images in the film are the means to depict the two conflicting characters and lifestyles.

Fig. 11-19
Von Sternberg putting his Blonde Venus through hoops: Dietrich as a sleazy whore.

Fig. 11-20
Von Sternberg putting his Blonde Venus through hoops: Dietrich as an international star.

Professor Rath's classroom is clean, bright, with desks arranged in geometric regularity; the Blue Angel club where Lola sings is smoky, hazy, chaotic, dim, and hung with entangling nets.

Professor Rath's ascetic life is sterile, schematic, so crammed with routine that it lacks the breath of life. Lola's sensual life is selfish and amoral; she is committed to love, not to loving someone—as her famous song, "Falling in Love Again," so clearly indicates. The film's business is not moral comment but the tragic story of what happens to a man from one life who tastes a drop of another. The wine that at first makes Rath drunk eventually poisons him. His final metamorphosis is into the kind of pathetic clown that he saw in Lola's dressing room when he first met her. That clown both foreshadows Rath's fate and implies that Lola's collection of human husks is endless. Rejected and humiliated, the shattered professor creeps back to his old classroom to die.

The von Sternberg–Dietrich American films are as dazzling visually as *The Blue Angel* (in fact, even more so), and like it they are suffused with a pervasive sexual energy. The best scene in *Morocco* (1930), the first of von Sternberg's Dietrich films made in America, shows Marlene's first appearance in the Moroccan nightclub. She is dressed as a man in tails; she sings, Eve-like, about selling apples, which she offers as she sings. A lesbian in the audience is obviously attracted to the male-clad performer. Marlene, knowing the woman's intentions, toys with her while singing and then matter-of-factly walks up to her and kisses her on the mouth. It is a stunning moment of sexual power.

The later von Sternberg–Dietrich films became progressively more bizarre. *Blonde Venus* (1932)—which contains enough plot for four films—features Marlene as loving wife, tempted adulteress, devoted mother, cheap whore in a border town, and international sensation of the music hall. Despite the film's wandering plot, it is redeemed by its moments of intensity and audacity: the sensuous opening scene as Dietrich swims in a shimmering stream (and as Herbert Marshall, impersonating a Boy Scout—at the age of 42!—voyeuristically watches her); the dusty, smoky chiaroscuro of the cheap dive in the Tex–Mex border town; the astonishing visual contrasts of the "Hot Voodoo" number,

in which the Blonde Venus, complete with platinum fright wig, pokes her head out of a gruesome gorilla costume; Dietrich in white top hat and tails, the masculine guise that attracts the adoration of her male admirers.

The coming of the Code and the Hays Office in no way inhibited the director's sexual fantasies but seemed to spur them to new heights. *The Scarlet Empress* (1934), his most sumptuous exercise in *mise-en-scène*, begins with the dreams of the sweet blonde seven-year-old Sophie who later becomes Catherine the Great of Russia. The child's nighttime visions are sadomasochistic fantasies, including the screams of tortured men on the rack and, in what may be the most de Sade–like image ever presented in a "respectable" Studio Era film, the hanging of a male body inside a huge bell, so that his swinging legs and heels can bang against the bell and send its peals out over the town and countryside.

Von Sternberg broke away from Dietrich to direct films without her after the ultimate study of Circean hypnosis, *The Devil Is a Woman*, in 1935. But his period of greatest influence—on both cinematic and cultural fashions—ended when he and Dietrich separated. In von Sternberg's hands, Dietrich became a modern goddess of Sexual Mystery—a celluloid icon of Circe, Aphrodite, Leda, Helen, and Galatea, all wrapped into a single key-lit face. And seven movies.

John Ford

John Ford continued the traditions of D. W. Griffith. Ford was an Irish Catholic born in Maine. He made westerns. Like Griffith's, Ford's values are traditional and sentimental: father, mother, home, and family; law, decency, democracy. Like Griffith—and Frank Capra—Ford was a populist. He praised the little people and damned those who twisted the system to grab money and power. More like Griffith than Capra, Ford emphasized visual images rather than talk and counterpointed violent dramatic action with rich comedy and wringing pathos. In his westerns, Ford used the settling of the frontier as his basic myth and central metaphor for the emerging American spirit—the bringing of civilization and fruitfulness to the savage wilderness. But Ford's films were neither naïve nor simple in their mythic vision. The "savage" could be very accomplished, evil could be awesomely

Fig. 11-21
The Scarlet Empress: *the spectacular wedding sequence.*

The Informer: *Ford's feeling for people is reflected in the strength and uniqueness of their faces.*

Fig. 11-22

powerful, and the forces of civilization could be stupid, rigid, and cruel.

The Ford films are as visually striking as von Sternberg's, but more direct and uncluttered. Unlike von Sternberg's Germanically moving camera, Ford's camera composes in space, in width and depth. Dominating Ford's films are the vast vistas of the plains, mountains, and sky, and the shots-in-depth of a group of faces or figures, tensely composed. But Ford never substituted picture taking for picture making. Although the films became complex allegories of good and evil—the lighting, the settings, the weather, the characterizations all supporting the symbolic structure—Ford never forgot the studio prescription that a film must tell a good story.

Ford's directorial career began in 1917 with a series of inexpensive program westerns starring the good badman, Harry Carey. He did not achieve wide recognition, however, until 1935 with *The Informer* (written by Ford's frequent collaborator, Dudley Nichols), which brought him the first of his many Academy Awards. In *The Informer*, Gypo (played by Victor McLaglen), a former member of the I.R.A., betrays his closest friend and former comrade to the hated British. The film traces the consequences of his succumbing to this weakness and eventually paying, both physically and mentally, for his betrayal. The film's power lies in Ford's achievement in making Gypo's tortured mind

manifest, in showing the man's hurts, hopes, fears, and conflicts.

Like many of Ford's prestigious projects of the late 1930s and early 1940s, *The Informer* was an adaptation of a respected literary work, a novel by Liam O'Flaherty. So were his adaptations of Eugene O'Neill's one-act plays about men at sea, *The Long Voyage Home* (1940), of John Steinbeck's *The Grapes of Wrath* (also 1940), and of Richard Llewellyn's *How Green Was My Valley* (1941). These adaptations were less impressive for their faithfulness to the original source material than for Ford's fondness for his characters and his feeling for the visual surroundings in which they worked, loved, and died. Whether indoors or out, Ford invests his faith in "the people"—working people, poor people, religious people, family people—never in commercial institutions like banks, mining companies, or government camps.

Ford poured his feelings for America—its history, its destiny, and its people—into his westerns. Two of Ford's major westerns—*Stagecoach* (1939) and *My Darling Clementine* (1946)—are allegorical studies of American history in the years just before and just after World War II.

The coach itself of *Stagecoach* becomes Ford's metaphor for "civilized" society. Like the trains in *The Iron Horse* (1924) and *The Man Who Shot Liberty Valance* (1962), the stagecoach is a manufactured vehicle the makers and

Fig. 11-23

Stagecoach: *Bringing white civilization to the wilderness. Fig. 11-23: Ford's stagecoach slices through the barren beauty of Monument Valley. Fig. 11-24: Inside a rustic shack, a microcosm of European-American society breaks bread.*

Fig. 11-24

occupants of which set out to tame the vast western wastes—in one of Ford's recurring metaphors, to plant a garden in the desert. In *Stagecoach* the key dramatic conflict is between the microcosm inside the coach and the "savagery" of the land and the Apaches outside it.

Inside Ford's stagecoach is a whole society of white people, of different social classes and mental habits: banker, sheriff, outlaw, salesman, doctor, prim wife, dance-hall "singer," gambler, stage driver. Ford and Dudley Nichols carefully distinguish

between the human traits of each: the gambler's chivalry and polish, the outlaw's sense of fairness, the delicate lady's shedding of her prejudices, and so on. Beneath their superficial tensions and differences, all these people (with one exception) eventually reveal an underlying warmth, kindness, and camaraderie that make them equally decent human beings.

The single unredeemed character in the film is Gatewood, the rich banker, who has stolen $50,000 from his own bank and is now running away with it. Despite his violation of the law, Gatewood is the most outspoken on the immorality of the doctor, singer, and outlaw and the most dogmatic in pontificating on the government's duty to protect his own self-important person. Ford's preference for the good-hearted, simple people over the evil-hearted rich is like Griffith's. Despite the exciting staging and cutting of the climactic battle with the Apaches, *Stagecoach* is primarily about character and values.

So is *My Darling Clementine*, although the enemy has shifted from Native American "savages" to savage members of the white race, and the battleground has shifted from the desert to a town. On its surface *My Darling Clementine* is an installment in the legend of Wyatt Earp. He and his brothers no longer enforce the law but live the private life of ranchers, out on the plains. The riot and disrule of a frontier town bring him back to "civilization" and its law. Earp, played by Henry Fonda, Ford's embodiment of American backwoods, self-educated social consciousness (Lincoln and Tom Joad), restores peace to the town. It builds a church and holds a dance, two of Ford's favorite emblems of communality, along with a gathering at a funeral, having a friendly fight, and sharing a meal.

Despite its western surfaces, the film's allegorical suggestions link it closely to the recent war in Europe and the Pacific.

The nighttime sneak attack of the vicious Clanton family on the youngest and unarmed Earp brother parallels the attack of the Japanese on Pearl Harbor or the Nazi invasion of Poland. Wyatt parallels the American fighting forces—peacekeeper in a former time (World War I), now withdrawn and isolated from the battle, steadily drawn into it when it engulfs him. Between the Earps and the Clantons stands Doc Holliday, a man of science (he is a doctor) and culture (he can quote Shakespeare), a former citizen of Boston (the most Eastern and European of American cities, and a favorite center of decadent mischief for Ford). Doc has fallen into the Slough of Despond—into decadence and drink. He no longer practices medicine but makes his living at cards; he has deserted the faithful woman back home, Clementine, for the dance-hall slut, Chihuahua; he is also dying of tuberculosis. Holliday seems the emblem of a sick and degenerate Europe, unable to defend itself, dependent on America—as Doc is dependent on Wyatt—to restore it to moral health.

Even the town's saloon is a mythic edifice: Row upon row of hanging lanterns stretch into the deep space of the frame, illuminating the perfectly planed and proportioned architecture of the building, which is less a frontier drinking place than a monument to civilization. The question of the film (and of many Ford westerns) is

Fig. 11-25

More civilization in the wilderness: the dance at the dedication of **My Darling Clementine***'s church.*

not how such a structure can be built but how civilization can be protected, how it can survive.

Ford's usual answer is that civilization requires a vigilant gunfighter to keep the peace.

My Darling Clementine expresses grave doubts whether a civilization can survive without the violent man of honor, the vigilant gunfighter and peacekeeper who carries the Law within him. Ford's westerns for the next 15 years (from the cavalry films—*Fort Apache*, 1948; *She Wore A Yellow Ribbon*, 1949; and *Wagon Master*, 1950—through *The Searchers* to *The Man Who Shot Liberty Valance*) would continue the exploration of this mythic theme.

Howard Hawks

If John Ford was the sound film's Griffith, Howard Hawks was its Ince. Compared with Ford's, Hawks's films are more brutal and less sentimental, more active and less mythic. Like Ince's, Hawks's movies are more striking in their driving narratives than in their examinations of psychology or emotional interaction. The psychological insight in a Hawks film functionally serves the narrative line. If Ince used his "soul fights" to move his narratives, Hawks showed that character motivates and is best judged by what one does. For all their verbal energy, his are films of action.

Howard Hawks is the most deceptively artless of the great Hollywood directors. His visual style lacks the tricky idiosyncrasies of a von Sternberg or a Lubitsch; his narrative style avoids the political and moral allegories of a Ford or a Capra. Direct and unsentimental, Hawks films merely seem to be well paced, well told, functionally shot genre pictures—gangster films, war films, westerns, screwball comedies, and the like. But the ultimate testimony to Hawks's powers and abilities may well be that he created at least one film that might serve as the very best representative example of almost every genre: the best gangster film (*Scarface*, 1930, released 1932), prison picture (*The Criminal Code*, 1931), racing picture (*The Crowd Roars*, 1932), western (*Red River*, 1948), backstage comedy (*Twentieth Century*, 1934), newspaper picture (*His Girl Friday*, 1940), whodunit (*The Big Sleep*, 1945, revised and released 1946), and screwball comedy (*Bringing Up Baby*, 1938). When a director succeeds so deeply and so broadly with these genre films, it is necessary to look more closely at the unique spirit and talent that created them.

That these films are at least arguably the very best examples of their genres is perhaps the result of two facts. First, Howard Hawks was not really a studio director, a staff member employed by a single studio (like Curtiz at Warners or Fleming at MGM). He was an independent producer for much of his career, and his films were released by various studios. He was not *assigned* genre pictures; he made the films he wanted to make in the way he wanted to make them. Second, Hawks was one of the greatest storytellers—perhaps the greatest—of the entire Studio Era. Hawks's special skill was an ability to convert plays and novels into cinematic narratives that were richer, tighter, more complex, and more perceptive than the originals.

The aesthetic of omission, of implying what is not explicitly and overtly stated, is an essential feature of Hawks's narrative mastery. Beneath the generic surfaces of his narratives lie complex tensions between the characters' verbal façades and their unverbalized feelings. In both the comedies and the adventure films, Hawks characters tend not to talk about their feelings overtly—first, because words can be hollowly manipulated; second, because Hawks characters attempt to protect themselves, either with silence or with torrents of chatter, not wanting to make the costly emotional mistake of investing their trust in someone unworthy of it. Most of the great Hawks films are stories of the evolution of trust, of growing faith in another human being, and the goal of the entire narrative is to reveal to the central pair (either two men or a man and a woman) that they have good reason to invest their faith in one another.

On the surface, *Twentieth Century* is a battle of wills, a study of two egomaniacal theatre people (played by Carole Lombard and John Barrymore) who fight to the egoistic death. Beneath the battle there is love (for they would not fight if they did not love), respect for each other's abilities, each other's strength, each other's egos. And in the same way, the scientist David (Grant) in *Bringing Up Baby* can free himself from his emotional and psychological cage only by experiencing the spontaneity and unpredictability of a Susan (Katharine Hepburn)

Fig. 11-26
Going screwball in Bringing Up Baby: *Katharine Hepburn and Cary Grant singing "I Can't Give You Anything But Love" to a leopard on a rooftop in Connecticut.*

rather than by working joylessly with his more proper fiancée, Miss Swallow. Although the plot of *Bringing Up Baby* seems to be a loony chase after dinosaur bones and escaped leopards, it really is an adventure in emotional education in which David learns how to be a complete human being.

Hawks's alterations of Raymond Chandler's *The Big Sleep* clearly reveal both his psychological interests and his thematic commitments. With the aid of screenwriters William Faulkner, Leigh Brackett, and Jules Furthman, Hawks builds the surface of the film as a maze of murders and bewilderingly proliferating names (Sean Regan, Eddie Mars, Joe Brody, A. G. Geiger, Carol Lundgren, Harry Jones) designed to lead the central pair, Marlowe (Humphrey Bogart) and Vivian (Lauren Bacall), to the knowledge that they can trust each other, if only because they work well together.

Despite its apparently different cowboy surface, *Red River* is a similar narrative. Thomas Dunson (John Wayne) builds an immense cattle spread from the mating of his bull with the calf of a young boy, Matthew Garth (Montgomery Clift). After the Civil War, it becomes necessary to drive the now huge herd a thousand miles to market, from Texas to Kansas City. During the drive, Dunson's inflexibility—his refusal to change his mind or alter a decision, his strict sense of

vengeful justice—threatens the success of the entire venture. Matthew usurps Dunson's authority and proves more flexible and more popular with the men he leads. The younger, "softer" man succeeds by altering the ultimate destination, bringing the herd to the new railroad line in Abilene and establishing the Chisholm Trail.

Instead of stealing the herd, Matt sells it for a good price and holds the money in trust for Dunson. His honorable, courageous, and professionally appropriate behavior answers the essential question Hawks asks of all his characters: "Are you *good enough*?"—good enough at who you are and what you do to be trusted. Dunson too is finally satisfied with Matt and promotes him to full co-owner of the herd, saying he's "earned it."

The film ends with an affirmation of love, friendship, fraternity, paternity, and marriage, as almost every Hawks film does.

As opposed to Ford, who saw American history as the movement of pioneers, prophets, and soldiers, followed by the spread of their civilized institutions—the law, the cavalry, the church, the dance, the home—Hawks saw American history as the assertion of individual wills. It is as Protestant an ethic of individualism and professionalism as Ford's is a Catholic view of fallible mortals within earthly institutions that invoke, interpret, and administer an ideal. While Ford's films test the responsiveness of those groups and institutions, Hawks's films test the firmness and responsiveness of human wills, both their resoluteness and their recognition of limits and limitations—the point at which they require the complementarity of another.

Alfred Hitchcock

Alfred Hitchcock was not a product of the American studio system at all, but a combination of the German studio style and the British studio industry. But the British film industry has maintained a symbiotic relationship with Hollywood since the end of World War I (Hitchcock's first film job was with a British branch of Paramount), made even more dependent by the common language after the conversion to sound. Hitchcock's affinity with the American system is clear in the popularity of his British films in America and in his smooth, effortless emigration from London to Hollywood in 1939.

Hitchcock served part of his apprenticeship as an art director at Ufa. Murnau gave him tips on staging and lighting. The German influence would persist throughout Hitchcock's career—in the murky shadows and studio-controlled Expressionist lighting of his black-and-white films, in the equally controlled universe of his color films, in the paranoia that consumes his characters and spreads to the audience, in the claustrophobic decor that confines his figures, in the inexorable and implacable sense of fate from which his characters cannot escape. Perhaps more British is Hitchcock's dry irony, which allows him to chortle at this doom and gloom that he finds as funny as it is alarming.

The 39 Steps is a prototype Hitchcock film of his British period. The plot is a mad chase from London to Scotland and back again. The chase throws the crime-tracking runners into the most wildly diverse and incongruous settings: a Scottish farmhouse, a plush manor, a vaudeville theatre. The action is a mad attempt to solve the film's great riddle (the narrative pretext that appears to motivate and integrate the film's intriguing incidents—a whatsit that, in the deep regions of character and irony where the film really operates, doesn't matter—which Hitchcock called the "MacGuffin"), the meaning of the "39 steps." The solution to that riddle is buried inside the head of the vaudeville performer, Mr. Memory, who, when publicly confronted with the question in front of an audience, is torn by his commitment to his art (he prides himself in knowing all) and his commitment to his fellow conspirators.

As in so many of his films, Hitchcock delights in showing the most horrible crimes taking place in the most public places: amusement parks, concert halls, trains. And like so many Hitchcock films, *The 39 Steps* is a completely apolitical story of political intrigue. He refuses to cloud a good story with ideology. For the same reason, Hitchcock films frequently take place in the world of the rich; they are divorced from such social–realist problems as poverty and hunger. The Hitchcock actors are smooth, slick males like Cary Grant, Ray Milland, and James Stewart and cold, sleek ladies (usually blonde with strong features) like Grace Kelly, Vera Miles, and Eva Marie Saint. *The 39 Steps* uses the slick Robert Donat and the cool Madeleine Carroll.

Fig. 11-27

Fig. 11-28
Subjectivity in Hitchcock's first sound film, **Blackmail***: The fleeing woman sees an electrified cocktail shaker become the knife with which she murdered her assailant.*

The Hitchcock films are a unique blend of story, style, mood, and a deceptively complex technique. Hitchcock mixes the macabre and the funny, mystery and whimsy, suspense and sardonic laughter. While the gripping story drives relentlessly forward, Hitchcock takes time out to focus on a subtle physical detail or ironic element. The plots revolve about the wildest improbabilities: vast international conspiracies; little old ladies who are really spies; psychotic killers who impersonate their dead mothers; chases that culminate on carousels, in concert halls, in a bell tower, on the Statue of Liberty, or on Mount Rushmore. Beneath almost every Hitchcock film is the structure of the chase, the accelerating rush

Subjectivity in **Strangers On A Train:** *the maniac as a tiny black blot on the white marble monuments of American values.*

Fig. 11-29

toward a climactic solution. But Hitchcock personalizes the improbable chase by making each of the racers surprisingly familiar and vulnerable, fallibly credible. The most intricate tales hang on the most trivial details—a rare brand of herb tea, a cigarette lighter, an inquisitive cocker spaniel. Frenzied suspense and wry understatement are the ultimate Hitchcock ingredients, bizarre psychological states beneath the most banal surfaces, the essential Hitchcock theme.

Hitchcock's two greatest technical tools are his command of editing and his control of what Pudovkin called the "plastic material." Hitchcock's films are rich in tiny yet revealing plastic details, from facial tics to physical objects, from the body in clothes to embodied dreams.

Hitchcock's awareness of the power of concrete detail is such that when the detail is not exactly right in its natural state, he fixes it up to emphasize it. In *Suspicion* (1941), to hypnotize us with a glass of milk that Joan Fontaine thinks is poisoned, Hitchcock puts a tiny light inside the glass to make the milk truly glow in the darkness. In *Spellbound* (1945), he makes a revolver dominate the foreground by photographing an immense, six-times-larger-than-life model. The power of these objects in Hitchcock films reveals the origins of his style in art direction and the

dependence of his technique on "storyboarding" his shots. After tight scripting, Hitchcock planned a film by having pictures drawn of exactly the way he wanted every image to look, then set up each shot to duplicate the drawing.

In an era of functional narrative cutting, Hitchcock's editing alone tightened the screws of suspense. As Sylvia Sidney slices roast beef at the dinner table in *Sabotage* (1936), Hitchcock's cutting shows her passion building until she drives the knife into her villainous husband. The same quick cutting creates the brutality of Janet Leigh's death in *Psycho* (1960) as Hitchcock cuts from shots of the victim's face, to shots of the slashing knife, to shots of the bloodstreaked water swirling down the drain of the shower.

Hitchcock films provide perfect examples of how to cut picture and sound together. In *The 39 Steps*, the charwoman walks into a room where she sees the shadow of a corpse; her eyes widen and her mouth begins to erupt into a scream. Hitchcock immediately cuts to the shriek of a train whistle and a shot of the train racing toward Scotland. The screaming train replaces the human scream and startles us with its unnatural shrillness.

The flair of Hitchcock's breathless construction and subtly ironic sequences is matched by

Fig. 11-30

Fig. 11-31

Fig. 11-32

The 39 Steps: *the sound-and-picture montage, from cleaning woman's discovery to train's scream.*

his complete control of craft. To underscore Mr. Memory's confusion about telling the audience the truth about the 39 steps, Hitchcock shoots the man's face in tight close-up from below and on a tilt; the composition of the shot dramatizes the tension in his mind. Hitchcock points the road back to Mr. Memory all along

because Robert Donat unconsciously whistles the theme song of the man's act throughout the film. But Donat, no Mr. Memory, cannot remember where he heard the tune that keeps running through his head.

The final scene of *The 39 Steps* is a brilliant synthesis of its action, irony, comedy, and psychology. Mr. Memory lies dying on the floor in the wings of the theatre. He insists on telling the police the complicated formula he has memorized—his pride in his work is that great. Meanwhile, a line of chorines dances on stage (in the background of the frame). Meanwhile, Robert Donat puts his arm around Madeleine Carroll (in the foreground), and suddenly we discover the same dangling handcuff on his wrist that has been there for the last hour of the film, during much of which Donat and Carroll have been cuffed together involuntarily. This final detail ironically undercuts the romance of the ending, a perfect indication of the British Hitchcock style and tone as well as a vivid anticipation of the endings of such American Hitchcocks as *Rear Window* (1954) and *North by Northwest*.

When he moved from England to America in 1939 at the invitation of producer David O. Selznick, Hitchcock turned the dry drollery of his English wit to observations of the American scene with even more corrosive subtlety. One of Hitchcock's favorite subjects became the superficial placidity of American life, whose clean, bright surfaces disguised the most shocking moral, political, psychological, and sexual aberrations: the wealthy members of an American cultural elite who happen to be Nazis (*Saboteur*); the small-town Americana wholesomeness that protects a psychopathic killer (*Shadow of a Doubt*, 1943). Beneath the surface, ordinary people and normal life were always "bent" for Hitchcock. This conviction would make him one of the most insightful and irreverent directors of the 1950s, when American culture retreated behind a façade of cheerful normality.

Orson Welles

Unlike Hitchcock, Chaplin, Hawks, or Ford, whose reputations rest on a great number of impressive films, critical respect for Orson Welles rests primarily on one film, *Citizen Kane* (1941), widely considered the greatest sound film ever made. *Kane*'s greatness can be discussed on several different levels: its technical innovation, structural complexity, complicated handling of narrative point of view, controversy as a biography of a famous American, philosophical search for meaningful values, sociological study of the "American Dream," acting, literacy, individuality. Orson Welles, the young sensation of both the stage and radio, had been invited to bring his Mercury Theatre group to Hollywood in 1939 to make any film he chose. Welles was 24 when he signed with RKO. The film, *Citizen Kane*, was both his first and the last he would ever be so free to make. Like an earlier *enfant terrible* of Hollywood, Erich von Stroheim, Welles insisted on participating in every production detail: acting, directing, writing, editing, sound, design. And like von Stroheim, Welles soon saw the Hollywood lords giving his negatives to other hands for slicing and later found the gates of the lords' studios locked against him.

From its opening sequence, *Citizen Kane* is no ordinary film. It begins in quiet and darkness: a wire fence with a "No Trespassing" sign; a series of tracking shots and dissolves past a weird menagerie that brings us closer to the creepy mansion, Xanadu, and eventually into the room of a dying man (Kane, played by Welles); his Expressionistic death, with the echoing, rasping sound of the word "Rosebud" on his lips; the glass ball dropping silently through snowy space before shattering; the distorted view of the nurse, seen through the curved glass of the fallen globe as she enters the room to attend to the dead man. From moody Expressionism, the film jumps to a brilliant parody of *The March of Time*: the musical fanfare, the booming "voice-of-God" narration, the overly descriptive printed titles, the purple prose, the diagrams and maps, the lifeless newsreel photography, the tendency to reduce motion pictures to stills that merely illustrate a verbal commentary. The newsreel ends as abruptly as it began and is followed by a scene in the projection room in which the reporters discuss the newsreel's defects as a biography of Kane, a scene played entirely in shadow, drenched in smoke, backlit by shafts of light from the projection booth. The scene is as garishly shadowed as the preceding news footage was flat and thin. Three sequences, three completely different film styles.

The film's technical brilliance continues throughout. Even today it seems striking in its extreme low-angle shots (how conscious were we that Hollywood sets before *Citizen Kane* had ceilings?), its consistently extreme contrasts of dark and light, its vast shots in depth revealing interaction between foreground and background. Welles was lucky to have the cinematic eye of Gregg Toland behind his camera and the designer's eye of Perry Ferguson in front of it. Toland had perfected his craft while working

Fig. 11-33

Citizen Kane: *dominated and distorted by the fallen glass ball, the Expressionistic and richly symbolic image of Kane's death.*

Fig. 11-34

The deliberate overexposure of the peeping news camera, trying to catch a glimpse of Kane (Fig. 11-34), and the shafts and shadows of the projection sequence, lit almost totally from behind (Fig. 11-35).

Fig. 11-35

with director William Wyler at Goldwyn on such pictures as *These Three* (1936), *Dead End* (1937), *Wuthering Heights* (1939), and especially *The Little Foxes* (released a few months after *Kane* in 1941), whose climactic scene he shot in deep focus; his last great work with Wyler was *The Best Years of Our Lives* (1946). Toland had further expanded his stylistic range through his rich, dark work for Howard Hawks (*The Road to*

Glory, 1936) and John Ford (*The Grapes of Wrath* and *The Long Voyage Home*, both 1940). For his work on *Citizen Kane*, Welles awarded Toland a credit equal to his own for directing; as much as Welles pushed Toland to devise even newer ways of shooting, Toland taught cinematography—and what he had learned about filmmaking from Freund, Wyler, Hawks, and Ford—to Welles.

Fig. 11-36
The shot in depth. Jed Leland (Joseph Cotten, left) and Bernstein (Everett Sloane) speak in the foreground while Charlie Kane (Orson Welles) dances with chorus girls in the background.

If Welles was learning the arts of camerawork and editing while directing *Kane,* he was also rapidly becoming their master. His genius for the cinema is evident in the editing, and again he learned from the person he was supervising—Robert Wise, who edited *Kane* before he became a director himself, and who was pushed by Welles into creating a pace and complexity never before attained in the sound film. One striking sequence—as much a matter of good writing and choice of camera position as it is of cuts, timing, and swish-pans—reveals the widening emotional gulf between Kane and his first wife (Ruth Warrick). As the two eat breakfast together at the dining table, Welles executes a montage series of vignettes, each of which shows the two moving farther apart physically. At the end of the sequence of breakfasts, the two, who had begun sitting next to each other, talking cheerily, sit at opposite ends of the long table, not talking at all; she is reading a competing newspaper—the supreme insult to a newspaper publisher.

Although it is full of quick cutting and has a narrative structure that functions as a dialectical montage, the visual style of *Citizen Kane* is primarily a triumph of camerawork and *mise-en-scène.* Welles often shoots long takes, composed in depth, and moves the actors and the camera from one composition to another within the same shot, instead of cutting from setup to setup.

Welles's control of sound is as careful as his manipulation of image. The years in radio made him aware of sound's dramatic power, an advantage he enjoyed over those directors who graduated to sound from the silents. The overloud narration of the news digest, the echoing emptiness of Thatcher's mausoleum–library, the flat tones of the ungifted opera singer, the echoing voices in the immense rooms of Xanadu, all are examples of an ear trained in the power of the microphone and the loudspeaker to create aural space. The sound field in this movie has as much depth as the deep-focus visual field.

Citizen Kane, one of the most complexly structured pieces of film narrative in cinema history, resembles an immense jigsaw puzzle (like the puzzles Susan, Kane's second wife, assembles in Kane's castle). Welles and screenwriter Herman J. Mankiewicz lead the audience through a seemingly chaotic collection of events and personal fragments until all the pieces of the puzzle are fitted together—the last piece being the identity of "Rosebud." Different pieces of Kane's story are supplied by the important people in his life. Thatcher, Kane's financial guardian, gives a cold accounting of Kane's childhood and fiscal irresponsibility in his memoirs. Bernstein, Kane's business associate, continues the narrative with admiration and affection. Jed Leland, Kane's embittered old college friend, speaks cynically about Kane's first marriage and his efforts to make

Fig. 11-37
Welles's "dissolve-montage." As Leland tells his story in the foreground, the events dissolve into the frame in the background—a technique borrowed from the stage.

Fig. 11-38   Fig. 11-39

The final views of Kane. Fig. 11-38: as a tiny dark figure, dwarfed by exotic arches. Fig. 11-39: as a mystery—holding the glass ball and walking between mirrors, his reflection multiplied to infinity.

Susan Alexander an opera star. Susan tells what it was like to be Kane's second wife. Even Kane's unctuous butler, Raymond, has a few parting shots to add. The whole film is framed by the movement of an objective camera that reveals what none of the characters sees or hears.

The film's key moral question is, What happened to Charles Foster Kane? What, if anything, went wrong? What destroyed his youthful hopes and excitement? The answer is a dark, sickly spot at the heart of Kane's values and, by implication, at the heart of the values of American life. The three abstract themes that constantly flow through *Citizen Kane* are wealth, power, and love. The questions that the film raises are whether the first two exclude the third and whether a life that excludes the third is worth living at all. Kane obviously has wealth; his wealth bought him newspapers, and his newspapers brought him power. But Kane thinks that money and power can buy him the affection of human beings. Kane is a man of quantities. He collects things in quantity: newspapers, *objets d'art*, "junk." When he runs for governor, he attempts to collect the people's hearts in the same way that he collects statues and paintings. The word "love" echoes through his whole political campaign. But hearts cannot be bought and stored like statues.

Failing to earn the people's love, Kane decides to demonstrate his power by making them love his creation, the opera singer Susan Alexander. But Kane fails to collect the people's hearts with

his creation much as he failed to get their votes. And so instead of collecting the hearts of the people *en masse*, Kane decides to collect a single human heart—Susan's. He becomes her absolute tyrant; he builds her a huge house, a private universe, where he is sole master of a single human destiny. The house becomes Susan's prison, and she merely one more piece of stuff that Kane has collected. Susan rebels; she leaves. Kane has not succeeded in collecting a single heart. The most appropriate epitaph at his death is the silent cellar full of crated marble and stone, the dead objects he has ravished with his checkbook from the museums, cathedrals, and chateaux of Europe.

Rosebud, the sled, is also an object. But it is an object of Kane's youth, an object that he did not buy, something he loved—and lost, given to him by parents he loved and lost. He kept Rosebud (from his mother's estate) because, like his mother's old woodstove, it had great sentimental value. And so Rosebud, in Kane's mind anyway, represented the opposite of everything his life had become, youth rather than corrupt maturity, genuine human emotion (with his mother particularly) rather than cash substitutes.

Like the hero of Marlovian tragedy, a Dr. Faustus or Tamburlaine, Kane is an immense human being with immense social power. Like Marlowe's Faustus or Shakespeare's Macbeth (a favorite Welles role), Kane is an overreacher, a man who dares the cosmos by seeking to accomplish more than a mortal can. The very virtues of such a figure—his energy, will, ambition—lead directly to his tragic flaw, as virtues do in classical tragedy. Finally, as in the classical tragedy, there is something inevitable about Kane's fate; elements inherent in the man's character and in the human condition itself conspire to produce the tragic result.

Citizen Kane was both shocking and confusing to its audiences in 1941. Instead of Hollywood's flat gloss, the film was sombre and grotesque. The action sprawled over more than 60 years, requiring its performers to make tremendous transitions in acting and appearance. There were no last-minute changes of heart, no romantic reconciliations. *Citizen Kane* followed its tragic premises to their logical, gloomy end. Even more disturbing for Hollywood was the enmity the film produced in the press, particu-

larly in the Hearst chain. William Randolph Hearst saw obvious and infuriating parallels between himself and Charles Foster Kane; between Susan Alexander and his own artistic protégée, Marion Davies; and between Kane's Florida castle, Xanadu, and his own California castle, San Simeon, where screenwriter Mankiewicz had been a regular guest. The pressures of the Hearst press—refusing advertisements for the film, pressuring theatres that showed it with threats not to print any future ads or notices—and the film's unspectacular showing at the box office led RKO to deny Welles total artistic control over his next project, an adaptation of Booth Tarkington's *The Magnificent Ambersons*. From then on, his life and career became a struggle to make films and have them released intact— which they virtually never were.

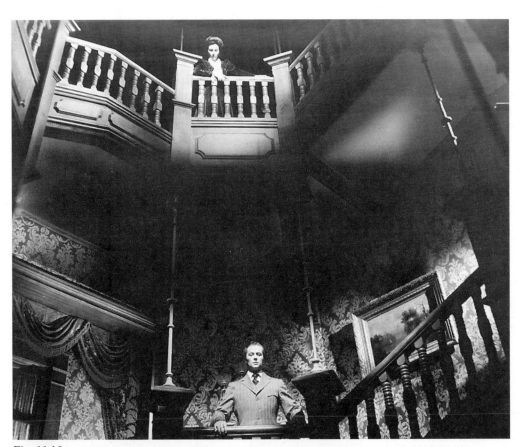

Fig. 11-40
The Magnificent Ambersons: *Agnes Moorehead and Tim Holt on the grand staircase.*

The Magnificent Ambersons (1942) might have been as great as *Kane* if Welles had not left the country—after he and Robert Wise, who also edited *Ambersons*, had assembled a rough cut—to shoot the ill-fated documentary *It's All True* (uncompleted; a 1993 documentary on the making of *It's All True* includes much of the footage). With the help of the cutting instructions Welles cabled from South America, Wise presented RKO with a lengthy masterpiece that flopped with preview audiences. Some new scenes were shot and old ones rearranged, disastrously wrapping up the film's last hour in a few rushed minutes. Like *Greed*, the complete *Ambersons* has proved impossible to restore, but what remains is extraordinary.

Its story of a vain, selfish brat (Tim Holt as George Amberson Minafer) who finally gets his "come-uppance" and sees the world more clearly once he has been brought down a peg allowed Welles to tell the larger, more nostalgic story of the old ways—incarnated in the rich, graceful, high-society Amberson family—that perished with the coming of the automobile. It was a movie designed for the moving camera (manned by Stanley Cortez, whom Welles taught much of what Gregg Toland had taught him); the great staircase in the Amberson mansion was built to facilitate the phenomenally varied use of a crane. As in *Kane*, scene elements moved fluidly from one to the other through changes of camera angle and composition, not with the previously obligatory cuts. Figures moved in and out of shadow, as if into their own ominous or unknown depths, as the camera kept pace with the action or stopped for an intense slow look. The superb cast included Dolores Costello, Joseph Cotten, and—in the performance of a lifetime—Agnes Moorehead.

Even without a Hearst seeking its destruction, the abridged version of *The Magnificent Ambersons* opened to dismal business. RKO relieved Welles of his duties on his next film, *Journey Into Fear* (1942), in the middle of production.

Later Welles films—*The Stranger* (1946), *The Lady from Shanghai* (1946, released 1948), *Macbeth* (1948), *Othello* (1952), *Mr. Arkadin* (1955), *Touch of Evil* (1958, restored 1998), *The Trial* (1962), and *Chimes at Midnight* (1966, also known as *Falstaff*)—are, like *Citizen Kane*, obsessed with the themes of the corrupting influence of power and money, with treachery and desire, with guesswork in a labyrinth, with egotism and gamesmanship, with the dark side of greatness and the limits of ambition and friendship. These later films also reveal Welles's unmistakable visual style, regardless of their budgets or their cinematographers: baroque, backlit contrasts of dark and light; claustrophobic interiors whose ceilings squash their occupants; a seem-

The Lady from Shanghai:
Orson Welles and Rita
Hayworth prove that love
has many angles.

Fig. 11-41

ingly infinite depth of field, often surveyed from a very low angle; and magnificently planned, complexly choreographed tracking shots.

The opening shot of *Touch of Evil* is one of the greatest and most complicated crane shots in cinema history. But the studio ran the opening credits over it and re-edited the rest of the film. Welles's editing remained as inventive as his camerawork. The climactic shootout in *The Lady from Shanghai*, as Everett Sloane and Rita Hayworth shoot repeatedly at each other's reflections in a house of mirrors, is one of the most memorable metaphors of cinematic death, translated into the shattering crash of glass and the annihilation of images.

Until his death in 1985, Welles was forced to contend with inadequate budgets and production schedules. He acted to make money to make films. Like Griffith and Gance and von Stroheim before him, he was a great artist rejected by the industry. Like Kane, he left many things unfinished. But even when the script, the budget, the producers, or the studios let him down, a Welles film never looked or sounded like anything other than a Welles film.

For Further Viewing

FILMS

DOROTHY ARZNER (1900–79)
Working Girls (1931)
Christopher Strong (1933)
Nana (1934)
Craig's Wife (1936)
Dance, Girl, Dance (1940)

TOD BROWNING (1882–1962)
The Unholy Three (1925)
Dracula (1931)
Freaks (1932)

FRANK CAPRA (1897–1991)
It Happened One Night (1934)
Mr. Deeds Goes to Town (1936)
Lost Horizon (1937)
Mr. Smith Goes to Washington (1939)
Meet John Doe (1941)
Why We Fight Series (1942–45)
Arsenic and Old Lace (1944).
    Completed 1941
It's A Wonderful Life (1946)

GEORGE CUKOR (1899–1983)
Dinner at Eight (1933)
David Copperfield (1935)
Camille (1937). Completed 1936
The Women (1939)
The Philadelphia Story (1940)
Gaslight (1944)
Adam's Rib (1949)
Born Yesterday (1950)
A Star Is Born (1954)
My Fair Lady (1964)

MICHAEL CURTIZ (1888–1962)
Mystery of the Wax Museum (1933)
Black Fury (1935)
Captain Blood (1935)
The Walking Dead (1936)
The Charge of the Light Brigade (1936)
The Adventures of Robin Hood (1938). Co-director, William Keighley
The Sea Hawk (1940)
Yankee Doodle Dandy (1942)
Casablanca (1942)
Mildred Pierce (1945)

WILLIAM DIETERLE (1893–1972)
A Midsummer Night's Dream (1935). Co-director, Max Reinhardt
The Story of Louis Pasteur (1936)
The Life of Emile Zola (1937)
The Hunchback of Notre Dame (1939)
Love Letters (1945)

W. C. FIELDS (1879–1946)
Shorts: *The Barber Shop, The Fatal Glass of Beer,* and *The Pharmacist* (all 1933)
Million Dollar Legs (1932)
Tillie and Gus (1933)
My Little Chickadee (1940)
The Bank Dick (1940)
Never Give a Sucker an Even Break (1941)

VICTOR FLEMING (1883–1949)
Lord Jim (1925)
The Virginian (1929)
Red Dust (1932)
Treasure Island (1934)
Captains Courageous (1937)
The Wizard of Oz (1939)
Gone With the Wind (1939)
Dr. Jekyll and Mr. Hyde (1941)

JOHN FORD (1895–1973)
The Iron Horse (1924)
The Lost Patrol (1934)
The Informer (1935)
The Plough and the Stars (1937). Completed 1936
Stagecoach (1939)
Young Mr. Lincoln (1939)
The Grapes of Wrath (1940)
My Darling Clementine (1946)
The Fugitive (1947)
Fort Apache (1948)
She Wore A Yellow Ribbon (1949)
The Quiet Man (1952)
The Searchers (1956)
The Man Who Shot Liberty Valance (1962)
Cheyenne Autumn (1964)

GRETA GARBO (1905–90)
The Story of Gösta Berling (1924)
The Joyless Street (1925)
Grand Hotel (1932)
Queen Christina (1933)
Anna Karenina (1935)
Ninotchka (1939)

HOWARD HAWKS (1896–1977)
The Dawn Patrol (1930)
Scarface (1932). Uncensored version
    completed 1930
Twentieth Century (1934)
Bringing Up Baby (1938)
"—only Angels have wings" or *Only Angels
    Have Wings* (1939)
His Girl Friday (1940)
Air Force (1943)
To Have and Have Not (1944)
The Big Sleep (1946). Shot 1944, revised 1945–46
Red River (1948)
Monkey Business (1952)
Gentlemen Prefer Blondes (1953)
Rio Bravo (1959)
Rio Lobo (1970)

ALFRED HITCHCOCK (1899–1980)
The Lodger (1926)
Blackmail (1929)
The Man Who Knew Too Much (1934)
The 39 Steps (1935)
Sabotage (1936)
Rebecca (1940)

Foreign Correspondent (1940)
Suspicion (1941)
Shadow of a Doubt (1943)
Lifeboat (1944)
Spellbound (1945)
Notorious (1946)
Rope (1948)
Strangers On A Train (1951)
Dial M for Murder (1954). 3-D, but released flat
Rear Window (1954)
To Catch a Thief (1955)
The Man Who Knew Too Much (1956)
Vertigo (1958)
North by Northwest (1959)
Psycho (1960)
The Birds (1963)
TV series: *Alfred Hitchcock Presents* (1955–62),
    The Alfred Hitchcock Hour (1962–65)

FRITZ LANG (1890–1976)
Fury (1936)
You Only Live Once (1937)
Scarlet Street (1945)
The Big Heat (1953)

VAL LEWTON (1904–51)
Cat People (1942, Jacques Tourneur)
I Walked with a Zombie (1943, Jacques Tourneur)
The Seventh Victim (1943, Mark Robson)
The Curse of the Cat People (1944, Robert Wise
    and Gunther Von Fritsch)
Isle Of The Dead (1945, Mark Robson)
The Body Snatcher (1945, Robert Wise)

**THE MARX BROTHERS (CHICO, 1886–1961;
    HARPO, 1888–1964; GROUCHO, 1890–1977;
    ZEPPO, 1901–79)**
The Cocoanuts (1929, Joseph Santley and Robert
    Florey)
Animal Crackers (1930, Victor Heerman)
Monkey Business (1931, Norman Z. McLeod)
Horse Feathers (1932, Norman Z. McLeod)
Duck Soup (1933, Leo McCarey)
A Night at the Opera (1935, Sam Wood)
A Day at the Races (1937, Sam Wood)

LEO MCCAREY (1898–1969)
Duck Soup (1933)
Ruggles of Red Gap (1935)
Make Way For Tomorrow (1937)
The Awful Truth (1937)
An Affair to Remember (1957)

LEWIS MILESTONE (1895–1980)
All Quiet on the Western Front (1930)
The Front Page (1931)
Rain (1932)
Of Mice and Men (1939)
A Walk in the Sun (1945)
The Strange Love of Martha Ivers (1946)

JOSEF VON STERNBERG (1894–1969)
The Docks of New York (1928)
The Blue Angel (1930)
Morocco (1930)
An American Tragedy (1931)
Shanghai Express (1932)
Blonde Venus (1932)
The Scarlet Empress (1934)
The Devil Is a Woman (1935)

PRESTON STURGES (1898–1959)
The Great McGinty (1940)
The Lady Eve (1941)
Sullivan's Travels (1941)
The Palm Beach Story (1942)
The Miracle of Morgan's Creek (1944).
   Completed 1943
Hail the Conquering Hero (1944)
Unfaithfully Yours (1948)

RAOUL WALSH (1887–1981)
What Price Glory (1926)
The Big Trail (1930). Wide screen
The Roaring Twenties (1939)
They Drive by Night (1940)
High Sierra (1941). Completed 1940
White Heat (1949)

ORSON WELLES (1915–85)
Citizen Kane (1941)
The Magnificent Ambersons (1942)
The Stranger (1946)
The Lady from Shanghai (1948). Completed 1946
Macbeth (1948)
Othello (1952)
Touch of Evil (1958). Reconstructed 1998
The Trial (1962)
Chimes at Midnight or *Falstaff* (1966)

WILLIAM A. WELLMAN (1896–1975)
Wings (1927)
The Public Enemy (1931)
Wild Boys of the Road (1933)

A Star Is Born (1937)
Nothing Sacred (1937)
The Ox-Bow Incident (1943)
Ernie Pyle's Story of G.I. Joe or *The Story of G.I. Joe* (1945)

MAE WEST (1892–1980)
She Done Him Wrong (1933)
I'm No Angel (1933)
Klondike Annie (1936)
My Little Chickadee (1940)

JAMES WHALE (1889–1957)
Frankenstein (1931)
The Old Dark House (1932)
The Invisible Man (1933)
Bride of Frankenstein (1935)
Show Boat (1936)

WILLIAM WYLER (1902–81)
Dodsworth (1936)
Dead End (1937)
Jezebel (1938)
Wuthering Heights (1939)
The Little Foxes (1941)
Mrs. Miniver (1942)
The Memphis Belle (1944)
The Best Years of Our Lives (1946)
Roman Holiday (1953)
Ben-Hur (1959)
The Collector (1965)

THE WARNER BROS. BUSBY BERKELEY (1895–1976) CYCLE
42nd Street (1933, Lloyd Bacon/Busby Berkeley)
Gold Diggers of 1933 (1933, Mervyn LeRoy/
   Busby Berkeley)
Footlight Parade (1933, Lloyd Bacon/Busby
   Berkeley)
Gold Diggers of 1935 (1935, Busby Berkeley)

THE RKO FRED ASTAIRE (1899–1987) / GINGER ROGERS (1911–95) CYCLE
Flying Down to Rio (1933, Thornton Freeland)
The Gay Divorcée (1934, Mark Sandrich)
Roberta (1935, William A. Seiter)
Top Hat (1935, Mark Sandrich)
Swing Time (1936, George Stevens)
Shall We Dance? (1937, Mark Sandrich)
The Story of Vernon and Irene Castle (1939,
   H. C. Potter)

Studio Era Miscellany

Little Caesar (1930, Mervyn LeRoy)

Grand Hotel (1932, Edmund Goulding)

I Am a Fugitive From a Chain Gang (1932, Mervyn LeRoy)

The Mummy (1932, Karl Freund)

Island of Lost Souls (1933, Erle C. Kenton). Completed 1932

King Kong (1933, Merian C. Cooper and Ernest B. Schoedsack)

The Black Cat (1934, Edgar G. Ulmer)

Manhattan Melodrama and *The Thin Man* (1934, W. S. Van Dyke)

Tarzan and his Mate (1934, Cedric Gibbons)

"G" Men (1935, William Keighley)

Mad Love (1935, Karl Freund)

Mutiny on the Bounty (1935, Frank Lloyd)

Flash Gordon (1936 serial, Frederick Stephani)

The Petrified Forest (1936, Archie Mayo)

Easy Living (1937, Mitchell Leisen)

The Good Earth (1937, Sidney Franklin)

Destry Rides Again (1939, George Marshall)

Gunga Din (1939, George Stevens)

Dark Victory (1940, Edmund Goulding)

Now, Voyager (1940, Irving Rapper)

Hellzapoppin' (1941, H. C. Potter)

The Wolf Man (1941, George Waggner)

The Pride of the Yankees (1942, Sam Wood)

Double Indemnity (1944, Billy Wilder)

Murder, My Sweet (1945, Edward Dmytryk)

The House on 92nd Street (1945, Henry Hathaway)

Detour (1945, Edgar G. Ulmer)

DVDs

Adam's Rib is in *Tracy & Hepburn* (see below).

The Big Sleep (1946, **Howard Hawks**). Warner Studios. Includes the 1944 pre-release version and the 1946 release version, with a documentary on their differences.

The Blue Angel is listed in Chap. 7.

Citizen Kane (1941, **Orson Welles**). Warner Home Video. Includes commentaries by critic Roger Ebert and Welles biographer Peter Bogdanovich, premiere newsreel, studio correspondence, storyboards, and a documentary.

Dr. Jekyll and Mr. Hyde (1932, **Rouben Mamoulian**, starring Fredric March). Warner Home Video. Also includes the 1941 version, directed by **Victor Fleming** and starring Spencer Tracy.

W. C. Fields: *Six Short Films* (1915 and 1930–33). Criterion Collection. Good prints—from original materials, some **restored**—of *Pool Sharks* (silent), *The Barber Shop, The Fatal Glass of Beer, The Pharmacist, The Golf Specialist*, and *The Dentist*.

42nd Street (1933, **Lloyd Bacon**). Warner Home Video. Includes 3 shorts and information on **Busby Berkeley**.

Freaks (1932, **Tod Browning**). Warner Home Video. Includes a documentary, a commentary by horror scholar David J. Skal, the reissue prologue, and 3 alternate endings.

Gone With the Wind (1939, **Victor Fleming**). Warner Home Video. Four-Disc Collector's Edition. The best **digital restoration** of this film yet, with hours of documentaries, newsreels, restoration information, and more.

It Happened One Night (1934, **Frank Capra**). Columbia TriStar. Commentary by Frank Capra, Jr.

The Lady Eve (1941, **Preston Sturges**). Criterion Collection. Commentary by film historian Marian Keane, introduction by Peter Bogdanovich, and the 1942 radio adaptation.

The Man Who Shot Liberty Valance (1962, **John Ford**). Paramount Home Video. Properly letterboxed (rare for this title).

*The **Marx Brothers** Collection*. Warner Home Video. Includes *A Night at the Opera, A Day at the Races, Room Service, At the Circus, Go West, The Big Store*, and *A Night in Casablanca*, with documentaries, shorts including **Robert Benchley** in *How to Sleep*, cartoons, and more.

*The **Marx Brothers** Silver Screen Collection*. Universal. Includes *The Cocoanuts, Animal Crackers, Monkey Business, Horse Feathers, Duck Soup*, and some extras.

The Mummy: The Legacy Collection (1932–44). Universal. Includes *The Mummy* (1932, **Karl Freund**) with commentary by film historian Paul Jensen, a documentary by horror scholar David J. Skal, and the Kharis sequels: *The Mummy's Hand, Tomb, Ghost*, and *Curse* (1940–44); the only extras for the sequels are their trailers. Other Legacy sets for *Dracula, Frankenstein*, and *The Wolf Man* include the originals and all their pre-Abbott-and-Costello sequels (though some sequels show up in surprising sets), with good extras and silly ones. Unfortunately, some of the films in these sets are not as sharp as the others (they were compressed at different **bit rates**; see Chap. 18). The *Dracula* set includes the **U.S. and Spanish versions**.

Notorious (1946, **Alfred Hitchcock**). Criterion Collection. Commentaries by film historians Rudy Behlmer and Marian Keane.

Rear Window (1954, **Alfred Hitchcock**). Universal. Collector's Edition. **Restored**, with a documentary on the production and restoration. The screenplay is in the DVD-ROM section.

The Scarlet Empress (1932, **Josef von Sternberg**). Criterion Collection. Includes a BBC documentary and essays by filmmaker **Jack Smith** and film critic Robin Wood.

Sullivan's Travels (1941, **Preston Sturges**). Criterion Collection. Includes 4 commentaries, interviews, a documentary, and Sturges singing a song and reciting a poem.

The 39 Steps (1935, **Alfred Hitchcock**). Criterion Collection. **Digitally restored**, with a documentary on Hitchcock's British period, the 1937 Lux Radio Theatre version, production design sketches, and a commentary by film historian Marian Keane.

Touch of Evil (1958, **Orson Welles**). Universal. The 1998 **restored** version, with Welles's memo regarding the editing of the picture.

Tracy & Hepburn: *The Signature Collection*. Warner Home Video. Includes *Adam's Rib* (1949, **George Cukor**), *Pat and Mike* (1952, **Cukor**), *Woman of the Year* (1942, **George Stevens**), and *The Spencer Tracy Legacy*.

Trouble in Paradise (1932, **Ernst Lubitsch**). Criterion Collection. Includes a Lubitsch 1917 short, *The Merry Jail*; a commentary by Lubitsch biographer Scott Eyman; and a 1940 radio show with Lubitsch, Jack Benny, Claudette Colbert, and Basil Rathbone.

Vertigo (1958, **Alfred Hitchcock**). Universal. Collector's Edition. **Restored**, with commentary by the restorers, Robert A. Harris and James C. Katz. Includes a documentary on the production and restoration**.**

White Heat (1949, **Raoul Walsh**). Warner Home Video. Part of Warner's Gangster series.

The Wizard of Oz Gift Set (1939, **Victor Fleming**). Warner Studios. Includes a printed reproduction of the script, printed posters and stills, outtakes, documentaries, excerpts from previous versions, radio broadcasts, recording sessions, and more.

12

Hollywood in Transition: 1946–65

In 1946 the American film business grossed $1.7 billion domestically, the peak box-office year in the 50-year history of the American film industry. Twelve years later, in 1958, domestic box-office receipts fell below a billion dollars; by 1962 domestic receipts had fallen to $900 million, slightly more than half the 1946 gross. And inflated ticket prices hid an even more devastating statistic: By 1953, weekly attendance at film theatres had fallen to about 25 percent of the 1948 figure. While box-office income steadily fell, production costs—unionized labor, new equipment, costly materials—steadily rose along with the nation's soaring, inflated economy. The two vectors of rising costs and falling revenues seemed to point directly toward the cemetery for both Hollywood and the commercial American film.

Yet in 1968, American box offices collected $1.3 billion (domestic box-office receipts having risen every year since 1963). In 1974, American theatres grossed almost $2 billion, and in 1983, over $3 billion. In 1989, domestic box-office grosses exceeded $5 billion for the first time. In 2000, they reached a new high of $7.7 billion, representing 1.42 billion tickets to studio movies that each cost, on the average, $54.8 million to produce. (In 1960, *Psycho* was produced for under $1 million, and only the makers of *Spartacus* could figure out how to spend more than $11 million.) Even if films are still attended by a much smaller percentage of Americans than went to the movies in 1946, and tickets cost about 20 times more than they did in 1946, the figures indicate that the American film industry emerged from a difficult transitional period and

solidified itself commercially by redefining its product and its audience. Between 1948 and 1963 lay 15 years of groping.

Enemies Within: Freedom of Association and Free Entertainment

Even before World War II, the two forces that would crush the old Hollywood had begun their assault. First, U.S. courts had begun to rule that the film industry's methods of distributing motion pictures represented an illegal restraint of open trade. Block booking was unfair to the individual competitive exhibitors, requiring them to book many pictures they did not want in order to get the few they did. Over the course of the 1920s and 1930s, the general tendency of American judicial and legislative pressure was to reduce the number of films the independent exhibitor could be forced to buy as a block. The studio-owned chains of theatres gave even greater monopolistic control of the market to the "Majors," the five biggest Hollywood production companies—MGM, Paramount, Warner Bros., 20th Century–Fox, and RKO—who could use their commercial and artistic power to control the industry's profits and practices. The industry knew that the day would come when the line that tied theatre to studio would have to be cut. The war postponed that day.

Second, by the mid-1930s a new electronic toy that combined picture and sound—television—had been demonstrated by its scientist creators. At first Hollywood laughed at the visually inferior upstart whose programs—like those of its parent, radio—were both live and free; by the late 1940s, Hollywood had begun to fight. In 1949, there were only a million television receivers in America. By 1952, there were 10 million; by the end of the decade, 50 million, and Hollywood had surrendered.

The world war helped postpone the domestic battle because fighting America needed movies to take its mind off the war. America also needed films for education: to train the soldiers to do their jobs, to teach them "why we fight."

While Hollywood did its part, its profits conveniently rose. The government added special war taxes to theatre tickets and sold bonds in the lobby; Americans who went to the movies not only enjoyed themselves, but also contributed to the war effort (see Fig. 11-7). Many Hollywood writers, directors, and producers took new pride in the educational and documentary projects. Frank Capra's *Why We Fight* series (1942–45), Ford's *The Battle of Midway* (1942), Ford and Toland's *December 7th* (1943), Wyler's *The Memphis Belle* (1944), Huston's *The Battle of San Pietro* (1945) and *Let There Be Light* (1946, released 1981), and Disney's *Victory Through Air Power* (1943) were among the most powerful wartime documentaries.

Even fictional feature films of wartime battles—Delmer Daves's *Destination Tokyo* (1943), Tay Garnett's *Bataan* (1943), Howard Hawks's *Air Force* (1943), Lewis Milestone's *A Walk in the Sun* (1945), William Wellman's *The Story of G.I. Joe* (1945)—borrowed the visual styles of documentary authenticity.

The government's Office of War Information established a Bureau of Motion Picture Affairs, while Hollywood responded with its War Activities Committee. After the war, the relationship between the industry and the government would not be so cozy.

The Supreme Court's 1948 decision in *U.S. v. Paramount Pictures, Inc.* was the ultimate in a lengthy series of court rulings that the studios must sell ("divest" themselves of) their theatres. The guaranteed outlet for the studio's product—good, bad, or mediocre—was closed. Each film would have to be good enough to sell itself. Meanwhile, more and more Americans bought television sets. The movies declared war on the box. Until 1956 (1954 for RKO), no Hollywood film could be shown on television; no working film star could appear on a television program.

So Americans stayed home to watch British and public-domain movies, their favorite radio stars made visible, and the new stars that television itself developed.

The Hollywood Ten and the Blacklist

These specific legal and commercial woes were accompanied by a general shift of American mood in the years following the war that also contributed to the ills of a troubled industry. The Cold War years of suspicion—dislike of foreign entanglements in general and the increasing fear of the "Red Menace" in particular—also produced a distrust of certain institutions within the United States. Because the film industry was so active in the war effort against the Nazis, because so many Hollywood producers and screenwriters were Jewish, because so many Jewish intellectuals seemed sympathetic to liberal political positions, and because the most extreme right-wing American opinion saw the entire war as a sacrifice of American lives to save the Jews in Europe and help the Soviets defend the Eastern front, it was not surprising that these rivers of reaction coalesced into an attack on the motion-picture industry as a whole. Whereas for four decades American suspicion had concentrated on Hollywood's sexual and moral excesses, in the decade following the war distrust shifted to Hollywood's political and social positions: to the subversive, pro-Communist propaganda allegedly woven—mainly by the writers—into Hollywood's entertainment films.

The first set of hearings of the House Un-American Activities Committee (or HUAC) in the fall of 1947, investigating Communist infiltration of the motion-picture industry, produced the highly publicized national scandal of the "Hollywood Ten." Asked "Are you now or have you ever been" a Communist, the Ten—screenwriters Alvah Bessie, Lester Cole, Ring Lardner, Jr., John Howard Lawson, Albert Maltz, Samuel Ornitz, and Dalton Trumbo; director Edward Dmytryk; writer–producer Adrian Scott; and director–producer Herbert J. Biberman—accused the Committee of violating the Bill of Rights by its existence. When the Ten were cited for contempt of Congress, the motion-picture industry reacted fearfully by instituting a blacklist—no known or suspected Communist or Communist sympathizer would be permitted to work in any capacity

Fig. 12-1
The Hollywood Ten: a 1950 demonstration.

on a Hollywood film. Convicted, their appeals denied, the Ten began to serve one-year sentences in 1950. (When he got out, director Dmytryk named names and went back to work.)

The second set of congressional hearings (1951–52) gave witnesses two choices. If they admitted a previous membership in the Communist Party, they were obligated to name everyone else with whom they had been associated at that time or suffer a contempt of Congress sentence as had the Hollywood Ten. The other choice was to avoid answering any questions whatever on the basis of the Constitution's Fifth Amendment guarantee against self-incrimination. Although "taking the Fifth" kept the witness out of prison, it also kept the witness out of work—thanks to the industry's blacklist.

A number of the blacklisted writers found work under pseudonyms. Many left Hollywood, and some left the country. In 1953, an independent film called *Salt of the Earth* was shot in New Mexico by three blacklistees: writer Michael Wilson, director Herbert Biberman, and producer Paul Jarrico. Wilson's script, the true story of a mining strike that lasted more than a year, was critiqued by and rewritten to the satisfaction of the hundreds of people who had participated in the strike, many of whom played themselves in the movie. *Salt of the Earth* rigor-

ously and dramatically analyzes a problem common to many political movements: that as the boss or tyrant treats the worker, so the male revolutionary often treats the female revolutionary. In this film the miners learn to stop treating their wives as underlings, and the newly unified community wins its battles. Completed despite concerted attacks, *Salt of the Earth* had practically no distribution in America, though it won awards and acclaim in both Western and Eastern Europe as well as the People's Republic of China. It was to become a cult film on American campuses during the 1960s and 1970s and is widely regarded now as a classic.

The result of the congressional hearings—and the controversial blacklist, the damaging publicity in the press, the threats of boycott against Hollywood films by the American Legion, the lists of suspected Communists or Communist sympathizers in publications such as *Red Channels*—was an even greater weakening of the industry's crumbling commercial and social strength.

By the late 1950s, the star system and the studio system were as good as dead. A minor studio like Columbia, with very few stars under contract, a small lot, and no theatres, stayed healthier in those years of thinner profits. The big movie houses suffered with the big studios. On a weeknight, only a few hundred patrons scattered themselves about a house built for thousands.

One by one the ornate palaces came down, to be replaced by supermarkets, shopping centers, and apartment buildings.

3-D, CinemaScope, Color, and the Tube

Television was not the sole cause of the film industry's commercial decay. The American demographic shift from the cities to the suburbs began just after the war. Movie theatres had always been concentrated in the city centers, and the multiplex cinemas of suburban shopping malls were two decades away. There were also many new ways to spend leisure time and the leisure dollar, including sports, travel, and music.

By 1952, Hollywood knew that television could not be throttled. If films and TV were to coexist, the movies would have to give the public what TV did not. The most obvious difference between movies and TV was the size of the screen.

Television's visual thinking was necessarily in inches, whereas movies could compose in feet and yards. Films also enjoyed the advantage of over 50 years of technological research in color, properties of lenses, and special laboratory effects; the infant television art had not yet developed color or videotape. Hollywood's two primary weapons against television were to be size and technical gimmickry.

One of the industry's first sallies was 3-D, a three-dimensional, stereoscopic effect produced by shooting the action with two lenses simultaneously at a specified distance apart. Two interlocked projectors then threw the two perspectives on a single screen simultaneously; the audience used cardboard or plastic glasses (with red and blue lenses for black-and-white films, polarized clear lenses for color films) to read the two overlapping, flat images as a single three-dimensional one.

Fig. 12-2
Hollywood executives watch 3-D dailies in 1952.

Despite the familiarity of the stereoscopic principle, to see it in a full-length, active feature film was a great novelty. The first 3-D feature was Harry K. Fairall's *The Power of Love* (U.S., 1922); Russia released its first 3-D film, *Day Off in Moscow*, in 1940. Hollywood rushed into 3-D production in 1952 with Arch Oboler's *Bwana Devil*, which was followed by pictures like *House of Wax*, *It Came From Outer Space*, *Fort Ti*, *Kiss Me Kate*, and *I, the Jury* (all 1953); *Creature from the Black Lagoon*, *The French Line*, and *Gog* (all 1954); and finally, *Revenge of the Creature* (1955). Audiences eagerly left their TV sets to experience the gimmick that attacked them with knives, arrows, avalanches, stampedes, vats of chemicals, Ann Miller's tap shoes, and Jane Russell's bust; the thrill of 3-D was that the formerly confined, flat picture convincingly threatened to leap, fly, or flow out of its frame at the audience.

Some blame the death of 3-D on the headache-inducing glasses that it required, but the more obvious cause of death was that any pure novelty becomes boring when it is no longer novel. 3-D was pure novelty; the thrill of being run over by a train is visually identical to that of being run over by a herd of cattle. Further, because 3-D required the theatre owner to make costly additions and renovations (in order to perform changeovers, mere startup costs included four projectors—two for each reel), the exhibitors declared a war of neglect against the process and hastened its demise. Business for 3-D films fell off so quickly that Hitchcock, who had shot *Dial M for Murder* (1954) in the new process—taking full advantage of the opportunity to compose in depth—released it in the conventional two dimensions.

A second movie novelty also promised thrills. Cinerama, unlike 3-D, brought the audience into the picture, not the picture into the audience. Cinerama originally used three interlocked cameras and four interlocked projectors (one for stereophonic sound). The final prints were projected not on top of one another (superimposed, as in 3-D), but side by side—with barely visible vertical lines where the images met. The result was an immense wraparound image that was really three images. The wide, high, deeply curved screen and the relative positions of the three cameras worked on the eye's peripheral vision to make the mind believe that the body was actually in motion. The difference between a ride in an

automobile and a conventionally filmed ride is that in an automobile the world also moves past on the sides, not just straight ahead. Cinerama's huge triple screen duplicated this impression of peripheral movement.

Like 3-D, the idea was not new. In 1927, Abel Gance had incorporated triple-screen effects, both panoramic and triptych, into his *Napoléon*. In 1938, Fred Waller, Cinerama's inventor, began research on the process. But when *This Is Cinerama* opened in 1952, audiences choked—quite literally—with a film novelty that sent them racing down a roller coaster track and soaring over the Rocky Mountains. A magnificent six-track (in later Cinerama films, seven-track) stereophonic sound system accompanied the thrilling pictures; sounds could travel from left to right across the screen or jump from behind the screen to behind the audience's heads.

Cinerama remained commercially viable longer than 3-D because it was more carefully marketed. Because of the complex projection machinery, only a few theatres in major cities were equipped for the process. Seeing Cinerama became a special, exciting event; the film was sold as a "roadshow" attraction with reserved seats, noncontinuous performances, and high prices. Customers returned to Cinerama because they could see a Cinerama film so infrequently. (The second, *Cinerama Holiday*, came out three years after *This Is Cinerama*.) And although Cinerama repeatedly offered its predictable post-card scenery and its obligatory rides and chases, the films were stunning travelogues.

Cinerama faced new troubles when it too tried to combine its gimmick with narrative: *The Wonderful World of the Brothers Grimm* (1962), *It's a Mad Mad Mad Mad World* (1963), *How the West Was Won* (1963). As with 3-D, what Aristotle called "Spectacle" (he found it the least important dramatic element) overwhelmed the more essential dramatic ingredients of plot, character, and ideas. In 1968, Stanley Kubrick's *2001: A Space Odyssey* subordinated a modified Cinerama (shot with a single camera but projected on a Cinerama screen) to the film's sociological and metaphysical journey, letting the big screen and sound work for the story rather than letting the story work for the effects. Despite the artistic and commercial success of *2001*, Cinerama was not the salvation that Hollywood thought.

Fig. 12-3
A contemporary diagram of Cinerama: the widest of screens broken into three frames with six-track stereo sound. The six-perf frames were taller than they appear here.

A third gimmick of the early 1950s also took advantage of the size of the movie screen. The new format, christened CinemaScope, was the most durable and functional of them all, requiring no extra projectors, special film, or special glasses. It did, however, require theatre owners to invest in "scope" or anamorphic projection lenses; wide, curved screens; and, in most cases, stereophonic sound systems. The action was recorded by a conventional movie camera on conventional 35mm film. A special anamorphic lens squeezed the image horizontally to fit the width of the standard film. When projected with a corresponding anamorphic lens on the projector, the distortions disappeared and a huge, wide image stretched across the curved screen. The first CinemaScope feature, Henry Koster's *The Robe* (1953), convinced both Fox and the industry that the process was viable. The screen had been made wide with a minimum of trouble and expense. A parade of screen-widening "scopes" and "visions" followed Fox's CinemaScope, notably VistaVision, which printed the image sideways on the celluloid strip, and Todd-AO, which widened the film to 70mm. The first 70mm film of the 1950s was *Oklahoma!* (1955), directed by Fred Zinnemann.

Ultimately it was size and grandeur that triumphed, not depth perception or motion effects. As early as 1930, Eisenstein advocated a flexible screen size, a principle he called the "dynamic square." He reasoned that the conventional screen, with its four-to-three ratio of width to height (an aspect ratio of 4:3, or 1.33:1), was too inflexible. The screen should be capable of becoming very wide for certain sequences, narrow and long for others, a perfect square for balanced compositions. But Eisenstein's principles were much closer to Griffith's use of masking or irising than to the wide screen's inflexible commitment to width. George Stevens complained that CinemaScope was better for shooting a python than a person. How could a horizontal picture frame, with a five-to-two ratio of width to height, enclose a vertical subject?

Like sound in the early years, the new technological invention was a mixed blessing, adding some new film possibilities and destroying many of the old compositional virtues. What many critics of the wide screen did not perceive at the time was that just as deep focus permitted con-trapuntal relationships between near and far within the frame (as in *Citizen Kane*), the wide screen permitted contrapuntal relationships among left, center, and right.

George Cukor's *A Star Is Born* (1954), a great remake of William Wellman's great 1937 melodrama, provides powerful proof of this potential. Two sequences demonstrate not only Cukor's mastery of the format, but also his awareness of its history and value. In one scene, Oliver Niles (Charles Bickford), the head of the studio, fires the aging matinee idol, Norman Main (James Mason). Main's popularity has been slipping and the studio itself has been slumping. The cause? Television. During this conversation, the men stand between two flickering black-and-white images on the far left and right edges of the frame. To the far left is a TV set; Niles has been watching the fights on TV (even a studio head cannot stay away from a TV screen). To the far right of the frame is a motion picture, projected in the next room for Main's party guests. The discussion between Main and Niles takes place precisely between a video image and a film image—a visual translation of the historical crossroads where all the studio heads and studio stars found themselves in 1954.

Cukor uses television again in the film's Academy Award ceremony. While Cukor shoots Vicky Lester's (Judy Garland) triumph with the CinemaScope lens in medium long shot, a TV monitor in the upper right-hand corner of the frame displays the moment in typical TV close-ups. The shot is simultaneously a long shot and a close-up, a wide-screen color image and a small-screen black-and-white TV image, a revelation of CinemaScope's visual power and television's cultural power, capable of bringing this moment, "live," into people's homes in close-ups.

The wide CinemaScope frame enabled Cukor to shoot whole scenes—even Garland's entire rendition of "The Man That Got Away"—in a continuous, complexly choreographed shot without a cut. (Of course, Welles and Toland had done that with the standard frame in *Citizen Kane*.) In the work of Cukor, Donen, Ophüls, Preminger, and others, the 1950s saw an explosion of interest in the uses of the wide screen, an interest that remained evident in the 1960s and 70s works of such directors as Lean, Kurosawa, Leone, Peckinpah, and Godard. By the mid-1960s, the wide-screen revolution was as complete as the sound revolution of the late 1920s, and the wide screen, like sound, would become the basis of a new generation's film aesthetics.

The battle with television was partially responsible for another technical revolution in the 1950s—the almost total conversion to color. From the earliest days of moving pictures, inventors and filmmakers sought to combine color with recorded movement. The early Méliès films were hand-painted frame by frame. Many silent films (Griffith's, Lubitsch's, and Gance's most notably) were bathed in color tints, adding a cast of pale blue for night sequences, sepia for interiors and yellow for sunlight, a red tint for certain effects, a green tint for others. Such coloring effects were obviously tonal, like the accompanying music, rather than an intrinsic part of the film's photographic conception. As early as 1908, Charles Urban patented a superb color photographic process, Kinemacolor. But opposition from the then-powerful MPPC Trust kept Kinemacolor off American screens.

Fig. 12-4

Fig. 12-5
Composition for the wide screen in A Star Is Born. *Fig. 12-4: Judy Garland surrounded by jazz musicians for "The Man That Got Away"; primary interest at center. Fig. 12-5: Garland, with Jack Carson, surrounded by the photographic faces of stardom; primary interest at the sides, in a CinemaScope approach to the two-shot.*

In 1917, the Technicolor Corporation was founded in the United States. Supported by all the major studios, Technicolor enjoyed monopolistic control over all color experimentation and shooting in this country. Douglas Fairbanks's *The Black Pirate* (1926) and the musicals *Rio Rita* (1929) and *Whoopee!* (1930) used the early Technicolor process, which added a garish grandeur to the costumes and scenery. In the 1920s, Technicolor was, like Urban's Kinemacolor, a two-color process: two strips of film exposed by two separate lenses, one strip recording the blue–green colors of the spectrum, the other sensitive to the red–orange colors, then bonded together in the final processing. But by 1933 Technicolor had perfected a more accurate three-color process: three strips of black-and-white film, one exposed through a filter to red, the second to blue, the third to green, originally requiring a bulky three-prism camera—with a single lens—for the three rolls of film, copies of which were used to transfer red, blue, and green dyes to a print. The first two-strip Technicolor feature had been *The Toll of the Sea* (1922); the one that used color most creatively was *Doctor X* (1932). The first film made in the three-strip process was Disney's cartoon *Flowers and Trees* (1932). RKO's *La Cucaracha* (1934) was the first three-strip Technicolor live-action short, and Rouben Mamoulian's *Becky Sharp* (1935) the first three-strip Technicolor feature. Hollywood could have converted to color at almost the same time it converted to sound. But expenses and priorities dictated that most talkies use black-and-white film, which was itself becoming faster, subtler, more responsive to minimal light, easier to use under any conditions. Color was reserved for cartoons or for lavish spectacles that could afford the slowness and expense of color shooting (for example, Michael Curtiz and William Keighley's *The Adventures of Robin Hood*, 1938; Victor Fleming's *Gone With the Wind* and *The Wizard of Oz*, both 1939).

World War II, which demanded that the film industry keep up production while tightening its belt, generally excluded the luxury of color filming—unless the film had propaganda value and was likely to improve morale. England put up the money for Laurence Olivier's *Henry V* (1944), whose splendid and complex use of color intensified the film's propagandistic appeal.

After the war, Hollywood needed color to fight television, which—at least until the 1960s—could offer audiences only black and white. Technicolor, formerly without competitors, had kept costs up and production down. Hollywood began encouraging a new, competing single-strip process, Eastmancolor. The new process was one of the spoils of war, a pirated copy of the German Agfacolor monopack. The monopack color film bonded three color-sensitive emulsions onto a single roll of filmstock. A color film could be shot with an ordinary movie camera. Color emulsions became progressively faster, more sensitive, more flexible. A series of new processes—DeLuxe, Metrocolor, Warnercolor—were all variations of Eastmancolor, which was less expensive and of lower quality than monopack Technicolor (introduced in 1942). What these monopack color processes gained over three-strip Technicolor in cheapness and flexibility they sacrificed in intensity and brilliance. (Technicolor's clean dyes were picked up and transferred directly onto the print by three strips or matrixes made from the camera's three strips, but the Eastman dyes were *in* the stock and had to go through chemical processing in the lab.) So unstable and impermanent were their color dyes that Eastmancolor prints of the 1950s have already faded badly.

During the 1950s, black and white gradually became the exception and color, even for serious dramas, little comedies, short subjects, and low-budget westerns, became the rule. As the technology of color cinematography became more flexible, film artists learned, as they did with sound, that a new technique was not only a gimmick, but also a way to fulfill essential dramatic and thematic functions.

Sound quality improved drastically after World War II, thanks to the introduction of magnetic tape (another of the spoils of war, invented in Nazi Germany). Until 1949, optical film was used to record all film soundtracks. From the 1950s to the present, a release print might have a magnetic or an optical soundtrack, but magnetic tape and magnetic film (called "mag stock") are used for virtually all analog sound recording, editing, and mixing. Even a computer's hard disk and digital tape record data magnetically.

Although the movies fought TV by offering audiences audiovisual treats that the tube lacked, Hollywood finally capitulated to TV by deciding to work with it rather than against it. If TV would not die, then it would need old movies and filmed installments of series to broadcast. Hollywood also lifted its ban against films and film stars appearing on TV. In 1954, RKO began to show its own movies on its own stations; as in a theatre, the "Million Dollar Movie" repeated the week's picture several times a day. In 1956, the other Hollywood studios first sold their films to TV, the sole provision being that the film had to have been produced before 1948. Since 1956, however, Hollywood has sold more and more recent films to the networks or cable stations; many of last year's movies appear on this year's television. In a sense, TV has replaced the old fourth- and fifth-run neighborhood movie houses, most of which had disappeared by 1965—much as the rentable video has nearly wiped out the revival house.

The theatre owners were hit hardest by a medium that could deliver entertainment directly to the home. Theatres countered by offering sights and sounds that televisions could not deliver. They still do. To see *Raiders of the Lost Ark* or *A Star Is Born* on TV—whether broadcast or on video—is not really to see it at all. The brightness, the brilliance, the immensity, the complex composition, the fullness of sound in the movie theatre remain basic reasons to go there. Although the most gimmicky innovations of 1952–53 have disappeared, the principle of supplying sights and sounds that TV cannot has dominated the feature film industry ever since.

By 1956, the war with TV was over, and although the armistice had clearly defined the movies' future relationship with its living-room audiences, the future with its audiences in theatres was still uncertain.

Films in the Transitional Era

With the collapse of the studio structure, the dictatorial head of production, and the quantitative demands of a large yearly output, producing films became similar to producing stage plays. Like the theatre producer, the new film producer concentrated on shaping and selling a single project at a time rather than a whole year's output of more than a dozen films. Like United Artists, David Selznick, and Samuel Goldwyn of earlier years,

Hollywood feature-film production, even within the studios, had "gone independent." The more independent producer selected the property, the stars, and the director; raised the money; and supervised the selling of the finished film. Perhaps the production company rented space on a studio lot; perhaps it used the studio's distribution offices to help sell the film. But the producer, not the studio, made the picture. With no lot, no long-term contracts with stars, no staffs of writers and technicians, the producer assembled a production company for a particular film, disbanded it when the film was finished, and assembled another for the next film.

Although independent production freed filmmakers from dictatorial studio heads, the new system had its own tyrannies. Veteran directors like Howard Hawks complained that they spent more time making deals than making movies. Now the director–producer handled all the petty problems—dickering to raise the money, compromising with bankers to get it—that a studio previously managed for him. And the large pool of expert studio craftsmen and technicians began to dry up—with fewer films to make and no way to know when or whether they would make them.

The individual producers, forced to make each film pay for itself, searched for stable, predictable production values. One of the axioms they discovered was that the most dependable films were either very expensive or very cheap. A very expensive film could make back its investment with huge publicity campaigns and high ticket prices at roadshow engagements. The theory translated itself into practice with big films like *The Robe, Oklahoma!, The Ten Commandments, The Bridge on the River Kwai, Ben-Hur*, and *Spartacus*. Even unpretentious directors of fast-paced action pictures like Howard Hawks and Nicholas Ray joined the parade of Colossal Spectacles (*Land of the Pharaohs*, 1955, and *King of Kings*, 1961, respectively). The biblical–historical dinosaurs disappeared after *Cleopatra* (1963) cost and lost more than any film ever had before.

But the 1950s were also the years of *I Was a Teenage Werewolf, Hercules, Not of This Earth, Joy Ride*, and *Riot in Juvenile Prison*. Joseph E. Levine built a commercial empire on Steve Reeves and a cast of Italians, films that were produced for under $150,000 in Italy and then dubbed into English. Roger Corman, the master of cheap monsters and outrageous scripts, enlarged his empire by teaming Vincent Price with Edgar Allan Poe. The inexpensive film could make back its investment in two weeks of saturation booking at neighborhood theatres and, most of all, drive-ins, a 1940s innovation that joined the 1950s war to pull people out of their living rooms.

For major productions, major producers became dependent on popular novels, musicals, and plays, properties that had excited the public in other forms and might excite it again. Lacking large, permanent staffs of screenwriters with original ideas, both studio and independent producers bought established, already written properties that simply required an artful, professional translation into film form: *The Caine Mutiny*, *Exodus*, *A Streetcar Named Desire*, *Tea and Sympathy*, and so forth. It was easier for a producer to raise money for a film that was considered "presold."

Because television applied even stricter moral regulations to its programs than the Production Code did to films, producers could lure audiences to the movie theatre with promises of franker, racier, "more adult" entertainment. Films adapted from novels like *Peyton Place*, *From Here to Eternity*, *Compulsion*, *Advise and Consent*, *Lolita*, and *Butterfield 8* could not possibly avoid references to adultery, fornication, or homosexuality, topics perfectly suited to Hollywood's audience war with television.

Freedom of Speech, Preminger, and the Blacklist

A landmark Supreme Court ruling, the so-called *Miracle* case of 1952 (formally, *Burstyn v. Wilson*), declared that movies were part of the nation's "press," entitled to Constitutional guarantees of freedom of speech.

The story of a simple-minded peasant woman, seduced by a stranger, who believes she has been impregnated by St. Joseph, Roberto Rossellini's *The Miracle* (1948) was condemned as sacrilegious by the archdiocese of New York and seized by New York's commissioner of police. After repeated losses in lower courts, Joseph Burstyn, the film's American distributor, took the case to the Supreme Court, which ruled that the term "sacrilegious" had no clear meaning and that films could no more be suppressed than any other forum for public debate. In addition to its liberating effect

on film exhibition, this ruling undermined the legitimacy of the Production Code, even if the PCA was not a government office. That it took a foreign "art film" to effect this important change in American law foreshadowed many other changes that "art films" would effect within the decade. Produced outside America and shown in little theatres whose owners were not members of the Motion Picture Association, these "art films" were never subject to the industry's Code.

The war against the Code began officially in 1953 with Otto Preminger's decision to release *The Moon Is Blue* without the Code's seal of approval. Not only was Preminger's the first major American movie since 1934 (when the first was awarded) not to bear a seal, it also demonstrated the commercial and publicity value of not receiving a seal of moral approval. The war declared by Preminger would end in 1968 with the elimination of the 1930 Production Code (already modified in 1966) and the adoption of the more flexible system of rating the "maturity" of a film's content.

Preminger, a Lubitsch protégé, had begun with ironic, unpretentious genre films at Twentieth Century–Fox (from *Laura* in 1944 to *River of No Return* in 1954) only to move toward more monumental, controversial, and socially conscious literary adaptations in the era of independent production. His *cause célèbre*, *The Moon Is Blue*, merely added a few "naughty" words (for example, *virgin* and *mistress*), leering eyebrows, and bedroom situations to a conventional comedy of manners. But his camerawork, his mastery of the crane and (beginning with *River of No Return*) the wide screen, never were conventional. Two of Preminger's steadily gripping adaptations, *The Man With the Golden Arm* (1955) and *Anatomy of a Murder* (1959), use quiet, understated acting and evocatively moody jazz scores (by Elmer Bernstein and Duke Ellington, respectively) to make the stories of drug addiction and rape more absorbing and the social commentary less obvious.

Preminger was instrumental in vanquishing the blacklist, as he had challenged the Code; he hired Dalton Trumbo, one of the Hollywood Ten, to write the script for *Exodus* (1960) under his own name. At approximately the same time, Kirk Douglas hired Trumbo to write *Spartacus* (1960), and the nearly simultaneous release of those two major spectacles broke the power of the blacklist.

Message Pictures: Kazan and Others

Stanley Kramer became the era's sentimental liberal. In *The Defiant Ones* (1958), he examined race relations by showing a black man (Sidney Poitier) and a white man (Tony Curtis) escaping from a southern prison. Chained together, they are forced to come to terms with one another. Although the terms, the problems, and their solutions are predictable from the moment the men flee, Kramer's loud and clear plea for racial tolerance would dominate his career from *Home of the Brave*, which he produced in 1949, to *Guess Who's Coming to Dinner*, which he directed in 1967.

The impetus for these socially committed films is clear enough—Kramer and his brethren wanted to do something meaningful, important, relevant. But some of their films lend unintentional support to one of Samuel Goldwyn's classic pronouncements: "If you want to send a message, go to Western Union." The tension between social consciousness and Hollywood cliché is uncomfortably strong in these message pictures.

Elia Kazan, originally a Cold War liberal in the era of Hollywood blacklisting, had the problem of making social-problem films that would neither offend an audience nor cost him his job. He solved the problem in his public life by co-operating with HUAC; he solved the problem in his films by turning social statements into "human" statements—*A Streetcar Named Desire* (1951), *Viva Zapata!* (1952), *On the Waterfront* (1954), *East of Eden* (1955), *A Face in the Crowd* (1957), *Splendor in the Grass* (1961)—all of which sustain their social issues with dynamic performances by Marlon Brando (the prototypic Kazan actor), Vivien Leigh, James Dean, Rod Steiger, and others. In these films Kazan brought to the screen the earthy, introspective "Method" acting style of the Group Theatre (founded in New York in 1931 by Lee Strasberg, Harold Clurman, and Cheryl Crawford) and of the Actors Studio (founded in New York in 1947 by Crawford, Robert Lewis, and Kazan; Strasberg was the key teacher and artistic director). Because of their intelligent writing, rich composition, and powerful acting, Kazan's literary adaptations of the 1950s—especially the CinemaScope masterpiece *East of Eden*—look better than his social-problem films of the 1940s (*Gentleman's Agreement*, 1947; *Pinky*, 1949).

Several other American filmmakers of the era also used New York styles to escape the studio clichés of Hollywood—in particular, the use of real New York locations and established New York actors (*Marty*, 1955; *12 Angry Men*, 1957; *A View from the Bridge*, 1962; *The Pawnbroker*, 1965). Many of these "New York films" owed their texture and impact not only to their director but also to their informal origins in television styles and to the apparent spontaneity of location shooting and lighting. The improvisational "look" of these New York films can often be attributed to Boris Kaufman, the cinematographer who shot many of them and who had demonstrated the same spontaneity in his collaboration with Jean Vigo two decades earlier.

The rise of New York in the early 1950s as both a production center and a production style suggested the growing uncertainty within the film industry itself. Not since before World War I had New York been a major center of American film production, although there had been a brief return to both New York studios and styles in the first years of synchronized sound. When Hollywood ran into trouble—as it did with the addition of dialogue or the loss of its audiences—it turned to New York for help.

In 1950, New York was not only the center of American theatre—as it had been for a century—but the center of American television production as well, with a large pool of talented actors, writers, and directors. Many of them would move from television to New Yorky "little" movies and then on to Hollywood itself.

Many important screenwriters of this generation came from television: Paddy Chayefsky (*Marty*, 1957), Reginald Rose (*12 Angry Men*), Abby Mann (*Judgment at Nuremberg*, 1961), Rod Serling (*Requiem for a Heavyweight*, 1962). A generation of new directors also came from television: Sidney Lumet, Arthur Penn (*Bonnie and Clyde*, 1967), Sam Peckinpah (*The Wild Bunch*, 1969), John Frankenheimer (*The Manchurian Candidate*, 1962). Although many of these directors would later adopt Hollywood's familiar genres, most of them were initially committed to detailed social and psychological portraits of people who are either very typical (like Ernest Borgnine in *Marty*) or atypical (like Kim Stanley in *The Goddess*).

Fig. 12-6

Fig. 12-7

Fig. 12-8

Fig. 12-9

Two films shot by Boris Kaufman. Kazan's On the Waterfront: *the realism of "Method" acting; Marlon Brando with Eva Marie Saint (Fig. 12-6) and Rod Steiger (Fig. 12-7). Sidney Lumet's* The Pawnbroker: *Steiger trapped in the cage of his pawnshop (Fig. 12-8) and in the cage of New York's modern architecture (Fig. 12-9, with Geraldine Fitzgerald).*

Adaptations and Values: John Huston and Others

A moralist with a taste for irony and for great literature, John Huston also faced the tension between cinematic style and significant statement. Some of his films, like *The Maltese Falcon* (1941, the first film he both wrote and directed) and *The Asphalt Jungle* (1950), match style and statement so unobtrusively that the results have classical status; others, like *Moulin Rouge* (1953), foreground their experiments at the expense of stylistic balance but remain of interest; and still others, like *Freud* (1962) and *Reflections in a Golden Eye* (1967), experiment in a manner that comes to seem pretentious. Most of his works are literary adaptations, and again it can be said that some, like *The Maltese Falcon* and *The Treasure of*

the Sierra Madre (1948), brilliantly convey the essence of their originals.

If Kazan's films revealed his background in the theatre, Huston's revealed his background as a screenwriter with their taut and subtle scripts. In Huston's films, the characters who survive are usually those who accept the limits of their humanity and navigate a moral crisis (the detective in *The Maltese Falcon*) or are flexible and resourceful enough to modify their projects (*The African Queen*, 1951). Those who fall—or fail, but remain of consuming interest—are obsessed, inflexible overreachers possessed by their projects (*The Man Who Would Be King*, 1975) or people who are too good at their jobs, or trapped in them, to give them up (*Prizzi's Honor*, 1985). The best of Huston's moral tales are both idealistic and

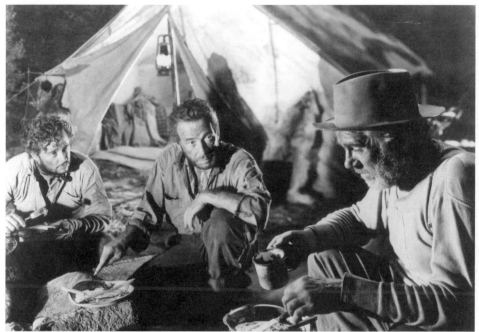

Fig. 12-10
The Treasure of the Sierra Madre: *from left, Tim Holt, Humphrey Bogart, and the director's father, Walter Huston.*

ironic; behind them one senses the shrewd, wry cackle of a student of the aspirations and failures of human nature.

Joseph L. Mankiewicz, whose brother Herman wrote *Citizen Kane*, adapted theatrical works as diverse as the tragedy *Julius Caesar* (1953), the musical *Guys and Dolls* (1955), the melodrama *Suddenly, Last Summer* (1959), and the comedy *Sleuth* (1972). His deceptively easy, controlled style made his *Caesar* one of the only films in which Shakespeare's poetry is delivered as natural dialogue with its rhythms intact. His skills as a writer and a director of sharp, ironic dialogue made his witty comedies of manners into grenades of manners and gave field days to great actors. One of the themes he returned to most often was the danger of celebrity, notably in *Julius Caesar*; in *Cleopatra* (1963), which gave him a second chance at Caesar, played this time by Rex Harrison, as well as a shot at the too-famous lovers Antony and Cleopatra, played by the too-famous lovers Richard Burton and Elizabeth Taylor; and in his masterpiece, *All About Eve* (1950), a tale of the theatre at its most brilliant and cruel, where celebrity

draws evil as well as attention, bringing out the worst in the worst people even as it lets a major actress (Bette Davis as Margo Channing) appropriately adopt, for as long as she chooses, the language, power, and magnitude of a star.

Film Noir and Other Genres

Although it was not apparent at the time, the most enduring Hollywood movies of the period wore the disguises of familiar genres. The two basic metaphors for American life—the open frontier and the dense modern city—had been the movie means for examining the promise and exposing the failures of American society since well before John Ford. The western provided the generic terms for mythifying American history, its aspirations in building a nation from a wasteland, the actions that hindered or furthered it. The gangster film established the generic terms for diagnosing the corruption and diseases of the present. It depicted America after the Fall, after the virgin wilderness had been cleared and densely packed with stone buildings and people.

Fig. 12-11
The children and the shadow of their pursuer: an Expressionistic moment from **The Night of the Hunter.**

The western remained one of the most exciting and entertaining genres of the transitional era: George Stevens's *Shane* (1953), Fred Zinnemann's *High Noon* (1952), Nicholas Ray's *Johnny Guitar* (1954). Some western films—most notably Anthony Mann's (*Winchester '73*, 1950; *Bend of the River*, 1952; *The Man from Laramie*, 1955) and Budd Boetticher's (*Decision at Sundown*, 1957; *The Tall T*, 1957; *Ride Lonesome*, 1959)—maintained the conventional attitudes of the genre toward violence and killing. Violence was a legitimate means of establishing law and civilization or a legitimate assertion of one's self and self-respect against elemental enemies. Like Ford's *Stagecoach* and Hawks's *Red River*, they were attempts to examine the essential human and social qualities that produced the American nation and its ideals in the first place.

But other westerns of the 1950s began bending the conventions of the genre to other ends. On the one hand, a filmmaker could use the mythic background of the Old West to attack contemporary American values (disguise was an especially useful ploy in an era of blacklisting). *High Noon*, in its attack on the timidity of the respectable majority and in its contempt for the think-alike, act-alike mentality, is clearly about the American social climate of 1952 and mixes contemporary moralizing with the western's setting and action. On the other hand, a filmmaker could take the violence of westerns as symptomatic of deranged behavior and imply that the forging of this "ideal" American nation was ruthless and corrupt from its very beginning: hence the nearly psychotic gunman in *Shane* and the rich man he works for.

The mystery and gangster films began turning very dark, concentrating on the inevitability of crime in urban America, on criminals who are not simply selfish and tough (like Little Caesar) but crazy (like the giggling maniac played by Richard

Widmark in Henry Hathaway's *Kiss of Death*, 1947), on policemen who are as diseased as their quarry, on lovers and partners who betray each other, and on visual images that are consistently shadowy, dark, and sharp. French critics coined the name for this genre—the *film noir*—a term derived from the black (*noir*) covers of crime novels in the French *Série noire*, many of which were translations of American novels by Dashiell Hammett, James M. Cain, Raymond Chandler, David Goodis, and Jim Thompson. But for all they owe to American crime fiction, both the style and the spirit of these *films noirs* were unmistakably German, from their fatalism to their looming shadows. Some were even directed by Germans (Wilder, Preminger, Ulmer, and Siodmak among them).

Edward Dmytryk's *Crossfire* (1947) is a dark mixture of murder, anti-Semitism, and homosexuality; almost everyone who worked on this film was targeted by the HUAC. Robert Rossen's

Body and Soul (1947) and Abraham Polonsky's *Force of Evil* (1948) both use John Garfield as a child of the slums facing the decision between an unprofitable honesty and lucrative dishonor. Garfield was a prototypic *film noir* hero (another was Robert Mitchum) and the "bad girl"—Gloria Grahame, Jean Hagen, Shelley Winters, the early Marilyn Monroe—its prototypically used and abused woman. Another prototypical *noir* figure is the *femme fatale:* the seductive woman who is deadly treacherous (Barbara Stanwyck in Billy Wilder's *Double Indemnity*, 1944).

Though anticipated by films ranging from *The Blue Angel* to *The Maltese Falcon*, the first true *noir* appears to have been Frank Tuttle's *This Gun For Hire* (1942), with the form fully defined by the time—and the example—of *Double Indemnity*. The last—the film that marked the end of the *noir* cycle—was Welles's *Touch of Evil* (1958).

Fig. 12-12
Out of the Past: *shadows in a world of traps and betrayals—the* **femme fatale** *(Jane Greer) left, the* **hero** *(Robert Mitchum) in a trenchcoat, and the* **blackmailer** *(Steve Brodie) speaking from the darkness; before the film ends, all three will die.*

An outgrowth of the *film noir* was a new genre that also showed marked affinities with the western. The "rebellious youth" films of the 1950s—particularly Laslo Benedek's *The Wild One* (1953) and Nicholas Ray's *Rebel Without a Cause* (1955)—were also a violent reaction against a decaying and diseased society. But whereas the gangster chose violence as a weapon against the brutal hardness of city life, the youths rebelled against the sterility, monotony, and conformity of normal adult life. "What are you rebelling against?" someone asks the smirking Johnny (Marlon Brando) on his motorcycle in *The Wild One*. "What'ya got?" he answers. The highway death of the young James Dean not only robbed Hollywood of a rich acting talent and translated an actor into a legend; it also seemed a symbol of the ultimate rebellion against what'ya got.

While a western looked at the past and a mystery or thriller at the present, science fiction looked at the future. Inspired by both the new fear of atomic annihilation and the hope of interplanetary travel, science fiction films brought atomic mutants and extraterrestrial visitors to Earth or sent Earthlings to the Moon, Mars, and the stars. In *The Thing From Another World* (1951), directed by Christian Nyby and produced by Howard Hawks, atomic science and outer space combine to produce a death-defying vegetable monster. But in *Forbidden Planet* (Fred M. Wilcox, 1956), Earthlings take their monster with them into space—a Freudian menace, emanating from the id of the scientist himself. Martians attack Earth in *The War of the Worlds* (1953), directed by Byron Haskin and produced by the great special-effects designer, George Pal. But in Robert Wise's *The Day the Earth Stood Still* (1951), a sage interplanetary visitor brings reason, sense, and peace to an Earth intent on destroying itself and everything else in the galaxy.

One of the most socially and politically revealing of the science fiction/horror films was Don Siegel's *Invasion of the Body Snatchers* (1956, from the novel by Jack Finney), in which vegetable pods from outer space replace the Earth's inhabitants, resembling the Earthlings in every

Fig. 12-13

Fig. 12-14

***Icons of 1950s rebellion. Fig. 12-13: Marlon Brando in* The Wild One; *Fig. 12-14: James Dean in* Rebel Without a Cause.**

way but one: They have no feelings. These pods seem (but were not meant as) a possible allusion to Communism: the way some Americans, who appear "normal," are really selfless agents of an evil foreign power—the Red Menace of the Cold War 1950s. But the pods also strongly suggest an indictment of American conformity, a uniform society that appears human but lacks the essential human qualities of emotion, moral judgment, and independent action. Either way, the point is that all the pods think alike. Don Siegel later said Hollywood was full of pods.

The newest comic performers were Danny Kaye at Goldwyn and Bud Abbott and Lou Costello at Universal. Abbott and Costello seemed to be built on the old physical premises of teams like Laurel and Hardy—one fat (Costello), one thin (Abbott); one clumsy, one suave. But despite their physical humor, Abbott and Costello were primarily verbal comics (their most famous routines, like "Who's on First?," originated on radio); the only other way to use them in a film was to plunge the bungling, cowardly, Lou into scary situations. And so Abbott and Costello went into jungles or the Army or met all the monsters under contract to Universal in an attempt to squeeze laughs from spine-tingling contrasts of humor and horror (*Abbott and Costello Meet Frankenstein*, 1948). The Danny Kaye films also juxtaposed comedy and danger, surrounding Kaye with rings of murderers, kidnappers, spies, and thieves who gave him his trademark comic jitters and stutters, which complemented his tongue-twisters (*The Court Jester*, 1956).

Succeeding Abbott and Costello in 1950 were Dean Martin and Jerry Lewis at Paramount, another team combining a zany clown and a slick "straight" man. Lewis and Martin contrasted both physically and mentally: the one brash, noisy, nasal, infantile; the other oily, loose, controlled. But their wacky personalities were frequently drowned in predictable, overplotted situation comedies.

Among the best postwar comedies of manners were Billy Wilder's, who with his co-author, I. A. L. Diamond or Charles Brackett, preserved the tradition of comic collaboration between director and scenarist. Wilder left Germany in 1933. His comedy juxtaposed verbal wit with a sinister, morally disturbing environment: the corruption of a postwar Berlin in rubble (*A Foreign Affair*,

1948), the dark estate of a psychotic has-been of the silent screen (*Sunset Boulevard*, 1950), a concentration camp (*Stalag 17*, 1953), the gangster underworld (*Some Like It Hot*, 1959), the corruption of Madison Avenue (*The Apartment*, 1960), and the Cold War in the now rebuilt and industrialized Berlin (*One, Two, Three*, 1961).

The Freed Musicals

Musicals in the postwar years were also undergoing a transition, one that produced Hollywood's greatest musical films. Before the war, Hollywood musicals were breezy concoctions that focused mostly on the doings of show folk. By the mid-1950s, however, filmed musicals, following the pattern of Broadway shows (which, of course, they were often adapting), became more realistic and psychological. World War II and street gangs had become subjects for Broadway musicals like *South Pacific* and *West Side Story*. The fluff of Rodgers and Hart had been replaced by the romantic seriousness of Rodgers and Hammerstein.

The "integrated" musical, as the Rodgers–Hammerstein type and its successors came to be known, tried to imagine under what conditions a human being might sing in reality—"feel a song coming on" or, in some cases, "think" a song. Although it was difficult enough to convince a Broadway audience that a group of juvenile delinquents would sing to each other before cutting each other's throats, the task was even more difficult for films. The stage, at least, enjoys the unreality of cardboard and plaster and paint and spotlight. The stage musical could draw on the conventions of two other theatrical forms—opera and the dance—as its stylized means of translating song and dance into a representation of reality. But how to make a film audience believe that a woman would sing a song standing on a real tugboat in the middle of New York harbor?

The director of early musical films did not have such problems. Musical films were obviously unreal, unserious spoofs that never tried to be credible. Busby Berkeley could twirl his camera, his dancers, their pianos, fiddles, and fountains in grandiose and grotesquely imaginative patterns precisely because his musical numbers owed no allegiance to either spatial logic or social reality.

Musical films just after the war, while they did become lavish, ornate, Technicolor spectaculars (as so many films did), maintained their stylized unreality. The MGM musicals produced by Arthur Freed in particular combined surrealistically imaginative musical numbers, pleasant scores, an exciting use of color, and funny, spoofing plots that often still revolved around showfolk.

Of the directors of musicals for Freed's unit, Vincenté Minnelli (professionally, Vincente) was the most conscious of the traditions of painting and modern art. His musicals (*Meet Me in St. Louis*, 1944; *An American in Paris*, 1951) are masterful in their attention to color and light, to details of costume and decor, and to their layering of perspectival space for the lens. Stanley Donen (with or without Gene Kelly) was most committed to defining visual space itself as an emanation and external projection of musical energy, movement, and feeling (*On the Town*, 1949; *Singin' In The Rain*, 1952; *Seven Brides for Seven Brothers*, 1954; *It's Always Fair Weather*, 1955).

The best of the Freed musicals were those with musical numbers conceived and choreographed by Kelly, particularly *An American in Paris* and *Singin' In The Rain*. In the former, Kelly's ballet, combining George Gershwin's tone poem with French Impressionist painting, received the most critical attention. Its integration of music, color, dance, decor, costumes, editing, and camera movement is as sensually and formally "pure" cinema as any that has ever been attempted.

Singin' In The Rain, co-directed by Donen and Kelly, boasts perhaps the funniest screenplay of any musical film, the best of Betty Comden and Adolph Green's many Hollywood spoofs, both in films and on the stage. Every musical number in *Singin' In The Rain* combines music and fun, pleasant movement and wry spoof—from the staging of the title song in which Kelly tap dances in rain puddles to the surrealistic ballet, "Broadway Melody," in which Kelly romanticizes a young entertainer's rise to the top.

Singin' In The Rain contains its own reflexive history of MGM musicals. The film's score is a virtual compilation of hit tunes from MGM musicals, from the 1929 *Hollywood Revue* and *Broadway Melody* through the succeeding *Broadway Melodies* and the Rooney–Garland "barnyard musicals," like *Babes in Arms*, of the 1930s and 1940s.

The Band Wagon is equally reflexive and retrospective. Its main character, Tony Hunter, is a veteran song-and-dance man whom modern fashion considers old and out of date. Hunter is played by Fred Astaire, about whom modern fashion held similar suspicions in 1953. The film's title is, not coincidentally, the same as that of Astaire's last Broadway show with his sister, Adele.

"That's Entertainment" is not only the most familiar new song written for this film but could well be the anthem for all of Freed's MGM musicals. Its lyrics clearly proclaim these film musicals as the contemporary American descendants of Shakespeare, melodrama, and farce, the true 20th-century art of the people. But there is also a sadness beneath the exuberant proclamation, a nostalgic realization that the tradition of entertainment sustained by these MGM musicals was coming to an end.

That the tradition was dead can be seen in the differences between the love song "You Were Meant for Me," of *Singin' In The Rain*, and the love song "One Hand, One Heart," of *West Side Story* (1961, Robert Wise and Jerome Robbins). In the earlier film, Gene Kelly leads his lady (Debbie Reynolds) onto a sound stage, turns on atmospheric colored lights and an artificial wind machine, then sings, surrounded by stylized unreality. In *West Side Story*, girl and boy pledge their troth in the bridal shop where she works, surrounded by the realistic artifacts of her trade, then consummate their "marriage" in a suggestive fadeout. Whichever style you prefer, the psychological and visual differences between them are obvious.

By the mid-1950s, MGM had already begun deserting original musical ideas, assigning Vincenté Minnelli to adapt stage shows like *Brigadoon* and *Kismet*. The original screen musical died with the original screenplay. It also died with the studio system that produced a certain number of musicals each year and kept a stable of musical talent stocked expressly for that purpose. The road for independent production was being cleared.

Things were changing, and not only for the musical. By the turn of the 1960s, there were signs that a powerful new sense of cinema was on the way—not just from the New Wave films arriving from Europe, but from such brave American black-and-whites as John Cassavetes's *Shadows* (1959), Alfred Hitchcock's *Psycho* (1960), Robert Rossen's *The Hustler* (1961), David Miller's *Lonely Are the Brave* (1962), and Frank and Eleanor Perry's *David and Lisa* (1963).

The exuberance of song and dance: Gene Kelly Singin' In The Rain.

Fig. 12-15

Surfaces and Subversion

To understand those American films of the 1950s that seem most interesting decades later requires a careful look at the differences between the clear values on their narrative surfaces and the more complicated social and psychological questions beneath. As a representative sample, or an intriguing set of films worth a closer look, consider *Rear Window*, *Rebel Without a Cause*, *The Searchers*, and *Imitation of Life*.

Unlike the American message films and European art films of the period, these Hollywood films wear thick disguises, masquerading as ordinary westerns or thrillers or weepies—the derogatory term for "women's pictures," itself a derogatory enough term. To wear a thick disguise

was an understandable strategy in an era of black-listing, when it was safer to make films with no apparent "message" at all. But these genre films, like those of the previous era, felt comfortable raising the important questions within the boundaries of familiar genres. Although few critics took even the best of these genre films seriously in the 1950s, most of the movies made money—accomplishment enough in that decade—and many of them have proved more durable than the critics who casually dismissed them.

Samuel Fuller

Beginning in 1949, Samuel Fuller directed, wrote, and often produced a series of inexpensive genre films that fell somewhere between

A and B pictures in their budgets, styles, stars, and shooting schedules: westerns (*I Shot Jesse James*, 1949; *Run of the Arrow*, 1957), gangster films (*Pickup on South Street*, 1953; *Underworld U.S.A.*, 1961), and disturbing melodramas (*Shock Corridor*, 1963; *The Naked Kiss*, 1964). Fuller's war films about the war in Korea (*The Steel Helmet* and *Fixed Bayonets*, both 1951) are shockingly violent and honest, and his *China Gate* (1957) is uncannily prophetic of the next Southeast Asian "conflict," the one in Vietnam. For the subject of his last war film, *The Big Red One* (1980), he returned to World War II. In 1982, he made a film about racism, *White Dog*, that was judged too controversial to release. In 1992, he made *Dead Pigeon on Beethoven Street* in Germany. Some of his pictures, including *Shock Corridor* and *The Naked Kiss*, were restored and re-released before he died, still full of energy and tough charm, in 1997. Sometimes instead of yelling "action," he fired his .45 in the air.

Late Hitchcock

Rope (1948) begins with an odd sexual climax—but the camera must wait outside a penthouse apartment, its curtains drawn, not permitted a view of the brutal homosexual murder, modeled on the sensational Leopold–Loeb murder case, in the dark. Only after the murderous climax can the camera and the light be invited inside, to permit the audience's identification with the two handsomely murderous boys, in the throes of the murder's postcoital exhilaration. The Code prohibited the depiction of explicit sexual and "unnatural" acts; still, Hitchcock implied a great deal. In a similar way, *Strangers On A Train* (1951) balances the audience's antipathies between a maniacal homosexual murderer, Bruno (Robert Walker), and a bland model of straight American normality, the tennis pro, Guy (Farley Granger).

In this decade committed to the "straight" and normal, Hitchcock's sly examinations of sexual aberration beneath the placid surfaces of 1950s American life were deliciously subversive. He took particular delight in exposing the dark sexual undersides of familiar movie stars—James Stewart and Cary Grant in particular—so familiar and safe as sexual beings: the calm rationality of Stewart, astonished that he has a libido; the graceful suavity of Grant, always verging on the hysterical and scatterbrained. Near the conclusion of *Vertigo* (1958), James Stewart grasps the female fantasy of his own construction, embodied by Kim Novak, in his arms. Hitchcock's sleazy hotel room begins spinning slowly, its walls, bathed in aqueous blue-green light, briefly replaced by Stewart's memory of that location where he last

The vertiginous kiss in **Vertigo**: *James Stewart almost remembers the last place he saw Kim Novak.*

Fig. 12-16

Fig. 12-17

Fig. 12-18

Fig. 12-19

Fig. 12-20

Fig. 12-21

Rear Window: *window frames as movie frames. The spectator–voyeur (James Stewart, Fig. 12-17) observes the framed stories of the newlyweds (Fig. 12-18), "Miss Lonelyhearts" (Fig. 12-19), "Miss Torso" (Fig. 12-20), and the murderer, Thorwald (Raymond Burr, Fig. 12-21).*

Fig. 12-22
Alfred Hitchcock on the set of The Birds.

encountered this fantasy woman before her apparent death. While the embracing couple stands at the center of this vertiginous circling (both they and the complex, rear-projected set turn), the erotic highpoint of 1950s cinema, Stewart pulls away slightly from Novak to glance over his shoulder, as if to ask, "Where the hell am I?" These great American stars didn't quite know where they were in Hitchcock films; like the audience, they were often kept off-balance.

Rear Window (1954), based on a story by Cornell Woolrich, puts all these disturbing themes together in a masterful comic thriller. A professional photographer, L. B. Jeffries (Stewart), confined to his apartment with a broken leg, has just one amusement during the hot summer days: gazing at the activity in the courtyard surrounding his apartment window. As he watches the activities of his neighbors through their open windows, he notices something wrong in one of the apartments: A woman mysteriously disappears. After a lengthy period of puzzling, spying, and piecing the evidence together, Jeffries exposes the missing woman's husband, Thorwald (Raymond Burr), as her murderer. Until the murderer comes after him, Jeffries's experience with the life outside his window is virtually identical to the spectator's experience at the cinema: looking through a rectangle at

the world, sometimes with the feeling that one is spying. Jeffries extends his vision with parallels to the movie camera—a pair of binoculars and his still camera's telephoto lens. This very long lens frequently sits in Stewart's inert lap—one of the slyest comic phalluses in Hitchcock's work.

The spectator gets into trouble when experience violates his voyeuristic privacy. When Thorwald discovers Jeffries's prying gaze (and, in person, his girlfriend Lisa's snooping), he steps out of the movie frame of his own apartment and into the auditorium of Jeffries's apartment. Unable to fight or run, Jeffries temporarily blinds Thorwald with flashbulbs, defending himself with characteristically photographic resources— but Thorwald throws him out the window. In a literal visualization of that classic movie metaphor, the "cliffhanger," Jeffries clings to the ledge—but over a metaphorical abyss that is more Hitchcock than Pearl White. If Hitchcock heroes often hang from such "cliffs" as the Statue of Liberty (*Saboteur*), the edge of a roof (*Vertigo*), or Mount Rushmore (*North by Northwest*, 1959), those who fall (as in *Vertigo*'s major dream sequence) lose their grip on more than a ledge, plummeting into the mystery of personal annihilation and secrets that are melodramatic and subconscious.

Hitchcock followed *Rear Window* with some of his greatest movies, disturbing even when they were comic and profoundly witty even in terror and despair. They include *Vertigo*, which many consider his masterpiece and which was certainly his best film since *Notorious* (1946). In black and white he made *The Wrong Man* (1956), a realistic tragedy, and *Psycho*, an Expressionist nightmare; like *Vertigo*, each went to the heart of his concerns with the nature of identity and guilt. Hitchcock's lifelong interest in Freudian psychology (about which one can never tell whether he is serious or has his tongue wedged in his cheek), seen in such earlier works as *Spellbound*, is a complex and ironic factor in *Vertigo*, *North by Northwest*, and *Psycho*—which were made in that order—as well as in the last of his great movies: *The Birds* (1963), in which he continued his demonstration that the apparently innocent and unnoticed can turn deadly; *Marnie* (1964), the "sex mystery," as he described it in the trailer, in which he took a deep look at the psychological links between sex and crime; and *Frenzy* (1972), which he returned to London to shoot and in which he showed more shocking and troubling (and, for once, unglamorized rather than elegantly stylized) violence than anyone had yet seen in a mainstream movie.

Nicholas Ray

A loner and a rebel, Nicholas Ray began making films in 1948. Ray became a director on the fringes of the Hollywood establishment with films that he often wrote himself. Although he began in the theatre and came to Hollywood as Elia Kazan's assistant, Ray would feel more comfortable with Hollywood genres than with theatrical ones: westerns (*Johnny Guitar*), war films (*Flying Leathernecks*, 1951), the combination of *film noir* and wild youth (*They Live By Night*, 1948, released 1949; *Knock on Any Door*, 1949). But like *Johnny Guitar*, his pictures often leave their genres behind.

Rebel Without a Cause (1955) is one of Ray's most personal works. The rebellion in the film's title is the only detail Ray borrowed from Robert Lindner's bestselling 1944 case study of a young psychopathic criminal. The title is a smokescreen for the film's real issue—the attempt of three outsiders, strangers alike to the materialistic values of their weak but rigid parents and the desperately insecure values of their teenage con-

temporaries, to form an alternative community of genuine human sympathy.

Jim Stark (Dean) begins the film as a hopeless drunk because he sees no value in a future represented by the enslavement of his father (Jim Backus—the voice of Mr. Magoo) to material possessions and a nagging wife. "Jimbo's" father is a man of no commitments or aspirations, except to keep the peace amongst the sterile bric-a-brac of his bourgeois home. Judy (Natalie Wood) also has problems with a father who spurns her confusedly provocative need for affection, sending her off in search of thrills and easy sensual power over boys her own age. Plato (Sal Mineo), the rich kid who never sees his divorced parents, is the most vulnerable and intellectual of the three, the most socially unskilled, and implicitly homosexual. Plato recognizes the fragility of human experience in a cold and awesome universe—suggested by the hypnotic planetarium show, a spectacle of sound and light analogous to movies. Plato, like Judy, searches for love and finds it in the same source—Jim.

Ray chronicles Jim's discovery of what it means to be a man and a responsible human being. The seeming alternative he sees to his father's emasculation is the world of his violent contemporaries, with their knife fights and chicken runs, car races that may be to the death. Jim, Judy, and Plato try to be good—and they are—but always seem to end up being called bad. Only love can unscramble their hearts, can give an uncontradictory message, can let them find themselves beyond the empty and unfulfilling hypocrisy of imposed social roles.

Rebel Without a Cause had great power for young audiences in the 1950s, urging them to abandon conformity to seek values that made personal sense. At the same time, it urged parents to face up to their own problems. The film's visual power—Ray's first in CinemaScope and color—contributed to its moral argument. The awesome horizontal sweep of the CinemaScope frame, as Ray used it, suggested a passion for openness that contrasted with the cramped and confined interiors of bourgeois homes. Ray described Dean's red jacket, in contrast with his black Mercury, as a danger sign, a personality about to explode. Ray consistently identified with oddballs and loners who saw themselves as different from everyone else.

Late Ford

Ethan Edwards of John Ford's *The Searchers* (1956) is another oddball and loner, different from everyone else. In *The Searchers*, Ford continued his mythic investigation of American history. Like Ford's postwar *My Darling Clementine*, the cavalry trilogy of 1948–50 (*Fort Apache, She Wore A Yellow Ribbon, Rio Grande*), and the 1962 *The Man Who Shot Liberty Valance*, *The Searchers* exposes the conflict of irresolvable historical forces between the struggle to establish and protect a civilization and the values of civilization that make it worth establishing and protecting. Both Ford and Wayne show the violence under the tightly controlled surface of a culture or a face. If the shadow of the recent world war fell darkly across *My Darling Clementine*, an even longer shadow—of World War II, Korea, and the Cold War—falls across *The Searchers*.

The searchers are Ethan Edwards (John Wayne), whose obsessiveness dominates the film, and Martin Pawley (Jeffrey Hunter), who is part Cherokee. Ethan's brother, Aaron, and Aaron's wife, Martha, whom Ethan may himself once have loved, are brutally slaughtered in a Comanche attack soon after the film begins. The Comanches carry off two daughters, Debbie and Lucy. Though Lucy is raped and murdered, Debbie remains among the Comanches. Ethan's search for Debbie, which consumes him for five years, is an act of determination and revenge: to murder the man responsible for the death of his kin (the Indian brave, Scar, played by Henry Brandon) and to rescue Debbie from the Comanches before she has suffered sexual contamination—or to murder her if he is too late (since, for Ethan, to be a white squaw is worse than death for a Christian woman). In this context, Martin's project is not only to find Debbie, but also to protect her from Ethan.

Ethan refuses to surrender the search, just as he has never surrendered any cause—he still reveres the sword of the Confederacy. Ethan and Martin pursue the search for years, living nomadically, like the Comanches they pursue. Ethan far more resembles the people for whom he searches than the "Texicans" he defends: He knows Comanche customs, habits, rituals, and strategies. He knows the way they think and thinks the way they do. Martin, however, strongly feels

the pull back toward home: His sweetheart, Laurie Jorgensen (Vera Miles), will not wait forever.

The film's dominant contrast is between those who settle and those who search. Ethan feels uncomfortable indoors, within the comforts of a home, covered by a ceiling. Ford's beautiful and parallel shots, which begin and conclude the film, looking outdoors into the glaring sunlight through the dark arch of a doorway, are visual metaphors for the contrasting regions—of indoors and outdoors, civilization and wilderness, garden and desert, settling and searching. In Ford's metaphor, these two regions are contiguous; the warm familial peace indoors cannot be secure without taming the threat from the outdoors. There can be no settlers without searchers.

In the film's climax, Ethan chases the fleeing Debbie (Natalie Wood). Martin runs after them, terrified that Ethan intends to kill her, but Ethan sweeps her into his arms, up on his horse, and simply says, "Let's go home, Debbie." Like the film's opening and closing shots, this action completes a circle, for Ethan had lifted Debbie in much the same way when she was a little girl. This act of loving acceptance makes the civilized family possible and brings Ethan's obsessive quest for revenge to an unexpected but appropriate solution.

Douglas Sirk

In contrast to Ford's complex, energetic, and mutually enriching opposition of the settler's hearth and garden and the loner's wide open spaces, Douglas Sirk shrinks the world into a modern, bourgeois interior that has been arranged and ordered to death. Born in Denmark, Sirk moved to Germany, where he began making films in the 1930s. A leftist, he left Germany in 1937 and arrived in America in 1939 to direct anti-Nazi war films (*Hitler's Madman*, 1943), *films noirs* (*Sleep My Love*, 1948), and domestic comedies (*No Room for the Groom*, 1952). Sirk's major work began in 1954 after his move to Universal, where he became a director of glossy melodramas (adult soap operas, at the time called weepies or women's pictures) under producer Ross Hunter.

The Sirk melodramas are odd mixtures of contradictory qualities. On the one hand, they seem slick depictions of the most tawdry values of materialistic, middle-class life. On the other hand, they seem brutally funny comments on this very tawdriness, on the values of bourgeois life that the characters automatically accept and on the values of movies and movie audiences that accept them just as automatically. To see a Sirk film, like *Imitation of Life*, in a 1959 movie theatre was a fractured experience: half the audience sobbing hysterically into wet handkerchiefs, the other half laughing hysterically in sheer disbelief. These same contradictory reactions have divided audiences of Sirk films ever since.

The reason is that Sirk films are powerful bourgeois melodramas and, at the same time, powerful comments on the assumptions of bourgeois melodrama. In *All That Heaven Allows* (1955, U.S. release 1956), an attractive, middle-aged widow (Jane Wyman) falls for a younger man (Rock Hudson), her own gardener, depicted as Thoreau's "man of nature." Her friends find the man unsuitable—not rich enough, not old enough, not a member of her own social class. The single attraction they see in him is physical— what they can see. She sees him as spiritually different. But if he is such a "natural spirit," why does nature play such a tame visual role in the film—embodied by one symbolic deer behind a plate-glass window in a sound-stage forest? "Nature" is a pitiful visual metaphor in many Sirk films, like the hurricane of paper leaves that opens *Written on the Wind* (1956); to say the least, we are not in Ford's Monument Valley. Why is almost every scene of nature in the supposedly Thoreauvian *All That Heaven Allows* so obviously an indoor imitation of the outdoors? Is it a

mere studio convention, or is Sirk debunking the convention—along with the contrast between nature and artifice on which the film depends? This question is always at the center of a Sirk film. We are never quite sure who is kidding whom.

Sirk shoots his bourgeois world filtered through reminders of Hollywood's presence. Doorways, partitioning screens, window panes, mirrors, reflective surfaces (even the glass screens of television sets) dominate Sirk frames, calling attention to the fact that we look not at life but at a frame. Unnatural prismatic lighting effects in Sirk's color films raise questions about the source and purpose of this oddly colored light. Is the *mise-en-scène* merely decorative, an exercise in cold good taste, or is Sirk "deconstructing" the very images he constructs (pointing out their internal contradictions)? Is he using Brechtian distancing devices to separate the audience from the illusion of the work? Or is he, without irony— and with or without contempt—simply giving the audience what it wants: the slickly artificial and maudlin?

Imitation of Life (1959) is the ultimate Sirk film—both his last and his most powerful at posing these questions. It is a story about race relations, one of the few serious social subjects that films could explore in the 1950s without fear of right-wing protests and boycotts. An unemployed white actress, Lora (Lana Turner), meets a black woman, Annie (Juanita Moore), early in the film while their daughters play together on a crowded beach. The actress rises to success, aided by the

Fig. 12-23

Fig. 12-24

Imitation of Life: *Whether in a dressing room (Fig. 12-23) or a kitchen (Fig. 12-24), Annie (Juanita Moore) finds it "natural" to become the maid of her friend and equal, Lora (Lana Turner).*

financial support and household service of Annie, who has moved in with her. Lora's daughter, Susie (Sandra Dee), enjoys a typical upper-middle-class adolescence (boarding school and college), while the black daughter, Sarah Jane (Susan Kohner), who looks white, suffers the pain of social exclusion. She tries to escape her black heritage, seeking sexual affairs with white boys, working as a showgirl in a white nightclub—but returns in the end for her mother's funeral to suffer orgiastic agonies of grief, accompanied by the sorrowful singing of Mahalia Jackson and the sobbing ecstasies of the film's audience.

In remaking this Fanny Hurst novel, Sirk and Hunter made a crucial change. While in the original (novel and film), Lora makes a public success of Annie's private recipe for pancake flour (a clear allusion to Aunt Jemima), the black woman in the 1959 film has no direct relation to the white woman's vocational success. The world of pancake mix has been abandoned for the glittering world of Broadway stardom. What happens to the black woman in this new world? Quite simply, she becomes Lora's maid.

There is no indication in the film of why this black woman—the social and financial equal of the white woman at its beginning—should automatically accept her "place" as the white woman's servant. Annie does all the household chores, supervises the kitchen, serves as Lora's dresser, arranges Lora's dinner parties without any agreement that she will be paid for these services. What she gets in return is room and board (an arrangement once called slavery). Lora wears an endless number (actually 34) of shapely, bright-colored, high-fashion outfits (designed by Jean-Louis), decked with rings, necklaces, bracelets, and earrings. But Annie wears drab, nondescript clothes with plain collars and little jewelry. However many of these outfits she wears, they all look the same and always suggest the domestic. Neither Annie nor Lora sees anything odd in this visual inequality (as if it were "natural" for a black woman to become or resemble the servant of a white woman). The question is, does Sirk? Is this a plea for interracial respect and personal authenticity, or a sentimental exaltation of the problems of racism and role playing? Although the white woman and the black women inhabit the same house, the same film, and the same frame, they don't inhabit the same universe. Class and race have nothing and everything to do with their friendship. Who's kidding whom here?

Whatever adjectives one might seek to describe these films by Fuller, Hitchcock, Ray, Ford, and Sirk, escapist wouldn't be one of them. The moral, economic, social, psychological, and sexual ambiguities of such films suggest an America that was itself as genuinely confused as it was superficially assured about its purpose and direction.

Finding the Audience

Despite the gimmicks, despite the wide screen, despite the sexual innuendos, despite the industry's claim that movies were better than ever, movie income and movie admissions continued to fall throughout the 1950s. In an effort to give the public what television could not, Hollywood had to discover who its public was. It could not assume, as studio moguls Mayer and Cohn did in the 1930s, that its public was all of the people all of the time.

The signs that would eventually point the way had begun to appear just after the war. A series of foreign films—with De Sica's *The Bicycle Thief* (1948) the first highly publicized import—proved that a particular kind of film, inexpensively produced, more obviously sociological and less idealized than the Hollywood film, could attract interested audiences to small theatres while slick Hollywood films played to empty houses in large ones. More and more little neighborhood theatres that could no longer do business as fourth-run houses for Hollywood films found a second life as "art houses" by replacing the popcorn machine with an espresso maker and showing foreign pictures like *Rashomon* (1950), *Seven Samurai* (1954), *La strada* (1954), *Diabolique* (1955), and *The Seventh Seal* (1956) as soon as they were released in the United States.

A foreign film was certainly unlike anything that the networks could or would present on television: introspective, with dialogue requiring the audience to read subtitles, sensitive to intellectual and political questions, treating sexual matters frankly, with refreshing insights into other cultures, other values, and other ways of seeing. And these foreign imports had never been required to submit themselves to the moral approval of the Hays Office Code. There had been a call for "art houses" and an "art movement" in the 1930s, which had been answered in a few major cities by a few theatres. But the small art house of under 500 seats, with its elite fare, ran contrary to the old financial tides of the 1940s, when the movie palaces of several thousand seats filled up every night with customers eager to see Cary Grant or Greer Garson. With television, however, the commercial tides had turned.

Hollywood discovered that movies had indeed become an elite as well as a popular art. Just as the legitimate theatre had been the art for *some* in the 1930s when movies were the art for *everyone*, so movies had become the art for some when television became the art for all. Whereas movies had been the casual everyday form of entertainment before the war, TV supplied that kind of entertainment after it. Movies, then, had to be aimed at the minority audience that wanted the kind of show that television could not or would not provide; *Psycho* found that audience in 1960, as did *Dr. Strangelove* in 1964, *Bonnie and Clyde* in 1967, *Faces* in 1968, and *Medium Cool* in 1969. The elitism of the movie audience by 1970 becomes clear when comparing the average cost of a ticket in 1946 and 1970. Although films grossed almost the same amount of money in both years, in 1946 the average movie seat cost about 40¢; in 1970, the average seat cost $2. By 1980, the average cost had risen to $3.50, and in 1990, it was normal to pay $5.50 (top big-city prices rose to $4 in 1978 and to $7 in 1989; in 2001, they reached $9.50). Movies were no longer the "nickel" entertainment, the easiest to get for the least cost, that they had been since the turn of the century. But the programs on TV, like those on radio, were free.

To keep any share of the entertainment market at all, the motion-picture industry needed to reflect about who still went to movies and why. Families were one answer; movies still provided an outing for the whole family. But the combined cost of four, five, or six tickets meant that the outing would be rare and special—perfect for those family-oriented "specials," like the biblical blockbusters of the 1950s or the musical blockbusters of the 1960s.

The professional college-educated elite, who still lived in the cities or frequently visited them, was another answer. A strongly committed moviegoing generation of upwardly mobile Americans had discovered the cultural importance of movies—both American and foreign, both classic and new—during their college days.

Finally, there were the young, aged about 14 and upwards, for whom movies were an essential part of the socialization process. These young people used movies to get out of the house, away from the society of their parents (increasingly symbolized by that TV set), into a society of their own contemporaries.

It was easy for the movie industry to attract members of these two groups—the cultural elite and the adolescent—away from the TV set. Hollywood aimed its films at their values, their interests, their styles, using their themes, their music, their moral codes.

Even before the days of MTV, the VCR, and digital video, the movies learned to coexist with television. They made TV movies and licensed their films to be shown on TV. They recruited directors, writers, and actors with TV experience. They scrapped their movie palaces and replaced them with 500-seat theatres that were easier to fill despite their high ticket prices. They chopped big theatres into two or three or even multiplex theatres on the same property, a much more economical use of land and space. In 1973 both the MGM and the Twentieth Century–Fox back lots were sold to make room for apartment houses, office buildings, stores, restaurants, and streets.

Television, which threatened to swallow the film studios, also subsidized them. Over 75 percent of the film footage shot in Hollywood today is for TV production. The old studios survived the years of drift and struggle—if they survived at all— thanks to the steady income from TV filming. The old economic hierarchy—specials, A pictures, programmers, and B pictures—of the Studio Era still determines types of theatrical and TV production: Theatrical movies are Hollywood's top, special product; the miniseries and made-for-TV movies parallel the A pictures and programmers; the weekly TV shows are Hollywood's B staples; and of course TV has its shorts, news, and cartoons.

Although the American film business—yearly gross, weekly admissions, audience vitality and interest—has been thriving in recent decades, the theoretical capital of that business, Hollywood, is no longer *the* production center of American theatrical films. With so many companies filming in or near New York, San Francisco, Toronto, Montreal, London, all over the continent of Europe, and even in developing regional production centers (where states have established film boards specifically to lure production companies), Hollywood is still the name of the American movie game. But it is no longer the only stadium where that game is played.

For Further Viewing

FILMS

JACK ARNOLD (1912–92)
It Came From Outer Space (1953). 3-D
Creature from the Black Lagoon (1954). 3-D
Tarantula (1955)
The Incredible Shrinking Man (1957)
The Mouse That Roared (1959)

ROGER CORMAN (1926–)
Not of This Earth (1957)
The Little Shop of Horrors (1960)
The Pit and the Pendulum (1961)
X or *X—The Man with the X-Ray Eyes* (1963)
The Masque of the Red Death (1964)

JULES DASSIN (1911–)
The Naked City (1948)
Night and the City (1950)
Rififi or *Du Rififi chez les hommes* (1955)

STANLEY DONEN (1924–)
On the Town (1949). Co-director, Gene Kelly
Royal Wedding (1951)
Singin' In The Rain (1952). Co-director,
   Gene Kelly
The Pajama Game (1957)
Bedazzled (1967)

JOHN FRANKENHEIMER (1930–2002)
The Manchurian Candidate (1962)
Seven Days in May (1964)
Seconds (1966)
The Iceman Cometh (1973)

SAMUEL FULLER (1911–97)
The Steel Helmet (1951)
Pickup on South Street (1953)
Underworld U.S.A. (1961)
Shock Corridor (1963)
The Naked Kiss (1964)
The Big Red One (1980)

JOHN HUSTON (1906–87)
The Maltese Falcon (1941)
The Battle of San Pietro (1945)
The Treasure of the Sierra Madre (1948)

Key Largo (1948)
The Asphalt Jungle (1950)
The African Queen (1951)
Fat City (1972)
Wise Blood (1979)
The Dead (1987)

ELIA KAZAN (1909–2003)
A Tree Grows in Brooklyn (1945)
Gentleman's Agreement (1947)
A Streetcar Named Desire (1951)
On the Waterfront (1954)
East of Eden (1955)
A Face in the Crowd (1957)
Splendor in the Grass (1961)

HENRY KING (1888–1982)
Tol'able David (1921)
The Song of Bernadette (1943)
Twelve O'Clock High (1949)
King of the Khyber Rifles (1953)
Carousel (1956)
Tender is the Night (1962)

STANLEY KRAMER (1913–2001)
The Defiant Ones (1958)
On the Beach (1959)
Inherit the Wind (1960)
Judgment at Nuremberg (1961)
Ship of Fools (1965)
Guess Who's Coming to Dinner (1967)

JERRY LEWIS (1926–)
The Bellboy (1960)
The Nutty Professor (1963)
The Patsy (1964)

JOSEPH LOSEY (1909–84)
The Boy With Green Hair (1948)
The Damned or *These Are the Damned* (1962)
The Servant (1963)
Accident (1967)
Mr. Klein (1976)

SIDNEY LUMET (1924–)
12 Angry Men (1957)
Long Day's Journey Into Night (1962)
Fail-Safe (1964)
The Pawnbroker (1965)
The Hill (1965)
Serpico (1973)

Dog Day Afternoon (1975)
Network (1976)
The Verdict (1982)

JOSEPH L. MANKIEWICZ (1909–93)
The Ghost and Mrs. Muir (1947)
A Letter to Three Wives (1949)
All About Eve (1950)
The Barefoot Contessa (1954)
Guys and Dolls (1955)
Suddenly, Last Summer (1959)
Cleopatra (1963)

VINCENTÉ MINNELLI (1903–86)
Cabin in the Sky (1943)
Meet Me in St. Louis (1944)
An American in Paris (1951)
The Band Wagon (1953)
Tea and Sympathy (1956)

OTTO PREMINGER (1906–86)
Laura (1944)
River of No Return (1954)
Carmen Jones (1954)
The Man With the Golden Arm (1955)
Porgy and Bess (1959)
Anatomy of a Murder (1959)
Exodus (1960)
Advise and Consent (1962)

NICHOLAS RAY (1911–79)
They Live By Night (1949). Completed 1948
Knock on Any Door (1949)
In A Lonely Place (1950)
Johnny Guitar (1954)
Rebel Without a Cause (1955)

DON SIEGEL (1912–91)
The Verdict (1946)
Invasion of the Body Snatchers (1956)
Dirty Harry (1971)
The Shootist (1976)

DOUGLAS SIRK (1900–87)
Magnificent Obsession (1954)
All That Heaven Allows (1955)
Written on the Wind (1956)
The Tarnished Angels (1957)
Imitation of Life (1959)

GEORGE STEVENS (1904–75)
Swing Time (1936)
Gunga Din (1939)

Woman of the Year (1942)
A Place in the Sun (1951)
Shane (1953)
Giant (1956)

BILLY WILDER (1906–2002)
Double Indemnity (1944)
The Lost Weekend (1945)
Sunset Boulevard (1950)
The Big Carnival or *Ace in the Hole* (1951)
Stalag 17 (1953)
The Seven Year Itch (1955)
Some Like It Hot (1959)
The Apartment (1960)
One, Two, Three (1961)

ROBERT WISE (1914–   )
The Curse of the Cat People (1944). Co-director, Gunther Von Fritsch
The Body Snatcher (1945)
The Set-Up (1949)
The Day the Earth Stood Still (1951)
West Side Story (1961). Co-director, Jerome Robbins
The Haunting (1963)
The Sand Pebbles (1966)

FRED ZINNEMANN (1907–97)
High Noon (1952)
From Here to Eternity (1953)
Oklahoma! (1955)
A Man for All Seasons (1966)
The Day of the Jackal (1973)

TRANSITIONAL ERA MISCELLANY
The Killers (1946, Robert Siodmak)
Crossfire (1947, Edward Dmytryk)
Out of the Past (1947, Jacques Tourneur)
Force of Evil (1948, Abraham Polonsky)
Home of the Brave (1949, Mark Robson)
Intruder in the Dust (1949, Clarence Brown)
Mighty Joe Young (1949, Ernest B. Schoedsack)
Gun Crazy (1950, Joseph H. Lewis). Completed 1949
The Thing or *The Thing From Another World* (1951, Christian Nyby)
Native Son (1951). With Richard Wright (Pierre Chenal)
Red Planet Mars (1952, Harry Horner)
My Son John (1952, Leo McCarey)

The Hitch-Hiker and *The Bigamist* (1953, Ida Lupino)

Salt of the Earth (1953, Herbert Biberman)

The Wild One (1953, Laslo Benedek)

The War of the Worlds (1953, Byron Haskin)

Invaders From Mars (1953, William Cameron Menzies)

House of Wax (1953, André de Toth). 3-D

Them! (1954, Gordon Douglas)

The Bridges at Toko-Ri (1954, Mark Robson)

The Caine Mutiny (1954, Edward Dmytryk)

Blackboard Jungle (1955, Richard Brooks)

Marty (1955, Delbert Mann)

The Night of the Hunter (1955, Charles Laughton)

Kiss Me Deadly (1955, Robert Aldrich)

This Island Earth (1955, Joseph Newman)

Forbidden Planet (1956, Fred M. Wilcox)

Sweet Smell of Success (1957, Alexander Mackendrick)

I Was a Teenage Werewolf (1957, Gene Fowler)

The Blob (1958, Irvin S. Yeaworth, Jr.)

Elmer Gantry (1960, Richard Brooks)

The Magnificent Seven (1960, John Sturges)

The Connection (1961, Shirley Clarke)

Lonely Are the Brave (1962, David Miller)

What Ever Happened to Baby Jane? (1962, Robert Aldrich)

David and Lisa (1963, Frank Perry)

Point of Order (1964, Emile de Antonio)

Dr. Strangelove Or: How I Learned To Stop Worrying And Love The Bomb (1964, Stanley Kubrick)

The World of Henry Orient (1964, George Roy Hill)

The Spy Who Came In from the Cold (1965, Martin Ritt)

DVDs

All That Heaven Allows (1955, **Douglas Sirk**). Criterion Collection. Includes BBC documentary with Sirk interview; **Fassbinder** essay, "Imitation of Life: The Films of Douglas Sirk"; and notes by film theorist Laura Mulvey. Blacklist data, interviews, and shorts are included with *Spartacus* (see Chap. 15 list).

The Day the Earth Stood Still (1951, **Robert Wise**). Twentieth Century Fox Home Video. Includes a 1951 Movietone newsreel, a commentary by Wise and Nicolas Meyer, a documentary, **restoration** comparisons, and the shooting script.

Dirk Bogarde Collection. Anchor Bay. **Dirk Bogarde** stars in *The Mind Benders* (1963, **Basil Dearden**), *The Servant* (1963, **Joseph Losey**), and *Accident* (1967, **Losey**).

Film Noir Classic Collection. Warner Home Video. Contains *Murder, My Sweet* (1945, **Edward Dmytryk**), *Out of the Past* (1947, **Jacques Tourneur**), *The Set-Up* (1949, **Robert Wise**), *Gun Crazy* (1949, rel. 1950, **Joseph H. Lewis**), and *The Asphalt Jungle* (1950, **John Huston**), with commentaries.

Film Noir Killer Classics. Questar. Includes *Detour* (1945, **Edgar G. Ulmer**), *Scarlet Street* (1945, **Fritz Lang**), *The Stranger* (1946, **Orson Welles**), *Too Late for Tears* as *Killer Bait* (1949, **Byron Haskin**), *D.O.A.* (1950, **Rudolf Maté**), 38 *film noir* **trailers**, posters, documentaries on *noir* and *femmes fatales*, and more.

From Here to Eternity (1953, **Fred Zinnemann**). Columbia TriStar. Includes documentaries, short biographies, and commentaries by Zinnemann's son and actor Alvin Sargent.

The Hitch-Hiker (1953, **Ida Lupino**). Kino Video. **Restored** from the Library of Congress print.

Invasion of the Body Snatchers (1956, **Don Siegel**). Republic Studios. Letterboxed (with the pan-and-scan for comparison), and with an interview with actor Kevin McCarthy.

The Manchurian Candidate (1962, **John Frankenheimer**). Metro-Goldwyn-Mayer. Special Edition. Includes commentary by Frankenheimer, interviews, and shorts.

On the Waterfront (1954, **Elia Kazan**). Columbia TriStar. Includes an interview with Kazan; short biographies of **Budd Schulberg**, **Marlon Brando**, etc.; a documentary; and commentaries.

Pickup on South Street (1953, **Samuel Fuller**). Criterion Collection. Interviews with Fuller, a poster filmography, trailers for 8 Fuller films, and a booklet with excerpts from his autobiography.

Rififi (1955, **Jules Dassin**). Criterion Collection. The best *noir* ever made in France, famous for its long, silent robbery sequence. Includes an interview with Dassin.

Singin' in the Rain (1952, **Stanley Donen** and **Gene Kelly**). Warner Home Video. Special edition, with a digital transfer from **restored** elements, a documentary on Freed musicals, other shorts and clips, and commentary by the screenwriters and cast. Looks good on DVD, but not when digitally projected.

Sunset Boulevard (1950, **Billy Wilder**). Paramount Home Video. Special Collector's Edition. **Restored**, with commentary by Wilder scholar Ed Sikov, documentaries, script pages for the original morgue prologue, a short on Edith Head's costume designs, and a map.

The Treasure of the Sierra Madre (1948, **John Huston**). Warner Home Video. New transfer from **restored** picture and sound elements; documentaries; cartoons; **Humphrey Bogart** trailers; a radio version; and commentary by historian Eric Lax.

West Side Story (1961, **Jerome Robbins** and **Robert Wise**). Metro-Goldwyn-Mayer. Special Edition Collector's Set. Includes a scrapbook with the complete working film script, memos, and reviews; a storyboard-to-film comparison; the intermission music (remastered); and a documentary with Natalie Wood's original recordings and new interviews.

13

Neorealism
and the New Wave

The French and Italian postwar cinemas revolutionized the values and aesthetics of the motion picture itself. The changes in content and style that began in Italy and culminated in France affected and influenced the entire world's cinema as much as Griffith, Murnau, or Eisenstein did in the Silent Era.

Italian Neorealism and the French New Wave were the two most important movements of the Sound Era. They forced filmmakers to rethink everything from the social value of movies to the realism of photography and from the politics of form to the metaphysics of cinematic time and space. They made the world care and think. They used film to investigate its own language. They used film to interrogate the world. They inspired and excited viewers with entirely new kinds of movies. As they rose to the defining challenges of political crisis and aesthetic opportunity, they urged the world to follow them into the next cinematic era.

After World War II, European directors did exactly what they did after the First World War. They climbed out from under years of wartime rubble and disrupted production, somehow scraped together enough money and film stock, and began making films that showed extraordinary sincerity, insight, and artistic control. While American films groped for a new identity, many of the films that struck audiences and critics as the best came from Europe. The European films seemed best not because they revealed portions of naked bodies, not because they were obscure, and not because Americans had become cultural snobs—as so many American film executives

claimed. The films seemed best because they raised the same questions in cinematic form that had been raised in the best novels, plays, poems, and philosophical essays of the 20th century. And the adult Americans who had become the new movie audience, those who found it easy to leave their TV sets, were precisely those who were reading the books.

It was not that American films were mindless but that the best films from Europe were so explicitly serious, more aggressively existential, Modernist, and adult than the familiar genres and attitudes of Hollywood. In the tradition of Mann, Proust, Pirandello, and Sartre (and, by the way, of Renoir, Eisenstein, Murnau, and Pabst), the new European film searched for meaningful, life-giving values in a world in which absolute values had crumbled. The social and psychological problems of these European films could not be solved by Hollywood's two most frequent forms of closure—the killing of a bad guy or the marriage of John and Jane. Many European films began with a marriage rather than ended with one.

The great films of postwar Europe, despite the individuality of the particular directors, shared several traits that contrasted with the typical American film. First, very few of them were adaptations of familiar books and plays. Most were original conceptions, carefully shaped by the director and scenarist working in unison.

Second, those postwar European films that reached American viewers continued the prewar tradition of structuring themselves around a theme or a psychological problem more than around a story.

Third, the focus on form and theme brought these films back into the mainstream of 20th-century thought and literature. The philosophical and psychological questions in these films, and to some degree the ways they were handled, from Bergman to the New Wave, were related to those in Kafka, Pound, Joyce, Proust, Mann, Woolf, Faulkner, Camus, Ionesco, and others.

Fourth, the films looked different from each other and from the product of Hollywood or any big studio. European directors discovered different ways to define film style, realizing that certain kinds of thematic inquiries or psychological states required a totally different handling of the *mise-en-scène*, camera, and soundtrack.

The postwar European cinema—especially the New Wave—brought the movies back into the mainstream of Modernism, the key 20th-century movement that produced nonrepresentational painting, atonal music, absurd drama, and the stream-of-consciousness novel. If the first major Modernist film was *Intolerance* and the best known for decades was *Battleship Potemkin*, the audiences of the 1950s and 1960s recognized the breakthroughs made by filmmakers from Rossellini to Resnais, and an invigorated social and intellectual discussion found the movies crucial both to art and to political analysis. The years after 1945 were a great period in film history, one in which wave after wave of European directors and writers had something to say and knew how to say it.

Italian Neorealism

Not since 1914 had Italy been an important international film power. Early Italian sound films traveled between the two poles of pro-Mussolini propaganda and of escapist comedies, historical spectacles, and musical romances. Mussolini extended considerable aid to the film industry, founding both a huge film studio (Cinecittà) and a film school (Centro Sperimentale). Although opposite the Soviets in ideology, Mussolini believed just as firmly in the persuasive power of cinema to shape a people.

After the overthrow of Mussolini and the expulsion of the Nazis, the Italian filmmakers, highly experienced in film production, used the new freedom to combine their skill in making pictures with the subjects about which they wanted to make pictures.

Roberto Rossellini

Even as the Nazis were evacuating Rome, Roberto Rossellini began to work on *Open City* (*Roma, città aperta*, 1945). An "open city" is one that is immune from attack because it has been declared demilitarized, as Rome was. Rossellini made the film under the most difficult conditions, closely resembling the early production problems of the Soviets: Raw film stock was scarce, money for constructing sets was even scarcer, actors were difficult to find, slickness and polish were impossible without the controlled lighting of studio filming. Rossellini turned defects into virtues. He willingly sacrificed polish for authenticity, sets for real locations, fiction for life. Rossellini often preferred laborers and peasants to actors (a parallel with Eisenstein and Pudovkin). He and cinematographer Ubaldo Arata carried their camera all over and fleetingly shot the real city on the run.

Open City (written by Sergio Amidei, Rossellini, and Fellini) contrasts the humane, committed, unified struggle of the Italian people for freedom—the unity of priests, workers, intellectuals, adults, children—with the brutality of the Nazi invaders, who used the most loathsome methods (torture, bribery, addiction) to enslave the weakest Italians or to force them to betray their fellows. The two styles of the film—the natural, open, realistic, crisply lit texture of the scenes with the Resistance figures and the cramped, artificial, shadowy texture of the scenes with the Nazis—support the film's thematic contrast.

At the end of the film a single member of the Resistance, a committed priest (Don Pietro, played by Aldo Fabrizi), is executed by the Nazi oppressors for his service to the people. This priest is a notable political exception (the Italian clergy generally supported Mussolini's Fascist government), and his alliance with the Resistance is also an alliance with the Communists who led it. As the partisan priest dies, Rossellini's camera captures the activities of the children of Rome and a far shot of the city itself, for from the death of this one man will come a solidarity that was to be the hope of the new Rome. *Open City* became the unofficial cornerstone of a new movement in Italian cinema—Neorealism, a "new realism" characterized by the use of nonprofessional actors and realistic dialogue, an emphasis on the everyday struggles of common people and the

Fig. 13-1   **Fig. 13-2**

Open City: *From the death of a single valiant priest (Fig. 13-1, Aldo Fabrizi), the boys walk back to the city, arm in arm.*

unvarnished look of nonstudio reality, and the determination to present the characters in relation to their real social environments and political and economic conditions.

Rossellini's next film, *Paisan* (1946), further defined his commitments. A collection of separate vignettes, each of the film's six sequences moves progressively north with the Allied invasion and Nazi retreat. Despite its documentary structure, mirroring the movement of the campaign, Rossellini concentrates on the human texture within each of the vignettes—some lighter and some more brutal, some dominated by the imagery of battle-scarred cities and some by the apparent placidity of the countryside. As is usual for Rossellini, he neither makes simple judgments nor takes simple positions, he is neither for nor against the insensitivities of the invading liberators and neither for nor against the Italians, themselves terribly divided by the struggle. Rossellini's camera, managed by Otello Martelli, records the luminous countryside in which the struggle takes place, seemingly unaffected by the brutal battle within it. The counterpoint between human action and the landscape that contains it would remain Rossellini's dominant visual technique and personal theme.

Rossellini completed this "War Trilogy" with *Germany Year Zero* (1947), in which he examined the rubble, hunger, and unemployment of postwar Berlin. He then tracked inward from cross-sectional surveys of an entire society to close studies of personal moralities and internal sensations. The best of these studies—*Stromboli*

(1949) and *Viaggio in Italia* (*Voyage to Italy,* 1953)—featured Ingrid Bergman, the great star who defied Hollywood propriety and world opinion by abandoning her husband to remain with Rossellini in Italy.

Rossellini's ability to render the moral, emotional, architectural, philosophical, and poetic power of sights and systems would make him a major influence on a new generation of directors in both Italy and France.

De Sica and Zavattini

Cesare Zavattini, who wrote virtually all of Vittorio De Sica's Neorealist films, defined the principles of the movement: to show things as they are, not as they seem, nor as the bourgeois would prefer them to appear; to write fictions about the human side of representative social, political, and economic conditions; to shoot on location wherever possible; to use untrained actors in the majority of roles; to capture and reflect reality with little or no compromise; to depict common people rather than overdressed heroes and fantasy role models; to reveal the everyday rather than the exceptional; and to show a person's relationship to the real social environment rather than to his or her romantic dreams. As can be seen from the last of these tenets, the movement was as opposed to Expressionism as it was to Hollywood. The Neorealist film developed the influence of the social environment on basic human needs: the need for food, shelter, work, love, family, sex, honor. In the tradition of Marxist thought

Fig. 13-3
The Bicycle Thief: *Father (Lamberto Maggiorani) and son (Enzo Staiola) search for the irreplaceable bicycle.*

(yet another parallel with the classic Soviet films), the Neorealist films repeatedly show that unjust and perverted social structures threaten to pervert or destroy essential human values.

Vittorio De Sica became the most popular Italian Neorealist with American audiences, probably because his melodramas effectively combined the political, the sentimental, and the traditional story—as opposed to the detached ironies, paradoxical observations, conceptual framing, and elliptical narratives of Rossellini. De Sica, a popular stage and film actor in the 1930s and director of escapist fluff films in the early 1940s, directed the Neorealist *Shoeshine* in 1946 (script by Zavattini), a brutally poignant study of the destruction of a pair of Roman boys by both the gangsters and the police who are using them. *The Bicycle Thief* (1948, Zavattini's most important script) is another study of degradation and pain. Its literal title, *Bicycle Thieves (Ladri di biciclette)*, is more appropriate than the accepted American translation because there are two thieves in the film: the man who steals the protagonist's bike and the protagonist himself (Antonio, played by Lamberto Maggiorani), who eventually becomes a bicycle thief out of necessity.

From the film's opening shots De Sica and Zavattini begin their relentless development of the kind of social environment that turns men into bicycle thieves: There are many men without work; there are very few jobs; the men have wives and children to support; the man with a bicycle is one of the lucky working few. To get his bicycle out of the pawn shop, Antonio's wife takes her wedding sheets to pawn in exchange for the bike. The poignancy of her sacrifice is underscored by De Sica's long shot of piles of pawned bridal sheets—others have been forced to make the same sacrifice. De Sica's camera emphasizes the quantities of people and things that are embraced by this story rather than implying that this is a tale of the exceptional few.

The film's powerfully simple narrative premise is Antonio's desperate need to find his stolen bicycle. Without the bicycle he has no job; without a job his family starves. The man and his young son, Bruno (Enzo Staiola), roam the streets, catching an occasional glimpse of the bike or the figure who stole it. Throughout the film the boy's relationship with his father serves as barometer of the effects of the agonizing search on the man's soul. Father and son drift further apart; the man even strikes the boy. When Antonio finally corners the thief, the thief's mother and neighbors protect him, and neither the police nor the local Mafia are any help, since Antonio has no evidence.

Realizing the impossibility of ever getting his own bicycle back, Antonio is tempted by the sight of the many unattended bikes around him. In desperation, he steals a bicycle himself, is swiftly caught, and then is beaten and abused by the angry citizens. Bruno sees his father's ultimate degradation. When the father tries to hurry away from the boy in shame, Bruno catches up with him and slips his hand inside his father's. Despite the terrible social humiliation, the humanity and affection of father and son have been restored. Then they disappear into a crowd of people who, the film implies, are struggling with analogous problems; this tragedy, made from such unglamorous materials, is one among thousands.

De Sica claims that an American producer offered him millions to make *Bicycle Thieves* with Cary Grant as Antonio. De Sica rejected both the money and the star. Instead, he cast a metal worker, a nonactor, as the desperate father. De Sica's preference reveals many of the principles of Neorealism: authenticity rather than pretense, earthiness rather than sparkle, the common man rather than the idol. Instead of Hollywood's bright sets and stylish clothes, these films showed primitive kitchens, squalid living rooms, peeling walls, torn clothing, streets that almost stank of urine and garbage. Instead of the Hollywood love goddess, the Neorealist heroine incarnate was Anna Magnani: coarse, fiery,

indefatigable, sexual, strong, sweaty. Zavattini claimed that the Neorealist film was as attached to the present as sweat was to skin.

The essential theme of the Neorealist film was the conflict between the contemporary common man and the immense social, economic, and political forces that determined his existence: first the war, after it the means of making a living and the struggle to keep a home and family together. In the late 1940s, many Italian directors developed their own variations on this essential theme.

But by 1950 Neorealism had either run or begun to change its course. The films became increasingly psychological and less sociological. The Italian film for the international market, while still valuing the realist actor and the realist milieu, had begun to use more polished scripts, more carefully constructed sets, more conventional fictional structures and themes, and highly professional actors. Even the original Neorealist directors wandered away from earlier styles and themes.

Luchino Visconti

The potential direction of Italian realism was predicted by a much earlier film: Luchino Visconti's *Ossessione* (*Obsession*, 1942, released 1943). Visconti's film, an unauthorized adaptation of James M. Cain's novel of sexual sordidness and murder, *The Postman Always Rings Twice*, uses squalid settings and realistic rather than romantic human types as background for its personal, psychological action. Social realism becomes the film's milieu, its soil, rather than its subject. Visconti's films consistently depart from the Zavattini definitions, using the social reality to define the personal problems of the characters rather than as the focus of the films themselves.

Of the three major Neorealist directors, Visconti had the most elegant visual sensibility, an almost sensuously formal approach to camera movement and composition. An aristocrat and Marxist, Visconti made the most uncompromisingly authentic of Neorealist pictures (*La terra trema, The Earth Trembles*, 1945—shot in a dialect most Italians could not understand) and the most artificial of grand romantic meditations (*Senso*, 1954; *Death in Venice*, 1971); the contradictions of his tastes and concerns were reconciled in the operatic approach he took to all his subjects. An excess of desire and a commitment to analysis characterized not only Visconti's films, but also those of the next generation of Italian masters, from Fellini to Pasolini.

Romantics and Antiromantics

Federico Fellini

Although Federico Fellini's apprenticeship was to Rossellini and Amidei on the screenplays for *Open City*, *Paisan*, and *The Miracle*, Fellini's own films reveal the flamboyant romantic. He preferred the places of mystery, magic, and make-believe—the circus, the variety theatre, the nightclub, the opera house—to the squalid slums of reality. His characters search for happiness, for love, for meaning, not for social security. If Anna Magnani or Ingrid Bergman is the soul of Rossellini's Neorealism, Giulietta Masina is the soul of Fellini, his wife offscreen—she survived him by only a few months—and the central figure of many of his films, including *La strada* (*The Road*, 1954) and *Nights of Cabiria* (1956), two of his greatest. Giulietta Masina, with the glowing eyes, the smirking mouth, the deep dimples, wildly joyful, wildly sad, is to Anna Magnani as a sunbeam is to a lion. In both *La strada* and *Cabiria* Masina plays a pure spirit of love, a being of the heart.

In the earlier film, she is Gelsomina, the clownish fool, apprenticed to the strong man, Zampanò (Anthony Quinn), who uses her as servant, performer, cook, and concubine—human chattel. Despite her rough treatment from the boorish animal–man, Gelsomina comes to love him. But he—afraid of human commitment, of emotional strings—betrays her, leaving her alone to die in the snow. Only after Gelsomina is dead, when the strong man hears the haunting, sweet–sad song that she once played on her trumpet, does the strong man learn how weak and alone he is as he sobs helplessly in a vast, cold, empty universe of sand, sea, and sky.

As Cabiria, Giulietta Masina plays once again the spirit of love trampled by the realities of human selfishness. Cabiria is the pure-hearted whore, forced to sell her love since no one wants it for nothing. The film opens with a boyfriend stealing her purse and throwing her in the river. Every sequence duplicates the disillusionment of this opening one.

But Cabiria does not die. In one of the most truly ironic and metaphorical endings in film history, the weeping Cabiria encounters a group of festive, singing youngsters as she walks on the road back to town (and, metaphorically, to life). They sing as she sobs; they do not notice her tears; their singing does not stop her tears, but she continues walking with them, participating vicariously in their song. The laughter and tears of Cabiria's life, of Everyman's life, have been brilliantly juxtaposed.

Fellini's greatest international success was *La dolce vita* (*The Sweet Life*, 1960; U.S. release 1961). In this wide-screen epic of the superficiality of modern life, with its unforgettable score by Nino Rota and stellar performance by Marcello Mastroianni, Fellini deserted Neorealism forever.

The contrast between sensuality and spirituality dominates *La dolce vita* from its first sequence, in which a helicopter pilot, towing a statue of Christ, looks down and waves at three women in bikinis, sunning themselves on a Roman roof. The film's themes are already clear: Christ has been petrified; he is a tool of the modern world (the helicopter); people have lost faith without finding an adequate substitute. Showing the effects of this moral superficiality, Fellini continues for three hours, contrasting sensual things—nightclubs, orgiastic parties— with the corruption of spiritual things—an intellectual commits suicide, children pretend to see a miraculous vision. But excess is part of his point, even this numbing excess of schematic examples. There is too much of everything in this film—everything but what the characters really need: some fulfilling kind of peace, simple beauty, self-knowledge. The hedonistic, narcissistic, highly publicized "sweet life" is an existential vacuum.

What characterizes and energizes Fellini's work is a romantic rebelliousness and an ambivalent reaction to the grotesque. A consistent Fellini target is the Roman Catholic Church. For Fellini, the Church is a hypocritical and empty show that bilks its public by playing on its insecurities and fears. The Church is the archsensualist masquerading as a spiritualist, hiding its confusion behind a mask of dogma and ritual. In *La strada*, Fellini photographs a solemn Church procession with a neon sign reading "Bar" in the foreground; in *Nights of Cabiria*, a society of human

Fig. 13-4
La strada: Gelsomina (Giulietta Masina) and Zampanò (Anthony Quinn). Love despite the obstacles.

unfortunates takes a desperate outing to a religious festival, where they are greeted by canned prayers on loudspeakers and greedy vendors hawking sacred candles and secular candies. In *8½* (1963), the Church offers the main character not spiritual guidance but a ritualistic structure of nostalgia and guilt. *Fellini Roma* (1972) includes a monstrously funny clerical fashion show.

Whereas Fellini treats organized religion with grotesque bitterness and comical contempt, he treats the glamorous world of the rich with a stylish grotesqueness that reveals both its emptiness and its fascination. The society party in *La dolce vita*, the patrons of the health spa in *8½*, the first-class passengers in *And the Ship Sails On* (1983), are all examples of the grotesque—in costume, make-up, gestures, features, shapes, sizes—that Fellini finds hauntingly attractive.

Fellini's greatest film, his most impressive synthesis of dramatic power, personal vision, and cinematic control, may well be *8½*. Perhaps the quintessential postwar Modernist feature, the subject of *8½* is simply itself. It is not merely about filmmaking; it is about the making of a film

very much like this one: a film the director finds impossible to make. The protagonist of *8½* (Guido, played by Marcello Mastroianni) is a director himself. Because of his nervousness and tension, he is relaxing, preparing for his next film, at a fashionable health spa. Preparing for the project, the director is flooded with images out of his film and memories out of his life, which get thoroughly and inextricably confused. The director's emotional problem in the film— and undoubtedly Guido represents Fellini here— is wondering whether he is successful at either life or art. His memories and fantasies not only intrude on the action but become it; the filmmaker's mindscreens and his moviemaking project unfold together, in a brilliantly integrated construct of stress and desire, analysis and nostalgia.

8½ begins with Guido's nightmare: He feels trapped inside a hot, smoky automobile during a mammoth traffic jam. He longs to escape from the car, to fly high above the earth. The remainder of the film works on the man's anxiety and longing, his desire to break free of the bonds of

8½: the artist (Marcello Mastroianni) among his memories and fantasies.

Fig. 13-5

his life, his desire to soar in life and art. He searches throughout for an actress to portray a pure lady in white, an illusory panacea that will make sense of both his personal relationships and his artistic purpose. By the end, Guido appears to renounce the search. He attends a gala party for his film. Unable to resolve his personal conflicts or to finish the film, he imagines crawling under a table and shooting himself. The party becomes a gigantic circus composing all the characters of his memories and his film. Fellini's camera swirls in an excited circle as the parade of Guido's creatures dances about a circus ring, that familiar Fellini setting. Guido stares at the dancing creatures; he then steps into their circle and joins the dance. The film that could not be made has been abandoned, but *8½* has been completed. Whatever Guido's (and Fellini's) deficiencies as a human being, he is a maker of films. That is his act in the big circus.

Michelangelo Antonioni

Like Fellini's, Michelangelo Antonioni's roots were in Neorealism. While Rossellini and De Sica were making their documentary-style features, Antonioni was making documentary shorts about the lives of street cleaners and

farmers. But Antonioni soon deserted the documentary for the highly polished and understated drama of personal sensations—of perceptions, emotions, epiphanies, moods—eventually to return to documentary filmmaking for the 1972 *Chung Kuo Cina*, shot in the People's Republic of China. Antonioni is as much an Abstract Expressionist painter as a documentary photographer. His series of 184 paintings, "Montagne Encantate" (Enchanted Mountain), reveals some of his visual values. These are colorful representations of living rocks, vaguely sensuous landscapes dominated by clashes of color and contrasts of forms. Such enigmatic shapes, charged with ambiguous significance, would dominate Antonioni's films as well, their evocative landscapes closer to Rossellini's disciplined psychological imagery (and, in France, Robert Bresson's pure, severe, unsentimental, understated intensity) than to Fellini's flamboyance or Zavattini's Neorealism. Whereas that Neorealism used the external social environment to define a human being, Antonioni found a way to present landscape and character as an integrated mystery—a subtle Expressionism in the service of psychological, sociological, and philosophical insight.

After making seven short documentaries (1943–50) and directing his first features, Antonioni achieved complete mastery over his method with *L'avventura* (*The Adventure*, 1960), the first film of a trilogy that includes *La notte* (*The Night*, 1960) and *L'eclisse* (*Eclipse*, 1962). In declaring a new Italian cinema, this trilogy was at least as significant as *La dolce vita* and *8½*, partly because the two filmmakers were so stylistically assured and such opposites. If Fellini's films are fast, flamboyant, grotesque, and richly emotional, Antonioni's are slow, spare, unwilling to draw pointed conclusions, and often about characters who are unable to feel deeply—or to be sure what it is they feel.

Antonioni's method concentrates as much on the scenic environment as on the people in the environment. The emotional resonances of the environment convey the internal states of the people within it. Antonioni's favorite photographic subjects include both nature—for example, the sea and rocks in *L'avventura*—and the slick, hard-surfaced materials of modern architecture: glass, aluminum, terrazzo. The beginnings of Antonioni films consistently use the scenic environment to define both the film's social milieu and its emotional climate.

A cliché of Antonioni criticism is that all his characters live lives that are boring and empty, meaningless and sterile and that his films are accordingly boring, sterile, and abstract. But *La notte* has a deep emotional power that sneaks up on you, and *Blowup* (1966) does not deny meaning but complicates our view of its nature. Most of the central Antonioni figures find some value that helps them live. And what they learn most often is how to live with ambiguity. Like the characters, the films struggle to communicate things that are almost impossible to put into words or express in actions and images. With great effort, Antonioni's movies communicate emotional and moral states that can never be entirely clear or resolved.

The real subject of the Antonioni films is education. In the course of their journeys, his characters learn the pervasiveness of emptiness and the possible if temporary ways of combating it. For such a theme, Antonioni's visual images are the only means of rendering each emotional stage of the journey convincingly and sensitively. These outer landscapes become inner ones. No other director of sound films is freer of words and more dependent on pictures than Antonioni.

L'avventura may be Antonioni's most completely realized film. It is at once rewarding and frustrating, stunning and boring, uplifting and depressing. When a group of friends go on an adventure to an uninhabited island, Anna (Lea Massari) disappears; her lover, Sandro (Gabriele Ferzetti), and her best friend, Claudia (Monica Vitti), try to find her. Sandro and Claudia eventually become lovers—and never do find Anna. Despite the impression that the plot wanders, it

The white wall in L'avventura: *Sandro (Gabriele Ferzetti) and Anna (Lea Massari).*

Fig. 13-6

travels steadily toward its final, ambiguous moment of reconciliation and compassion in which Claudia can feel sympathy for the weakness of Sandro and in which Sandro can feel the terrible pathos of his need to betray Claudia. The plot is a series of betrayals. Anna betrays Claudia by making her wait downstairs while she viciously devours Sandro in an afternoon of casual lovemaking. Sandro has betrayed his talent as an architect by selling out to the pressures of finance. Antonioni shows Sandro's bitterness as the former architect deliberately spills ink on a young architectural student's careful line drawing of the town's cathedral. Sandro's betrayals are also sexual. He betrays Anna by lusting after Claudia before Anna disappears. And even after the touching, fulfilling moments with Claudia, he callously flirts with the tasteless American publicity seeker in the very hotel where Claudia waits in bed for his return.

But if Sandro's education is to discover the human weakness that makes betrayal so inevitable, Claudia's education is to discover that betrayal is a fact of human life. "Human" and "fallible" are unfortunately synonymous; any meaningful human relationship must start from that definition. *L'avventura* is a journey and adventure that bring Sandro and Claudia to that potential starting point, but their relationship may be over. The ending of the film is both open and final; *L'avventura* leaves many questions unanswered—What happened to Anna? What will happen to Sandro and Claudia?—and is complete. It offers figures in a landscape that is often more interesting than they are, and it has no interest in genre or formula. For all its emotional complexity, it is beyond the characters that *L'avventura*, like other Antonioni films, finds a coherence that can be expressed only by the camera.

Pasolini and Bertolucci

The two most interesting and influential Italian *auteurs* to emerge in the 1960s were Pier Paolo Pasolini and Bernardo Bertolucci. Like most of the earlier Neorealists, both were Marxists who sought to combine a passion for politics with a passion for cinema. But if Bertolucci is a romantic, Pasolini is profoundly antiromantic.

Pasolini began his career as a street bum and a poet. All his life, he wrote poetry and interrogated systems. He was expelled from the Italian Communist Party in 1949 because of his homosexuality. "Rational and irrational to the utmost," as he said of himself in a poem, he began making films in the Neorealist mode—the protagonist of *Accattone* (*Beggar*, 1961) is a poor, brash young man in a Roman slum, trying to earn enough money to survive—but soon was questioning and exploding its conventions. Abandoning Neorealism but not the poor and not the question of power, Pasolini made elliptical, satiric, and often brutal films about moral and political degradation and the poetry of rebellion.

Bertolucci's first major success, *Before the Revolution* (1964), set the pattern for his more famous films to follow—a study of the interrelationship between political structures and sexual or emotional fulfillment. While Pasolini's films are more abstract, more complexly structured, and more ferociously aggressive moral–political investigations, enlivened and propelled by dazzling bursts of unforgettable imagery, Bertolucci's conform to a more familiar narrative pattern, which combines political events in a particular society with richly rendered characters, emotionally expressive color settings, and carefully structured strings of narrative action, sinuous but linear (like the rich movements of his camera).

In Pasolini's *Teorema* (*Theorem*, 1968), its very title informing us that it is a logical demonstration, a beautiful young man—a kind of angel—succeeds in blasting apart the apparently solid foundations of a bourgeois family by making every member of it fall in love with him—the maid, daughter, artist son, mother, and high-finance businessman father. At the end of the film, the businessman has been so overwhelmed by his passion, his commitment to a forbidden, antibourgeois love, that he wanders about the town's railroad station, seeking to pick up hustlers. The grand bourgeois has been stripped of all the moral, social, and political apparatus by which he lived his life. The theorem that underlies this stripping process is, quite simply, that sexual passion knows no moral or social boundaries and that those who least know this truth—the grandest, *hautest* bourgeoisie—are most easily overwhelmed by the discovery of the flimsy assumptions on which their lives are based.

Salò (1975) was Pasolini's last film before he was murdered in a sexual incident that might well have occurred in one of his films. Based on

Salò: *sexual slavery as a metaphor for moral and political bondage.*

Fig. 13-7

the Marquis de Sade's *The 120 Days of Sodom* and named for the northern lake town that was Mussolini's last capital, *Salò* is an even more extreme, aggressive, and repellent allegorical theorem than *Teorema*. In this piece of cinema cruelty (in Antonin Artaud's sense of the term), the audience is subjected to a horrifying vision of political totalitarianism disguised as sadomasochistic sexuality. In 1943, four pillars of Italian fascistic society—a duke, a priest, a judge, and a banker—gather a specially selected group of beautiful boys and girls in a mansion and then proceed to make them perform every imaginable sexual atrocity for their own pleasure. The young people are permitted to indulge in any sexual wish, so long as it is not a natural or tender one. Pasolini fills the screen with orgies of sexual torture and oppression. And yet this cruel, obscene, ironic film is uncompromisingly ethical. Presenting fascism in all its horror and absolutely rejecting it, the film refuses to express a conventional, holier-than-thou preference for the "normal"; instead it problematizes the normal. His other films, all of which rejected studio values, varied greatly in structure and tone, alternating among the shattering allegorical mode of *Salò* (*Porcile*, 1969); a neo-Neorealism with speed, humor, and bite (*The Gospel According to St. Matthew*, 1964; *Hawks and Sparrows*, 1966); and fabulous, intricate experiments in narration that

were inspired by great literary sources, *The Decameron (*1971) and *The Canterbury Tales* (1972).

The political films of Bernardo Bertolucci are more sensuous, more meticulous in their stylish attention to visual detail, and less schematic in their abstract arguments. As a result, they are also much more popular. In *Before the Revolution, The Conformist* (1970, based on a novel by Alberto Moravia), and *Last Tango in Paris* (1972), Bertolucci examines the interrelationship between political issues and sexual drives not, as Pasolini does, by revealing the radical anarchic power of sexual passion but, instead, by showing that political and sexual commitments weave together in complex and mysterious ways. The rich, bored dilettantes are no more committed to Marxist ideology than they are to their own lusts and seductions in *Before the Revolution.* They play around with both and succeed in fulfilling neither. In *The Conformist*, the central figure's ideological emptiness is intimately connected with his lack of sexual identity, his need to assert his masculine *machismo* while evading his unacknowledged homosexuality. *Last Tango in Paris* was not one of Pasolini's abstract sexual theorems but an intimate and detailed portrait of human carnality, dominated by the pervasive lust and persuasive confusion of the lost American portrayed by Marlon Brando, in one of his greatest screen roles.

Fig. 13-8
Stefania Sandrelli and Dominique Sanda dance in The Conformist.

In *1900* (1976), an epic history of Italy in the 20th century, Bertolucci shifts his personal focus from lust to friendship—a study of the limits on and the possibilities for friendship of two men, born on the same day on the same estate in 1900 but in the opposite classes of landowner (Robert De Niro) and peasant (Gérard Depardieu). Bertolucci examines the closeness of the two boys (their comradely discoveries of nature, sex, and death together; the genuine emotional ties that bind them) and the barriers to that friendship (their different financial, educational, and moral backgrounds; their different romantic decisions; their different attitudes toward the phenomena of the century—two wars; the rise and fall of fascism; the labor, union, and workers' movements—and toward private property itself).

Politics and sexual politics continued to concern Bertolucci in a series of extravagant international co-productions: *The Last Emperor* (1987), *The Sheltering Sky* (1990), *Little Buddha* (1993). *The Last Emperor*, like *1900*, is an epic with real political intelligence and carefully observed human drama. *The Sheltering Sky* is his most sensually complex work since *Last Tango*, and it opens the return to romance in his later films, *Stealing Beauty* (1996) and the more ambitious and political *Besieged* (1998).

Germi, Leone, and Others

Pietro Germi was Italy's greatest film satirist of the postwar period. Germi made several Neorealist films just after the war, the most interesting of which was *In the Name of the Law* (1948), a contrast between social hypocrisies and the underlying moral realities in a Mafia-dominated Sicily. This contrast of the appearance and the reality, the external show and the internal emotion, later became Germi's dominant theme in his great satirical comedies, *Divorce—Italian Style* (1961, U.S. release, 1962), *Seduced and Abandoned* (1963), and *The Birds, the Bees, and the Italians* (1966; literal title, *Ladies and Gentlemen*).

The paths of Neorealism took several other directions. Marco Bellocchio satirically examined the clumsy attempts of the bored rich to carve a meaning out of their lives by dabbling in romance and Marxist politics in *China Is Near* (1967). And Lina Wertmüller, who served her apprenticeship with Fellini, sought to combine broad satire with sharp political analysis. Her major films (*The Seduction of Mimi*, 1972; *Love and Anarchy*, 1973; *Swept Away . . .* , 1974; *Seven Beauties*, 1976) reveal both a Marxist analysis of contemporary social problems and an exuberant comic sensitivity to the dilemmas of sexuality, power, morality, and survival. In *The Battle of Algiers* (1966), Gillo Pontecorvo combined a Neorealistic tale of political resistance with a visual style that suggested newsreel actuality—to "document" the Algerian struggle for freedom from the French.

Most Neorealistic of the second-generation postwar directors was Ermanno Olmi. In *Il posto* (*The Job*, also called *The Sound of Trumpets*, 1961), Olmi studies an adolescent boy's absorption into the machinery of bureaucratic industrialized society.

Olmi's masterpiece, *The Tree of Wooden Clogs* (1978), set in Northern Italy around 1900, relates economic conditions and "minor" subjects to the crucial concerns of real life as relentlessly as any of its Neorealist predecessors. A rigorously shot color study of a year in the lives of three peasant families, it focuses on the story of a man who cuts down a small tree to make a new pair of clogs for his son.

Fig. 13-9
The Battle of Algiers: *political fiction as newsreel reportage.*

A third generation of Italian masters emerged in the 1970s—Ettore Scola, Paolo and Vittorio Taviani, and Francesco Rosi—all of them fully conscious of their Neorealist roots. Scola is the subtle ironist and comic stylist of the group. Like many of his contemporaries, Scola is dedicated to exploring the processes of history: political history, like the French Revolution (in *La Nuit de Varennes*, 1982), or cinema history, like Scola's explicit homage to De Sica (*We All Loved Each Other*, 1974) and the succeeding quarter century of Italian film styles.

The Taviani brothers closely examine Italian social structures within periods of historical crisis. *Padre Padrone* (1977) is a careful dissection of Italy's paternalistic familial structures, collapsing beneath the attack of modern literacy. *The Night of the Shooting Stars* (1982) pays explicit homage to Rossellini and *Paisan*. The Tavianis capture a child's magical and mythic recollection: a memorable night and day, over three decades earlier, of civil-war brutality in the last hours of Mussolini's Italy—much as the Taviani brothers themselves recall the magic of seeing such battles in *Paisan* as children.

The films of Francesco Rosi (*Salvatore Giuliano*, 1962; *The Mattei Affair*, 1972; *Christ Stopped at Eboli*, 1979; *Three Brothers*, 1981)

are also attracted to periods of historical crisis. As a political tragedy, *Salvatore Giuliano* has been compared to *Julius Caesar* and *Citizen Kane*; its realism is masterful.

In the 1960s, a series of Italian "spaghetti westerns," the best of which (*For a Fistful of Dollars*, 1964) starred Clint Eastwood and were directed by Sergio Leone, not only made money but attracted a cult of admirers. Leone's success with the cheap violent western—and the wide screen—was so great that he was given the chance to shoot a major high-budget western, *Once Upon a Time in the West* (1968), which may be the slowest paced, most naturalistically detailed, and most visually intense collection of western clichés ever assembled—but with a difference (Henry Fonda smiles as he shoots a child . . .). The West is demystified, shown in all its grossness, while Leone weaves a new myth.

The reflexivity of the Italian film did not end with *8½* and *We All Loved Each Other So Much*. Giuseppe Tornatore's movie about watching and projecting movies, *Cinema Paradiso* (1989), touched audiences around the world, and Maurizio Nichetti's *The Icicle Thief* (1989) may be the funniest picture ever made about the problems of showing a film on television.

The Italian traditions of comedy and romance were well represented in the 1990s. *Il Postino* (*The Postman*, 1994, directed by Michael Radford), an Italian–French co-production, combined tones and genres—a tragic romantic comedy about words and life, sex and the sea, politics and celebrity, recording and remembering—in its story of a man whose only job is to deliver the mail to an exiled poet. Roberto Benigni, a comic actor and screenwriter, wrote, directed, and starred in *Johnny Stecchino* (1991), a comedy that broke all Italian box-office records, followed by *The Monster* (1995) and *Life is Beautiful* (1998), which set further records. Benigni is as adept at silent comedy as he is at words, the only total comic working in film today.

France—Postwar Classicism

The postwar Italian film sprang from the reality that the filmmaker sought to capture with camera and film; the postwar French film sprang from the filmmaker's stylistic concern with the way a camera can capture reality. That the postwar French cinema should be committed to style and form is not surprising; the prewar French cinema was just as committed to formal experiment. To approach consciousness and reality through the manipulation of style and form has been an aesthetic premise of the French creative mind from Racine to Proust to Ionesco. The postwar French cinema is very much in the same tradition.

Cocteau and Others

The most important surviving directors of the 1930s—Clair, Renoir, and Cocteau—continued to make films after World War II. René Clair combined fantasy, song, and social satire like *Beauty and the Devil* (1949), an ironic treatment of the Faust legend; and *Beauties of the Night* (1952), the romantic reveries of a daydreaming musician.

Renoir made at least three films that are arguably as great as his masterpieces of the 1930s. The three films—*The River* (his first in color; shot 1949–50, released 1951), *The Golden Coach* (1952, shot in Italy), and *French Cancan* (1954, shot in France)—are a kind of trilogy. All three use color as a metaphoric and thematic element in their investigations. Their primary duality is the familiar Renoir conflict between art and nature, but in these late films the conflict

becomes a communion as the very artfulness of the films themselves—their visual beauty as well as their structural complexity—reveals how one can indeed make life into art.

Jean Cocteau, whose only prewar film was the 1930 *The Blood of a Poet* (an experimental, personal attempt to "picture the poet's inner self"), made several films in strikingly different though equally formalistic film styles: the claustrophobic realism of *Les Parents terribles* (1948), a complicated tangle of sexuality, incest, parental rivalry, and jealousy; the poetic symbolism of *Orphée* (*Orpheus*, 1950), a Surrealistic study of the artist's ambivalent relationship with love and death as well as a rich realization of some of the ways that poetry and film can work together; and *Beauty and the Beast* (1946), a perfectly realized fairy tale that mixed Cocteau's surreal romanticism and evocative symbolism quite effectively in the story of Belle's growing love for the physically ugly yet humanly loving beast. The impression of these stylistically eclectic Cocteau films is that they are the works of a cinematic amateur (in the original sense of the word). The artist, having given birth to his personal and symbolic world on the stage, on the page, and on canvas, also decided to people the screen with his personal fantasies, images, motifs, and symbols. Cocteau felt that only the work of art was capable of effecting a synthesis of the conflicting demands of art and nature, of form and freedom.

Max Ophüls

Of the new directors of French cinema in the 15 years following the war, the three greatest were Max Ophüls, Robert Bresson, and Jacques Tati. All three of them had made films in the Clair–Carné–Renoir tradition; all three had, in fact, made films before 1945. Whereas the end of the war signaled a shift in an entirely new direction for the Italian film, the end of the war in France extended an earlier one. The break with French tradition came in 1959, and, as we shall see, it was not a complete break at all.

Max Ophüls made films in Italy, Holland, and the United States after fleeing his German homeland and Hitler in 1933 (he was Jewish). Ophüls's reputation today rests primarily on the last films he made in America (*Letter From An Unknown Woman*, 1948; *Caught* and *The Reckless Moment*, both 1949) and the four he directed and co-wrote

Cocteau's union of opposites in Beauty and the Beast—*loveliness (Josette Day as Beauty) and ugliness (Jean Marais as the Beast), human and animal, nature and artifice, animate and inanimate (note the candelabra's arm).*

Fig. 13-10

in France before his death: *La Ronde* (1950), *Le Plaisir* (1952), *Madame de . . .* (*The Earrings of Madame de . . .*, 1953), and *Lola Montès* (1955, shot in Paris and Munich); all the French films were shot by Christian Matras and are noted for their fluid, highly charged camerawork. *Lola Montès* features a wide-screen camera whose movements are so graceful and comment with such authority on the action that they have been considered the best of the 1950s, the great experimental period of anamorphic camerawork (Ray, Kazan, Preminger, and many others). Ophüls is clearly an international rather than a French director. And yet he found a place in French studios at a particularly apt time for his talents— a time when French film values favored the literate, almost theatrical script and the ornate, carefully styled studio production.

The last Ophüls films all revolve around sexual intrigue in conflict with social regulations. The Ophüls characters continue to carry on their intrigues while either hypocritically ignoring the social tensions (as the liars do in *La Ronde* and *Madame de . . .*) or openly defying social convention (as Lola does). In developing a consistent theme, Ophüls also prefers consistent stylistic conventions. Each film's plot is less a single driving narrative than a string of vignettes, held together by the setting (the Vienna of *La Ronde*,

the circus tent of *Lola Montès*), by an object (the earrings of *Madame de . . .*, which are passed from person to person in a fatal circle), or by a concept (in *Le Plaisir*, which retells three stories by Guy de Maupassant, how pleasure is found easily but happiness is elusive). Ophüls's deliberate choice of an artificial, theatrical setting (the soundstage in *La Ronde*, the circus tent in *Lola Montès*) provides a nonrealistically appropriate setting for Ophüls's comedies of sociosexual manners and also raises intentional questions about the shams of real human activity and the realness of acting and impersonation. Lola Montès, for example, is put on display to act the role of herself.

La Ronde is one of the finest translations of a stage work (Arthur Schnitzler's *Reigen*) into film. The film is both theatrical and cinematic. The setting in *La Ronde* is both an undisguised soundstage and the city of Vienna around 1900. The camera wanders about the soundstage at will between the two poles of obvious stage set and realistic bedroom, between a metaphorical carousel, symbolic of the film's everturning dance of sexual relationships (a conjugal merry-go-round in which A loves B who loves C who loves A), and a real boudoir. Ophüls keeps the camera perpetually on the move; his German heritage is especially clear in his use of the moving camera and emphasis on *mise-en-scène.*

Fig. 13-11

Max Ophüls's urbane narrator–chorus (Anton Walbrook) with the whore (Simone Signoret) and the metaphoric carousel of La Ronde.

The gliding photography adds not only visual energy but also continuity between the vignettes. And Ophüls's wandering camera has an ally: The director has invented a narrator, a character who does not exist in the original play, who speaks directly for the filmmaker to the audience. The urbane, perceptive, witty narrator (Anton Walbrook) wanders, as the camera wanders, as he speaks for Ophüls. Director, camera, and narrator are one.

Ophüls preserves the intentions of Schnitzler's witty play—even finding cinematic equivalents for the asterisks, usually handled on the stage by dimming and then brightening the lights. His cleverest device is the sequence in which the film abruptly stops and cuts to the narrator holding up a strip of film and a pair of editing scissors, shaking his head in concern over the lewdness of the scene he is about to censor. The narrator snips the sensual strip from the reel, and the film jumps back to the two sated lovers.

La Ronde poses a moral tension between natural human responses and unnatural social restrictions. The result is that the only time the characters cannot lie to each other is when they are lying with each other, during the unshown "asterisks" of each scene.

The same antithesis between authentic experience and convention propels *Lola Montès*, but

Lola (Martine Carol) resolves the contradiction by remaining unflinchingly true to her feelings, regardless of the risk, regardless of the consequences. The story of Lola is the fictional biography of a real person, a notorious courtesan of the 19th century, who took a series of brilliant lovers—a famous composer (Liszt) and a ruling Bavarian prince (Ludwig) among them. But Lola falls on evil fortune; she becomes a circus performer, forced to parade her life's story before a crass and ogling audience, selling gossip and letting her hand be kissed for a dollar. Lola has, on the surface, fallen from great lover to romantic exhibit; once free, she is now controlled. Her new lover is the slimy ringmaster (Peter Ustinov) who salaciously revels in Lola's past, his present mastery over her, and the money he makes from her life. Lola's conquerors are circumstance and time, as her sick and aging body requires more whisky to keep it going.

But *Lola Montès* is more than an examination of a romantic lifestyle. It is one of the most dazzling of visual shows—in both color and Cinema-Scope. Each of the sequences has its own unique color and tone: the warm browns, oranges, and ambers of the rustic affair with the composer; the cold whites, silvers, and pale blues of the affair with the prince; the dazzling reds and golds of the circus, glowing in the blackness of the tent.

Fig. 13-12
Lola Montès: *composition for the wide screen—contrapuntal verticals (Martine Carol and Anton Walbrook).*

The film's composition is as dynamic as its color. Ophüls was one of those early directors to compose not *in* the wide screen but *for* the wide screen. The big shots—in the circus tent, in the palace—truly fill the frame. Ophüls's turning camera, his metaphorical setting, and the very structure of *Lola Montès* turn all human experience into a vivid circus and all spectators in the movie theatre into spectators in the circus tent.

Robert Bresson

Robert Bresson, though equally careful with narrative structure, details of decor, and pictorial composition, was a completely different kind of filmmaker. Subdued rather than flamboyant, introspective rather than extrovertedly spectacular, Bresson's films are as far apart from Ophüls's as Brittany is from Vienna. Bresson made only 15 films in 40 years. He died in 1999 at the age of 98. His slowness and care as a craftsman seem to mirror the quietness, the slow pace, the austere rigor, the internalized probing of his films. Like

Antonioni, Ozu, and Dreyer, Bresson was a purist and a perfectionist. Whereas the Ophüls films are dizzying visual shows, the Bresson films feel more like ascetic, introspective novels. Like the novelist, Bresson could tell his story through an omniscient third person (*Les Dames du Bois de Boulogne*, 1945) or a confessional first person (*Diary of a Country Priest*, 1950). Most of his stories seem to be trying to find ways to tell themselves. Like the films of Dreyer and Antonioni, Bresson's are often about expressive silence. And some of his characters are caged into silence, while others choose it as a discipline.

Bresson's primary theme is the battle of spiritual innocence with the corruption of the world. Bresson, a devout Roman Catholic, sought spiritual meaning and salvation in a world that had lost touch with them. In *Diary of a Country Priest*, a young, innocent curé faces the worldly evils about him: A cynical, nihilistic doctor commits suicide; a wealthy count substitutes money and influence for morality and faith; the

Fig. 13-13
Diary of a Country Priest.

faith of the count's wife wavers at the loss of her son; the count's neurotic daughter viciously implicates the priest in the countess's death; the peasants of the countryside remain indifferent and hostile. As a priest, the man fails. He succeeds only in bringing a moment of faith and peace to the countess. The other members of his parish remain tied to their selfish cares and material concerns. But as a man, the priest succeeds completely. He dies of cancer, unshaken in his faith to the end, certain that "all is grace."

Tati, Clouzot, and Clément

Jacques Tati was the great comic of the French film, probably the greatest film mime and visual comic since Chaplin and Keaton. Like Bresson, Tati worked slowly, controlling every detail of the film himself from script to cutting; like Bresson, Tati refused to compromise with either technicians or producers. As a result, though Tati's first film appearance was as early as 1932, he made only six feature films: *Jour de fête* (1949), *Mr. Hulot's Holiday* (1953), *My Uncle* (1958, his first

in color), *Playtime* (1967, in 70mm), *Traffic* (1970), and *Parade* (1973).

Like Chaplin and Keaton, Tati plays essentially the same character in each picture: a charming fool whose incompetence is preferable to the inhuman competence of the life around him. Tati's Mr. Hulot (even the name Hulot recalls Charlot) merely goes about his business, totally unaware that the world around him has gone mad and that his naïve attention to his own business turns its orderly madness into comic chaos. Tati's Hulot neither looks nor moves like anyone else in the universe. He leans forward at an oblique angle—battered hat atop his head, pipe thrusting from his mouth, umbrella dangling at his side, trouser cuffs hanging two inches above his shoes—an odd human construction of impossible angles, off-center and off-kilter. His bouncy walk implies an elastic spring, ready to launch him into space and off the earth, where he simply doesn't belong.

For *Mr. Hulot's Holiday*, his second feature film, Tati created Monsieur Hulot, an apparently conventional, pipe-smoking, easygoing, middle-class gentleman who comes to spend a conventional week at a completely conventional middle-class resort. Hulot, again like Chaplin and Keaton, runs afoul of objects. His troubles with bathers on the beach, with his sputtering little car, even with the twang of the hotel's dining-room door, reduce the conventional, routinized tourist resort to unconventional hysteria. Tati's comic attack exposes the resort—supposedly a place devoted to leisure and fun—as the domain of the dull and monotonous. M. Hulot is the force who enlivens the dead place of play by bombarding it with uncanny objects, sounds, and movements. We in the theatre, like those few vacationers who take the time to notice Hulot's spontaneous, disruptive activities, also discover what genuine, active fun really is.

Playtime brings a group of American tourists to Paris. Hulot, more a passive observer than the central figure of this film, accompanies the group on their tour of a modern industrial exposition and a fancy nightclub that has just been glued together for fashionable Parisians and American tourists. Tati ridicules the slick surfaces of modern life with hilarious visual gags: The tiles of the dance floor have been pasted down so recently that they stick to the dancers' high-stepping shoes; a plate-glass door has been cleaned so well—to the point of invisibility—that the customers cannot tell whether the doorman actually opens the door or merely mimes it.

Like *Mr. Hulot's Holiday*, the underlying theme of *Playtime* is the creative use of leisure and the genuine fun that can result from active perception rather than the passive acceptance of planned and canned routines. Shot in 70mm, its geometric modern city planned and constructed by Tati himself (humorously called "Tativille," its cost drove him into bankruptcy, from which he never recovered), *Playtime* invites us to explore its vast spaces without a dictatorial guide. There is not a single close-up in the film; our eye must pick out visual and comic significance for itself. In their blend of social satire, wry charm, imaginative physical gags, and the creative use of the visual and aural devices of the cinema itself, the films of Jacques Tati have not been surpassed by those of any other postwar film comic, French or otherwise.

Two other major French directors of the years just following the war were Henri-Georges Clouzot and René Clément. Clouzot is, like Hitchcock, an assured director of extremely suspenseful melodramas. Both *The Wages of Fear* (1953) and *Les Diaboliques* (*Diabolique*, 1955) mix chills, horror, sexual intrigue, and taut suspense. *Diabolique* is the more celebrated of the two, a story of sexual intrigue and shocking cruelty. But *The Wages of Fear* is a purer representative of the Clouzot method: an agonizingly tense, long journey of two trucks transporting nitroglycerin through the jungles of South America. Audiences that screamed at *Diabolique* sat frozen with tension through *Wages*.

Clément's most important film is *Forbidden Games* (1952), a wartime story of two children who are both affected and infected by the murderous world of their elders. A young girl's parents and puppy are machine-gunned by a strafing German airplane. The girl, horrified by the death of her parents, fixes her fascination on the dead puppy, refusing to believe it is dead; she tries to keep it and play with it. She is adopted by a family of Pyrenees farmers who, through their young son, teach her that dead things must be buried. The girl buries the puppy. She becomes so fascinated with burying things that she and the young boy go about the countryside killing things so they can bury them. Eventually their private cemetery is discovered; they are punished for their activity, which ironically merely mimics that of their elders.

1959 and After

In the years following the war a new generation of the French became addicted to the movies. Many of these *cinéastes* first became film critics rather than filmmakers. These cinephiles did not like the film establishment's ornately staged, heavily plotted, unspontaneous films. In *Cahiers du cinéma*, the journal founded by film theorist André Bazin, the young critics François Truffaut, Jean-Luc Godard, and Claude Chabrol ripped apart the films of Clément and others for what they considered the same literary, talky, tasteful, studio-crafted, theatrical type. It was Roberto Rossellini, one of the idols of these critics, who urged them to stop writing about films and start making them.

These *Cahiers* critics retreated a generation, to the 1930s of Clair, Renoir, and Vigo, where they found the zest and spontaneity of what they considered the authentic French tradition. Just as the French directors of the 1920s leaped backward to the primitive exuberance of Cohl, Zecca, and Méliès, the French directors of the 1960s leaped backward to the films of the 1920s and 1930s. Just as the French films of the 1920s combined echoes of the past with bizarre innovations for the future, the films of Truffaut and Godard were to be full of echoes of Vigo, Bogart, Hitchcock, Feuillade, Hawks, Welles, and more, combined with ingeniously elliptical techniques. The year 1959 was the year that the critics, heeding Rossellini's advice, became filmmakers—the year of Truffaut's *The 400 Blows*.

The New Wave

The New Wave ("*la nouvelle vague*") was a term coined in France to describe the sudden appearance, on many fronts, of brilliant films by new directors. Although there were several directors (such as Louis Malle) affiliated with neither camp, the New Wave consisted primarily of two parts: the *Cahiers* group of critics-turned-directors (Claude Chabrol, Jean-Luc Godard, Jacques Rivette, Eric Rohmer, and François Truffaut) and the "Left Bank" group of Chris Marker, Alain Resnais, and Agnès Varda, who had gone directly into filmmaking. The Left Bank group has often been characterized as taking literature, philosophy, politics, and the possibilities of documentary more seriously than the *Cahiers* group. They were also the more professionally experienced filmmakers, and Varda's *La Pointe-Courte* (shot and privately premiered in 1954, released in 1956, and edited by Resnais) has been called by some the first New Wave film; it is certainly the crucial precursor, as *Ossessione* prepared the way for Neorealism.

In France as well as abroad, the perceived crest of the New Wave was *The 400 Blows*, which was completed and released in France in 1959 and—something almost unprecedented— released in America that same year. America saw *The 400 Blows*, *The Lovers*, *Look Back in Anger*, and *Room at the Top* in 1959; *Hiroshima mon amour* and *Shoot the Piano Player* in 1960; *Breathless*, *La dolce vita*, and *L'avventura* in 1961; and *Jules and Jim* and *Last Year at Marienbad* in 1962—and perceived itself in the midst of something new and exciting: A wave of films

was breaking on its shores, a wave of films from England, Italy, and especially France.

François Truffaut

The young François Truffaut, like the young Vigo and the young Renoir, built his early films on the central artistic idea of freedom, both in human relationships and in film technique. Truffaut's early protagonists are rebels, loners, or misfits who feel stifled by the conventional social definitions. Antoine Doinel (Jean-Pierre Léaud), the 13-year-old protagonist of *The 400 Blows* (*Les Quatre cents coups*: to raise hell or make mischief), must endure a prison-like school and a school-like prison, sentenced to both by hypocritical, unsympathetic, unperceptive adults. Charlie Kohler (Charles Aznavour) of Truffaut's *Shoot the Piano Player* (1960) has deliberately cut himself free of the ropes of fame and fortune as a concert pianist, preferring his job in a small smoky bar, where he thinks he can remain—uncommitted, unburdened, unknown. Catherine (Jeanne Moreau) of *Jules and Jim* (1961, released 1962) feels so uncomfortable with all definitions—wife, mistress, mother, friend, woman—that she commits suicide. Truffaut's early cinematic style was as anxious to break free as his characters were. The early films are dazzlingly elliptical, omitting huge transitional sections of time and emotional development. These narrative leaps—and a camera that moved unpredictably but always effectively, as if possessed by a vision of cinema and its renewed possibilities—gave the Truffaut films an intensity, a spontaneity, a freshness that other films lacked.

Jules and Jim (based on the novel by Henri-Pierre Roché) is a cinematically fresh study of the relationship of love and life. Catherine refuses to live any longer than she can love, feel, respond freely, act impulsively. She travels with a bottle of vitriol as a potential means of escape from a life that might one day hang too heavily about her neck. She is a creature of whim, of impulse, of change. She can dress up like a Jackie-Cooganesque kid; she can race across a bridge; she can dive into the Seine to shake up her complacent companions. Her face and smile match those of the statue of the love goddess that Jules and Jim first encounter in a friend's slide show, then track down. But the pure spirit of love has difficulties surviving in the real world of

Fig. 13-14
The 400 Blows: *Antoine Doinel (Jean-Pierre Léaud) in the classroom. Both the feeling and the candid style of Vigo's* **Zéro de conduite.**

geographical boundaries, marriage laws, child-bearing, and political wars. Though Catherine enjoys supremely sunny moments with Jim (Henri Serre), with Jules (Oskar Werner), and with her daughter, the moments lose their sunlight when they become months and years. She cannot remain happy with anyone for very long. And so she cuts the rope that binds her both to life and to Jules and Jim by driving her car off a pier, taking Jim with her, while Jules can only watch.

The Truffaut filmography splits into two unequal halves—a group of early films in black and white (which earned him his initial respect and reputation) and two decades of films in color (which, despite their craft and subtlety, have never achieved the critical recognition of his first three films). The two recurrent themes of Truffaut's later films are education and art, both of which grow out of his earliest work. After several transitional pieces in a variety of styles—the realistic love triangle of *The Soft Skin* (1964),

a repressive, antiliterate world of the future in *Fahrenheit 451* (1966, based on the novel by Ray Bradbury), and a Hitchcock dissertation in *The Bride Wore Black* (1968, based on the novel by Cornell Woolrich, and made after he published his book-length interview with Hitchcock)— the more commercial, less experimental half of Truffaut's career begins with the return to Antoine Doinel in *Stolen Kisses* (1968).

Antoine Doinel is Truffaut's alter ego; his adventures on film parallel Truffaut's own personal experiences as a child and young man; the maturing of the actor who plays Doinel, Jean-Pierre Léaud, parallels the maturing of the film director behind the camera who discovered the young boy and nurtured his early career. Léaud is Truffaut's spiritual son, much as Truffaut claimed André Bazin as his own spiritual father.

In *Stolen Kisses*, young Doinel blunders at both love and work, clumsily groping toward self-fulfillment in both. In *Bed and Board* (1970),

Antoine is married, with a child of his own as well as a mistress; he is still a half-committed blunderer, the consistent trait of his adult life. And in *Love on the Run* (1979), Antoine gets divorced, but his novel has finally been published (his own creation of a work of art)—a novel that is really an auto-biographical exploration of his own experiences with women, transmuted into art.

The Wild Child (1969, released 1970), Truffaut's only black-and-white film after *The Soft Skin*, is also devoted to education. A late 18th-century scientist succeeds in taming a wild boy—a child who had spent his entire early life in the forest—and introduces him to the luxuries of civilization: speech, clothes, shelter, discipline, and love—which make him unfit for life in the wild. That the film is much closer to the Doinel cycle than it might seem from its case-history surface can be seen in Truffaut's dedication of the film to Jean-Pierre Léaud; that Truffaut himself played Dr. Jean Itard, the scientist who taught the boy; and that the Truffaut–Léaud relationship is unmistakably significant to *The Wild Child*. Just as both the boy and the scientist are changed as the result of the educational process in *The Wild Child*, both Truffaut and Léaud, themselves outlaws and outcasts, grew in the process of creating works of art, the ultimate product of civilization.

The central Truffaut theme had evolved into one that was quite close to Renoir's: the relationship of art to nature and the ability of art to contain nature and to become its own nature.

This tension between art and nature propels *Day for Night* (1973), whose subject is the process of filmmaking itself. As in *The Wild Child*, Truffaut plays a role in his own film—a similar role—the patient, paternal teacher–master who is responsible for the success of a complex project. As in *The Wild Child*, the film develops the conflict and resultant synthesis of art and nature, for the commercial filmmaking process is one of converting the arranged and the artificial into the seemingly natural. A film produces candle effects with electric lights, rain and fire with valves and hoses, snow with suds of foam. The term that gives the film its title, *day-for-night* (in French, *la nuit américaine*—"American Night"), is itself a contradiction and an artifice that transforms nature, the term that Hollywood coined in the era when the movies produced the effect of nighttime by shooting during the day with a filter

or with the lens opening reduced. Art and nature approach a synthesis in the twist—reminiscent of late Renoir—that the dedication to art becomes natural for people who define themselves as being artists. Truffaut's director dreams of how the commitment to art turns the fears of death into a celebration of life.

Truffaut was never a committed political filmmaker. Like Renoir, he was too much the sympathetic but detached observer and ironist who saw the validity of competing ideological positions. And like Ophüls, he was too much the romantic and formalist in his quest for emotional satisfaction and artistic perfection. Truffaut faced his evasions directly in *The Last Metro* (1980), his most political film and his most successful—commercially and critically—in France. The director of a Parisian acting ensemble during the Nazi Occupation (Catherine Deneuve) insists on continuing business as usual, performing the escapist plays the public and the authorities expect of her, refusing to take a stand against the anti-Semitic regulations that devastate her own acting company. Although her detachment angers the new leading man of the troupe (Gérard Depardieu), he discovers that her apolitical stance is a ruse to protect her own husband, the company's former director and leading man, who is hunted by the Occupation authorities and hiding in the basement of the theatre.

Here Truffaut made two points about his own apolitical films—in response to the activism of his colleague and contemporary, Jean-Luc Godard, who took quite the opposite path. First, the genuine political effects of art are frequently unknowable on the surface; second, the business of artists is to make art. The artist who rejects his *métier* for explicit political and rhetorical programs might produce bad art.

Jean-Luc Godard

Jean-Luc Godard took the idea for his first feature film, *Breathless* (*A bout de souffle*, shot in 1959 and released early in 1960), from Truffaut. Michel Poiccard, the gangster–lover–hero of the film, is very much a Truffaut figure, a synthesis of Charlie, Catherine, and Antoine Doinel. Except for the fact that the cinema was both directors' ultimate subject, *Breathless* was as close as Godard's films ever came to Truffaut's. Whereas Truffaut's films are consistent in both theme and technique, the

Godard films are consistent in their inconsistency, their eclecticism, their mixing of many different kinds of ideas and cinematic principles.

Godard, paradoxically, supports several contradictory ideas and filmic methods at the same time. He finds human experience irrational and inexplicable: many of his films end in sudden, almost arbitrary deaths. But we do not cry over these deaths, from which we are distanced by the director's unsentimental treatment. Godard embraces Brechtian devices and politics, and Brecht's premise was that both art and human problems must be viewed as strictly rational and hence solvable.

Like Truffaut's, Godard's film career breaks into two parts—the works preceding and following 1968. But Godard's films never evolve toward Truffaut's synthesis of life and art; instead, Godard's films progressively reflect a fear that the familiar solutions of art are precisely antithetical to the necessary solutions for life, particularly political life. Bourgeois films cannot solve bourgeois problems, let alone Marxist and Maoist ones; such films cannot even ask the right questions. One cannot think with these films. The old forms provide their own oversimplified answers. And so Godard's films become not more whole and dramatic but more fragmented and questioning, in search of "new forms for new contents." Rather than resolving his contradictions, Godard's evolving work seeks to explore and analyze them. To the extent that he characteristically presents a dialectic rather than its resolution and that he

thinks so deeply about the cinema as a language, Godard may well be considered the filmmaker who picked up where Eisenstein left off.

Breathless remains the strongest narrative of the Godard films. Godard examines the life of Michel Poiccard (Jean-Paul Belmondo), alias Laszlo Kovacs. Poiccard is indeed a petty crook in the B-picture tradition, a casual car thief who kills a policeman virtually by chance, gets emotionally entangled with his girl (Jean Seberg), whom he wants to run away with him, and is eventually gunned down by the police after the girl tips them off. The remarkable thing about the film is not just its simple story and the choppy, exciting, refreshing way it is told, but its Bogartesque character: brazen, charming, free, refusing to warp emotions into words or conduct into laws.

To like Godard for *Breathless* is perhaps to wish he were another Truffaut. But even in *Breathless* the unique Godard devices—the logical assault against logic, the sudden and abrupt event, the Brechtian detachment of the viewer from the illusion of the film—control the work. As Michel drives the stolen car, his monologue on life and the countryside is addressed directly to us, an artifice that Godard emphasizes with his jump cutting, which destroys— or excitingly charges—the visual continuity of time and space.

The primary strength of Godard's early films is his ability to catch flashing, elusive moments of passion, joy, or pain with the most surprising and unconventional narrative techniques. *Vivre*

Breathless: Michel (Belmondo) and Patricia (Jean Seberg) in the bedroom.

Fig. 13-15

sa vie (1962) is a cold and moving, compelling and detached study of a woman (Nana, played by Godard's first wife, Anna Karina), who drifts into prostitution (a consistent Godard metaphor for the relationships of people under capitalism) and is shot to death when one pimp tries to sell her to another (in an understated, realistic scene of almost arbitrary violence—as far from a big "Hollywood ending" as possible).

Masculine Feminine (1966) includes touching moments as well as hard-edged analyses. Godard seeks to capture the world, the politics, the vitality of the young, the generation of "Marx and Coca-Cola." Godard relies on improvisational interviews with his central figures, whose charm, spontaneity, and honesty in front of the camera are infectious. Godard again handles death anticlimactically. We discover that the boy has fallen off a building to his death only when his girlfriend reports the accident to the police. The clicking clatter of the bureaucratic typewriter recording the account in the coldest, most mechanical manner contrasts poignantly with the breathing, vital energy of the living boy. Life and death, radical energy and officious indifference are that close and that far apart in the world of Godard.

If Godard's overall career reveals a consistent pattern, it is that he began by using bizarre devices of cinematic perception as a means to tell rather conventional narratives—the means to bring his characters to life—and he became progressively more concerned with a critique of cinematic perception as an end in itself.

Three of Godard's pre-1968 films are most clearly committed to a study of image making. *Contempt* (1963) is a film explicitly about the making of film images (with Fritz Lang in the role of a director and Brigitte Bardot as a sex-object star); *A Married Woman* (1964) is an analysis of the commodification of women, marriage, "beauty," and "romance" in modern society. *2 or 3 Things I Know About Her* (1967) is a return to the milieu of prostitution of *Vivre sa vie* but with the emphasis on the milieu (cafés, cars, city streets, architecture) and the cultural, political, and economic system of which prostitution is an integral part and for which it is a valid symbol. It is also about the problem of knowing, defining, and filming anything—a major investigation of the phenomenology and epistemology of the filmed world. As his films moved toward 1968, Godard became increasingly convinced that one cannot make movies—or any other kind of artwork—without first understanding how one is making them and why.

The Paris riots of May–June 1968 intensified Godard's political commitments, leading him to organize a political cell (he and co-founder Jean-Pierre Gorin called it the Dziga Vertov film

Vivre sa vie: *sudden, meaningless death during a business transaction.*

Fig. 13-16

collective, after the Soviet innovator of *Kinó-Pravda*) for making films, in opposition to the Apollonian, bourgeois model of the individual artist–creator. The character played by Yves Montand in *Tout va bien* is, like Godard, a film director who explains that he could no longer continue making auteurist films after the events of 1968. But Montand's choice becomes a cynical one; he decides to shoot the most vapid and exploitative television commercials exclusively. Unlike this character, Godard has decided to become the analyst rather than the manipulator of modern cultural packaging.

The investigation of language is an aspect of every Godard film, but it reaches its philosophical peak in *2 or 3 Things* and its political apex in *Wind from the East* (1969). Beginning in 1968, Godard also made films for TV about language (*Le Gai savoir*, released 1969); with Anne-Marie Miéville, he made two important series for TV, the 1976 *Communication* (*Six fois deux/Sur et sous la communication* [*Six Times Two*]) and the 1978 *France/Tour/ Détour/Deux/Enfants*. After *Sauve qui peut*, Godard made a number of richly theatrical films that investigated art, religion, and genres and that ranged from the commercial (*Detective*, 1985) to the sublime (*Passion*, 1982; *First Name: Carmen*, 1983; *Hail Mary*, 1985).

Extending the investigation of self, divination, and spirit begun in *Passion* and *Hail Mary*, and facilitating the leap from *Germany Nine Zero* (1991) to *For Ever Mozart* (1996), *Hélas pour*

Fig. 13-17
France/Tour/Détour/Deux/Enfants: *Godard and Miéville put "truth" ("vérité") on TV.*
Photo by Erika Sudeuburg.

moi (*Alas for Me*, or *Woe is Me*, 1992, released 1993) is a meditation on mortality and disappointment. If Wittgenstein was the philosopher most important to *2 or 3 Things*, *Hélas pour moi* extrapolates the work of Jacques Derrida—seeking the traces of a god in a legend and in the ordinary contemporary world, while knowing that the traces can lead to no final knowledge and that there can be no absolute universal center or foundation of knowledge. Nevertheless, Godard meditates from a kind of center (which he calls *ici-bas*, or "here as over there," a pun on *là-bas*) in which he finds that things are "absent—but nowhere else." As in *2 or 3 Things*, which ended at "cinema degree zero" (a reference to Roland Barthes), Godard is still investigating objects and trying to construct a basis for the cinema; he is also still doing a lot of quoting. Even if, as he admits, parts of the world and his subject refuse to be told, Godard's mature understanding of distance allows him to continue to probe the nature of engagement.

Alain Resnais

The tension between formal experiment and political commitment is also central to the work of Alain Resnais. Although Resnais has been consistently linked with both Truffaut and Godard, he is a completely different kind of filmmaker. Ten years older than Truffaut and Godard, Resnais began his career in films not as *cinéaste* and critic but as film editor and documentary filmmaker. His most important early films were documentaries that studied the works of artists (Van Gogh, Gauguin, Picasso's *Guernica*) or examined the horrors of the Nazi concentration camps (*Night and Fog*, 1955). But as with Truffaut, 1959 was the year of Resnais's first feature, *Hiroshima mon amour*, and critics considered his work part of the same "wave" despite the differences in his films.

Resnais begins with a far more literary premise than Truffaut or Godard. His films are neither improvised nor spontaneous. Like Bresson and Renoir, Resnais begins with detailed, literate, highly polished scripts. Although Resnais does not adapt novels into films, he asks novelists to write his original scripts: Marguerite Duras, Alain Robbe-Grillet, Jean Cayrol. Resnais respects literateness, complex construction, and poetic speech. His films are thoughtful, astonishing, tightly controlled, and operatic in comparison with the breezy, erratic, makeshift feeling of the early Truffaut and Godard films. Because one of the key Resnais themes is the effect of time, the interrelation of past, present, and future, of memory and event, his narratives are frequently elliptical, cutting in time and space even more freely than Truffaut's or Godard's.

In *Hiroshima mon amour* (1959), written by Marguerite Duras, a French woman and a Japanese man try to build something more between them than a single night in bed. She is an actress who has come to Hiroshima to make a peace film; he is an architect trying to build the ruined city up from its ashes. But they are separated by more than cultural distance. Between them is the past. For him, there is Hiroshima, the burned-out home of his youth; for her, Nevers, the little French town where she loved a German soldier in the occupation army whom the villagers murdered when the Nazis evacuated. Both have burned-out pasts.

To show the intrusion of these pasts into the present, Resnais, the sensitive editor, continually cuts shots of Nevers and the Hiroshima carnage into the shots of the present. At the film's opening, the two embracing lovers' arms seem to be covered with radioactive dust. As they make love, Resnais's camera tracks through the Hiroshima war museum, showing the burnt buildings and mutilated bodies. When the woman (Emmanuelle Riva) glances at the twitching hand of her sleeping lover (Eiji Okada), Resnais cuts to a short, sudden flash of her experience in Nevers: the moment she held her German lover and saw his hand twitch as he died. The result of this assault of the past on the present is an emotional gulf between them that can never be bridged.

In *Last Year at Marienbad* (1961), every event is ambiguous. A man (X, played by Giorgio Albertazzi) meets a woman (A, played by Delphine Seyrig) at what may or may not be an elegant resort near the town of Marienbad; he may or may not have met her there or at a different resort one year before. He relentlessly implores her to leave the resort with him, to flee the man (M, played by Sacha Pitoeff) who may or may not be her husband. At the end of the film, she may or may not remember having met him (X may have convinced her of a lie), and they may or may not leave the chateau together.

In this maze of time and faces, several dominant themes are quite clear. One is the contrast between sincere emotional interaction and stifling artificial conventions. A more important theme is time itself. The man claims to have met the woman last year, but what exactly is a year? She has photographs in her room, clear mementos of the past, but the pictures seem to be of her in the present. At one point in the film a man bumps into a woman and spills her

Emmanuelle Riva and Eiji Okada in **Hiroshima mon amour.**

Fig. 13-18

Fig. 13-19

Fig. 13-20

Fig. 13-21
Framing and space in **Last Year at Marienbad.**
Fig. 13-19: X, the suitor (Giorgio Albertazzi),
watches a couple we see framed in a mirror;
Fig. 13-20: a board game against a painted
checkerboard; Fig. 13-21: the woman, A
(Delphine Seyrig), poses in front of a formal
garden that might be either real or **trompe l'oeil.**

drink. Some 45 minutes of film time continue
from this point. Then Resnais returns to the
spilled-drink sequence, with the characters in
exactly the same positions as when the drink

was spilled. Has Resnais equated 45 minutes of
screen time with an instantaneous flash
of thought and feeling in a character's
mind? And if it is a subjective flash, whose is it?
Although the film's structure resembles the
stream-of-consciousness narration of modern
fiction, it is difficult to determine whose consciousness is streaming in the film—the man's,
the woman's, the director's, the writer's, or that
of the film itself.

Resnais followed *Marienbad* with *Muriel or
The Time of a Return* (1963), his first feature in
color. *Muriel* sticks to the present as its characters attempt to deal with the past. Even as the
characters remember and talk about the past,
and figures from the past show up (some with
lies and some with the hidden truth), forcing all
of them to deal with old political atrocities and
romantic betrayals, *Muriel* shows how they and
the city in which the action is set (Boulogne—
like Hiroshima, reconstructed after World War II)
are part of a system. As cold and intellectual as
some people find such systematic, formally perfect films, they are deeply romantic and intensely
political in addition to being philosophically profound. Like Godard and Chris Marker, Resnais is
someone who thinks with film.

After returning to black and white to make a
relatively accessible story of love and politics in
the context of the long-lost Spanish Civil War,
La Guerre est finie (*The War is Over*, 1966),
Resnais concentrated on formal color style
pieces. Many of Resnais's later films, including
Providence (1977), *Mon oncle d'Amérique*
(1980), and *La Vie est un roman* (1983), continue his experiments with narrative, contribut-
ing to the library of world cinema some of the
most vigorously crafted, intellectually provocative movies ever made.

Chabrol, Rohmer, and Rivette
Many important directors—though not of the
stature of Godard, Truffaut, and Resnais—also
contributed to the reputation of the French film
in the 1960s. Claude Chabrol was the first of the
Cahiers critics to make a feature film (*Le Beau
Serge*, 1958). In films such as *Les Cousins* (1959),
Les Bonnes femmes (1960), *Les Biches* (1968),
Le Boucher (1970) and *Violette* (1978), Chabrol
reveals—rather like Hitchcock, whom he often
emulates—a superb contrapuntal tension

between the sexual passions of his characters and the carefully detailed social environment.

Eric Rohmer began making his "Six Moral Tales" in 1962 and found a worldwide audience with the fourth one, *My Night at Maud's* (1969), a tale of love and religion and serious conversation. The mental battle over desire was joined again, almost as memorably, in the last two films in the series, *Claire's Knee* (1970) and *Chloe in the Afternoon* (1972). In 1976 he turned his austere eye to literature, adapting Heinrich von Kleist's *The Marquise of O . . .*, and in 1978 he retold Chrétien de Troyes's 12th-century version of the legend of the grail-seeking Parsifal according to the conventions and in the imagery of medieval art (*Perceval*). He then began another cycle, "Comedies and Proverbs," which includes *The Aviator's Wife* (1981), *Le Beau mariage* (*The Perfect Marriage*, 1982), *Pauline at the Beach* (1983), and *Full Moon in Paris* (1984). *A Tale of Winter* (1992) is part of another series, "Tales of Four Seasons," begun in 1989 with *A Tale of Springtime* and completed with *Autumn Tale* in 1998.

Of the five *Cahiers* critics-turned-filmmakers, Jacques Rivette has had the least commercial success, but his long, labyrinthine explorations of the nature of film and the paradoxes of narration are central to the New Wave's spirited reinvention of the cinema. His first feature was *Paris nous appartient* (*Paris Belongs to Us*, released in 1961); produced by Truffaut, it's the picture the family goes to see in *The 400 Blows*. Using both narrative and antinarrative methods, Rivette dramatized and analyzed narration itself in *L'Amour fou* (1968), *Out one* (1971, nearly 13 hours), *Out one: Spectre* (1974, a different film made from the footage of *Out one*), and especially the mysterious, intricate, and playful *Céline and Julie Go Boating* (1974).

Varda, Marker, and the Documentary

The "Left Bank" group of Chris Marker, Alain Resnais, and Agnès Varda worked in the documentary as well as the feature film, and they often worked together. Marker and Resnais co-wrote and co-directed *Les Statues meurent aussi* (1953)—and both concentrated in their later works on the problems of time, politics, and the nature of truth; both also learned much about stasis and editing from comic books, and both turned at some point to science fiction in search

of the freedom to explore their ideas about memory and time. In 1954 Resnais edited Varda's *La Pointe-Courte*, which as previously mentioned was either the first of the New Wave features or the film that most decisively anticipated the movement. But Varda was also connected with a New Wave filmmaker who belonged to neither the Left Bank nor the *Cahiers* group: her husband, Jacques Demy.

Demy might be considered the Busby Berkeley of the movement. In *The Umbrellas of Cherbourg* (1964), which introduced Catherine Deneuve to the screen, Demy took the tritest of melodramatic plots (boy loves girl; he goes into the army; she marries a rich suitor; he returns; their love can never be again), decorated it with the richest frosting he could find, and made audiences weep. The film is 100 percent all-singing; even the most banal ideas—needing a penicillin shot, asking for a liter of gas—get the benefit of Michel Legrand's lush score in what may be the first opera written for the cinema.

Agnès Varda is a totally different kind of filmmaker: probing, thoughtful, intellectually sensitive to the problems of the artist and the difficulty of living fully. Her first film, *La Pointe-Courte*, was inspired by William Faulkner's *The Wild Palms*, a novel written in what Eisenstein would have called parallel montage (two short, systematically opposite novels about the nature of love and freedom, presented in alternating chapters), two of whose characters leave the city to nurture their love in the woods.

The film that made Varda famous was *Cléo from 5 to 7* (1961), which follows a woman (Corinne Marchand) in virtually real time while she confronts the possibility that she has cancer. *Le Bonheur* (*Happiness*, 1965), shot in deliberately beautiful color, tells the moral tale of a happily married man who has a happy extramarital affair and decides to share his happiness with his wife, who takes the news rather badly. *Daguerréotypes* (1975), one of Varda's many documentaries, presents the people who live on her street, which is named after Daguerre. (All her documentaries are personal as well as objective; the most moving is *Jacquot de Nantes*, 1991, a film about Demy.) *One Sings, the Other Doesn't* (1977) returns to fiction to examine, in feminist terms, a long friendship between two women. The personal and careful way she studies what

Fig. 13-22
Cléo from 5 to 7: *a look at life and death (Corinne Marchand, right).*

she gathers is clear in the title of her documentary *The Gleaners and I* (2000). A true *auteur*, Varda writes, directs, and edits or co-edits her films, which are characterized by her great eye for strong compositions and colors and by the complex, painful problems with which she forces her characters to deal.

Chris Marker established himself as an author and world-traveled journalist before co-directing his first documentaries with Resnais in the early 1950s. Some of his narrative films are as much fiction as nonfiction; what drives them is narration itself. Even his science fiction short, *La Jetée* (1962, released 1964)—perhaps the best film ever made on the subject of time—is told in words, voice-over, as much as it is shown, and it is shown almost entirely in a paradoxically cinematic succession of stills. In the early 1960s Marker experimented with *cinéma vérité* (*Le Joli mai*, 1962, released 1963). In the mid-1960s he organized the

SLON film cooperative (the Society for the Launching of New Works), through which he produced several highly political compilation films and released such controversial films as the long, powerful documentary *The Battle of Chile* (directed by Patricio Guzmán; Parts I and II, 1973–77).

One of the greatest films ever made about one filmmaker by another is his study of Tarkovsky's directing, *One Day in the Life of Andrei Arsenevich* (1999). Since 1998, he has done a great deal of his work on CD-ROM.

In 1960, ethnographic filmmaker Jean Rouch, in collaboration with sociologist Edgar Morin, made *Chronique d'un été (Paris 1960)* (*Chronicle of a Summer*, released 1961), the first and most influential film in the French documentary movement that was another contribution of the New Wave, *cinéma vérité*. In *cinéma vérité*—made possible by the invention of portable 16mm sync-sound equipment—the primary drama is the

Fig. 13-23

Chris Marker's Sans soleil: *a travelogue through the culture of images in an attempt to define the self, the other, and actual others.*

Fig. 13-24

A frozen moment from La Jetée.

interaction of the unrehearsed subject, warts and all, with the camera, whose presence is always acknowledged.

Marcel Ophuls created his own form of the investigative documentary, characterized by a cagey, well-informed style of interviewing. Sometimes playful, sometimes sarcastic, and sometimes devastating, Ophuls's montage intrusions are the release valve for the tensions accumulated during his long, patient interviews. In *The Sorrow and the Pity* (1969) he exposed the ways many of the French felt all right about collaborating with the

Nazis during the Occupation. In *The Memory of Justice* (1976), the most powerful and demanding of his works, he compared the war crimes, and the military trials and investigations that followed, in World War II, the Algerian War, and the Vietnam War—finding, to no one's surprise, that the French lawyers were harder on the Nazis than they were on the French officers who committed atrocities in Algeria.

Inspired by Ophuls's work, Claude Lanzmann made *Shoah* (1985), a 9½-hour documentary about the Holocaust. Lanzmann's extremely long

Shoah: *Simon Srebnik, a survivor of the Holocaust, meets with the Polish gentiles who remember him from 40 years ago and listens—outside the town church where Jews were rounded up—to their reminiscences and unexamined prejudices.*

Fig. 13-25

interviews stick rigorously to the present; there is no archival footage, only an intense look at what remains. As Lanzmann noted, his approach was precisely the opposite of that adopted by Spielberg in his 1993 *Schindler's List*, which took the easier and more sentimental route of historical re-creation and bourgeois drama.

Malle and Others

Louis Malle was one of the most eclectic of the New Wave directors. After studying political science and then filmmaking, he virtually co-directed Jacques-Yves Cousteau's underwater documentary *The Silent World* (1956), which won an Academy Award; then he assisted Bresson on *A Man Escaped*. His first feature, *Elevator to the Gallows* or *Frantic* (1957, released 1958), was a thriller with a score by Miles Davis, starring Jeanne Moreau, and shot by Henri Decaë. In later years he would make a multipart documentary on India as well as two of the best movies ever to attempt to sort out the moral complexities of living in France under the Nazi occupation: *Lacombe Lucien* (1974) and *Au revoir les enfants* (1987). His first contribution to the New Wave was *The Lovers* (1958), a graceful and erotic tale of the manners and world of the rich, culminating in the woman's throwing over both industrialist husband and polo-playing lover to leave with the young student with whom she spends the night. *Zazie dans le Métro* (1960) is a delightfully breezy, illogical, spirited film that uses cinematic tricks to re-create the literary and linguistic gags of Raymond Queneau's novel. Malle would later desert his French environment for the American scene—*Pretty Baby* (1978),

Atlantic City (1980, a Canadian–French co-production), *My Dinner with Andre* (1981), *Damage* (1992)—a prime example of the internationalization of film production since the late 1970s. The last film he completed before his death in 1995 was *Vanya on 42nd Street* (1994).

Four women directors joined the post–New Wave generation of French filmmakers—two of whom worked within the French film industry, and two of whom worked very much outside it. Diane Kurys (*Peppermint Soda*, 1977; *Entre nous*, 1983; *C'est la vie*, 1990) and Nelly Kaplan (*A Very Curious Girl*, 1969; *Néa*, 1976; *Charles and Lucie*, 1979) moved from apprenticeships with Gance, Resnais, and Truffaut to direct their own relatively commercial, industry-backed films, frequently concentrating on young women or maturing adolescents at turning points in their lives. The novelist Marguerite Duras went from writing scripts for Resnais (*Hiroshima mon amour*) to writing and directing films, often based on her own novels and plays (*Destroy, She Said*, 1969; *Nathalie Granger*, 1973; *India Song*, 1975; *Le Camion*, 1977). She died in 1996 at the age of 81. Like her novels, Duras's films experiment with both narrative form and psychological representation—often in the interplay between minimal visual imagery and densely rich soundtracks. Chantal Akerman is influenced by experimental filmmakers on both sides of the Atlantic—Godard, Michael Snow, Stan Brakhage. In her first 10 years as a filmmaker, she directed 17 movies. Her films (especially *Jeanne Dielman / 23 quai du commerce / 1080 Bruxelles*, 1975, and *Meetings with Anna*, 1978) reduce plot and

Fig. 13-26

Lacombe Lucien: *Lucien (Pierre Blaise), a French peasant who becomes a German agent during the Occupation, practices his slingshot in front of a portrait of Marshal Pétain, the head of the Vichy government.*

Fig. 13-27

Z: *the synthesis of spy thriller and revolutionary political document.*

dialogue, emphasizing the power of sounds, the duration of uninterrupted temporality, and the resonance of spaces in depicting moments of action, sensation, and recollected experience. Like Varda, these directors have given France the claim to the longest of woman-centered cinematic narrative traditions, one that goes back to Alice Guy, Germaine Dulac, and Marie Epstein.

In the 1990s, France remained a major presence on world screens, thanks not only to the new films of Akerman, Chabrol, Godard, Resnais, Rohmer, Varda, and other established artists, but also to the compelling and fully realized works of many newcomers. *Microcosmos: The People of the Grass* (1996, a French–Swiss–Italian co-production) showed a day in a meadow—created by Claude Nuridsany and Marie Pérennou out of years of extreme close-ups—as it might be experienced at ground level, primarily by insects. Gaspar Noé, who was born in Argentina and signs his films "Noe," took psychological and social horror to new extremes with a short (*Carne*, 1991) and a feature (*Seul contre tous* or *I Stand Alone*, 1998) about a horsemeat butcher whose life is destroyed by his

Fig. 13-28
Amélie (Audrey Tautou) watches a movie.

violence, his sweeping hatred, and his love for his daughter. Noé's next feature, *Irreversible* (2002), starts with the butcher but soon abandons him to tell the story of an extraordinarily vicious rape and a misguided revenge.

Alain Berliner's *Ma vie en rose* (*My Life in Pink*, 1997, a Belgian–French–British co-production) is a sex comedy about a boy who wants to be a girl; the film asserts the power of imagination to transform life—the look and even some of the reality of oneself and the world. In *Irma Vep* (1996), Olivier Assayas portrays the attempt of an obsessed director, played by Jean-Pierre Léaud, and a real martial arts star, Maggie Cheung, to create something perfectly new and old, a shot-for-shot remake of Feuillade's silent serial *Les Vampires*—as a nervous breakdown. In *The Dreamlife of Angels* (1998), Érick Zonca offers an unforced, realistic look at what it is like, in the cities of northern France, for two young women to find and lose a job, a place to live, and someone to care about. Chilean filmmaker Raul Ruiz made the best film yet adapted from Marcel Proust's overwhelming novel, *A la recherche du temps perdu* (*In Search of Lost Time*). Patrice Leconte won audiences over with his tales of a knife-thrower (*Girl on the Bridge*, 1999) and a guillotine (*The Widow of Saint-Pierre*, 2000). The team of Jean-Pierre Jeunet (*metteur-en-scène*) and Marc Caro (artistic director—i.e., production designer) crammed the screen with vibrant, deeply colored images in complex compositions; their fast cutting, poetic writing, surreal comedy, and exhilarating special effects (by far the best computer work in France)

made their wild, dark fables, *Delicatessen* (1991) and *The City of Lost Children* (1995), as entertaining as they were demanding. (Jeunet and Caro were in some ways the French complement of England's Michael Powell and Emeric Pressburger, the most inventive team of the 1940s.) On his own, Jeunet directed the squirmy *Alien Resurrection* (1997— the fourth in the series) in America, then returned to France to make the most positive film he could dream up, the popular and endearing *Amélie* (2001).

Currently the elder statesman of the new generation of French directors, Bertrand Tavernier is the most conscious of uniting the traditions of past and present cinema. Although a committed leftist, Tavernier, like Renoir of the 1930s, gives ordinary citizens their dignity in their attempts to understand the political, social, and military structures that contain them, for "everyone has his reasons." Although the middle-class clockmaker (*The Clockmaker*, 1974) cannot understand his son's acts of political radicalism, he comes to understand that his son must have a reason for them. His greatest commercial success of the 1980s was *Round Midnight* (1986), an evocative realization of the jazz scene in 1950s Paris; it experimented with jazz rhythms in its own structure and starred Dexter Gordon as an expatriate master of the tenor sax. But the most impressive of all his films may be *L.627* (1992), a realistic look at the problems of drug use, the legal system, and police work in contemporary France.

Among the New Wave characteristics these later films share are their careful rendering of the textures of sensations and experiences, their anti-studio look, their interest in political analysis (including the politics of gender), and their elliptical narrative structures that emphasize thematic development rather than a linear, chronological presentation of events.

For Further Viewing

FILMS

ITALY

MICHELANGELO ANTONIONI (1912–)
Il grido (*The Cry*, 1957)
L'avventura (*The Adventure*, 1960)
La notte (*The Night*, 1960)
L'eclisse (*Eclipse*, 1962)
Il deserto rosso (*Red Desert*, 1964)
Blowup or *Blow-Up* (1966)
The Passenger (1975)

BERNARDO BERTOLUCCI (1940–)
Before the Revolution (1964)
The Conformist (1970)
Last Tango in Paris (1972)
1900 (1976)
The Last Emperor (1987)
The Sheltering Sky (1990)

VITTORIO DE SICA (1902–74)
Shoeshine (1946)
The Bicycle Thief or *Bicycle Thieves* (1948)
Miracle in Milan (1950)
Umberto D. (1952)
Two Women (1960)
A Brief Vacation (1973)

FEDERICO FELLINI (1920–93)
La strada (*The Street* or *The Road*, 1954)
Nights of Cabiria (1956)
La dolce vita (*The Sweet Life*, 1960)
8½ (1963)
Juliet of the Spirits (1965)
Fellini Satyricon or *Satyricon* (1969)
Amarcord (1973)
Casanova (1976)

SERGIO LEONE (1921–89)
Fistful of Dollars or *A Fistful of Dollars* or *For a Fistful of Dollars* (1964)
For a Few Dollars More (1965)
The Good, the Bad and the Ugly (1966)

Once Upon a Time in the West (1968)
Once Upon a Time in America (1984)

PIER PAOLO PASOLINI (1922–75)
Accattone (*Beggar*, 1961)
The Gospel According to St. Matthew (1964)
Hawks and Sparrows (1966)
Teorema (*Theorem*, 1968)
Porcile (*Pigpen* or *Pigsty*, 1969)
Medea (1969)
The Decameron (1971)
The Canterbury Tales (1972)
The Arabian Nights (1974)
Salò or The 120 Days of Sodom (1975)

ROBERTO ROSSELLINI (1906–77)
Open City or *Rome, Open City* (1945)
Paisan (1946)
Germany Year Zero (1947)
Stromboli (1949)
Europa '51 (1951)
Viaggio in Italia (*Voyage to Italy*, 1953)
India (1958)
General Della Rovere (1959)
The Rise to Power of Louis XIV (1966)

ETTORE SCOLA (1931–)
We All Loved Each Other So Much (1974)
A Special Day (1977)
La Nuit de Varennes (1982)

LUCHINO VISCONTI (1906–76)
Ossessione (*Obsession*, 1943)
    Completed 1942
La terra trema (*The Earth Trembles*, 1948)
Rocco and His Brothers (1960)
The Leopard (1963)
The Damned or *Götterdämmerung* (1969)

ITALIAN MISCELLANY
Salvatore Giuliano (1962, Francesco Rosi)
Il posto (*The Job* or *The Sound of Trumpets*, 1961, Ermanno Olmi)
Divorce, Italian Style (1961, Pietro Germi)
Seduced and Abandoned (1963, Pietro Germi)
The Battle of Algiers (1966, Gillo Pontecorvo)
Swept Away . . . or *Swept away by an unusual destiny in the blue sea of August* (1974, Lina Wertmüller)
Seven Beauties (1976, Lina Wertmüller)
Padre Padrone (1977, Paolo and Vittorio Taviani)
The Tree of Wooden Clogs (1978, Ermanno Olmi)

The Night of the Shooting Stars (1982, Paolo and Vittorio Taviani)

KAOS (*Chaos*, 1984, Paolo and Vittorio Taviani)

Cinema Paradiso (1989, Giuseppe Tornatore)

Life is Beautiful (1998, Roberto Benigni)

The Son's Room (2001, Nanni Moretti)

My Mother's Smile (2002, Marco Bellocchio)

Best of Youth (2002, Marco Tullio Giordana)

FRANCE

ROBERT BRESSON (1901–99)

Les Dames du Bois de Boulogne (1945)

Diary of a Country Priest (1950)

Un Condamné à mort s'est échappé (*A Man Escaped*, 1956)

Pickpocket (1959)

Mouchette (1967)

CLAUDE CHABROL (1930–   )

Le Beau Serge (1958)

The Cousins (1959)

Les Biches (1968)

The Beast Must Die or *This Man Must Die* (1969)

Le Boucher (1970)

Wedding in Blood (1973)

JEAN COCTEAU (1889–1963)

The Blood of a Poet (1930)

Beauty and the Beast (1946). Asst. director, René Clément

Les Parents terribles (1948)

Orpheus (1950)

JEAN-LUC GODARD (1930–   )

Breathless (*A bout de souffle*, 1960). Shot 1959

Vivre sa vie or *My Life to Live* (1962)

Les Carabiniers (1963)

Contempt (1963)

Bande à part (*Band of Outsiders*, 1964)

Alphaville, A Strange Adventure of Lemmy Caution (1965)

Pierrot le fou (1965)

Masculine Feminine (1966)

2 or 3 Things I Know About Her (1967)

La Chinoise (1967)

Weekend (1967)

One Plus One or *Sympathy for the Devil* (1968)

Wind from the East (1969). Co-director, Jean-Pierre Gorin

Tout va bien (1972). Co-director, Gorin

Communication (6 parts, 1976). Co-director, Miéville

France/Tour/Détour/Deux/Enfants (1978). Co-director, Miéville

Sauve qui peut/La vie or *Every Man for Himself* (1980)

Hélas pour moi (*Woe is Me*, 1993). Completed 1992

JLG/JLG: Self-Portrait in December (1994)

For Ever Mozart (1996)

Histoire(s) du cinéma (8 parts, video, 1998–99)

Our Music (2004)

LOUIS MALLE (1932–95)

The Silent World (1956). Co-director, Jacques-Yves Cousteau

The Lovers (1958)

Zazie dans le Métro (1960)

Murmur of the Heart (1971)

Lacombe Lucien (1974)

Atlantic City (1980)

My Dinner with Andre (1981)

Au revoir les enfants (1987)

CHRIS MARKER (1921–   )

Le Joli mai (1963). Completed 1962

La Jetée (1964). Completed 1962

Sans soleil (1982)

The Last Bolshevik (1993)

Prime Time in the Camps (1994)

One Day in the Life of Andrei Arsenevich (1999)

MARCEL OPHULS (1927–   )

The Sorrow and the Pity: Chronicle of a City under the Occupation (1969)

The Memory of Justice (1976)

MAX OPHÜLS (1902–57)

Letter From An Unknown Woman (1948)

Caught (1949)

La Ronde (1950)

Madame de . . . or *The Earrings of Madame de . . .* (1953)

Lola Montès (1955)

ALAIN RESNAIS (1922–   )

Night and Fog (1955)

Hiroshima mon amour (1959)

Last Year at Marienbad (1961)
Muriel or The Time of a Return (1963)
La Guerre est finie (1966)
Je t'aime, je t'aime (1968)
Mon oncle d'Amérique (1980)
Smoking/No Smoking (1993)

JACQUES RIVETTE (1928–   )
Paris nous appartient (Paris Belongs to Us,
    1961). Shot 1957–59
Out one (1971)
Out one: Spectre (1974)
Céline and Julie Go Boating (1974)

ERIC ROHMER (1920–   )
My Night at Maud's (1969)
Claire's Knee (1970)
Chloe in the Afternoon or Love in the Afternoon
    (1972)
A Tale of Springtime (1990)
A Tale of Winter (1992)
A Summer's Tale (1996)
Autumn Tale (1998)

ALAIN TANNER (1929–   )
La Salamandre (1971)
Jonah Who Will Be 25 in the Year 2000 (1976)

JACQUES TATI (1908–82)
Jour de fête (1949)
Mr. Hulot's Holiday (1953)
Mon oncle (1958)
Traffic (1970)

BERTRAND TAVERNIER (1941–   )
The Clockmaker (1974)
A Sunday in the Country (1984)

FRANÇOIS TRUFFAUT (1932–84)
The 400 Blows (1959)
Shoot the Piano Player (1960)
Jules and Jim (1962). Completed 1961
Stolen Kisses (1968)
The Wild Child (1970)
Day for Night (1973)
The Last Metro (1980)

AGNÈS VARDA (1928–   )
La Pointe-Courte (1956). Completed 1954
Cléo from 5 to 7 (1961)
Le Bonheur (1965)

Daguerréotypes (1975)
One Sings, the Other Doesn't (1977)
Documenteur: An Emotion Picture (1981)
Vagabond or Sans toit ni loi (1985)
Jacquot de Nantes (1991)
The Gleaners and I (2000)

FRENCH MISCELLANY
Forbidden Games (1952, René Clément)
The Wages of Fear (1953, Henri-Georges
    Clouzot)
Du Rififi chez les hommes or Rififi (1955,
    Jules Dassin)
Bob le flambeur (1955, Jean-Pierre Melville)
Les Diaboliques or Diabolique (1955, Henri-
    Georges Clouzot)
The Red Balloon (1956, Albert Lamorisse)
Black Orpheus (1959, Marcel Camus)
Chronique d'un été (Paris 1960) (1961, Jean
    Rouch). Co-director, Edgar Morin
The Umbrellas of Cherbourg (1964, Jacques
    Demy)
King of Hearts (1966, Philippe de Broca)
Le Samouraï (1967, Jean-Pierre Melville)
Z (1969, Costa-Gavras)
State of Siege (1973, Costa-Gavras). Completed
    1972
India Song (1975, Marguerite Duras)
*Jeanne Dielman / 23 quai du commerce / 1080
    Bruxelles* (1975, Chantal Akerman)
Entre nous (1983, Diane Kurys)
Shoah (1985, Claude Lanzmann)
Jean de Florette and *Manon of the Spring* (1986,
    Claude Berri)
Delicatessen (1991, Jean-Pierre Jeunet and Marc
    Caro)
Three Colors (3 parts, 1993–94, Krzysztof
    Kieślowski). *See* Poland
The City of Lost Children (1995, Jean-Pierre
    Jeunet and Marc Caro)
Microcosmos (1996, Claude Nuridsany and Marie
    Pérennou)
Irma Vep (1996, Olivier Assayas)
Seul contre tous or I Stand Alone (1998, Gaspar
    Noé)
The Dreamlife of Angels (1998, Érick Zonca)
Time Regained (1999, Raul Ruiz)
The Captive (2000, Chantal Akerman)
Belleville Rendez-vous or The Triplets of Belleville
    (Sylvain Chomet, 2003)

DVDs

ITALY

L'avventura (1960, **Michelangelo Antonioni**). Criterion Collection. Includes Antonioni's statements on the film after its premiere, selected Antonioni writings read by Jack Nicholson, a documentary, and more.

The Battle of Algiers (1966, **Gillo Pontecorvo**). Criterion Collection. Includes an informative booklet and many documentaries (one narrated by postcolonial theorist Edward Said) on Pontecorvo, the making of the film, Algerian history, terrorism, etc. One documentary shows French soldiers recalling the torture and execution of rebels.

Blow-Up (1966, **Michelangelo Antonioni**). Warner Home Video. Commentary by film historian Peter Brunette.

Deep Red (1975, **Dario Argento**). Anchor Bay. This director's cut (126 min.) improves on the uncut release version (120 min.); includes a documentary and filmographies.

L'eclisse (1962, **Michelangelo Antonioni**). Criterion Collection. Includes a documentary on Antonioni as well as essays, a commentary, and a short about *Eclipse*.

8½ (1963, **Federico Fellini**). Criterion Collection. Includes Fellini's documentary *Fellini: A Director's Notebook*, a booklet with essays by Fellini and others, a documentary on composer **Nino Rota,** and many interviews.

The Leopard (1963, **Luchino Visconti**). Criterion Collection. **Restored**; includes both versions (the European original and the American release cut—with **Burt Lancaster**'s voice instead of the previous dubbed one), a commentary by film historian Peter Cowie, a documentary, interviews, and newsreels.

Medea (1969, **Pier Paolo Pasolini**; starring **Maria Callas**). Vanguard Cinema. Compare with the von Trier–Dreyer version (see Chap. 14 list).

Open City (1947, **Roberto Rossellini**). Image Entertainment. The same company offers *Paisan* and *Germany Year Zero*.

Pier Paolo Pasolini Collection: Volume 2 (1961–66, **Pier Paolo Pasolini**). Water Bearer Films. Contains Pasolini Foundation prints of *Accattone, The Gospel According to St.*

Matthew, and *Hawks and Sparrows*; includes a documentary on Pasolini. Volume 1 includes *Porcile*.

Il posto (1961, **Ermanno Olmi**). Criterion Collection. Includes an interview with Olmi; an Olmi short, *La cotta*; a **restoration** demonstration; and a deleted scene.

Salvatore Giuliano (1962, **Francesco Rosi**). Criterion Collection. An essential set, with a **restored** print, an exemplary commentary by film historian Peter Cowie, part of a 1950 newsreel about Giuliano's death, a documentary about Rosi, an interview with Rosi about realism, written tributes by Coppola and Fellini, and more.

Umberto D. (1952, **Vittorio De Sica**). Criterion Collection. Includes a documentary on De Sica and writings about the film by De Sica, novelist and theorist Umberto Eco, and others.

I vitelloni (1953, **Federico Fellini**). Criterion Collection. **Restored**, with a documentary.

FRANCE

The Adventures of Antoine Doinel (1957–79, **François Truffaut**). Criterion Collection. Includes all the Doinel films—*The 400 Blows, Antoine and Colette* (from *Love at Twenty*), *Bed and Board, Stolen Kisses,* and *Love on the Run*—and the early short *Les Mistons*, along with **Jean-Pierre Léaud**'s screen test and many documentaries, TV-show excerpts, commentaries, and interviews.

Band of Outsiders (1964, **Jean-Luc Godard**). Criterion Collection. Includes interviews with Godard, cinematographer **Raoul Coutard**, and star **Anna Karina**, and a silent comedy by **Agnès Varda**.

Bob le flambeur (1955, **Jean-Pierre Melville**). Criterion Collection. Includes a radio interview with Melville.

Les Carabiniers (1963, **Jean-Luc Godard**). Fox Lorber. Many important Godard films, including this one, are on DVD with few or no extras. *2 or 3 Things I Know About Her* is available only on VHS (New Yorker).

Cléo from 5 to 7 (1961, **Agnès Varda**). Criterion Collection. Varda **restored** the opening color sequence and supervised the digital transfer.

Diary of a Country Priest (1950, **Robert Bresson**). Criterion Collection. **Digitally restored**, with a commentary by film historian Peter Cowie.

Eyes without a Face (1960, **Georges Franju**). Criterion Collection. **Digitally restored**; includes Franju's short documentary, *Blood of the Beasts*, and an interview with Franju about the fantastic and horror.

The Gleaners and I (2000, Agnès Varda).

Hiroshima mon amour (1959, **Alain Resnais**). Criterion Collection. Includes excerpts from writer **Marguerite Duras**'s script notes, interviews with Resnais and star **Emmanuelle Riva**, commentary by film historian Peter Cowie, and more.

Jules and Jim (1962, **François Truffaut**). Criterion Collection. **Digitally restored**; includes interviews with Truffaut, cinematographer **Raoul Coutard**, and others; commentaries by star **Jeanne Moreau**, Truffaut collaborator **Suzanne Schiffman**, co-writer **Jean Gruault**, editor **Claudine Bouché**, and others; a discussion between film scholars Dudley Andrew and Robert Stam; TV-show excerpts; and more.

Mon oncle (1958, **Jacques Tati**). Criterion Collection. **Restored**, with a 1947 Tati short.

Night and Fog (see Chap. 1 list).

The Orphic Trilogy (**Jean Cocteau**). Criterion Collection. Includes *The Blood of a Poet*, *Orpheus*, and *The Testament of Orpheus*; a documentary on Cocteau; a collection of Cocteau's writings on the trilogy; a filmography; and a Cocteau short, *Villa Santo Sospir*.

Rififi (see Chap. 12 list).

Shorts 2: Dreams (anthology). Warner Studios. Includes **Chris Marker**'s *La Jetée*.

Tout va bien (1972, **Jean-Luc Godard** and **Jean-Pierre Gorin**). Criterion Collection. Includes their film *Letter to Jane* and several interviews with both directors.

14

National Cinemas 1: 1945–

The flourishing of the French and Italian cinemas was not an isolated postwar occurrence. Forces similar to those of the New Wave affected cinemas of many other countries. First, the postwar period encouraged personality and individuality in the cinema—new things to say and new ways to say them—because the old formulas and stylistic assumptions were breaking down. Second, the audience, the technology, and the world were all changing. Times of instability and change tend to encourage originality rather than formula. Third, the American film industry was in severe trouble artistically and commercially. Prizes at international film festivals (a new sign of the times) brought not only honor to previously unknown film artists and industries, but also, and perhaps more important, bookings. American films were no longer powerful or attractive enough to keep foreign films off the screen, either abroad or in America.

Finally, feature film production has been either directly or indirectly supported by government policies in almost every country except the United States. Foreign governments have established quotas to limit the importation or exhibition of American films, have levied exorbitant taxes on profits from showing American films or limited the currency that American companies could export, and have invested directly in film production or invested indirectly through state-supported television systems. While the American film industry has always had to sink or swim on its own, in the lean postwar years of shrinking feature-film production, the American government let the

Hollywood industry sink, while other governments kept their industries afloat.

In the mid-1970s, the wheel came full circle. By adopting the styles and assumptions of the foreign film movements, the American cinema not only became strong enough again to keep most foreign competition off American screens—clearly a loss for the audience—but began winning the prizes at the international film festivals as well.

Sweden and Denmark

The name of Ingmar Bergman is as synonymous with the new cinematic directions of the second half of the 20th century as those of Fellini, Antonioni, Resnais, or Godard. Like them, Bergman is the product of a rich national film tradition. The Swedish film industry, though never producing a great number of films, enjoys a long history. Bergman, an actor, playwright, and stage director, learned his film craft from Alf Sjöberg, Sweden's most important director in the first two decades of sound production. And Sjöberg learned his craft in the Silent Era of Victor Sjöström and Mauritz Stiller. Bergman also learned much from the films of Denmark's Carl Theodor Dreyer.

Stiller and Sjöström combined the visual and poetic power of the northern landscapes with stories of realistic passions and mystical influences—much as Bergman would do 40 years later. The three consistent traits of the Swedish silents were: first, their use of natural imagery to evoke and convey human passions as in Sjöström's use of the sea in *A Man There Was* (1916, released 1917) and Stiller's use of the snow and mountains in *The Story of Gösta Berling* (1924, starring Garbo); second, their satirical and critical condemnation of social hypocrisies and injustices, as in Sjöström's *The Outlaw and His Wife* and Stiller's *Erotikon* (1920); third, also Dreyer's great theme, the influence of cosmic, metaphysical forces in human affairs. The eerie, ghostly carriage that comes for the tramp who dies at precisely midnight on New Year's Eve in Sjöström's *The Phantom Chariot* (1920, released 1921) is the ancestor of the hearse that comes for Isak Borg in Bergman's *Wild Strawberries*; Sjöström's figure of death is an ancestor of Death in Bergman's *The Seventh Seal.* The metaphorical unity in the Swedish film tradition is striking, for Victor Sjöström—Sweden's first film master—played the role of the old doctor in Bergman's *Wild Strawberries.*

Much as the Swedish cinema looks back to Sjöström, the Danish cinema takes continuing inspiration from Dreyer, every one of whose films was a fresh experiment. As in his French *The Passion of Joan of Arc* (1928) and his German *Vampyr* (1932), a central theme in the works Dreyer made when he returned to Denmark is the intersection between the mortal and the immortal. In *Vampyr*, humans are touched by the supernatural—a vampire—and the realm of shadows, reversals, and dreams into which evil turns the world is transcendental and terrifying. In *Day of Wrath* (1943), it is hard to be sure whether what may be supernatural intrusions come from Satan, God, or the characters' immersion in religion and its sexual politics; the film is plotted and shot in such a way that the main character might or might not be a witch; no modern view completely dispels the belief the filmed world has in witchcraft. The divine intervenes directly in *Ordet* (*The Word*, 1954, released 1955), as the satanic does in *Vampyr.* Dreyer's last planned film was a life of Jesus; his last completed film was *Gertrud* (1964), which is purely about the mortal world and the importance of believing in love. Dreyer's subtle work with actors and bold, insightful camerawork—from his absolute mastery of lighting to the camera movements that almost seem conscious—remained at the height of the art; the few movies for which he was able to

obtain funding secured his place as the most interesting mind on film.

Three decades after Dreyer's death, the Danish director best known to international audiences was the audacious Lars von Trier (born Lars Trier), who delighted in making up rules—like those in the Dogme95 manifesto, discussed below, most of which he wrote—and breaking them to arrive at new forms of expression: using theatrical and realistic sets—and black and white and color—in the same scene, as in *Zentropa* (released in 1991 as *Europa*) or turning the rigid expectations of religious and sexual convention against themselves, as in *Breaking the Waves* (1996).

Where von Trier differs from Dreyer is in the range of his style, which can be flamboyant and full of effects or ruggedly low-budget and antiartistic, and in the quality of his vision: He parodies vision instead of being possessed by the real thing. Even so, his parodies of crazy visionaries are terrific. If, like the characters in his 1998 film *The Idiots*, one nurtures one's "inner idiot," the results may well include the orgiastic, the stupid, and the brutal, in any order and in no conventional hierarchy. In the worlds of Lars von Trier, you never know what will save you (*Breaking the Waves*) or that nothing will (*Zentropa*).

In 1995, von Trier convinced directors Thomas Vinterberg, Søren Kragh-Jacobsen, and Kristian Levring to take a "Vow of Chastity" and agree to film according to a strict set of rules; they took the vow and formed the movement, Dogme (or "dogma") 95, written Dogme95. They vowed not to shoot in black and white (too "artistic") or use filters, not to make genre films or include murders and similar "superficial action," to follow the actors with a hand-held camera, and to observe other stringent rules that would, as von Trier put it, "force the truth out of the characters and settings." Most of them shot their movies with camcorders. The first of the Dogme95 films were released in 1998: Vinterberg's *The Celebration* and, shortly after it, *The Idiots.*

Ingmar Bergman

Bergman directed his first film, *Crisis*, in 1945. For ten years Bergman and his first cinematographer, Gunnar Fischer, felt their way together within the film form, discovering how to synthesize the theatre (Bergman's first love) with the visual image, building a stock company of actors sensitive to each other and to the director: Max von Sydow, Gunnar Björnstrand, Eva Dahlbeck, Ingrid Thulin, Harriet Andersson, Bibi Andersson, Gunnel Lindblom. Later regulars would include Liv Ullmann and Erland Josephson. *Smiles of a Summer Night* (1955) was probably Bergman's first fully mature work.

But it was *The Seventh Seal* (1956, released 1957) that first conquered audiences throughout the world, and soon Bergman had released two more films, *Wild Strawberries* (1957) and *The Magician* (*The Face*, 1958), to cement his reputation. These three films are a central unit in the Bergman canon, a pool of ideas and images from which all his later work seems to be drawn.

The Seventh Seal is the story of a medieval knight who returns home from the crusades only to encounter Death waiting for him on a desolate, rocky beach. The knight (Antonius Blok, played by Max von Sydow) challenges Death (Bengt Ekerot) to a game of chess, knowing the inevitable result but playing for time. He wants the time for one reason: to discover the value of living. Everywhere around him he sees death: from the crusades, from the plague, from flagellation and superstition.

Fig. 14-1
The Seventh Seal: *Death as confessor. The equation of black, death, darkness, restraints, and the Church; from left, Bengt Ekerot and Max von Sydow.*

Fig. 14-2
The Seventh Seal: *Mary (Bibi Andersson) and Joseph (Nils Poppe), two actors in the sunlight.*

At the end of the film, the knight loses the chess game, and Death overtakes him and his party. But as the knight himself says, the delay has been most significant, for he has found some good people and learned, partly through them, to value life and hope, and he has helped a young family escape Death. This innocent, happy family of father (named Joseph), mother (named Mary), and infant becomes the film's trinity of life. At the end of the film, they stand in the sunlight as Joseph watches Death lead the knight and his party across a hilltop in shadow.

The film's central contrast is the opposition of the ways of life and the forces of death. The Church—organized, dogmatic religion—becomes emblematic of superstition and death. The Church

instigated the deadly crusades. The Church decorates its walls with pictures and statues of death. The Church inspires people to frenzies of prayer and mourning and mortification. The Church burns human scapegoats. The men of the Church wear black, the color of death. In fact, the knight mistakes the figure of Death for a priest when he makes confession.

Opposed to the film's dark moments are its moments of life, clarity, and light. The scenes between Joseph (Nils Poppe) and Mary (Bibi Andersson)—the two strolling players—are slightly overexposed, brilliantly bathed in light. The scene in which the knight partakes of their happiness, when the group sits in the sunshine to eat wild strawberries, is natural, peaceful, and bright. The real religion, the real humanity in the film stems from the sincere, unselfish feelings of the characters for one another.

Wild Strawberries puts the same theme in modern dress. The film begins with a vision of death, the old man's dream in which he sees a hearse roll down a desolate street, in which he sees himself inside the hearse's coffin. Bergman increases the dream's impression of bleakness and desolation by overexposing the whole vision. Then the old doctor wakes up. Since he perceives the closeness of death, he is haunted by questions about the value of the life he has lived. Ironically, this doctor, Isak Borg (played by Sjöström), aged 78, is about to be honored by society for the value of his life's work; a university is to award him an honorary degree. Despite the university's assessment of his life's worth, the doctor is not so certain about it. The rest of the film shows him groping for an answer, through his memories and through the events of the day (as well as a final dream).

When Borg examines his present relationships, he sees nothing but empty sterility. He has tyrannized his old housekeeper of some 40 years, taking her completely for granted. Borg's great legacy to his son has been to transfer his nihilism, his contempt for life. So successfully has Borg passed on this dowry that the son and daughter-in-law are in danger of separating. The son hates life so bitterly that he refuses to bring children into it.

The two groups that Borg encounters on the road are diametric opposites. The young hikers are shining, vital, energetic; they devour life with a callous yet honest robustness (Ibsen called it the Viking Spirit), unfettered by social convention, disillusionment, and failure. The middle-aged couple are tied to one another by habit, by argument, and by the need to share futility. Both encounters trigger Borg's visions. The pair with blasted lives evokes Borg's bitterest dream, in which he attends a hell-like school (the scene echoes the school scene in Strindberg's *A Dream Play*) and fails an examination administered by the husband. Uncompassionate and guilty, he must learn to ask forgiveness.

But the hikers, particularly the young woman (Bibi Andersson), stimulate Borg to dream of his childhood, his summers at the family summer house, where he felt both disappointment in romance and the happiness of youth. Bergman shoots these scenes with a clarity and a whiteness that echo the scenes between Mary and Joseph in *The Seventh Seal.* Summer and sunshine—not overexposure, which he saves for nightmares—are consistent metaphors for moments of happiness in *Smiles of a Summer Night, Monika, Summer Interlude* (1950, released 1951), and even the violent *The Virgin Spring* (1959, released 1960, where the metaphor is used ironically, turned against itself to intensify a sunlit horror).

Like the knight of *The Seventh Seal*, Isak Borg translates his vision into action, primarily by offering to ease his pressure on his son and, in effect, reconciling son and daughter-in-law to one another. By the film's end, Borg has taken a journey toward life and finally helped his son do the same.

In *The Magician* (literally, *The Face*), Bergman turns from the relationship of death to life to examine the relationship of art to life. A 19th-century magic lanternist (who is also a "mesmerist," or hypnotist) and his assistants travel by coach to a town where they are stopped by the local authorities. These bureaucratic devotees of reason are anxious to see the lanternist display his wares, to see whether his illusion is powerful enough to unsettle their conventional understanding of reality. The magician's art is indeed powerful enough to drive one spectator to hang himself and another to the point of madness. And yet the bureaucrats judge the man's performance a failure. In the midst of his dejection, word comes to the illusionist that his presence is desired at court. In an unexpected mood of triumph and sunshine, the magician's coach sets out for the court.

The great power of *The Magician* is that it operates on two levels simultaneously. There are two magicians: Vogler, the lanternist (played by Max von Sydow), and Bergman, the filmmaker. Both Vogler and Bergman work on the principle that the trick, the mask (a false face), the illusion can seize the mind more powerfully than the expected reality. Vogler's life is a web of lies and tricks. He is not mute as he pretends to be; his assistant is not a boy but his wife. Everything about the man is false—a game of mirrors and deceptive appearances like his lantern show. But Bergman plays tricks on *his* audience just as Vogler plays them on his: by making us think a character has died, by switching from gloom to sunshine as if switching on the lights in a theatre. His ultimate trick on us is also the magician's ultimate trick on the bureaucrat: Vogler lures the official to an attic, locks him in, and then reduces him to absolute terror with thumping sounds, invisible attacks, and the vision of a detached eyeball swimming in an inkwell. Bergman scares us too; the sequence is inexplicable, evocative of the powers of the unknown, tensely controlled in its rhythm of sounds and cutting. The irrational, the weapon of the artist (certainly of Bergman and Vogler), has an undeniable power; its appearances can capture not reason but feelings and the imagination. Loving and imagining, as both *The Seventh Seal* and *Wild Strawberries* assert, are the essential human functions, and the cinema is, like the title of Bergman's favorite Strindberg work, a dream play.

The later Bergman films return often to the same ground as these central three. The films that Bergman designated as his trilogy—*Through a Glass Darkly* (1961), *Winter Light* (*The Communicants*, 1962), and *The Silence* (1963)— all seek meaningful, sometimes spiritual values in a world in which life has no absolute purpose and there are many barriers to communication. *Cries and Whispers* (1972) shows how the awareness of an impending death defines the values of living. And *Persona* (1965, released 1966) combines the self-conscious cinematic tricks of *The Magician* with a psychoanalytic and metaphysical study of a person who, like Isak Borg, views the experience of living as a bleak and terrible lie.

But despite the similarities of these to the earlier films, the Bergman cinematic style had altered radically, becoming less theatrical and more elliptical. Bergman's stylistic shift was partly the result of his switching to a more experimental cinematographer, Sven Nykvist, who replaced Gunnar Fischer in the 1960s. The late Bergman films are increasingly concerned with psychology—the fears, anguish, and even mental diseases of individuals—and painful relationships. The characters are caught in institutions through which they can fulfill or destroy themselves but which they can never fully understand: the church, the theatre, marriage.

Persona is Bergman's masterpiece, his most complex and reflexive film, and his truest display of technical virtuosity. On its surface, the film is the story of a cure, a psychological case study of Elisabeth Vogler (Liv Ullmann), an actress who went blank onstage during a performance of *Electra* and has refused to speak since. Her refusal to communicate is symptomatic of her feeling that human existence is merely a collection of lies. For Elisabeth, to speak is to lie. She is treated in a mental hospital by a young, energetic, and dedicated nurse, Alma (Bibi Andersson), and later to a seaside home of the hospital's head psychiatrist. At that seaside retreat, where the nurse does all the talking, and the two women share moments of intimacy and hatred. The end of this process is the actress's apparent return to communication, to her life on the stage and with her family, and Nurse Alma's return to her job, shaken by the experience but continuing on her way.

What complicates the case study is Bergman's elliptical and nonlinear way of telling this story, which gives rise to several motifs that extend far beyond a simple examination of a neurotic artist. Bergman presents *Persona* not as a record of events but (1) as a film and (2) as a kind of mental movie screen on which the "events" appear. The film repeatedly refers to itself—at one point appearing to stop, rip, and burn in the projection gate.

Bergman calls attention to the film as a film because he wants to emphasize that what follows is a fiction, an illusion—a sequence of light and shadow on a flat screen. The audience has entered the world of art and chimera—of magic and theatre, not of nature and reality. But Bergman's film then gives this clear dichotomy another twist, for is the world of nature—or personal identity itself—any more solid, any more real than the one of artistic illusion?

Persona was followed by the grim, powerful, nightmarish trilogy of *Hour of the Wolf* (1966, released 1968), *Shame* (1967, released 1968), and *The Passion of Anna* (1969), all of which starred Liv Ullmann and Max von Sydow. After several more emotionally painful works—notably *Cries and Whispers* and *Scenes from a Marriage* (1974, condensed from the 1972 TV version)— Bergman returned to the sustaining vision of theatricality. Most of his later films reaffirm his faith in illusion, in the imagination, in art, and in

A SHORT HISTORY OF THE MOVIES

Fig. 14-3

Persona. *Merging two personae into one: the joining of Elisabeth Vogler (Liv Ullmann, left column) and Sister Alma (Bibi Andersson, right column). As the two women face each other across a table, the scene is side lit, from Alma's right and Elisabeth's left, leaving complementary halves of each character's face in darkness; at the end of the last shot, with the illuminated side of Alma's face on the left side of the screen, the dark half is filled in with the lit side of Elisabeth's face.*

magic. The three-part structure of *Fanny and Alexander*, fashioned from a longer version made for Swedish TV, seems Bergman's own spiritual autobiography. It begins happily, surrounded by family, in the theatre—the place where Bergman began, the place of joyous illusion, of smiles and light. It then plunges into a middle section of dark despair, dominated by Calvinist severity and mortification—which parallels Bergman's despairing black-and-white films of the 1960s. But it escapes once again into the light, back to the celebration of magic and theatre—and the performance of Strindberg's *A Dream Play*.

After *Fanny and Alexander*, Bergman officially retired from filmmaking, but he continued to work in television and theatre, and he wrote movie scripts for others to direct (*The Best Intentions*, by Bille August, and *Sunday's Children*, by his son Daniel Bergman, both 1992; *Faithless*, by Liv Ullmann, 2000). In 2003 he wrote and directed the film he announced was his very last: *Saraband*. A sequel to *Scenes from a Marriage*, again starring Liv Ullmann as Marianne and Erland Josephson as Johan, it is emotionally grueling and ultimately enlightening.

Although Bergman was the unquestioned directorial star of the postwar Swedish industry, several later lights have appeared: the lush, pictorial, fatalistic romanticizing of Bo Widerberg's *Elvira Madigan* (1967); the close, affectionate observation of Swedish immigrants in Jan Troell's two-part epic, *The Emigrants* (1971) and *The New Land* (1972); and the disciplined realism of Sven Nykvist's *The Ox* (1991).

England

With certain notable exceptions, the British film never quite recovered the experimental uniqueness of the era of Hepworth, Smith, and Williamson. The common language made England—the center of filmmaking activity in the British Isles—such a Hollywood colony that in 1927 the British government passed quota laws to protect the native cinema. A British theatre owner was obliged to show a certain quota of British-made films. These quotas produced a flood of cheapies—called "quota quickies"—that served as second features (sometimes screened at 10 A.M.) for the American films that everyone came to see.

If a British film did score an international success in the 1930s—such as Alexander Korda's *The Private Life of Henry VIII* (1933) or Hitchcock's *The 39 Steps*—its director or star almost immediately departed for Hollywood. Cary Grant (born Archibald Leach in Bristol), Laurence Olivier, John Gielgud, Ralph Richardson, Jack Hawkins, Stan Laurel, Charles Chaplin, Boris Karloff, and Leslie Howard were as much a part of the Hollywood of the past as Richard Burton, Sean Connery, Maggie Smith, Julie Andrews, Anthony Hopkins, Richard Attenborough, Peter O'Toole, Ben Kingsley, Daniel Day-Lewis, Kate Winslet, Judy Dench, and Emma Thompson have been of the "Hollywood" of the recent past.

Postwar Masters

David Lean's first great film was the restrained, deeply moving romantic drama *Brief Encounter* (1945); he followed it with two of the most highly regarded of all Dickens adaptations, *Great Expectations* (1946) and *Oliver Twist* (1948). He then began directing a series of spectacles, literate and long, that were overwhelmingly pictorial, organized around complex characters, and designed to explore moral questions under pressure. The best of these were *The Bridge on the River Kwai* (1957) and *Lawrence of Arabia* (1962, shot by Frederick A. Young), followed by *Doctor Zhivago* (1965) and *A Passage to India* (1984).

Carol Reed made his mark with economical, precisely observed films as diverse as *The Stars*

Fig. 14-4
Olivier's Henry V: *France as an English Renaissance audience might have imagined it while watching Shakespeare's play, thanks to an art direction based on the art of the period.*

Look Down (1939) and *Outcast of the Islands* (1951). He did his very best work in two tightly constructed, haunting thrillers: *Odd Man Out* (1947) and *The Third Man* (1949). One of his last pictures was the screen adaptation of *Oliver!* (1968), a relatively extravagant film for Reed, even if it was more efficiently and effectively directed than other big musicals of the time.

For the 15 years after World War II, British film seemed synonymous with four kinds of movies, all carefully crafted. London was—and still is—the world capital of a style of English theatre and literature that has evolved over many centuries. These literate, well-spoken films displayed the taste, style, grace, and intelligence that also account for the popularity of programs like *Masterpiece Theatre* on television.

First, there were the polished, fluently acted adaptations of literary classics: Lean's films of Dickens, Anthony Asquith's adaptations of Rattigan (*The Winslow Boy*, 1948; *The Browning Version*, 1951) and Wilde (*The Importance of Being Earnest*, 1952), and Olivier's later adaptations of Shakespeare (*Hamlet*, 1948; *Richard III*, 1955). Olivier's *Henry V* (1944) had created much of the momentum for this genre: More than an effective wartime propaganda film, it showed how cinematically original a literary adaptation could be; beyond that, its bold use of color and artificial sets put it in the company of the fantasy films of Powell and Pressburger.

Second, there were the tightly edited, intelligently written contemporary dramas, many of which adopted the terms of familiar genres. Some of these concerned themselves with wartime military assignments or postwar political cabals, but the majority were romances (*Brief Encounter*), thrillers (*Odd Man Out*), mysteries (Sidney Gilliat's *Green For Danger*, 1946), and horror films (*Dead of Night*, 1945).

Third, there were the biting, richly dry and satiric "little" comedies made at the Ealing Studios by Robert Hamer (*Kind Hearts and Coronets*, 1949), Alexander Mackendrick (*The Ladykillers*, 1955), Charles Crichton (*The Lavender Hill Mob*, 1951), and Anthony Kimmins (*The Captain's Paradise*, 1953). Many of these masterpieces of comic construction, irony, and understatement—including some not made at Ealing, such as

Ronald Neame's *The Horse's Mouth* (1958)—featured the protean performances of Alec Guinness, who could transform himself into any kind of comic character—fuddy-duddy scientist, bohemian painter, old lady.

And fourth, there were the elegant Technicolor spectacles produced by the Archers, an independent company formed by Michael Powell, who directed the films, and Emeric Pressburger, who wrote them. The Archers were best known for their intense use of color, their spectacular fantasies, and their social and psychological boldness. Their key works include *The Life and Death of Colonel Blimp* (1943, an epic satire), *A Matter of Life and Death* (1946, a fantasy released in the U.S. as *Stairway to Heaven*), *Black Narcissus* (1947), and *The Red Shoes* (1948). *The Red Shoes* was no fairy-tale backstage musical, but a beautiful, disciplined, adult film made with absolute artistic control. Like the ballet danced within it— "The Red Shoes," based on Hans Christian Andersen's story—*The Red Shoes* tells of a woman (Moira Shearer) who puts on the red shoes, cannot take them off, and dances to her death. She is torn between two men, the impresario who offers her the great career she wants and deserves, and the young composer who wants her to quit dancing and love him. Neither of these men will give her a break, and the conflict they represent is, in any case, between the lover and artist in herself; the choice proves impossible, and she is destroyed—in a moment that intricately represents the triumph of artifice. Powell and Pressburger collaborated from 1938 to 1957; Powell went on to direct the savage, brilliant *Peeping Tom* (1960). *Peeping Tom*, released earlier in the same year as Hitchcock's *Psycho*, is, like *Psycho*, a forerunner of the slasher film, a disciplined masterpiece, and an ironic mixture of voyeurism and murder—reflexively linked by the making of images literally taken from life.

The general traits of all four of these British categories were a subtle understatement, expert acting, detailed decor, and a firm control of taut narrative construction.

Among the most distinctive and significant work in the British film between the era of Charles Urban and 1959 was the documentary film movement of the 1930s and 1940s.

Fig. 14-5

Fig. 14-6
Black Narcissus: *two worlds. Fig. 14-5: Sister Clodagh (Deborah Kerr) tries to find comfort in the well-organized Christian world of her office, where everything fits within the frame assigned to it. Fig. 14-6: Having renounced her vows, Sister Ruth (Kathleen Byron) runs through the rich darkness of the old palace, losing her scarf on a Hindu wall sculpture. Production designed by Alfred Junge.*

Fig. 14-7
Peeping Tom: *Carl Boehm as the photographer who, spied on and abused as a child, has become obsessed with recording the ultimate private moment—the confrontation with one's own fear at the point of death. In the background, Anna Massey as his observant friend.*

Sponsored by the government and directed by filmmakers like John Grierson, Paul Rotha, Basil Wright, Harry Watt, Edgar Anstey, and Humphrey Jennings, the British documentaries developed the craft of capturing the surfaces of reality to illuminate the essences beneath them. The realist texture that seemed to distinguish British fictional films from Hollywood's was especially obvious in the purely realist documentary films. To some extent, the new British film of 1959—which found a ready international market as part of the generalized new wave of European cinema—began with a similar premise. This new British film was the product of several influences: of the British documentary tradition; of the new class-conscious British novels and plays by authors like John Osborne, Alan Sillitoe, and Alun Owen; of the Italian Neorealist films; and of the new spirit of free cinema that was emerging in France at the same time. The result of these

many influences was a series of films that were radically different from the polished, elegant films of Asquith and Reed.

Another New Wave

The new British films, like the Italian Neorealist ones, emphasized the poverty of the worker, the squalor of working-class life, the difficulty of keeping a home and keeping one's self-respect at the same time, the social assumptions that sentence a person with no education and a working-class dialect to a lifetime of bare survival. British directors turned their cameras on the oppressive smoke of factories, the dull and drizzly weather at their stifling seaside resorts, the dingy and smoky feel of the pubs, the faded austerity of the rooms they can afford to rent. In the midst of this intentionally barren and gray world, the directors focus on a common man reacting to his surroundings—bitter, brutal, angry, tough. These heroes of the films, traditionally labeled "angry young men" (a term first applied to the writers and antiheroes of the plays on which many of these films were based), react in one of two ways to the working-class prisons of their lives: They try to grab some of the swag of the upper-class life for themselves, or, failing that, they get nasty, yell at women, and break things. Their tragedy is usually that their only talent is struggling to love, and society does not reward that kind of talent. Angry young men aside, Tony Richardson's *A Taste of Honey* (1961) and Bryan Forbes's *The L-Shaped Room* (1962) were among the best of the new films whose central characters were female.

Jack Clayton's *Room at the Top* (1959) was the first of the working-class British films to earn an international reputation and to make money. Clayton came to films not as a young rebel but as a tireless perfectionist who had worked his way up in the British film industry. Joe Lampton (Laurence Harvey), an ambitious young man with a provincial accent and a provincial education, takes a job at Brown's factory in a northern industrial city. Joe quickly learns the economic facts of life. He believes the old line that there is always "room at the top." He becomes enamored of a posh residential area of the city known as the "top," a hill that dominates the town. Most attractive of all the houses on the "top" is that of Mr. Brown (Donald Wolfit), the owner of the factory and commercial lord of the industrial town.

Joe sets his sights on Susan (Heather Sears), Brown's daughter, a pretty but emotionally shallow young woman who responds to affection with the same intensity as to a brisk set of tennis. Then Joe meets Alice (Simone Signoret), an older, warmer woman who reveals to him what two people are capable of feeling for one another. Just when Joe has decided that the relationship with Susan is valueless, she becomes pregnant, and her father compels Joe to marry her. When Joe tells Alice that he is going to marry Susan, she kills herself in a car accident. And so Joe marries Susan. He gets what he wanted—makes it to the top—but no longer wants it.

In 1959, Tony Richardson directed the film version of John Osborne's *Look Back in Anger*, three years after he had directed the sharp, tongue-lashing stageplay at London's Royal Court Theatre. Within three years Richardson had directed three similar films: two adaptations of realist, class-conscious plays (*The Entertainer*, 1960, starring Laurence Olivier,

from the play by John Osborne; *A Taste of Honey*, starring Rita Tushingham, from the play by Shelagh Delaney) and an adaptation of Alan Sillitoe's antiestablishment, class-conscious novel *The Loneliness of the Long Distance Runner* (1962, starring Tom Courtenay). *The Loneliness of the Long Distance Runner* is the most adventurous of the films cinematically; the freeness of the novel and the influence of the French New Wave helped Richardson escape the tyrannies of stage dialogue and stage setting, of stage time and stage place. It remains the best example of the social realism of the period.

Richardson's collaboration with playwright John Osborne indicates that English fashions in its cinema are inseparable from fashions in its theatre. As British playwrights moved away from working-class characters and themes, so did British cinema. A parallel movement can be seen in the collaboration of playwright Harold Pinter and the blacklisted American director Joseph Losey, who emigrated to England. While Pinter began writing plays that arose from his own working-class background, his later plays were paradoxical studies of upper-middle-class characters who suffer from sexual doubts, moral dilemmas, and ambiguous power struggles. Losey turned a number of similar Pinter screenplays into elegantly acted, coolly mysterious, and psychologically insightful films—*The Servant* (1963), *Accident* (1967), *The Go-Between* (1971)—that had nothing to do with angry young men, let alone with Joe McCarthy's America.

From *A Hard Day's Night* to *Masterpiece Theatre*

One obvious exception to this school of social realism is the work of Richard Lester, an American expatriate who united the Beatles with the cinematic ellipticality of Truffaut and Resnais. The results—*A Hard Day's Night* (1964) and *Help!* (1965)—were buoyant romps through the fields of illogic. Lester does best when the parts propel a whole that is conceived as an elliptical string of bits—from the Beatles films and *How I Won the War* (1967) to *The Three Musketeers* (1974), *The Four Musketeers* (1975), and *Superman II* (1981; uncredited co-director, Richard Donner).

Fig. 14-8
**The Servant*: Dirk Bogarde and James Fox (right) as the manservant and master who exchange roles in Losey and Pinter's brilliant study of decadence and power.*

From the Renaissance stage to the music hall, the British have enjoyed a witty and often outrageous comedic tradition. In the 1950s, some of the best working talent was on the radio, as it was on television in the 1970s, and the stars of these shows often went on to significant film careers. The BBC's *The Goon Show*, one of the most bizarre and hilarious programs in the history of radio, starred Spike Milligan, Harry Secombe, and Peter Sellers. Lester's first comedy, *The Running, Jumping and Standing Still Film* (1960), was a short that starred the Goons; its sheer craziness and comic energy led straight to *A Hard Day's Night*. Peter Sellers, whose voice was as protean as Lon Chaney's face, became one of England's great screen comedians, starring in films as diverse as *The Mouse That Roared* (1959), *Lolita* (1962), *The Pink Panther* (1964) and *Dr. Strangelove* (1964).

Just over a decade after the Goons, the BBC's silliest and most creative comedians were the Pythons: Graham Chapman, John Cleese, Terry Gilliam, Eric Idle, Terry Jones, and Michael Palin. They broke into film in 1972 with *And Now For Something Completely Different* (directed by Ian McNaughton), an anthology of routines from their TV show, *Monty Python's Flying Circus*. Their first original feature, *Monty Python and The Holy Grail* (1974)—which made cinematic, literary, and historical jokes with equal skill in an outrageous sendup of the Arthurian legend—was directed by Terry Jones and Terry Gilliam (an American and the troupe's animator); the ones after that were directed by Jones alone and include *Monty Python's Life of Brian* (1979), the tale of a fellow whose life runs parallel to that of Jesus, and *Monty Python's The Meaning of Life* (1983), a guide for the perplexed. Cleese, Idle, and Palin went on to establish themselves independently as actors and writers in such films as Richard Loncraine's *The Missionary* (1982) and Charles Crichton's *A Fish Called Wanda* (1988), and Gilliam became a controversial director with his wildly grotesque dystopia, *Brazil* (1985). The

Fig. 14-9
King Arthur (Graham Chapman, central foreground) and his knights receive their mission from God in Monty Python and The Holy Grail.

Pythons ceased to exist as a troupe after the death of Graham Chapman in 1989.

Economically and internationally, England's biggest hit was the James Bond series, based on the spy novels of Ian Fleming and starring Sean Connery (succeeded by Roger Moore and others). Released through United Artists and becoming one of that company's chief assets, the Bond films have, since the 1960s, offered sophisticated adventure, witty dialogue, state-of-the-art gadgetry, spectacular sets, elaborate action sequences, and generous helpings of sex and death.

Hammer Films also attracted loyal audiences worldwide with its boldly colored, bloody horror films, beginning with Terence Fisher's *The Curse of Frankenstein* (1957). But Britain still turned out a number of restrained, relentless, black-and-white chillers—such as Jacques Tourneur's *Curse of the Demon*, 1957—that were at least as effective as the gruesome color pictures.

Not every British filmmaker moved to America as Hitchcock did; there was a lot of traffic both ways. Many who rushed to see that very English import, *The Servant*, did not realize Joseph Losey was American. Tony Richardson, Karel Reisz, Lindsay Anderson, and John Schlesinger all made films in the United States. In spite of all this crossover, there will always be an England, and no one would mistake a British heist comedy like *The Lavender Hill Mob* for an American heist comedy like *Take the Money and Run.*

Since the beginning, when the Brighton group led the world in narrative complexity and momentum—anticipating a cinema that would range from *Peeping Tom* to *Dr. No* (1962), respectively—and certainly throughout the Sound Era, the British cinema has excelled in comedy, mystery, drama, literary adaptation, social realism, fantasy, and documentary. Through every period of its history, even when it was reduced to quota quickies, the British produced memorable pictures in all these areas. But from a longer perspective, taking the comedies and mysteries as constants, the thesis and antithesis of British cinema, the extremes where the action is, are social realism and triumphant artifice. If the 1940s offered audiences a choice between the artificial worlds of Powell and Pressburger and the realistic dramas of Carol Reed, and if the social realism of the 1960s was balanced by Hammer's elegant period horror films, it is no surprise that the British cinema since 1970 has been divided between the social realists, led by Ken Loach and Mike Leigh, and the fantasists, led by Peter Greenaway.

Some of the directors who established themselves in the 1970s continued to do important work for decades. Ken Loach, a compassionate realist whose work is free of embellishment or overstatement, keeps his camera on a developing scene, no matter how painful, or on a character's truthful expression, no matter how unpleasant, until his look—his decision to keep shooting and not edit out—becomes in itself a moral statement, a commitment to the abused and the excluded, the confused and the graceless, the silenced and the rebellious who are all utterly valuable and who are surrounded by cruel and stupid people. They are surrounded by powerful, destructive people in their own families (*Family Life*, 1971, also called *Wednesday's Child*, the first insightful film about schizophrenogenic families), in the courts and the welfare system (*Ladybird Ladybird*, 1994, based on the true story of a woman whose children were repeatedly taken from her by the social services, one of them virtually in the delivery room), and on the battlefield (*Land and Freedom*, 1995, the only narrative film about the Spanish Civil War that can stand up to the documentaries). Loach's matter-of-fact, grueling, and at times horribly funny pictures are crucial works in the history of realist cinema.

In marked contrast to a grim master like Loach, Ken Russell is the most audacious and gaudy British stylist, a director with a brilliant sense of decor and a gift for big cinematic flourishes. Russell, whose training came in filming biographies for TV, directed his first highly acclaimed film in 1969, *Women in Love*. The solidity of the D. H. Lawrence characters and the effectiveness of the novel's symbolism helped anchor Russell's visual flights of fancy in solid fictional ground. His film of *The Boy Friend* (1971) was as pure a style piece as has ever been made, a self-contained history of the musical film. Russell's "psychological" studies of Tchaikovsky (*The Music Lovers*, 1970) and medieval religious fanaticism (*The Devils*, 1971) were not very convincing as psychology, but they were stylistically astounding—especially *The Devils*.

Fig. 14-10

In Ken Loach's Ladybird Ladybird, *Crissy Rock stars in the true story of a woman's struggle against the social-service system and the courts to keep her children and live as she sees fit.*

Fig. 14-11

Gorging on desire: Peter Greenaway's The Cook The Thief His Wife & Her Lover. *In contrast to the psychological, social, and political realism and the flat, unstylized look of Loach, Greenaway probes artificial worlds structured by the rules of games, especially games of power, numbers, sex, and art.*

John Schlesinger was a completely different kind of stylist, more verbal and more psychologically credible. For Schlesinger, "abnormal," "aberrant" people live lives that make perfect sense from their point of view, and the Schlesinger films develop precisely this subjective point of view. The young man's erratic and erotic fantasies in *Billy Liar* (1963), the complex desires and problems of those who live *Far from the Madding Crowd* (1967), based on Thomas Hardy's novel, and the bisexual triangles in *Sunday, Bloody Sunday* (1971) are not examples of human freaks but of people trying to satisfy the most common human needs: security and love.

Lindsay Anderson remained the British director most devoted to rebellion against a stagnant and repressive bourgeois society and mentality. Anderson's rebellion was embodied by his violent central characters, who usually want to attack the elements in society that oppress and restrict them: Richard Harris in *This Sporting Life* (1963) and Malcolm McDowell in *If . . .* (1969) and *O Lucky Man!* (1973). Anderson's rebellion determined his cinematic style: violent attacks on the continuity of space, time, and action.

Nicolas Roeg was a cinematographer who moved to directing. His dominant interests are sexual ambiguity, scientific paradox, the power of the otherworldly, and the mystical influence of cultural myth—sometimes featuring rock stars (Mick Jagger in *Performance*, 1970, which Roeg co-directed with Donald Cammell; David Bowie in *The Man Who Fell to Earth*, 1976). His superb horror film, *Don't Look Now* (1973), intercuts subjective and objective visions as rapidly and complexly as it intercuts the past, present, and future; the daring, originality, and narrative significance of montage in his films put Roeg in the tradition of Eisenstein and Resnais. But he is also, as *Don't Look Now* plainly reveals, a master of *mise-en-scène*. His Australian production, *Walkabout* (1971), proved enormously influential, suggesting themes and images that the new Australian feature-film industry would explore later in the 1970s, particularly in films such as Peter Weir's *The Last Wave* (1977).

Peter Watkins, who began as an editor for the BBC, is the most distinguished British documentarist of the past 40 years. His *The War Game* (1965) was so powerful an indictment of atomic competition and British vulnerability to its terrifying consequences that it was banned from British television and has never been shown on the BBC. Watkins's biographical re-creation of the life of painter *Edvard Munch* (1974) is its formal opposite—one of the most tactile cinematic examinations of a painter's creative activity. His politically radical fiction films—which often deal, much as *The War Game* does, with the urgency of finding, circulating, and preserving an image of the truth, despite government censorship.

After Roeg, the most labyrinthine and intellectual of the British directors is Peter Greenaway; his *The Draughtsman's Contract* (1982) elicited as many attempts at summary or symbolic explanation as *Blowup* had. As cold and as sensual as Roeg, Greenaway has pursued the trails of desire and formal signification through films that are constructed as elegant, dangerous puzzles.

Greenaway organizes all of his films by taxonomy (classification and list making), using numbers (*1–100*, 1978), alphabets (*H is for House*, 1973), alphanumeric puns (*A Zed & Two Noughts [ZOO]*, 1985), menus (*The Cook The Thief His Wife & Her Lover*, 1989), postcards (*5 Postcards from Capital Cities*, 1967), books (*Prospero's Books*, 1991; *The Pillow Book*, 1996), and other systems of linear and nonlinear narrative.

Provoked by the sexually and politically conservative regime of Prime Minister Margaret Thatcher, Stephen Frears made films that took homosexuals for their central characters (*Prick Up Your Ears*, 1987), portrayed the nihilistic, anarchistic spirit of England's new rebels (*Bloody Kids*, 1983), and examined racial and economic conflicts (*My Beautiful Laundrette*, 1985; *Sammy and Rosie Get Laid*, 1987).

Three of the newer directors are quite different in style and temperament. Mike Leigh makes slice-of-life black comedies about misfits, some of whom are endearing oddballs (*High Hopes*, 1988; *Life Is Sweet*, 1991), while at least one is the terminal "angry young man" whose ideas are as bleak and violent as his behavior (*Naked*, 1993). One of his most popular films was *Secrets & Lies* (1996), a comic family melodrama full of sexual, racial, and emotional surprises. Some directors did their most important work in the 1980s but became famous in the 1990s, including Kenneth Branagh (*Henry V*, 1989; *Much Ado About Nothing*, 1993), Mike Hodges (*Croupier*, 1998), and Terence Davies (*Distant Voices, Still Lives*, 1988).

The upscale British film keeps its roots in the theatre for the simple reason that British stage actors, directors, and playwrights remain expert delineators of a lengthy English-language tradition. From Laughton, Olivier, and Guinness to the Redgraves, Maggie Smith, Ben Kingsley, and Jeremy Irons, British actors are among the most proficient in the world. Later British films maintained this theatrical "Tradition of Quality": *The Dresser* (Peter Yates, 1983) and *Betrayal* (David Jones, 1983, with a great script by Pinter) were both adapted from plays. *Chariots of Fire* (Hugh Hudson, 1981) and *Gandhi* (Richard Attenborough, 1982) brought England two successive Academy Awards for Best Picture, and *A Room with a View* (directed by James Ivory and produced by Ismail Merchant, 1985) did nearly as well—perfect examples of the Masterpiecery that impresses many Americans as "best."

Central and Eastern Europe

The Czech Golden Age

No cinema better demonstrates the interrelationship of film art and political freedom than the cinema of Czechoslovakia, a country that may have been invaded, occupied, and liberated more times in the 20th century than any other. In January 1993, it became two countries: the Czech Republic and Slovakia; though the Czech Republic now has the more active industry, both parts of the former Czechoslovakia contributed to its Golden Age. The Czech Golden Age of cinema (or "Czech film miracle" or "Czech New Wave" as it has also been called) was an extremely short one—roughly, 1961 to 1969—during which time over a dozen Czech films won major awards at the important international film festivals, including the Academy Awards for Best Foreign Language Film of 1965 (*The Shop on Main Street*) and 1967 (*Closely Watched Trains*, Czech release 1966). The years of Czechoslovakian film mastery coincided with the only years since the Munich Agreement of 1938 that the Czech people and Czech artists enjoyed a measure of intellectual and creative freedom. Before this brief eruption, the Czech cinema was one of promising beginnings cut short by political repression and artistic censorship.

During the decades of occupation and repression, two significant institutions were founded that would later contribute to the greatness of the Czech film. The noted Czech film school, the F.A.M.U., was founded in 1947, and the Barrandov Studios were built into one of the best-equipped production facilities in Europe during the Nazi occupation. (Both were in Prague.) The great Czech films and filmmakers would come from this film school (five intensive years of training at state expense) and film studio as soon as the filmmakers were free to combine their artistic imaginations with their technical capabilities.

The Czech masterpieces were of four general types, including two that had undergone a transformation in the previous years of Soviet repression. First, there was the tale centered on resistance to the Nazi occupation, a safe subject in the Stalinist era since opinion of the Nazis was quite unanimous. But under the Soviets, the Czech resistance film mirrored the values of Socialist Realism, primarily by presenting a positive, heroic, almost superhuman figure as the embodiment of political resistance—like Shchors and Chapayev in those Stalinist Soviet sound films. In the mature Czech films of the 1960s, however, the central figures of resistance are frequently weak, lazy, and comic—nonheroic, ordinary, all-too-human figures who eventually choose or are forced to take a political stand. Such a study of the comic antihero confronted by the demands of war is a tradition in Czech literature, perhaps most memorable in Karel Hašek's novel *The Good Soldier Schweik*.

Such are the "heroes" of Jiří Weiss's *The Coward* (1961), the study of a cowardly rural schoolteacher who eventually decides to sacrifice himself rather than to select ten of his fellow townspeople to be slaughtered by the Nazis, and of Zbyněk Brynych's *The Fifth Horseman Is Fear* (1964), the story of the tenants of an apartment house in Nazi-occupied Prague, particularly an old Jewish doctor who must choose between protecting himself and helping a fugitive who has dedicated himself to helping the doctor's people; as well as of both *The Shop on Main Street* and *Closely Watched Trains*.

A second genre, the historical costume drama, also popular during the years of suppression, was less popular in the 1960s. As in Hitler's Germany and Mussolini's Italy, a film could avoid delicate political issues by avoiding contemporary life altogether. In the 1960s this escapist tendency continued, but of special note are František Vláčil's *Markéta Lazarová* (1967), a mammoth and carefully detailed historical spectacle set in 13th-century Bohemia, and Jiří Weiss's *The Golden Fern* (1963), a beautiful adaptation of a Czech fairy tale.

The third of the Czech genres of the 1960s—the film of contemporary life—had a very different analogue in the era of Soviet suppression. Under the Soviets, Czech cinema eulogized the noble worker, sang the praises of the collective society, depicted the beauty of the factory, and dedicated itself to the proposition that with hard work and cooperation Life Would Be Beautiful. The mature Czech films of the 1960s doubted the values of collectivization, suggested that work did not equal happiness, refused to glamorize the everyday, and implied that the essential human problems were personal rather than societal.

Věra Chytilová, among the most important and accomplished women directors of postwar Europe, made careful studies of feminist problems (*Ceiling*, 1961; *Daisies*, 1966; *The Fruit of Paradise*, 1970). Jaromil Jireš's *Joke* is explicitly anti-Stalinist and anti-Soviet, the story of a man who seeks revenge for his earlier imprisonment in the 1950s era of the purges.

A strong tendency of the contemporary films is to concentrate more on character than on politics, to study the human comedy. These "experiential" films—studies of experience—represent one of the truly unique and most influential accomplishments of the Czech cinema: personal, subtle, touching, probing. The purest expressions of these "experiential" films are the sympathetic satires by Miloš Forman (*Black Peter*, 1963; *Loves of a Blonde*, 1965; *The Firemen's Ball*, 1967) and the delicate, perfectly constructed comedy *Intimate Lighting* (1965), by Ivan Passer.

Precisely the same is true of the fourth genre of Czech films of the period, the surreal or futuristic allegory. Jan Schmidt's riveting, postapocalyptic *The End of August at the Hotel Ozone* (1966, released 1968) is a brutal and frightening odyssey of survivors of an atomic holocaust, all of them women, roaming about the countryside on horseback, killing.

Perhaps the most anarchic and surreal director of the era was Juraj Jakubisko, a Slovak. Like some of the works of Dovzhenko, Jakubisko's films (*Deserters and Nomads*, 1968; *Birds, Orphans, and Fools*, 1969) seem anarchically poetic: a series of striking images that mix a blunt sexuality, politics, religion, audacious visual stunts, and experiential frenzy, cohering neither in plot nor in temporal continuity. As in many Czechoslovakian films there is also an undercurrent of fatalism and nihilism in Jakubisko. It is no wonder that Juráček and Jakubisko, two of the most daring and pessimistic of the period's directors, were not permitted to make films by the new authorities.

Although the Czech filmmakers usually preferred to shoot in real locations, the dominant imagery of this cinema is not nature but the human face. By keeping the camera much closer to the faces of the actors, who were often nonprofessionals, the Czech films achieved a feeling of naturalness, imperfection, spontaneity, and authenticity.

Another trait of these films is their intermingling of humor and seriousness, producing films that were quite remarkable in their range of emotions, from hilarity to pathos to sudden horror. In their seriocomic blend the Czechs distilled the tragic modern history of their tyrannized nation

Loves of a Blonde: comic stabs at adolescent love and tenderness (Vladimír Brecholt and Nana Brechkova).

Fig. 14-12

into a positive vision of life that saw humor in even the darkest moments and that (with a few exceptions) refused to surrender its faith in exertion, commitment, and integrity.

Jiří Menzel's *Closely Watched Trains* (1966) is a good example of this Czech spirit. The film's story (scripted by Bohumil Hrabal, from his short story) is of a comical young man, Miloš Hrma, who has taken a job as an apprentice at a train station during the Nazi occupation—primarily to avoid any serious or difficult labor. Despite its wartime setting, the film is a sex comedy, concentrating on the failures and fears of the inexperienced boy.

But beneath the sexual comedy are darker elements, even while Menzel refuses to desert his comic spirit and pratfalls. The boy attempts to ease his sexual failure and frustration by slashing his wrists in a steamy bathtub. But even the suicide has a comic balance, for the boy's final act of bidding the world goodbye is to remove his precious cap (he doesn't want to dishonor it), and Miloš is saved from death when a comically clumsy workman punches a hole in the bathroom wall.

Of the pure comedies, Miloš Forman is the master. An affectionate satirist who pokes fun at human folly, he also realizes that folly is what makes people human. Two of Forman's Czech films (*Black Peter, Loves of a Blonde*) and three of his American films (*Taking Off*, 1971; *Hair*, 1979; *Amadeus*, 1984) are youth films that deal with self-discovery and the generation gap. His other major films, *The Firemen's Ball* and *One Flew Over the Cuckoo's Nest* (1975), as well as the later *Ragtime* (1981), *The People Vs. Larry Flynt* (1996), and *Man on the Moon* (1999), keep in touch with the bad-boy spirit of *Black Peter* while they examine the follies of adulthood.

One further contribution of the Czech cinema that cannot be overlooked is its accomplishments in cel animation and in puppet cinema, most notably the work of Jiří Trnka (*The Hand*, 1966), Karel Zeman (*Christmas Dream*, 1945; *On a Comet*, 1970), and Jan Švankmajer (*Dimensions of Dialogue*, 1982; *Conspirators of Pleasure*, 1996).

Poland

The other cinemas of Eastern and Central Europe endured the same Stalinist and anti-Stalinist twists and turns as the Czech cinema, producing similar periods of fertility and barrenness.

The most fertile period of the Polish cinema preceded the Czech era by almost a decade (1955–64), produced primarily by the founding of another major film school (the Lódź Film School in 1948) and the splitting of the Polish industry into individual artistic production units in 1955. (One of the greatest films made before these changes was *The Last Stop*, 1947, which Wanda Jakubowska shot in Auschwitz—where she herself had been a prisoner.) These smaller production units granted the Polish directors a new freedom and allowed the exercise of more individuality; the two most talented directors, Andrzej Wajda (of the KADR unit) and Roman Polanski (of the KAMERA unit), took advantage of this new opportunity.

As in Czechoslovakia, the Nazi occupation and the resistance to it were favored subjects of the Polish cinema, and no one made more powerful films on the Occupation era than Andrzej Wajda, whose first feature, *Generation* (1955), became the first work of the new "Polish school." As opposed to the seriocomic, intimate style of the Czech war films, Wajda's style is more active, more violent, more baroque, and less internalized. The greatest early Wajda films (*Kanal*, 1957; *Ashes and Diamonds*, 1958) consistently use arresting, grotesque visual imagery (for example, the claustrophobic Warsaw sewers in *Kanal*), often dwelling on shots of rubble, ashes, and garbage, but these images can turn suddenly beautiful and unforgettably disturbing, as do the sheets hung out to dry in *Ashes and Diamonds*, which become a deadly labyrinth even as they wave neutrally in the breeze.

Wajda's filmmaking career is itself a miniature of the political history of Poland over four decades. With the constriction of Polish freedoms in the mid-1960s, Wajda's work became more introspective and more ambiguous in its treatment of politics. But with the return of Polish dissent in the 1970s, symbolized by Lech Walesa's Solidarity organization of workers and intellectuals, Wajda's films again became openly political. He identified strongly with Solidarity in *Man of Marble* (1977, also influenced by *Kane*) and *Man of Iron* (1980).

Roman Polanski's career represents another kind of historical metaphor, centered on horror; though he has attempted to flee from it and deny its power, along with that of the state, horror and trouble have found him in one country after

Ashes and Diamonds: *the death of a political assassin (Zbigniew Cybulski).*

Fig. 14-13

another. From *Repulsion* to *Rosemary's Baby*, his characters don't escape, and as in *Chinatown*, the state is too corrupt to do any good. Even in his early Polish films, Polanski's primary theme is not the rubble of war but the ominousness of the universe itself. Polanski's black-and-white films use a simple situation and very few characters (two men carry a wardrobe out of the sea in *Two Men and a Wardrobe*, 1958; three people sail a boat out to sea in *Knife in the Water*, 1962). But Polanski charges the universe with a menacing spirit that turns the simplest events into terrifying combats of great magnitude.

Polanski's visions of cosmic malevolence, mortal power games, and psychological ambiguity were incompatible with any socialist theory of justice. Imprisoned as a child of eight in a concentration camp, where his mother died, Polanski could resolve his nihilistic conflict with a repressive state only by escaping to a more indulgent West to make films in England, France, and the United States (*Repulsion*, 1965, made in England; *Cul-de-Sac*, 1966, a devastating black comedy; *Rosemary's Baby*, 1968, a straight-forward, glossy horror film and his first American picture; *Macbeth*, 1971, a version of Shakespeare's play that is short on poetry and—perhaps because it was the first film he made after his pregnant wife, Sharon Tate, was murdered by the Manson "family"—long on violence; *Chinatown*, 1974, a classic mystery and a latter-day *noir*; *Tess*, 1979, from the novel by Thomas

Hardy; and *Death and the Maiden*, 1994, a tale of political revenge).

Jerzy Skolimowski was, like Polanski, a younger-generation filmmaker who fled Poland. After serving as scriptwriter for both Wajda and Polanski, he wrote and directed *Walkover* (1965) and *Barrier* (1966) in Poland, *Le Départ* (1967) in Belgium, *Deep End* (1970) in Germany, and *Moonlighting* (1982) in England.

An intellectually demanding director whose films explore moral and philosophical dilemmas, Krzysztof Zanussi is, after Wajda, the most important Polish filmmaker still working in the country (though he was forced out of Poland after the fall of Solidarity and worked in Germany for much of the 1980s). His characters—often scientists (Zanussi's degree was in physics)—struggle with ideas and intuitions within networks of social and moral codes; his major works include *The Death of a Provincial* (1966), *Camouflage* (1977), *The Constant Factor* (1980), *Contract* (1980), and *Life As a Fatal Sexually Transmitted Disease* (2000).

For various reasons, by choice or compulsion, the three most important new Polish filmmakers of the 1980s and 1990s did not work in Poland. For directing *Interrogation* (1982)—the relentless, compelling story of a woman (Krystyna Janda) who is imprisoned and questioned for years and develops a complex relationship with her Stalinist inquisitor—Ryszard Bugajski found his film immediately banned, not to be shown until 1990, and himself a political exile. Working in Canada, he made such important films as *Clearcuts* (1991). Agnieszka Holland studied under Forman, was jailed in 1968 after the Prague Spring, collaborated on several films with Wajda, and then became internationally famous with *Europa Europa* (1991), a French–German co-production that told the true story of a Jewish youth who survived the war by pretending to be an Aryan Nazi. Her next films were made in France (*Olivier Olivier*, 1992) and America (*The Secret Garden*, 1993).

Krzysztof Kieślowski also made important films in Poland before finally settling in France: *Camera Buff* (1979) and the ten-part *Dekalog* (*The Decalogue*, 1988, for TV), each of whose probing and ironic, roughly hour-long tales was based on one of the Ten Commandments. Working in France and Poland, Kieślowski and his regular co-writer, Krzysztof Piesiewicz, went on to make *The Double Life of Veronique* (1991), an intuitive study of two women, living in different countries, who are virtually identical. They climaxed their exploration of the almost inexpressible connections between people with the Swiss–French–Polish trilogy *Three Colors*, whose parts—*Blue* (1993), *White* (1993, released 1994), and *Red* (1994)—are named after the colors of the French flag and ironically investigate liberty, equality, and fraternity. Color-coded to the core and insightfully interrelated, these three films marked Kieślowski as the long-sought heir of Antonioni and Bergman—but at the premiere of *Red*, he announced his retirement. He died in 1996.

Hungary

The best-known international representative of the new Hungarian cinema of the 1960s and 1970s was Miklós Jancsó (*Cantata*, 1962; *The Red and the White*, 1967; *The Confrontation*, 1968). Jancsó's films combine Hungarian folk tales and history with extremely lengthy and carefully planned tracking shots that choreograph cinema space as complexly as those of Orson Welles; his use of the wide screen, especially in *The Red and the White*, is among the most impressive in the history of the art. István Szabó, originally a member of Balázs's experimental workshop, makes psychologically detailed portraits of citizens who must make

difficult choices between the personal and the political. The actor of *Mephisto* (1981, starring Klaus Maria Brandauer) refuses to take a stand against the Nazi oppressors because he's "only an actor." He indeed becomes the slave of his satanic role, both onstage and off. *Colonel Redl* (1985), the next film in a Brandauer trilogy that concluded with *Hanussen* (1988), explores what it means to care only about power.

One of Hungary's women directors, Ildikó Enyedi, achieved international recognition with *My 20th Century* (1988), a playful, moving exploration of the nature of light (as starlight, electric light, movies) and communication (wireless telegraphy, homing pigeons) as two sisters lose and find each other while the young century also tries to find its way through a maze of sexual, political, and technological changes.

The Balkan States

Of all the countries known collectively as the Balkan States, Greece and the former Yugoslavia have had the greatest impact on world cinema.

When it was still called Yugoslavia, the country built its international cinematic reputation with the productions of the Zagreb studio, the most innovative and influential source of animated films in the world since 1957. Its best known director of feature films, particularly in the late 1960s and 1970s, was the irreverent satirist Dušan Makavejev, whose movies resist narrative continuity and test taboos (*WR—Mysteries of the Organism*, 1971); he also made satiric montages that are primarily political (*Innocence Unprotected*, 1968) and sociopolitical tragicomedies full of unpredictable twists (*Montenegro, or Pigs and Pearls*, 1981).

In 1991 and 1992, the former Yugoslavia split into separate countries: Bosnia–Herzegovina, Croatia, Tfyrom (The Former Yugoslav Republic of Macedonia), Slovenia, and the Federal Republic of Yugoslavia (which includes Serbia and Montenegro). Ethnically driven civil wars broke out in 1992, and in the context of the new map it became significant that Emir Kusturica was a Bosnian Muslim, Makavejev a Serbian. In Bosnia–Herzegovina during the 1990s, most of the filming was done by news cameras. Kusturica, who had won audiences around the world with two occasionally surreal coming-of-age films— *When Father Was Away on Business* (1985) and

Time of the Gypsies (1989)—shot *Arizona Dream* (1993) in the United States. Like the most important Romanian film of the period (*An Unforgettable Summer*, 1994, the first film Lucian Pintilie had been allowed to make in 30 years) and the first film made in Tfyrom (Milcho Manchevski's circularly structured *Before The Rain*, 1994), *Arizona Dream* was a French co-production. Foreign money also helped Kusturica make his next pictures in Prague and Belgrade (*Underground*, 1995) and on the Danube in Yugoslavia (*Black Cat, White Cat*, 1998).

Greek cinema came to international attention in the early 1960s, thanks primarily to *Never on Sunday* (1960) and three films by the Cyprus-born Michael Cacoyannis: *Stella* (1955), which introduced Melina Mercouri in the role of a woman who loves deeply but defies marriage—a significant break with Greek social and artistic conventions; *Electra* (1961), which starred Irene Papas and remains the greatest cinematic adaptation of a Greek tragedy; and *Zorba the Greek* (1964), which was a popular hit based on a novel by Nikos Kazantzakis. Like *Electra*, the strongest of Cacoyannis's later films—*The Trojan Women* (1971) and *Iphigenia* (1977)—are Greek tragedies set not on the stage but in the rough natural world. Cacoyannis creates a convincing picture of the ancient world in which the tragedies unfolded, an approach exactly opposite to the spectacular approach of the Hollywood "epic."

Never on Sunday, a comedy about a prostitute (Melina Mercouri) with a mind of her own, was a worldwide hit; its director, Mercouri's husband, was the blacklisted American Jules Dassin. If some directors, like Dassin, came to Greece in the 1950s and 1960s, others left—notably Costa-Gavras, who went to France, where he learned the trade and eventually made his great film about political assassination, fascism, and the struggle for truth in Greece, *Z* (1969).

The most stylistically rigorous of the new Greek directors is Theodoros Angelopoulos. Episodic, ambiguous, and slow-paced, his films present the "other Greece"—not the one of stunning beaches and crowded cities, the *Never on Sunday* Greece, but the rhythmically different land of peasants, refugees, nomads, and soldiers, a place where continuity (emphasized in the long takes and following shots) is the essential structure of life and perception, while the definitions according to which people attempt to organize their lives prove elusive and sometimes destructive. His works include the trilogy *Days of '36* (1972), *The Traveling Players* (1975, his most challenging and important film, an *Oresteia* that cuts back and forth across decades of political turmoil in modern Greece), and *The Hunters* (1977); as well as *Ulysses' Gaze* (1995); *An Eternity and a Day* (1998); and *Trilogy: The Weeping Meadow* (2004), which begins the story of a woman whose tragic life is an image of 20th-century history.

These Central and Eastern European films suggest that no matter how the map of Europe might be drawn, moral, psychological, and stylistic concerns transcend political borders even as they respond to political conditions.

Cinemas East

Japan

The Japanese cinema first conquered the West when Akira Kurosawa's *Rashomon* won the Golden Lion at the Venice Film Festival of 1951. In the wake of *Rashomon* followed a series of imaginative and impressive films from Japan, directed by Kurosawa and by other masters of a cinema that had previously been unknown to most Western audiences: Kenji Mizoguchi, Yasujiro Ozu, Teinosuke Kinugasa, Kon Ichikawa, Hiroshi Inagaki, Masaki Kobayashi, Tadashi Imai, Mikio Naruse. The decade of the 1950s proved to be Japan's richest cinematic era—both commercially and artistically—as a result of many of the same forces that stimulated the new Western film industries in the same period: the receptivity to new forms of film expression, the new market for non-American films, and the new period of political and intellectual freedom. As in many European nations, the Japanese cinema emerged from over a decade of political constraints caused by World War II and its aftermath of normalization. The awards given to *Rashomon* restored the esteem of a defeated generation, the warriors who had lost the war. What surprised Western audiences was not simply the maturity of Japanese films in this decade but the richness and depth of the Japanese film tradition: Mizoguchi and Kinugasa had been directing since the 1920s, and the 1930s had been a great period.

The Japanese cinema developed under conditions that kept it approximately ten years behind the cinemas of the West, a lag that worked in its favor in the 1950s, for the Japanese film industry felt the crippling effects of television almost a decade later than the industries of America and Europe. So, too, the early period—in which Japanese narrative and philosophical traditions developed along native lines into a unique cinematic syntax—lasted a decade longer in Japan, at least into the mid-1920s. The primary reasons for this delay were aesthetic. First, women did not appear in Japanese films until the mid-1920s, women's roles being played by female impersonators called *oyama*. This tended to prevent the Japanese cinema from asserting the kind of naturalness and spontaneity that gradually evolved in the films of the West between 1905 and 1915.

Second, the Japanese cinema used a narrator to explain the film to the audience. Called the *benshi*, this narrator's presence eliminated the need for printed titles and partly accounts for the way the Japanese cinema developed its own cinematic grammar and rhetoric. In Japan, where the commentary of a narrator was a convention of Kabuki theatre, some films became so dependent on a human speaker that the cinema itself did not need to "speak" in its own unique and powerful terms. (On the other hand, the absence of intertitles let the best of the Japanese filmmakers achieve a scroll-like flow of carefully chosen images.)

Third, while Western cinematic conventions evolved from enacted and written storytelling, the indigenous Japanese cinema evolved from the stylizations of its theatrical and visual arts. Many Japanese film stories derive from expectations about these two opposite types of actors: strong, powerful, virile men (called *tateyaku*) and the slighter, sweeter, milder figures (the *nimaime*—literally, the "second lead") of Kabuki.

The confining Japanese cinematic traditions died slowly and unwillingly. The *oyama* disrupted film production in 1922 by calling a strike when they saw they were to be replaced by women. The *benshi*, who had made themselves into one of the primary attractions of the Japanese cinema, fought extinction even more vigorously.

The coming of sound to Japan nearly a decade later than it did to the West was quickly followed by the coming of war, and the Japanese government demanded that the film industry support the war effort with films reflecting national militaristic policies. An equally repressive policy restricted the Japanese film industry after the war when the American Occupation Forces created a cultural "reorientation" committee, which banned certain subjects (for example, all Japanese period dramas because they were feudalistic and militaristic) and demanded others (for example, the values of peaceful living and democratic institutions).

On the other hand, the Japanese film industry had developed a number of practices and traditions that would work for rather than against it when a period of commercial, technical, and political equality would enable it to compete on the world's screens. The Japanese film industry, like the American one, was composed of several competing commercial companies, with their own writers, directors, actors, and technicians working under contract, which were in the business of conceiving, making, and selling films. The four Japanese studios that became most familiar to Western audiences were Nikkatsu (the oldest, founded in 1912—Ichikawa's studio); Shochiku (founded in 1920 and for three decades the commercial leader—Ozu's studio); Toho (founded in the 1930s by the amalgamation of several smaller companies—Kurosawa's primary studio and the exploiter of Japanese monster pictures, like *Godzilla*; and Daiei (founded during the war— producer of *Rashomon; Gate of Hell*, 1953; and Mizoguchi's later films).

The Japanese studio system avoided many of the evils of the American system, but it produced others. A primary advantage was that the system was built around the director rather than the producer or star. The Japanese "producer" is comparable to the production manager in Hollywood who manages production details but makes no creative decisions. The Japanese director is a more powerful audience attraction than a film's star. As a result, Japanese stars earn less money than their counterparts in the West and enjoy far less power. The Japanese director is the paternalistic head of his own production "family." The disadvantages of such a system—more comfortable and less competitive than Hollywood's—are, first, that talented directors must serve long apprenticeships to work up the ladder (in the case of a mentorship under a great senior director, this may be an advantage). Japan does not import instant talents from outside its studio system—no Rouben Mamoulians or Bob Fosses who come from the theatre; no Jean-Luc Godards or Lindsay Andersons who come from film journals. A second disadvantage is that the paternalistic system keeps women from rising to positions of authority.

Japanese films tend to bunch themselves in clear-cut genres and cycles. The basic division is between the *jidai-geki*, a period or costume film set in Japan's past (in most cases, in the feudal period before the emperor returned to power in the 1868 Meiji Restoration), and the *gendai-geki*, a film of modern life. But within these two basic genres there are many subgenres.

Two consistent structural traits do seem to dominate the best Japanese films, and both are descendants of the Japanese theatrical traditions of the Kabuki and the Noh. The first trait is an economical concentration on the central theme; the second is a concern for symmetry, for parallels and contrasts that find a balance. But no single consistent stylistic trait dominates the Japanese cinema. Those three directors who, at least from a Western perspective, appear to be Japan's greatest film artists—Akira Kurosawa, Kenji Mizoguchi, and Yasujiro Ozu—have three completely different visual senses and are unique, individual stylists.

Akira Kurosawa is the Japanese director most popular in the West—perhaps because he was so obviously influenced by films of the West. He is one of the only filmmakers to have made effective movies in both the *jidai-* and *gendai-geki*. Kurosawa's *samurai* films are closely related to American westerns (and have been remade as westerns), and he was clearly influenced by Western cinematic styles.

Rashomon (1950) clearly demonstrates Kurosawa's thematic concerns and stylistic maturity (he had been directing films since 1943). The film is famous as the essential cinematic demonstration of the relativity and subjectivity of truth—and that it is. But it is also notable for Kurosawa's stylistic control and for what he says people should do, given the problematic nature of truth and the imperfection of human beings.

Rashomon uses what might be described as six different cinematic styles, six separate camera strategies, each corresponding to one of the levels of the film's realities. Two of the six sections are "frames," not the central incident itself but ways of telling or finding out about the incident. One of these two frames is primary: two men telling a third about the incident as they sit beneath the ruins of the Rashomon Gate during a rainstorm; the other is, in effect, a frame-within-a-frame: the testimony of the three participants in the incident to a judge who is attempting to discover what happened. The remaining sections are four different versions of what happened and why, three told at the inquest and one told later, each of them mirroring the attitudes, perceptions, and personality of the witness. The one known fact is that a man lies dead in the forest; but what emerges as worse, the real moral problem, is that the inquest has been filled with immoral lies. Since people need to assign a cause, to see a reason for a catastrophic fact, the film becomes a search for answers and reasons: how he died, why they lied, and whether people are any good.

Many of Kurosawa's films are battles with despair, and like the majority of Japanese films (even those with "happy endings"), they end on a sad or emotionally mixed note. *Seven Samurai* (1954) ends with a shot of the graves of the heroes who fell in battle, rather than a shot of the survivors. If *Rashomon* gives us a happy ending, it is only after showing us that the search for truth must lead to ambiguity; that people can be cowardly, vain, and immoral; that ideals, codes of honor, and roles may not be lived up to; and that nostalgia for goodness and honor is a sad emotion, since for every moral success one finds many more moral failures and brutal acts. These points are made with equal conviction in Kurosawa films from *Ikiru* (*To Live*, 1952) to *Ran* (*Chaos*, 1985).

Kurosawa's two most interesting *samurai* films—*Seven Samurai* and *Yojimbo* (*Bodyguard*, 1961)—work the theme of existential action into two opposite situations, both borrowed from the western. *Seven Samurai* is a variation on the farmers-against-the-ranchers western, except in Kurosawa's film they are the farmers against the bandits. *Yojimbo* is the story of the paid gun (sword) for hire who rides (walks) into a small town that is split between two warring but equally crooked rival factions and succeeds in cleaning up both sides. *Seven Samurai* develops the theme of assertion and action through

Fig. 14-14

Fig. 14-15
Rashomon. *Fig. 14-14: husband (Masayuki Mori), bandit (Toshiro Mifune), and swords;*
Fig. 14-15: husband, wife (Machiko Kyo), and knife.

cooperation; *Yojimbo* develops the theme of self-assertion and individual integrity. Kurosawa paid his debt to the American western when both *Seven Samurai* and *Yojimbo* were made into westerns (John Sturges's *The Magnificent Seven*, 1960, and Sergio Leone's *Fistful of Dollars*, 1964, respectively). His *samurai* films also had a significant effect on another genre: The plot of George Lucas's *Star Wars* owes as much to Kurosawa's *The Hidden Fortress* (1958) as it does to *The Wizard of Oz*, and the editing and pace of both *Star Wars* and *The Empire Strikes Back* (1980) were strongly influenced by the fast wipes and stirring editing of *Seven Samurai*.

Kurosawa's most important *gendai-geki* is *Ikiru*, a story of the assertion of dignity through significant action. *Ikiru*'s hero is a petty bureaucrat (played by Takashi Shimura) who has wasted most of his life and who discovers that he is dying of cancer. He finally decides to dedicate his last days to accomplishing one important thing—which is discussed at his wake in the film's second part. *Ikiru* is as sensitive as the *samurai* pictures are active and violent.

But perhaps no two films reveal Kurosawa's stylistic range so well as his two films of 1957, both of them film adaptations of Western classics of the drama: Shakespeare's *Macbeth* (*Throne of Blood*) and Maxim Gorky's *The Lower Depths*. The two literary texts pose opposite cinematic problems: Shakespeare's magnificent language and sprawling terrain; Gorky's claustrophobic, discursive, and philosophic study of a social mass rather than a single protagonist. Kurosawa solved these opposite stylistic problems in opposite ways. He dispensed altogether with Shakespeare's text and turned the spirit of the play's theme and poetry into an interconnected set of rich visual symbols; he kept the text of the Gorky play almost verbatim and shot the entire film in confined and cramped settings.

Kurosawa continued to make great films until his death in 1998. *Dodes'ka-den* (1970) is an Expressionist color study of the lives and dreams of the homeless. *Dersu Uzala* (1975), a Japanese–Soviet co-production, contrasts the values of a hunter who dwells in the forests, living close to the land and its creatures, with the aimlessness of modern, indoor city dwellers who have lost their contact with nature and even with the power of dreams. And *Kagemusha* (1980) is a return in color to the feudal world of *Seven Samurai* and *Yojimbo*, more critically dissecting the political inequities, class distinctions, and illusions of identity that supported feudal society.

Five years after *Kagemusha*, *Ran*, Kurosawa's adaptation of *King Lear*, appeared to worldwide praise. In this version, Lear has three sons rather than daughters, and several of Shakespeare's characters are condensed and combined. Visually gorgeous and philosophically bleak, *Ran* was as pessimistic as *Lear* and at times as action packed as *Seven Samurai*.

Kenji Mizoguchi was a director of an earlier generation whose career came to its artistic culmination as Kurosawa's began to expand. Compared with Kurosawa, Mizoguchi employs a more consistent visual style, a more consistent theme and setting, and a much narrower range of emotion and tone. Mizoguchi specializes in period dramas, and his milieu is not simply the past but the past as seen in folk legends, plays, and paintings. Mizoguchi develops the distant mildness and stateliness of the past as well as some of its harsher realities. His primary attraction to the past is its apparent synthesis of art and nature—a synthesis that is fundamental to the motion picture. Many of Mizoguchi's central figures are artists: the actress Taki no Shiraito in the 1933 silent film of the same name; the troupe of Kabuki players in *The Story of the Last Chrysanthemum* (1939); the artist Utamaro in *Utamaro and His Five Women* (1946); the potter in *Ugetsu* (1953). For Mizoguchi, the business of the artist is the conversion of life into the perfection and precision of art, and the business of the cinema is both the conversion of life into art and the reverse conversion of art (a folk tale, for example) into the "living" vitality of cinema. No clearer blending of the domains of art and nature exists than in the opening of *Ugetsu*, which begins with paintings of nature and dissolves into shots of nature.

In his photographic style Mizoguchi mirrors this art-as-nature-as-art synthesis, which is typical of Japanese aesthetics. Where Kurosawa often uses a traveling camera and deep focus, Mizoguchi uses a generally fixed camera (when it travels, it does so slowly and gracefully) and softer focus. Mizoguchi's shots of Japanese settings—fields, mountains, lakes—are much softer and flatter than Kurosawa's shots of nature, deliberately turning these natural settings into evocations of Japanese prints and paintings.

Fig. 14-16

Ugetsu: *Mizoguchi's elegantly balanced composition as the potter enjoys a picnic with a ghost.*

Mizoguchi tends to use back- and side-lighting for these outdoor shots, not only softening them and reducing the depth of field but also giving them a hazy, limpid glow. Even in the moments of human agitation (for example, the sister's suicide in *Sansho the Bailiff,* 1954), nature remains soft, still, and quiet. The woman drowns herself in a placid pool of glassy water, framed by statuesque, motionless, and gauzy trees that do not react (as opposed to Kurosawa's nature whose tumult mirrors human agitation).

In his structure, Mizoguchi is also more classical than Kurosawa; Mizoguchi's major films are perfect examples of the Japanese sense of symmetry. Mizoguchi's primary structural device is the separation of the leading characters, each of them traveling different paths—quite literally, since the journey is essential to many Mizoguchi films. *Taki no Shiraito* traces the separate paths of the actress and the young law student until fate draws the paths together; *Utamaro* follows the artist's "journey" as well as that of each of the women; *Sansho* is a series of separations and eventual reunions with both the living and the dead. The symmetry of *Sansho* is so perfect that there are two fathers in the film (Sansho and Zushio's father), two sons (Taro and Zushio), two separations (the mother from Zushio and Anju; Zushio from Anju), two children (Zushio and Anju), two reunions with the living (Zushio with Taro and Zushio with his mother), and two reunions with the dead at their shrines (Zushio at his father's tomb and at the lake where Anju drowned).

Ugetsu is a perfect Mizoguchi film in structure, theme, visual style, and tone. There are four central characters—a potter and his wife, the potter's brother and his wife—each of whom travels a separate path and comes to a different end. The men, pursuing the false goals of money, fame, and lust, both discover the worthlessness of these goals, primarily because the wives—in many respects, the main characters—trod a road that led to their undoing (one is murdered by soldiers, the other becomes a prostitute). Mizoguchi brings the film to life by the elegance of this symmetry and the magnificence of his visual technique, which dissolves nature into the mystical and concretizes the mystical into nature.

Far more than Kurosawa, Mizoguchi—whose moral system is relatively conventional—values the traditional Japanese virtues of patience, honor, self-control, humility, and resignation. But there is nothing naïve or automatic about his moral judgments, which are no less insightful than those of Kurosawa.

Yasujiro Ozu, Mizoguchi's contemporary, is the master of the *shomin-geki*—films about ordinary, modern-day people, often but not always comedies. Ozu's primary subjects are the surfaces, forms, rituals, and processes of middle-class and lower-middle-class life. His films are dominated by scenes of conversing and eating, both at home and in restaurants; scenes at the office; scenes of men drinking together in bars. They are films about the central social processes: work, marriage, family life, friendship—and life and death.

As a stylist Ozu challenges most of the West's cinema theory. He abjures the visual conventions of Western cinema—traveling shots, montage, movement within the shot, dissolves, fades, even the boundary of the 180° line, whose crossing within a Hollywood scene is thought to confuse the viewer. The titles of many of Ozu's films are so similar that they are hard to keep straight (*Late Spring*, 1949; *Early Spring*, 1956; *Late Autumn*, 1960—a color remake of *Late Spring*; *End of Summer*, 1961; *An Autumn Afternoon*, 1962). In truth, their subjects are similar—parents and children; whether, when, and whom to marry—and the actors recur from one film to another (as in the work of Griffith or Bergman). His films are visually spare, use many long takes, and have a similar tone: an understated pathos and comedy that play against one another in delicate counterpoint. And their endings are more likely to be wistful and complexly balanced than

simply "happy"; virtually all of them share an attitude or tone the Japanese call *mono no aware:* a wistful acceptance of the evanescence of all things. But for all that they share, the films are unique, and the differences between them construct a multifaceted view of life.

There is more talk in Ozu's films than in most Japanese films, but there are also moments of contemplation and silence. Sometimes the camera will hold for as long as 10 seconds on a room the characters have left; on the other hand, many of his shots are only 5–7 seconds long. Ozu's style is as spare, rigorous, and subtly flexible as Bresson's. Ozu's editing is functional, and the camera rarely moves—but when it does move, the shot is momentous. The camera is very often put at a low eye level—as if it were the view of someone sitting on the floor in a Japanese house—but even if it has been invited, so to speak, to sit at the family table, it remains neutral, an impersonal but not unkind observer (see Fig. 14-17).

Ozu's masterpiece, *Tokyo Story* (1953), is a film about ordinary life that must be called extraordinary. It tells of an elderly couple—Shukichi, the father, played by Chishu Ryu, and Tomi, the mother, played by Chieko Higashiyama—who take their first trip to the big city to visit their children. Shortly after their arrival in Tokyo, it becomes clear that the son and daughter are far

Tokyo Story: *Noriko (center) extends her hospitality to her parents-in-law; from left, Chishu Ryu, Setsuko Hara, and Chieko Higashiyama. Note the position of the camera.*

Fig. 14-17

more interested in their own problems than in devoting respectful, loving attention to their parents. Only Noriko (Setsuko Hara), the widow of their second son, is genuinely glad to see them, spends time talking with them, and sincerely extends them the proper hospitality. In the loud, fast world of the town, Noriko is a rarity; much of the film concerns the differences between old and modern ways as well as between small town and big city living *and* between generations, and all these themes become especially clear, both intellectually and emotionally, in the scenes with Noriko and her parents-in-law.

The son and daughter send their parents to a resort—obviously to get rid of them, but supposedly because the old couple will enjoy themselves more there. The mother's strength, which has been failing, takes a turn for the worse, and shortly after they reach home, she dies. Now it is the children's and in-laws' turn to travel from Tokyo to the small town (a good example of symmetry in Ozu's work); they pay their respects, but leave soon enough. Noriko stays longer, to comfort the father and keep him company, but he tells her that she needs to get on with her life and that he is content to be alone. His acceptance of life and the solitude to which it has brought him— *mono no aware*—is profound and unforgettably moving.

After Kurosawa, Mizoguchi, and Ozu, Kon Ichikawa is among the most interesting directors of that generation. Ichikawa savagely and openly criticizes political, social, and personal corruption as he examines the depravity of the human animal. Ichikawa's first noted film, *The Burmese Harp* (1956), is one of his milder studies: the examination of a soldier in Burma (now Myanmar) in the final days of World War II who first disguises himself as a priest in order to survive and then becomes a true convert to the priestly values. *Fires on the Plain* (1959), which has been called the most powerful antiwar film ever made in Japan, concentrates on the horrors of the last days of the war, on a man's determination to survive (although he is ill with consumption), even if it means murdering and eating other people.

Kinugasa's *Gate of Hell* and Inagaki's *Samurai* (both 1953) were two of Japan's first color films and are magnificent in their application of splendid color photography to the *jidai-geki*. Inagaki

went on to make a color, wide-screen version of the Legend of the Loyal 47 Ronin (a favorite subject of the Japanese drama for hundreds of years), the 1962 *Chushingura*. Hiroshi Teshigahara's *Woman in the Dunes* (1964) is remarkable for its tactile examination of a change of heart. A man from a modern city on vacation in the dunes is imprisoned by the people who live there in pits, forced to serve as the husband of a woman who lost her previous one. He begins by trying to escape, loathing the omnipresent sand. Eventually, he comes to care about the woman, but only when he ceases to fight the sand and decides to study it (he calculates a way to distill precious water from the sand) does his prison become a home.

Masaki Kobayashi's first great work was the 9½-hour trilogy *Human Condition* (1958–61), a wide-screen epic, in black and white, about the treatment Manchuria received at the hands of the Japanese and the efforts of the powerfully beset Japanese hero, an idealist around whose pre-war and wartime experience the trilogy is organized, to escape a prison camp and walk home. The best of his later films are *Harakiri* (1962), told through flashbacks, of an atrocity and a revenge that are both covered up—and *Kwaidan* (1964), a widescreen, Expressionist color anthology of beautiful and scary ghost stories adapted from the writings of Lafcadio Hearn. In 1983, he made a documentary, *The Tokyo Trial*, about the tribunal on war crimes committed by Japan during World War II, a film that was unpopular at home.

The Japanese film industry, like the industries of the West, underwent severe commercial changes in the decade following 1950. The Japanese discovered that many of their cheaper productions—monster pictures (*Godzilla*, *Rodan*), invasions from outer space (*The Mysterians*)—could make money abroad. And so Japan was continually invaded by prehistoric monsters or visitors from space who stomped or incinerated models of Japan's cities before they were repulsed by some new weapon or by each other. As the Japanese bought (and manufactured) more and more TV sets, Japanese film attendance dropped. The Japanese film industry had learned from the West, however, that this was one monster that could not be repulsed. Japanese studios began production for TV from the start—and even began operating TV stations. Then the Japanese invented the VCR . . .

Of the generation of directors influenced by the New Wave, Nagisa Oshima, who mixes radical film techniques, radical politics, and a radical sexuality, may have worked in the most styles and tones. Like the films of Godard, *The Man Who Left His Will on Film* (1970) is both a deconstruction of cinema and an essay on the context of film images. *Death by Hanging* (1968) is a Brechtian attack on easy definitions of social crime and personal identity in bourgeois society. *Cruel Stories of Youth* (1960) links big business and crime. *Boy* (1968) is the dispassionate story of a boy whose parents have trained him to get hit by cars so that they can extort money from the drivers. *In the Realm of the Senses* (1976), a Japanese–French co-production, is pornographic, feminist, and obsessively romantic.

Shohei Imamura seems a descendant of both Ozu, for whom he worked, and Godard, whom he admires. Called the "cultural anthropologist" of modern Japanese cinema, Imamura's films (*The Pornographers*, 1966; *Black Rain*, 1989; *The Eel*, 1997; *Dr. Akagi*, 1998) often mix fictional and documentary styles, dissecting characters and societies that either resist or suffer modernization.

Late in the 1980s, having cornered the world market on televisions and video equipment, the Japanese reached out to acquire several American studios in order to have more films, of demonstrated quality, to own, license, and duplicate for playback on all those machines.

The 1990s saw the generation that followed Oshima begin to take shape. For some, like Kore-eda Hirokazu, that meant finding a way to build on the work of Mizoguchi, Ozu, and Naruse; for Takashi Miike, it meant testing or breaking the rules of logic, taste, and respect; for Takeshi Kitano, who performs in his movies and others' under the name Beat Takeshi and who is particularly good at turning from quiet to violent, it meant finding a way to work in the art film and the genre film at once, violating expectations while subtly or brutally controlling the mood of a scene (*Boiling Point*, 1990; *Hani-bi* or *Fireworks*, 1997; *Zatoichi*, 2003); and for the animators, many of whom worked with computers, it meant giving Japan an epic cinema charged with conservationist messages while deepening their treatment of character and perfecting their skills (*Princess Mononoke*, 1997, and *Spirited Away*, 2001, both directed by Hayao Miyazaki).

Anime filmmakers work closely with the epic and romantic traditions of the Japanese cinema while seeking to create a revitalized hero. That leaves the artfully observed psychological film in the hands of Kore-eda, whose interest in memory led him to make *After Life* (1998), a sad, funny, reflexive, and touching film about having to choose one moment, and only that moment, to remember from your whole life, and *Maborosi* (1995), an extraordinarily beautiful, slow, and quiet film about a woman who tries to understand why her husband killed himself—why he succumbed to the lure of the eternal and unknown, compared by one of the characters to a *maborosi*, a strange enticing light out at sea. He followed those with a realistic human-interest picture, *Nobody Knows* (2004), based on the true story of a woman who abandoned her children in the big city. However differently Kore-eda, Miike, Miyazaki, and Kitano approach the questions of filmmaking and of human nature, they are all major stylists in a cinema with an exceptionally rich stylistic history.

India

The West discovered the Indian cinema much as it did the Japanese. Satyajit Ray's *Pather Panchali* (*Song of the Little Road*, 1955) won a prize at the 1956 Cannes Film Festival, and his next film, *Aparajito* (*The Unvanquished*, 1956) won the Golden Lion Award at Venice the following year. *Apur Sansar* (*The World of Apu*, 1959) completed the trilogy. Unlike the Japanese cinema, Indian cinema offered no rich unknown cache of artistry. Not that the Indian film industry was not prolific: India produced some 300 feature films in 1958, second only to Japan in the quantity of feature production. In the 1970s, India became the world leader in the number of feature films produced each year. In the 1980s and 1990s, India remained the world's top producer, releasing an average of two films a day (one fifth of all the features made worldwide). But several causes—unique both to Indian society and to its film industry—keep quantity up and quality down, generally confining distribution of many Indian films to local markets. It should be noted, however, that some of the most formulaic, mass-market Indian films are exported to more than 100 nations—primarily in the Third World—where they have long proved extremely popular.

First, India is a vast nation of over 900 million people, and movies remain the only form of popular entertainment accessible to the masses. Although the videocassette industry is very much on the rise, there are still relatively few TV sets in India per capita. The pressure on the studios to provide film after entertaining film for a huge, uneducated audience has led to a consistent mediocrity, a devotion to formula and convention, and a fear of experimentation. The dominant narrative formula calls for a lengthy love story, many problems standing in the way of the lovers' happiness (he might be from the wrong caste, she might be kidnapped by gangsters . . .), endless musical numbers, a great deal of violence, a happy ending in which all problems are resolved, and three hours of footage.

Second, and even more difficult for the film industry, India is a nation without a common language. There are over a dozen Indian languages, not counting dialects—every one of them a mystery to the speakers of the others—the most common of which are Hindi, Urdu, Bengali, Telegu, Marathi, and Tamil. This language barrier caused little difficulty in the Silent Era. The Indian silent film industry, effectively established in 1913 by the magical, mythological films of Dadasaheb Phalke and developed by pioneers such as Dhiren Ganguly, Debaki Bose, and Chandulal Shah, may well have been more artistically advanced than the silent Japanese cinema. But the coming of sound, which liberated the Japanese cinema from the *benshi*, imprisoned the Indian cinema in the Tower of Babel.

Most films for the all-India market are now made in Hindi in the commercial film capital, Bombay. In Madras and elsewhere, many films— some more mainstream than others—are made in regional languages for regional and, in some cases, international distribution. The art film, or "alternative cinema," has flourished in Bombay and Calcutta and runs parallel to the commercial film establishment, never touching it. This New Indian Cinema produces work of considerably greater interest than the Hindi popular melodramas, finds little distribution in India, and acknowledges the inspiring example of Ray (most of whose films were shot in Bengali, adopted a lyrical realist aesthetic, and found a worldwide audience).

Third, the Indian cinema has been subject to ruthless government intervention and censorship. Under the British, themes of independence were forbidden; under the government of free India, "decadent" Western influences were forbidden. Kissing scenes first appeared in the 1970s. In addition to limiting its artistic freedom, the Indian government taxes the film industry heavily; its huge audiences provide handsome revenues, even with the low ticket prices. Further, the government has levied severe import quotas that restrict the supply of raw film stock. Even more ironic, an Indian print that has been shown abroad is subject to duty as an "imported" film upon returning home. If the government restricted the movement of commercial films, it encouraged alternative production by financing personal films. Satyajit Ray's first films—as well as those of Mrinal Sen, Shyam Benegal, and Aparna Sen—were supported by the Indian government.

Fourth, the Indian film industry itself is a victim of corrupt profiteering practices. Independent producers who want to make a quick killing, rather than established film companies, are the rule. In the 1930s, however, India's studios were more solid organizations; the most famous of them, Bombay Talkies, was a cooperative familial studio—modeled on Germany's Ufa, where Bombay Talkies' married owners, Himansu Rai and Devika Rani, had worked. But the independent speculator, who usually did not have enough money to complete a film once it was started and therefore needed to beg, borrow, deal, and swindle more as the shooting went along, came to dominate the industry in the 1940s.

The speculator could get that money only because, fifth, the Indian film industry has been totally dominated by the star system since the familial studios collapsed in the 1940s. And it has been a star system with a vengeance, making the power and salaries of the Hollywood luminaries look puny. Because only a producer with a major star could get the money to finish a film, stars became so popular and enjoyed such power— even political clout—that they commanded immense salaries (at least half of it paid under the table in untaxable "black money") and might work on as many as two dozen films at once, dropping in periodically on each of the production units as the star's schedule and inclinations permitted. Music was the supporting "star" of an

Indian film (the music director is the second highest paid position in the Indian film industry); for decades, of the hundreds of films shot each year in India, there was *not one* without singing and dancing. The Indian film became so conventional that its foremost historians (Barnouw and Krishnaswamy) described the formula succinctly as "a star, six songs, and three dances." These formulaic Hindi films are called *masala* films; "masala" means a mixture of spices, and the sense of the term is that these films consist of a number of standard ingredients in combinations that vary only slightly from film to film—as if one were adding a little more garlic to a successful recipe or substituting turmeric (pirates) for fenugreek (gangsters).

To such assumptions and conventions Satyajit Ray was, and remained, a stranger. His father was a friend of Rabindranath Tagore, the greatest Indian poet of the 20th century. Well read in Indian literature and philosophy, Ray studied painting after receiving a degree in economics.

Fig. 14-18
Pather Panchali: *the worlds of youth and age.*
The young Apu (Subir Banerji).

But Ray was also a *cinéaste*; with Chidananda Das Gupta, Ray was co-founder of the first film society in India, the Calcutta Film Society, in 1947. So one might see Ray as uniting the traditions of Indian literature, painting, and music with those of Western cinema. The meeting of Western and Indian values is one of his recurring subjects. The influence of European films is unmistakable in Ray's films, particularly Italian Neorealism and the French cinema of the 1930s—though when he was a young man, he preferred Hollywood movies. Ray was particularly influenced by observing Jean Renoir make *The River* in Calcutta in 1949–50, when he spoke frequently with the classical French director. Although Ray, who died in 1992, was a Bengali, his outlook was always international.

In the Indian cinematic tradition, the two dominant genres are "socials" and "mythologicals." The mythologicals, as the name suggests, use the cinema to bring to life the traditional tales and settings of Indian folklore, ancient literature, and myth. The socials, or contemporary melodramas, address social problems but use them primarily as plot complications. In the most general sense, Ray's films could be classified as socials. Though he is not hostile to the mythologicals and once hoped to make one, he does poke gentle fun at the genre in the film-within-a-film sequence of *The World of Apu*, which parodies a mythological but also shows the audience's intense devotion to the movie. *Pather Panchali*, which he was inspired to begin after seeing *Bicycle Thieves* in London, had no star (in the manner of the Soviets and Italians, Ray even used some nonprofessional actors), no songs and dances (although there was an instrumental score by Ravi Shankar), a cinematographer who had never shot a motion picture before (the still photographer Subrata Mitra)—and it was shot on location. Ray's film wanted to have as much to do with reality as possible.

Ray's Apu trilogy (*Pather Panchali*, *Aparajito*, and *Apur Sansar*, commonly referred to as *The World of Apu*), adapted from two mammoth novels by Bibhutibhusan Banerjee (*Pather Panchali*, which covers the first film, and *Aparajito*, which covers the last two), employs a complex, careful structure that is apparent in the unity of the individual films as well as in the overall conception of the trilogy. The subject of

Fig. 14-19
Pather Panchali: *the worlds of youth and age. The old aunt (Chunibala Devi).*

the trilogy is the growth of a young Indian boy (Apu) from his peasant, rural youth to a mature and educated adulthood in the city—an Indian *Bildungsroman.* The three films devote themselves to childhood, adolescence, and adulthood, respectively.

At the end of *Pather Panchali*, the remaining family members leave their village to try to live better in the city (Benares). At the end of *Aparajito*, Apu pulls himself together after the death of his mother and takes the path back to the city (Calcutta) and the university. At the end of *The World of Apu*, Apu is back on the road, returning to Calcutta again, his son on his back.

Perhaps Ray's essential theme may be found in his ultimate commitment to life, to human exertion, and to the cycles of nature of which man is a small and uncomprehending part. Ray's films acutely show that life is often painful, that people can be petty, that sorrow is inescapable and death inevitable, and that nature is an ever-present mystery.

Ray's other films are equally interesting in their careful views of Indian life and are often quite as effective. In *The Music Room* (1958) Ray examines the collapse of the old India—its traditions and its art—and the rise of the new bourgeoisie. *Devi* (*The Goddess*, 1960) is also a clash of old and new, a study of the old religious prejudices and fanaticism that can destroy happiness. *Mahanagar* (*The Big City*, 1963) examines family life in the new Calcutta, particularly the new status of women. *The Chess Players* (1977), Ray's first film in Urdu rather than Bengali, is the chilling–amusing story of two men who concentrate so much on the chess games they play with each other that they do not notice—or pretend to be above—how the political world is playing games with them. All of these films, and others not yet mentioned, are memorable for their careful and sensitive development of human relationships, their social analysis, their understated camerawork, and their subtle philosophical psychology.

Ray's are not the only nonmainstream films made in India. One of his most significant contemporaries, in many ways his opposite (loud sound effects, jarring editing, a ruthless vision of the interconnected evils of the world), was Ritwik Ghatak, whose masterpiece is *Meghe Dhaka Tara* (*The Cloud-Capped Star*, 1960); he followed that with *Komal Gandhar* (*E Flat*, 1961), *Subarnarekha* (1962), and *Jukti Takko ar Gappo* (*Reason, Debate, and a Tale*, 1974), then drank himself to death. Ray's other great contemporary, Mrinal Sen, is a Marxist whose denunciations of the exploitation of the poor (*Akaler Sandhaney/In Search of Famine*, 1980) and of women (*Ek Din Pratidin/And Quiet Rolls the Day*, 1979) and whose attacks on middle-class hypocrisy (*Khandhar/The Ruins*, 1983) have found an international audience.

Apart from this trio, the most acclaimed filmmaker in India today is Adoor Gopalakrishnan, whose films draw on the history and culture of his native Kerala in south India. Kerala's transition from feudalism to modernity serves as a backdrop to his complex meditations on the psychology of power, the nature of oppression, the corruption of patriarchy, and the coexistence of the modern and the feudal in post-Independence democratic India. *Elippathayam* (*The Rat Trap*, 1981), his masterpiece, vividly captures the descent into paranoia of a man trapped within his feudal universe. In *Mukhamukham* (*Face to Face*, 1984), a study in failed idealism, a Communist leader gives up on revolution and decides to go to sleep instead. Gopalakrishnan's more recent films—*Mathilukal* (*The Walls*, 1989) and *Kathapurushan* (*Man of the Story*, 1995)—display a new concern with interiority and reflexivity, foregrounding time, memory, consciousness, and the nature of storytelling.

A significant movement, the New Cinema, began in the late 1960s. As mentioned before, this parallel or alternative cinema is completely distinct from the artificial worlds of the Hindi romances and violent adventures—whose color and camerawork are flashy, whose sets range from the studio-realistic to the theatrical and fantastic, and whose heroes spring up from vicious beatings as free from permanent damage as the heroes of cartoons. The New Cinema examines social problems (often from a Marxist perspective), prefers to shoot on location, seeks to create a Neorealism for the expression of Indian reality, rejects formulaic narrative structures, uses the camera subtly and effectively, occasionally uses Brechtian and reflexive devices, and promotes the concept and creative authority of the *auteur*. None of these notions has any place in Bombay's mainstream industry.

The New Cinema began with Mrinal Sen's *Bhuvan Shome* (*Mr. Shome*, 1969), an irreverent comedy that had been financed by a loan from the government's Film Finance Corporation (FFC). When *Bhuvan Shome* proved to be a critical and popular success, the FFC made more money available for quality, low-budget films, much as the French government helped to finance the New Wave. The key *auteurs* fall into two groups, those in Bombay and those in the south of India. In Bombay are Shyam Benegal (*Ankur/The Seedling*, 1974; *Manthan/The Churning*, 1976), Ketan Mehta (*Mirch Masala/Spices*, 1986), and Kumar Shahani (*Maya Darpan/Mirror of Illusion*, 1972; *Tarang/The Wave*, 1984). In the south are Malayali G. Aravindan (*Chidambaram*, 1985), Girish Karnad (*Kaadu/The Forest*, 1973), and Pattabhi Rama Reddy (*Samskara*, 1970). To this list must be added a group of gifted filmmakers from Bengal: Buddhadeb Dasgupta (*Duratwa/Distance*, 1978; *Phera/The Return*, 1986; *Tahader Katha/Their Story*, 1992), Gautam Ghosh (*Dakhal/The Occupation*, 1982; *Paar/The Crossing*, 1984), and Rituparno Ghosh (*Unishe April/Nineteenth April*, 1994; *Dahan/Crossfire*, 1997).

The New Cinema has brought new opportunities for women directors. Aparna Sen was already a famous actress when she directed *36 Chowringhee Lane* (1981), the carefully detailed story of an Anglo–Indian schoolteacher (played by Jennifer Kendal) who must come to terms with loneliness and old age. Mira Nair's first feature, *Salaam Bombay!* (1988), which is "Dedicated to the children on the streets of Bombay" and whose profits funded shelters for homeless children, is the story of a nice, honest boy (Krishna, played by Shafiq Syed) who tries, while making a living on the street at menial jobs, to save enough money to go home to his family and village. Like the homeless kids in *The 400 Blows* and *Shoeshine*, Krishna and his friends endure rough times until they are taken under the care of the social services, which make things worse. Nair's later films include

Mississippi Masala (U.S., 1992), the controversially sexy *Kama Sutra: A Tale of Love* (1996), and *Monsoon Wedding* (2001).

China

Japan and India are by no means the only film-producing nations across the Pacific. The People's Republic of China, founded in 1949, has for the most part encouraged film production. Between 1949 and the beginning of the Cultural Revolution (1966–76), the state abolished commercial filmmaking and then nationalized and completely subsidized the industry, ten major studios were built, and the number of theatres increased from 646 to 20,363. As in the Soviet Union, the films' essential task was to communicate the ideals of the revolution to a huge and far-flung population; not surprisingly, the best Chinese films have been works of art as well as of propaganda. Zheng Junli's *Lin Zexu* (1959), for example, told a patriotic war story *and* attempted to find visual equivalents for the subtle tropes of Chinese poetry. During the Cultural Revolution, censorship was at its most formidable, many filmmakers were sent away from the cities and studios to learn from the peasants, and very few pictures were made. By 1978, however, the "rehabilitated" filmmakers were back at work, determined to make artistic movies, and they encountered no government opposition. In the early 1980s, the studios were given the responsibility of planning their own budgets, working with only partial government financing, and raising the rest of their production money at the box office. In 1983, an astounding 27 billion movie tickets were sold. In 1984, Wu Tianming's *Life* portrayed both peasants and intellectuals as good characters. Things were opening up.

The first major work of "the Fifth Generation" —a group of younger directors who were the fifth set to graduate from the Beijing Film Academy—appeared late in 1984: Chen Kaige's *Yellow Earth*, a magnificently photographed, complexly constructed drama about a soldier who goes to a remote feudal village to learn folk songs that he can adapt for use by the army; the effect he and the villagers have on each other; and a young woman who must choose between going through with an arranged marriage (the old ways of the peasants, which—as most Chinese films emphasize—tend to oppress women) and

leaving the village and her world to join the army, for which she would very much like to write inspiring songs. As so many Chinese films do, *Yellow Earth* dramatizes the confrontation of new and old ways, presenting the military representative of the Socialist revolution (the film is set in 1937) as the bringer of new information and attitudes.

The Fifth Generation's evolution from an artistically sophisticated social realism to an outright art cinema that denounced tyranny and outraged the censors can be seen in the differences between *Yellow Earth* and Chen's 1993 international hit, *Farewell to My Concubine* (released, after full-length premieres at film festivals, in a shortened version called *Farewell, My Concubine*). Rather than concentrating on what the Revolution has to offer the peasants, the later film emphasizes how much is lost when the old ways—especially the traditions of Chinese art— are destroyed by military and political groups who are sure of the new way things ought to be done. The rich artistic tradition of the Beijing Opera is set against over 50 years (1924–77) of political upheaval, culminating in the Cultural Revolution's complete purge of the "Old Society." These events are witnessed by two boys, originally trained for the opera, whose lives are interwoven with each other, with their operatic roles, and with the rough cloth of recent Chinese history.

After *Farewell to My Concubine* shared the top prize at Cannes (with Jane Campion's *The Piano*), it played for one day in Beijing before being banned for its treatment of homosexuality. Within two months, the ban was lifted—no reason given. But another masterful film that showed the destructive effect of Maoism, this time on an urban family—Tian Zhuangzhuang's *The Blue Kite* (1993)—was banned permanently; not only that, Tian (who had made one of the most beautiful and starkly moving, practically nonverbal films of the new Chinese cinema, the 1985 *Horse Thief*) first was not allowed to edit the film and then was forbidden to make films in China. By that time, ticket sales were down to 10.6 billion, the studios had been entirely cut off from government support (forcing them into numerous productions bankrolled by Taiwan and Hong Kong), and the new Chinese films had been recognized—everywhere but in China—as the most consistently excellent works of the late

Fig. 14-20

New and old ways and values meet in Yellow Earth.

Fig. 14-21

Farewell to My Concubine: *Leslie Cheung (left), Zhang Fengyi (center), and Gong Li (lower right).*

1980s and the 1990s. Chen Kaige, Tian Zhuangzhuang, Wu Tianming, and especially Zhang Yimou had taken their place beside the world's great directors.

Wu Tianming, who headed the Xi'an studio for most of the 1980s and helped to make it the center of Fifth Generation filmmaking, directed *Old Well* in 1987, a film that not only told the story of a Party member with a better idea for a well and a village woman who cuts her ties to the dowry system, but also made extraordinary use

of the only true Technicolor lab in the world, which happened to be in China. The colors in *Old Well* and in Zhang Yimou's *Red Sorghum* (1988) are intense beyond words.

Red Sorghum has an additional level of intensity, however: outright exuberance. Although like virtually all Chinese films it keeps sexual activity offscreen, *Red Sorghum* is full of raw sexual energy, which it celebrates along with life, love, the earth, action, resistance. Although the movie is, like most Chinese art, subtly and carefully

Fig. 14-22
Red Sorghum: *Gong Li (right, as Nine) carries food for the resistance fighters through a field of sorghum.*

structured, it pulls no punches: Its violent scenes are absolutely violent, its scenes of collective action are irresistibly inspiring, its humorous scenes are outrageous, its tender moments and fine characters ring true, and its wild beauty is stunning and uncompromised. In the summer of 1988, when Chinese politics were at their most liberal, young people expressed their idealism, energy, determination, and revolutionary optimism by humming and singing the songs from *Red Sorghum*. But in the summer of 1989, when a pro-democracy demonstration, held primarily by students in Beijing's Tiananmen Square, was brutally put down by the government, China entered another oppressive phase. "Stupid Old People Should Resign Quickly," read one banner hung in Tiananmen Square; they didn't. The Xi'an studio was virtually shut down. Wu Tianming left the country. And Zhang Yimou's next film, *Ju Dou* (1990, co-directed with Yang Fengliang), which is both more politically critical and more sexually frank than *Red Sorghum*, became another hit at the festivals but was not allowed to be shown in China.

Gong Li, who played the heroine in *Ju Dou*, was a big box-office draw. In Zhang's next film, *Raise the Red Lantern* (1991), she played one of several wives who compete for their husband–master's sexual attention and the power that gives them; set well before the Revolution, the film dramatized how women were oppressed not only by polygamy and by limited options in life, but also by each other. This rigorously composed and richly photographed film had none of the earthiness of the earlier films but was every bit as moving. It was followed by *The Story of Qiu Ju* (1993), the heroic but unglamorous struggle of a peasant woman (Gong Li) seeking justice through the contemporary legal system. Zhang's next film, *To Live* (1994), which took a dim view of what the Chinese have had to endure in order to survive recent Chinese history, was followed by *Shanghai Triad* (1995). Each of these films met fierce government opposition and world-wide critical acclaim.

In 1999 Zhang made two films about teachers, both produced in China: *Not One Less*, about a girl put in the role of teacher and told not to allow any truancy, and *The Road Home* (released 2000). The latter tells the story of a young woman transfixed by love for the village teacher and their romance as it is remembered by their son 40 years later. The father has died, and the old mother wants his body carried back on "the road home" to the village so that his soul will know the way back; this is a "superstitious" custom not practiced since the Cultural Revolution. As it urges China to keep in touch with its past—a pre-Revolutionary custom and the indelible face of Zhang Ziyi as the mother when she was young—*The Road Home* offers an integrated vision of how life can be complete.

Taiwan

After the founding of the People's Republic of China in 1949, the former Chinese government and many of the commercial filmmakers—particularly those who had worked in the Shanghai industry—set up shop on the island of Taiwan. Not surprisingly, the industry that developed in Taiwan was formulaic and commercial, emphasizing martial arts films and melodramas. An art cinema appeared in the 1980s; its two most important directors were Edward Yang (*That Day, On the Beach*, 1983) and Hou Hsiao-hsien (*City of Sadness*, 1989), whose films examined what it meant to live in a country that was continually changing hands, where cultural backgrounds and languages were diverse but not shared, and where urban life was a maze of contradictions that could be intimate or general, exhausting or perilous. Both have continued to do important work and to win international attention. In the late 1990s, Chinese reviewers were debating Hou's apparent turn away from the "nostalgia" of his earlier films—the intellectually rich, perfectly composed long takes that explored moments of crisis and transition in childhood, the family, and the history of Taiwan (*A Summer at Grandpa's*, 1984; *A Time to Live and a Time to Die*, 1985; *City of Sadness*; and the first film he shot with synchronized sound, *Puppet Master*, 1993)—in favor of a rougher but still long-take look at contemporary Taiwan. Meanwhile, Yang's fans were trying to unravel *A Confucian Confusion* (1994) and studying how he managed to cover 40 or more characters in the mere four hours of his urban epic of disaffected youth, *A Brighter Summer Day* (1991). In *Yi Yi* (2000), a little boy uses his still camera to shoot the backs of people's heads, to show what they haven't seen; one needs a camera like that boy's or like Yang's to venture into the complexity of others' points of view and into unsuspected or forgotten regions of one's own experience.

If the dominant theme of the new Taiwan cinema has been the ways people adjust to cultural conflict and change, the films of Ang Lee (*The Wedding Banquet*, 1993; *Eat Drink Man Woman*, 1994; *Sense and Sensibility*, 1995; *The Ice Storm*, 1997; *Crouching Tiger, Hidden Dragon*, 2000) might be considered an extension of the movement, even if most of them are accessible comedies of manners co-produced and sometimes shot in the United States. *The Wedding Banquet* presents the "two men and a girl" triangle with a difference: the lovers are the two men, and the cross-cultural and cross-generational hurdles leaped in the course of winning the Taiwanese man's parents' approval of the household he sets up with his American lover and pregnant Chinese wife are both universal and culturally specific. *Eat Drink Man Woman* also uses food and family gatherings to define and catalyze emotional and cultural conflicts, but it is far more sophisticated in structure and ambitious in concept; like

a Jane Austen novel, it finds in its focus on a chef and his daughters an intimate, concentrated way to organize within a work of art practically everything that matters about living. The aptness of the comparison with Jane Austen was confirmed in his next picture, *Sense and Sensibility*, a U.S./U.K. co-production based on a masterful screenplay by Emma Thompson—by far the most faithful and spirited of Austen adaptations, a 1995 film immersed in the look and rules of the dawn of the 19th century.

Lee described his next film as "*Sense and Sensibility* with martial arts." As choreographed by Yuen Wo-Ping (also the martial arts director for *The Matrix*, 1999) and shot by Peter Pau, the result, *Crouching Tiger, Hidden Dragon*, goes where the martial arts film has gone and beyond. Nothing in this picture is entirely new, but its wire-work and camerawork and fast, graceful action (the chase across the walls and roofs, the fight in the waving trees) are integrated with more beauty, rigor, and complexity than the genre usually affords; the reach into the depths of character and decisive action is deeper; and the open ending gives the image and the story an awe-inspiring, transcendent reach.

In the 1990s, as previously mentioned, money from Taiwan and Hong Kong fueled much of the film production on mainland China. For some of these capitalist producers, China became a low-rent backlot whose spectacular range of landscape could not be duplicated in the choked streets of Hong Kong or on the island of Taiwan. The first entirely Taiwanese film to be shot entirely in China was Huang Jianxin's *The Wooden Man's Bride* (1994), an action-packed tale of forbidden romance. But many things were changing by then: Trade borders opened even as political borders hardened (Tibet) or were redefined (Hong Kong became part of China again in 1997, with a limited degree of self-regulation and the promise of economic continuity).

Hong Kong

The most single-mindedly commercial and artificial cinema in the world, that of Hong Kong, is also one of the world's largest (with the United States and India) and most flamboyant. Whether they are gritty and gory or sentimental and magical, whether they are gangster stories or fairy tales or martial arts spectaculars, the films defy the limits of space and time and endurance and even gravity in a realm of impossible wonders where dreams turn real, honor matters, style and skill are one, and every action and skill is an expression of good or evil.

Loyalty—to a friend, a teacher, a ritual, a code—is a recurring theme in these films, and it is tested by deception and contamination at every turn. Romantic, even chivalric, and directed entirely toward exciting and entertaining the audience, these films adapt the conventions of Cantonese opera to the cinema (one source of the colorful costumes and aerial choreography) and create a shamelessly fantastic and action-oriented universe in which ideals are as real as corruption.

These values are expressed in the urban comedy–dramas (Wong Kar Wai's *Chung King Express*, 1994, a film that is complex, obscure, downbeat, and exciting) and in the martial arts films. Examples of that central genre range from Chang Cheh's *The One-Armed Swordsman*, 1968, to Lo Wei's *The Chinese Connection*, 1972—starring Bruce Lee, who consistently portrayed a figure of pride and power and who was also a superb fight choreographer—to Jackie Chan's *Drunken Master II* (1994, directed by Liu Chia-Liang, *a.k.a.* Lau Ka Leung; released in the United States in 2000 as *The Legend of Drunken Master*). These values are just as evident in the supernatural extravaganzas (Ronny Yu's stunning *The Bride with White Hair*, 1993), in the buddy films—also known as the "Masochistic Flaming Brother genre" (John Woo's *The Killer*, 1989),

and in the police/gangster thrillers (Ringo Lam's *City on Fire*, 1987). Some of the films break new ground, like Woo's *Bullet in the Head* (1990, about three friends whose civilian experiences in Vietnam test their loyalty and values) or Wong Kar Wai's *In the Mood for Love* (2000), a beautifully composed romance about two people who do *not* get together. But genre and formula have always been at the heart of Hong Kong cinema—and have continued to be, even after the British left in 1997 and the former Crown Colony came under Chinese control—providing structures within which the creative imagination can run wild.

Korea

Largely isolated for 500 years, the "Hermit Kingdom" of Korea was traumatically wrenched into modernity at the end of the 19th century as Japanese, Russian, and Chinese territorial ambitions began to be played out across the peninsula. Annexed by the Japanese in 1910, it remained occupied until the liberation in 1945, but the Korean War (1950–53) brought division and new occupation, leaving the North in the Soviet sphere and the South dependent on the West—a most brutal experience of the Cold War that persists to the present. All the films produced under the Japanese occupation were lost during the wars of the mid-century, and about the films made in the North we know little more than that they have adhered to Kim Il-Sung's policies of self-reliance and the aesthetic of Socialist Realism. But recently, the South Korean cinema has been revitalized, forming an internationally

The "unusual killer" (Chow Yun-fat, left) and "unusual cop" (Danny Lee), who both believe in honor and justice and keeping promises—and whose guns almost never run out of bullets—in John Woo's The Killer, *whose original title, literally translated, is* A Pair of Blood-Splattering Heroes.

Fig. 14-23

Sop'yonje: *Lifting their spirits in a bad time, the soloist (Oh Jung-Hae, left), drummer (Kim Kyu-Chul), and teacher (Kim Myung-Gon) sing a folk tune in the Korean countryside. Reproduced with the permission of the Korean Cultural Center, Los Angeles.*

Fig. 14-24

recognized New Korean Cinema, paralleled in many ways to the contemporary art cinemas of China and Taiwan.

The South Korean cinema had its heyday in the 1960s, producing as many as 200 films a year, most of them genre pictures for domestic consumption. With the increasing popularity of TV in the 1970s, a decline set in, and the country was flooded with foreign imports. But opposition to the military dictatorship and the subsequent political liberalization that culminated in democratic presidential elections in 1993 led to a renewal of the cinema. Its core was a group of directors debuting in the mid-1980s, including Chung Ji-Young, Bae Yong-Kyun, Jang Sun-Woo, Park Kwang-Su, and Park Jong-Won. They used innovative narrative structures and camera styles to approach Korea's troubled history with a directness that had previously been censored. Park Kwang-Su has best sustained the impetus of this group with *To the Starry Island* (1994), about wartime social conflicts on one of Korea's remote islands, and *A Single Spark* (1996), about a young man whose suicide ignited the labor movement in Korea. But the chief figure behind this renewal and the one who brought Korean cinema to the world's attention was Im Kwon-Taek, who had been making films since the 1960s.

Born in 1936, Im began as a set builder, eventually became an assistant to an action-film director, and debuted with his own first film in 1962. He made almost 70 features in the next 15 years, most of which were routine genre productions. By his own testimony, he first discovered his personal style in *Genealogy* in 1978, a film about the worst excesses of the Japanese occupation just before World War II. Since then his work has followed two main currents. One current continued the genre films' box-office orientation, culminating in the enormously successful *The General's Son* (1990), a martial arts epic, again set in the period of the Japanese invasion, that spawned two sequels. Generally the financial success of works like these has subsidized the other current, a series of works meditating on the ordeals of modern Korean history, often using an abused woman character as a figure for Korea and attempting to translate into film the qualities of traditional Korean culture. These include *Mandala* (1981), *Gilsottum* (1985), *Ticket* (1986), *Surrogate Mother* (1986), *Sop'yonje* (1993), *Festival* (1996), and *Chunhyang* (2000).

Set in the period after the Korean War, *Sop'yonje* is about *p'ansori*, a traditional form of folk opera practiced since the 19th century by itinerant musicians. The film is a seamlessly integrated mosaic of flashbacks, distinguished by the melancholy beauty of both *p'ansori* singing and the Korean countryside. *Sop'yonje* was a major cultural event in South Korea, occasioning a storm of media attention, breaking all previous box-office records, and sparking a national revival of interest in traditional arts. In the West, *Sop'yonje* did for Korea what *Rashomon* had done, so long ago, for Japan.

For Further Viewing

FILMS

SWEDEN AND DENMARK

INGMAR BERGMAN (1918–   )
The Naked Night or *Sawdust and Tinsel* or *The Clown's Evening* (1953)
Smiles of a Summer Night (1955)
The Seventh Seal (1957). Completed 1956
Wild Strawberries (1957)
The Magician or *The Face* (1958)
The Virgin Spring (1960). Completed 1959
Through a Glass Darkly (1961)
Winter Light or *The Communicants* (1962)
The Silence (1963)
Persona (1966). Completed 1965
Hour of the Wolf (1968). Completed 1966
Shame (1968). Completed 1967
The Passion of Anna (1969)
Cries and Whispers (1972)
Scenes from a Marriage (1974). TV version 1972
The Magic Flute (1974)
Fanny and Alexander (1982)
Saraband (2003)

CARL THEODOR DREYER (1889–1968)
The Passion of Joan of Arc (1928)
Vampyr (1932)
Day of Wrath (1943)
Ordet (1955). Completed 1954
Gertrud (1964)

SWEDISH AND DANISH MISCELLANY
A Man There Was (1917, Victor Sjöström). Completed 1916
Erotikon (1920, Mauritz Stiller)
The Phantom Chariot (1921, Victor Sjöström). Completed 1920
The Story of Gösta Berling (1924, Mauritz Stiller)
Torment (1944, Alf Sjöberg)
Elvira Madigan (1967, Bo Widerberg)
The Emigrants (1971, Jan Troell)
The New Land (1972, Jan Troell)
My Life as a Dog (1985, Lasse Hallström)
Babette's Feast (1987, Gabriel Axel)
Pelle the Conqueror (1988, Bille August)
Medea (1988, Lars von Trier). Script by Dreyer
The Ox (1991, Sven Nykvist)

Zentropa or *Europa* (1991, Lars von Trier)
The Celebration (1998, Thomas Vinterberg)
The Idiots (1998, Lars von Trier)
Mifune (1999, Søren Kragh-Jacobsen)
Faithless (2000, Liv Ullmann)
The Five Obstructions (2003, Lars von Trier and Jørgen Leth)

ENGLAND

LINDSAY ANDERSON (1923–94)
This Sporting Life (1963)
If . . . (1969)
O Lucky Man! (1973)

JACK CLAYTON (1921–95)
Room at the Top (1959)
The Innocents (1961)
The Pumpkin Eater (1964)

DAVID LEAN (1908–91)
Blithe Spirit (1945)
Brief Encounter (1945)
Great Expectations (1946)
Oliver Twist (1948)
The Bridge on the River Kwai (1957)
Lawrence of Arabia (1962)
Doctor Zhivago (1965)
A Passage to India (1984)

RICHARD LESTER (1932–   )
The Running, Jumping and Standing Still Film (1960)
A Hard Day's Night (1964)
Help! (1965)
How I Won the War (1967)
Petulia (1968)

KEN LOACH (1936–   )
Family Life or *Wednesday's Child* (1971)
Ladybird Ladybird (1994)
Land and Freedom (1995)

LAURENCE OLIVIER (1907–89)
Henry V (1944)
Hamlet (1948)
Richard III (1955)

MICHAEL POWELL (1905–90)
The Thief of Bagdad (1940). Co-directors, Ludwig Berger and Tim Whelan
The Life and Death of Colonel Blimp (1943). Co-director, EMERIC PRESSBURGER (1902–88)
Black Narcissus (1947). Co-director, Pressburger

The Red Shoes (1948). Co-director, Pressburger
Peeping Tom (1960)

CAROL REED (1906–76)
The Stars Look Down (1939)
Kipps (1941)
Odd Man Out (1947)
The Third Man (1949)
Trapeze (1956)
Oliver! (1968)

KAREL REISZ (1926–2002)
Saturday Night and Sunday Morning (1960)
Morgan! or *Morgan, a Suitable Case for Treatment* (1966)
The Loves of Isadora (1968). Condensed as *Isadora*
The French Lieutenant's Woman (1981)

TONY RICHARDSON (1928–91)
Look Back in Anger (1959)
The Entertainer (1960)
Sanctuary (1961)
A Taste of Honey (1961)
The Loneliness of the Long Distance Runner (1962)
Tom Jones (1963)

NICOLAS ROEG (1928–   )
Performance (1970). Co-director, Donald Cammell
Walkabout (1971)
Don't Look Now (1973)
The Man Who Fell to Earth (1976)
The Witches (1990)

KEN RUSSELL (1927–   )
Women in Love (1969)
The Music Lovers (1970)
The Devils (1971)

JOHN SCHLESINGER (1926–2003)
Billy Liar (1963)
Far from the Madding Crowd (1967)
Midnight Cowboy (1969)
Sunday Bloody Sunday or *Sunday, Bloody Sunday* (1971)

THE EALING COMEDIES
Kind Hearts and Coronets (1949, Robert Hamer)
Tight Little Island or *Whisky Galore!* (1949, Alexander Mackendrick)
The Lavender Hill Mob (1951, Charles Crichton)

The Man in the White Suit (1951, Alexander Mackendrick)

UNITED KINGDOM MISCELLANY
Dead of Night (1945, Alberto Cavalcanti, Charles Crichton, Basil Dearden, and Robert Hamer)
The Importance of Being Earnest (1952, Anthony Asquith)
The Horse's Mouth (1958, Ronald Neame)
Tunes of Glory (1960, Ronald Neame)
The L-Shaped Room (1962, Bryan Forbes)
Dr. No (1962, Terence Young)
Lord of the Flies (1963, Peter Brook)
Zulu (1964, Cy Endfield)
The War Game (1965, Peter Watkins)
Marat/Sade or *The Persecution and Assassination of Jean-Paul Marat as Performed by the Inmates of the Asylum of Charenton Under the Direction of the Marquis de Sade* (1966, Peter Brook)
The Ruling Class (1972, Peter Medak)
Monty Python and The Holy Grail (1974, Terry Jones and Terry Gilliam)
Edvard Munch (1974, Peter Watkins)
The Rocky Horror Picture Show (1975, Jim Sharman)
My Beautiful Laundrette (1985, Stephen Frears)
High Hopes (1988, Mike Leigh)
The Cook The Thief His Wife & Her Lover (1989, Peter Greenaway)
Life is Sweet (1991, Mike Leigh)
The Remains of the Day (1993, James Ivory)
Trainspotting (1996, Danny Boyle)
Secrets & Lies (1996, Mike Leigh)
The House of Mirth (2000, Terence Davies)
Iris (2001, Richard Eyre)

CENTRAL AND EASTERN EUROPE

THEODOROS ANGELOPOULOS (1935–   )
Days of '36 (1972)
The Traveling Players (1975)
Landscape in the Mist (1988)
The Suspended Step of the Stork (1991)
Ulysses' Gaze (1995)
Eternity and a Day or *An Eternity and a Day* (1998)

MILOŠ FORMAN (1932–   )
Loves of a Blonde (1965)
The Firemen's Ball (1967)

One Flew Over the Cuckoo's Nest (1975)
Hair (1979)
Amadeus (1984)

MIKLÓS JANCSÓ (1921–   )
Cantata (1962)
The Red and the White (1967)
The Confrontation (1968)

KRZYSZTOF KIEŚLOWSKI (1941–96)
Dekalog or *The Decalogue* (10 parts, 1988).
    Made for TV
The Double Life of Veronique (1991)
Three Colors: Blue (1993)
Three Colors: White (1994). Completed 1993
Three Colors: Red (1994)

ROMAN POLANSKI (1933–   )
Knife in the Water (1962)
Repulsion (1965)
Rosemary's Baby (1968)
Macbeth (1971)
Chinatown (1974)
The Tenant (1976)
The Pianist (2002)

JERZY SKOLIMOWSKI (1938–   )
Walkover (1965)
Barrier (1966)
Le Départ (1967)
Deep End (1970)
Moonlighting (1982)

ANDRZEJ WAJDA (1926–   )
Generation or *A Generation* (1955)
Kanal (1957)
Ashes and Diamonds (1958)
Man of Marble (1977)
Man of Iron (1980)
Danton (1982)

MISCELLANY: FORMER CZECHOSLOVAKIA, POLAND, HUNGARY, FORMER YUGOSLAVIA, GREECE
The Last Stop (1947, Wanda Jakubowksa)
Stella (1955, Michael Cacoyannis)
Electra (1961, Michael Cacoyannis)
The Fifth Horseman Is Fear (1964, Zbyněk
    Brynych)
Intimate Lighting (1965, Ivan Passer)
Closely Watched Trains (1966, Jiří Menzel)
Daisies (1966, Věra Chytilová)
The End of August at the Hotel Ozone (1968, Jan
    Schmidt). Completed 1966

WR—Mysteries of the Organism (1971, Dušan
    Makavejev)
Iphigenia (1977, Michael Cacoyannis)
The Constant Factor and *Contract* (1980,
    Krzysztof Zanussi)
Mephisto (1981, István Szabó)
My 20th Century (1988, Ildikó Enyedi)
Time of the Gypsies (1989, Emir Kusturica)
Interrogation (1990, Ryszard Bugajski).
    Completed 1982
An Unforgettable Summer (1994, Lucian
    Pintilie)
Before The Rain (1994, Milcho Manchevski)
Underground (1995, Emir Kusturica)
Conspirators of Pleasure (1996, Jan
    Švankmajer)
The Wounds (1998, Srdjan Dragojević)
Cabaret Balkan or *The Powder Keg* (1998, Goran
    Paskaljević)
Kontroll (2003, Nimrod Antal)

JAPAN, INDIA, CHINA, TAIWAN, HONG KONG, KOREA, AND VIETNAM

CHEN KAIGE (1952–   )
Yellow Earth (1984)
Life on a String (1991)
Farewell to My Concubine (1993). Shorter
    version, *Farewell, My Concubine*
The Emperor and the Assassin (1999).
    Completed 1998

HOU HSIAO-HSIEN (1947–   )
A Summer at Grandpa's (1984)
A Time to Live and a Time to Die (1985)
City of Sadness or *A City of Sadness* (1989)
Puppet Master or *The Puppetmaster* (1993)
Goodbye South, Goodbye (1996)
Coffee Time or *Café Lumière* (2004)

KON ICHIKAWA (1915–   )
The Burmese Harp (1956)
Fires on the Plain (1959)
The Makioka Sisters (1983)

IM KWON-TAEK (1936–   )
Genealogy (1978)
Mandala (1981)
Sop'yonje (1993)
Chunhyang (2000)
Chihwaseon or *Painted Fire* (2002)
Lower Class Life (2004)

AKIRA KUROSAWA (1910–98)
Rashomon (1950)
Ikiru (*To Live*, 1952)
Seven Samurai (1954)
The Lower Depths (1957)
Throne of Blood (1957)
The Hidden Fortress (1958)
Yojimbo (1961)
High and Low (1963)
Dodes'ka-den (1970)
Dersu Uzala (1975)
Kagemusha or *Kagemusha, The Shadow Warrior* (1980)
Ran (*Chaos*, 1985)

ANG LEE (1954–)
The Wedding Banquet (1993)
Eat Drink Man Woman (1994)
Sense and Sensibility (1995)
Crouching Tiger, Hidden Dragon (2000)

KENJI MIZOGUCHI (1898–1956)
Osaka Elegy and *Sisters of the Gion* (1936)
The Story of the Last Chrysanthemum (1939)
The 47 Ronin (2 parts, 1941)
Utamaro and His Five Women (1946)
The Life of Oharu (1952)
Ugetsu or *Ugetsu Monogatari* (1953)
Sansho the Bailiff (1954)
Chikamatsu Monogatari (*A Story from Chikamatsu*, 1954)

NAGISA OSHIMA (1932–)
Death by Hanging (1968)
Diary of a Shinjuku Thief (1969)
In the Realm of the Senses (1976)
Merry Christmas, Mr. Lawrence (1983)
Gohatto (*Forbidden*, 2000)

YASUJIRO OZU (1903–63)
I Was Born, But . . . (1932)
Woman of Tokyo (1933)
A Story of Floating Weeds (1934)
Tokyo Story (1953)
Floating Weeds (1959)
Late Autumn (1960)
End of Summer (1961)
An Autumn Afternoon (1962)

SATYAJIT RAY (1921–92)
Pather Panchali (*Song of the Little Road*, 1955)
Aparajito (*The Unvanquished*, 1956)

The Music Room (*Jalsaghar*, 1958)
Apur Sansar (*The World of Apu*, 1959)
Devi (*The Goddess*, 1960)
Charulata (*The Lonely Wife*, 1964)
Days and Nights in the Forest (*Aranyer Din Ratri*, 1970)
Distant Thunder (*Ashani Sanket*, 1973)

WONG KAR WAI or WONG KAR-WAI (1958–)
Chung King Express (1994)
Fallen Angels (1995)
Happy Together (1997)
In the Mood for Love (2000)
2046 (2004)

ZHANG YIMOU (1950–)
Red Sorghum (1988)
Ju Dou (1990). Co-director, Yang Fengliang
Raise the Red Lantern (1991)
The Story of Qiu Ju (1992)
To Live (1994)
Not One Less (1999)
The Road Home (2000). Completed 1999
Hero (2002)
House of Flying Daggers (2004)

ASIAN MISCELLANY
A Page of Madness or *Crazy Page* or *A Page out of Order* (1926, Teinosuke Kinugasa)
Gate of Hell (1953, Teinosuke Kinugasa)
Two Acres of Land (1953, Bimal Roy)
Godzilla, King of the Monsters (1954, Ishiro Honda). U.S. version, with new material by Terry Morse, 1956
Rodan (1956, Ishiro Honda)
Chushingura (1962, Hiroshi Inagaki)
Harakiri (1962, Masaki Kobayashi)
Kwaidan (1964, Masaki Kobayashi)
Woman in the Dunes (1964, Hiroshi Teshigahara)
The Pornographers (1966, Shohei Imamura)
Double Suicide (1969, Masahiro Shinoda)
Bombay Talkie (1970, James Ivory)
Horse Thief (1985, Tian Zhuangzhuang)
A Chinese Ghost Story (1987, Ching Siu-tung)
Old Well (1987, Wu Tianming)
Akira (1988, Katsuhiro Otomo)
The Killer (1989, John Woo)
The Bride with White Hair (1993, Ronny Yu)
Cyclo (*Xich Lo*, 1995, Tran Anh Hung)
Maborosi (1995, Kore-eda Hirokazu)
Hana-bi or *Fireworks* (1997, Takeshi Kitano)

Princess Mononoke (1997, Hayao Miyazaki)
After Life (1998, Kore-eda Hirokazu)
Yi Yi or *A One and a Two . . .* (2000, Edward Yang)
Spirited Away (2001, Hayao Miyazaki)

DVDs

SWEDEN AND DENMARK

The Celebration (1998, **Thomas Vinterberg**). Focus Features/Umvd. Marked "Dogme #1" on the cover.

Dreyer Box Set (1943–64, **Carl Theodor Dreyer**). Criterion Collection. Contains *Day of Wrath*, *Ordet*, and *Gertrud*; interviews with Dreyer and others; a biographical essay by Dreyer scholar Edvin Kau; and a documentary by Torben Skjødt Jensen, *Carl Th. Dreyer— My Métier*, with outtakes.

A Film Trilogy by Ingmar Bergman (1961–63, **Ingmar Bergman**). Criterion Collection. Contains *Through a Glass Darkly*, *Winter Light*, and *The Silence*, with discussions and essays by Bergman scholar Peter Cowie and others.

The Five Obstructions (see Chap. 1 list).

Häxan (1922, **Benjamin Christensen**). Criterion Collection. Contains the 1922 version **restored** by the Swedish Film Institute, running at 20 fps, with the original music and some outtakes; a gallery of "diabolical" images and other sources Christensen consulted; a commentary by Danish-film expert Casper Tybjerg; and the 1968 recut version, *Witchcraft Through the Ages*, narrated by novelist **William S. Burroughs**.

The Ingmar Bergman Special Edition DVD Collection (1966–77, **Ingmar Bergman**). MGM Home Entertainment. Contains the uncensored, original Swedish versions—in their correct aspect ratios, with readable subtitles—of *Persona* (whose opening includes an erection, in case one needs a warning), *Hour of the Wolf*, *Shame*, and *The Passion of Anna*, as well as, for some reason, *The Serpent's Egg*. Also includes several interviews with Bergman; new, important interviews with stars **Bibi Andersson**, **Erland Josephson**, and **Liv Ullmann**; the original Swedish trailers; interpretive shorts and commentaries; and documentaries on Bergman, his island, and cinematographer **Sven Nykvist**.

Medea (1988, **Lars von Trier**; script by **Dreyer**). Facets Video. Compare with the Pasolini–Callas version (see Chap. 13 list) and von Trier's later films.

The Passion of Joan of Arc (see Chap. 10 list).

The Seventh Seal (1957, **Ingmar Bergman**). Criterion Collection. **Restored** from the camera negative; includes a **restoration demonstration**, an illustrated filmography, and a commentary by Bergman scholar Peter Cowie.

Wild Strawberries (1957, **Ingmar Bergman**). Criterion Collection. With a commentary by Peter Cowie and a documentary by Jörn Donner, *Ingmar Bergman on Life and Work*.

ENGLAND

*The **Alec Guinness** Collection*. Anchor Bay. Contains *Kind Hearts and Coronets*, *The Lavender Hill Mob*, *The Man in the White Suit*, *The Captain's Paradise*, and *The Ladykillers*.

Billy Liar (1963, **John Schlesinger**). Criterion Collection. Includes commentary by Schlesinger and actors **Tom Courtenay** and **Julie Christie**.

Black Narcissus (1947, **Michael Powell** and **Emeric Pressburger**). Criterion Collection. The excellent commentary track is a conversation between Powell and **Martin Scorsese**.

The Edge of the World (1937, shot 1936; **Michael Powell**). Image Entertainment. Includes Powell's 1978 follow-up documentary, *Return to the Edge of the World*; a Powell short, *An Airman's Letter to His Mother*; the original press kit, in the DVD-ROM section; and commentaries by **Thelma Schoonmaker Powell**, film historian Ian Christie, and others.

A Hard Day's Night (1964, **Richard Lester**). Miramax Entertainment. Includes many interviews and, in the DVD-ROM section, the first draft of the script.

Henry V (1944, **Laurence Olivier**). Criterion Collection. Remastered from Technicolor elements, with information on the kings of England and a commentary by film historian Bruce Eder.

The Horse's Mouth (1958, **Ronald Neame**). Criterion Collection. Includes a **D. A. Pennebaker** short, *Daybreak Express*, and an interview with Neame.

Lawrence of Arabia (1962, **David Lean**). Columbia TriStar. Superbit Collection. **Restored**. Mastered at a higher **bit rate** than most DVDs, leaving no room for extras but giving a better image and single-frame capability. The only DVD that approaches the correct colors and the sharp, rich look of **Robert A. Harris**'s 70mm restoration (the basis of most DVD editions), this is the best available substitute for Criterion's out-of-print laserdisc.

Peeping Tom (see Chap. 1 list).

Richard III (1955, **Laurence Olivier**). Criterion Collection. **Restored**; includes a 1966 interview with Olivier.

The Ruling Class (1972, **Peter Medak**). Criterion Collection. The original, uncut version, with a commentary by Medak, star **Peter O'Toole**, and writer **Peter Barnes**.

The Third Man (1949, **Carol Reed**). Criterion Collection. **Digitally restored**; includes an episode from **Orson Welles**'s radio series, *The Lives of Harry Lime*; the Lux Radio Theatre adaptation of *The Third Man*; a reading of part of **Graham Greene**'s treatment; and **Joseph Cotten**'s alternate voice-over opening for the U.S. version.

The 39 Steps (see Chap. 11 list).

Walkabout (1971, **Nicolas Roeg**). Criterion Collection. Director's original, uncensored cut (5 minutes longer than the release version); includes an essay by film critic Roger Ebert and a commentary by Roeg and star **Jenny Agutter**.

CENTRAL AND EASTERN EUROPE

Ashes and Diamonds (1958, **Andrzej Wajda**). Facets Video.

Black Peter (1963, **Miloš Forman**). Facets Video.

Daisies (1966, **Věra Chytilová**). Facets Video.

The Decalogue (1988, **Krzysztof Kieślowski**). Facets Video. Includes interviews with Kieślowski and writer **Krzysztof Piesiewicz**, a visit to the set, and more.

Everything for Sale (1969, **Andrzej Wajda**). Vanguard Cinema.

The Firemen's Ball (1967, **Miloš Forman**). Criterion Collection. Includes an interview with Forman and a look at the **digital transfer** process.

Kanal (1957, **Andrzej Wajda**). Facets Video.

Knife in the Water (1957–62, **Roman Polanski**). Criterion Collection. Includes *Two Men and a Wardrobe*, *The Fat and the Lean*, and 6 other Polanski shorts; the feature, with new subtitles by Polanski; and an interview with Polanski and co-writer **Jerzy Skolimowski**.

Mephisto (1981, **István Szabó**). Anchor Bay. Includes a documentary featuring Szabó and actor **Klaus Maria Brandauer**.

The Red and the White (1967, **Miklós Jancsó**). Facets Video.

Stella (1955, **Michael Cacoyannis**). Fox Lorber. Includes filmographies.

Three Colors Trilogy (1993–94, **Krzysztof Kieślowski**). Buena Vista Home Video. Contains *Blue*, *White*, and *Red*.

Ulysses' Gaze (1995, **Theo Angelopoulos**). Fox Lorber. *The Traveling Players* is available only on VHS (Facets Video).

Underground (1995, **Emir Kusturica**). New Yorker Video. Includes an interview with Kusturica.

JAPAN, INDIA, CHINA, TAIWAN, HONG KONG, KOREA, AND VIETNAM

Audition (1999, **Takashi Miike**). Chimera Entertainment. The unrated director's cut (avoid the poorly labeled R version), plus an interview with Miike and a partial commentary by him.

Bullet in the Head (1990, **John Woo**). Tai Seng Video.

Chunhyang (2000, **Im Kwon-Taek**). New Yorker Films.

Chushingura (1962, **Hiroshi Inagaki**). Image Entertainment. Compare with *The 47 Ronin*.

Crouching Tiger, Hidden Dragon (2000, **Ang Lee**). Columbia TriStar. Includes a commentary by Lee and writer–producer **James Schamus**, an interview with star **Michelle Yeoh**, and a making-of documentary.

Cyclo (1995, **Tran Anh Hung**). New Yorker Films.

The Emperor and the Assassin (1999, **Chen Kaige**). Columbia TriStar. Commentary by Chen. *Yellow Earth* is not on DVD, and *Farewell to My Concubine* is available only in the shortened version (Miramax).

Fireworks (1997, **Takeshi Kitano**). New Yorker Films. Includes a making-of documentary.

The 47 Ronin (1941, **Kenji Mizoguchi**). Image Entertainment. Contains both parts. Compare with *Chushingura*.

Goodbye South, Goodbye (1996, **Hou Hsiao-hsien**). Fox Lorber.

Hero (2002, **Zhang Yimou**). Buena Vista Home Video. Includes storyboards, a short about the film, and a conversation between **Quentin Tarantino** and star **Jet Li**.

The Hidden Fortress (1958, **Akira Kurosawa**). Criterion Collection. **Digitally restored**; includes an interview with **George Lucas**.

Ikiru (1952, **Akira Kurosawa**). Criterion Collection. **Digitally restored**; commentary by film scholar Stephen Prince; includes documentaries on the film and on Kurosawa, one featuring several interviews with him.

In the Mood for Love (2000, **Wong Kar Wai**). Criterion Collection. Includes interviews with Wong, deleted scenes with his commentary, a making-of documentary, a short by Wong (*Hua Yang de Nian Hua*), biographies, a press conference, and the electronic press kit.

The Lower Depths (1936, **Jean Renoir**; 1957, **Akira Kurosawa**). Criterion Collection. Contains both movies, **digitally restored**, with new subtitles. Kurosawa's version has a commentary by film historian Donald Richie, and Renoir's version is introduced by Renoir.

Maborosi (1995, **Kore-eda Hirokazu**). New Yorker Films.

Pather Panchali (1955, **Satyajit Ray**). Columbia TriStar. The same company also offers *Aparajito* and *The World of Apu*.

The Pornographers (1966, **Shohei Imamura**). Criterion Collection. **Digitally restored**.

Rashomon (1950, **Akira Kurosawa**). Criterion Collection. **Digitally restored**. Includes the original short stories "In a Grove" and "Rashomon"; newly translated subtitles; and a commentary by the film historian who knew Kurosawa best, Donald Richie.

The Road Home (2000, **Zhang Yimou**). Columbia TriStar.

Seven Samurai (1954, **Akira Kurosawa**). Criterion Collection. **Restored**. The 207-minute original, longer and better than the version shown outside Japan in the 1950s.

A Story of Floating Weeds/Floating Weeds (1934 and 1959, **Yasujiro Ozu**). Criterion Collection. **Digitally restored**, with new subtitles; contains the silent and sound versions of the film. *A Story of Floating Weeds* has an exemplary commentary by Ozu scholar Donald Richie; *Floating Weeds* also has an excellent commentary by film critic Roger Ebert.

Tokyo Story (1953, **Yasujiro Ozu**). Criterion Collection. **Digitally restored**, with new subtitles, a commentary by film scholar David Desser, a documentary on Ozu (*I Lived, But . . .*), and a short in which directors such as **Hou** and **Wenders** talk about him.

15

Hollywood Renaissance: 1964–76

It is not entirely certain when the old American movie reawakened as the new American cinema: *Bonnie and Clyde* (1967)? *Seconds* (1966)? *The Pawnbroker* (1965)? *Dr. Strangelove* (1964)? *David and Lisa* (1963)? *Lonely Are the Brave* (1962)? *The Hustler* (1961)? *Psycho* (1960)? Hollywood arose for its fifth era, its renaissance, gradually, just as it had slipped into its transitional fourth phase—quite unlike its sudden leaps into the second era of the feature film and the third era of synchronized sound.

All eight of these films (of which only *Bonnie and Clyde* is in color) contain seeds of the period's values: the offbeat antihero protagonists; the sterile society that surrounds them; the explicit treatment of sexual conflicts and psychological problems; the mixing of the comic and the serious; the self-conscious use of cinematic effects (slow motion, quick cutting, stylized memory and dream sequences, and so forth).

Most of the films give evidence of the two clichés that critics used to describe films of the era: sex and violence. But films have always used sex, whether it was the sexiness of Griffith's Friendless One, of Valentino's Sheik, of Dietrich's veiled face in a key light, or of bare breasts and buttocks in a Paris apartment. And films have always been violent—whether it was violent death on a Civil War battlefield in *The Birth of a Nation*, the violent death of a hoodlum on the cathedral steps in *Little Caesar*, or the violent deaths on the highway in *Easy Rider* (Dennis Hopper, 1969). The question is not whether a movie includes sex and violence but how it uses them. The graphic sex and violence of this "new" Hollywood cast a cynical look back on the genre films of the old Hollywood, suggesting that their assured and optimistic conclusions simplified the unresolved divisions in American life.

This new cinema in America evolved for several reasons. The first was a negative cause: The old, regular movie patrons now stayed home to watch television. The industry had to find new regular customers, not those who would go to the occasional movie that seemed special enough but those who would go every week—who still liked movies and considered them important to their social and leisure experience, and who appreciated the adult dialogue and treatment TV was forbidden to offer.

For another, the new cinema of Europe eventually converted American producers. The innovations of Godard, Truffaut, and Antonioni, along with those of Kurosawa and Bergman, had already conquered the rising generation of young filmmakers and audiences at the art houses. Even more convincing, Truffaut and Fellini could make money. The years 1959–61 were as important as any to the future American film: the years of *Breathless*, *The 400 Blows*, *L'avventura*, *La dolce vita*, *Through a Glass Darkly*, and *Hiroshima, mon amour*.

Third, though Hollywood repeatedly scoffed at the Underground Cinema, the underground crawled up to enjoy the last laugh. Not only did underground filmmakers succeed financially—for example, Andy Warhol, Robert Downey, and Brian De Palma—but the underground films conditioned a whole generation of young filmgoers (precisely those who became the steady

Fig. 15-1
*Love, thrills, and bullets. Michael J. Pollard, Faye Dunaway, and Warren Beatty (right)
in* **Bonnie and Clyde.**

customers for Hollywood films) to understand
and accept innovations in cinematic form, visual
stimulation, and elliptical construction.

Fourth, the film industry pushed its discovery
of the elitism of the new film audience to its limits.
Rather than attempting to make all of the films
for all of the people, producers and exhibitors
realized they must appeal to very special tastes.
They made a few family pictures to serve that
special need. They capitalized on the racial
make-up of urban audiences by making
"blaxploitation" cops-and-robbers films (Gordon
Parks's *Shaft*, 1971, and its descendants). They
made "sexploitation" films for that special audience—not "stag" shorts but full-length movies:
The Devil in Miss Jones (1973), *Deep Throat*
(1972), and *Boys in the Sand* (1971) were three
of the most commercially successful pornographic features. (For a horrifying account of the
making of *Deep Throat*, read Linda Lovelace's
autobiography, *Ordeal.*) There were even special

cult films shown at midnight for late-night "film
freaks" in the cities. Among the most popular of
these cult films were Andy Warhol's *Sleep* (1963),
Russ Meyer's *Faster, Pussycat! Kill! Kill!* (1966),
Alexandro Jodorowsky's *El Topo* (1969), John
Waters's *Pink Flamingos* (1971), Hal Ashby's
Harold and Maude (1971), Jim Sharman's *The
Rocky Horror Picture Show* (1975), and David
Lynch's *Eraserhead* (1977). There were also old
films that attracted cults (*Casablanca*) and cult
films that never became "midnight movies."

In the same way, the American industry aimed
its "art films" (those directed by Arthur Penn,
Mike Nichols, and others) at the minority audience that liked such films. These films, however,
found a wide audience and were precisely those
that served as America's best examples of film art
and the key representatives of its fifth era.

Finally, the values of these new American
"art films" reflected the sexual and social values
of American film audiences in the period. The

American college student, the core of this audience, had discovered politics, drugs, and premarital sex, and protested against the covert and overt policies of the government as well as the racism, materialism, and hypocrisy of American society. The vision of reality on the screen did not entirely shape its audience; as in the 1930s, the screen still reflected the values of those who sat in front of it. Those values had changed.

Arthur Penn's *Bonnie and Clyde* was perhaps the first full statement of the new cinema's values; it was so popular that many of its daring innovations became conventions in the years that followed. In most cases, the protagonists of the films were social misfits, deviates, or outlaws; the villains were the legal, respectable defenders of society. The old bad guys became the good guys; the old good guys, the bad guys. The surprising element in *Bonnie and Clyde* (and *Easy Rider, Cool Hand Luke, The Wild Bunch, Butch Cassidy and the Sundance Kid, Thieves Like Us*, et cetera) was not simply that the protagonists were criminals, for films had depicted their Little Caesars and Bonnie Parkers for decades. The surprise was that these new murderers were also charming, exciting, compassionate, and funny—and that the violence was much more graphic. The pursuers with badges were the cruel ones; even the pursuers without badges—as in *The Graduate* (Mike Nichols, 1967) and *Easy Rider*—had no sense of humor, of fair play, of love. The new obligatory ending was unhappy (*Joe*, 1970) or open (*Billy Jack*, 1971) rather than happily resolved (a rare exception among counterculture movies was Alan Myerson's *Steelyard Blues*, 1973).

The crucial thing about the new antihero heroes was not that they died violently, nor that the Establishment vanquished them, but that how they lived and what they stood for were validated. Even if evil regularly triumphed over goodness, rationality, and freedom, the American film was still essentially romantic and Manichean, just as it was in the 1920s and 1930s. There were still film characters who lived beautiful lives and others who lived vile ones; it was clear who the good guys were, even if they would have been called bad guys in the 1950s and even if they lost.

Rather than effacing the film's artfulness, as a Ford or Hawks intentionally did, the new directors threw in as many cinematic tricks as possible, which both intensified the film's moods and reminded the audience that it was watching a film. Slow motion, grainy filmstock, jump cutting, splitting the wide screen, self-conscious camerawork, mixtures of black and white and color were all standard tricks of the new trade. There was an emotional power in the visual assaults of the medium itself. And the flashes both forward and backward in time as well as into and out of a character's private mental experience broke down the definitions and distinctions of time and space, of now and then, of reality and fantasy, of "proper" linear continuity.

The new films played as trickily with sound as they did with images. Gone was the old principle of studio scoring—to underscore a scene with music that increases the action's emotional impact without making the viewer aware of the music's existence. In the new films, there was little of this kind of background music. If there was to be music, it had to be either clearly motivated (playing on a radio or record player nearby) or deliberately artificial (a song on the soundtrack that existed specifically to be noticed and played either in harmony with or in counterpoint to the sequence's visuals). Coppola's *Apocalypse Now* (1979) starts with the Doors' "The End." In Haskell Wexler's *Medium Cool* (1969), the patriotic speeches and songs inside the Democratic Convention hall accompany the sounds of the riots in Grant Park. Most of the new films used rock music heavily (the scores of Martin Scorsese's *Mean Streets* and George Lucas's *American Graffiti*, both 1973, were anthologies of highly relevant rock hits), for rock was the other artistic and social passion of the young audiences who supported the movies.

Fewer films were shot on soundstages; directors preferred the authenticity of shooting on location. Whereas the old Hollywood style was devoted to eliminating the imperfections of reality —uneven lighting, unwanted noise—the new films required accident and imperfection for their visual style and human credibility. The lighting styles of Bergman's Sven Nykvist and of the New Wave cinematographers (Raoul Coutard, Nestor Almendros, Henri Decaë), who bounced light off the ceilings of rooms and caught it as it poured through windows, influenced a new generation of American cinematographers—Haskell Wexler, Gordon Willis, Vilmos Zsigmond, John Alonzo.

Inside the old studios, the only light that poured through a window flowed from an electric pitcher.

The new American films were gladly influenced by French films, Italian films, Czech films, British films, underground and avant-garde films, and even rediscovered films. Many of the new American films, like the new European films, depicted how actions *felt*, not just actions, so that character became more important than plot; they also tackled big issues, much as the Europeans did.

However Europeanized the fifth American era had become, it still maintained its old inclination toward rigid genres and marketable cycles. Producers still felt safer with a formula that had succeeded before, and so a series of films about compassionate thieves followed *Bonnie and Clyde*, a series of films about the last violent gasp of the old frontier followed *The Wild Bunch*, the chase scene in *Bullitt* was topped by the chase in *The French Connection*, and so forth. Despite their new experiential and stylistic commitments, the new films were descendants of the old genres: the western, the gangster, the *policier*, the screwball comedy, and the rest. The basic generic division in the new films was between city films and country films. Beyond these lay the road films (*Easy Rider*), the wilderness of horror (George Romero's *Night of the Living Dead*, 1968), and the world of fantasy (*Willy Wonka and the Chocolate Factory*, 1971, directed by Mel Stuart).

Many of the city films developed a thematic opposition between the unnaturalness and brutality of the city and the freedom and openness outside the city. While the *noir* city films shove law and crime, promise and corruption up against one another in tempting proximity, the city films of the "new" Hollywood suggest a seething human hell, augmented by location shooting and gory "effects" make-up. The cities breed paranoid fantasies, whether the sounds of San Francisco (*The Conversation*, 1974) or the sights of New York viewed through a windshield—smoke, steam, and brimstone rising from the entrails of the city itself (Martin Scorsese's *Taxi Driver*, 1976).

Close cousins to the city films, thematically as well as geographically, were the suburb films—such as *The Graduate* and Romero's *Dawn of the Dead* (1978, released 1979). If, compared with the densely packed older cities, these suburb–cities

were clean, bright, and new, they were also rootless and soulless. They lacked a center—either geographical or moral.

The new "experiential" western—for example, Sam Peckinpah's *The Wild Bunch* (1969) and George Roy Hill's *Butch Cassidy and the Sundance Kid* (1969)—was more violent, sensual, and antiestablishment than earlier westerns. For the new films, the vast plains and deserts were (like the highways in road movies) the last outposts of the free spirit of America. Both *The Wild Bunch* and *Butch Cassidy* were set in an era when the Old West was crumbling, when the city's values were swallowing the country's. The heroes of both films prefer to remain anachronisms rather than surrender to "decency" and the machine. If the new western differed from the old one, it was not because it had a higher body count. But in the old western the audience merely saw a man shot dead. The new western amplified the bloody details and turned the moment of death and the causing of death into the emotional epiphany.

The new gangster film mirrored the same basic generic division between past and present, city and country, rural criminals and urban criminals. The country-crime genre was essentially a subgenre of the new western. Whereas the protagonists of the western depended on their horses, the central figures of *Bonnie and Clyde*, *Thieves Like Us*, and Terrence Malick's *Badlands* (1973) used the automobile as their means of slicing through the country. In *Easy Rider* they used motorcycles; the open road was romantic and free, but sullied, and corruption and bigotry won in that movie's shockingly violent ending.

If the upsetting death sequence was obligatory in the western and country-crime films, as well as many urban dramas, the assaultive chase was obligatory in the city-crime films. The essential technical tool of the city film was editing—rather than composition as in the country films—and a familiar subjective device was the violent rushing of the traveling or hand-held camera. Cops in the city-crime films (Peter Yates's *Bullitt*, 1968; William Friedkin's *The French Connection*, 1971; Don Siegel's *Dirty Harry*, 1971) usually faced two sources of tension: within themselves (are they just doing their job or are they neurotically driven to violence and sadism?) and within their own departments (the pressures of politicians, bureaucrats, and incompetents). The *film noir* of the Transitional Era (for example, Lang's *The Big Heat*, 1953) was a truly transitional link between the detective films of the Studio Era in which the cop fought crime and of the new era in which a cop fought himself and cops fought each other (Lumet's *Serpico* and *Prince of the City*).

The most obvious link with the old Hollywood was the one "new" genre of the 1970s—what might be called the genre genre. These Postmodern films parodied the plots, conventions, and stars of Hollywood Past, usually by compiling a reflexive catalogue of Studio Era clichés—the Neil Simon–Robert Moore comedies (*Murder by Death*, 1976), Stanley Donen's *Movie Movie* (1978), some of the early Woody Allen films (*What's Up, Tiger Lily?*, 1966; *Take the Money and Run*, 1969; *Play It Again, Sam*, 1972, written by Allen but directed by Herbert Ross), and, of course, almost everything by Mel Brooks, the writer–director of *The Producers*, 1968; *Blazing Saddles*, 1974; *Young Frankenstein*, 1974; *Silent Movie*, 1976; and *High Anxiety*, 1977.

If a single American film of the 1970s put all these themes together, it was *Chinatown* (1974). Like many of the most perceptive film dissections of American society—from Chaplin's to Lang's to Hitchcock's—*Chinatown* was not directed by an American. Roman Polanski—whose view of life, American or otherwise, stretched from a Nazi concentration camp to Bel Air and the brutal Manson murder of Sharon Tate, Polanski's wife—directed the film from a masterful script by Robert Towne. The film explored American political corruption in a supposedly saner, cleaner social era of "wholesome values"—the 1930s of Frank Capra and the New Deal. While the 1930s films reaffirmed the myths of American purpose and destiny (after serious setbacks and struggle), *Chinatown* exposed the myths themselves as naïve falsehoods.

The period that began with the assassination of one president ended with the disgrace of another. The national mood of anger, doubt, and distrust understandably differed from the optimism, commitment, or vigilance of prewar, wartime, and postwar America. Not every American shared that mood, but the most vocal Americans against the war and in favor of civil rights—who marched on Washington in immense numbers and disrupted college campuses—were the ones who went to the movies. The American film business—much leaner than it had been a decade earlier—could afford to play a central role in this national debate.

Not coincidentally, the old Hollywood Production Code, which had always been a hypocritical compromise between the facts of life and the pressures of public opinion, came to an end as this era began. After several years of hedging, of making exceptions for prestige films like *Lolita* (1962) or *Who's Afraid of Virginia Woolf?* (1966), in 1968 the Motion Picture Association of America (MPAA, formerly the MPPDA) finally replaced the PCA (Production Code Administration) with the CARA (Classification and Rating Administration). The new board—which, as a service to parents, rated the "level of maturity" a film assumed of its audience rather than prohibited certain kinds of material altogether— instituted four categories: originally, G (for all audiences), M (suggested for mature audiences—which became GP, then PG), R (restricted to audiences of 18 years and older, except when accompanied by an adult), and X (restricted to audiences of 18 and over). PG-13, a warning stronger than PG (parental guidance suggested) but weaker than R, was added in 1984. In 1990, the new NC-17 (no children under 17) rating replaced the X. In CARA's first 20 years, half of the nearly 9,000 features rated received an R, one third a PG.

While the new MPAA ratings system unleashed more explicit sexual talk and activity and a more open critical attack on society's norms than had ever been seen in American movies before, there was still plenty of uncertainty, bargaining, and hypocrisy. Who was to say what a 17-year-old did or should know? CARA repeatedly re-vised the guidelines and the age limits. Since young people made up such a large share of the movie audience, just to drop the cutoff age one year, from 18 to 17, translated into a major increase in a film's potential audience. There was considerable bargaining between film producers and CARA over what a film might cut to receive a more commercially "desirable" rating—just as there had always been bargaining between producers and the PCA over what a film could show or say.

To distinguish rated films with adult content from unrated films brimming with prurient sex, the MPAA instituted the NC-17, hoping that certain films could be rated "adults only" without falling prey to the many ordinances that prohibited X-rated films from advertising in local papers or playing in local theatres. But many organizations simply boycotted NC-17 films. Another 1990 change in the ratings system was that CARA was required to give the reasons (sex, violence, language) a picture had been rated R. The industry's new rating system changed the shape of public debate about personal morality and public exhibition but certainly did not end the discussion.

The New American *Auteurs*

Like the film industries of Europe and Japan, the American cinema became more a directors' cinema, granting proven directors a higher measure of control over the scripting, production, and editing decisions, allowing them more freedom in selecting their projects and giving them more credit for their contributions than the studios once did in the era of the moguls. A film was frequently labeled *by* or *of* its director, whose name often appeared above or before the film's title. The American director became one of the film's stars, and it is significant that many 1970s directors were allowed to make films without any major star at all (*The Last Picture Show, Thieves Like Us, Days of Heaven*), an unheard-of practice for major studio films.

When François Truffaut in France and Andrew Sarris in America developed the "*auteur* theory" (or *auteur* policy), they did so as a means of distinguishing directorial individuality in the Studio Era, since individuality was often buried beneath the decisions of producers and the scripts of the story department. The new American *auteurs* are film authors in the full sense of a Griffith, Gance, Dreyer, Ford, Hitchcock, Godard, Fellini, Bergman, or Kurosawa—the ones who control the responsibility for the entire project so that their own personal visions and visual styles get recorded on film. Though the following list of American *auteurs* must necessarily be tentative (most of them are still in mid-career), each has created a large body of work that demonstrates considerable power and imagination as well as a clear consistency of style and vision.

John Cassavetes

John Cassavetes got his start in television, but as an actor. Like Orson Welles, he acted in features (*Rosemary's Baby, The Dirty Dozen, The Fury*) primarily to pay for the films he directed, the most significant of which are *Shadows* (1959; improvised version shown 1958), *Faces* (1968), *Husbands* (1970), *Minnie and Moskowitz* (1971), *A Woman Under the Influence* (1973, released 1974), *The Killing of a Chinese Bookie* (1976, recut 1978), *Opening Night* (1978), and *Love Streams* (1984). His films reveal a unique fusion—of narrative cinema, candidly documentary shooting styles, confessional explorations of character, and an unswerving commitment to filmmaking as personal statement—that remained fresh, experimental, honest, and intense throughout his career (he died in 1989). As a director, he was an actor working with actors, trying to get them to reveal the essential being and unstylized behavior of their characters; as a writer, he strove to present the ways people really talk and behave; as a complete filmmaker, he sought an invisible style that would not be arty, pretty, or in the way. His wife, Gena Rowlands, and his friends Seymour Cassel, Peter Falk, and Ben Gazzara gave their finest performances in his films, probing their own, their characters', and Cassavetes's vital energies and personal mysteries in an atmosphere that was kept utterly free of artificiality, phoniness, and formulaic solutions.

However deeply personal its sources, experience is public and social. Cassavetes's characters function within a force field of social "influences" that can never be escaped or avoided. The only course of survival is to master these ever-shifting, often fiercely predatory forces; the alternatives are misery and destruction. As his characters maneuver for position, power, and self-knowledge within volatile networks of mutual responsibility, Cassavetes reveals just how complex living can be. The intricacy of Cassavetes's depiction of his characters' negotiations with each other—along with the deliberately unpolished quality of the shooting and editing—give his scenes the appearance of having been improvised, but the fact is that all these hesitations, ellipses, and obliquities of expression were scripted and rehearsed in advance.

Although the relentless pressures and the fierce conflicts in his work gave Cassavetes the reputation of being a pessimist, he argued that he was celebrating his characters' heroic capacities of creative response to the dangers and problems they confront.

That heroic creative response is one Cassavetes shared with his characters. A Hollywood outsider fighting the studios, distribution systems, and publicity machinery for his vision of the feature film not as a commercial product but as a personal expression, this fiercely independent, embattled filmmaker was not discouraged but challenged and energized by the forces that sought to destroy or dismiss his uniquely demanding, historically significant work.

Woody Allen

Woody Allen is the American comic *auteur* who is most conscious of the older American comic-film tradition that he inherits. His glasses create a "glass character" who resembles Harold Lloyd, his physical clumsiness and unattractiveness parallel Harry Langdon's, and his dryly quiet, off-beat comic ironies suggest the flavor of Buster Keaton and the wit of Groucho Marx. But more than anyone else, Allen resembles Chaplin as an observer and chronicler of the contemporary American social scene. Although his characters wear different names (Fielding Mellish in *Bananas*, 1971; Miles Monroe in *Sleeper*, 1973; Boris Grushenko in *Love and Death*, 1975; Alvy Singer in *Annie Hall*, 1977), a device that parallels Keaton's different names and costumes, Woody Allen's comic persona is a single, familiar, established being, like Charlie, who wanders across the landscape of modern urban life, contrasting that persona with the less observant, less sensitive—and probably married and employed—characters who surround him. One might call Woody Allen's entire *oeuvre* "Modern Times," and if the problem for Allen's city dwellers has shifted from the external one of finding a job and founding a home to the internal one of feeling secure enough to survive between appointments with the analyst, that shift is symptomatic of almost seven decades of change in American life. Like Charlie (the British tramp), Woody (the Jewish *schlemiel*) is out of tune and out of step with the society that threatens and excludes him but that he wants to join and comically reflects.

Allen's cinematic technique in his earliest films was casually flippant, and he leapt from gag to gag, often wearing out the audience (and his ideas) before the end of the film. But Allen's three late-1970s films (*Annie Hall*; *Interiors*,

1978; *Manhattan*, 1979) show far more care and consciousness of cinematic style and "art."

After *Love and Death*, Allen's movies became increasingly reflexive, committed to exploring the condition of comic movies rather than his own fixed comic persona. *Love and Death* alluded to Soviet cinema—from Eisenstein's images to Prokofiev's film scores—as often as to 19th-century Russian fiction. *Stardust Memories* (1980), like Fellini's *8½*, which it deliberately echoes, shows the way a popular artist can be trapped by his own success and the expectations of fans and critics. *A Midsummer Night's Sex Comedy* (1982) combines Shakespeare's *A Midsummer Night's Dream* and Bergman's *Smiles of a Summer Night*. *Zelig* (1983) is virtually an entire movie in the style of *Citizen Kane*'s newsreel—an ironic examination of the way American hype converts anonymous nonentities into media superstars. Some of his best later films are nostalgic and engaging looks at show business (*Radio Days*, 1987; *Bullets Over Broadway*, 1994) or formal experiments, but the major theme of his work since *Annie Hall* has continued to be the nature of contemporary intimate relationships (*Manhattan*; *Hannah and Her Sisters*, 1986; *Crimes and Misdemeanors*, 1989; *Husbands and Wives*, 1992; *Mighty Aphrodite*, 1995; *Deconstructing Harry*, 1997), with an emphasis on the problems of authenticity and performance.

Robert Altman

Robert Altman made 15 feature films in the 1970s alone. It is clear that he would rather make movies than masterpieces, a large number of attempts rather than a few polished gems.

Altman's work comes in two narrative sizes. The first is a smaller, closer study of people who lead bizarre lives or are possessed by their dreams—the boy who wants to become a bird and fly in the great *Brewster McCloud* (1970), the thieves who want to rob enough banks to settle down to respectable lives in *Thieves Like Us*, Nixon in a room (*Secret Honor*, 1984).

The second Altman narrative structure requires a much larger canvas. It is a broad study of a particular American institution, built from a great number of interwoven characters, adding up to a cross-sectional view of American life. *MASH* (1970), Altman's first major success, used the sexy, funny, gory activities of a group of American medics in Korea to examine (at the height of the Vietnam crisis) American attitudes toward war, particularly wars against other races in distant parts of the world; the script was by Ring Lardner, Jr., one of the Hollywood Ten. *MASH* led to a hit TV series, *M*A*S*H*, and to more advanced experiments in complex film soundtracks. *Nashville* (1975), probably Altman's most solid and respected film, used the American country-and-western recording industry—and all the people it touched or who wanted to be touched by it—to investigate American political, sexual, and economic structures, as well as the American dreams of fame and success.

One of Altman's consistent strengths is the compelling spontaneous authenticity of the moments of human interaction. Altman works improvisationally with his actors, and the scenes they build together (between Donald Sutherland and Elliott Gould in *MASH*, Julie Christie and Warren Beatty in *McCabe & Mrs. Miller*, Gould and Sterling Hayden in *The Long Goodbye*, Barbara Harris or Lily Tomlin and everybody else in *Nashville*) are hypnotic encounters with acting that feels like life.

The second Altman strength is his perceptive scrutiny of American social institutions, which he explores with haunting and startlingly memorable images. *Brewster McCloud* is dominated by images of the bare, sterile Astrodome. In *A Wedding* (1978) the unforgettable visual splendor of a totally mirrored bathroom converts it into a gleaming temple for the worship of the shiny, the surface, and the body. The brilliance of Altman's perceptive, evocative imagery frequently overcomes the dreamlike meanderings of his weaker narratives.

Fig. 15-2
McCabe & Mrs. Miller: *no idealized civilization in this wilderness. The dirty frontier town of Presbyterian Church, blanketed by perpetual snow, rain, and mud—its church spire barely visible in the background.*

Consistent with the spirit of the era, Altman's work attacked the myths of American life as articulated in the genres of American movies. *McCabe & Mrs. Miller* does to the western what *The Long Goodbye* does to the detective film: explodes its assumptions and picks up only a few of the pieces. In this ragged frontier town, ironically named Presbyterian Church, there is no mythic showdown between good and evil in the glaring light of high noon. The "good guy," McCabe, is a drunken profiteer from gambling and prostitution, who shoots his assailants in the back. Mrs. Miller, reveals no heart of gold when trouble comes but retreats into her opium haze.

This is a western concerned not with decency but with sanitation—obsessed with the way people smell, belch, fart, and rid themselves of bodily wastes. Despite the town's name, its church, that great icon of civilization in John Ford westerns, is only half-built. Its major purpose in the film is to catch fire and distract the town's citizens from the real battle between McCabe and the hired killers—just as western movies, Altman perhaps implies, distracted American citizens from political realities with mythic façades.

After the mid-1970s and the passing of that era's attack on movie myth, Altman found it increasingly difficult to finance projects and please audiences. His most ambitious and disturbing films of the 1980's—*Jimmy Dean, Fool for Love* (1985, written for the screen by playwright Sam Shepard), and *Vincent & Theo* (1990, the story of the brothers Van Gogh)—attracted critics and audiences but still failed to convince producers that Altman could be trusted to turn out a commercially viable project; during this period Altman lost several assignments when he told studio heads that he intended to make an Altman film rather than, for example, an MGM film. But in 1992 he made a genuine comeback with *The Player*, a relentless satire of the Hollywood food chain.

Francis Ford Coppola

If Robert Altman was a foe of movie myth and industry during the 1970s, Francis Ford Coppola virtually *was* the American film industry in this period. Coppola is less a film director than an all-around man of the movies. He began as an assistant to Roger Corman—where he learned to cut, dub, write, and direct films. He has written scripts for other directors (notably the Oscar-winning *Patton*, 1970, for Franklin Schaffner, co-written by Edmund H. North), and he has become a producer or co-producer of others' films. More than anything else, Coppola is committed to the cinema—to its past and its future, its genres and its possibilities. He is the single most important film figure of his generation, a combination of D. W. Griffith and Thomas Ince.

For his personal projects, Coppola's films tend to be either big commercial epics (*Finian's Rainbow*, 1968; *The Godfather*, 1972; *The Godfather Part II*, 1974; *Apocalypse Now*, begun in 1976 and finally released in 1979; *The Cotton Club*, 1984; *The Godfather Part III*, 1990) or smaller, more offbeat style pieces (*The Rain People*, 1969; *The Conversation*, 1974; *The Outsiders*, 1983; *Rumble Fish*, 1983). *The Conversation*, with its clever use of sound as both the central subject and the dominant stylistic device of the film, with its furtive *cinéma vérité* sequences shot in Union Square that are an exact visual equivalent of the sound-recording process, with its effective settings, is the most profound and disturbing of his "smaller" films as well as the most highly respected. Like the *Godfather* films that came just before and after it—the greatest of his "big" movies—*The Conversation* is morally intense and intellectually solid. One might see the film's theme as the clash between a person's craft and conscience, the pure devotion to artisanship as opposed to the moral responsibilities of engaging in any business that affects the lives of other human beings.

The first two parts of *The Godfather*, adapted from Mario Puzo's bestselling novel, constitute a monumental American epic about the conflict between doing business and living according to meaningful values—a conflict built into the very familial and economic structure of American society. *The Godfather* opens with a wedding—a family celebration of fertility, union, and the future—and it ends just after the bride (Talia Shire) has become a widow. Vito Corleone (Marlon Brando) spends his time not outdoors, in the bright and open sunlight, but in his dark cavelike office, where he does business with his wedding guests. Although his may seem a special, unethical business (using his power and influence to do "favors" for his "friends"), he is no different from other American businessmen, who often discuss business at weddings.

The negotiations indoors represent the dark underside of the brightly visible activity outdoors; for Coppola, every American business has this dark underside. As an Italian American, Coppola is terribly conscious of the suspicion that all Italian and Sicilian immigrant families are branches of the illegitimate Mafia tree. Instead, Coppola argues that no American and no American business, of whatever ethnic extraction, can escape the conflict between business dealings and personal values. The Mafia is not a disease within American life; it is a symptom of American life itself.

The Godfather Part II extends the examination historically into both past and future—an epic chronicle of debasement and degradation, the dissolution of the American Dream that brought immigrants to the United States in the first place. The temporal leaps in Coppola's narrative—late-19th-century Sicily, the arrival of immigrants at Ellis Island, life in New York's Little Italy in the 1910s and 1920s, Batista's corrupt Cuba of the 1950s, Las Vegas of the 1960s—produce a political conversation between the simple hopes of the past and the complex corruption of the present, as the stories of Vito's and Michael's careers are cross-cut. Like the Ricos and Tony Camontes of Hollywood Past, Michael Corleone (Al Pacino) accumulates wealth and power at the expense of losing everyone close to him—associates, friends, wife, children, brother. Unlike those earlier gangsters, Michael himself does not lose his life but remains—a lonely, tragic, coldly powerful head of a corporation of crime.

The Godfather Part II, widely considered the best sequel ever made, is so different in style and structure that the two parts form a genuine historical dialectic. Although no Marxist, Coppola's dialectical method within and between the two films suggests a historical analysis of the assumptions of Old and New World capitalism and is a vivid way to dramatize the rise and fall of the family and all that it stands for.

In *Part III*, Michael completes his project of shifting all the family's business interests to legitimate activities—but everywhere he turns, even the Vatican, he encounters corruption and more enemies. After confessing his sins to an insightful cardinal, Michael asks God for an opportunity to atone for killing his brother (Fredo, at the end of *Part II*—the most important of his sins, since it was against the family), and he gets it: Michael loses the person he loves the most—his daughter, who is shot to death right in front of him. His silent scream as he holds her body is the beginning of his penance. While not a complete betrayal of the first two parts, *The Godfather Part III* is nowhere near them in power and range. It has a few excellent scenes but no *necessary* ones.

Coppola's Vietnam epic, *Apocalypse Now*, had a stunning surround soundtrack, many unforgettable sequences, and a muddled ending. Coppola's foe is again the system itself, the military mentality that produces a Kurtz (Brando), insane with power; a Willard (Martin Sheen), who must search for Kurtz by becoming Kurtz; and a Kilgore (Robert Duvall), who can make little distinction between the fun of surfboarding and the fun of napalming. Coppola's metaphoric journey upriver—adapted from Joseph Conrad's *Heart of Darkness*—is dominated by powerful images: Playboy bunnies entertaining the troops (deliberately reminiscent of those Bob Hope GI shows), the psychedelic nighttime carnival in which Willard wanders through an eerie wasteland of stoned soldiers, the collection of severed human heads that decorates Kurtz's camp, and many more. The story became more comprehensive, and more comprehensible, when Coppola and the great sound designer and editor Walter Murch recut and expanded it into *Apocalypse Now Redux* (2000, released 2001).

Coppola's musicals (*Finian's Rainbow, One from the heart, The Cotton Club*) are stylistic exercises that explore the central paradoxes of the musical as a genre—the relation of convention to credibility, stylization to reality, number to story, and entertainment to social commentary. Unfortunately, these musicals have at times (despite that title) very little heart—the ultimate element that gives a musical its artistic sense. *Bram Stoker's Dracula* (1992—and not a faithful adaptation of the novel, despite *its* title) has an analogous problem: It is a horror film that is not scary—drenched in romantic imagery, overwhelmed by style and getting nowhere, and sunk by a ridiculous ending. But when Coppola's romantic energy and grand imagination are

Fig. 15-3
Apocalypse Now: *the grotesque juxtaposition of surfboards and napalm.*

focused by a compelling subject, as they were in his four great films of the 1970s—*The Godfather, The Conversation, The Godfather Part II,* and *Apocalypse Now*—his mastery of style is beyond challenge.

Martin Scorsese

Martin Scorsese brings a tense urban sensibility and a vision of spiritually charged moral conflict to the Italian-American film. He puts his characters through explosive scenes that have the flavor of improvisation and chaos but are profoundly determined. Scorsese seems to succeed most with carefully textured psychological portraits of people who are entangled in their detailed social environments —New York's Little Italy (*Mean Streets,* 1973), a diner in the American Southwest (*Alice Doesn't Live Here Anymore,* 1974), New York street life (*Taxi Driver,* 1976; *Bringing Out the Dead,* 1999), late-19th-century high society (*The Age of Innocence,* 1993), mid-19th-century slums

(*Gangs of New York,* 2002). *Raging Bull* (1980) was an interpretive biography of boxer Jake La Motta, but it went much deeper. Combining Italian Neorealism and the visual style of 1950s New York films (set in that period, shot primarily in black and white), *Raging Bull* related the violence of boxing to sexual violence in general, as well as to the limits of theater and the beginnings of religion.

As fast and violent as Scorsese's films often are, they are also intensely meditative; many also have thoughtful voice-over narrators. He moves the camera with more zest and authority than any American now making movies. He is scrupulously attentive to technical quality and wildly excited about the work of classic directors like Michael Powell—or Lean, Rossellini, Welles, Bresson, Hawks, Hitchcock, Cassavetes—because this is one director who knows film history and loves watching movies as well as making them. The visceral editing (often by Thelma Schoonmaker), the evocative music, and beyond all that the

Fig. 15-4
Mean Streets: *Charlie (Harvey Keitel) in church, crossing himself before the lighted candles and thinking of "the pain of Hell," the burning heat "from a lighted match increased a million times. Infinite."*

ironies and depths of Scorsese's films have vaulted him to the first rank of American directors.

"I'm God's lonely man," says Travis Bickle (Robert De Niro), the psychopathic taxi driver who wants to cleanse the world of sin—and many of Scorsese's central characters are isolated (often within the limits of an obsession, whether it be an idea, a desire, or a view of the world) and do think about God. At the beginning of *Mean Streets*, Charlie (Harvey Keitel) observes, voice-over, "You don't make up for your sins in church. You do it in the streets; you do it at home." Charlie would like to do penance for his sins on his own, in his own terms, with actions rather than words. For a character like Jake La Motta (De Niro) in *Raging Bull*, punishing himself and impulsively, blindly seeking redemption might mean screaming at and fighting with everyone he loves or getting punched to a pulp in the ring and destroyed through all his mistakes. There are times, however, when his movies are dragged down by their religious symbolism: In

spite of its superb sets, costumes, and other period details—and a major performance by Daniel Day-Lewis—*Gangs of New York* pursues an Old Testament vs. New Testament allegory that is unnecessary and even offensive.

After two diversions, *The King of Comedy* (1983) and *After Hours* (1985), Scorsese returned to the world of *Mean Streets* with *GoodFellas* (1990), the true story of a boy (Ray Liotta) who grew up to join the "wiseguys"—the friendly brotherhood of criminals who ran his neighborhood—and thought it was great until some of the crazy murderousness of his buddies (Joe Pesci, Robert De Niro) got out of hand. Highly charged, fast paced, full of sudden violence, and very funny, its tones and rhythms masterfully varied and controlled, *GoodFellas* presents the work and home life of its gangsters in a realistic, understated manner (unlike the romanticized *Godfather*)—at 100 miles an hour and changing direction without warning. *GoodFellas* and *The Age of Innocence*

Fig. 15-5
Raging Bull: *Jake La Motta (Robert De Niro), at home, fighting with his first wife (Lori Anne Flax).*

(faithfully adapted from the novel by Edith Wharton) reveal the absolute stylistic control and the emotional range of the films of his maturity.

Malick, De Palma, and Others

Terrence Malick, who has been influenced by Murnau as much as by George Stevens, and who once taught philosophy, is the film poet of this generation. Until he made a comeback in 1998 with a meditative war film, *The Thin Red Line*, Malick had directed only two features: *Badlands* and, five years later, *Days of Heaven* (1978). Both these films manipulate several complexly contrapuntal lines; both juxtapose violent narrative events with a spectacularly lush and rhythmically languid series of stunning visual images; both use ironic, immature voice-over narrators (Sissy Spacek in *Badlands*, Linda Manz in *Days of Heaven*) who understand, to varying degrees, the events they are involved in and whose unpolished voices contrast tonally with the rigorous,

magnificent shots. Both films are parables of good and evil, but *Badlands* is flatter—and for that, funnier and more frightening; its love anthem is the strange rock song "Love Is Strange," and its narrator thinks in clichés (which, as we compare what she says with what we see, generate narrative complexity). The narrator of *Days of Heaven*, however, is a reliable commentator whose remarks are on target and have their own poetry and wit, without being the least bit arty.

Paul Schrader, like Coppola and Scorsese, came to filmmaking from film school. His scripts for Scorsese (*Taxi Driver*), Brian De Palma (*Obsession*), Sidney Pollack (*The Yakuza*), and others led to directing his own scripts. Raised in a strict Calvinist home and not permitted to see a movie until he was 18 (a background reflected in his *Hardcore*, 1979), Schrader's films explore the repressions and guilt of characters with enormous sexual appetites and inflexible moral codes, characters who are fanatically attracted to ritual and seek redemption through discipline and violence or find it through grace. His first feature, *Blue Collar* (1978), took a sharp and intensely political look at labor unions and at the "divide and conquer" strategy that frustrates class awareness in America. The later films have been more redemptive and philosophical than political, and extremely self-conscious in their rich use of *mise-en-scène*; the finest of these are *American Gigolo* (1980) and *Mishima* (1985). Most of his work is concerned with the expression of spirit in a fallen world.

Brian De Palma began with offbeat projects (*Greetings*, 1968; *Dionysus in '69*, 1970). He graduated to reflexive parodies (*Phantom of the Paradise*, 1974), wonderful horror films (*Carrie*, 1976; *The Fury*, 1978), overproduced gangster pictures (*Scarface*, 1983; *The Untouchables*, 1987), and ingenious thrillers combining Hitchcock psychoses with Roger Corman atrocities (*Sisters*, 1973; *Obsession*, 1976; *Dressed to Kill*, 1980; *Raising Cain*, 1992). His best slow-motion sequence, the one you can't look away from, is in the middle of *The Fury*. His best reflexive intrusion and the first of his major statements on voyeurism and moviemaking is at the end of *Greetings*. His *Carrie* may be the best adaptation of a Stephen King novel. But he went into a big-movie slump. After a string of vacuous big-budget pictures including *Mission: Impossible* (1996), De Palma regained some of his audience with the opening of *Snake Eyes* (1998), a 20-minute sequence shot as remarkable for its sound editing as for its bold, intricate camerawork.

In De Palma's *Mission to Mars* (2000) two historically significant shots define the surround sound field precisely: The first shot, just over half a minute long, rotates a fixed sound source (a video monitor) around to the right of the theatre, not in a square but in a circle, as the camera pans to the left across a cylindrical meeting area in a space ship. At the start of this shot, the camera swings past the monitor, whose sound comes from the front center, and it pans 180° until a character speaks on camera, his voice heard from the front, while the monitor is heard from directly behind. Then there is a reverse-angle cut to the monitor that also reverses the sound field so that the monitor is heard from the front. These were not the first shots to define the sound field's left/right/surround orientation

in terms of the left/right orientations of what was seen on screen, but they were the most exact and deliberate, the most like a map. The earliest stereo and surround fields maintained a consistent orientation regardless of where the camera was pointed; in an auditorium, for instance, the left front side's sound would always come from the left front speaker, and the right front from the right, whether the camera showed the front of the room or the rear; this kept the auditorium a consistent sound environment in the theatre, even if for the second shot in that example the left/right/front/ rear relations of the sound should have been reversed. The surround sound field developed relatively conservatively, took longer to evolve to a shot-specific, changing field—a sound field whose changes (in this example, bouncing the front and rear of the auditorium across the theatre to match a shot/reverse-shot conversation) were at first expected to confuse the audience.

Doubling and disguise are running themes in his work, whether the linked figures are twins, look-alikes, or parts of a multiple personality. His films do not question reality so much as question our knowledge of it. How we know anything about ourselves or each other or the network of danger within which we may be forced to act is the natural subject of the thriller, at which De Palma excels, and an invitation to explore some of the ways of knowing that for him have the greatest cinematic resonance: identification, psychoanalysis, and voyeurism.

Peter Bogdanovich was strongly influenced by the *auteur* theory and its application to the old Hollywood movie. Like many of the French New Wave directors, Bogdanovich began as a film critic, his favorite subjects being Hawks, Ford, and Welles. Bogdanovich's first film, *Targets* (1968), in many ways his cleverest, is a film buff's film, taking its style from the Roger Corman low-budget terror factory (Corman produced the film), complete with Boris Karloff as its star. For *The Last Picture Show* (1971) and *Paper Moon* (1973) Bogdanovich re-created the dry, dusty look of America's rural past—of the 1950s and 1930s, respectively. He also used the textures of American films of those decades, in particular his radical decision to use black and white. The danger of Bogdanovich's pure universe of art and homage is clear in *What's Up, Doc?* (1972) and *At*

Long Last Love (1975), heavy-handed attempts to combine 1930s musical and screwball comedy with contemporary acting techniques and production values. Unlike the *Cahiers* critics who became filmmakers in France, Bogdanovich seems to have little to make movies about except movies or Hollywood.

William Friedkin was the tightest and most impersonal technician of the new directors. Among the problems he has posed himself are translating talky stage plays into cinema (*The Boys in the Band*, 1970); translating the violence of urban police life into kinetic imagery (*The French Connection*, 1971); bringing the devil to the screen with convincing effectiveness (*The Exorcist*, 1973); and capturing the atmosphere of New York's sadomasochistic homosexual underworld (*Cruising*, 1980). Friedkin described his own intention in all his films as that of producing powerful but crude emotional effects—terror, tension, suspense. With the exception of *To Live and Die in L.A.* (1985), most of Friedkin's later films—*Deal of the Century* (1983), *The Guardian* (1990)—have struck audiences as more crudely leaden than crudely exciting.

One of the period's great satirists, Mike Nichols (*Who's Afraid of Virginia Woolf?*; *The Graduate*; *Catch-22*, 1970; *Carnal Knowledge*, 1971), a very successful director of comedies on the stage, made his most important film in 1967 when *The Graduate*—released a few months after *Bonnie and Clyde*—seemed to summarize the attitude of the younger generation toward the hypocritical world of bourgeois adulthood. In the 1980s, Nichols spent most of his time back in the theatre but made two commercially successful films, *Silkwood* (1983) and *Working Girl* (1988). Elaine May, his partner in the 1950s nightclub-and-LP comedy team Nichols and May, has directed several films, the most biting and funny of which are *A New Leaf* (1971) and *The Heartbreak Kid* (1972).

Arthur Penn is a director of the old school (*The Miracle Worker*, 1962) who came to the movies from television dramas and became one of the central figures of the new school. His dominant interest is the creation of folk legends out of outsiders, rebels, and misfits (*Bonnie and Clyde*; *Alice's Restaurant*, 1969; *Little Big Man*, 1970), a concern that, like *The Graduate*, made its greatest impact on younger audiences in the antimyth late 1960s and early 1970s.

Sidney Lumet began as an off-Broadway director, then became a highly efficient TV director. His first movie was typical of his best work: a well-acted, tightly written, deeply considered "problem picture," *12 Angry Men* (1957). Since then, Lumet has divided his energies among idealistic problem pictures (*The Hill*, 1965; *Serpico*, 1973; *The Verdict*, 1982), literate adaptations of plays (*Long Day's Journey Into Night*, 1962) and novels (*The Pawnbroker*, 1965), big stylish pictures (*The Wiz*, 1978), and New York–based black comedies (*Network*, 1976). Lumet's sensitivity to actors and to the rhythms of the city have made him America's longest-lived descendant of the 1950s Neorealist tradition and its urgent commitment to ethical responsibility. *The Hill* is one of the most politically and morally radical films of the 1960s. Beneath the social conflicts of Lumet's films lies the conviction that love and reason will eventually prevail in human affairs, that law and justice will eventually be served—or not.

Like Lumet and Penn, John Frankenheimer directed for TV before making movies. His best picture, *The Manchurian Candidate* (1962, from the novel by Richard Condon), was withdrawn from distribution after the assassination of President Kennedy because it includes a number of political assassinations, one virtually at the presidential level. When it was re-released in 1987, the industry was surprised that audiences would be so interested in an old black-and-white movie that took politics seriously and played games with perception (near the beginning, it cuts between what is seen by characters who have been hypnotized and by those who have not). The best of his later works is *Seconds* (1966), a cautionary tale about the desire to recapture one's youth. Others that merit a look include *Seven Days in May* (1964), *The Fixer* (1968), *The Iceman Cometh* (1973), and *Black Sunday* (1977).

Sam Peckinpah also came to films from television, where he was primarily a writer. Without question, he made the greatest westerns of the 1960s. Peckinpah's three best films study the old men (Randolph Scott and Joel McCrea) who personify the last gasp of the Old West (*Ride the High Country*, 1962), the necessity of defining one's relation to violence (*Straw Dogs*, 1971), and the role of honor in a crummy world (*The Wild Bunch*, 1969).

Most of Peckinpah's films were recut by the studios before release—even *The Wild Bunch* lost ten crucial minutes. Charlton Heston once stood outside the cutting room with a rifle so that Peckinpah could edit *Major Dundee* (1965) without interference—but the film was simply recut after Peckinpah delivered it. The final film of this artist who was, in his own way, an embattled last survivor of the Old West—and whose work amounted to much more than rapid cutting and bloody, slow-motion death sequences—was *The Osterman Weekend* (1983); to see it was not only to feel that it could have been better but to know that it *had* been better.

Whether they are set in the wide open spaces or modern cities, the films of Clint Eastwood are westerns. Like the classic westerns, they define moral stature through the assertion of individual will and the exercise of personal style, and as they pit civilians and outlaws against each other, they examine the values of civilization. From the 1960s "spaghetti westerns" directed by Sergio Leone (*Fistful of Dollars*; *For a Few Dollars More*; *The Good, the Bad and the Ugly*) through the "Dirty Harry" city-crime films of the 1970s and 1980s directed by Don Siegel (*Dirty Harry*, 1971), Ted Post (*Magnum Force*, 1973), and Eastwood himself (*Sudden Impact*, 1983), the Eastwood films depict a society ungovernable by laws, lawmakers, procedures, and bureaucrats.

Eastwood is an accomplished director of action films (*The Enforcer*, 1976), westerns (*High Plains Drifter*, 1973), and thrillers (*Play Misty for Me*, 1971) who also has a serious interest in jazz (*Bird*, 1988). Like *Unforgiven* and *A Perfect World* (1993), most of his pictures show that the world is imperfect and corrupt; his heroes *and* villains seek what order they can. They know when things feel right (*The Bridges of Madison County*, 1995); feel just (*Sudden Impact*); or feel sick, cruel, crazy, and wrong (*Misty*). But sometimes, beyond any question of how they feel, his protagonists *are* wrong; a film of Eastwood's maturity, *Mystic River* (2003), investigates the actions, social forces, and assumptions that distort the world into a place where violence appears the only way to set things right. When a gun is fired in *Mystic River*, the action is tragic rather than fulfilling.

Eastwood's status as a total filmmaker was confirmed when he picked up two Oscars—one as producer and one as director—for the film

voted best picture of 1992, *Unforgiven*, a western that showed the unglamorous reality behind the myth of the gunfighter—and then, without contradicting itself, reaffirmed the power of that myth.

A new generation of horror directors appeared during this period, though some (in America, John Carpenter and Wes Craven; in Canada, David Cronenberg; in Italy, Dario Argento) were not widely known until after 1976. While studio pictures from *Rosemary's Baby* and *The Exorcist* to *Jaws* (Steven Spielberg, 1975) and *Carrie* kept the genre alive in the mainstream, independently produced films catered to the drive-in crowd with explicit gore (Herschell Gordon Lewis's *Blood Feast*, 1963, was the first gore film), sadistic sex and violence (Wes Craven's *The Last House on the Left*, 1972), and troubling fantasy (Herk Harvey's *Carnival of Souls*, 1962).

The most important American horror film since *Psycho* was George A. Romero's *Night of the Living Dead* (1968), a gory, low-budget, black-and-white, tightly organized shocker that remains as frightening and revolting as it is thought-provoking. *Night of the Living Dead* takes a hard look at the world that is in danger of being taken over by flesh-eating zombies, and few of the living measure up; most are selfish, violent, stupid. The strongest, smartest, most resourceful character is played by a black man (Duane Jones), and though he survives the night, he is shot and burned the next morning by a redneck posse—shown in grainy stills and brief shots that resemble 1960s news coverage of racist incidents in the South. The Vietnam War and the civil rights movement made their presence felt in this film, though it did not set out to be a political or racial allegory and simply happened to express—as Expressionist horror often does—the tension of the time with unprecedented force.

The Texas Chain Saw Massacre (1974) was another independent first feature made far from Hollywood (in Texas; *Night of the Living Dead* came from Pittsburgh) that put its director, Tobe Hooper, in the permanent annals of the genre. A deranged family melodrama that lives up to its title, *The Texas Chain Saw Massacre* is painfully violent, grossly repulsive, and full of ghoulish art (like *Psycho*, it was inspired by the case of Ed Gein, the Wisconsin ghoul), for one of its principal subjects is the art of horror.

Fig. 15-6
Kept back by fire, but not for long: the flesh-eating zombies of George Romero's **Night of the Living Dead.**

Stanley Kubrick

Discussions of science fiction in this period inevitably come around to one film: Stanley Kubrick's *2001: A Space Odyssey* (1968), released one year before the first moon landing but still offering a completely realized vision of outer space—which is not surprising, since Kubrick was always such a meticulous and demanding artist. In the early 1960s, Kubrick detached himself from the constraints of American studios to produce films in England, where he died in 1999. A perfectionist who decided on every detail of the film himself, from scripting to editing—with the advantage of being his own producer—Kubrick worked very slowly. His reputation rests on only ten films: *The Killing* (1956), *Paths of Glory* (1957), *Lolita* (1962), *Dr. Strangelove Or: How I Learned To Stop Worrying And Love The Bomb* (1964), *2001, A Clockwork Orange* (1971), *Barry Lyndon* (1975), *The Shining* (1980), *Full Metal Jacket* (1987), and *Eyes Wide Shut* (1999). Kubrick's

early films, *Fear and Desire* (1953) and *Killer's Kiss* (1955), are melodramatic apprentice work, and on *Spartacus* (1960) Kubrick was not the primary director, having been brought in halfway through production by Kirk Douglas.

From the *noir* world of *The Killing* to the military world of *Full Metal Jacket*, the essential Kubrick theme is man's love affair with death. Kubrick seems to be a social critic in that his films consistently rip apart the hypocrisies of polite society: the military society of World War I France (*Paths of Glory*), the pseudointellectual society of suburbia (*Lolita*), the political society of the White House and Pentagon (*Dr. Strangelove*), the sterilized banality of a society of the future (*2001* and *A Clockwork Orange*), the elegant hypocrisies of Europe's 18th-century aristocracy (*Barry Lyndon*). As with Renoir, Kubrick's social evils are human evils; the problem is with human nature. Without a society, men slaughter each other individually, as they do in "The Dawn of Man" sequence in *2001* after the first ape/man discovers the use of a weapon. With society, men slaughter each other *en masse* under the pretext of patriotism, military justice, potency, or national defense.

Kubrick's great cinematic gift is not just his ability to develop this bitterly ironic theme but his gift for finding the right ironic tone—part horror, part humor, a cold mixture of burlesque and Grand Guignol—for developing it. Unlike Renoir, Kubrick does not always appear to care about his characters; sometimes it is as if he puts them in boldly decorated freezers, to calculate their behavior and cackle at their struggles. But there is compassion, even vulnerability, in his long look at the married couple in *Eyes Wide Shut*; there is sorrow in *Full Metal Jacket*, rage in *Paths of Glory*, awe in *2001*. There is a tone of sympathy in *Barry Lyndon* that modifies the cold irony—but the merciless, cynical, sardonic, ironic tone is relentless in *Lolita, A Clockwork Orange, The Shining*, much of *2001*, all of *Dr. Strangelove*, at the end of *Full Metal Jacket*, and wherever else it pleased Kubrick to weave it into his work, from the cold vantage point of his masterfully controlled compositions.

Dr. Strangelove is the fullest and the least ponderous expression of the Kubrick theme and tone. The film begins with an audacious visual joke: Two jet planes, one refueling the other in mid-air, appear to be copulating. Kubrick emphasizes the gag by underscoring the planes' passion with a lush romantic version of the popular tune, "Try a Little Tenderness." As it turns out, the whole film synthesizes copulation and death. The American general, Buck Turgidson (George C. Scott) acts the same in the bedroom with his sweetie as he does in the War Room discussing the bomb crisis. The crazed army commander, Jack Ripper (Sterling Hayden), develops his whole theory about the Commies attacking his "precious bodily fluids" with fluoridated water based on how depleted he felt after making love. The American pilots in the atomic bomber work feverishly to drop their bomb on the Rooskies although the plane has been critically damaged. When they finally succeed in dropping it, the plane's commander (Slim Pickens) rides the bomb down to his destruction, whooping like a cowboy on a bronco, the bomb looking exactly like an enormous surrogate phallus.

For decades people have made films about the threat of nuclear war. If *Dr. Strangelove* still seems as fresh and pointed as any of them, that is because it never deserts its caustic analysis of causes for the effects of pathos (*On the Beach*), heavy dialogue (*Fail-Safe*), realistic horror (*The War Game*), or reassuring solutions.

2001: A Space Odyssey really is two films, one mystical, one cynical, which Kubrick holds in balance. On the one hand, Kubrick's astronauts travel toward the meaning of life itself, the life force that has specifically planted metal slabs on Earth, beneath the surface of the moon, and near

Fig. 15-7

Fig. 15-8
Full Metal Jacket: *Kubrick's relentless parody of the Vietnam War takes the recruits from the point where they are taught by the machine to be part of the machine (Fig. 15-7) to their survival or death in combat (Fig. 15-8, one of the few images to acknowledge the high number of black casualties in the war).*

Jupiter at the "dawn of time," in order to influence human progress—and reward it at the correct stage, for in order to find the moon's monolith, human technology would have to have developed to the point of landing people on the moon. Thus the mysterious silent slabs are both beacons and goads, and the central theme of the film is evolution. The first slab provokes the discovery of the first tool, a discovery that culminates in the invention of rocket ships and computers. Kubrick's brilliant cut from the soaring bone to the floating space shuttle visually establishes the connection between these tools. The second slab provokes the Jupiter Mission, which takes human beings to their next stage of evolution, "beyond the infinite." After some form of education and maturation in a strange room, the life mystery sends the reborn astronaut back to Earth in a different kind of space capsule— a womblike bubble. Another stage of evolution begins with this starchild. This metaphysical theme

Fig. 15-9

Dr. Strangelove: *Farcical madmen decide the fate of the world. Dr. Strangelove (Peter Sellers, Fig. 15-9) and General Buck Turgidson (George C. Scott, right, Fig. 15-10) in the War Room.*

Fig. 15-10

necessarily remains elusive; the monoliths and the force behind them are never explained—which leaves the feeling of metaphysical mystery intact.

The Independent American Cinema

The Independent American Cinema has been called by many names: the American Underground, the American Avant-Garde, the New American Cinema, and the Experimental American Cinema among them. By whatever name, an alternative cinema tradition has existed in the United States since the 1920s with a series of assumptions that differ markedly from those of the commercial American cinema. This cinema is highly personal and individual (often one person literally makes the entire film); like poetry, it has virtually no commercial aspirations; and it is necessarily revolutionary in structure, or visual technique, or intellectual attitude, or all three. These personal, experimental films first attracted wide attention in the late 1950s. Nevertheless, the American avant-garde, independent, poetic cinema was not particularly a 1950s or even a 1960s movement. Rather, a tradition of avant-garde filmmaking that had grown along with, and been influenced by, the avant-garde cinema of Europe since the 1920s, and that had its own major films and figures and movements all along, went through a particularly creative phase just when public interest in film as an art was at its height.

There are three conflicting critical attitudes about the Independent American Cinema. For some, it represents the narcissistic visual scribblings of the lunatic fringe whose work is ultimately irrelevant to the development of serious film art (that is, commercial, narrative, feature-length "art films"). In support of this position, it is probably true that a vast majority of American filmgoers has never even heard of the most respected Independent filmmakers. A second position finds the Independent American Cinema a fertile testing ground for techniques and devices that are later absorbed and practiced by the mainstream of filmmaking (that is, commercial, feature-length narrative films). In support of this position one can point to the influence of the French avant-garde on the later features of Clair, Epstein, Cocteau, and Buñuel (all of whom came out of the avant-garde), as well as the fact that

many of the stylistic devices and moral attitudes of the commercial films of the 1960s and 1970s (their sensuality, the use of slow motion, multiple exposure, accelerated motion, rock music, *musique concrète*, computer graphics, shock cutting, split screen) were first seen in Independent films. Yet a third position finds the Independent American Cinema the only significant and serious works of film art in America. In support of this position, they observe that these are the only films free of commercial pressures, totally dependent on the vision of a single artist, and totally aligned with the parallel movements in modern painting, music, and poetry. The business of these independent films is perception: the way the devices of an art can aid, extend, and complicate one's ability to perceive inner and outer realities. That goal might be taken as the ultimate intention of all the Modernist arts.

Early History

Rather than engaging in this controversy of values, it would be useful simply to trace the history of this movement, to define its principles and principal types, and to mention the accomplishments of its most distinctive filmmakers. The tendency of the earliest avant-garde American films (in the 1920s and 1930s) was to avoid the Hollywood assumptions by making films of pure visual form, films that were, in effect, moving paintings. Ralph Steiner's H_2O (1929), which is composed exclusively of images of light reflecting on water, begins with beautiful and recognizable images (say, raindrops splashing in a rippling stream) and steadily becomes more abstract, so that the shots of light and shimmering water cease to look like anything except waving abstractions (a sort of moving Klee or Pollock painting).

The best early films of pure form, movement, rhythm, and (later) music were made not in America, however, but in Europe. In the Silent Era, Hans Richter and Viking Eggeling excelled in rhythmically moving forms that also manipulated the restrictions of black and white. For example, Richter's *Rhythmus 21* (1921) features a variety of kinds of rhythmic movement: Rectangular shapes move about the screen, they change their sizes and shapes (expanding and contracting into lines, squares, trapezoids, and so forth), and they change their shades (shifting from white on black to black

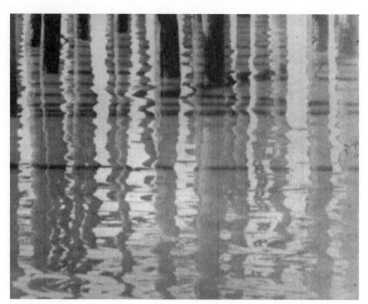

*H₂O: the abstract play of
moving light and water.*

Fig. 15-11

on white to gray on black, etc.). Fernand Léger's *Ballet mécanique* (1924) was another film that strongly influenced the Americans. In effect, these films became dances of color and shape. Other European filmmakers of the 1920s and 1930s—along with the Americans Man Ray (who worked in Europe) and Webber and Watson—whose influence on later independent film poets was strong include Buñuel and Dalí, Alberto Cavalcanti, René Clair, Jean Cocteau, Marcel Duchamp, Dimitri Kirsanov, and Walter Ruttmann.

The most important American independent filmmaker of the 1940s was Maya Deren (born Eleanora Derenkowsky in Kiev), who combined her interests in dance, in voodoo, and in subjective, phenomenological psychology in a series of surreal perceptual films. *Meshes of the Afternoon* (1943) uses a series of repeating dreamlike motifs—a shadow walking down a garden path, a flower, a key, a knife, a telephone receiver, attempts to mount a flight of stairs—that prefigure the use of similarly repeating motifs in *Last Year at Marienbad* almost two decades later. Deren attacks objective reality by metamorphosizing the knife into the key, the flower into the knife, and by combining suggestions of chastity, sexuality, and death without the audience's ever being able to pull the complexly

woven themes apart to make solid sense of them. The motifs weave together musically and subconsciously rather than rationally, tangling the viewer in a systematic labyrinth of unresolvable resonances. As such, the film serves as a clear bridge between the Surrealism of *Un Chien andalou* and the dream-realities of *Marienbad, Persona*, and *8½*. Her very brief *A Study in Choreography for Camera: Pas de Deux* (1945), which, like most of her films, is silent, combines Deren's two dominant interests—the movement through space of dance and the movement of space through editing—to reveal how editing may create the impression of continuous motion through discontinuous space.

The New Film Poets
Greatly influenced by Maya Deren and Marie Menken, the American avant-garde began building itself into a movement in the mid-1950s—aided by the expanding availability of 8mm and 16mm equipment—with the recognition of the work of a great many major filmmakers. Joseph Cornell and Harry Smith, who preceded Deren, made their first films in 1939. Mary Ellen Bute began work a decade before that. Marie Menken started as the cinematographer of *Geography of the Body* (1943), directed by

Fig. 15-12
Maya Deren meets herself in **Meshes of the Afternoon.**

her husband, Willard Maas, whom she photographed with his male lover. She soon began her own career with sweeping hand-held images of sculptor Noguchi's works, followed by a series of gently critical visions of her husband's homosexual life, metaphorically using everything from microscopic sperm to the huge Versailles. Her epic "city film" *Go! Go! Go!* (1964) was imitated by filmmakers as diverse as Godfrey Reggio (*Koyaanisqatsi*, 1983) and Jonas Mekas.

American independents who began to make films in the 1940s, and of course continued to work for decades, include Kenneth Anger, James Broughton, Rudy Burckhardt, Douglas Crockwell, Maya Deren, Dwinell Grant, Alexander Hammid, Curtis Harrington, Hy Hirsch, Willard Maas, Gregory Markopoulos, Marie Menken, Sidney Peterson, Frank Stauffacher, James Whitney, and John Whitney. European film poets starting at the same time included Georges Franju and Humphrey Jennings.

The 1950s saw the first films of Jordan Belson, Stan Brakhage, Robert Breer, Shirley Clarke, Bruce Conner, James Davis, Robert Gardner, Ian Hugo, Ken Jacobs, Larry Jordan, Helen Levitt, Christopher MacLaine, Ron Rice, and Stan VanDerBeek. In Europe novelist Jean Genet was making films, as were Jean Isidore Isou, Kurt Kren, and Peter Kubelka; in Canada there was Jack Chambers.

In the 1960s, they were joined by Bruce Baillie, Robert Beavers, Les Blank, Nathaniel Dorsky, Ed Emshwiller, Hollis Frampton, Ernie Gehr, James Herbert, Will Hindle, George Kuchar, Mike Kuchar, George Landow, Saul Levine, Adolfas Mekas, Jonas Mekas, Richard Meyers, Gunvor Nelson, Robert Nelson, Andrew Noren, Pat O'Neill, Peter Rose, Carolee Schneemann, John Luther Schofill, Paul Sharits, Jack Smith, Chick Strand, Michael Wallin, and Andy Warhol. Takahiko Iimura was working in Japan; Dr. Noel Brinckmann, Werner Nekes, and Dore O were in Europe; and Keewatnin Dewdney, David Rimmer, Michael Snow, and Joyce Wieland were in Canada.

Since the 1950s, the Independent Cinema has tended to gravitate toward four vague but recognizable "genres": the formal, the social–satirical, the sexual, and the reflexive, although these categories are neither rigid nor mutually exclusive.

The film of pure form, one of the oldest experimental styles of cinema, persisted in the American Underground, much of it influenced by the earlier work of Fischinger, Léger, and Lye. Among the outstanding formal dances are the computer films of John Whitney, who, like Fischinger, combines his ceaselessly changing color-forms with synchronized music (*Catalog*, 1961; *Permutations*, 1968; *Matrix*, 1971).

Other films in the formal tradition include those of Jordan Belson (*Mandala*, 1953; *Allures*, 1961; *Re-Entry*, 1964; *Phenomena*, 1965; *Samadhi*, 1967), whose meditational colors and forms flowed into the commercial mainstream with the astronaut's shimmering visions in Philip Kaufman's *The Right Stuff* (1983). Many of the animated films of Robert Breer are sorts of spatial dancing: *Blazes* (1961), which smashes the viewer with 24 different images per second (more an attack than a "dance"); *66* (1966), another sequence of evolving forms and colors.

Bruce Conner is the funniest and most reflexive of the social satirists; he is essentially an editor, and his best films (*A Movie*, 1958; *Cosmic Ray*, 1961; *Report*, 1963–67; *Marilyn × Five*, 1965) cleverly splice together existing stock footage to make their satirical point. Conner's movie implies that the business of the movies is to chronicle and eroticize catastrophe. Humans are his machines (and the movie is also the product of a machine), and the machines produce death and disaster. Stanley Kubrick's juxtaposition of stock footage with ironic music in the closing sequence of *Dr. Strangelove* clearly derived from Conner's *A Movie*.

Equally satirical is Stan VanDerBeek's *Breath-death* (1963), which combines his interest in collage and cartooning with his own apocalyptic vision of a society warring, breathing, and boring itself to death. Tom DeWitt's *Atmosfear* (1967) is a satirical view of "pollution": of the air, of the landscapes (with ugly factories and smokestacks and architecture), of the cities (with repressive and restrictive signs), and, ultimately, of the mind.

Yet another kind of satirical "underground" film burlesques the business of aboveground movie making (also an implication of the Bruce Conner films), for society's art mirrors society's values. The comical, usually camp films in this tradition are those of the Kuchar brothers (*Sins of the Fleshapoids*, 1965, by Mike, and *Hold Me While I'm Naked*, 1966, by George) and some of the early films of Andy Warhol (*Harlot*, 1965; *The Chelsea Girls*, 1966).

The satires are close cousins to the sexually oriented films, whose studies of "abnormal" sexuality often comment satirically on society's concepts of normality. The master in the field was Kenneth Anger, the son of a famous Hollywood agent of its Golden Age.

Anger's most important film, *Scorpio Rising*, is an examination of the practices, perversions, and paraphernalia of the motorcycle "man." The motorcycle freak's worship of the macho external is, Anger implies, a literal cover-up of his homosexual essence, and Anger uses the soundtrack to comment contrapuntally (and comically) on this gap between self and projected self-image. Popular rock-and-roll tunes of the era (a clear precursor of *Easy Rider*) dominate the soundtrack, and at one point, as the cyclist adoringly dons his macho Levi's, the song goes, "She Wore Blue Velvet." Anger's film served as the basis for several of the country's crucial obscenity test cases, first seized and then judged not obscene by the State of New York in 1965. This film alone was responsible for the demise of that censorship board, a reminder that "underground" films, because of their artistic seriousness, have played a major role in American social history as test cases for definitions of pornography.

Fig. 15-13
Kenneth Anger seeks to complete himself in Fireworks.

Ken Jacobs has made films in the sexual—social–satirical tradition (*The Death of P'town*, 1961; *Blonde Cobra*, 1963), though he is better known for his Structuralist, reflexive films (*Little Stabs at Happiness*, 1963; *Soft Rain*, 1968; *Tom, Tom, the Piper's Son*, 1971).

The fourth kind of Independent film, the cinematically self-conscious, reflexive one, also attacks the commonly accepted assumptions of what a movie is or ought to be. As the term *reflexive* (or the redundant but widely used *self-reflexive*) implies, these films are meditations on themselves—as works of film art. As meditations, these films consciously test the possible definitions of cinema and its processes, revealing the different purposes to which cinema can be put.

Stan Brakhage is the most lyrical, poetic, and romantic of the reflexive filmmakers. Brakhage combines the Romantic's investigation of nature, innocence, and experience with the Modernist's meditation on the processes and materials of his art. For Brakhage, the love of film intensifies the love of life and nature, and his films simultaneously celebrate both the world and the remaking of the world with cinema. Brakhage treats celluloid itself as a living, organic substance—growing mold on it (which he calls "a little garden"), baking film in the oven, cutting individual frames of film into pieces and reassembling them as celluloid collages, scratching and painting directly onto the celluloid, assembling an entire film (*Mothlight*, 1963) by scattering bits of leaves, flowers, seeds, and moths' wings on pieces of Mylar splicing tape and then printing the results.

One of Brakhage's most important works is *Dog Star Man* (1961–64), a 79-minute silent work (allowing exclusive concentration on the dense visual imagery) in four parts plus a Prelude. This mythic film combines an adoration of nature (mountains, forests, snow, moon, mists, clouds, sun) with the tortuous journey of a man (Brakhage himself) and his dog up a mountainside to create Brakhage's cosmological view of man's relation to the universe, shaped by his ability to translate his visions into works of art. Perhaps the most stunning of his later achievements is *The Dante Quartet* (1982–87), a series of four hand-painted films that takes the viewer from Hell to Paradise: *Hell Itself*, *Hell Spit Flexion* (on 35mm stock), *Purgation* (on 70mm stock), and *existence is song* (on Imax stock, each frame a nearly 3-inch by 4-inch layered painting, up to ⅛-inch thick). These short, silent, hypnagogic films are fast, gripping, visionary. The title of one of Brakhage's major works, *The Text of Light* (1974), a lengthy abstract study of the prismatic play of light beams in a glass ashtray, might serve as the key to all his texts of light.

After nearly dying of cancer and going through chemotherapy in the mid-1990s, Brakhage said that he wished "to leave something like a snail's trail in the moonlight." He abandoned the paints and dyes it had turned out his body was unable to tolerate, but he did not give up on the "hand-tooled film." Although he made some films with a camera (*Commingled Containers*, 1997, a tight, macrophotographic look at underwater air-bubble formation, contrasted with the surface of the rushing stream), most of his energy went into a primarily handmade film begun in 1996 and called ". . ." (or, for convenience, *Ellipsis*). This long film is divided into reels, not parts, that can be shown in any order; some are in black and white, some are in color, some have sound, some are collaborations. In this "effort to avoid language," Brakhage scratched film leaders of various colors (and some photographed footage), then printed them—superimposed, in negative,

and so forth—to create a further variety of color. Unlike Len Lye and others who scratched animation, in ". . ." Brakhage was scratching "moving visual thinking." Right up to his death in 2003, his efforts and artistic passions remained romantic and analytic, documentary and fantastic, phenomenological and synaptic, pursuing, as Gertrude Stein did, a simultaneous perception and expression of the exact, changing nature of being.

Although strongly influenced by Brakhage and by Ken Jacobs, Phil Solomon's work is original. He has made all of his films on an optical printer, one multilayered frame at a time, in a meditation whose time is measured by the vertical line of sprocket holes, not by the circle of hours. They include *What's Out Tonight Is Lost* (1983), *The Secret Garden* (1988), and *Remains To Be Seen* (1989, revised 1994).

Bruce Baillie combines Brakhage's romantic consciousness of nature with the social analyst's perception of the corruption of modern life. *Mass for the Dakota Sioux* (1964) and *Quixote* (1964–65) examine the ways in which the pioneer spirit of America—as symbolized by its original inhabitants—has been corrupted by the building of cities, the buying and selling of food, the digging and erecting of edifices by machines. Just as Brakhage recorded his own life in a cinema diary, *Scenes from Under Childhood* (1967–70), Baillie constructed his own autobiographical cinema diary, *Quick Billy* (1967–71). Perhaps the most dedicated of the film diarists is Jonas Mekas, who seeks subjective and objective authenticity with the concentration of a jazz musician on the moment, recording his life and the course of his art: *Diaries, Notes and Sketches (Walden)* (1968); *Lost Lost Lost* (1976).

The films of Hollis Frampton were more logical exercises than romantic quests. *Zorns Lemma* (1970), a complex, three-part, hour-long film, was probably Frampton's most important—and most difficult—work. The first section of the film uses sounds without images—dominated by blackness; the second, images without sounds—dominated by colors; its third part combines word and image—dominated by whiteness—in a single, apparently unbroken 12-minute shot (whereas the second part used editing extensively—2,592 images of 1 second each). A man,

Clepsydra: *Phil Solomon's frame-by-frame meditation on time and memory, light and water, and the fight for clarity under a torrent of interference and emotion.*

Fig. 15-14

woman, and dog cross a snowy white field as a group of female voices recites a visionary text according to a strict, 1-second, metronomic beat (the aural equivalent of 24 frames per second). The point of Frampton's mathematical and alphabetical games is to reveal how insidiously our vision and knowledge are constricted by our methods of seeing and knowing. To create a new alphabet of images is to see the world and the means of recording it differently.

Perhaps the most celebrated and controversial of the reflexive films came from Canada rather than America: Michael Snow's *Wavelength* (1967)—the film credited with establishing the Structuralist film movement—which is, on its surface, nothing more than an agonizingly slow 45-minute zoom shot through a single loft. In the course of this inexorable forward zoom, human figures wander into the space of the frame—two men who move a bookcase, two women who listen to the radio, a man who breaks into the loft and collapses on the floor, a young woman who uses the telephone—but all of these humans leave the frame (or the frame leaves them—as it does the man on the floor, when it zooms past his body), never to return. These people, and whatever pattern of narrative causality has brought them

to this particular space, are never developed, investigated, or explicated. The usual center of human interest for the usual movie is not at all central to this film.

Wavelength takes its chosen space as its most important subject (and the most important characteristic of any framed image); what else does a frame frame other than space itself? So for Snow, human actions are significant only when and if they happen to intersect with that framed space—and they are no more important than anything else in that space.

A film like *Wavelength* once again raises the question about the significance of the Independent American and Canadian Cinema. On the one hand, the critic can respond to *Wavelength* with a "So what?" Space that lacks human significance is empty and boring. Cinema space is meaningful only if it has been invested with meaning. On the other hand, the critic can respond to *Wavelength* as one of the most perfect expressions of the cinema condition (that movies necessarily frame spaces) as well as one of the most perfect means of educating us about the human condition—that cinema can provoke viewers to perceive the mystery, the expressiveness, and the variety of the shapes around them, not only in the frame but in the world.

For Further Viewing

FILMS

WOODY ALLEN (1935–   )
What's Up, Tiger Lily? (1966)
Bananas (1971)
Sleeper (1973)
Love and Death (1975)
Annie Hall (1977)
Manhattan (1979)
Stardust Memories (1980)
Zelig (1983)
Broadway Danny Rose (1984)
Hannah and Her Sisters (1986)
Crimes and Misdemeanors (1989)

ROBERT ALTMAN (1925–   )
MASH or *M*A*S*H* (1970)
Brewster McCloud (1970)
McCabe & Mrs. Miller (1971)
The Long Goodbye (1973)
Nashville (1975)
Vincent & Theo (1990)
The Player (1992)

PETER BOGDANOVICH (1939–   )
Targets (1968)
The Last Picture Show (1971)
Paper Moon (1973)

MEL BROOKS (1926–   )
The Producers (1968)
Blazing Saddles (1974)
Young Frankenstein (1974)
High Anxiety (1977)
Spaceballs (1987)

JOHN CASSAVETES (1929–89)
Shadows (1959). Earlier version shown 1958
Faces (1968)
Minnie and Moskowitz (1971)
A Woman Under the Influence (1974).
    Completed 1973
The Killing of a Chinese Bookie (1976). Recut 1978
Opening Night (1978)
Love Streams (1984)

FRANCIS FORD COPPOLA (1939–   )
The Godfather (1972)
The Conversation (1974)
The Godfather Part II (1974)

Apocalypse Now (1979)
One from the heart or *One From The Heart*
    (1982)
Rumble Fish (1983)
The Godfather Part III (1990)
Apocalypse Now Redux (2001). Completed
    2000

BRIAN DE PALMA (1940–   )
Obsession (1976)
Carrie (1976)
The Fury (1978)
Blow Out (1981)
Body Double (1984)
Mission to Mars (2000)

CLINT EASTWOOD (1930–   )
Play Misty For Me (1971)
Bird (1988)
Unforgiven (1992)
Mystic River (2003)
Million Dollar Baby (2004)

STANLEY KUBRICK (1928–99)
The Killing (1956)
Paths of Glory (1957)
Spartacus (1960)
Lolita (1962)
*Dr. Strangelove Or: How I Learned To Stop
    Worrying And Love The Bomb* (1964)
2001: A Space Odyssey (1968)
A Clockwork Orange (1971)
Barry Lyndon (1975)
The Shining (1980)
Full Metal Jacket (1987)
Eyes Wide Shut (1999)

TERRENCE MALICK (1943–   )
Badlands (1973)
Days of Heaven (1978)
The Thin Red Line (1998)

MIKE NICHOLS (1931–   )
Who's Afraid of Virginia Woolf? (1966)
The Graduate (1967)
Catch-22 (1970)
Carnal Knowledge (1971)
Primary Colors (1998)

ALAN J. PAKULA (1928–98)
Klute (1971)
The Parallax View (1974)
All the President's Men (1976)

Sophie's Choice (1982)
The Pelican Brief (1993)

SAM PECKINPAH (1925–84)
Ride the High Country (1962)
Major Dundee (1965)
The Wild Bunch (1969)
The Ballad of Cable Hogue (1970)
Straw Dogs (1971)

ARTHUR PENN (1922–)
The Miracle Worker (1962)
Bonnie and Clyde (1967)
Alice's Restaurant (1969)
Little Big Man (1970)

PAUL SCHRADER (1946–)
Blue Collar (1978)
Hardcore (1979)
American Gigolo (1980)
Mishima (1985)
Affliction (1998). Completed 1997

MARTIN SCORSESE (1942–)
Mean Streets (1973)
Taxi Driver (1976)
The Last Waltz (1978)
Raging Bull (1980)
The Last Temptation of Christ (1988)
GoodFellas (1990)
The Age of Innocence (1993)
Gangs of New York (2002)

HOLLYWOOD RENAISSANCE MISCELLANY
To Kill a Mockingbird (Robert Mulligan, 1962)
Cool Hand Luke (1967, Stuart Rosenberg)
The Dirty Dozen (1967, Robert Aldrich)
Point Blank (1967, John Boorman)
Night of the Living Dead (George A. Romero, 1968)
In Cold Blood (1967, Richard Brooks)
Bullitt (1968, Peter Yates)
Planet of the Apes (1968, Franklin J. Schaffner)
Salesman (1968, Albert Maysles, David Maysles, and Charlotte Zwerin)
Easy Rider (1969, Dennis Hopper)
Medium Cool (1969, Haskell Wexler)
Midnight Cowboy (1969, John Schlesinger)
Butch Cassidy and the Sundance Kid (1969, George Roy Hill)
True Grit (1969, Henry Hathaway)
Putney Swope (1969, Robert Downey)

The Learning Tree (1969, Gordon Parks)
Bob & Carol & Ted & Alice (1969, Paul Mazursky)
Woodstock: 3 Days of Peace & Music (1970, Michael Wadleigh)
Beneath the Planet of the Apes (1970, Ted Post)
Patton (1970, Franklin J. Schaffner)
Five Easy Pieces (1970, Bob Rafelson)
Dirty Harry (1971, Don Siegel)
The French Connection (1971, William Friedkin)
Shaft (1971, Gordon Parks)
Sweet Sweetback's Baad Asssss Song (1971, Melvin Van Peebles)
Billy Jack (1971, Tom Laughlin)
Little Murders (1971, Alan Arkin)
Willy Wonka & the Chocolate Factory (1971, Mel Stuart)
Tomorrow (1972, Joseph Anthony)
The Heartbreak Kid (1972, Elaine May)
Sounder (1972, Martin Ritt)
Deliverance (1972, John Boorman)
The Sting (1973, George Roy Hill)
The Exorcist (1973, William Friedkin)
The Way We Were (1973, Sydney Pollack)
The Texas Chain Saw Massacre (1974, Tobe Hooper)
The Front (1976, Martin Ritt)
Mikey and Nicky (1976, Elaine May). Shot 1973
The Omen (1976, Richard Donner)
Rocky (1976, John G. Avildsen)
Leadbelly (1976, Gordon Parks)
Being There (Harold Ashby, 1979)

AMERICAN INDEPENDENT CINEMA

The Fall of the House of Usher (1928, James Sibley Watson and Melville Webber)
H₂O (1929, Ralph Steiner)
Allegretto (1936, Oskar Fischinger)
Meshes of the Afternoon (1943, Maya Deren). Soundtrack added 1959
Ritual in Transfigured Time (1946, Maya Deren)
Fireworks (1947, Kenneth Anger)
Mother's Day (1948, James Broughton)
Begone Dull Care (1949, Norman McLaren, Canada)
Loony Tom the Happy Lover (1951, James Broughton)
Mandala (1953, Jordan Belson)

Analogies #1 (1953, James Davis)
The Wonder Ring (1955, Stan Brakhage)
Anticipation of the Night (1958, Stan Brakhage)
A Movie (1958, Bruce Conner)
Cosmic Ray (1961, Bruce Conner)
Guns of the Trees (1961, Jonas Mekas)
Allures (1961, Jordan Belson)
Blazes (1961, Robert Breer)
Blonde Cobra (1963, Ken Jacobs)
Scorpio Rising (1963, Kenneth Anger)
Mothlight (1963, Stan Brakhage)
Sleep (1963, Andy Warhol)
Flaming Creatures (1963, Jack Smith)
Little Stabs at Happiness (1963, Ken Jacobs)
To Parsifal (1963, Bruce Baillie)
Breathdeath. A Trageede in Masks (1963, Stan VanDerBeek)
Mass for the Dakota Sioux (1963–64, Bruce Baillie)
Dog Star Man (1961–64, Stan Brakhage)
The Art of Vision (1961–65, Stan Brakhage)
Oh Dem Watermelons (1965, Robert Nelson)
Relativity (1966, Ed Emshwiller)
The Chelsea Girls (1966, Andy Warhol)
Wavelength (1967, Michael Snow, Canada)
Pas de deux (1967, Norman McLaren)
Trash (1968, Andy Warhol and Paul Morrissey)
Diaries, Notes and Sketches (Walden) (1968, Jonas Mekas)
←——→ (1969, Michael Snow)
The Man Who Envied Women (1985, Yvonne Rainer)
The Dante Quartet (1982–87, Stan Brakhage)
Moon Streams (2000, Mary Beth Reed)
Occam's Thread (2000, Stan Brakhage)
The Jesus Trilogy and *Coda* (2001, Stan Brakhage)

DVDs

by **Brakhage**—*an anthology* (see Chap. 1 list).
Chinatown (1974, **Roman Polanski**). Paramount Home Video. Widescreen Collection. Includes interviews with Polanski, writer **Robert Towne**, and producer **Robert Evans**.
A Clockwork Orange (1971, **Stanley Kubrick**). Creative Design Art Inc. Limited Edition Collector's Set. Includes a frame of 35mm film and a booklet; letterboxed (unusual for this title).

Dawn of the Dead Ultimate Edition (1978–79, **George A. Romero** and **Dario Argento**). Anchor Bay. Includes all three versions: the release cut (127 min., Romero's favorite), the European cut re-edited by Dario Argento (118 min.), and the extended edition premiered at Cannes (139 min., preferred by many), along with several documentaries (including *Document of the Dead*), commentaries by all concerned, an original commercial for the Monroeville Mall, many shorts, and more.
Dr. Strangelove Or: How I Learned To Stop Worrying And Love The Bomb (1964, **Stanley Kubrick**). Columbia TriStar. 40th Anniversary Special Edition. Includes the feature with the correctly changing aspect ratios; documentaries on Kubrick and Sellers; interviews with Robert McNamara and others; an essay by film critic Roger Ebert; and a split-screen interview with stars **Peter Sellers** and **George C. Scott**.
Easy Rider (1969, **Dennis Hopper**). Columbia TriStar. Includes commentary by Hopper and a documentary featuring interviews with star **Peter Fonda**, Hopper, and others.
The Fall of the House of Usher is in *Treasures from American Film Archives* (see Chap. 1 list).
The French Connection (1971, **William Friedkin**). Twentieth Century Fox. Includes a commentary by Friedkin, deleted scenes, a BBC documentary, and scene-specific comments by stars **Gene Hackman** and **Roy Scheider**.
The Godfather DVD Collection (1972–90, **Francis Ford Coppola**). Contains the three features; the extra scenes included in the chronologically re-edited *Godfather Saga*; a making-of documentary; shorts on the music, cinematography, etc.; and a Corleone family tree.
John Cassavetes: Five Films (see Chap. 1 list).
Martin Scorsese Collection (1969–90, **Martin Scorsese**). Warner Home Video. Contains *Who's That Knocking At My Door, Mean Streets* (Special Edition), *Alice Doesn't Live Here Anymore, After Hours*, and *Goodfellas* (2-disc Special Edition), all with commentary by Scorsese.
Medium Cool (1969, **Haskell Wexler**). Paramount Home Video. Commentary by Wexler and others.

Nashville (1975, **Robert Altman**). Paramount Home Video. Commentary by Altman.

Night of the Living Dead (1968, **George A. Romero**). Elite Entertainment. Millennium Edition. Includes the final interview with star **Duane Jones**, commentary by Romero and several cast members, and early commercials and shorts by Romero.

OffOn is in *Treasures from American Film Archives* (see Chap. 1 list).

Salesman (1968, **Albert Maysles**, **David Maysles**, and **Charlotte Zwerin**). Criterion Collection. **Digitally restored**. Includes an interview with Albert and David Maysles, commentary by Albert Maysles and Zwerin, filmographies, and the original trailer.

Spartacus (1960, **Stanley Kubrick**). Criterion Collection. The only DVD offering **Robert A. Harris**'s complete **restored** edition. Includes deleted scenes; interviews with stars **Peter Ustinov** and **Jean Simmons**; the first **Blacklist** documentary, *The Hollywood Ten*, and further information on the Blacklist; storyboards by **Saul Bass**; a **restoration** demonstration; writer **Dalton Trumbo**'s scene-by-scene analysis; and a commentary by novelist **Howard Fast**, star–producer **Kirk Douglas**, Peter Ustinov, Robert Harris, Saul Bass, and others.

Straw Dogs (1971, **Sam Peckinpah**). Criterion Collection. Includes a documentary on Peckinpah.

Targets (1968, **Peter Bogdanovich**). Paramount Home Video. Commentary by Bogdanovich.

The Texas Chain Saw Massacre (1974, **Tobe Hooper**). Pioneer Video. Includes a commentary by Hooper, cinematographer **Daniel Pearl**, and star **Gunnar Hansen**.

To Kill a Mockingbird (1962, **Robert Mulligan**). Universal. Commentary by Mulligan and producer **Alan J. Pakula**.

The Wild Bunch: The Original Director's Cut (1969, **Sam Peckinpah**). Warner Studios. Contains the 145-minute cut (longer than the release version) and a documentary.

Young Frankenstein (1974, **Mel Brooks**). Twentieth Century Fox. Special Edition. Commentary by Brooks.

16

National Cinemas 2: 1968–

As in the first two decades after the Second World War, new national cinemas have attracted international attention since the political upheavals of the late 1960s, promoted by the international film festivals, supported by their governments or national television systems, and welcomed by audiences and critics. The most exciting new movements were those in Germany, Australia, and that collection of developing nations vaguely called the Third World, although the increasing internationalism of film production was as striking as any single national movement.

Das neue Kino

For 35 years, from 1932 to 1967, Germany produced very few films of international significance. Among the scattered postwar German films to be exported were Kurt Hoffmann's *Aren't We Wonderful?* (1958), a terrific political comedy, and Swiss-born Bernhard Wicki's *The Bridge* (1959), the story of a group of German schoolchildren who were killed while defending a worthless bridge in the last days of the war. Volker Schlöndorff's *Young Törless* (1966), which parallels sadomasochistic torture in a boy's school with the moral and psychological conditions for Nazism in Hitler's Germany, was either the last of these occasional German films to achieve international recognition or the first representative of the new and genuine German film movement.

In 1960 the German film industry produced some 70 feature films, almost exclusively for local consumption in their simple themes and conventional styles. The Oberhausen Manifesto, formulated by 26 German screenwriters and directors at the Oberhausen Film Festival of 1962, called for a "new German cinema," free from the stifling habits and conventions of the German film industry. Through its leaders, especially Alexander Kluge (*Yesterday Girl*, 1966; *Strongman Ferdinand*, 1975), the group successfully pressured the West German legislature to set up a film board and allocate subsidies for film production in 1967. The new German cinema flowed from these subsidies.

In the late 1960s and early 1970s appeared the first feature films of three young German filmmakers—Werner Herzog (*Signs of Life*, 1968), Rainer Werner Fassbinder (*Love Is Colder Than Death*, 1969), and Wim Wenders (*Summer in the City*, 1970; *The Goalie's Anxiety at the Penalty Kick*, 1971). All three were born within a few years of one another (Herzog in 1942, Wenders in 1945, Fassbinder in 1946); each was about 24 when his first feature appeared; each was supported by government subsidy, either directly through the Film Subsidies Board, or indirectly through subsidized television production. These three directors, who steadily achieved international recognition, formed the nucleus of one of the most interesting and productive new national film movements since the French New Wave.

Although American and European critics and festivals had realized as early as 1972 that something important was happening in West Germany, American audiences did not take to the New Cinema (*das neue Kino*) as rapidly as they had to the films of the New Wave. There were both cultural and commercial reasons for

373

the slow American reception of the New German Cinema. First, in the 1970s fewer small "art cinemas" in America were devoted to showing foreign-language films than there had been in the 1950s and 1960s (in the 1990s there were even fewer). The reduced number of theatres meant a much smaller audience for such films than in the period when significant numbers of American filmgoers first turned eagerly to the European imports. As in the 1990s, many audiences seemed content with Hollywood's offerings and unwilling to read subtitles. Second, the new German films were not more difficult to understand than previous European films, but they were difficult in a different way—colder, harder edged, more ironic, and less charming than the films of Fellini or Truffaut.

The surprising commercial success of Fassbinder's *The Marriage of Maria Braun* (1979) accompanied international financing for English-language productions by Fassbinder (*Despair*, 1977), Wenders (*The American Friend*, 1977; *Paris, Texas*, 1984) and Herzog (*Fitzcarraldo*, 1982). The major American publicity campaigns for these films, Wenders's collaboration with Coppola and playwright Sam Shepard, and the posthumous interest in Fassbinder's last films—from the epic *Berlin Alexanderplatz* (1980, 15½ hours, made for TV) to *Querelle* (1982)—indicated that these filmmakers had attracted the critical attention and the audiences they deserved in the United States.

That the New German Cinema initially made little impact in America was ironic, for one of its traits was a conscious debt to the American cinema. Wenders, Fassbinder, and Herzog all paid homage to American genres (melodrama, film noir, the western) and directors (Douglas Sirk, Nicholas Ray, Sam Fuller) in their movies. They acknowledged their debt to French filmmakers like Max Ophüls and Jean-Luc Godard as well. But these three Germans also owed much to a native German film tradition—the Expressionist masterpieces of the 1920s. The Fassbinder films often evoke the stylized, statuesque, highly patterned visual world of Fritz Lang.

Herzog's works recall the spiritual, mystical aspects of such films as *Caligari*, *Destiny*, and *Nosferatu*—the last one quite literally, since Herzog modeled his *Nosferatu* (1979) on Murnau's.

Although Wenders is the most apparently realist of the three directors (in the sense that Fassbinder is theatrical and Herzog is visionary), his work can be compared with such German classics as the more realistic works of Murnau and Pabst. Yet Fassbinder could present a world as *grossly* realistic as the opening of *The Love of Jeanne Ney.*

Rainer Werner Fassbinder

Rainer Werner Fassbinder was the most prolific of the new German directors until his death from a drug overdose in 1982. Directing some 40 feature films in a dozen years, in addition to producing television programs and radio plays, as well as writing and staging theatrical productions in the same period, he worked—and ate and drugged—himself to death.

Fassbinder's work is consciously Brechtian; even the title of one of his films, *Mother Küster's Trip to Heaven* (1975), is a deliberate echo of Brecht's *Mother Courage.* The Fassbinder narratives, like those of Brecht, develop a detached irony that prods the audience to examine the political, psychological, or moral implications of the tale rather than to become intimately attached to the feelings and fortunes of its central characters. Fassbinder's parables, however melodramatic (and in that sense un-Brechtian) they may become, tend toward the allegorical and take the form of complex and explicit elaborations of a simple moral–political lesson.

Fassbinder's roots, like Ingmar Bergman's, were in the theatre, and his films never deserted the theatre's elegant, economical stylization. Like Bergman and D. W. Griffith, Fassbinder preferred the theatrical method of working with an acting ensemble rather than with individual types and stars, and over the 1970s the faces of the Fassbinder players became almost as familiar as the Griffith or Bergman stock companies—Irm Hermann, Margit Carstensen, Hanna Schygulla, Brigitte Mira, Kurt Raab, Volker Spengler, Marquard Böhm, Harry Baer. Despite the speed of his production and shooting, Fassbinder's style and control evolved slowly and steadily into a consistent look and tone.

There are three primary Fassbinder visual and social settings: the stifling, tawdry world of the working and middle class—their apartments, bars, and shops (*The Merchant of the Four Seasons*, 1971); the hard, shiny world of the rich and famous (*Petra von Kant, 1972*); and the detached elegance of the world of the near or distant past (*Effi Briest*, 1974). The visual characteristic that links these three social realms is their unrelenting hardness and coldness, their lack of comfort or human charm. Both private homes and places of public habitation become uninhabitable in the Fassbinder world; they are mausoleums. Whether cutely cluttered or chicly bare, Fassbinder films are set in the Land of the Dead.

The central theme of Fassbinder's work is power—social power, economic power, psychological power, erotic power, often translated into specific scenes of sadomasochistic dominance and subservience. The characters in Fassbinder films exercise terrible power over others, just as the filmmaker exercises a terrible power over the audience. *Satan's Brew* begins and ends with a quotation from Antonin Artaud, and the union of Artaud and Brecht, the theatre of cruelty with the theatre of ideas, mental punishment with political discussion, is as important to Fassbinder as it was to Pasolini and Polanski. Appropriately enough, one of Fassbinder's final works was an adaptation of Jean Genet's *Querelle de Brest*, for Genet, like Fassbinder, evolved a radical politics

based on sadomasochistic, homosexual alternations of dominance and subservience. Many central Fassbinder figures are completely mistaken in the power they think they possess—the sexual power of Effi Briest is much lighter than the social and economic power that engulfs her, and the mercantile power of the merchant of the four seasons is equally illusory and inadequate. As in the plays of Jean Genet, the characters in Fassbinder films love to dominate and to be dominated, and many of the films chronicle the economic, social, political, and romantic revolutions of this sadomasochistic circle.

Ali: Fear Eats the Soul (in German, ungrammatically—as Ali would say it—*Fear Eat the Soul*) is one of Fassbinder's most popular and accessible works, the strange love story of a middle-aged widow and a young, moody, black Moroccan who meet, marry, confront the societal rejection and isolation, and try to deal with anxiety. The film is clearly based on Sirk's *All That Heaven Allows*, but the differences between the Sirk film and the Fassbinder show a degree of psychological perceptivity and artistic courage in the German work that the American one either did not or could not achieve. Sirk's middle-aged widow, Carrie, is an upper-class, graceful, and attractive woman (played by Jane Wyman);

Ali: Fear Eats the Soul: *Emmi (Brigitte Mira) and Ali (El Hedi Ben Salem) as Fassbinder's radically odd couple.*

Fig. 16-1

Fassbinder's widow, Emmi, is an old, wrinkled, frumpy, working-class cleaning lady (played by Brigitte Mira, who plays most of Fassbinder's matrons). Sirk's young sexual male, Ron, was impersonated by Rock Hudson, who played a gardener (which put him in a lower social class from those whose trees he pruned, but also gave him a "natural" dignity—a quality that the film emphasized by frequently mentioning Thoreau's *Walden*). Although Sirk's film made it clear (or as clear as a 1955 Hollywood film could) that the gardener was an attractive sexual object, his embodiment by the picture-perfect Hudson converted the sexual male into a pretty mannequin. Fassbinder's Ali (El Hedi Ben Salem), on the other hand, is a total social outcast and a target of extreme social pressure (a black, unlettered stranger in a strange land) but a very powerful, graceful male presence, seething with energy and sexuality— and an anxiety that eats him alive. Whereas the central narrative question in Sirk was, "Can she marry this man?"—a marriage opposed by all her friends, family, and social set—Fassbinder goes beyond to a more ironic problem: Can they stay married? How can they maintain their affection without living under pressure in a world of their own?

Werner Herzog

Werner Herzog makes both documentaries and fictional feature films, but the differences between them are not nearly so great as such terms imply. Even Herzog's documentaries are far less concerned with the objective recording of events, processes, or conditions than with the subjective and symbolic aspects of undergoing a particular event, process, or condition. *Fata Morgana* (1970) is a transcendental documentary shot in the Sahara and as concerned with creation myths as it is with looking at the desert through new eyes. *Land of Silence and Darkness* (1971) attempts to re-create the sensation of experiencing the world as a blind and deaf person (quite a task for film, whose two tools are images and sounds). In *Little Dieter Needs to Fly* (1997), Herzog makes it very clear—by taking him back to the jungles and prison camp from which he had escaped during the Vietnam War—exactly why Dieter, now a claustrophobic whose house is stocked with food, *needs* to fly, free in his plane in the unbounded space of the air. Even if his words,

whether voice-over or in dialogue, are richly significant, Herzog depends finally on the poetic evocations of his visual imagery, distinguished by its intense silence, its haunting colors, its hypnotic slowness, its stare through the surface of light.

Among Herzog's favorite images are natural settings that are mysterious and untamed. He once said that he searches this planet for extraterrestrial landscapes. The lushly dense Amazonian jungle of *Aguirre, the Wrath of God* and *Fitzcarraldo*, or the dusty Wisconsin plains of *Stroszek* are some of the environments to which Herzog's German characters have been transported. Herzog's soundtracks are as careful as his visual imagery; he gives particular attention to music and to the musical scoring of both speech and noises—the repetitive use of intense silences; the calls, cries, and hoots of birds; the use, in film after film, of music by South American Indians.

At the center of most Herzog narratives is a character who follows his single-minded determination to an ironic and irreversible end. The Herzog characters are driven by destinies or inner compulsions that can be neither softened nor averted. Aguirre (played by Klaus Kinski, whom Herzog once called the only true demon of the cinema and about whom he made a documentary, *My Best Fiend*, in 1999), the Spanish conquistador, is driven to seek the mythical city of El Dorado in the depths of the South American jungle. He tyrannically and unswervingly pushes his steadily dwindling band of Europeans into the heart of the unknown continent, refusing to alter his determination despite the poisoned darts, the devastating heat and diseases, the dense forest, and the angry uncharted waters. Aguirre ignores the arguments of men and the evidence of nature. The result is complete catastrophe: the death of everyone on the raft that Aguirre—the stranded imperialist, the demon of European power, the self-proclaimed wrath of God, a Hitler before his time—has forged to tame the continent.

Other Herzog figures attempt to mold the physical world according to the shapes of their imagination. Like Aguirre, the residents of a small town in *Heart of Glass* (1976) become obsessed with a mythical quest that leads to death and destruction—not the search for El Dorado but the attempt to rediscover a secret formula for making

Aguirre, the Wrath of God:
Aguirre (Klaus Kinski)
demonically enclosed in
his universe of one.

Fig. 16-2

the ruby-red glass for which the town is famous. Like Aguirre, the innocent child–man Kaspar Hauser (played by Bruno S., who had been institutionalized as a schizophrenic before Herzog starred him in *Kaspar Hauser* and *Stroszek*) sees the universe with a singleness of personal vision that clashes with the assumptions of all those citizens who teach him to see it differently by teaching him to speak. Fitzgerald (Kinski again), of *Fitzcarraldo*, is determined to haul his ship up and over the top of a mountain—a feat that had to be duplicated by Herzog and his crew—contrary to gravity and common sense, so that he can bring the voice of Enrico Caruso to the jungle and raise money for an opera house. The journey of that ship—all to create an edifice for art, the opera house Fitzgerald envisions—seems an emblem for Herzog's art and for Herzog himself: fixing one's sights on an impossible task and refusing to look away from it until the film is finished and the limits of experience have been challenged and extended once again.

Wim Wenders

Many of Wim Wenders's films are about American movies and the pervasive force of American cul-

ture in the former West Germany. Characters in Wenders films drink Jack Daniel's whiskey, listen to American rock, discuss American novels, drive American cars, delight in American names, and attempt to re-create the lifestyles and values of characters in American films. The goalie in *The Goalie's Anxiety* attends a showing of Howard Hawks's *Red Line 7000* (1965), and a newspaper in *Alice in the Cities* (1974) announces the death of John Ford. If Wenders's films glorify—and investigate and critique—American culture and American movies, they also pay homage to cinema itself. French directors Jean Eustache and Gerard Blain play roles in *The American Friend*, as do American directors Ray and Fuller.

The vocation of one of the two major characters in *Kings of the Road* is to service motion picture projectors, maintaining the machines that allow the cinema to exist. The shadow-show that the two friends mime behind a movie screen, their three-dimensional bodies converted into two-dimensional silhouettes by the worklight behind them, is a tribute both to the magic of silent comedy (their routine echoes Laurel and Hardy) and to the hypnotic image of cinema in general (their antics captivate a group of noisy children,

Fig. 16-3 **Fig. 16-4**
The American Friend: *the framemaker (Bruno Ganz, Fig. 16-3) and the cowboy (Dennis Hopper, Fig. 16-4), each framed within the frame.*

impatient for the equipment to be repaired and the film to begin, into adoring silence). This "live" shadow-show becomes itself a piece of cinema—two-dimensional, moving, silent silhouettes on a white screen, created by the power of light.

Wings of Desire (1987; literally, *The Heavens over Berlin*), a French–German co-production, was written by Wenders and novelist Peter Handke (author of *The Goalie's Anxiety*). It tells of two angels (Bruno Ganz and Otto Sander), assigned to Berlin since prehistoric times, who move through the city in 1987, eavesdropping on people's thoughts and wondering what it would be like to be human, to live in time rather than eternity. Since the angels can remember everything that ever happened on a particular street, Wenders can show that street in the present, then during the Third Reich, then in the present again or after an Allied bombing, summarizing all that Berlin has been, has done, and has endured. The movie takes the long view of history and of the fates of individuals, but it also moves in close to show all the concerns and uncertainties of the present and of individuals—and so does the camera, which may look at Berlin from above or at people straight on. What the angels see is in black and white, while mortal experience is in color; angels hear the thoughts of others (sometimes the soundtrack is a chaos of minds), while people hear only themselves. The ultimate questions this movie raises about life are posed by Rainer Maria Rilke, one of whose poems is quoted repeatedly, and by the everyday/cosmic attitude the movie adopts with such calm, authority, and love. It turns out that some angels may become mortal; Peter Falk plays one of these "former angels," and the film is dedicated to three more: Ozu, Truffaut, and Tarkovsky. *Wings of Desire* is certainly the *It's A Wonderful Life* of the 1980s, but it is also a movie that feels on the verge of some great historic change. A film about the present and for the future, it ends on a note of setting out on the adventure of life, its story to be continued. When Germany was reunified in October 1990, after 45 years of division, that seemed to fit perfectly into the film's worldview—and rather than become dated, *Wings of Desire* became even more relevant and inspiring.

After making another long road movie, *Until the End of the World* (1991), Wenders returned to Berlin to tell the story of the other angel (Otto Sander) in *Far Away, So Close!* (1993), the companion film to *Wings of Desire* (Wenders insisted it was not a sequel). Six years later, Wenders and the angel find Berlin an increasingly hostile place whose citizens are disoriented and disunited, but the film suggests they may be healed—perhaps if they discover compassion and learn to use their eyes (especially in the loving look) not only to take and to take in, but also to give. As a female angel puts it, "They've forgotten that light enters the heart through the eye and then shines back out through the eye from the heart."

Von Trotta and Others

The new German cinema has not been confined to its three major voices. Alexander Kluge has already been mentioned. Volker Schlöndorff excels in stylish literary adaptations—of Heinrich von Kleist (*Michael Kohlhaas*, 1969), Heinrich Böll (*The Lost Honor of Katharina Blum*, 1975), Günter Grass (*The Tin Drum*, 1979, the most popular German film of all time in Germany), and Margaret Atwood (*The Handmaid's Tale*, 1990). He also excels at the political melodrama, bringing out the irony and the commitment in a story like that of Katharina Blum or the heroine of *The Legends of Rita* (2000). His then wife, Margarethe von Trotta, wrote Schlöndorff's scripts, co-directed *Katharina Blum*, and writes and directs films that are often confrontationally and controversially feminist (*Marianne and Juliane*, 1981; *Rosa Luxemburg*, 1985; *Three Sisters*, 1988). By the time she made the political thriller *The Long Silence* (Italy, 1993) and a romance about lovers separated by the Berlin Wall, *The Promise* (Germany, 1994), von Trotta was recognized as one of the world's most versatile and forceful directors. Though all of the 26 filmmakers who signed the Oberhausen Manifesto were men, many women directors are now active in Germany, notably Helma Sanders-Brahms (*Germany Pale Mother*, 1979), Doris Dörrie (*Enlightenment Guaranteed*, 2000), and Monika Treut (*Didn't Do It for Love*, 1998).

The husband–wife team of Jean-Marie Straub and Danièle Huillet, the most radical filmmakers at work in Germany, have been influenced by Bresson as well as by Brecht and Godard. They are committed to deconstructing both the ordinary processes of film narrative and the usual strategies of film imagery. Straub/Huillet, as they are usually referred to, together write, produce, and direct their films, which include *Chronicle of Anna Magdalena Bach*, 1967; *History Lessons*, 1972; *Class Relations*, 1983; and *The Death of Empedocles*, 1987. Films from the "Berlin Underground" include Frank Ripploh's *Taxi zum Klo* (1981), an amusingly frank account of Germany's gay subculture. At the opposite extreme, Hans-Jürgen Syberberg makes operatic films on an epic scale. While his *Parsifal* (1982), a staging of Wagner's opera, recalls the German traditions of Romanticism and Expressionism, *Our Hitler* (1977) more directly confronts those traditions and German history in search of the roots of Nazism.

It remains to be seen just how the reunification of Germany will finally affect the film industries on either side of what used to be the Berlin Wall. East–West co-productions can be expected, and perhaps even a unified industry, but the biggest difference may be made by the fact of a unified audience—the kind that got behind the work of a new filmmaker, Tom Tykwer, made his *Run Lola Run* (or *Lola Runs*, 1998) a hit in Germany, and launched its international success.

Third World Cinemas

The term "Third World film" does not so much describe a national tradition as provide a heading for many politically and economically related but geographically scattered national cinemas: those films from the underdeveloped emerging nations of Africa, Asia, and Latin America that explicitly examine the political, social, and cultural issues of those nations. Although Brazil is one of those countries that has produced Third World films, the popular romantic–erotic fantasy *Dona Flor and Her Two Husbands* (Bruno Barretto, 1978), with its escape from social realities, would probably not be considered one of them. Nor would either the personal, psychological studies of Satyajit Ray or the spectacles and action films produced for India's vast popular audience (but the films of Mrinal Sen would). Nor would the Kung Fus from Hong Kong. On the other hand, some European films (*The Battle of Algiers*, *State of Siege*) and some American black or Latino films (like Melvin Van Peebles's *Sweet Sweetback's Baad Asssss Song*, 1971; John Singleton's *Boyz N the Hood*, 1991; and Anna Thomas and Gregory Nava's *El Norte*, 1983) have been considered spiritual products of the Third World even though the films were produced or directed by Americans or Europeans. Michel Khleifi's *Wedding in Galilee* (1987), officially an Israeli production, was made primarily with money from Belgium and France, has a distinctly Palestinian point of view, and is usually discussed as a Third World Palestinian picture (much like the films Khleifi did produce in Palestine, again with European money but without the participation of Israel), with a flavor of having been made under the nose of the enemy and a running theme of having to get Israeli approval for everything. *Yol* (1982), a realistic, socially critical Turkish film directed by Şerif Gören and written by Yilmaz Güney—who wrote the script while in jail and had to smuggle it out—is certainly a Third World film. To keep an already muddy metaphor from becoming any more murky, it would make sense to define a Third World film by both its national origin and its cultural content.

These developing, often postcolonial countries produce films either to educate their own citizens about the cultural history and contemporary conditions of the nation or to present that nation's problems and positions to the citizens of the rest of the world—sometimes both. To make feature films up to the technical standards of the international market costs a lot of money, particularly for countries with limited economic resources. Those Third World films that have been widely screened outside local markets must pass a strict test of social utility—serving a country's national and international interests—or they must be artistically striking enough to do well at film festivals and find distribution, which brings prestige to the country and support for its film industry.

Whether or not they are films of revolt, almost all of them are films of national and cultural self-definition. Their clearest historical analogy is to the Soviet silent classics of the 1920s. Like the new Soviet Union, these nations are emerging from decades or even centuries of cultural exploitation. As in the new Soviet Union, films could be used to educate an audience unable to read and ignorant or dubious of the goals and methods of a new government. As in the Soviet Union, films could be projected in remote regions of these often topographically tortuous countries with the aid of portable power supplies. As in the Soviet Union, films could combine their political lessons with moving stories of human action, often mingling native symbols and folk elements with their didactic tales of social values.

No clearer parallels with the early Soviet movement can be found than in several specific devices of these Third World films. The ending of the Cuban film *The Last Supper* (1976), directed by Tomás Gutiérrez Alea, reflects the influence of Pudovkin: A montage of metaphoric cross-cuts links the uprising of an oppressed people with the inevitable and irreversible processes of nature. The ending of Miguel Littin's Chilean film *The Promised Land* (1973; never released in Chile), like Pudovkin's *Mother*, shows a failed revolution of the past passing on its spirit to the future and, like Dovzhenko's *Arsenal*, develops the mystically unkillable power of the people. Finally, like the Soviet cinema, the cinema of the Third World includes many works that are mere propaganda (telling the audience what to think) and many that present ideas for the audience to think about (comparable to a Brechtian theatre of ideas). Third World cinema is both an international phenomenon and a set of national cinemas, bursting with important movements (*cinema novo* in Brazil) and exciting director/theorists (Solanas and Getino in Argentina, Glauber Rocha in Brazil, Tomás Gutiérrez Alea in Cuba) and essential films (Rocha's 1969 *Antonio das Mortes*) whose international influence has been enormous.

Emerging Cinemas, Emerging Concerns

The methods and goals of film production in these Third World countries can be divided into three very broad categories. First, one country, Cuba, with a well-developed, sophisticated, and nationalized film industry, can rival the industries of all but a few countries of the world in the quality of its output. Like Lenin, Fidel Castro declared the cinema the most important and socially useful of the arts; as a result, the Cuban government, like the Soviet Union, founded and funded a national film school and film production company (ICAIC—Instituto Cubano del Arte e Industria Cinematograficos). Although ICAIC produces mainly documentaries, it also makes several narrative feature films each year, for the Cubans discovered, as did the Soviets, that the populace preferred Hollywood-style stories to didactic documentaries. These feature films, too, help Cuba forcefully argue its case abroad—particularly in Paris, where there is less political resistance to them than in New York.

Second, several Third World countries make a small number of feature films for both national consumption and international distribution (for example, Senegal, Egypt, Ethiopia). Because the population of many of these countries is small, these films seek international distribution to expand their impact and justify their cost. And because the governments of some of these

Fig. 16-5

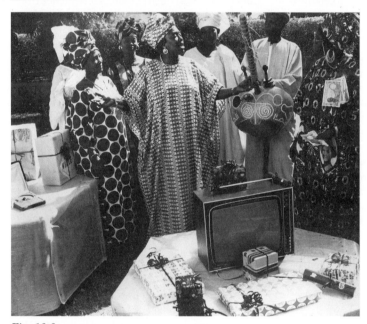

Fig. 16-6

Clashes of cultures. Black African song and a sleeping white aristocrat in **The Last Supper** *(Fig. 16-5); traditional African dress with Westernized gifts at the wedding in* Xala *(Fig. 16-6).*

countries are still politically repressive, the political content of these films is often guarded and metaphoric—more ironic, less radical, less explicitly Marxist, less dominated by revolutionary rhetoric than the films of Cuba or those of the third group.

That third group of films comprises those from countries with such repressive totalitarian governments that the films become underground acts of rebellion and sedition in themselves—films from Argentina, Chile, Bolivia, Peru. Because these films are so dangerous to make, they could never be shown in the countries that produced them without a revolutionary change in their governments; two outstanding examples are *The Hour of the Furnaces: Notes and Testimonies on Neo-Colonialism, Violence and Liberation* (Fernando Solanas and Octavio Getino, 1968) and Parts I and II of *The Battle of Chile* (Patricio Guzmán, 1973–77). These films have been produced almost exclusively for international distribution, to rally international opinion against the ruling regimes.

It was not then and still is not dangerous to make a nonpolitical film in a country like Argentina, especially when the international film market is hungry for good new work; in 2001 alone, Argentina released Lucrecia Martel's *La Ciénaga*, an independent film whose production funds were raised almost entirely through international grants, and Fabián Bielinsky's *Nine Queens*, a wonderfully twisted drama about con artists that was produced because its script won a national contest. Not every Argentinean film, let alone every Latin American or African film, is Third World; not every one is subversive, experimental, radical, and charged with an urgent message to its country and the world.

Despite these differences in the methods of their production and distribution, Third World films share several general themes. The first is an attack on the dominating cultural presence of the more affluent nations of Europe and America—the British presence in *The Night of Counting the Years* (Egypt, 1969), a film by Shadi Abdes-Salam, the French presence in the films of Ousmane Sembene (Senegal), the American presence in South American films.

A second major theme is the crushing, unimaginable poverty of vast segments of the peasant population—whether of the Andes Indians of Jorge Sanginé's *Blood of the Condor* (Bolivia, 1969), the feudal farmers of Haile Gerima's *Harvest: 3000 Years* (Ethiopia, 1975), or the impoverished street children in the Rio de Janeiro slums of Hector Babenco's *Pixote* (Brazil, 1981).

A third theme, like the title of Eisenstein's 1929 film, might be called "Old and New," the contrast of the old backward ways of farming, living, thinking with newer, more progressive ones—the conflicts of ancient and modern customs in *Xala* (1974), and of the general patterns of historical evolution in the Cuban fictional classic, *Lucía* (1968). Some of these films celebrate the old ways, the founding rituals and unique look of their land and culture—as Souleymane Cissé treats Africa in *Brightness* (Mali, 1987). Others say that it is about time for a change in customs: A powerful example is Ousmane Sembene's *Moolaadé* (2004), a study of female circumcision that is revolutionary, compelling,

and easy to understand; the last point is important because Sembene went from writing novels to making movies so that he could reach more people in more direct, clear terms.

A final theme that unites many of these films is the implication that these scattered countries, continents, and peoples are indeed united by common cultural problems and goals—that the exploited peoples of the Middle East, Africa, Cuba, and many other places share a common need and common enemy.

Instructive Dramas

Like Humberto Solás's *Lucía*, many of these Third World films have been recognized as contemporary classics from world-class directors. *Lucía* is a film in the tradition that stretches from Griffith's *The Birth of a Nation* to Bertolucci's *1900*: the political epic that juxtaposes personal dramas with immense historical events and sociopolitical processes. Solás divides his epic into three periods—1895, 1932, and 196 . . . —each of them reflecting a particular political struggle of the Cuban people (first, the War of Independence from Spain; next, the first Cuban political revolution against the dictator Machado; finally, the continuing worker's revolution under Castro). Uniting the film is a woman named Lucía—or rather, three different women with the same name. In each of the film's eras, there is a conflict between Lucía's romantic love and the political events that surround and threaten that love.

The 1895 Lucía surrenders to her sexual passion for Rafael, although such a passion is forbidden in the proper, highly Europeanized upperclass world of 1895 Cuba. Her Rafael, an undercover Spanish agent, seduces Lucía as a means of capturing an arsenal held by the Cuban guerrilla army. The result is that Lucía becomes the unknowing cause of her country's defeat, of her brother's death, and of her own horrifying rape. The 1932 Lucía is a member of the *haute bourgeoisie* who falls in love with and marries Aldo, a young radical student. She supports his political struggle by, in effect, joining the working class (she goes to work in a factory) and participating in the street demonstrations of the Cuban women. After the success of the insurrection against Machado, Aldo discovers that their revolution has become corrupt (this was, after all, an insurrection of the bourgeoisie—and Batista would be its end product).

Aldo continues his fight against the new status quo, machine-gunning the mayor of Havana on the steps of the city hall (this assassination is a piece of Cuban history), himself dying in the struggle. Lucía remains alone with her personal and political futures shattered.

The 196 . . . Lucía is a member of the working class who has recently married her very energetic and attractive Tomás. Unfortunately, Tomás, in addition to his masculine charm, is also enslaved by the old masculine ways of thinking; he converts his new wife into his domestic prisoner, refusing to allow her to work in the fields, to be seen in public, or to learn to read and write, all because

of his sexual jealousy and macho possessiveness. Lucía rebels and deserts him, but the two live very unhappily apart. (This section sets itself the propagandistic problem of supporting marriage while opposing the enslavement of the wife.) In the film's final shot, after their reunion, Lucía continues to insist on her right to be free and Tomás on his right to possess her. The film ends on this unresolved argument—implying that the battle has not been won and that the struggle of Cuban women still continues.

In its individual narratives and its general political philosophy—that it is impossible to be happy in love without also being happy in a just

Fig. 16-7

Fig. 16-8

*Lucía: **political history as pictorial history. Fig. 16-7: the 1895 Lucía (Raquel Revuelta) surrounded by the formal elegance and symmetry of her aristocratic world. Fig. 16-8: the 1960s Lucía (Adela Lagra) and her Tomás (Adolfo Llaurado) surrounded by the bustling vitality of her worker's world.***

society—the film is certainly no richer or clearer than Griffith's *Intolerance*. But also like the Griffith film, *Lucía* gets its power from the broader intellectual plan that integrates the individual tales and, especially, from the careful visual style, texture, and detail that convey each of the historical periods—even the cinema of each period. For if *Lucía* is a history of Cuba from 1895 to 196 . . . —particularly in its steady descent of the class ladder, from upper-class plantation dwellers to the urban *haute bourgeoisie* to working-class rural laborers—it is also a history of film lighting, film stocks, and cinematic visual values—from high contrast to soft contrast to deep focus. The 1895 section is set in the year the Lumière brothers first projected their films. And the 196 . . . section is shot with fast panchromatic film in deep focus, mirroring the visual values of both contemporary cinema and, not coincidentally, Italian Neorealism. The film mirrors the problems of contemporary life by capturing the look of contemporary cinema.

Nelson Pereira dos Santos's *Vidas secas* is in a very different style and single key—a hard, close, unflinching look at the desperate poverty of a single family of "Nordestinos," the rural peasants of Brazil's Northeast, in 1940. This family—husband, wife, two boys, and faithful dog—roams the barren, burned plains in search of a farm or ranch where they can earn their keep. The couple's great goal in life is to save enough money for a leather bed—a bed with a sheet of leather to cover the bony wooden branches that serve as its mattress. Fabiano, the very hard-working husband, runs into trouble with a petty government policeman, but rather than take the path of rebellion (he gets the opportunity both to join a band of guerrillas and to murder this toad in uniform), he remains the hard-working docile slave. The film's setting in the past implies that the man's political docility is a sign of an incompletely evolved political consciousness.

One of the film's remarkably effective devices is its brilliantly cinematic use of available light for both indoor and outdoor sequences. The scorching, blazing power of the sun, the cause of the land's dryness, is also the film's central metaphor and the source of its absolutely authentic depiction of people living in the midst of their genuine surroundings, either outdoors when exposed to its pitiless glare or indoors when trying to escape into the temporary shade of rooms and houses.

Although the film pretends to be set in the past (many radical Brazilian films, like *Antonio das Mortes*, must masquerade as apolitical and unconnected to the present), it nevertheless successfully implies that the journey of such people continues, unsolved and unresolved, into the present.

Documentaries

The Third World political documentaries, like Solanas and Getino's *The Hour of the Furnaces*, have a very different kind of artistic power and political purpose. *The Hour of the Furnaces* is a three-part, 260-minute analysis of the political, economic, and cultural landscape of Argentina, past and present. Part 1 examines Argentinean political–cultural life in the present and the roots of that life in the past—the dependence on foreign investments and capital, the domination by foreign culture and customs, the concentration of wealth in the hands of the few, the political alienation of the working class, and the extreme impoverishment of the native Indian population. Part 2 examines Perónism, which the film calls the only genuine working-class political movement in Argentinean history—first, the decade of Perón rule, 1945–55, then the decade of underground Perónist sentiment and activity following the coup that overthrew the Perón regime. Part 3 is a call to arms, urging armed revolution and resistance as the only way to establish a just and equitable government in Argentina. The film's three parts exhibit the three-part argument of Marxist dialectic: thesis, antithesis, and synthesis.

The Hour of the Furnaces is interesting on a number of levels and for a number of reasons. First, like the great political documentaries of Marcel Ophuls (*The Sorrow and the Pity*, *The Memory of Justice*), the film shakes its audiences—regardless of their political convictions—with the sense of witnessing and participating in a series of historically important and humanly shattering events. The film presents the country's social chaos and cultural antagonisms so sharply, so clearly, and so comprehensively that audiences from more stable, less divided cultures in happier times can only marvel at a spectacle with the intensity of historical fiction but the authenticity of historical fact. Second, the film adopts the stance of Marxist (rather than fascist) rhetoric—asking the audience to think about the issues it has presented, to discuss them

Fig. 16-9
The Hour of the Furnaces: *testament to political oppression and social violence.*

(indeed there are sections where the film abruptly breaks off and asks the audience to have a discussion), to formulate questions and to argue about them. This request for conscious and active participation seems antithetical to the fascist propaganda strategy, also common to bourgeois cinema, of hypnotizing viewers by manipulating ideologically loaded plots (where only the right people get the happy endings or the audience's sympathy) and symbols that strike beneath the viewer's threshold of conscious awareness.

A great documentary that makes its case with precision and force is Guzmán's two-part, 191-minute *The Battle of Chile* (released in 1977; a third part was added in 1979), which chronicles the six months of social agitation that led to the military *coup d'état*—the bloodiest in South American history—against the constitutionally elected left-wing government of Allende in 1973. Less than a decade later, Costa-Gavras's *Missing* (1982) could make commercial Hollywood fiction—but not a Third World film—from almost as radical an interpretation of the same political events (as long as it was primarily the story of an American victim; otherwise there would have been no studio interest in the project).

Unlike the Ophuls documentaries, these Third World chronicles tend to be ideologically one-sided. Ophuls is painfully aware of the complexities and ironies in the commitment to any single political position. These enriching ironies and complexities are luxuries that only pluralistic democratic nations can usually afford. Two Third World directors, Tomás Gutiérrez Alea of Cuba, who received his cinema education at Italy's Centro Sperimentale, and Ousmane Sembene of Senegal, a novelist who was educated in France and studied filmmaking in Moscow, reveal many of the same broader ironies and complexities of a more international outlook.

Alea and Sembene

Alea's first major work to be seen in the United States, *Memories of Underdevelopment* (1968), is an ironic portrait of a member of the bourgeoisie (Sergio Corrieri) who, unlike many other members of his class, remains in Cuba after the fall of Batista. This highly influential film carefully and comically reveals the man's difficulty in finding a place for himself in the new society. His sexual tastes (rather graphically recorded), his cultural tastes (in books, paintings, music)

Memories of Underdevelopment: *the bourgeois intellectual surrounded by books, physical embodiments of his attitudes and values; the book in his hands is* Lolita.

Fig. 16-10

simply do not belong in the new Cuba, and the film simultaneously condemns the man's spiritual emptiness and ironically sympathizes with his isolation.

Strawberry and Chocolate, co-directed by Alea and Juan Carlos Tabío, was a film about different tastes in sex, politics, and ice cream. Completed in 1992, it was shown at a Cuban festival in 1993 and immediately banned; the producer was forced to leave the country. The film attacks the homophobia of the Castro regime and outlines many of the failures of the revolution by allowing a character who is both intellectual and gay (Diego, played by Jorge Perugorría) to express his view of the world to a party-line heterosexual (David, played by Vladimir Cruz) who comes to care about him and to understand—even to share—some of his perspective. This consciousness-raising film, in which a radical becomes aware of a new radical agenda (a new sexual politics and an openness to world culture and new ideas), attempts to advance the essence of social and political revolution while opposing the limited vision of the dominant regime. In other words, it is a Third World film that appears counterrevolutionary only to a gov-

ernment that sees the revolution as a fixed and established entity, rigid in its political and cultural agendas and social attitudes.

Ousmane Sembene, the most important director in sub-Saharan Africa, has been adapting his own stories and novels into films since 1966 when he made *Black Girl,* a study of an African woman who feels stifled, deceived, and corrupted when brought to the South of France to work as a cleaning lady. Born in Senegal, he became a dockworker and union activist in France in the 1950s before turning to writing and—thanks to a scholarship to the Moscow film school in 1962—to filmmaking. One of Sembene's most complex films is his adaptation of his novel *Xala,* an ironic study of the difficulty of exercising power well after having seized it. The prologue is a comic allegory of political change—the native-dressed black Africans enter a marble-halled, mausoleum-like European-style building, the Chamber of Commerce, and jauntily evict its white occupants and their symbols—busts of European figures, army boots, institutional paintings—spouting rhetoric about "Africa for the Africans." But in the very next shot, the African deputies sit in the Chamber's conference room, dressed in European tuxedos and tail-coats; in succeeding shots, a white commander, one of those previously expelled from the Chamber, directs a perfect line of metronomi-cally marching black policemen; two other for-merly expelled white deputies present attaché cases stuffed with greenbacks to each of the current deputies, who sit in perfect symmetrical lines around the conference table. (Sembene deliberately uses the unnaturally straight line and the overperfection of sharp, rectangular compositions as satiric devices.) The prologue's point is clear: A group of Africans throw the rascals out of the Chamber of Commerce and become the rascals themselves.

The rest of *Xala* tells the story of one of those bureaucratic deputies, a respected businessman, whose business, significantly, is importing food. This minister has decided to indulge his sexual appetite by taking a third wife. (Sembene ironi-cally reveals that the sexist Africans have pre-served those vestiges of African culture that suit their pleasure under the guise of perpetuating "Africanness.") The wedding party is a curious mixture of African customs (the groom need not even attend the church service) and Western ones (the guests drink cocktails and Coca-Cola; gifts include African ones, like gold jewelry, and a Western one, a red-ribboned automobile; a band plays a terrible but funny pastiche of pop-rock music). This marriage begins the minister's downfall—he sinks steadily into debt, beggary, and social disgrace.

Unfortunately, the minister is mysteriously incapable of sexual arousal with this new young bride he took for sexual purposes. The minister believes that someone has put a curse—a *xala*—on his virility. So he seeks a variety of native magical cures (again Sembene shows that these Westernized Africans become very Africa-conscious when it suits their needs), but his impotence is incurable. At the end of the film, the minister has fallen lower than the outcast poverty of a group of beggars and cripples that has wan-dered symbolically through the film—beggars who have been swindled out of the food they need to survive by the minister's own economic machinations. The man's true *xala* is that he is a stranger to his own people—not white and not black, not traditional and not modern, not African and not Western. Like all of the hypocritical

swindlers and thieves in the outwardly respectable Chamber of Commerce, he is a not.

In *Xala*'s ironic contrasts of black and white, old and new, male and female, Africa and Europe, Third World and Western World, political justice and political repression, economic freedom and economic dependence, the film brilliantly, ma-turely, comically, perceptively summarizes the es-sential issues of Third World cinema as a whole.

Other English-Language Cinemas

If the British film industry has been a Hollywood colony, ruled by the common language, the English-language film industries of former British colonies—from Australia to Canada (which also has a French-language industry)—have faced even greater difficulty. While England possessed the resources to develop projects that Hollywood could not do at all or as well, the industries of the former colonies struggled to find the economic means and cultural distinctiveness to flourish as alternatives to both London and Hollywood.

Australia
Australia's film-production problem paralleled that of any Third World nation—with important differences. Founded by the British as a penal colony in 1788 (which it remained until 1840), not federated as a commonwealth until 1901, Australia has a population most of which de-scends directly from Britain. While an emerging country of Africa or Latin America could draw upon its own native culture, customs, and lan-guage that had been usurped by colonizers, the dominant customs and language of Australia came from the colonizers, from England, and it was this culture that would produce its films.

Given its direct British descent, Australian culture is not without its parallels to America's. As opposed to the verdant unity of the English countryside, Australia remains a largely untamed frontier continent with awesome topographical contrasts—plains, seas, mountains, deserts, forests. Like modern America, it has both vast modern cities and vast open spaces. Also like America, it has an indigenous culture that the European white settlers pushed back and pushed aside but could neither ignore nor assimilate. The clash of European immigrants and Australian aborigines paralleled that between white pioneers and Native Americans. While some Australian films (notably Peter Weir's *The Last Wave*, 1977) set Australian whites in the context of aboriginal culture, as colonizers who need to learn from or at least stop oppressing the natives, the majority (like Weir's *Gallipoli*, 1981) celebrate white Australian culture in itself and bitterly resent the ways Australians are treated by *their* imperialist oppressors, the stuck-up and sometimes cruel British. The Australian films of the 1970s defined their identity by combining local themes with models from both London and Hollywood: British traditions of literary elegance and polished acting (many Australian actors and directors have trained at the London dramatic academies and have apprenticed in British repertory companies) with the vitality of American images and Hollywood genres.

Before there could be films, there had to be budgets. Shot in Australia, Nicolas Roeg's British film, *Walkabout* (1971), was among the first to demonstrate the power of Australian themes and visual imagery (the contrast of white and aboriginal children's worldviews in the frontier Australian Outback). If the British could make such films (or a Canadian—Ted Kotcheff's harrowing *Outback*, also 1971), why couldn't Australian directors make them as well? As in so many film production centers outside America, the stimulus came from governmental subsidies for feature films with "local content," consistent with international standards of technical expertise and stylistic polish, through the Australian Film Development Commission, established in 1970 (which became the Australian Film Finance Corporation, or FFC).

Although many Australian films try to sort out modern Australian life (for example, Gillian Armstrong's comic rock-musical, *Star Struck*, 1983, or Stephan Elliott's *The Adventures of Priscilla, Queen of the Desert*, 1994), some impressive Australian films look back at the nation's history—particularly the two decades between the Boer War in South Africa and World War I, the very period of Australian confederation. Australian troops had fought for the British in both wars, with great loss of life and little Australian gain—except for clichés like defending the Empire, serving the Queen, or protecting the "race" against the "wogs." Australians had been

Fig. 16-11
Edward Woodward in 'Breaker' Morant.

forced to fight British economic wars against colonial insurgents very much like themselves. Bruce Beresford's *'Breaker' Morant* (1980) and Peter Weir's *Gallipoli* are two powerful depictions of the Australian soldier as hero and cannon fodder, under the yoke of sneering British superiors.

'Breaker' Morant picks up the debate in John Ford's cavalry films between the laws of peace and the necessities of war. Morant's platoon had been specially trained to fight the Boer guerrillas by using the enemy's informal and improvisational tactics rather than the rules of British military protocol. But when Morant's Australian platoon performs one of the actions for which it was expressly created, the British disown it for political and diplomatic reasons, court martial Morant and his fellow officers as criminals, and execute two of them on a beautiful morning.

The films Beresford later directed in America include several distinguished "small" films like *Tender Mercies* (1983) and *Driving Miss Daisy*

(1989). With Beresford's move to Hollywood, the filming of "rough" Australian types was left to Paul Hogan and Peter Faiman, whose *Crocodile Dundee* (1986) was an international hit.

Gillian Armstrong's *My Brilliant Career* (1979), set in the same period as *'Breaker' Morant* and within the same visual environment, is a *Bildungsroman*—the coming of age of Australia's first major woman novelist (Miles Franklin, played by Judy Davis). The film examines both the social disadvantages of women in colonial Australia and the cultural prejudices against Australian thought and art within the entire British Empire. The woman's lowly status in her patriarchal culture mirrors the country's lowly status in the Empire. Her growing maturity and confidence suggest the growth and confidence of Australia in the same period—and of creative, powerful women in any period. From *Star Struck* to her most popular American film, *Little Women* (1994), Armstrong's movies have continued to explore the ways her female characters learn to define and express themselves.

Both Peter Weir and Fred Schepisi have contrasted Australia's Europeanized culture with that of its aboriginal natives. Schepisi's *The Chant of Jimmy Blacksmith* (1978) is a study of a brutally disturbing incident in Australian history. Jimmy Blacksmith is a native Australian who gives up his values, his customs, even his name to serve the whites. When he discovers that he has been betrayed, he goes berserk and murders as many white settlers as he can find. He is of course sentenced and executed by white courts of law. Schepisi's film is both a political plea for the rights of Australia's exploited aborigines as well as a warning about inevitable retribution—a persistent fear of British colonialism. Schepisi later made a number of fine films in America, including *Roxanne* (1987, with Steve Martin as Cyrano), *A Cry in the Dark* (1988, with Meryl Streep; a U.S.–Australian co-production based on an Australian infanticide case), and *Six Degrees of Separation* (1993).

Peter Weir's *The Last Wave* also envisions aborginal retribution—not as overt violence but as

Fig. 16-12
Richard Chamberlain in The Last Wave: *discovering his own fate—and face—while probing an aboriginal mystery.*

a quietly subversive power, more psychic and metaphysical than conventionally political. In contrast to the modern man of law (Richard Chamberlain), Weir's aborigines are in touch with the "dreamtime" and with supernatural influences capable of summoning a wave that will drown the puny white civilization. More than any other Australian director, Weir suggests the doubt beneath the surfaces of Australian culture—that "modern," "rational," "civilized" white European society is a mere shadow and delusion in the mystical eyes of Australia's original inhabitants—the ones who were there *ab origine*, "from the beginning." *Picnic at Hanging Rock* (1975) is a very elegant mystery—the inexplicable disappearance of three girls and a teacher from a proper boarding school during an outing, leaving no physical traces behind. Set in the same period as *'Breaker' Morant*, *Picnic at Hanging Rock* contrasts the rational, orderly appearances of repressive white European society (the school itself) with the operations of an inexplicable universe—just as *The Last Wave*, his best film, does in modern dress.

Gallipoli and *The Year of Living Dangerously* (1982) were the last films Weir made in Australia. His American films have been well received (*Witness*, 1985; *Dead Poets Society*, 1989; *Master and Commander*, 2003), except when they depart markedly from Hollywood formulas (*The Mosquito Coast*, 1986).

George Miller's Mad Max films—*Mad Max* (1979), *The Road Warrior* (*Mad Max 2*, 1981), and *Mad Max Beyond Thunderdome* (1985, co-directed by George Ogilvie)—are futuristic fantasies that combine several genres and traditions while creating an original myth; together they constitute an epic. The central character, Max (American-born Mel Gibson, who emigrated to Australia with his parents), is an "enforcer" like Dirty Harry, a searcher and a loner like Ethan Edwards, a wanderer of the wasteland like an Arthurian knight, a founder like Aeneas, a fighter like Achilles, and a wily if not amoral survivor like Odysseus. He makes his own rules and establishes his own loyalties. Max is incapable of settling down but makes vital contributions to the pockets of civilization that are humanity's only alternative to an age of barbarism. *The Road Warrior* tells how Max helps a besieged group—occupying a refinery that resembles a fort in a western but also echoes the tiny, walled city of Troy—escape to found "the great northern tribe" (much as the Trojans were said to have founded Rome), and *Thunderdome* ends with a foundation story that is also a creation myth. The Mad Max films draw, then, on classic genres and images with uniquely modern and Australian issues: What would happen to an immense, isolated continent like Australia after an atomic war, in a world already plagued by oil embargoes?

Among Australian directors who did their first significant work in the 1980s and 1990s, Baz Luhrmann (*Strictly Ballroom*, 1992; *Moulin Rouge!*, 2001) is the most flamboyant stylist; Ray Lawrence (*Lantana*, 2001), the most intense choreographer of complex characters; and Rob Stich (*The Castle*, 1997), the most congenial and outrageous comedian. Paul Cox was born in the Netherlands but made his mark as an Australian filmmaker (*Man of Flowers*, 1983; *A Woman's Tale*, 1991; *Innocence*, 2000). And continuing the trend of those who, like Weir, direct their most original and daring works in Australia only to make what are for the most part less interesting films in America, Phillip Noyce left after the brilliantly realistic drama *Newsfront* (1978) and the fiercely tense *Dead Calm* (1989) to make such pictures as *Clear and Present Danger* (1994) and *The Bone Collector* (1999). He returned to Australia to make *The Quiet American* (2001, released 2002) and *Rabbit-Proof Fence* (2002), which are among his finest works.

New Zealand

New Zealand was settled by the Maori, a people of Polynesian origin, in the 10th century and by Europeans in the 17th and 18th centuries. The Maori called the country Aotearoa—and still do. A British colony since 1840, it became self-governing in 1907 and has been an independent member of the Commonwealth since 1947. While the Maori continued to control their own lands, white New Zealanders nurtured their Britishness along with their independence. The film industry, given a boost by the founding of the New Zealand Film Commission in 1978, is independent and original as well as linked with the industries of Great Britain, America, and Australia.

For some time, the most important filmmakers from New Zealand were *from* New Zealand and did their major work in England or the

United States—notably Len Lye, whose *A Colour Box* (1935) made the first great use of painting directly on celluloid and is considered a British film. Beginning in the late 1970s, however, Roger Donaldson drew attention to New Zealand filmmaking with his *Sleeping Dogs* (1977) and *Smash Palace* (1981). Like Lee Tamahori's *Once Were Warriors* (1994), whose main characters are Maoris living in the big city, *Smash Palace* is a violent family melodrama about the conflict between the way things are and the way heroes and antiheroes think they ought to be; there is a tendency in both films to revert to the old codes in the face of the wreck of everything important. The black comedies and outrageous horror films of Peter Jackson (beginning with *Bad Taste* in 1987) became cult favorites and prepared audiences for his horrific family melodrama, *Heavenly Creatures* (1994), the true story of two infatuated, murderous girls. Jackson went on to make an authoritatively phony documentary about early film history, *Forgotten Silver* (1996, co-directed with Costa Botes), and his first big-budget horror film, *The Frighteners* (1996), in which he revealed a gift for managing large teams and a command of slick special effects, rich visuals, solid performances, and relatively good taste, all of which he put to use in his next major project, the three-part/three-year adaptation of J. R. R. Tolkien's trilogy, *The Lord of the Rings*. Its first part, *The Fellowship of the Ring*, was released in 2001 to critical acclaim and increased book sales. The second part, *The Two Towers* (2002), and the final part, *The Return of the King* (2003), were even more impressive. With each film, Jackson and his New Zealand effects teams broke new ground. Although produced with American money, the trilogy was made in New Zealand.

The hero of Niki Caro's *Whale Rider* (2003), a modern version of an ancient story, is Paikea, a young Maori whose brother, who was supposed to become the next leader, died at birth. Although the boys are educated in their culture and rituals, Paikea (Keisha Castle-Hughes), as a female, is barred from the teaching sessions. At the climax, she rides a whale, re-creating the journey of her ancestor, celebrated in myth, who rode a whale to bring his people to Aotearoa, and she is accepted as the new leader. A feminist film as well as a

Fig. 16-13
Maori boys are taught the history and rituals of their culture in Whale Rider.

mythic one, *Whale Rider* brought another powerful woman director to world attention; she joined Jane Campion as one of New Zealand's vital artists.

Jane Campion was born in New Zealand and made her first films in Australia: several shorts and *Passionless Moments* (1984); the TV film *Two Friends* (1986); and her first theatrical feature, *Sweetie* (1989). She returned to New Zealand to make *An Angel at My Table* (1990, originally for TV) and to shoot the Australian–French–New Zealand co-production that made her famous, *The Piano* (1992, released 1993). Most of Campion's films are about women whose means of expressing themselves are met with rejection and incomprehension.

Sweetie is about a dysfunctional family dominated by a spoiled, obnoxious daughter who, the audience finally realizes, was probably sexually abused by her father and has been expressing, in her own way, all the tension and chaos the family denies. Her language is to explode. *An Angel at My Table*, based on the autobiographies of Janet Frame, who became one of New Zealand's most famous authors, tells how Frame's shy ways, coupled with a nervous breakdown, were misdiagnosed as schizophrenia and led to her being incarcerated for eight years of shock treatment. She was saved from brain surgery only when the stories she had been writing were published and the authorities around her realized that she had a rich and sane inner life. If the withdrawn person she presented to the world seemed hard to know, isolated in some private space, her language—written words—got

Fig. 16-14
Harvey Keitel and Holly Hunter in **The Piano:**
love in another language.

through the barrier. The woman in *The Piano*, who can speak but until the end of the story does not (a decision she has held to since childhood), has her language too: music.

Canada

If Australia and New Zealand struggled with or adapted to the cultural imperatives of British domination before developing original cinemas, they enjoyed the cultural oddity of isolation as Western societies in the oceans south of Southeast Asia. Even more severe have been the cultural handicaps on a Canadian cinema, not only a former British colony, but also a former French colony, a nation of two cultures and two languages, just across the border from the country with the West's most powerful film industry. The earliest Canadian feature was *Evangeline* (1913), directed by E. P. Sullivan; the earliest that survives is *Back to God's Country* (1919), directed by David M. Hartford and starring the

woman who masterminded the project, Nell Shipman (see Chapter 6).

For decades, Canadian cinema was synonymous with the National Film Board of Canada, founded by the British documentarist John Grierson in 1939. Government-supported and famous for the experimental films of Norman McLaren (*Neighbours*, 1952; *Pas de deux*, 1967), the Film Board was committed almost exclusively to short films—documentary or animated, in English or in French. Canada's international prestige rested on its animated films and documentaries, as well as on the avant-garde films of Michael Snow (*Wavelength*, 1967), Bruce Elder (*The Book of All the Dead*, 1975–95), and others. Many feature-oriented Canadian directors (Norman Jewison, Arthur Hiller) and actors (Donald Sutherland, Christopher Plummer) left to work south of the border, as Mack Sennett had.

The changes in Canadian feature-film production began in 1978, stimulated (as usual) by government policy—seed money for film investment through the Canadian Film Development Corporation (established in 1967) and new tax laws that attracted film projects from outside.

Finding Canadian subjects for Canadian films has been more difficult. Ted Kotcheff's *The Apprenticeship of Duddy Kravitz* (1974), based on a bestselling Jewish–Canadian novel and supported by the Canadian Film Development Corporation, was the first thoroughly Canadian feature film to make a great deal of money outside Canada.

One of the first French–Canadian directors to reach an international audience was Claude Jutra with his small-scale *Mon oncle Antoine* (1971) and grand-scale *Kamouraska* (1974). In the late 1980s, the most popular French–Canadian films were those of Denys Arcand: *The Decline of the American Empire* (1986), a witty, sexy comedy of manners, and *Jesus of Montreal* (1989), a reflexive satire about the production of a Passion Play; he also had great success with the sequel to *Decline, The Barbarian Invasions* (2003), in which the characters deal with a death. In the late 1990s, Montreal's bravest director was Denis Villeneuve, whose *August 32nd on Earth* (1998) broke the rules of continuity editing and narrative connection to explore the paradoxical ways people nearly connect, rather like an episode of *The Twilight Zone* based on *L'Age d'or*.

Fig. 16-15

"From The System of Dante's Hell, *the first region of* The Book of All the Dead. *One who lives with the knowledge of death—of the deaths of love, desire, and creative power—abides from moment to moment with the horrible question, 'Am I acceptable to the Creator?' and so must constantly reaffirm his poetic capacities. Out of this urgency has emerged a long, and densely allusive text, that like Pound's* Cantos, *after which it is fashioned, seeks to fashion a* paradiso terrestre.*"—Bruce Elder*

Many of the newer English-language directors established their reputations with Canadian features and continued to pursue the themes of their early works in the films they made in the United States and elsewhere. Kotcheff left Canadian TV to make films in England (*Life at the Top*, 1965) and Australia (*Outback*, 1971—a richly atmospheric and disturbingly violent film, certainly his best) before returning to Canada to make *Duddy Kravitz.* His most successful American film, *First Blood* (1982), inaugurated the Rambo series but was more thoughtful and intense than its sequels. The heroes of all these films are at war with the world around them, either because they have been forced to fight groups they would rather ignore (*Outback, First Blood*) or because they have chosen to "conquer" groups they want to join (*Life at the Top, Duddy Kravitz*).

The horror films of David Cronenberg are even more tightly interrelated, taking for their essential subject the nature of evolution, both of "the flesh" and of consciousness. The changing body is a cancerous horror in some of his films, a paradox in others, and it is often accompanied by a scary but fascinating change in mental ability and sexual behavior. There is no thematic break between his major Canadian films (*Shivers*, 1975,

released in the United States, with cuts, as *They Came From Within*; *Rabid*, 1977; *The Brood*, 1979; *Scanners*, 1980, released 1981, his first international hit), his Canadian/U.S. co-productions (*Videodrome*, 1982, released 1983, and *Dead Ringers*, 1988), his American pictures (*The Dead Zone*, 1983; *The Fly*, 1986; *M. Butterfly*, 1993), and his Canada-based international co-productions that have included France, the United Kingdom, and sometimes Japan (*Naked Lunch*, 1991; *Crash*, 1996; *eXistenZ*, 1999). They all fit and advance together on a dramatic definition of the nature and psychology of flesh, the metaphoric and sometimes gory route he takes into the study of people in bodies. In *The Brood*, the story of a woman whose angry thoughts cause her to give birth to little monsters who kill her enemies—so that they are the children of her anger, "the shape of rage"—the horror is characteristically mental and physical. The protagonist in *Spider* (2002) suffers mental anguish, and the audience shares his painful, contradictory visions and memories. The hero of *Videodrome* (Max) attains a new level of consciousness partly as the result of a brain tumor induced by a video signal, and the hero of *The Dead Zone* (one of the best Stephen King adaptations and the first Cronenberg film not based on his own story) gains telepathic abilities, from brain injuries, that allow him to save the world. In the original version of *The Fly* (Kurt Neumann, 1958), the scientist ends up with the fly's head and arm immediately, as soon as the teleportation experiment goes wrong; in Cronenberg's version, the emphasis is on the scientist's slow evolution into a man–fly and on the way he learns to enjoy, as his body changes, the way a fly thinks. The characters in *Crash* attempt to merge flesh and metal, lust and death, through the power of sheer erotic will. And the end of *Scanners* shows two brothers in one body (one's mind and voice in the other's body), as *Dead Ringers* examines the problem of twin brothers with disturbingly separate minds in disturbingly similar bodies, who come together to die.

Of course, not every Canadian director has commuted or emigrated to Hollywood. Atom Egoyan, born to Armenian parents in Egypt in 1960, remained in Toronto even after *Exotica* (1994), *The Sweet Hereafter* (1997), and *Felicia's Journey* (1999) made him famous. One of his most personal films, *Ararat* (2002), told the little-known story of the mass murder of Armenians in 1915, the Armenian genocide still denied by those who carried it out. Egoyan's characters are always looking at each other, sometimes in person but usually through some kind of mediator: the phone, a video camera, a TV set, a surveillance camera, a movie, a movie on tape. They peek into others' lives, usually maintaining an excited, voyeuristic distance but sometimes involving themselves with the people they have met through the camera, whom they sometimes cannot even see without a camera (in *Family Viewing*, 1987, one character becomes introspective only when looking at herself on closed-circuit video). Some of Egoyan's characters depend on films and tapes to maintain their real or imagined relationships with the dead. In *Felicia's Journey* a man whose late mother hosted a cooking show from her own kitchen keeps the kitchen just as she had it and watches her old shows on a TV set in that kitchen, following her instructions exactly in an effort at last to win—or at least be worthy of—her approval.

Transience is one of Egoyan's central themes: the ephemeral nature of commitments, relationships, places to live, and life. Capturing life with a video camera is a transient (erasable) way to stay partly in touch with all that one has lost or will lose. Nevertheless, the woman in *Family Viewing* (Arsinée Khanjian) who is given a tape of her mother's funeral, who was deprived of the ritual of the family viewing—strictly defined—and the chance to bury her mother in person, tosses the tape away, to the incomprehension of the youth who thought that she would be as comforted by watching the tape as by having been there; in other words, Egoyan knows the difference between media and life, but some of his characters don't. Beyond video, another way to spy on life and create a record of it is to investigate: not to tape people but to question them, getting a thrill of connection from probing their wounds while doing all one can to restore their losses (*The Adjuster*, 1991; *The Sweet Hereafter*). The latter film—adapted from the novel by Russell Banks and the first of his pictures for which Egoyan did not write an original story—makes it especially clear that the ambulance-chasing lawyer is trying to get a life by getting other people's lives, that some secrets will always be kept private, and that some losses cannot be restored. When the Academy nominated Egoyan for an Oscar as best director for *The Sweet Hereafter*, it was, for once, not trying to lure a Canadian to Hollywood but honoring a major artist of the Canadian cinema.

Ireland and Elsewhere

The United Kingdom comprises Wales, Scotland, and Northern Ireland as well as England; the Republic of Ireland is a separate country. The island with England, Scotland, and Wales is called Britain. This survey of alternative English-language cinemas is happily obliged to call attention to the small but developing industries of Wales (Paul Turner's *Hedd Wyn*, 1992), Scotland (Bill Forsyth's *Gregory's Girl*, 1981; Danny Boyle, an Englishman whose first success was made in Scotland—*Shallow Grave*, 1994—and whose next was shot in Edinburgh but financed in England—*Trainspotting*, 1996), and Ireland (Jim Sheridan's *My Left Foot*, 1989), as well as independent productions such as Jamie Uys's *The Gods Must Be Crazy* (1981), from Botswana.

Hedd Wyn (pronounced "Heth Win") was not only the first Welsh feature, but also one of the best films ever made about poetry, the story of a prize, a chair, and a war. It was shot in Welsh and bore English subtitles, a way of honoring the language and its poets. One of the most important of the early Scottish pictures was an Irish co-production; *The Magdalene Sisters* (Peter Mullan, 2003) was so controversial a study of Catholic institutions for supposedly wayward Irish women that it had to be produced primarily outside the country.

The most developed of these new cinemas is that of the Republic of Ireland. In the late 1980s and the 1990s, its two best known directors were the Irish novelist Neil Jordan, most of whose films were produced in England but who often drew on Irish materials, and the Irish playwright Jim Sheridan, who put the industry on the map with *My Left Foot*, in which Daniel Day–Lewis played Christy Brown, who became a writer and painter in spite of the cerebal palsy that left him able to move only one foot.

Sheridan's next picture, *The Field* (1990), starred Richard Harris as an Irish farmer, best described as an "angry old man," who becomes crazy and destructive when a field he has rented and improved for years is sold to an outsider. Sheridan took a deeper look at the Irish family—and at the politics of Irish rebellion and British injustice—in the largely factual *In The Name Of The Father* (1993), a melodrama in which power, strength, and renewal come from getting the truth told rather than letting the liars win.

Neil Jordan applies his lush visual imagination and sneaky wit to genre materials that only at first appear to be familiar. *The Butcher Boy* (1997) cast the then notoriously anti-papal Sinéad O'Connor as the Virgin Mary; one of the most violent and stylistically assured of his films, it may be the funniest family tragedy ever made, the story of the making of a crazy, likable killer who is perfectly OK with himself. The characters in *Mona Lisa* (1986) surprise the audience as much as each other, and the film manages to be funny and tough, with a romantic undertow. Much the same can be said of *The Crying Game* (1992), in which Stephen Rea (Fergus), Jaye Davidson (Dil), Forrest Whitaker (Jody), and Miranda Richardson (Jude) negotiate a wilderness of sexual and political twists, and what begins as a story about a gang of Irish terrorists turns into an adult examination of race and sex, a witty and elegant game with the nature of barriers and distinctions in general.

Russia and the Former Soviet Union

After the death of Stalin, Soviet culture and filmmaking "thawed" under Nikita Khrushchev, and a number of cinematically fresh and emotionally engaging movies won critical acclaim at home and abroad: Mikhail Kalatozov's *The Cranes Are Flying* (1957), Sergei Gerasimov's *The Quiet Don* (1957), Grigori Chukhrai's *Ballad of a Soldier* (1959), Alexei Batalov's *The Overcoat* (1959), and Josef Heifitz's *Lady with a Dog* (1960). Other important and powerful films appeared in the next decade—Kalatozov's *I Am Cuba* (1964), Andrei Konchalovsky's *The First Teacher* (1966), Sergei Bondarchuk's 8½-hour *War and Peace* (1967), Grigori Kozintsev's *Hamlet* (1964) and *King Lear* (1971). But under Khrushchev's successors, especially Leonid Brezhnev, the late 1960s and 1970s became an increasingly difficult period in which to work. Filmmaking was subsidized, but many films were not approved for production; art films were entered in festivals but rarely shown in Moscow or other big cities. Some filmmakers were persecuted under the Brezhnev regime, and some left the country. Even so, enough great films were made to justify world attention to a Soviet Renaissance, whose most important directors were Sergei Paradjanov (born Sarkis Paradjanian) and Andrei Tarkovsky.

Paradjanov, Tarkovsky, and Others

Sergei Paradjanov was born in Georgia, was tutored by Dovzhenko, made most of his films in Ukraine (some in Georgia and Armenia), and died in Armenia in 1990. A musician, painter, and connoisseur of folk tales, Paradjanov became world famous with the Ukrainian *Shadows of Forgotten Ancestors* (1964), a lyrical explosion disguised as a movie. Set in the Carpathian mountains among a tribe "forgotten by God and men," *Shadows* episodically relates a folk tale of undying love. Its combination of realism and mythology evokes what is at once a vivid natural world and a magical realm brimming with the power of characters who are both simple and bigger than life (as in the folk legend and myth) and with psychological and supernatural forces that erupt into the wild daylight. Like the people it examines, its "prosaic days are for work, holidays for magic." But this world that has been so carefully re-created, both in its look

Fig. 16-16
Shadows of Forgotten Ancestors: *doomed lovers in a folk legend.*

and in its worldview, is observed by an utterly up-to-date camera that rushes to frame the action or follows it fluidly, or circles within or around the action. From its swish pans to its slow motion, from its constantly changing music to its abrupt shifts in narrative tone, from its rough realities to its brilliant dreams, *Shadows of Forgotten Ancestors* was the most important Soviet film since *Ivan the Terrible, Part II*. Though Paradjanov was hailed as a new Dovzhenko, he ran into trouble when the film was accused of formalism—the demon of the old Stalinist censors—and of promoting Ukrainian nationalism. In 1968 he made a controversial film—*Sayat Nova*, also known as *The Color of Pomegranates*—that evoked the poems and the inner life of an 18th-century Armenian monk through a series of stunning images; when he refused to revise the film to

suit authorities, it was recut by someone else and shelved. While he was serving four years at hard labor in the Gulag, an early, unfinished (1971) version of *Sayat Nova* was seen by filmmakers and shown at festivals outside the country; Paradjanov completed the film in 1978, when he got out of prison. His last major works were *The Legend of the Suram Fortress* (1984, co-directed by Dodo Abashidze) and *Ashik Kerib* (1988).

Andrei Tarkovsky, who died in 1986, was an astounding creator of worlds: worlds that had been (*Ivan's Childhood* or *My Name is Ivan*, 1962; *Andrei Rublev*, also spelled *Roublyov*, 1966—Soviet release 1971) and worlds that could never be (*Solaris*, 1972; *Stalker*, 1979, released 1982). And these worlds are transformed by the imagination: in *Andrei Rublev*, the attempts of medieval Russians to transcend their limits,

Fig. 16-17

Tarkovsky's
**Andrei
Rublev.**

whether by flying in a balloon or by discovering the secret of casting a perfect bell, and the icons painted by Rublev; in *Solaris*, the memories and dreams of a crew in orbit around a remote planet, a virtual sea of thought, that can materialize what they imagine. The most surreal of his films are full of cool, clean shots of nature, often of leaves and stones seen through running water (*Stalker*); his most natural films are never far from subjective vision (*Mirror*, 1974). Although Tarkovsky was allowed to make these films, which brought Russia international prestige, he was frustrated that they were so rarely, if ever, shown in his homeland for their intended audience. *Andrei Rublev*, based on the life of a major icon painter, used its central character—a monk whose wanderings and painting take him across a brutal stretch of 15th-century Russia—to focus its study of the relations between the suffering and grime of the world and the transcendent, almost impossible achievements of art and obsession; though it was shown abroad after winning a prize at Cannes in 1969, it was shown only once in Russia—in 1966—before it was grudgingly released there in 1971.

Among the many other filmmakers who came to prominence in this period, three more stand out: Larissa Shepitko, Nikita Mikhalkov, and Tenghiz Abuladze. Larissa Shepitko was recog-nized as Russia's major woman director before she died in a car accident in her early 40s. Her best known works are *Wings* (1966), *You and I* (1971), and a harrowing, black-and-white, personal, poetic film called *The Ascent* (1977).

Nikita Mikhalkov made the warmest and most inventive art-house hit the Soviets had produced since the days of Sputnik: *A Slave of Love* (1976), a reflexive romantic comedy that was exuberant and moving. His *Oblomov* (1980) was a solid adaptation of the classic Russian novel, and *Dark Eyes* (1987, made in Italy) adapted Chekhov to the talents of Marcello Mastroianni. It is Mikhalkov who mastered the new way to succeed in Soviet filmmaking: to direct international co-productions that sell tickets abroad and win prizes at festivals.

Tenghiz Abuladze, who died in 1994, came from and worked in Georgia. He is best known for the great trilogy on which he labored for nearly 20 years: *Molba* (*Prayer*, 1967, released 1969), a black-and-white drama full of winter, raw violence, and poems (read voice-over); *The Wishing Tree* (1978), a color film that could pass for a Czech tragicomedy if it were not such a Russian fable; and *Repentance* (1984, released 1987), a surreal black comedy about an official who resembles Stalin and who will not stay buried after his death, because someone repeatedly digs him up.

Glasnost and After

Repentance was shown to acclaim abroad and huge lines of patrons at home when it finally was released, its uncompromising and darkly amusing anti-Stalinism proof that a new openness (*glasnost*) was indeed beginning to flourish as the Cold War (1945–90) drew to a close.

For there had been a change in command. Mikhail Gorbachev began in 1985 a policy of restructuring (*perestroika*) and openness. Restrictions on Soviet art were virtually eliminated, and studio productions were expected to help pay for themselves. Subsidized production dropped; co-production, especially with companies abroad, substantially increased. Shelved films were released. New ideas were welcomed. The shadows of Brezhnev and stagnation were gone. Filmmakers replaced bureaucrats in key industry positions. And out of this, in the short-lived *glasnost* era (roughly 1985–92), came some daring and remarkable films, among the most influential of which were *Is It Easy to be Young?* (Juris Podnieks, 1987), an interview–documentary that traces the fortunes of several teenagers across two years; *Little Vera* (Vassili Pitchul, 1988), a sexually frank and sometimes depressing, almost Neorealist look at a young woman's options under the oppressive sexual, economic, and political systems that are as inescapable as her family; and *Get Thee Out!* (Dmitri Astrakhan, 1990), the first Soviet film about the pogroms. The script of *Little Vera* (by

the director's wife, Maria Khmelik) went unproduced for four years but was approved under *glasnost*; its production and *Repentance*'s 1987 release indicated that the old restrictions on content and treatment truly were gone.

Perestroika opened the door to free enterprise, but also to inflation and food shortages; Soviet society became more vital, but also more threatened. In December 1991, the Soviet Union was disbanded, and its republics became separate countries; Russia, or the Russian Federation, remained the largest and was headed by its first elected president, Boris Yeltsin. Yeltsin called for a completely free-market economy and even tried to ban the Communist Party. Subsidized filmmaking was at an end. Mosfilm, the industry's largest studio, suffered so drastically from the loss of government backing that by 1993 its output had dropped from 45 to 7 pictures a year. An impossible thing had happened: Soviet filmmakers, who were supposed to focus on ideology rather than the box office, suddenly became post-Soviet filmmakers who had to make movies that would make money.

The problem is that the post-Soviet Russian movie business is no place to make money. Tickets are cheap, but very few people go; in theatres they most enjoy American films, and at home they watch videotapes and soap operas. According to a 1993 poll taken in Moscow, only four percent of the respondents had any interest in seeing movies about daily life in Russia.

Tenghiz Abuladze's Repentance.

Fig. 16-18

This is not to suggest that the Russians have given up on making masterpieces and reconsidering the past. Alexander Sokurov's *Mother and Son* (1997) ranks with the best of Tarkovsky and Paradjanov; its muted colors, distorted perspectives, and slow tempo give the death of a mother the time it demands and make possible the rigorous search for the right images, images that seem to come from another world but go to the heart of ours.

As the studios in Russia sought to make it on their own, studios and independents in the former republics began to develop self-supporting national cinemas. If it had always been important to know from which region of the USSR a Soviet filmmaker came (Dovzhenko was Ukrainian to his bones), it now became appropriate to speak of Noughmanov's *Wild East* (1993) as a film from Kazakhstan, in fact part of the "Kazakh New Wave." From the breakup of the Soviet Union came more than a dozen emerging national cinemas, each of them starting from scratch.

Iran

The Islamic Republic of Iran has produced state-supported and independent films of extraordinary quality; it also has a conventional film industry that is, in the words of director Abbas Kiarostami, "across the street" from where the real filmmaking is going on. Before the 1979 revolution that overthrew the shah, Iran had produced a total of 1,300 films, including a brief New Wave in the early 1970s; since 1984 it has produced at least 50 "Superior Iranian Films" every year, partly by making low-budget grants available for films that would teach worthwhile lessons and whose artistry would bring international prizes and bookings.

There were, of course, restrictions. Because a woman had to be covered when she left her house, even to go to a movie set and play an indoor scene, she still had to be covered in that indoor scene; one result was that the majority of new Iranian films with adult characters were shot outdoors, even in cars like so many of Kiarostami's, to avoid shooting unrealistic indoor scenes in which, for example, a fully clothed couple talk things over in bed.

One of the most remarkable things about the Iranian cinema of the mid-1980s and later is that

without portraying violence or sexual activity, let alone a woman's uncovered head, these pictures have revived Neorealism, the fable, and the children's film all at once. Many of these movies are about children and take them more seriously than adults, though they pretend to treat adults as equals. Most of them are about an ordinary person with a single big problem—a legacy of the most influential of all imports, *The Bicycle Thief*—and many are shot outdoors with nonprofessionals. The best have a solid sincerity and an apparent simplicity that sneaks the overwhelming into the frame, whether they are as matter-of-fact as Kiarostami's or as ugly and beautiful as those of Makhmalbaf (a radical sent to prison in the days of the shah), little tales with good advice, or focused celebrations of human decency.

Abbas Kiarostami, an accomplished director of commercials, was asked to start the filmmaking branch of the Institute for the Intellectual Development of Children and Young Adults. Kiarostami began to write and direct short films in 1970, features in 1974 (*The Traveler*). He also wrote screenplays—treatments, really, with room for the actors to improvise the dialogue—that were directed by others but often edited by him; the most widely available of these are *The Key* (1986, Ebrahim Forouzesh) and *The White Balloon* (1995, Jafar Panahi). *The Key* is about a four-year-old boy who manages, when he figures out what the neighbors are yelling about, to save his baby sister and himself from a gas explosion in their locked apartment. *The White Balloon* is about a little girl who wants to buy a special goldfish for the New Year, the people who scare her, and the people who help her, especially her brother and a refugee who gives up the chance to sell his last balloon—the white one—to help her get her money from under a street grate. In 1987, Kiarostami directed *Where is the Friend's Home?* (or *Where is My Friend's House?*, as the French release title translates), a completely involving movie about a boy, Ahmad, who has accidentally picked up the school notebook of his friend, Mohammad Reza, and *has* to return it, in spite of the fact that he doesn't know where his friend lives.

In *Life, and Nothing More . . .* (1992, also called *And Life Goes On*) a man like Kiarostami tries to drive with his son to that remote area, on roads that are mostly blocked, to find out

Shaghayegh Djodat in Mohsen Makhmalbaf's Gabbeh.

Fig. 16-19

whether the children he filmed are all right. *Through the Olive Trees* (1994) is a fictional film about the shooting of *Life, and Nothing More . . . .* This series of films is consistently realistic and increasingly reflexive.

Taste of Cherry (1997) is about a man who drives around looking for a stranger who will help him commit suicide—either by burying him or, if he's changed his mind and is alive, by pulling him out of the pit where he will or will not have killed himself by the next morning. The film ends while he is in the pit; it refuses to take a stand on suicide and leaves the issue to the audience. Most of Kiarostami's films are Neorealist in spirit, structure, and method, but they are never violent, hysterical, or sentimental; they are as flat as Godard's but do not lecture. While dealing with the problems of everyday life, they address and leave open the questions of life itself.

Mohsen Makhmalbaf has worked in a variety of styles, from Neorealism to Expressionism, from raging satire to poetic mystery. His formal masterpiece, *Gabbeh* (1996), is a film of rich color and interwoven narrative lines; as a structure, it is woven. A *gabbeh* is a rug that shows a story; it is made of wool grown and sheared, dyed and woven, by a nomadic tribe in southeastern Iran. The Handicraft Industries Organization asked Makhmalbaf to make a movie about these weavers, expecting a documentary. Instead he made the story of a rug in the form of a rug. An old couple washes their prized blue wedding car-

pet in a stream; the *gabbeh* shows a distant horseman and a woman living with a tribe. The old man asks the *gabbeh* to tell its story, and a young woman in blue (Shaghayegh Djodat) materializes out of the rug; her name is Gabbeh, and her father is Weave of the Wool. She tells the old woman, who is dressed in the same blue, how she is waiting for her father to allow her to marry the man who waits for her, on his horse, in the distance. We see this romance played out, and the story of Gabbeh's uncle's search for a wife, while the old couple washes the rug. The old man wants Gabbeh to love him, but she of course is not interested; she prefers her lover, who howls like a wolf. At one point the uncle teaches a class, essentially to us, about color. He reaches out of the shot into another shot of a yellow, flowering field and pulls back a bunch of yellow flowers; he reaches out of the shot into the sky, and his hand comes back painted blue. "Love is color," says Gabbeh. At last the lovers run away, the father only pretends to kill them—and the old man howls his romantic longing like a wolf. The old couple may *be* the lovers in the story— the movie has just that kind of interreferential structure—or the point could be simply that the *gabbeh* renews a couple's affection as they clean it and identify with its story.

The Apple (1998) was written and edited by Makhmalbaf but directed by his 18-year-old daughter, Samira Makhmalbaf. It is the true story, re-enacted by the actual family, of an overprotective man who refuses to let his blind wife and their two daughters leave their small, high-walled dwelling, and what happens when a social worker lets the kids out. But it ends with a sense of perfect, formal closure when the mother herself, left alone for the first time, finally walks outside and touches an apple, a piece of the richness of life, dangled by a playful neighbor.

The New Internationalism

The most striking change in film commerce since the mid-1960s has not been the introduction of individual national traditions but a leveling of national boundaries that has created a truly international market. The extent of international distribution, the extent of American investments in foreign production and foreign investments in American production, the number of international co-productions, the number of international film festivals, and the number of directors working outside their native industries have become more significant than any particularly national statistics.

To take only one example, *Crouching Tiger, Hidden Dragon*, which won Taiwan the Oscar for Best Foreign Language Film of 2000—while it was, simultaneously, in the running for Best Picture—was produced by companies in Mainland China, Hong Kong (where much of it was shot), the United States, and Taiwan. The director himself, Ang Lee, has worked across the world while maintaining a base in New York—the site of his first pictures, *Pushing Hands* and *The Wedding Banquet*—making films like *Eat Drink Man Woman* in his native Taiwan, *Sense and Sensibility* (a U.S./U.K. co-production) in England, and *The Ice Storm* in the United States. He is an international director, and each country in his co-productions has added a significant presence, not just backing, as can plainly be seen in the contributions England made to *Sense and Sensibility*, from the Jane Austen novel and the Emma Thompson screenplay to the cast and the landscape. And if *The Ice Storm* is strictly American drama, *Crouching Tiger* is a film immersed in all of China, leaping from one region to another as gracefully as its characters bound across rooftops and basing itself in literature and in fable as well as in the history of Chinese cinema.

Directors had, of course, changed residence before: both Billy Wilder and Fred Zinnemann left Germany for Hollywood, as Hitchcock left England, and stayed, while Lang and Renoir worked in Hollywood for a while and then left. But in the 1970s and later it became more common to find directors working in several countries—like Louis Malle, who continued to make films in France after he began directing in America, or Wim Wenders, who made *Paris, Texas* in America, then hit the road for Tokyo (to make the documentary *Tokyo-Ga*, 1985) and Berlin. International crews and casts flourished as filmmakers satisfied the desire to work with the right people in the right place (Tarkovsky wanted his Swedish film, *The Sacrifice*, to be shot by Sven Nykvist) and learned from one another: Pavel Lungin's Soviet–French *Taxi Blues* was one of the first Soviet films to be shot with live sound—because it had a French sound crew.

It also became far more common to find films financed by groups or industries in several countries: international co-productions such as the Italian–British–Chinese *The Last Emperor* (1987), which was directed by Bertolucci and shot by Vittorio Storaro (both Italian) on location in China—notably in the Forbidden City, where no Westerners had previously been allowed to film—and which starred John Lone (from Hong Kong), Joan Chen (from Shanghai), and Peter O'Toole (from Connemara).

A film may be co-produced because the filmmakers are living and working in different countries (Kieślowski's Swiss–French–Polish *Three Colors*), because economic opportunities arise (the 1987 co-production treaty signed by Canada and Hungary), because another country or industry has the facilities—or politics—without which the project could not be realized (the controversial Chinese films co-produced in Taiwan and Hong Kong); and because some projects require a great deal of funding from industries unable to support them single-handedly (*The Last Emperor*).

It should be remembered that most films—made by studios or by independents, made in Hollywood or co-produced by people and industries in different countries—earn significant profits (or break even) only when they are exhibited worldwide. Alfonso Arau's *Like Water for*

Fig. 16-20
The Pearl: a Mexican classic written by John Steinbeck, directed by Emilio Fernandez, and shot by Gabriel Figueroa.

Chocolate (1991, released 1992, script and novel by Laura Esquivel) was a hit in Mexico, but abroad it sold more tickets than any Mexican film yet made. Mexico's Alfonso Cuarón, the director of *Y Tu Mamá También* (2001), is also well known for his U.S. pictures, which include *A Little Princess* (1995) and *Harry Potter and the Prisoner of Azkaban* (2004).

International filmmaking has cross-fertilized the cinema. When John Ford decided to film *The Fugitive* (released in 1947) in Mexico, he hired a Mexican cinematographer, Gabriel Figueroa. Figueroa had been trained in Hollywood and had been particularly impressed by the style and example of Gregg Toland—not just in *Citizen Kane* but also in the films Toland shot for Ford and Wyler. One result was that *The Fugitive* looks almost as if Toland had shot it for Ford, but it also reveals Figueroa's own rich, developing style. Figueroa brought his international eye to many of the films he shot in Mexico, from Buñuel's *Los olvidados* and *The Exterminating Angel* (1962) to John Huston's *Under the Volcano* (1984). He also worked regularly with the greatest Mexican director of the 1940s, Emilio Fernandez, shooting—among others—his *María Candelaria* (1943) and

the dramatically powerful, visually stunning *The Pearl* (1946). *The Pearl* was itself the product of an international collaboration, for John Steinbeck wrote its script for Fernandez before rewriting it as a short novel. And Fernandez passed some of his tricks along to Peckinpah, for whom he played the role of General Mapache in *The Wild Bunch*.

There have always been three reasons for film production to cross national boundaries—political, economic, and thematic. The first exodus of filmmakers from their homeland for political reasons was of Germans and other Europeans (Renoir and Clair, for example) from Hitler's Europe. Blacklisted American directors left the United States in the 1950s for England (Joseph Losey) or Greece (Jules Dassin), while the young Costa-Gavras left Greece to study and make films in a more politically receptive France (*Z*) and the United States (*Missing; Music Box*, 1989). After the mid-1960s, the major political exodus was from Eastern Europe: Miloš Forman, Roman Polanski, Agnieszka Holland, Krzysztof Kieślowski, Ryszard Bugajski, and Ivan Passer are among the many Eastern Europeans who deserted native production—temporarily or permanently—for the West. Related to the history of exodus is that of return. Renoir returned to Europe after the war, and Hitchcock went back to England long enough to shoot *Frenzy*. But there are also filmmakers who go back home to risk shooting controversial material under native conditions. Barbet Schroeder was born in Iran, spent part of his childhood in Colombia, and established himself as a filmmaker in France, first working with Rohmer and then shooting his own features (*The Valley Obscured by Clouds*, 1972; *Reversal of Fortune*, 1990) and documentaries (*Idi Amin Dada*, 1974) wherever his camera took him. But in 1999 he returned to the streets and apartments of Medellín to make a violent, tender, realistic movie about love (and drugs, and fame, and—as is usual for him—the meaning of life and death) in contemporary urban Colombia: *Our Lady of the Assassins* (2000), a Colombian–French co-production that was shot with small video cameras to minimize the security risks.

International co-productions also solve economic problems. Through this internationalism flows American investment capital for a Kurosawa to make a film deemed too extravagant and unpopular for the Japanese studios to support (*Kagemusha*); capital also flows the other way, allowing American filmmakers to raise money wherever they can find it (as Paul Schrader did for his Italian–American *The Comfort of Strangers*, 1990). International co-productions often imply international casts—such as Robert De Niro, Burt Lancaster, Donald Sutherland, Dominique Sanda, Stefania Sandrelli, Sterling Hayden, and Gérard Depardieu in Bertolucci's *1900*—which may give the picture box-office appeal in more than a single country.

Finally, some filmmakers shoot outside native boundaries because thematic commitments require the alternative visual or social environment. Peter Weir inspects American culture, while Werner Herzog requires savage and alien landscapes. *The Last Emperor* was a much better film for having been shot on location in China; conversely, the only place Terrence Malick could find the look of 1916–17 Texas for *Days of Heaven* was on the plains of Canada.

Luis Buñuel

Perhaps the model for this internationalism is the career of the vagabond director Luis Buñuel, for 50 years a man without a cinematic country—

making films in France, working as an editor and translator in America, then making films in Mexico, returning again to France, and only occasionally making a film in his native Spain.

Although the Spanish have a rich tradition of painting, poetry, theatre, and fiction, decades of political repression constrained the country's filmmakers until the death of Franco in 1975 and the emergence of three of the greatest directors in modern cinema: Victor Erice (*Spirit of the Beehive*, 1973; Carlos Saura (*Blood Wedding*, 1981; *Carmen*, 1983; *El amor brujo*, 1986— choreographed by Antonio Gades—and more recently, *Tango*, 1998), and Pedro Almodóvar. Almodóvar is most interested in melodrama, approached from a variety of angles, some of them skewed; he can be outrageous (*Women on the Verge of a Nervous Breakdown*, 1988), symbolic (*Matador*), relatively realistic (*What Have I Done to Deserve This!!*, 1984), novelistic (*Live Flesh*, 1997), or subtly ironic (*The Flower of My Secret*, 1995), but he always gets top performances from his actors, who manage to be at home in—and, while performing, to comment on—a vast spectrum of roles. *Bad Education* (2004), for example, was a daring treatment of pedophilia, but it was more about role-playing and what some people will do to make it in the film business; like *Live Flesh* and others, it shows how he links comedy, tragedy, and history in melodrama. Saura is most interested in theatre, particularly the dance, and has made color and camera movement part of an all-embracing choreography. And Erice is most interested in light; his films are evocative and careful, intimate and shrouded, symbolic and direct, reminiscent of the works of Werner Herzog and Zhang Yimou at their most romantic, but also of the intense and meditative pictures of Carl Dreyer. Other Spanish directors working today include Bigas Luna (*Jamón jamón*, 1992), whose films might be said to explore masculinity or just to take its extremes for granted, and Alejandro Amenábar (*Thesis*, 1995; *Open Your Eyes*, 1999), who excels at cerebral horror. No work like this was going on in Spain in Buñuel's time.

Buñuel, a descendant of the Surrealism of Paris in the 1920s where he learned his craft from Jean Epstein, made films in a variety of styles. Through these differing styles over an amazingly long career shine the consistent Buñuel traits: the

Stirrings of a new Spanish cinema: two internationally popular examples. Fig. 16-21: Antonio Gades and Laura Del Sol in Carlos Saura's Carmen; *Fig. 16-22: Carmen Maura (right) in Pedro Almodóvar's* Women on the Verge of a Nervous Breakdown.

Fig. 16-21

Fig. 16-22

Surrealist's perception of the insubstantiality of reality coupled with the Surrealist's savage humor; the psychologist's interest in sexual fantasies and personal visions of experience that violate all the norms of the realists, the professional psychologists, and the Church; and, finally, his satiric, hostile preoccupation with the Church itself. (He was educated by the Jesuits.)

The first event in Buñuel's first film, *Un Chien andalou* (1929), was a close-up of a razor slicing an apparently human (actually a dead animal's) eyeball. The brutality, the nausea, the visceral attack of this first action dominate the Buñuel canon. One of the most unflinchingly sadistic and brutal scenes ever filmed is in the assault of the juvenile delinquents in *Los olvidados* (*The Forgotten Ones*; U.S. title, *The Young and the Damned*, 1950) on a legless beggar. The delinquents pull the cripple out of his cart, kick him, then gleefully send the empty cart careening down the street. The young hero ends up dead on a pile of garbage. As realistic as this depressing, nasty movie is, it still contains Surrealistic dream sequences—and a certain perverse tone—that make it utterly unlike any of the other children of Neorealism.

Viridiana (1961), one of Buñuel's richest works as well as one of his most blasphemous, was filmed in Spain. It begins in a monastery with the music of Handel's *Messiah*; it ends in the bedroom of a young lecher with rock 'n' roll music. The young woman, Viridiana (Silvia Pinal), feels her soul strengthened by this Christian–communist colony in which everyone works together and no one goes hungry. But one day when Viridiana and the other masters leave on an excursion, the peasants break into the house, set out the fancy linen and china, and begin to devour a banquet of their own. They raucously break furniture and dishes; they drunkenly bloody the white linen with wine. One of the beggars takes a "picture" of the loathsome group; they pose in the positions of the disciples in da Vinci's "The Last Supper"; the beggar woman "snaps the picture" of the gathering by raising her skirt and exposing her naked groin. This lewd burlesque of the sacred scene deflates any hope that this human scum can be converted or helped by any means whatever. Viridiana has failed at both faith and charity. Seeing no hope at all, Viridiana wanders into the bedroom of her sensual cousin where he "plays cards," as he euphemistically puts it. As Viridiana sits down at the card table, her cousin tells her that he has always known she would one day play cards with him. Buñuel's allegory of the spirit and flesh is complete.

After *Viridiana*, Buñuel returned to Mexico (*The Exterminating Angel*, 1962) and finally to France. *The Discreet Charm of the Bourgeoisie* (1972) develops the gap between the simple concrete reality that the bourgeois expectations assume (the banality of property, success, money, social intercourse, and, especially, eating dinner) and the complex levels of superrealities

The beginning of Buñuel's film career and of Un Chien andalou—*the filmmaker (Buñuel himself).*

Fig. 16-23

Fig. 16-24
Alfonso Mejía as Pedro in Buñuel's Los olvidados, *one of the greatest of his Mexican features; cinematographer, Gabriel Figueroa.*

(wishes, dreams, imaginings, fancies) that actually exist. Expectations are memorably reversed in *The Phantom of Liberty* (1974), where friends chat and defecate at a "dinner table" but excuse themselves to eat in a little room in private. One of the cleverest and most challenging of the late Buñuel films is *The Milky Way* (1969), named after the route of pilgrimage from Paris to San Sebastian in Spain, where Christian pilgrims of the Middle Ages traveled to view the tomb of St. James. Buñuel's film is more a pilgrimage in time than in space, for as his two modern "pilgrims" (one old, one young; both of them tramps) make the same journey, their "stopping places" are a series of religious heresies that have been debated and banned over the past five centuries. Buñuel's editing, audacity, and philosophical logic—the demands of the argument, realized as scenes—make it completely natural for the two

20th-century pilgrims to meet two young men who continually walk back and forth between centuries.

Even if filmmakers have always been able to make the fictitious appear real, Buñuel pushes this freedom into the realm of absurdity and contradiction. For example, the single female object of desire in *That Obscure Object of Desire* (1977) cannot possibly be embodied by two different women, but there the two women concretely are, both of them the single beloved the man would like to possess. The fact that she is two—and played by two actresses who do not resemble each other—underscores the impossibility of ever fulfilling the desire to possess, let alone define, another human being. For Buñuel the cinema has always been the realm of the impossible actual: Phenomena, which in the reality of time and space cannot possibly occur, can occur before the viewer's eyes because the cinema is free of reality's time and space. But for Buñuel this feature makes the cinema *more* like life and experience, not less, for reality is composed of thoughts, dreams, ideas, and desires as much as of tangible objects. The old heresy staged in a farmhouse *is there* on that Milky Way just as clearly as that farmhouse is there. The alternating objects of abstract desire—one cool and virginal, the other fiery and sensual—are there, just as clearly as each of those actresses is there. In Buñuel's view, only when people realize the insubstantiality of our supposedly "objective reality" and of our opinions based on it will we be able to avoid doing violence both to reality and to one another. It was a view Buñuel maintained ferociously for five decades, in country after country, until his death in 1983.

For Further Viewing

FILMS

THE NEW GERMAN CINEMA

RAINER WERNER FASSBINDER (1946–82)
Why Does Herr R. Run Amok? (1969)
The Bitter Tears of Petra von Kant (1972)
Ali: Fear Eats the Soul or *Fear Devour the Soul* (1973)
Effi Briest (1974)
Fox and His Friends (1974)
Mother Küster's Trip to Heaven (1975)
The Marriage of Maria Braun (1979)
Berlin Alexanderplatz (1980)
Lola (1981)
Veronika Voss (1981)

WERNER HERZOG (1942–)
Signs of Life (1968)
Fata Morgana (1970)
Aguirre, the Wrath of God (1972)
Everyone for Himself and God Against All or *The Mystery of Kaspar Hauser* (1974)
Heart of Glass (1976)
Stroszek (1977)
Nosferatu: Phantom of the Night (1979)
Woyzeck (1979)
Fitzcarraldo (1982)
Little Dieter Needs to Fly (1997)

VOLKER SCHLÖNDORFF (1939–)
Young Törless (1966)
The Lost Honor of Katharina Blum (1975). Co-director, Margarethe von Trotta
The Tin Drum (1979)
The Ninth Day (2004)

MARGARETHE VON TROTTA (1942–)
The Lost Honor of Katharina Blum (1975). Co-director, Volker Schlöndorff
Marianne and Juliane or *The German Sisters* or *The Leaden Time* (1981)
Sheer Madness or *Friends and Husbands* (1982)
Rosa Luxemburg (1985)

WIM WENDERS (1945–)
The Goalie's Anxiety at the Penalty Kick (1971)
Kings of the Road or *In the Course of Time* (1976)
The American Friend (1977)
Paris, Texas (1984)
Wings of Desire or *The Heavens over Berlin* (1987)
Far Away, So Close! (1993)
Buena Vista Social Club (1999)

GERMAN MISCELLANY
The Captain from Koepenick (1956, Helmut Kautner)
Aren't We Wonderful? (1958, Kurt Hoffmann)
Chronicle of Anna Magdalena Bach (1967, Straub/Huillet)
Moses and Aaron (1974, Straub/Huillet)
Our Hitler (1977, Hans Jürgen Syberberg)
Das Boot (1981, Wolfgang Petersen)
Parsifal (1982, Hans Jürgen Syberberg)
Class Relations (1983, Straub/Huillet)
Run Lola Run or *Lola Runs* (1998, Tom Tykwer)

THIRD WORLD CINEMA

CUBA
Lucía (1968, Humberto Solás)
Memories of Underdevelopment (1968, Tomás Gutiérrez Alea)
The Other Francisco (1975, Sergio Giral)
Alicia (1976, Victor Casaus)
The Last Supper (1977, Tomás Gutiérrez Alea)
Strawberry and Chocolate (1993, Tomás Gutiérrez Alea and Juan Carlos Tabío)
Who the Hell is Juliette? (1997, Carlos Marcovich)

Latin America

The Pearl (1946, Emilio Fernandez; Mexico)

Vidas secas (1963, Nelson Pereira dos Santos; Brazil)

The Hour of the Furnaces: Notes and Testimonies on Neo-Colonialism, Violence and Liberation (1968, Fernando Solanas and Octavio Getino; Argentina)

El Topo (1969, Alexandro Jodorowsky; Mexico)

Blood of the Condor (1969, Jorge Sanjinés; Bolivia)

Antonio das Mortes (1969, Glauber Rocha; Brazil)

How Tasty Was My Little Frenchman (1972, Nelson Pereira dos Santos; Brazil)

Xica (1976, Carlos Diegues; Brazil)

The Battle of Chile (1973–79). Part I released 1975, Parts I and II released together in 1977, Part III released 1979 (Patricio Guzmán; Chile)

Pixote (1981, Hector Babenco; Brazil)

Sugar Cane Alley (1983, Euzhan Palcy; Martinique/France)

Kiss of the Spider Woman (1985, Hector Babenco; Brazil)

Rodrigo D. No Future (1990, Victor Gaviria; Colombia). Completed 1989

Like Water for Chocolate (1992, Alfonso Arau; Mexico). Completed 1991

Central Station (1998, Walter Salles; Brazil)

Our Lady of the Assassins (2000, Barbet Schroeder; Colombia/France). Completed 1999

Amores Perros (2000, Alejandro González Iñárritu; Mexico)

Y Tu Mamá También or *And Your Mother Too* (2001, Alfonso Cuarón; Mexico)

La Ciénaga (2001, Lucrecia Martel; Argentina)

Nine Queens (2001, Fabián Bielinsky; Argentina)

City of God (2002, Fernando Meirelles; Brazil)

Africa and the Middle East

Abbas Kiarostami (1940–)

Where is the Friend's Home? or *Where is My Friend's House?* (1987)

Close-Up (1990)

Life, and Nothing More . . . or *And Life Goes On* (1992)

Through the Olive Trees (1994)

Taste of Cherry or *The Taste of Cherries* (1997)

Mohsen Makhmalbaf (1957–)

The Cyclist (1989)

Gabbeh (1996)

The Silence (1998)

Kandahar (2001)

Ousmane Sembene (1923–)

Black Girl (1966)

Xala or *The Curse* or *Impotence* (1974)

Guelwaar (1992)

Faat Kiné (2000)

Moolaadé (2004)

African and Middle Eastern Miscellany

The Gods Must Be Crazy (1981, Jamie Uys; Botswana)

The Wind (1982, Souleymane Cissé; Mali)

Yol (1982, Şerif Gören and Yilmaz Güney; Turkey)

Yeelen or *Brightness* (1987, Souleymane Cissé; Mali)

Wedding in Galilee (1987, Michel Khleifi; Israel/Belgium/France)

The White Balloon (1995, Jafar Panahi; Iran)

Guimba, un tyrant une époque or *Guimba the Tyrant* (1995, Cheick Oumar Sissoko; Mali)

The Apple (1998, Samira Makhmalbaf; Iran)

Genesis (1999, Cheick Oumar Sissoko; Mali)

The Circle (2000, Jafar Panahi; Iran)

Blackboards (2000, Samira Makhmalbaf; Iran)

Osama (2003, Siddiq Barmak; Afghanistan)

At Five in the Afternoon (2003, Samira Makhmalbaf; Iran)

Australia, Canada, Ireland, and New Zealand

Bruce Beresford (1940–)

'Breaker' Morant (1980)

Tender Mercies (1983)

Driving Miss Daisy (1989)

Jane Campion (1955–)

Sweetie (1989)

An Angel at My Table (1990)

The Piano (1993). Completed 1992

David Cronenberg (1943–)

Shivers (1975). U.S. version, *They Came From Within*

Scanners (1981). Completed 1980

Videodrome (1983). Completed 1982
The Dead Zone (1983)
The Fly (1986)
Dead Ringers (1988)
Crash (1996)
eXistenZ (1999)
Spider (2002)

ATOM EGOYAN (1960–   )
Family Viewing (1987)
The Adjuster (1991)
Exotica (1994)
The Sweet Hereafter (1997)
Felicia's Journey (1999)
Ararat (2002)

PETER JACKSON (1961–   )
Bad Taste (1987)
Heavenly Creatures (1994)
The Frighteners (1996)
The Lord of the Rings: The Fellowship of the Ring (2001)
The Lord of the Rings: The Two Towers (2002)
The Lord of the Rings: The Return of the King (2003)

PETER WEIR (1944–   )
Picnic at Hanging Rock (1975)
The Last Wave (1977)
Gallipoli (1981)
The Year of Living Dangerously (1982)
The Truman Show (1998)

AUSTRALIA, CANADA, IRELAND, NEW ZEALAND MISCELLANY
The Story of the Kelly Gang (1906, Charles Tait)
Back to God's Country (1919). With Nell Shipman (David M. Hartford)
Nobody Waved Goodbye (1964, Don Owen)
Outback (1971, Ted Kotcheff)
The Apprenticeship of Duddy Kravitz (1974, Ted Kotcheff)
The Picture Show Man (1977, John Power)
Newsfront (1978, Phillip Noyce)
Mad Max (1979, George Miller)
My Brilliant Career (1979, Gillian Armstrong)
The Road Warrior or *Mad Max 2* (1981, George Miller)
Man of Flowers (1983, Paul Cox)
The Company of Wolves (1984, Neil Jordan)

Crocodile Dundee (1986, Peter Faiman)
The Decline of the American Empire (1986, Denys Arcand)
My Left Foot (1989, Jim Sheridan)
The Crying Game (1992, Neil Jordan)
Once Were Warriors (1994, Lee Tamahori)
The Adventures of Priscilla, Queen of the Desert (1994, Stephan Elliott)
The Ugly (1996, Scott Reynolds)
The Castle (1997, Rob Stich)
The Butcher Boy (1997, Neil Jordan)
Maelström (2000, Denis Villeneuve)
Innocence (2000, Paul Cox)
Moulin Rouge! (2001, Baz Luhrmann)
Atanarjuat the Fast Runner or *The Fast Runner* (2001, Zacharias Kunuk)
Rabbit-Proof Fence (2002, Phillip Noyce)
Whale Rider (2003, Niki Caro)
The Barbarian Invasions (2003, Denys Arcand)

THE FORMER SOVIET UNION

TENGHIZ ABULADZE (1924–94)
Molba (*Prayer*, 1969). Completed 1967
The Wishing Tree (1978). Completed 1977
Repentance (1987). Completed 1984

SERGEI PARADJANOV (1924–90)
Shadows of Forgotten Ancestors (1964)
Sayat Nova or *The Color of Pomegranates* (1968–78). Shot 1968; early version released 1971; completed 1978
The Legend of the Suram Fortress (1984). Co-director, Dodo Abashidze
Ashik Kerib (1988)

ANDREI TARKOVSKY (1932–86)
Ivan's Childhood or *My Name is Ivan* (1962)
Andrei Rublev or *Andrei Roublyov* (1966). Shown abroad since 1969; Soviet release, 1971
Solaris (1972)
Mirror (1974)
Stalker (1982). Completed 1979
Nostalgia or *Nostalghia* (1983)
The Sacrifice (1986)

POST-STALINIST AND POST-SOVIET MISCELLANY
Boris Godunov (1955, Vera Stroyeva)
The Quiet Don (3 parts, 1957, Sergei Gerasimov)
The Cranes Are Flying (1957, Mikhail Kalatozov)
The Overcoat (1959, Alexei Batalov)
Ballad of a Soldier (1959, Grigori Chukhrai)
Lady with a Dog (1960, Josef Heifitz)

Hamlet (1964, Grigori Kozintsev)
I Am Cuba (1964, Mikhail Kalatozov)
The Wish (1966, Larissa Shepitko)
The First Teacher (1966, Andrei
Konchalovsky)
War and Peace (1967, Sergei Bondarchuk)
King Lear (1971, Grigori Kozintsev)
A Slave of Love (1976, Nikita Mikhalkov)
The Ascent (1977, Larissa Shepitko)
Oblomov (1980, Nikita Mikhalkov)
Come and See (1985, Elem Klimov)
Little Vera (1988, Vassili Pitchul)
Freeze, Die, Come to Life (1990, Vitaly
Kanevsky)
Burnt by the Sun (1994, Nikita Mikhalkov)
Window to Paris (1994, Yuri Mamin)
Mother and Son (1997, Alexander Sokurov)
Outskirts (1998, Petr Lutsik)
Russian Ark (2002, Alexander Sokurov)

SPAIN

PEDRO ALMODÓVAR (1951–)
What Have I Done to Deserve This!! (1984)
Women on the Verge of a Nervous Breakdown
(1988)
Live Flesh (1997)
All About My Mother (1999)
Bad Education (2004)

LUIS BUÑUEL (1900–83)
Un Chien andalou (1929). Co-director, Salvador
Dalí
L'Age d'or (1930). Co-director, Salvador Dalí
Las Hurdes or *Land Without Bread* (1932)
Los olvidados or *The Young and the Damned*
(1950)
Viridiana (1961)
The Exterminating Angel (1962)
Belle de jour (1967)
The Milky Way (1969)
The Discreet Charm of the Bourgeoisie
(1972)
The Phantom of Liberty (1974)
That Obscure Object of Desire (1977)

VICTOR ERICE (1940–)
Spirit of the Beehive (1973)
El sur or *The South* (1983)
El sol del membrillo or *The Sun of the Quince*
or *Dream of Light* (1992)

CARLOS SAURA (1932–)
Cría or *Cría cuervos* (*Raise Ravens*, 1975)
Blood Wedding (1981)
Carmen (1983)

SPANISH MISCELLANY
La aldea maldita (*The Accursed Village*, 1929,
Florián Rey)
Marcelino, Bread and Wine (1954, Ladislao Vajda)
Death of a Cyclist (1955, Juan Antonio Bardem)
To a God Unknown (1977, Jaime Chávarri)
Jamón jamón (1992, Bigas Luna)
Open Your Eyes (1999, Alejandro Amenábar)
The Others (2001, Alejandro Amenábar)

DVDs

THE NEW GERMAN CINEMA
Aguirre, the Wrath of God (1972, **Werner
Herzog**). Anchor Bay. Commentary by Herzog.
Ali: Fear Eats the Soul (1973, **Rainer Werner
Fassbinder**). Criterion Collection. Includes a
short about the film, a 1976 BBC documentary
on New German Cinema, and interviews.
The American Friend (1977, **Wim Wenders**).
Anchor Bay. Commentary by Wenders.
The BRD Trilogy (1979–81, **Rainer Werner
Fassbinder**). Criterion Collection. Contains
The Marriage of Maria Braun, Lola, and
Veronika Voss, along with a documentary on
Fassbinder (*I Don't Just Want You to Love
Me*) and a long interview with him, a docu-
mentary on actress **Sybille Schmitz**, com-
mentaries by Wenders and others, and more.
BRD stands for Bundesrepublik Deutschland.
Buena Vista Social Club (1999, **Wim Wenders**).
Artisan Entertainment. With additional con-
cert footage, information about the musicians,
and a commentary by Wenders.
Heart of Glass (1976, **Werner Herzog**). Anchor
Bay. Commentary by Herzog.
Lightning Over Water (1980, **Nicholas Ray** and
Wim Wenders). Anchor Bay. With a lecture by
Ray and a commentary by Wenders.
The Lost Honor of Katharina Blum (1975,
Volker Schlöndorff and **Margarethe von
Trotta**). Criterion Collection. Includes an in-
terview with the directors.
Run Lola Run (1998, **Tom Tykwer**). Columbia
Tri-Star. Commentary by Tykwer and star
Franka Potente.

The Tin Drum (1979, **Volker Schlöndorff**). Criterion Collection. **Digitally remastered**; commentary by Schlöndorff. Includes deleted scenes; author **Günter Grass** reading from the novel in 1987; interviews with Schlöndorff, Grass, co-writer **Jean-Claude Carrière**, and others; the original ending of the script; and a documentary on the lawsuit.

AFRICA, CUBA, LATIN AMERICA, THE MIDDLE EAST, AND THIRD WORLD CINEMA

Amores Perros (2000, **Alejandro González Iñárritu**). Studio Home Entertainment. Includes a production commentary, music videos, and behind-the-scenes footage.

Central Station (1998, **Walter Salles**). Columbia TriStar. Commentary by Salles and others.

La Ciénaga (2001, **Lucrecia Martel**). Studio Home Vision Entertainment.

Close-Up (1990, **Abbas Kiarostami**). Facets Video. Includes an interview with Kiarostami and filmographies for him and **Mohsen Makhmalbaf**.

The Cyclist (1989, **Mohsen Makhmalbaf**). Image Entertainment.

The Devil's Backbone (2001, **Guillermo del Toro**). Columbia TriStar. Commentary by del Toro.

Genesis (1999, **Cheick Oumar Sissoko**). Kino International.

Osama (2003, **Siddiq Barmak**). MGM. Includes a documentary, *Sharing Hope and Freedom*, featuring Barmak.

Our Lady of the Assassins (2000, **Barbet Schroeder**). Paramount Home Video.

Pixote (1981, **Hector Babenco**). New Yorker Films.

Rodrigo D. No Future (1990, **Victor Gaviria**). Facets Video.

Sembene's works are not available on DVD.

Strawberry and Chocolate (1993, **Tomás Gutiérrez Alea** and **Juan Carlos Tabío**). Buena Vista Home Video.

Sugar Cane Alley (1983, **Euzhan Palcy**). New Yorker Films.

Taste of Cherry (1997, **Abbas Kiarostami**). Criterion Collection. Includes an interview with Kiarostami.

Wedding in Galilee (1987, **Michel Khleifi**). Kino International.

Who the Hell is Juliette? (1997, **Carlos Marcovich**). Kino Video.

Yeelen (1987, **Souleymane Cissé**). Kino International.

Y Tu Mamá También (2001, **Alfonso Cuarón**). MGM/UA. Unrated edition; includes a commentary by the cast members in Spanish, a short (*Me la Debes*), a making-of documentary, and deleted scenes.

AUSTRALIA, CANADA, IRELAND, AND NEW ZEALAND

The Company of Wolves (1984, **Neil Jordan**). Hen's Tooth Video.

Dead Ringers (1988, **David Cronenberg**). Criterion Collection. Includes information on the medical instruments; a demonstration of the twinning/motion-control effects; the electronic press kit; and commentary by Cronenberg, star **Jeremy Irons**, and others.

Family Viewing / Next of Kin (1987 and 1984, **Atom Egoyan**). Zeitgeist Video. Contains both movies, with commentaries by Egoyan.

The Fast Runner (see Chap. 18 list).

Innocence (2000, **Paul Cox**). Columbia TriStar.

The Lord of the Rings: The Fellowship of the Ring, The Two Towers, and *The Return of the King* (2001–03, **Peter Jackson**). New Line Home Entertainment. Platinum Series. Special Extended DVD Editions. One 4-disc set for each film in the trilogy, containing the extended version of the movie, commentaries by all concerned, and hours of documentaries and features about the background and production of the film, with especially good coverage of **digital effects**, **production design**, and the use of New Zealand **locations**. Even those who prefer the theatrical release versions will find the extras offered in these sets to be comprehensive, entertaining, and extremely informative.

Mad Max (1979, **George Miller**). MGM/UA. Special Edition. Includes the original Australian-language track, shorts on star **Mel Gibson** and the series, and more.

The Magdalene Sisters (2003, **Peter Mullan**). Miramax Home Entertainment. Includes a 1997 Channel Four documentary about the Magdalene Asylums, *Sex in a Cold Climate*.

Moulin Rouge! (2001, **Baz Luhrmann**). Twentieth Century Fox. Commentary by Luhrmann and others.

Picnic at Hanging Rock (1975, **Peter Weir**). Criterion Collection. Director's cut (3 minutes shorter than the release version). Unlike the director's cut of *The Last Wave* (Criterion), which changes the ending, this one is an improvement.

Rabbit-Proof Fence (2002, **Phillip Noyce**). Miramax Home Entertainment. Includes a making-of documentary and a commentary by Noyce, author **Pilkington Garimara**, and others.

The Sweet Hereafter (1997, **Atom Egoyan**). New Line Home Entertainment. Commentary by Egoyan and writer **Russell Banks**.

Videodrome (1983, **David Cronenberg**). Criterion Collection. Includes *Fear on Film*, a 1982 discussion of horror by Cronenberg, **John Carpenter**, and others; the unrated cut of the film; a documentary and an interview about the effects; a 2000 Cronenberg short, *Camera*; the uncut Videodrome footage with Cronenberg's remarks; and commentaries on the feature by Cronenberg and by stars **James Woods** and **Deborah Harry**.

THE FORMER SOVIET UNION

Andrei Rublev (1966, **Andrei Tarkovsky**). Criterion Collection. The complete director's cut (205 minutes), new subtitles, a commentary and an essay by film scholar Vlada Petrić, and a timeline of Russian history and Rublev's life.

Ashik Kerib (1988, **Sergei Paradjanov**). Ruscico.

Come and See (1985, **Elem Klimov**). Kino Video. Includes interviews with the cast and crew, filmographies, and archival materials on Nazi brutalities and Belarus partisans.

Little Vera (1988, **Vassili Pitchul**). Water Bearer Films.

Mother and Son (1997, **Alexander Sokurov**). Fox Lorber.

Outskirts (1998, **Petr Lutsik**). Facets Video.

Russian Ark (2002, **Alexander Sokurov**). Wellspring. Includes an excellent making-of documentary, interviews with Sokurov and others, filmographies, and more.

Sergei Eisenstein: The Sound Years (1935–46, **Sergei Eisenstein**). Criterion Collection. Contains *Alexander Nevsky* and *Ivan the Terrible, Parts I and II* (with deleted scenes); a stills-based reconstruction of *Bezhin Meadow*; an essay by film historian David Bordwell; and multimedia essays on Eisenstein's visual vocabulary, his collaboration with composer **Sergei Prokofiev**, and more.

Solaris (1972, **Andrei Tarkovsky**). Criterion Collection. Includes 9 deleted and alternate scenes, many interviews, an essay by Tarkovsky scholars Vida Johnson and Graham Petrie, and an excerpt from a documentary featuring author **Stanislaw Lem**.

Stalker (1979, **Andrei Tarkovsky**). Image Entertainment. Includes an excerpt from Tarkovsky's diploma film, *The Steamroller and the Violin*; a documentary about Tarkovsky's home; and interviews with the cinematographer and the production designer.

SPAIN

L'Age d'or and Un Chien andalou (see Chap. 9 list).

Cría (1976, **Carlos Saura**). Miracle Pictures.

The Discreet Charm of the Bourgeoisie (1972, **Luis Buñuel**). Criterion Collection. Includes two documentaries on Buñuel.

Erice's works are not available on DVD.

Live Flesh (1997, **Pedro Almodóvar**). MGM/UA.

Talk to Her (2002, **Pedro Almodóvar**). Columbia TriStar. Commentary by Almodóvar and star **Geraldine Chaplin**.

Tango (1998, **Carlos Saura**). Columbia TriStar. Includes a making-of documentary and a commentary by producer **Juan Carlos Codazzi** and star **Mia Maestro**.

That Obscure Object of Desire (1977, **Luis Buñuel**). Criterion Collection. Includes an interview with writer **Jean-Claude Carrière**, the text of an interview with Buñuel, and excerpts from a 1929 silent adaptation of the same source novel.

Thesis (1995, **Alejandro Amenábar**). New Yorker Films.

What Have I Done to Deserve This!! (1984, **Pedro Almodóvar**). Wellspring.

17

The Return
of the Myths: 1977–

At some point in the late 1970s, the American cinema abandoned its attack on the genres of American movies and the myths of American life to embrace them both again. Though some critics sneeringly compared the new films to computerized video games, American movies were born as close cousins to the electrical and mechanical novelties in amusement arcades. The new films self-consciously defined movies as both the repository for cultural myths and the contemporary medium for their dissemination. They saw the movies as myth machines. The new films viewed these myths and mysteries not with the jaded eye of adulthood but with the hope and wonder of childhood; they set out to recapture or invent a kind of innocence.

In this period, muscular heroes in T-shirts, robots with hearts of gold, tough cops, resourceful teens, and benevolent masters rose up to vanquish purely evil villains, and what came from outer space could be endearing. Instead of the intellectual and emotional complexity of such previous big films as *Lawrence of Arabia* and *The Godfather*, the typical blockbuster became a wide-screen, color, stereophonic *ride*, full of action and special effects, constructed for speed and thrills rather than contemplation, and with a simple, forceful, unthreatening message (for example, cheaters never prosper); examples range from Steven Spielberg's *Indiana Jones and the Temple of Doom* (1984) to Jan De Bont's *Speed* (1994). Many audiences and most producers preferred what were called "feelgood" movies to "downers" and "bummers"; by far the majority of films had heroes to root for, villains to hate, and

happy endings. Movies fit once more into recognizable genres and embraced their conventions, even while harmlessly making fun of them.

Films that tackled difficult political or psychological material (or were considered too negative, like Ridley Scott's *Blade Runner*, 1982) sometimes had their endings changed by executives—although a few subversive, questioning films did sneak by. It was the period of the blockbuster, the sequel, the Dolby soundtrack, the videocassette and laserdisc and DVD, the direct-to-video release, the camcorder, the computer, and the all-powerful talent agent—a time that began with the science fiction spectacles of George Lucas and Steven Spielberg and grew to include the creepy ironies of David Lynch and the political fables of Spike Lee. This period of American film history has continued into the 2000s, so that its end remains unknown, but its aesthetic, technical, and economic elements are already clear enough. It is not an extension of the Hollywood Renaissance but an entirely new period: technically advanced and politically in retreat, devoted utterly to entertainment but afraid of ideas and risks, with films that are innovative but rarely new. For a capsule version of the difference, compare the spiritual scenes in *Mean Streets* and in *Field of Dreams* (Phil Alden Robinson, 1989).

The late 1970s saw major changes in the film industry, film technology, and film content. The film business adopted a "blockbuster mentality," preferring to finance and distribute a few big films with the potential for enormous profits rather than a larger slate of modest films with modest profits. One "monster hit" a year could

Fig. 17-1

From Kinetoscope parlors to video arcades. **WarGames presents the War Room as the ultimate arcade (Fig. 17-1) and makes explicit the long kinship between movies and novelty arcades (Fig. 17-2; with Matthew Broderick, right).**

Fig. 17-2

keep a studio in business and help to pay for the flops and the less expensive movies it also produced. *The Godfather, Jaws, Star Wars, Close Encounters of the Third Kind, Grease,* and *Superman,* all from the 1970s, were among the top-grossing films of all time—as were their 1980s cousins *The Empire Strikes Back, E.T., Raiders of the Lost Ark, Return of the Jedi, Beverly Hills Cop, Ghostbusters,* and *Batman.* The 1990s added *Terminator 2, Jurassic Park, The Lion King, Forrest Gump, Men in Black, Titanic,* and others to that list. Although *The Birth of a Nation, Snow White,* and *Gone With the Wind* may still be considered more commercially suc-

cessful than most of these blockbusters—they made more profit in relation to their cost, and in more valuable dollars—even when the figures are adjusted for inflation, *Titanic* (James Cameron, 1997) is ahead of them all. In the hope of repeating that kind of success introduced by *Jaws* in 1975, the studio attitude became to spend a lot of money to make a lot of money. *Titanic* cost and made so much that it confirmed this attitude all over again. At $200 million, it was the most expensive movie yet made, and it was the first to earn over $1 billion at the worldwide box office ($600 million domestic). A *blockbuster* is a picture that takes in over $100 million at the U.S. box office. "Small" films with relatively low budgets—many of which were "picked up" from independent producers and simply released by the studio—were given smaller openings and often had to make their profits overseas or on video. (Video itself made a difference, to be discussed later.) Given the cost of these spectacles—as high as $100 million or more, when to produce the average feature cost $11 million in 1981, $34 million in 1994, $55 million in 1997, and $64 million in 2003—the films required tremendous advertising campaigns, which cost even more, and the theatre owner had to send a higher percentage of ticket earnings back to the distributor. Blockbuster or not, a movie that cost $90 million to make and $110 million to distribute but that grossed only $120 million would be in the red until the foreign box office, and perhaps even video, raised its earnings. Theatres learned to make their profits at the concession stand, not at the box office. Theatres also were remodeled, or built, to house 2 or 4—or 16—screens; the multiplex cinema marked the era's biggest change in the practice of theatrical exhibition.

While the cost of the studio film rose, independent producers and distributors proved that they could still make profits with good low-budget pictures. Rebellious and creative directors found maverick producers and made their own films without "help" from the bottom-line studio bureaucrats. As recently as 2001, Todd Field's *In The Bedroom* was produced for $2 million. Robert Rodriguez became a medical test subject and maxed out his credit cards to raise the $7,000 it cost him to make *El Mariachi* (1992), doing the writing, directing, shooting, and editing himself. By 2000, shooting on digital video, editing on a computer, and distributing on disc and over the Internet had brought ministudios to individual desktops, yielding projects that could be transferred to film in a lab and might lead to a job making a feature for a studio or an independent producer.

The major technical advances of the late 1970s were the introduction of the Dolby noise-reduction process, which drastically improved sound quality whether the final soundtrack was optical or magnetic; the Dolby Stereo Variable Area (SVA) soundtrack, which allowed 35mm prints to have four-track stereophonic *optical* soundtracks that had a subtlety, clarity, depth, and range previously possible only with magnetic sound; and the Steadicam, which combined the mobility of the hand-held camera with the smoothness of the old Mitchell studio camera mounted on a dolly. Just as it became normal, in the course of the 1960s, for features to be shot in color, stereo (usually with one or two surround channels that came from the sides and back of the auditorium) became the norm by 1980.

Finally, a new cultural attitude—a conservatism associated with but not limited to the presidency of Ronald Reagan—seems to have produced a shift in film content. The antiestablishment types who dominated American films from *Bonnie and Clyde* and *Midnight Cowboy* to *MASH* were replaced by more ordinary citizens—like Donald Sutherland and Mary Tyler Moore in Robert Redford's *Ordinary People* (1980)—who sought to find a meaningful place within conventional society. With the final singing of "God Bless America," the working-class, small-town protagonists of Michael Cimino's *The Deer Hunter* (1978) reintegrate themselves, both as individuals and as a group, into the fabric of American moral and social life, despite the agony their country has forced them to endure. The working-class hero of John Badham's *Saturday Night Fever* (1977) also seeks some meaningful place in American social life, beyond the escapist dream-dance world of the disco and the narrow moral and political provinciality of Bay Ridge. The Dustin Hoffman of *Kramer vs. Kramer* (Robert Benton, 1979), who just wants to live lovingly with his son, would not give a dime on a cold day to the Dustin Hoffman of *Midnight Cowboy*.

The young welder of *Flashdance* (Adrian Lyne, 1983), who is not a feminist, wants to exchange her blue-collar job for the opportunity to express herself in ballet. The majority of 1980s studio pictures reflected a movement away from social rebellion and toward something else: something not to be angry about but to believe in. What might have been hissed or laughed off the screen in the politicized late 1960s and early 1970s became the stuff of dreams in the 1980s. As the song in *Flashdance*—and President Reagan—repeatedly asserted, anyone with determination and talent could "have it all," and that sweet hope fit well into a culture in which people tried to fulfill all the roles they thought they should (wife– mother–executive); in which they were encouraged to want more and buy more, even on credit; and in which poverty, disappointment, and suffering (the homeless could not "have it all") went unacknowledged.

Stars Wars and the New Mythology

These developments took place throughout the industry and across the country, but if any single film can be credited with opening the era—as *The Jazz Singer* cleared the way for the talkies—that film is George Lucas's *Star Wars* (1977), whose unprecedented use of Dolby Noise Reduction from the beginning to the end of production and whose Dolby SVA soundtrack led to what has been called the "second coming of sound," a complete revolution in the technology and aesthetics of film sound; whose use of a computer to control the camera was equally unprecedented; whose special effects changed the look not only of science fiction but of the fiction film in general—not to mention what they and the film's sound effects did to video games (in a way bringing the cinema back to the arcades where it began); whose phenomenal earnings led the industry to concentrate on big films designed for young audiences; whose creative interest in sequels was clear from the start, when *Star Wars* declared itself "Episode IV" of an otherwise

unproduced series; and whose successful integration of Zen philosophy, of Joseph Campbell's researches into mythology and heroism, of serials and their heroes, of fantasy, of science fiction, and of fast-paced action and adventure announced the Return of the Myths.

Set "a long time ago" and as rooted in old movies as it was in the far older traditions of the saga and romance, this futuristic fantasy made the past new, a goal aspired to by the next two decades of American film, from the significantly named *Raiders of the Lost Ark* (1981) and *Back to the Future* (1984) to *Pulp Fiction* (1994)—not to mention an avalanche of sequels to hits, remakes of classics, and big-budget B pictures in familiar genres.

Supermen, Slashers, and Cops

In addition to the *Star Wars* series and Spielberg's *Close Encounters* and *E.T.*, whose mythic figures come from outer space—and Lucas and Spielberg's Indiana Jones series, whose myths come from ancient and biblical mythology or from the movies—two other films helped to form the mythic consciousness of this period: Richard Donner's *Superman* (1978) and John G. Avildsen's *Rocky* (1976). The comics have a presold audience of readers and their own mythology, and the perfect, moral, likable, mighty Superman—an Achilles whose "heel" is his vulnerability to Kryptonite—

Star Wars: *left to right, Peter Mayhew, Mark Hamill, Alec Guinness, Harrison Ford.*

Fig. 17-3

was a refreshing figure in whom the audience wanted to believe. *Rocky*, a small film that became an unexpected hit, created its own life-sized but mythic hero in Rocky (Sylvester Stallone), the underdog who won't quit. Rocky became the prototype for working-class overachievers like the heroine of *Flashdance* and, from Stallone's own Rambo to Sigourney Weaver's Ripley (the *Alien* series), at least 25 years of winners. There were very few films about losers.

The mythic, often escapist films generally had high production values, impressive stunts and special effects, and attractive heroes—many of whom, in this conservative period, were police. The hero of *RoboCop* (Paul Verhoeven, 1987) is both a man and a machine, and both are good cops. The hero of *Blue Thunder* (John Badham, 1983) is a good cop and the skillful pilot of an armed surveillance helicopter. The hero of *Top Gun* (Tony Scott, 1986) is a hotshot jet pilot who wins tests of skill and gets the girl. The hero of

True Lies (James Cameron, 1994) is a virtually invulnerable secret agent who blows terrorists away with high-tech weapons and saves his marriage. Some heroes did not work for the police force—that is, who were not sheriffs and gunslingers in what were essentially the period's westerns. There were real-life heroes (Steven Soderbergh's *Erin Brockovich*, 2000), metaphysical heroes (Andy and Larry Wachowski's *The Matrix*, 1999), ordinary people forced to rise to extraordinary demands (Andrew Davis's *The Fugitive*, 1993), and people who had heroic fantasies (Alan Parker's *Fame*, 1980).

Not every myth was of a hero; mythic villains were part of the same system. (After all, the Force has a Dark Side, and there are good and bad Terminators.) The young stockbroker in *Wall Street* (Oliver Stone, 1987), who wins morally even if he suffers, must defeat a tremendously powerful antagonist, a takeover artist who incarnates every evil known to capitalism. The "other woman" in

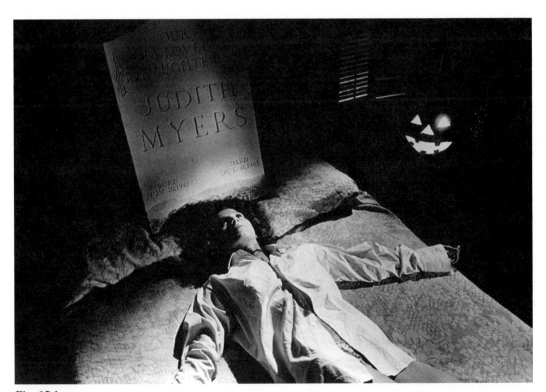

Fig. 17-4
Halloween: *The ritual of formally arranged bodies, later imitated by* Friday the 13th, *creates an atmosphere of eerie significance (Nancy Loomis as Annie).*

Fatal Attraction (Adrian Lyne, 1987) has to be rejected, drowned, and shot at close range before the threat she represents can be destroyed. Although many of these films simply had nasty but mortal bad guys, others presented villains who might look human but were almost impossible to defeat or kill (James Cameron's *The Terminator*, 1984). The most common unstoppable villain of the era was the slasher, the compulsive madman (occasionally a woman) who kills one person after another—with a knife, with his bare hands, or with whatever happens to be around. The slasher film was defined and codified by John Carpenter's *Halloween* (1978), which brought together the essential elements of obsession, madness, immortality (previous slashers could be killed), one-by-one teenage victims, hints of the mythic and supernatural (the killer, who is compared to the boogeyman, is fueled, at least in part, by the energy and folklore of Halloween, when the dead are said to come home), the butcher knife, the mask, the unspeaking killer, the resourceful female survivor, and sex (that is, sex scenes that are associated with bloody death). *Halloween* was cloned by its own sequels as well as by countless low-budget independent productions, but its most famous imitator was the *Friday the 13th* series. The next major slasher series, one of the most creative, began with Wes Craven's *A Nightmare on Elm Street* (1984), whose slasher attacks his victims in their dreams.

Feelgood Movies and Bummers

Two baseball pictures, Phil Alden Robinson's *Field of Dreams* (1989) and John Sayles's *Eight Men Out* (1988), clearly demonstrate that in this period, the escape from politics was a step into fantasy and mythmaking, and to confront political and economic corruption was to dismantle a myth. In *Field of Dreams*, an Iowa farmer (Ray, played by Kevin Costner) obeys a voice that tells him, more or less, that if he builds a baseball field on his property, the great "Shoeless" Joe Jackson will come there to play. Jackson had been one of the "Black Sox," members of the Chicago White Sox who conspired to throw the 1919 World Series and were barred forever from professional baseball; he represents a scandal this film would like to heal. In fact, the movie sets out to forgive and heal all of the failings of the 20th century, both personal and political. The key is to believe

in one's dreams, to follow them with the innocent part of one's heart. And in this definitively mythic film, every dream comes true. When Ray builds the baseball diamond, the ghosts of Shoeless Joe and his teammates do appear; their suspension from the game has, in this magical time and place, been lifted, their sins forgiven. Given this second chance, the Sox think the Iowa field must be heaven, because heaven is where dreams come true. In this film, to believe in the dream is to undo the failures of the past (the fixed World Series, Watergate) and set aside everything that has divided us (the hero's unfortunate fight with his father). The myth of America—the genuine America, as unspoiled as the ideal of baseball, which can be a "heaven" where dreams come true—is renewed, and whatever was bad about the bad old times, including all those disruptive political struggles, is forgiven and forgotten; the past has been given back its innocence, and the present looks better too.

Eight Men Out tells the true story of the Black Sox scandal in a firm, realistic style. If the myth of baseball is taken down a peg—the players are workers, the boss is cheap, and even the gamblers treat the players unfairly—the spirit of the game still comes across. Because of the depth with which it treats betrayed idealism, *Eight Men Out* manages to deal authentically with idealism. America, like baseball, is presented in a less-than-mythical light—a place that can be so hypocritical and economically corrupt that it is almost a fixed World Series in itself, full of betrayed, believing fans. The moral conflicts and disasters this film explores are intense, and the film argues that they need to be understood, not set aside—as history needs to be remembered and learned from. Erasing history is no way to defend or recapture the essence of an ideal. *Field of Dreams*, which did much better at the box office, is a *feelgood* movie; *Eight Men Out* is a *bummer*. Studio executives used those words at the time. Distrustful of official institutions, refusing to offer simplistic solutions, and taking legendary figures with a grain of salt, *Eight Men Out* is an example of the period's "anti-myth" movies.

Some of the anti-myth films were low-budget independent productions; a few were studio extravaganzas. Kubrick's *Full Metal Jacket* (1987), a war film; Ridley Scott's *Alien* (1979), a horror film set in outer space; and Michael Cimino's *Heaven's Gate* (1980), a western, spent their big budgets on unflattering portraits of militarism and big capitalism. *Full Metal Jacket* fired a metaphoric bullet at the myths of the Vietnam War and closed with an image of marching soldiers singing the "*Mickey Mouse Club* Song." *Alien* has a strong, intelligent, fast-acting hero (Ripley, played by Sigourney Weaver), a metamorphosing monster as indestructible and rapacious as Ripley is heroic, and a bad-guy robot, all of which would seem to make this a mythic film. But the real villain—undefeated at the end—is the company that owns the spaceship and wants it to bring back the Alien, even at the cost of the crew, as a specimen from which to develop new weapons and troops.

Heaven's Gate told the story of the Johnson County Wars in 1890s Wyoming, drawing explicit political connections between the federal government and the rich cattlemen who, in the course of the film, exterminate the peasant immigrants whose desire to work the land stands in the way of the cattlemen's plans. Read as "cattlemen vs. farmers," this is a standard western conflict, waiting for its Shane. But the Cattlemen's Association (Sam Waterston as Frank Canton) is far better organized than the marshal, as well as cruel and cold, prejudiced and patrician. *Heaven's Gate* makes the Old West the site of a class war in which the cavalry rides to the rescue—of the bad guys.

Heaven's Gate was a big box-office disaster. Painfully re-evaluating the myths of the western, of fair government, and of the hero, Cimino's critique pushed the anti-myth position too far for its time. Its clearly articulated leftist message, which just as clearly referred to the social, economic, and political problems of the present, may have offended studio executives (as Cimino's arrogant behavior on the set certainly did) or may have been too out of step with current attitudes. By contrast, that same year, Lucas's *The Empire Strikes Back* (1980, directed by Irvin Kershner) took creative mythology even beyond the achievements of *Star Wars* and took the box office along for good measure.

Fig. 17-5
Raiders of the Lost Ark: *Indiana Jones (Harrison Ford) in a mythic world of old serials, ancient artifacts and forces, state-of-the-art effects, and up-to-date irony.*

Popular Heroes and Postmodern Irony

But the debate over mythic values continued throughout the 1980s and into the 1990s, well after *Heaven's Gate* had closed. At a climactic point in *Lethal Weapon* (1987), a villain smugly says there are "no heroes left"—and Mel Gibson rushes in to save the day. Incarnated by Harrison Ford, Arnold Schwarzenegger, Sylvester Stallone, and others, the heroes of action–adventure films affirmed the power of the myths. The most cinematically impressive of these were *Raiders of the Lost Ark* (Spielberg, 1981), which started the Indiana Jones series; *First Blood* (Ted Kotcheff, 1982), which started the Rambo series; and *The Terminator* and *Terminator 2: Judgment Day* (James Cameron, 1991). Two personal and ambitious pictures, Spike Lee's *Malcolm X* (1992) and Spielberg's *Schindler's List* (1993), showed with minimal fictionalizing how real people, gifted and determined but not superhuman, could grow into heroes. On the other hand, a film like Eastwood's *Unforgiven* (1992) suggested that there may never have been any heroes, at least the way we like to think of them and the media (in *Unforgiven*, a writer who chronicles the exploits of gunfighters) like to construct them. The way the media create heroes was analyzed—deconstructed, but with heart—in Oliver Stone's *Natural Born Killers* (1994), whose latter-day Bonnie and Clyde are killers with style. If that film was to be the period's *Bonnie and Clyde*, its *Graduate* was *Forrest Gump* (Robert Zemeckis, 1994), in which Tom Hanks plays a character elevated to mythic status without developing mythic consciousness, a blank that audiences filled with their own nostalgia for innocence.

Leading Directors

Lucas and Spielberg

The master mythmakers of the era are George Lucas and Steven Spielberg. They are also the most powerful creative figures in the contemporary American film industry. Like P. T. Barnum, they are producers, showmen, masters of the revels; like Hitchcock, they are known by those who might not recognize the names of any other directors. As a producer who controls a vast, multifaceted creative enterprise and whose cinematic fantasies have had an immense influence on more than a generation of children, Lucas has become the next Disney. As the director of the

world's most popular spectacles, Spielberg has been called the next DeMille, but he also combines elements of Thomas Ince and Victor Fleming.

Lucas's first feature was *THX-1138* (1971), a stylized science-fiction drama about a passionless, mechanized, regimented dystopia. *American Graffiti* (1973), a comedy about teenagers cruising the streets of a small town, was a major hit. His next film combined the adolescent coming-of-age drama with science fiction: *Star Wars*. Giving up directing to concentrate on producing, Lucas followed *Star Wars* with *The Empire Strikes Back* (1980, directed by Irvin Kershner) and *Return of the Jedi* (1983, directed by Richard Marquand); they are the fourth, fifth, and sixth episodes, or central trilogy, of a nine-part epic conceived as three trilogies. (By 2004, plans for the third trilogy had been abandoned.) Late in 1998 Lucas announced that he would direct the next episode himself (*Star Wars: Episode I—The Phantom Menace*, released 1999) and that it would introduce a new surround-sound format (Dolby Digital–Surround EX) with an additional rear-center channel that would allow sounds to be placed more precisely. In 2001 he announced that the shooting of the next picture (*Star Wars: Episode II—Attack of the Clones*, 2002) had been completed without exposing a foot of film, using high-definition digital video cameras: the new 24p (24 fps progressive-scan) camera, developed in 1997 by Sony with help from Panavision, that gave nearly filmlike results. (This technology is discussed in the next two chapters.) Shooting with a 24p allowed Lucas to avoid any loss of information when transferring a film original to digital for effects and editing; he simply started with a 24 fps digital original. This was comparable to his much earlier decision to use Dolby Noise Reduction throughout the first *Star Wars*.

Raiders of the Lost Ark and its sequels were co-produced by Lucas and directed by Spielberg. With their cliffhangers and nonstop action, the mythic Indiana Jones films owe even more to the 1930s and 1940s serials and pulp fiction than *Star Wars* does. One of the most entertaining and imaginative action pictures of the 1980s, *Raiders* deserves to be ranked with the greatest films ever made in the genre of action–adventure. *Indiana Jones and the Temple of Doom*, a more violent film with a less interesting heroine (Kate Capshaw instead of *Raiders'* Karen Allen), took an "anything goes" attitude that encouraged more reflexive jokes and nonstop action. *Indiana Jones and the Last Crusade* (1989) set archaeologist Jones (Harrison Ford) on the trail of the Holy Grail, in the company of his father—played by Sean Connery, who as James Bond was the definitive hero of the action–adventure spectacle that leapt from one big action scene and exotic location to another, and thus *was* the cinematic father of Indiana Jones.

From *Duel* (1971) to *Temple of Doom*, it is Spielberg who established the movie as ride. *Jurassic Park* (1993), about dinosaurs and chaos theory and a theme park that gets out of control, is itself a theme park that offers the thrills of chaos

Fig. 17-6

Close Encounters of the Third Kind: *the wondrous sight of the Mother Ship's landing (Fig. 17-6) and the wonder of childhood vision (Fig. 17-7, Cary Guffey).*

Fig. 17-7

but never slips out of control. His control of tension and pace is both tight and expansive; he may be better at grand, sweeping effects than any director since David Lean; and he has a firm, efficient sense of narrative structure. Spielberg's one flaw—which in some of his films works as a strength—is his belief that scenes have to be "big" to work. Certainly the D-Day sequence in *Saving Private Ryan* (1998) is big and works. But overstatement and out-of-control sentimentality derail the climax of *Schindler's List. A.I. Artificial Intelligence* (2001; onscreen title, *Artificial Intelligence AI*), the project he inherited from Kubrick, has big scenes that are emotionally relentless, like the one in which the mother abandons her adopted robot child in a forest as threatening as that in any fairy tale; it has other fairy-tale moments that are involving without turning sentimental; and it has an uncharacteristically subtle, quiet ending. A disturbing film that did not do well at the box office, *A.I.* may be his masterpiece, not only in theme (a robot who wants to be a real boy so the mother will love him and who ends up surviving the human race) but also in execution (the seamless integration of the worlds of live action and effects.) It is an emotionally rich and ironic tragedy, a *Pinocchio* for adults. His earlier science-fiction pictures—which were, unlike *A.I.*, definitively mythic—were big entertainments that kept in touch with individuals and their feelings: *Close Encounters of the Third Kind* (1977, revised 1980) and *E.T.—The Extra-Terrestrial* (1982) are engrossing spectacles whose visions are awesome and whose domestic, terrestrial scenes are well observed. In the best of his early films, *Jaws* (1975), and in sequences like the silent drowning of the slaves in *Amistad* (1997), his style has the authority and economy of a master.

Like Lucas, Spielberg is also a producer. Though he rarely interfered with their directors, his creative stamp is evident on the films he produced, the best of which were *Poltergeist* (1982), directed by Tobe Hooper; *Gremlins* (1984), directed by Joe Dante; and *Back to the Future* (1985), directed by Robert Zemeckis.

Dark Satire: Lynch, Waters, and Others

Nobody ever got lost trying to follow a Spielberg or Lucas film, but the films of David Lynch are something else. A unique stylist with a unique vision, Lynch has a fearlessly bizarre approach to the aesthetic challenges of narrative tone and structure. Whether set in the past or outer space or small-town America, the world he presents is—as his characters often remark—a strange place. Of all the major directors whose first features appeared during or after 1977, Lynch is by far the most experimental.

An abstract painter and something of a cartoonist, Lynch learned a great deal from the avant-garde. His emphasis on intriguing, unexplained images whose presence not only *is* a mystery but also points obliquely to related mysteries can be traced back to the poetic devices of avant-garde cinema in general. The sound for Lynch's first four films—*Eraserhead* (1977), *The Elephant Man* (1980), *Dune* (1984), and *Blue Velvet*—was designed by Alan Splet, whose complex, ominous sound composites perfectly complement Lynch's haunting images.

Lynch's films—along with *Twin Peaks* (pilot, 1989; series broadcast 1990–91), the enigmatic TV series he created with Mark Frost—present and rework a number of recurring themes and images. Life has a mystery. What lurks below the surfaces of ordinary reality may be horrible, unbearable (*Eraserhead, Blue Velvet*). Or there may be a secret knowledge, to uncover which is to solve a problem, grow in spiritual power, and fulfill one's destiny (*Dune, Twin Peaks*). The human body, though it may be kept squeaky clean (*Twin Peaks*), can be seen as fundamentally repulsive (*Eraserhead, The Elephant Man, Dune*). Sex is dangerous, unpredictable, and uncontrollable (*Eraserhead; Blue Velvet; Wild At Heart*, 1990). Children want love and suffer horribly (*Eraserhead, The Elephant Man*). Following a mystery to its end can lead one into a dark and paradoxical space where personal identity is at risk—characters can even switch roles—while the official mystery remains unsolved (*Lost Highway*, 1996; *Mulholland Drive*, 2001). What one discovers in a Lynch film about people's private lives is usually awful. The innocent look of too-ordinary reality is clearly hiding something. The secret—the vision of the way life really is—may be the stuff of soap operas (*Twin Peaks*), of cosmic poetry (*The Elephant Man*), of *noirs* (*Blue Velvet*), or of sexual labyrinths (*Eraserhead*), and the ironic tone may be clean-scrubbed or gross, metaphysical or melodramatic. In most of his pictures, characters find out who they really or paradoxically are.

At the climax of Eraserhead, *Henry (Jack Nance) watches as the mysterious "planet" cracks open.*

Fig. 17-8

Eraserhead makes love and marriage, intercourse and reproduction, food and life all utterly horrible. Henry Spencer (Jack "John" Nance), who is "on vacation," marries Mary X (Charlotte Stewart) after they have a baby—although the hospital staff isn't sure that it is a baby: a skinless, screaming, goatlike head, linked by its skinny neck to a torso held together with swaddling. Mary is pitifully unhappy, makes weird sounds in her sleep when she can sleep, can't stand the baby's constant painful crying, and finally goes home to her nutcase parents. Henry, who has a dream in which his brain is made into erasers, eventually kills the baby (after it frightens away a beautiful woman Henry has had sex with, then *cackles*—the only time it's done anything but cry or eat) and perhaps ends up with the girl of his dreams, a tiny imaginary lady with huge cheeks whom he has watched perform on a stage inside the radiator. This is not the stuff of Hollywood romance. Its outdoors is geometric and muddy and bleak, its indoors claustrophobic and depressing, its characters maddening and unattractive and hurting badly. Dreams of creativity are squished in this wildly creative black-and-white black comedy, which became a major cult hit, often shown by itself at midnight on Fridays and Saturdays.

Blue Velvet was Lynch's most popular film and the ancestor of another complicated mystery set in a strange small town, *Twin Peaks*. At the beginning of the film, everything is bright and clean and in peaceful slow motion—until a man who has been watering his lawn suddenly falls, stricken with an ailment that is never identified. His son, Jeffrey (MacLachlan), comes home from school to work in the family store; he falls for a sweet girl, Sandy (Laura Dern), and everything is apple-pie normal—or, more precisely, heightened apple-pie normal—until Jeffrey finds a man's ear on the ground and sets out, with Sandy's help, to solve the mystery it poses. The key figures in that mystery are a violent psychopath named Frank (played by Dennis Hopper) and a sexual masochist named Dorothy (Isabella Rossellini). Dorothy does whatever Frank wants—sings "Blue Velvet," for example—because Frank and his cohorts have kidnapped her husband (whose ear Jeffrey found) and child. Sandy and Jeffrey have a love theme, played on a church organ; it is heard under their first kiss and under the scene in which Sandy expresses her hope that everything will be all right again, which will happen magically when the robins come back. The countertheme, "Blue Velvet," is the song of irresistible sexuality and dark, violent, obsessive perversity.

When sung by Rossellini, it is a siren song that leads, so to speak, through a severed ear into the darkness that everyone hides.

Mulholland Drive started as a pilot for a Disney series. When the studio rejected it, Lynch shot new footage to make what had been an anemone of stinging loose ends into a finished feature—in some cases, splicing the loose ends into Postmodern loops, so that one road led to another, one self to another, one clue to another, and so that the only answer to the mystery would be, as is often the case with Lynch, the whole film—a structure that is an answer to itself, a complete work of art that may have but does not require any external reference, that sets its own balance and its own definitions of identity in spite of the normal world, that reveals the beauty of the labyrinth.

Jim Jarmusch is a minimalist who constructs his films according to strict formal principles. *Stranger Than Paradise* (1984) was conceived as a black-and-white film consisting of nothing but sequence shots (each scene is presented in a single long take) linked by blackouts. While the scenes in *Stranger Than Paradise* follow one another in chronological order, those in *Mystery Train* (1989) are presented in an artificial order—simultaneous events are presented one after the other—that reflects a formalized approach to time. *Night on Earth* (1991) consists of five cab rides in five cities. Each of his films is a self-conscious response to a formal problem, almost in the manner of Godard; each patiently observes the so-called minor, aimless, and boring stretches of everyday life, almost like a Czech comedy; and each has a deadpan wit, an uncrowded *mise-en-scène*, and a love of rock 'n' roll.

Jarmusch is a minimalist in another sense as well; to quote him: "My aesthetic is minimal. I make films about little things that happen between human beings." He avoids putting in too much, refusing to burden the film with extra props and dialogue and events that would get in the way of the subtleties that interest him—the peculiar, fortuitous way things happen. Very little takes place in his mundane scenes, but as they grow on you, they become very funny. Steering away from what Hollywood calls "action," he spends narrative time with matters Hollywood would skip over. Jarmusch rejects Griffith's aesthetic of cutting out the inessential (and of calling attention to what is important in a scene through

editing and camerawork) to dramatize what is, in another way, essential. He avoids cutting within scenes in order to present them in real time while reminding the audience—which gets restless when denied continuity editing—that it is watching a movie. In this period, the narrative filmmakers most unlike each other are Jarmusch and Spielberg, who might be considered a maximalist.

John Waters is an ironist, like Lynch and Jarmusch, a writer–director of satirical comedies that at first were cult films in bad taste, then crossed into the mainstream when Waters restrained himself to what he calls "good bad taste." Shot and set in Baltimore, his home town, many of his films starred his childhood friend, the transvestite actor Divine (Harris Glenn Milstead), who died shortly after starring in *Hairspray.* Among their first films together were *Multiple Maniacs* (1971), *Pink Flamingos* (1972), and *Female Trouble* (1975), milestones in the history of trash art. Waters established the outer limits of cinematic taste in *Pink Flamingos* (which ends with an unfaked shot of Divine eating dog excrement), then moved on to the sense of smell in *Polyester* (1981), which was released in "Odorama." Each viewer of *Polyester* was given a card. In one of the cleverest gags in the history of film/viewer interaction, Divine reaches for some flowers, and a number flashes on the screen instructing the audience which area on the Odorama card to scratch off; the audience scratches, expecting flowers and dropping its guard (some of the earlier odors were vile), then smells instead the disgusting thing that is suddenly thrust in Divine's face. The viewer literally shares the character's sense of surprise as well as her unpleasant experience—a real step toward Bazin's "myth of total cinema." Waters's eleventh film, *Hairspray* (1988), was his first hit with those who go to the movies before midnight.

Hairspray, set in Baltimore in the spring and early summer of 1963, takes a nostalgic *and* parodistic look at the clichés of the period—but if that were all it did, it might have been nothing more than another *Grease*. However, into this apolitical world of dancing, romancing, feuding teenagers come the social and political struggles of the early 1960s. It is as if we were seeing a 1963 teen picture that dealt with the turbulent real world of 1963, something no such film ever did. The result is a humanistic political fable that is also a Postmodern satire.

Each of the Coen brothers' features concentrates on a separate genre—*Blood Simple* (1983), the *film noir*; *Raising Arizona* (1987), the romantic comedy; *Miller's Crossing* (1990), the gangster melodrama; *Barton Fink* (1991), the Hollywood-insider black comedy (imagine *Sunset Boulevard* directed by Polanski); *The Hudsucker Proxy* (1994), the rags-to-riches story; *Fargo* (1996), the cop picture; *The Big Lebowski* (1998), the buddy picture; *O Brother, Where Art Thou?* (2000), the Homeric epic; and *The Man Who Wasn't There* (2001), the period film. Each of the genres they parodied and enriched became jumping-off places for their twisted comic imaginations, offering not formulas for action and dialogue, but *occasions*— as the formula that the police officer's romantic life must figure in the cop picture let the Coens make up, for *Fargo*, the policewoman's husband and their sweet, offbeat marriage. But nothing ever compels them to stick to one genre at a time—*Lebowski* is also a sports picture, a cowboy legend, and a parody of *noir*—and no genre dictates or constrains the eruptions of cockeyed Expressionism in their work.

Joel Coen directs, Ethan Coen produces, and they write the scripts together. Although their tight, witty films are primarily concerned with style, calling attention to their clever camerawork, rich detail, and self-conscious distance from their subjects, each movie is also a genuine, effective genre work with strongly defined characters.

The plot of *Blood Simple* is so complex, so full of betrayals and misunderstandings, that none of the characters ever completely figures it out. To the audience, however, it makes perfect sense. As when watching a Hitchcock film, one is rewarded for paying attention to details—in this case, for keeping track of a cigarette lighter and a pearl-handled .38, which are narrative elements as central as the main characters: an unnamed detective who narrates the film (M. Emmet Walsh); bar owner Julian Marty (Dan Hedaya); Marty's wife, Abby (Frances McDormand); and Abby's lover, Ray (John Getz). The violence, passion, pessimism, and look of *noir* are all here, and the tone is set at the start, as the detective observes voice-over that "nothing comes with a guarantee"—anybody can have something just go all wrong. When things do go wrong for the detective and he lies dying in the bathroom of Abby's apartment, shot

with the last bullet in the revolver, the film ends with a tight death image. Lying on the floor, the narrator–detective looks up at the underside of the sink, which has been dripping throughout the climax; taking as long as the rest of his life, another droplet begins to form, grows—and falls, with a cut to black, as his tale necessarily ends.

Jonathan Demme has also worked in a number of genres, sometimes with an ironic edge and sometimes with scrupulous neutrality. In his concert films, *Stop Making Sense* (1984) and *Swimming to Cambodia* (1987), the camera observes the performers—the Talking Heads and Spalding Gray, respectively—and lets their own styles come through directly. This is not something that can be achieved simply by turning the camera on and recording the show; it requires discipline and clarity as well as a perfect understanding of the performer's aesthetics. Demme's stylistic integrity is clear from his films but not foregrounded by them. His gangster comedy, *Married to the Mob* (1988), has none of *The Godfather*'s rich romanticism or *GoodFellas*'s muscular precision, but a sharply ironic touch and a zippy pace of its own. His thriller, *The Silence of the Lambs* (1991, from the novel by Thomas Harris), is full of ferocious, gruesome characters and events, portrays them without compromising their horrific nature, and becomes troubling without being troubled. In all his works Demme appears to like and care about his central characters as well as to understand them. That understanding, authorial transparency, and restrained balance had a great deal to do with the impact of *Philadelphia* (1993), one of the first mainstream features to deal with AIDS.

Darren Aronofsky made a strong cautionary tale about the abuse of legal and illegal drugs, the scary and sharply edited *Requiem for a Dream* (2000), but he is better known for his first feature, π (or *Pi*, 1998), a dark comedy about the search for the meaning of the universe at the intersection of mathematics and Jewish mysticism. Mary Harron demonstrated her skills in realism and tragicomedy in *I Shot Andy Warhol* (1996), but it was her scrubbed-white, violent satire *American Psycho* (2000, based on the novel by Bret Easton Ellis) that scored a new high for black comedy as a vehicle of cultural analysis.

Terry Gilliam, the American member of England's Monty Python group, first became well known as the creator of the animated sequences in their TV series, *Monty Python's Flying Circus*, and as the co-director (with Terry Jones) of *Monty Python and The Holy Grail*. After directing another two British pictures (*Jabberwocky*, 1977; *Time Bandits*, 1981), Gilliam shot two American-backed pictures in Europe—*Brazil* (1985) and *The Adventures of Baron Munchausen* (1989)—then returned to the United States for *The Fisher King* (1991) and *Twelve Monkeys* (1995). *Brazil*, shot in 1984, is a dark social satire based loosely on George Orwell's novel *Nineteen Eighty-Four*. *Brazil*'s dystopia is an oppressive "free society" that spies on its citizens—a huge, inefficient, ruthless bureaucracy devoted to red tape. The government has been under terrorist attack for 13 years but dismisses that as "beginner's luck." Crude instruments and cheap furniture dominate the cramped, ugly work environment; ducts are everywhere, and it is a crime to have anything fixed without going through Central Services (Robert De Niro plays an outlaw repairman, Harry Tuttle). The hero (Sam Lowry, played by Jonathan Pryce) begins by tracking down a bureaucratic error—a

Fig. 17-9
Brazil: *Dr. Jaffe (Jim Broadbent) tries a new kind of plastic surgery on the hero's mother, Mrs. Lowry (Katherine Helmond).*

fatal typo—and ends by falling in love with a terrorist (Jill Layton, played by Kim Greist). Sam meets his fate in Gilliam's version of Orwell's "Room 101," where a friend tortures him; Sam's escape is to retreat mentally—forever—to an idyllic fantasy inspired by the song "Brazil." Taking an ironic, prodigiously creative look at stupidity, incompetence, vanity, and short-sightedness, the drab and dull and confused—with an undercurrent of passion and rebellion—*Brazil* is the best representative yet of Gilliam's satiric side, as *Time Bandits* remains the best of his fantasy—adventures. The battles over releasing *Brazil* were a dreadful window on the film industry, which needs its rebels but often is comfortable destroying their work.

The Comic Edge: Burton, Zemeckis, and Others

Some of the period's comedies broke away from standard sex-role constructs, satirized contemporary society, or knowingly portrayed the traumas of growing up. Many of the latter were "teenpix," made for a target audience of adolescents. Among the more successful teenpix were those written and directed by John Hughes, whose *The Breakfast Club* (1985) spent a day in detention with five adolescents as they raised and lowered their social and personal shields until they came to understand each other and themselves. Although some of his comedies were silly without being funny, and some were entertaining without touching the nerve of self-recognition, one of them—*Home Alone* (1990), directed by Chris Columbus, written and produced by Hughes—became the highest grossing comedy yet made, a record held until 1994 and *Forrest Gump*. Bolder talents took up the genre of young-adult *Angst*, and social and economic pressures: Whit Stillman's *Metropolitan* (1990), Richard Linklater's *Dazed and Confused* (1993), Kevin Smith's *Clerks* (1994), and Terry Zwigoff's *Ghost World* (2001).

While most of the comedies were strictly boy-meets-girl, a few explored the complexities of sexual identity. Reversals of sexual roles and clothes are common motifs of films such as *Victor/Victoria* (Blake Edwards, 1982), *Tootsie* (Sydney Pollack, 1982), and *All of Me* (Carl Reiner, 1984), which consciously descend from screwball comedy. *Victor/Victoria*, set in the

Paris of Lubitsch (a Hollywood soundstage calling itself Paris), refers explicitly to the Lubitsch "touch" of suppressing visual information from the frame. The year of the film's action, 1934, is the very one in which Hollywood enforced its Production Code. *Victor/Victoria* seems a conscious return to the explicit sexual matters that the pre-Code Lubitsch had treated so deftly.

Carl Reiner, who was Sid Caesar's straight man on 1950s television and a cohort of Mel Brooks, also directed—among many other works—*The Comic* (1969) and *Oh, God!* (1977, in which George Burns is convincing as God, a role never previously filmed with any success). His son, Rob Reiner, began as an actor on the TV show *All in the Family*, then went into directing with *This Is Spinal Tap* (1984), a parody of a rock documentary; that and *When Harry Met Sally . . .* (1989) may be his funniest comedies, and they share with his two best dramas (*Stand By Me*, 1986, and *Misery*, 1990—both adapted from works by Stephen King) and

his great tale of romantic adventure, *The Princess Bride* (1987), an unfailing ability to strike the right note at the right time, be it sad or uproarious, frightening or wistful. In both the Reiners' films, from *All of Me* to *Stand By Me*, interpersonal relationships are deeply explored, and what results is a moving understanding of the ways people bond together, the comedy and the drama of acceptance.

If Roger Corman can be credited with discovering and apprenticing Bogdanovich, Coppola, Dante, Demme, Sayles, and Scorsese—to name just a few—Spielberg's top discoveries to date are Frank Marshall (*Arachnophobia*, 1990; *Alive*, 1993) and Robert Zemeckis (*Romancing the Stone*, 1984; *Back to the Future*, 1985; *Who Framed Roger Rabbit*, 1988; *Back to the Future Part II*, 1989, and *Part III*, 1990; *Forrest Gump*, 1994; *The Polar Express*, 2004; and the less successful *Contact*, 1997, and *What Lies Beneath*, 2000). Zemeckis's comedies are intricately plotted, full of zingy jokes and impressive special

Fig. 17-10
Who Framed Roger Rabbit*: Detective Eddie Valiant (Bob Hoskins) finds himself in the same frame—and desk—as Roger.*

effects. *Romancing the Stone* pits fantasy against reality as deftly as *Back to the Future Part II* juxtaposes versions of the same character from different temporal continua. And just as *Forrest Gump*, a bit like Woody Allen's *Zelig*, puts its hero in the same frame as a president, *Who Framed Roger Rabbit* puts live actors and cartoon figures ("toons") in the same shots. *Roger Rabbit* called on an extraordinary spectrum of major talents to create the most technically advanced and visually seamless cartoon-with-people ever made. The 1940s Los Angeles of this film still has its streetcars, a reliable system of public transportation ("Who needs a car in L.A.?"). The villain—like the villain of *Chinatown*, who wants to control the city's expansion and the region's water—has a vision of shopping centers and gas stations, freeways and pollution, and wants to begin creating that Los Angeles on the site of Toontown. The villain is destroyed, the mystery is solved, Toontown and the streetcars are saved—but anyone familiar with today's Los Angeles must find this happy ending dark and sly, since the streetcars are gone, freeways and smog are everywhere, and no Toontown can be found on the maps. Alternate realities are indeed central to the comedies of Robert Zemeckis.

The boldly designed films of Tim Burton, who once worked as an animator at Disney, turn to bright and dark subjects with equal zest. His lightest were *Pee-wee's Big Adventure* (1985), in which the childlike Pee-wee Herman (Paul Reubens) sets off in search of his stolen bicycle, and the science fiction comedy *Mars Attacks!* (1996); his darkest was the blockbuster *Batman* (1989), whose look and mood were inspired not by the early Batman comics but by the later, more pessimistic Batman graphic novels. *Edward Scissorhands* (1990), a fable about why it snows, stars Johnny Depp in a brilliant re-imagining of *Frankenstein*. A film with heart and wit, *Edward Scissorhands* is set in a bland modern suburb that happens to adjoin a gothic castle inhabited by an old inventor (Vincent Price) and his creation, Edward (Depp). The inventor, as much a lonely, loving Gepetto as a Dr. Frankenstein, dies before he can give Edward normal hands; instead

Fig. 17-11
Tim Burton's **Edward Scissorhands.**

Edward's fingers are shears and blades—the tools of his art (sculpting) and the fate that separates him from others, whom he cannot readily embrace without cutting. In the end, when this sensitive artist has been exiled to the castle by a Tupperware torch party, Edward uses the scissors—the sign of his origin—to express his love in art, shaving ice sculptures to make the snow that falls on his beloved.

Two comedies stood out for their original uses of basic cinematic elements: *Being John Malkovich* (1999, directed by Adam Spiegel under the name Spike Jonze) let subjective camera and sound give the impression that characters—and the audience—could temporarily be, or at least share the experience of, the famous actor; *Groundhog Day* (1993, directed by Harold Ramis) used straight cuts and an alarm clock to start the same day over and over until the jerk of a hero (Bill Murray) learns how to use the day in the best possible way.

The definitive late-1980s comedy of manners was independent Steven Soderbergh's first feature, *sex, lies, and videotape* (1989). (His later works include *Erin Brockovich*, 2000 and *Traffic*, 2000.) This film did for the video generation what *Carnal Knowledge* and *Trouble in Paradise* had done for their generations—addressed the present terms of intimacy—using a video camera to mediate between relationships.

Politics, Insight, and Violence: Lee, Carpenter, and Others

The years since 1977 have also produced some filmmakers interested more in political and social problems than in the irrational, ironic, reflexive, comic, and fantastic.

Michael Cimino's works are not devoid of irony, but he appears to have no sense of humor. What he does have is a rich, grand, grave style—style to spare. In his big films, the politically conservative *The Deer Hunter* and the politically radical *Heaven's Gate*, this style works brilliantly, from the intelligently moving camera to the overwhelming sense of place. *The Deer Hunter* is sophomoric in its symbolic use of Russian roulette, not to mention the deer, but it is a very good movie about friendship and postcombat stress. *Heaven's Gate*—speaking always of the uncut version—is careless about conveying essential narrative information, but it is visually magnificent, has the range of an epic novel rather than (like so many movies) that of a short story, and is the only great western of the 1980s. In the later films, however, his style not only gets in the way but is unmotivated and irritating, vain and pushy. *Year of the Dragon* (1985) has problems with psychological and narrative credibility, revealing a shallow understanding not just of character but of people—but it is more disciplined and watchable than the films that followed (*The Sicilian*, 1987; *Desperate Hours*, 1990). *Year of the Dragon* is the

Fig. 17-12

Momentarily turning the tables, Ann (Andie MacDowell) takes charge of the camera in sex, lies, and videotape.

interesting work of a showoff trying to keep a low profile after the disaster of *Heaven's Gate*, the masterpiece for which he had to apologize.

Oliver Stone began as a screenwriter, receiving an Oscar for Alan Parker's *Midnight Express* (1978), then writing De Palma's ham-fisted remake of *Scarface* (1983) and Cimino's *Year of the Dragon*. All this time he was trying to sell *Platoon*, a script based on his experiences in Vietnam. After directing *Salvador* (1986), a buddy film whose view of the politics of El Salvador was left of center, he was given the chance to direct *Platoon* himself; released in the last days of 1986, it quickly attracted large audiences who proclaimed it the first film to portray accurately the experience of the American foot soldier in Vietnam. Although there are many characters in *Platoon*, the most important is first-timer Chris (Charlie Sheen). Like many of Stone's heroes, Chris is torn between two fathers, a good one (Sgt. Elias, played by Willem Dafoe) and a bad one (Sgt. Barnes, played by Tom Berenger). The good one opposes the massacre of civilians, takes care of his men, and even smokes dope with them. The bad one takes care of his men too, but he is contemptuous and ruthless; "There's the way it ought to be, and there's the way it is," he says to Chris, making the usual, lazy argument against idealism and incarnating "the way it is." After Barnes kills Elias, Chris kills Barnes; his conclusion about the war is that Americans were really just fighting each other on foreign soil. Politics aside, *Platoon* does convey the experience of protracted jungle warfare, putting the audience through a long, rough tour of duty.

With his Vietnam movies (*Platoon*; *Born on the Fourth of July*, 1989, which starred Tom Cruise as a paralyzed veteran who becomes an activist; and *Heaven & Earth*, 1993, based on the autobiographies of a Vietnamese woman) and his powerfully edited *JFK* (1991), Oliver Stone has positioned himself as a vigorous rhetorician, whether he is acting as a trippy culture critic or as a political moralist.

Natural Born Killers (1994), Stone's richest satire and boldest cinematic experiment, is the story of Mickey and Mallory Knox (Woody Harrelson and Juliette Lewis), lovers on a killing spree who become celebrities. Mickey and Mallory express what is chaotic, destructive, amoral, and crazy about America, and the film mirrors the chaos of its subject with a controlled, apparent chaos of constantly shifting images that is a filmlong montage. The camera, often tilted and hand-held, is sharp and restless; the rapidly edited images jump cut from color to black and white, from fine grain to grainy (some shots were taken on Super8 film and blown up), from film to video or animation or tinted stock; and the background readily becomes a rear-projection screen that allows the lovers to drive through the clouds or may flash their violent memories and thoughts. The world that is shown here is falling apart, but it is capable of being healed by love and by cultivating a harmony with the good spirits in nature; unfortunately, there is great power in nature's evil spirits (Mickey's rabbit) and in the demons that possess not only Mickey, but also the incarnation of the media, Wayne Gale (Robert Downey, Jr.), who is most responsible for nurturing the tabloid and reality-TV cult that surrounds the killers and to whom they give a fatal lesson in reality.

Quentin Tarantino got most of his film education as a clerk in a video store. After he sold two scripts (later rewritten by others, a norm in the industry) to Oliver Stone (*Natural Born Killers*) and Tony Scott (*True Romance*, 1993), Tarantino became famous as the director of two stylish, violent, smart genre pictures: *Reservoir Dogs* (1992) and *Pulp Fiction* (1994). Unlike the films of Cimino and Stone, Tarantino's are unfettered by big messages; like them, they are cinematically intense, self-consciously *auteurist*, and swimming in testosterone. If *Reservoir Dogs* is dominated by its sources (especially a Hong Kong police drama called *City on Fire*), it also has a dark energy that is convincing on its own. And *Pulp Fiction* is an original: bright, audacious, enigmatic, witty, violent, and surprising, with an unchronological narrative line that cleverly interrelates the events and characters in a triumph of style. Too hip to be *noir* and too slick to be pulp, *Pulp Fiction* is not an homage to the 1930s or 1940s but a 1990s Postmodern film in which words and images play in a self-referential field that has no definable underlying absolutes; unlike *film noir* and totally unlike pulp fiction, it doesn't care that there is no moral center. Whether or not it was misnamed, *Pulp Fiction* became one of the most influential films of the decade, a model of formal complexity and stylized tone.

Tarantino has encouraged new directors and arranged for theatrical revivals of films most of today's viewers have seen only on video. He also brought Zhang Yimou's *Hero* (2002) to the U.S. in 2004, a film people strongly wanted to see but that had not yet found a Western distributor. His great enthusiasm for martial-arts pictures led to his fourth film (after *Jackie Brown*, 1997, a crime caper starring Pam Grier as a feisty flight attendant), which was released in two parts: *Kill Bill Vol. 1* (2003) and *Kill Bill Vol. 2* (2004). Tarantino's powerful sense of rhythm in action, music, and editing made *Kill Bill* a nonstop experience charged with strength and cunning, pain and beauty, though its superb pacing could slow down at any time for an impressive silence or for a long, tense scene. It starred Uma Thurman as a mythic hero who overcomes incredible obstacles with immense energy, skill, and determination in her quest for revenge. As pure an action film as one could want—until the very ending turns cute—*Kill Bill* also made deeper use of his love of movies and had an absolute authority of style.

John Sayles is an insightful writer with a good ear for dialogue and a director whose style is understated, meticulous, economical, and evocatively realistic. Sayles's understanding of character and his leftist politics are central to all his works, from his novel *Union Dues* and his first feature, *Return of the Secaucus Seven* (1979, released 1980), a comedy about a reunion of 1960s radicals, to *Men With Guns* (1997), about a doctor who finds out how brutal the police state in his Latin American country really is. Sayles puts his characters in situations where they have to figure themselves out (*Baby It's You*, 1982, released 1983; *Lianna*, 1983; *Passion Fish*, 1992), which they cannot really do without figuring out the social, economic, and political systems in which they live (*City of Hope*, 1991; *Lone Star*, 1996). *Matewan* (1987)—a film about coal miners in the 1920s—may be the most compelling pro-labor film of the 1980s. Sayles also has a talent for comic horror with a sociopolitical twist—evident in his brilliant script for Dante's *The Howling* (1980, released 1981, co-written by Terence Winkless). His science-fiction fable, *The Brother from Another Planet* (1984), performs a twist on *E.T.* for good reason: Sayles was one of *E.T.*'s uncredited writers, dropped from the project because he disagreed about the direction it should take. So he made

his own *E.T.*, in which the visitor from outer space is black.

Through the mid-1970s, the most respected and accomplished African-American director was Gordon Parks. After 20 years as a photographer and reporter for *Life*, he made *The Learning Tree* (1969), which he produced, directed, and adapted from his own autobiographical novel; he also wrote the music. *The Learning Tree*, which was among the first group of 25 films selected in 1989 by the Library of Congress for its Hall of Fame, the National Film Registry, is a realistic, humanistic, visually rich, and often tender coming-of-age film set in Kansas in the 1920s. Parks's biggest commercial success was *Shaft* (1971), a witty and violent film that inspired a commercial wave of "blaxploitation" pictures. Melvin Van Peebles had a festival hit in *The Story of a Three-Day Pass* (*La Permission*, 1967, made in France) and a box-office smash in the sexually frank and politically revolutionary *Sweet Sweetback's Baad Asssss Song* (1971); his son, Mario Van Peebles, made one of the most vivid, violent, and stylish of the inner-city crime dramas, *New Jack City*, in 1991.

In the late 1980s and early 1990s, so much attention was paid to the work of Spike Lee, John Singleton, and the Hughes brothers that one of the greatest African-American directors, Charles Burnett, was overlooked in the rush. Part of the reason for this may be that Burnett's films do not focus on the problems of crime and violence; instead, he makes poetically charged, dramatically resonant movies that are often about black families dealing with some destructive force that has to be identified and purged. His first film, *Killer of Sheep* (1973, released 1977), examined the stress a man brings home from his job in a slaughterhouse. It was added to the National Film Registry in 1990, the year he released *To Sleep With Anger*, a moral, convincingly acted film about a black family that lives in South Central Los Angeles but keeps in touch with its biblical and Southern rural roots, and what happens to them when Harry (Danny Glover), an old friend of the father, Gideon (Paul Butler), comes to visit. Harry is a superstitious con artist full of the wild, bad ways of the old life, and like the serpent in Eden, he seductively tests the weak spots in the family until violence and illness and buried resentments erupt.

Spike Lee, son of jazz musician Bill Lee, was born in Atlanta; as a graduate student in NYU's film program, he made a thesis film—*Joe's Bed–Stuy Barbershop: We Cut Heads* (1983)—that won a Student Academy Award. Now an independent filmmaker based in New York—writing, producing, directing, and usually acting in his "Forty Acres and a Mule" productions, many of which have been backed and distributed by major studios—Lee is the most prominent black filmmaker of his generation. His frank, caustic, committed, reflexive style can best be described as "in your face."

Like *Bed–Stuy Barbershop*, a realistic drama about a barber who is more interested in cutting hair than in letting his shop be a front for the numbers racket, many of Lee's films are set and shot in the Bedford–Stuyvesant section of Brooklyn. His films tackle the clichés about black character and experience that pervade American culture, investigating and radicalizing them until the clichés are dismantled and—in the best of his works, but not all—the personal and social realities step forward. His first two fea-

tures, *She's Gotta Have It* (1986) and *School Daze* (1988), addressed the images blacks have of each other, while the next, *Do The Right Thing* (1989), looked at interracial constructs. *School Daze*, a big-studio but low-budget musical, attacked assimilation and black fraternity life while exploring the prejudices that sometimes divide light- and dark-skinned blacks. *She's Gotta Have It* is about a woman who repudiates the clichés that surround her and refuses to be controlled by blacks or whites.

Do The Right Thing is set on a single block in Bedford–Stuyvesant on the hottest day of the year. Although it is a black neighborhood, there are no black-owned businesses, only a market owned by Koreans and a pizzeria owned by Italians (Sal, played by Danny Aiello, and his two sons). The Koreans are newcomers, but Sal has been in business for 25 years; although it is not his neighborhood, Sal is proud that its residents have grown up on his pizza. When Sal confides his pride and his dreams to his sons, sappy family-melodrama music can be

Fig. 17-13. **Do The Right Thing:** *Radio Raheem (Bill Nunn, left) and Buggin Out (Giancarlo Esposito).*

heard beneath the dialogue; when Da Mayor (Ossie Davis) and Mother Sister (Ruby Dee), two of the neighborhood's older residents, remark how hot it is, the music plays variations on "Summertime"; this is one way that the movie identifies artistic and social stereotypes reflexively, urging the audience to recognize the clichés and think.

The heat provokes confrontations and brings out latent racial antagonisms. Buggin Out (Giancarlo Esposito) demands that Sal add pictures of African Americans to the pizzeria's Wall of Fame, which has pictures only of famous Italian Americans; Sal refuses, and Buggin Out tries to organize a boycott. Mookie (Spike Lee), who delivers Sal's pizzas and has no developed political consciousness, unsuccessfully tries to defuse the suddenly growing antagonism between Buggin Out and Sal. At one point Da Mayor gives Mookie the simple, venerable advice, "Always do the right thing." "That's it?" says Mookie, who will find, along with the audience, that it is not always simple to know what the right thing is. Mookie's best friend, Radio Raheem (Bill Nunn), carries his prized portable stereo (a boom box) wherever he goes, loudly playing Public Enemy's "Fight the Power," a call to "fight the powers that be."

As tensions increase, Sal and the police are clearly revealed as the powers that be. The film ends in an escalating chain of violent acts and two dialectically opposed quotations, one from Martin Luther King Jr. and one from Malcolm X. King argues against violence as a way of achieving racial justice. Malcolm advocates violence in the cause of self-defense, calling it "intelligence." Yet there is something on which King and Malcolm agree: the need to recognize oppression and take an unalterable stand against it. Despite their opposing positions, a synthesis is implied by the photo of the two together, which fades in just before the quotations have finished scrolling up the screen and is the movie's final image.

Lee's project in *Do The Right Thing* is to expose the structure of racism. And as in all his films, his rude, upfront, catalytic technique is to come right out with what many people leave unsaid, or live with in silence—in this case, the injustice and racism that underlie the politics of contemporary America and determine its social conflicts. He also explores these conflicts in the epic biography *Malcolm X* (1992); in the romantic melodrama *Jungle Fever* (1991), which also addresses the crack epidemic; and in the satire *Bamboozled* (2000), which plays like a cross between *The Producers* and *Putney Swope* while suggesting that both satire and sincerity are doomed in the image-controlling world of contemporary media.

The most profitable movie of 1991 was not *Terminator 2* but John Singleton's *Boyz N the Hood*, which earned 10 times its $6 million cost. For this realistic, intelligent film about kids, young adults, and parents—all of them vividly conceived human beings—who try to survive the violence and pressures of family and street life in South Central Los Angeles, Singleton became the youngest person and the first African American ever to be nominated for an Oscar for best director. The success of *Boyz* encouraged producers and studios to back and release the work of many new young black filmmakers. One of the most dramatically intense and cinematically inventive of those films was *Menace II Society* (1993), directed by Allen and Albert Hughes from a story by them and screenwriter Tyger Williams. Unceremoniously violent (because, unlike the majority of "violent" filmmakers, who lead insulated lives, the Hughes brothers know how unglamorous it is) and perfectly paced, *Menace II Society* takes the coming-of-age film up a blind alley, allowing the characters virtually no escape and killing the hero at the moment he finally gets it together. The most highly praised American film of 1994 was a coming-of-age documentary about black basketball players, *Hoop Dreams*, by Steve James, Fred Marx, and Peter Gilbert.

Luis Valdez, the founder of El Teatro Campesino, began as a playwright and stage director. Working with his brother, Daniel Valdez, who composed the music and played one of the two leads (Henry Reyna), Luis Valdez wrote and directed *Zoot Suit*, a Brechtian musical about Chicano consciousness. Rewritten for the screen and directed by Luis Valdez, *Zoot Suit* (1987) was set and shot in a theatre; sometimes it shows the audience watching the play, sometimes it is a movie with stage sets, and sometimes it is a movie shot as if the event were happening on location. It employs theatrical transitions, devices, and conventions as well as cinematic ones, all of which work together in a reflexive

Fig. 17-14
Zoot Suit: *Alice (Tyne Daly, left) offers her help to Henry Reyna (Daniel Valdez, center) and his co-defendants (in the background: Mike Gomez, left, and Kelly Ward). At the far right, in a skeptical mood, is El Pachuco (Edward James Olmos).*

and blazingly cinematic style. *Zoot Suit* is also one of the most colorfully designed, strikingly choreographed, and rhythmically edited films of the decade, with an extremely sophisticated narrative structure and a direct, engaging tone. Politically intense in its portrayal and analysis of the 1942 Sleepy Lagoon murder case, which was exploited in a racist anti-"Mexican" campaign that unjustly sent many *pachucos* (who today would call themselves Chicanos) to prison, the film is also irresistibly energetic and sardonically, boldly funny. One of the few significant musicals of the period (only Bob Fosse's *Cabaret* and *All That Jazz* approach it), the most important Chicano film of the 1980s, and one of the most brilliantly conceived conjunctions of theatre and cinema in film history, *Zoot Suit* was given a very limited theatrical release. Valdez's next movie, *La Bamba* (1987), was a more conventional approach to the mythic theme of Chicano heroism, a biography of rock star

Ritchie Valens that was made in simultaneously released Spanish and English versions.

Both racial and sexual politics are explored in the understated, elliptical films of Wayne Wang (*Chan is Missing*; *Eat a Bowl of Tea*, 1989; *The Joy Luck Club*; *Smoke*, 1994, released 1995; *Chinese Box*, *1998*) and the sensitive dramas of Robert M. Young (*Short Eyes*, 1977; *The Ballad of Gregorio Cortez*, 1982; *Dominick and Eugene*, 1988—and, as cinematographer and co-director, Michael Roemer's *Nothing But a Man*, 1964). These honest and unassuming filmmakers explore characters, and their relationships and options, with great and delicate skill. In their different ways, Wayne Wang and Bob Young are the most humanistic of the new independent directors.

Feminist politics significantly affected American film theory as well as the makers of avant-garde and short narrative films in this period, but the feature-length narrative films, including those made by women, rarely were programmatically feminist. Mainstream cinema responded to the feminist movement of the 1960s and 1970s by creating more roles for strong women (or superficially revising the old roles) and putting sexism in the same "sensitive" category as racism—not to be treated in an offensive manner. But that was a far cry from exploring a gynocentric cinema, as women directors in Germany and France—and in the American avant-garde—were doing. Feminism was a subtext and a secondary concern in the American features directed by women, the majority of whom were fighting their way into the studio system with films that would entertain mainstream audiences—which is certainly one route to power in Hollywood, and often the only way to get a chance to direct *again*. But there were also brilliant directors, like Mary Harron (*American Psycho*) and Julie Taymor (*Titus*, 1999; *Frida*, 2002), who made their mark by being stylistically daring and ultimately subversive. Among the unprecedented number of women directors to have come to prominence since the mid-1970s are Allison Anders (*Gas, Food Lodging*, 1992; *Mi vida loca*, 1994), Lizzie Borden (*Born In Flames*, 1983; *Working Girls*, 1986, wide release 1987), Sofia Coppola (*Lost In Translation*, 2003, for which she won the Oscar for best original screenplay and was nominated for best director), Julie Dash (*Daughters of the Dust*, 1991), Nora Ephron (*Sleepless in Seattle*, 1993), Amy Heckerling (*Fast Times at Ridgemont High*, 1982; *Clueless*, 1995), Barbara Kopple (*Harlan County, U.S.A.*, 1976; *Wild Man Blues*, 1997), Kasi Lemmons (*Eve's Bayou*, 1997), Penny Marshall (*Big*, 1988), Susan Seidelman (*Smithereens*, 1982; *Desperately Seeking Susan*, 1985), Joan Micklin Silver (*Hester Street*, 1975), Barbra Streisand (*Yentl*, 1983; *The Prince of Tides*, 1991), Betty Thomas (*The Brady Bunch Movie*, 1995), and Claudia Weill (*It's My Turn*, 1980).

Four British directors joined the American industry in the 1980s, making pictures that were, for the most part, either hotly debated (Ridley Scott, Alan Parker) or uncritically enjoyed (Tony Scott, Adrian Lyne). The courses of their careers were determined by what their respective audiences demanded, and so they become interesting as a guide to the Reagan era itself. When Tony Scott and Adrian Lyne uncharacteristically made intricate, resonant, risk-taking films that departed

from conservative mythic formulas and included unpleasant material, audiences stayed away; such was the fate of Tony Scott's *The Hunger* (1983, starring David Bowie and Catherine Deneuve as vampires) and Lyne's *Jacob's Ladder* (1990). And when Ridley Scott made empty spectacles (*1492: Conquest of Paradise*, 1992) or Alan Parker carelessly rewrote history (*Mississippi Burning*, 1988), *they* lost fans in droves. Even though Ridley and Tony Scott are brothers, the audiences for Tony's *Top Gun* (1986) and Ridley's *Blade Runner* (1982) were distinct camps: the former, much larger and more self-centered, looking to be blatantly entertained and subtly reassured; the latter preferring artistically ambitious films that tackled significant matters in complex, revealing, *and* entertaining ways.

All four directors had made commercials in Britain before turning to features; Tony Scott's fast-moving, seamlessly edited commercials were extremely influential in America, as were those of Adrian Lyne. Lyne's first major hit, *Flashdance* (1983), was the standard-bearer for the Reagan era, a movie that seductively preached that anyone who worked and dreamed hard enough could have everything she wanted. With its music-video colors and rhythms, likable heroine (Jennifer Beals), and denial of political and socioeconomic realities, *Flashdance* encouraged its audience to be uncritical. Tony Scott's big films (*Top Gun*; *Days of Thunder*, 1990; *True Romance*) also had the look and pace of feature-length music videos and a feelgood reliance on formula, but they were not as programmatically antifeminist as Lyne's; nevertheless, they reinforced conventional sex roles and demonstrated by their good box office that the mainstream audiences of the period were happy with clichés. Fortunately, Tony Scott made other films that were politically intriguing (*Enemy of the State*, 1998) and, like *The Hunger*, stylistically ambitious.

Alan Parker's often violent and menacing films showed the dark side of dreams: a vacation that lands its drug-smuggling hero in a Turkish prison (*Midnight Express*), the nightmare of crazy divorce at the end of a marriage (*Shoot the Moon*, 1982), a murder case whose successful solution destroys the detective (*Angel Heart*, 1987).

Ridley Scott's first picture, *The Duellists* (1977, British), was based on a story by Joseph Conrad; like most of his films, it was superbly

Fig. 17-15
Alien: *A search party from the "Nostromo" finds the remains of a nonhuman pilot, the "space jockey"*
who radioed a warning. Production Design, Michael Seymour; Director of Photography, Derek
Vanlint; Costume Design, John Mollo; "Alien" Design, H. R. Giger; Art Directors, Les Dilley, Roger
Christian; Set Decorator, Ian Whittaker; Concept Artists, Ron Cobb, Jean Giraud, Chris Foss; Visual
Design Consultant, Dan O'Bannon.

designed and shot in Panavision and color.
The ore-laden ship in his next film, *Alien*, was
named the "Nostromo" in reference to Conrad's
Nostromo (part of whose plot concerns the
corrupting effect of a hoard of silver), an allusion
that identified the greedy, colonialist owners of
the ship as the primary villains. His next picture,
Blade Runner, was based loosely on a dystopic
novel by Philip K. Dick. *Thelma & Louise* (1991)
struck that perfect balance of genre (the road
movie), politics (sexual), and look (engrossing)
that characterizes his best films, whatever the
politics or the genre. A master of *mise-en-scène*,
Ridley Scott has worked with some of the best
cinematographers, production designers, art
directors, concept artists, and special-effects
wizards in the business. The look of *Blade
Runner*—a neo-*noir* set in Los Angeles in 2019—
with its towering buildings, endless rain, in-

escapable ads, richly dark color scheme, low-key
lighting, and awesome special effects, survives
in the release version despite many unfortunate
changes made by producers. Fortunately, the director's cut of *Blade Runner* restored Scott's original version when it was released in 1992.

Science fiction has seen a great many imitations of *Star Wars*, *Alien*, and *Blade Runner*,
from their action to their *mise-en-scène*. But
there have been many original science-fiction
films since the late 1970s, among the best of
which are Douglas Trumbull's *Brainstorm*,
James Cameron's *The Terminator*, Paul
Verhoeven's *RoboCop*, Alex Proyas's *Dark City*
(1998), and Spielberg's *A.I.* Two films that are
not science fiction but do put their heroes in odd
relationships with time are *Groundhog Day*,
where a man repeatedly starts the same day but
has a complete memory of all the days he has

done this, and *Memento*, where a brain injury keeps a man from forming short-term memories and thus causes him to begin each new day or sequence with no memory of the days or even the hours that have come before. Because the character in *Memento* cannot remember what just happened, the film unfolds in reverse chronological order, so that the audience does not know what happened in the "previous" (next to be shown) scene or sequence and shares the character's predicament.

A tremendous number of horror movies were released in the late 1970s and 1980s, the majority low-budget slasher films in which victims were picked off by mortal or immortal psychopaths. The immediate paradigms for this subgenre were *Halloween, Friday the 13th*, and *Friday the 13th Part 2*; models within the previous two decades included *Peeping Tom, Psycho, The Texas Chain Saw Massacre*, and *Black Christmas* (Bob Clark, 1974, Canada). More significant than the slasher clones, major horror pictures continued to appear from George Romero, John Carpenter, Wes Craven, David Cronenberg, Tobe Hooper, and many others. Among the most interesting English-language horror films to have appeared since 1977 are *The Evil Dead* (Sam Raimi, 1983), *The Return of the Living Dead* (Dan O'Bannon, 1985), *Henry: Portrait of a Serial Killer, Aliens, A Nightmare on Elm Street 3—Dream Warriors* (Chuck Russell, 1987), *Candyman* (Bernard Rose, 1992), *Bride of Chucky* (Ronny Yu, 1998), *The Blair Witch Project* (Daniel Myrick and Eduardo Sánchez, 1999), *American Psycho*, and Friedkin's expanded version of *The Exorcist* (2000). The "gore boom" that lasted from the 1970s to the mid-1980s was dampened by CARA, which began to make it much more difficult for violent horror films to get an R rating; in the late 1980s, producers afraid of the X—like those of the *Friday the 13th* series—left in the sex scenes but drastically trimmed the kill scenes.

Hollywood Boulevard (1976), directed by Joe Dante and Allan Arkush, is a fine example of the comedies Roger Corman produced, full of outrageous gags and film jokes and clearly made fast and on the cheap. Dante's next picture for Corman was *Piranha*, a parody of *Jaws* (and at least ten other movies) and a violent nibble at the military, the Vietnam War, Bob Hope, and capitalist priorities. Horror, reflexivity, and comedy are the mainstays of his movies, and they reinforce each other perfectly in *Gremlins* (1984), the first of Dante's films produced by Spielberg.

Wes Craven's first film was the utterly shocking, ruthlessly violent *The Last House On The Left* (1972, produced by Sean Cunningham), a remake of Ingmar Bergman's *The Virgin Spring*. The rape and murders—and water symbolism— of Bergman's film are all in *Last House*, but stripped of Bergman's civility; updating the story to the bourgeois American present, Craven vividly shows the cruelty that is possible in the world. Most people consider this film terminally sick, but it is a crucial example of the realistic horror film and a key to the most important of Craven's later films, anticipating *A Nightmare on Elm Street* and *The Hills Have Eyes* (1977). Like it or not, *Last House* is as significant in the historical development of the genre as *Night of the Living Dead* and *The Texas Chain Saw Massacre*.

John Carpenter proved himself as a wide-screen action director with the tightly paced *Assault on Precinct 13* (1976), then became famous with *Halloween*. Carpenter writes or co-writes the music for his films—and often writes their screenplays, using his own name or various pseudonyms. *The Thing* (1982), his best film since *Halloween* and until *Prince of Darkness* (1987), was a remake of the 1951 film produced by Hawks, directed by Christian Nyby, and homaged in *Halloween* as it plays on the late show: *The Thing From Another World*. It is one of the very few remakes in this period that compares favorably with its original. In *Prince of Darkness*, an interracial team of professors and graduate students work together to prevent the triumph of Satan. The ending, and the ending implied beyond that one, are frightening and moving with all the complexity of great horror, as we realize that love may be responsible for a spiritual and metaphysical catastrophe.

They Live, Carpenter's most richly conceived picture—and in many respects the most political American film of the 1980s was the first film to portray the hardships of blue-collar workers and others who lost their homes and jobs during the Reagan era, while big capitalism flourished.

It argues that a revolution can be brought about by, and consists of, a new way of seeing— having the veil lifted and seeing things as they are.

Fig. 17-16
Aliens disguised as riot police attack the rebels: a black-and-white shot from They Live.

Both politically and reflexively, Carpenter argues, movies are a site of vision, while TV is a lulling realm of sleep, empty diversion, socio-economic conditioning, and false reassurance. When *They Live* begins, the audience and the characters see a false vision that is in color and appears normal. With special glasses (later, contact lenses), we and the heroes see a black-and-white vision that is more truthful; for the next hour, we look at the color world and imagine the hidden black-and-white reality. At the end, we see a truthful vision in color. Our ability to see correctly, and film's to record correctly, have been restored; the film has rescued vision.

For Further Viewing

FILMS

CHARLES BURNETT (1944–   )
Killer of Sheep (1977). Completed 1973
My Brother's Wedding (1983)

To Sleep With Anger (1990)

JAMES CAMERON (1954–   )
The Terminator (1984)
Aliens (1986)
Terminator 2: Judgment Day (1991)
Titanic (1997)

JOHN CARPENTER (1948–   )
Halloween (1978)
The Thing (1982)
They Live (1988)

JOEL (1955–   ) AND ETHAN (1958–   ) COEN
Blood Simple (1983)
Fargo (1996)
The Big Lebowski (1998)
O Brother, Where Art Thou? (2000)

WES CRAVEN (1939–   )
The Last House on the Left (1972)
The Hills Have Eyes (1977)
A Nightmare on Elm Street (1984)
Scream (1996)

JONATHAN DEMME (1944–)
Swimming to Cambodia (1987)
Married to the Mob (1988)
The Silence of the Lambs (1991)

BLAKE EDWARDS (1922–)
Breakfast at Tiffany's (1961)
Days of Wine and Roses (1962)
The Pink Panther (1964)
10 (1979)
Victor/Victoria (1982)

BOB FOSSE (1927–87)
Sweet Charity (1968)
Cabaret (1972)
All That Jazz (1979)

JIM JARMUSCH (1953–)
Stranger Than Paradise (1984)
Down By Law (1986)
Mystery Train (1989)
Night on Earth (1991)

SPIKE LEE (1957–)
She's Gotta Have It (1986)
Do The Right Thing (1989)
Jungle Fever (1991)
Malcolm X (1992)

GEORGE LUCAS (1944–)
THX-1138 (1971)
American Graffiti (1973)
Star Wars (1977)
The Empire Strikes Back (1980, Irvin
   Kershner)
Raiders of the Lost Ark (1981, Steven
   Spielberg)
Return of the Jedi (1983, Richard Marquand)
Star Wars: Episode I—The Phantom Menace
   (1999)
Star Wars: Episode II—Attack of the Clones
   (2002)

DAVID LYNCH (1946–)
Eraserhead (1977). Completed 1976
The Elephant Man (1980)
Blue Velvet (1986)
Twin Peaks: Fire Walk With Me (1992).
   Completed 1991
Lost Highway (1997). Completed 1996
Mulholland Drive or *Mulholland Dr.* (2001)
TV series: *Twin Peaks* (pilot, 1989; broadcast
   1990–91). Co-producer, Mark Frost

JOHN SAYLES (1950–)
Return of the Secaucus Seven (1980).
   Completed 1979
Baby It's You (1983). Completed 1982
The Brother from Another Planet (1984)
Matewan (1987)
The Secret of Roan Inish (1994)
Men With Guns (1997)

RIDLEY SCOTT (1939–)
The Duellists (1977)
Alien (1979)
Blade Runner (1982). Director's cut released 1992
Thelma & Louise (1991)

STEVEN SPIELBERG (1946–)
Duel (1971). Made for TV
Jaws (1975)
Close Encounters of the Third Kind (1977).
   Revised 1980
Raiders of the Lost Ark (1981)
E.T.—The Extra-Terrestrial (1982)
Indiana Jones and the Temple of Doom (1984)
Jurassic Park (1993)
Schindler's List (1993)
Amistad (1997)
Saving Private Ryan (1998)
A.I. Artificial Intelligence or *Artificial
   Intelligence AI* (2001)
Minority Report (2002)

OLIVER STONE (1946–)
Platoon (1986)
JFK (1991)
Natural Born Killers (1994)

QUENTIN TARANTINO (1963–)
Reservoir Dogs (1992)
Pulp Fiction (1994)
Jackie Brown (1997)
Kill Bill Vol. 1 (2003)
Kill Bill Vol. 2 (2004)

JOHN WATERS (1946–)
Pink Flamingos (1972)
Polyester (1981)
Hairspray (1988)
Serial Mom (1994)

ROBERT ZEMECKIS (1952–)
Romancing the Stone (1984)
Back to the Future (1985)
Who Framed Roger Rabbit (1988)

Back to the Future Part II (1989),
  Part III (1990)
Forrest Gump (1994)

DVDs

The Adventures of Indiana Jones (1981–89,
  Steven Spielberg; co-produced by **George
  Lucas**). Paramount Home Video. **Digitally
  restored** prints of *Raiders of the Lost Ark*,
  Indiana Jones and the Temple of Doom,
  and *Indiana Jones and the Last Crusade*.
  Includes a making-of documentary and
  shorts on the films' stunts, sound, music,
  and effects.
Alien (1979, **Ridley Scott**). Twentieth Century
  Fox. 20th Anniversary Edition. Includes the release version, a commentary by Scott, storyboards, other artwork, and deleted scenes.
  The director's cut and the extended version of
  the film are available on the more recently released *Alien: The Director's Cut* (Fox;
  Collector's Edition), which includes deleted
  scenes and many making-of documentaries
  and interviews.

A.I. Artificial Intelligence (2001, **Steven Spielberg**). DreamWorks Home Entertainment. Special Edition. Includes two making-of documentaries; storyboards; interviews with Spielberg, the ILM effects group, and others; and more.

Back to the Future: The Complete Trilogy (1985–90, **Robert Zemeckis**). Universal. Includes commentaries by Zemeckis, writer **Bob Gale**, and star **Michael J. Fox**; deleted scenes; a making-of documentary and a short about the special effects; and screen tests.

Brazil (1985, **Terry Gilliam**). Criterion Collection. Includes the director's cut of the film (142 minutes) as well as the "Love Conquers All" edited-for-TV version (the U.S. theatrical release version is not included); a making-of documentary emphasizing the battles over releasing the picture; interviews with writers **Tom Stoppard** and **Charles McKeown**, production designer **Norman Garwood**, costume designer **James Acheson**, and composer **Michael Kamen**; storyboards; and a commentary by Gilliam.

Daughters of the Dust (1991, **Julie Dash**). Kino Video. Deluxe Edition.

Do the Right Thing (1989, **Spike Lee**). Criterion Collection. Includes a commentary by Lee, cinematographer **Ernest Dickerson**, and others; a making-of documentary; a visit to the locations; Lee's music video of **Public Enemy**'s "Fight the Power"; an interview with editor **Barry Brown**; storyboards; and the 1989 Cannes press conference with Lee and stars **Ossie Davis**, **Ruby Dee**, and **Joie Lee**.

Down By Law (1986, **Jim Jarmusch**). Criterion Collection. Includes interviews with Jarmusch, cinematographer **Robby Müller**, and others; the 1986 Cannes press conference with Jarmusch and stars **Roberto Benigni**, **Nicoletta Braschi**, and **John Lurie**; outtakes; unusually good production and location stills; and Jarmusch's phone calls with singer **Tom Waits**, Benigni, and Lurie.

Eraserhead (1977, **David Lynch**). Available only from the davidlynch.com store. Includes a terrific print of the film and a long interview with Lynch. The same Web site offers a selection of his shorts.

Fargo (1996, **Joel and Ethan Coen**). MGM/UA. Special Edition. Includes a documentary, an interview with the Coens and star **Frances McDormand**, and more.

Halloween (1978, **John Carpenter**). Anchor Bay. Divimax 25th Anniversary Edition. Includes a commentary by Carpenter, writer–producer **Debra Hill**, and star **Jamie Lee Curtis**; a documentary with many interviews; and a visit to the original location.

The Hills Have Eyes (1977, **Wes Craven**). Anchor Bay. Includes a commentary by Craven and producer **Peter Locke**; the alternate ending; storyboards; a documentary on Craven's career featuring interviews with him and many actors, including **Robert Englund**, **Neve Campbell**, and **Meryl Streep**; and, in the DVD-ROM section, the screenplay.

Jaws (1975, **Steven Spielberg**). Universal. 25th Anniversary Widescreen Collector's Edition. Includes a making-of documentary, storyboards, and deleted scenes.

The John Waters Collection (1972–98, **John Waters**). New Line Home Entertainment. Contains *Pink Flamingos*, *Female Trouble*, *Desperate Living*, *Polyester*, *Hairspray*, and *Pecker*, with commentaries by Waters.

Memento (2000, **Christopher Nolan**). Columbia TriStar. Limited Edition. Remastered in high definition; includes a commentary by Nolan, the shooting script (with links to completed scenes), and puzzles that unlock information.

Men With Guns (1997, **John Sayles**). Columbia TriStar. With a commentary by Sayles.

O Brother, Where Art Thou? (see Chap. 19 list).

Se7en (1995, **David Fincher**). New Line Home Entertainment. Platinum Series. Includes commentaries by all concerned, an exploration of the opening title sequence, storyboards, alternate endings, and more.

Titus (1999, **Julie Taymor**). Twentieth Century Fox. Includes a making-of documentary, information about the costumes, articles on the film from *American Cinematographer*, a short about creating the nightmare sequences, and a Q&A between Taymor and students at Columbia.

18

Conglomerates and Cassettes: 1975–

While filmmakers from Spielberg and Lucas to Scorsese and Lynch were pushing the American cinema to new levels of expression, many important developments took place in the business and technology of film. These changes were so extreme that by the beginning of the 21st century, almost every major studio had become part of a gigantic media corporation, the average studio picture cost more than $60 million to produce, an unprecedented number of films were sequels rather than risk-taking originals, and video— first analog, then digital—had become a viable medium for watching and even shooting motion pictures.

It's A Wonderful Deal

The Hollywood Renaissance ended shortly after the film industry became more interested in making deals than in making movies. Ironically, this change was motivated by the success of several key Renaissance films, notably the great sequel *The Godfather Part II* and the blockbuster *Jaws*. Movies began to earn such high profits that more expensive films were made, designed specifically to make even more money. With higher costs came higher risks, so the movies became more formulaic and exciting, driven by increasingly sophisticated effects and calculated to be pleasing rather than disturbing, offbeat, or thought-provoking. Movies were built around marketable elements—especially the stars, the book or picture the film would be based on, and the director—linked in a deal, often before there was a final script and sometimes when there was only a vague notion of what the movie would be about. It was the package of stars and the genre, producers believed, that people went to see.

The reins of production passed into the hands of several kinds of executives: young business majors fresh out of school, former talent agents, corporate bigwigs, and producers of recent hits. Most of these new decision makers thought they were skilled at identifying projects that could turn into hits, but almost none of them had any visual training, on-the-set filmmaking experience, or grasp of film history (Chaplin, *Casablanca*, and *2001* about covered it). They rarely thought about what would make a good *film*, not just a good story or a good business opportunity. And they were desperate for appealing, entertaining, sure-fire projects.

Sequels and Blockbusters

Most film ideas were approved for production on the basis of market research and guesswork rather than experience and confident instinct. New ideas were rare, and when they succeeded, they were repeated in sequels. No period in film history ever saw so many sequels. Nor so many remakes—attempts to discover the old magic in old ideas, updating what had worked before. *The Big Clock* (as *No Way Out*), *The Blob*, *Dawn of the Dead*, *D.O.A.*, *Out of the Past* (as *Against All Odds*), *Planet of the Apes*, and *Stella Dallas* (as *Stella*) were just a few of the films that were remade, sometimes with a lame change of title and rarely with success. Screenwriter and novelist William Goldman summed up the studio mentality of the period with the motto, "NOBODY KNOWS ANYTHING."

Studio executives listened as writers pitched stories, producers outlined projects, and agents presented packages; put 100 projects into development when they knew they would make only 12; and ordered changes in completed films in response to the reactions of preview audiences and other executives. The great goal was to reach the desired (*target* or targeted) audience and earn its repeat business, then to reach other age and population groups—ideally, to see a picture with *legs* (the ability to grow in popularity on its own, without needing extra advertising, and to move from a few theatres to many) do so well that it became a blockbuster that could be kept in release a long time, be profitably distributed overseas and profitably licensed for TV and DVD, be the basis of a sequel, and perhaps even be re-released.

For Hollywood executives, the new world began in 1975, when *Jaws* made money faster than any movie since *The Birth of a Nation*, catalyzing the blockbuster mentality and identifying teenagers and young adults as the audience to please. Decades of teenpix came from this conception of the primary audience, but so did an unprecedented interest in and development of new sound technologies and special effects. *Star Wars* confirmed these priorities: special effects, young audiences, open endings leading to sequels, and impressive soundtracks. And *Rocky*, released between *Jaws* and *Star Wars*, showed that the right medium-budget movie could make zillions and that the public was looking for heroes. *Rambo: First Blood Part II* (George P. Cosmatos, 1985) provided what for many executives was the final revelation: that a sequel could earn more than the film on which it was based ($79 million, compared with *First Blood*'s $23 million).

Conglomerates

But not every studio executive was in Hollywood, or even in a studio. Beginning in the 1960s, many studios were taken over by bigger corporations whose executives saw filmmaking as part of their company's business rather than all of it, and strictly as a profit-making venture. (Imagine the difference it would have made if Mayer and Thalberg had had to answer to General Motors.) Universal-International was taken over by MCA (1962), Paramount by Gulf + Western (1966),

United Artists by Transamerica (1967), Warner Bros. by Kinney (1969), and Columbia by Coca-Cola (1982)—and all of them went on to change hands. Even before *Titanic*, vast amounts of money rushed into the industry, which began to take in billions. Studios were valuable producers of salable entertainment, and when the dust had settled, most of them had been absorbed by media *conglomerates:* huge corporations made up of many diverse companies.

In 1994, the media conglomerate Viacom bought Paramount Communications, which included Paramount Pictures, Paramount Television, Simon & Schuster, and Madison Square Garden. Viacom owned the cable channels MTV, Nickelodeon, Showtime, and The Movie Channel, and by 2000 it had acquired CBS. That meant that in 2000 a Paramount movie could play in a Viacom theatre (Famous Players and United Cinema International; divestiture laws have long kept the studios from owning theatres, but many media conglomerates included theatre chains anyway; significantly, no one objected in 1997 when Sony Corp. and Cineplex Odeon merged their theatre businesses to form Loews Cineplex Entertainment) and then go to cable on a Viacom cable outlet (Showtime), to stores in Viacom's video outlet (Blockbuster), and to network TV on a Viacom TV network (CBS), while the underlying novel was reissued by a Viacom publisher (Pocket Books), with ads for all of these showings and products going out on Viacom's TV and radio stations.

The conglomerates were not monopolies but slices through the culture, communications structures that included some of the country's books, some of its newspapers, some of its channels, some of its cables and phone lines, some of its movies, some of its toys. By cutting out the middleman and controlling virtually all aspects of production, distribution, and exhibition, the studios brought back vertical integration, only it was not the studio in charge but the conglomerate, which owned all the companies including the studio.

For Sale: Studio

Some studios were bought and sold repeatedly, even by the same people. Consider the fate of MGM. Investor Kirk Kerkorian gained control of MGM in 1969 and United Artists in 1981, forming the MGM/UA Entertainment Company. In 1985 Ted Turner, the owner of several major cable-TV stations, bought MGM and UA, but in 1986 he sold them back to Kerkorian, keeping the films. In 1986, Turner also sold the MGM lot and laboratory to Lorimar. Kerkorian sold MGM again in 1990 to Giancarlo Parretti of Pathe Communications (no relation to the legendary Pathé Frères). Parretti rang down the curtain on UA and formed MGM-Pathe, but he ran the studio for less than six months. (Like Turner's, Parretti's was a highly leveraged buyout. Little of the $1.3 billion Parretti paid Kerkorian for his 80 percent interest in MGM/UA was cash—the rest a transfer of paper assets, borrowed money, and anticipated revenues pledged by other companies for rights to the not-yet-owned films—and when it came to running the studio, the Italian financier had trouble paying the bills.

Although the studios survived, they no longer had permanent staffs of skilled artists and artisans—no Script Department with its group of experienced writers, no pool of directors, no costumers who worked for the studio on film after film and both understood and helped to create the studio's style, and not even the costumes themselves. Studios emptied their warehouses of props and costumes, from "Rosebud" to the dresses worn in *Gone With the Wind*. Just one result of this housecleaning was that far fewer period pictures were made; most films were set in the present, using costumes and props that could be bought in ordinary stores or rented from a supply house. A more significant result was that filmmakers became freelancers: Everyone was hired to work on a specific project—and without a project was out of work, hoping for a call.

There was no studio staffed like the old MGM, which had actors like Judy Garland, Mickey Rooney, Clark Gable, and Spencer Tracy on the payroll, available to work on anything, as it had writers like Jules Furthman and Frances Marion, designers and choreographers who knew how to make an MGM musical, acres of outdoor sets, and even its own film laboratory. The MGM lab, Metro-color, was closed in the late 1980s. The old MGM back lot was sold long ago (by Kerkorian) to real estate developers, and the rest of the lot, with its soundstages and office buildings, passed from control of MGM/UA to Lorimar-Telepictures to Warner Bros. to Columbia, which itself was finally

bought by Sony. Even a highly successful studio like Disney, which has never changed ownership, began to hire "talent" on a film-by-film basis, only in rare cases going so far as to offer a contract to an actor or director for a set number of pictures.

In the Studio Era, a Paramount picture was approved, made, and released by Paramount, whether or not it was shot on the Paramount lot. Today a Paramount picture is just as likely to have been made by an independent production company and "picked up" (as *Friday the 13th* was) by Paramount for release as "A Paramount Picture." In a *negative pick-up* deal, an independent producer sells the completed negative—the finished film—to a studio, thus recouping the costs of production and in most cases securing the rights to a portion of the film's earnings. But the deal may be made earlier, even before the film is shot, with the studio paying some or most of the cost of production; in this case, the filmmakers get more of their money at the "front end" of the deal—that is, right away—and are entitled to less of the film's profits. Generally, those who spend their own money or defer their compensation, whether they are producers, studios, directors, or actors, receive more money at the "back end" of the deal, after the film has been released. All of the studios make pick-up deals—and there's no secret about it; it's made plain in credits like "MGM presents a GMT Production . . ." or when a studio logo (such as MGM's shot of the roaring lion) is followed by "An Acme Film." The important thing to realize here is that the studios themselves are not producing as many films as it appears; they have been working in partnership with independents for dedades.

Throughout this period, a number of studio heads and major producers were former talent agents who brought their clients along with them. But the talent agencies themselves soon became as powerful as the studios. The sales of Columbia and Universal—whole studios—were arranged by talent agents. With virtually everyone working on a contract basis—contracted to work on *a* film, with a profession but not a regular job—agents assembled prominent "elements" into a *package*, which in business terms was package deal and the talent it bound: the basic idea and the key people who would make the film and attract the audience. This constituted putting a picture together, constructing the picture-as-deal and deciding, as studio producers alone once did, which movies would be made by whom. Indeed, the major agent's list of clients, from whom the package of writer, director, and stars typically was selected, was the period's version of the studio's "stable" of talent. If Mickey Rooney and Judy Garland appeared together in a new picture, it would be because they had the same agent, not because they worked for the same studio.

The Budget Explosion

The cost of making films went up throughout the period; it was not simply a matter of inflation when the average *negative cost* of a studio feature (the expenses involved in producing the negative—in other words, the cost of making the movie before any copies are struck) jumped from $11 million to over $20 million in the 1980s, then hit $50 million in the 1990s. In 2003 it cost Hollywood $64 million to make the average film and $103 million to distribute it; included in the latter figure was $39 million for prints and ads.

The blockbuster mentality fed on itself. If a star's last picture had cost $10 million and earned $50 million, his or her fee on the next picture would be at least $1 million, possibly $20 million. If a picture was expected to do well—perhaps because it was the sequel to a hit—it appeared a safe investment, and more money was spent on it; thus, *Die Hard 2* (1990) cost much more than *Die Hard*. Studios spent more in the hope of making more. But if one spends $70 million on a *Die Hard 2*, and if conventional practices dictate that a film must take in three times its negative cost at the box office to break even (to cover the costs of prints, advertising, distribution, exhibition, and interest as well as the cost of production), that overburdened sequel would have to sell at least $210 million in tickets before earning a penny.

Studios hedged these enormous bets by selling *subsidiary rights* even before a picture was shot: licenses to distribute the film theatrically in other countries, to show it on cable, to broadcast it on network TV, to reproduce and sell it on videocassettes and laserdiscs (and later, DVDs), to distribute it nontheatrically in 16mm, to sell a novel based on its plot, to consider it for a TV series, and to make toys and clothes inspired by its characters as well as many other trademarked items, from party napkins to

computer games. These secondary revenues, especially the ones from video, could equal or surpass those taken in at the box office, and they had an effect on the way the film was shot: to play well in a theatre and acceptably on a TV set.

Another commercial practice that had a marked effect on film content was *product placement*, which amounted to selling advertising space within the movie. Sometimes the product would show up subtly—everyone in the movie just happened to drink Budweiser or drive a Ford—but it could also make its presence felt blatantly. When a father and son go shopping in *Manhunter* (Michael Mann, 1986), the boy asks his dad what kind of coffee he likes, then says "You like that Folgers stuff, don't you? Mom likes it too."

The studios were no longer the only game in town, though they remained extremely powerful. Many independent producers, directors "shopping projects" (trying to interest studios in them), and writers with finished scripts "written on spec" (*on speculation*—that is, on one's own, with no guarantee that anyone would buy the work) visited the studios in the hope of selling an idea or a script, obtaining co-financing to produce a film, or convincing the studio to make a film. But many independents made films with no guidance or interference from any studio—films that usually cost under $10 million to produce and could turn out to be more profitable than any studio product. *The Blair Witch Project* cost the original filmmakers, who used both film and video, $60,000. For $1.1 million, it was acquired by Artisan, which put another $300,000 into post-production polishing, so that its final cost was under $1.5 million—and it made $140 million at the U.S. box office, over 95 times its cost (or 2,333 times the cost of the original version). Then it made even more on video and internationally.

Independent filmmakers who felt strongly about what they made could make pick-up deals with studios when the film was completed, on a take-it-or-leave-it basis, refusing to make cuts, but it was more common for them simply to deal with smaller releasing companies or independent distributors. Many other independent filmmakers struck co-financing deals with studios, instantly raising much of the production money they needed, gaining prestige, validating the payroll, and getting rid of the worry of finding a distributor in one fell swoop. Or they let the studio finance the project completely and more or less take over. The biggest problem independent artists found in working with studios on a creative level was that once they had sold their scripts or seen their productions become studio productions—subtly or grossly, the studio made its own version of the film, not theirs. It was often said that the only way to keep a good script from being rewritten was not to sell it.

Executive Decisions

The most frustrating pre-production experience any writer, producer, or director underwent at the hands of post-1970 studios was called "development hell," a good description of the years one might spend waiting for a studio to make up its mind to produce a project, ordering rewrites and other substantial but tentative revisions in the meantime—until one found that the project had been put in *turnaround*, offered to any other studio that might want it in exchange for reimbursement of the project's cost so far . . . where the cycle of indecision could begin again.

Yet the studios needed these outsiders—the writers, who gave them ideas, and the independents, who gave them films. If Hollywood demonstrated anything at the end of the 20th century, it was a hunger for ideas; it didn't seem to know what to make. It wanted the new–old. It wanted sequels to documented hits (*The Godfather Part III*); it wanted updated remakes of classics (*Cape Fear*) and Americanized remakes of overseas hits (*3 Men and a Baby*); it wanted revitalized genres (*Body Heat* and the "new *noir*"). The art of the sequel is one of *repetition with variation*, and the same can be said of the remake, the genre revival, and—according to conservative Hollywood—the aesthetics of the sure-fire investment. "Do it again, but differently," executives demanded, looking for a film idea that would "grab them" and thus, they assumed, would interest an audience.

The art most anxiously but consistently pursued by producers and agents in this period, whether or not they were also executives, was that of putting creative people together to work on viable projects. In many respects, the package was the movie. Entertainment lawyers made fortunes. Cinematography, sound, editing, and other cinematic matters were rarely considered; to hire a director was to indicate a preference for a certain style and pace. Since the agents and executives saw movies simply as stories acted out by stars in a repeatable medium, it was enough for them to determine the story, the stars, and the director, which were not only the key elements of the film as they saw it, but also the basis of its marketing campaign. And if overseas and video markets were willing to commit to this film, and if Chrysler wanted to donate all the cars for the chase scenes, so much the better. Even if the executives couldn't quite envision the movie they were approving, they *could* see the deal and knew precisely how to evaluate it.

Theatres

The conditions of film exhibition changed drastically in the course of the 1980s. Thanks to Dolby Stereo, theatres with optical sound projectors could present movies in four-channel stereo (before, stereo required a magnetic sound projector). The theatrical sound experience became more important, and sound editing and mixing became far more sophisticated than ever before, both technically and aesthetically.

The battle of the aspect ratios, which began with the wide-screen revolution of the 1950s, was settled in favor of two formats: American widescreen, a flat (nonanamorphic) format with an aspect ratio of 1.85 to 1 (written 1.85:1, it means that the screen is 1.85 times as wide as it is high), and Panavision, a scope (anamorphic) format with an aspect ratio of 2.35:1, later 2.4:1. (Early in the 1970s, Panavision widened its anamorphic aspect ratio to 2.4:1, while some other scope films continued to be shot at 2.35:1. See "Aspect ratio" in the Glossary. Also note that in Europe, flat widescreen is 1.66:1.) In the 1990s, with the rise of high-definition television (HDTV), 16:9 or 1.78:1, also written 16×9, emerged as a film as well as a TV format.

The *cineplex* (or *multiplex cinema*), now found in most cities, standing alone or in shopping malls, houses at least four—usually six or more—small theatres, each an auditorium with a big stereo and a relatively small screen. In the 1980s, virtually no new theatres were built except multiplexes. The new exhibition spaces were smaller, but they were easier to fill than the cavernous single-screen theatres that had been built in times when far more people went to the movies.

A 1990 study found that only 25 percent of Americans went to more than five films a year. The price of admission crept ever higher; by 1990 most theatres were not allowed to sell tickets for less than $5 except at bargain matinees. To take a family to the movies became an expensive proposition. The big films with big soundtracks were, audiences judged, worth seeing and hearing in big theatres—or in a multiplex, even with the sound turned down so it wouldn't be heard in the other theatres, because even if the screen was small, what one saw on it was a *movie*, not a video.

In the 1980s and 1990s, audiences saw motion pictures in big theatres with state-of-the-art projection and sound equipment, in multiple-screen theatres with their many selections, in the older single-screen theatres that kept alive the "ordinary" moviegoing experience, or at home. Trading quality for convenience and economy, a family could rent a video of a recent movie, watch it on TV, and save $20 or $30. At that rate, a videocassette recorder–player (*VCR*) could pay for itself with a few skipped movies. By the early 2000s, when the laserdisc had come and gone, there were more DVD players than VCRs, and tickets cost $9 or more, people chose to watch a movie at home far more often than in a theatre.

Studio Shakeups

The drama of buying, selling, merging, and taking over studios reached a historic climax in the late 1980s when Columbia and Universal were bought by Japanese companies and Warner Bros. merged with Time Inc. Movie companies had long been corporately linked with the publishing and recording companies that had, like them, been absorbed by conglomerates. Now the conglomerates renamed themselves "communications" enterprises and flung their nets of information and entertainment across the globe. Time, which owned several publishing and recording companies as well as Home Box Office (HBO, which showed new movies on cable), merged with Warner Bros. Communications in 1989 to form Time Warner, the world's largest communications conglomerate; in 1996, they acquired Turner Broadcasting in a merger. Time Warner also founded a TV network and went on to acquire and develop the country's second-largest system of cable lines (after AT&T). In 2000 Time Warner and the Internet service provider America Online (AOL) announced a merger—really a takeover in which AOL acquired Time Warner—that would form the largest media conglomerate in the world; the deal creating AOL Time Warner was approved in 2001. Now the Internet was part of the conglomerate's package. With the improvement of broadband technology, it became possible to download and watch a digital copy of a movie (versions suitable for saving onto a DVD could be sent aross the Internet by the year 2001). AOL Time Warner had a mammoth base of subscribers (from AOL to *Sports Illustrated*) and the cables to deliver, with the high-speed technologies of the future, digitized content not just from the Turner stations but from Warner Bros., New Line, and the other studios that had become part of Time Warner. Beyond being the largest company, it was the one that appeared most prepared for a digital future; however, AOL was dial-up and remained so for too long. Another media colossus had been created in 1994, when Viacom Inc., as previously mentioned, completed its acquisition of Paramount, making it possible to send *Star Trek* to audiences in almost any conceivable form. The Walt Disney Company stayed Disney—and eventually bought ABC.

But the other four majors were acquired by foreign companies. In 1985, Twentieth Century–Fox was bought by Rupert Murdoch's News Corporation, which is based in Australia; in the process Fox dropped its dash. Within a few years, the television arm of Fox had launched its own broadcasting network. As previously discussed, MGM was bought and sold all around the world, ending up in 1996 where it started, in California, as part of MGM/UA, and not owned or controlled by any other company. (A decade later, however, it was part of Sony.) Columbia, which had merged with TriStar early in 1989, signed a merger agreement with Sony late in the year, and Columbia Pictures Entertainment became a Sony company—as did CBS Records soon after; now Columbia and TriStar were listed under Sony. Finally, in 1990, Matsushita Electric Industrial Co. Ltd. bought MCA Inc., the parent company of Universal as well as of many recording companies, a TV division, and a publisher. Matsushita also owned Panasonic, Quasar, and Technics, which manufactured stereo and video equipment. When Columbia and Universal passed into Japanese hands, the new owners made it clear that they did not want to influence or supervise the studios' filmmaking activities. Their primary interest was the *software* for their hardware: the music for their CDs and CD players, the movies for their videocassettes and VCRs, laserdiscs and laser players (and after them the DVDs and DVD players), monitors and TV sets—much as Time and HBO needed movies for their video and cable operations. Sony, the inventor of Betamax (the first popular VCR and its half-inch video format), and Matsushita, its archrival and one of the chief developers of VHS (the competing format that took over the half-inch video market), now had studios to supply them with new films and old, grist for the mills of video.

But in 1995 Matsushita got out of the film and music business and sold MCA to the Seagram Company; they did not, however, get out of the video business. In 2000 Seagram merged with Vivendi (a French company with extensive holdings in publishing, advertising, and waste management) and Canal Plus (or Canal+, which has a film production entity—Studio Canal—and the largest pay-TV channel in France); the core of the deal was the sale of MCA, with all its music holdings as well as Universal Studios, to Vivendi. In 2001 Seagram bowed out, and the resulting company was named Vivendi Universal. So at the turn of the millennium, this is how it stood: the huge Disney, the new DreamWorks, the new Pixar, and the small MGM were self-owned; Columbia and TriStar were part of Sony; Fox was part of News Corp.; Paramount was part of Viacom; RKO was long gone; Universal was part of Vivendi Universal; and Warner Bros. was part of AOL Time Warner.

In 2003, when America Online had become less powerful and was no longer seen as the key to the integrated digital future, AOL Time Warner changed its name back to Time Warner. As the MPAA listed them early in 2004, the seven *majors*—the major producers and distributors of movies in the U.S. at the time—were Buena Vista Pictures Distribution (The Walt Disney Company), Metro–Goldwyn–Mayer Studios, Paramount Pictures Corporation, Sony Pictures Entertainment (its status as a major continuing Columbia's), Twentieth Century Fox Film Corporation, Universal City Studios, and Warner Bros. Entertainment. But by the end of 2004,

even if the studios still had those names, things had changed: Universal was no longer controlled by Vivendi, and Sony had put in a bid, accepted in September, to buy MGM and UA. It was not immediately clear whether the MGM lot, which had been renamed the Columbia lot and then the Sony lot, would be renamed the MGM lot.

NBC Universal was formed in May 2004. According to the deal, announced in 2003, Vivendi owned 20 percent of the new company, and General Electric—the parent company of NBC—owned 80 percent. Once again, a movie studio and a TV network had come together as parts of a gigantic business entity. It is ironic and significant that one of the two companies that had gone into the forming of General Electric in 1892 had been Edison General Electric. Thus GE's buying Universal might be thought of as the return of the Wizard in the age of the media conglomerate. A company descended from Edison now controlled Universal, one of the original independents. Edison's spirit would be glad, no doubt, to be at the head of a media revolution based on the electronic storage and transmission of data, running a company with a global reach.

Movies in the Age of Video

From the late 1970s to the present, video has played important roles in the production, consumption, and destruction of feature films.

The studios found themselves with two actively competitive and lucrative markets for their classics and new features—network TV (which is broadcast: sent through the air to all antennas) and cable TV (which is a restricted-access system whose signal is sent directly, via electronic cables, only to paying subscribers; cable can transmit stereo as well as data and phone calls). At the same time, public TV stations became the chief subsidizers of independent documentary filmmaking. Typically, studios and independents licensed their new features to be shown first on cable and then on network TV, obtaining some of the production money they needed by pledging these exhibition rights.

By 1994, more than 85 percent of the American homes that had TVs also had VCRs. By then it was typical for a new film to be released first to domestic theatres, then to foreign theatres, then to video manufacturers and outlets, then to cable, then to 16mm distributors (a step often skipped), and then to network TV. In some cases, video distribution became as important to the studio as theatrical exhibition (in the U.S. and abroad, because every country that had TVs had VCRs). If a film was not expected to do well, it might open for as little as a week (to get reviews and earn theatrical status), or it might be released "direct to video" without appearing in theatres at all. The film companies found that the sale of video copies of hit films could realize tremendous amounts of money. Disney's *Lady and the Tramp* (1955) made $50 million in theatres—counting its first release and all revivals—but it made $90 million on video.

Analog and Digital Information

Videotape is a magnetic medium that can store movies and other information in either analog or digital form. *Analog* information is continuous, like a sound wave, with differences signaled by having more or less of something. *Digital* information is discrete. The digital world is binary, offering a choice between polar alternatives: on or off, yes or no, present or absent. An electronic switch can be open or closed. In the electronic and mathematical language of computers, a *one* (the equivalent of "yes" or "on") opens a switch, letting current flow through it as if through a sluice, and a *zero* ("no" or "off") closes it, stopping the flow. A character, say, "T," can be stored as a *byte* of information, a unit consisting of 8 adjacent bits that are processed together. Each *bit* (a contraction of "binary digit") is a minimal unit of information—or the memory needed to store it—in the form of a zero or a one. A binary number such as 10101101 could be an 8-bit byte recognized by a computer as a particular letter—or as the amount of red in a colored dot in a picture. A kilobyte (*KB*) is 2^{10} or 1,024 bytes; a megabyte (*MB*) is 2^{20} or 1,048,576 bytes; and a gigabyte (*GB*) is 2^{30} or 1,073,741,824 bytes, which is 1,024 MB or about a billion bytes. A megabit (abbreviated *Mb*) is 2^{20} bits.

Sampling and Conversion

What in analog might be a gradual curve would, if it was converted to digital information, be a staircase. The more steps there are, and the tinier and closer together they are, the more the staircase in this example will resemble a single curved line—that is, the more closely the digital version will sound or look like the analog original. The size and closeness of the steps depends on how often and at what level of detail the source—in this case, the curve—is checked. In a process called *sampling*, an analog signal is converted into digital form (*digitized*) by dipping into the analog flow at regular intervals and encoding each discrete sample of the curve as a step in the digital staircase (that is, put into the digital *code* of zeros and ones). In the case of a frame, what is sampled is a picture. Sampling resembles a movie camera's regularly shooting discrete frames that show unmoving parts of a continuous motion.

The number of samples gathered per second is the *sampling rate* or *sampling frequency*. The higher this rate, and the more information in a sample (measured in bits), the more clearly a digital copy will resemble its analog original.

Videotape Recorders, Cassettes, and Discs

Videotape was developed in America in the early 1950s, and the video recorder with it. Although the idea for video recording was patented by a Russian scientist in 1922, he never built a working instrument. German scientists had used magnetic sound recordings on tape as early as 1935, using it to repeat radio programs during World War II, but it was the Americans who first used tape to store data in 1951.

The first practical color videotape recorder (VTR) was developed in 1957. When portable VTRs were invented in the 1960s, more and more news events were shot on video, not on 16mm. "Canned"—as opposed to live—TV shows continued to be shot on video or on film for decades, though by the early 21st century most were shot on digital video. In the late 1960s and 1970s, portable VTRs that used reel-to-reel tape were widely used not only by TV news crews, but also by traveling activists who brought material the official media ignored ("the video underground") and by video artists.

In 1965, Sony marketed the world's first VTR for home use, and a color version followed in 1966. Sony offered the world's first truly portable VTR in 1967. But it was not until Sony invented the *videocassette*—which kept videotape prethreaded in a plastic case, as audiocassettes did, rather than on open reels—that it revolutionized video recording and playback, not only in the home, but also for film and TV professionals. Sony's U-Matic cartridge, invented in 1971, used ¾-inch tape that recorded for one hour. Sony introduced the consumer *videocassette recorder* (VCR) in 1975; it used ½-inch tape and was called the Betamax. The Beta format proved to be convenient and of high quality. A year later, JVC introduced the VHS (Video Home System) format, which also housed ½-inch tape in a cassette but could record for a longer time and produced a relatively inferior image; both VHS and Beta were color systems. RCA joined Matsushita, whose brand names included Panasonic and JVC, in the development of VHS tapes and VCRs.

The VHS format proved more popular than Beta and eventually replaced it in the home market (following the "format wars" of the 1980s). It first became widely available in the U.S. in 1977—the same year that Twentieth Century–Fox, sensing a trend, licensed Magnetic Video to sell its films on videocassette.

From 1976 to 1984, Sony was in court, accused—primarily by Disney—of encouraging copyright infringement on a massive scale by facilitating the home recording of TV programs and particularly of movies. The Supreme Court finally ruled that home taping was a legal technology as long as the copies were only for personal use. That 1984 decision made it legal for people to build their own collections of video copies of films, taping them off the air for purposes of entertainment and reference. (Buying legally prerecorded cassettes never posed copyright problems.) It was also in 1984 that Woody Allen's *Manhattan* was released on video, at his insistence, in what became known as the *letterbox* format: the complete, original wide-screen image, with black bars above and below, as if one were looking through the rectangular door of a mailbox. As VCRs were improved, so that later models could scan and locate images rapidly, record and play back in stereo, and display a single frame for several minutes, they became very useful tools for the study of motion pictures.

Even more versatile and useful was the *laserdisc* player, developed throughout the 1970s by Philips (in the Netherlands) and MCA—with both companies apparently building on the "optical disc" technology first patented in 1967 by American inventor David Gregg—and finally put on the market in 1978. Its single-frame display (on the standard-play or CAV discs) was perfectly steady, and the visual quality of the laserdisc image far surpassed anything possible with tape, as did the theatrical quality of its sound (the laserdisc is the ancestor of the compact disc or *CD*, introduced in 1982). Even an extended-play or CLV laserdisc could display single frames, though not as well as a CAV disc. A competing product, the grooved videodisc, came and went in the early 1980s. The laserdisc's fatal competition in the late 1990s was the *DVD* (which doesn't stand for anything, because its creators couldn't decide between *digital video disc* and *digital versatile disc*). As optical discs, the laserdisc, CD, and DVD were not magnetic media; they could be stamped out like phonograph records, whereas videotapes had to be recorded in real time—which cost more. (Floppy disks, computer tape, and hard drives or hard disks are magnetic. Magnetic disks are spelled with a *k*, optical discs with a *c*.)

DVDs

The DVD went on sale in Japan in 1996 and in the U.S. in 1997. By 2000, it had made the laserdisc (which produced a better image) obsolete, and DVD players were outselling VCRs. In the U.S., the discs began to outsell prerecorded videos in 2002; the next year, more DVDs than tapes were rented. In the first six months of 2004, Americans spent 84 percent of their video budgets renting and buying DVDs—a record $10.7 billion, more than the film industry had collected at the U.S. box office in all of 2003. Because of their high storage capacity, which began at 4.38 GB per side, soon nearly doubled, and would increase even more in the next generation of discs, DVDs could offer movies in an interactive format with a choice of versions and a full complement of background material.

Consumers enjoyed the DVD's visual quality and digital sound, which were much better than the picture and sound on a VHS tape; the DVD's instantaneous random access, which was inspired by the laserdisc and impossible with film or tape; and the supplemental materials with which DVDs were crammed, which built on the practice of the laserdisc but included more material. DVDs could include trailers, deleted scenes, interviews, detailed "making-of" documentaries and interactive demonstrations, other relevant films such as shorts by the filmmakers or newsreels, and more. DVDs also had subtitles that could be in different languages or could be turned off (film and all earlier video formats had had either one set of subtitles or none) as well as dubbed and original soundtracks, solving the problem of which version to buy; now one could play whichever version was appropriate for the immediate audience. Some DVDs included both full-screen and wide-screen versions. Some offered a "director's cut" made before or after the film was released, a version that might differ significantly from the one shown in domestic theatres. Some had running scene-by-scene and shot-by-shot commentaries by film scholars, and the majority had at least one running commentary track made by the filmmakers or constructed from interviews with them.

Because DVDs were digital, their data could be compressed, and because they were the size of a CD, the data had to be compressed, usually by a factor of 30 or more. In the most common method of compression used for DVDs (the MPEG-2 compression scheme), parts of the image that, in the computer software's view, did not change from frame to frame—perhaps the sky, a wall, or a range of mountains—could become image fragments repeated for each affected frame. This method saved storage space but usually left only one of every 12 frames in the form of a complete picture with full image data. So most DVDs could not—unlike standard-play laserdiscs— precisely access and completely display, with full detail and resolution, any frame one desired; instead, they would show that frame or a nearby one as fully as possible. True frame-by-frame viewing of a movie was possible on DVD, but few DVD publishers were willing to commit the extra time, care, bits, and money required.

Out of the Vaults

As a home-video format, DVD was strikingly different from tape in one respect: When introduced, it was only for playback. Although as rental items both tapes and DVDs were prere-

corded and designed only to be played back, the first DVD players did not record, and every VCR did. Standard blank videocassettes, which in the late 1970s had cost $30 apiece, were popular enough to drop as low as $1 by the early 2000s. Even if one had only a single tape and cycled it till it wore out—because a distinct advantage of magnetic recording, whether of sound or picture or data, is that as new material is recorded, old material is erased, allowing the tape or other medium to be reused—one of the first appeals of the VCR had been that it allowed people to time-shift for themselves. They could record what they wanted and watch it when they wanted. They could erase it or keep it. They could skip commercials. Thus the VCR gave viewers control over the schedules and priorities of broadcast, cable, and satellite TV. So did its digital offspring, marketed in the early 2000s: a hard drive for time-shifting (a DVR) coupled with a DVD recorder for saving.

In much the same way, renting or buying a video gave viewers control over both TV and theatrical movie programming—not just scheduling. No longer dependent on what the theatres happened to book or the stations happened to show, audiences could choose from a multitude of recent releases, nostalgia items, cult films, classics, favorites of all kinds that would never again play in theatres and might not even be shown on TV, subtitled movies, and even pornographic movies (video's first big hit). Around the world, renting a movie to watch at home became one of the most common private and social pastimes, and seeing new movies on video became normal in cities— or countries—that could maintain only one or two 35mm theatres, if any.

In the video revolution, which by the end of the 20th century had completely changed people's access to movies, it was the rental outlet that first made available that great number and variety of pictures, movies that could be seen at will. People were able to see more old movies and more movies from around the world. In the rental and sales outlets taken as one big electronic cinémathèque, a great deal of film history—perhaps 10 percent of the world's surviving films—was in the video equivalent of "release" all at once. A brilliant video clerk like Tarantino could march into filmmaking with a staggering background, his years of watching films augmented by thousands of tapes and discs. In spite of the fact that a movie's date of publication has almost always been its release date, it could be said that movies were *published on video* instead of being kept only on film, in archives and studio vaults, the way that paintings had been kept in museums and castles—until inexpensive, inferior copies had finally become widely available in the form of printed pictures. The cheap technology of video let ordinary people rent and buy movies. If one wanted to watch a particular film, getting a video copy of it became as simple as getting a book off the shelf of a personal or public library.

Home video also changed how people studied films. It became easy to examine a scene shot by shot, to capture a frame for printing, to check a detail, to compare different versions of a picture, and so on. In many cases, descriptions and citations of films became more accurate, less dependent on memory. Of course, memories of films are interesting in themselves, but it was good to be able to be exact even when one didn't have access to a 16mm or 35mm print—when quoting dialogue, for instance, or analyzing a composition. The movies were out of the vaults.

Pixels and Lines
They were not exactly the movies, however. They were electronic copies. No video can truly reproduce a film image. The film frame contains far more information than all but the most advanced video frame. Film grain is finer than TV's dots and is not arranged in lines. Film colors are dyes. To explain the fundamental ways in which film and video differ, one needs words like "pixel" and "scan."

A *pixel*, or picture element, is a single unit of an electronic image, one colored box or dot. Each pixel has red, green, and blue values that are sampled when the image is digitized—unless it is simply played or broadcast in analog—with at least 256 levels for each of the three component colors. (The component colors of a negative are yellow, cyan, and magenta.) Often, however, a pixel is not a single dot but a tight triangle of dots on a screen, one for each of the R, G, and B values; it can also be a tiny square whose colors have been mixed. By rough equivalence, the term can be applied to film, as if the frame were composed of—or could be broken down into—regular, minimal areas.

Pixels are lined up in rows that run horizontally across the frame. These rows, called *scan lines*, can also be scanned across the screen of a cathode-ray tube (a conventional TV picture tube) or onto other surfaces—for example, the raw stock in a *film recorder*—one line at a time, to generate a frame.

A video camera or display has two kinds of *lines of resolution*: the stack of horizontal lines (the scan lines or *lines of vertical resolution*, sometimes simply called "lines") and, running perpendicular to them, the *pixel lines*, or *lines of horizontal resolution*, which are virtual vertical lines created by the pixels that are directly above and below one another. The number of pixel lines in a frame is the same as the number of pixels in a scan line. Each pixel in a line can also be called a *horizontal sample* of the image, because a pixel is *not* a one-for-one equivalent of the same area on the film, but a representation of an electronic sampling of that area. Pixel lines are responsible for a picture's horizontal resolution, scan lines for its vertical resolution. The number of piled-up scan lines gives the frame's height, while the number of pixels in each scan line gives its width. Multiplying the number of scan lines by the number of pixels in each line gives the frame's resolution and its area as the number of pixels in it, a figure that is usually expressed in megapixels (Mp; a *megapixel* is one million pixels) and that gives a general indication of image quality at a particular size. The information is tentative because the number of Mp does not indicate how much information has been supplied for each pixel (which depends on sampling and other matters), and it is related to the size of the display because a blown-up image does not have more pixels than the original; one needs more pixels for a larger image at the same level of detail. Enlarged too much, a video image becomes *pixelated*, clearly showing each pixel as a separate unit.

At the turn of the 21st century, worldwide, there were at least six primary TV systems, of which the most significant were NTSC, PAL, SECAM, and HDTV. The most common conventional systems were NTSC, used in the U.S., Japan, etc.; PAL, used in China, most of Europe, etc.; and SECAM, used in France, Russia, etc. Each system uses a different scheme of lines and pixels.

High-definition television (HDTV, an advanced set of standards—incorporating Dolby digital stereo—for digital television, or DTV) debuted in the late 1990s. In the early 2000s, HDTV offered several high-definition formats. HDTV was widescreen, with an aspect ratio usually referred to as 16×9 or 16 × 9 (1.78:1) as opposed to conventional TV's 4×3 (1.33:1). HDTV could letterbox-wide movie images to preserve their original shapes—usually 1.66:1, 1.85:1, or 2.4:1—or it could deform them to its own 16×9, in which its shows and a growing number of movies were shot. With HDTV, television became widescreen to come closer to the aspect ratios of most new movies. As film had led TV to be in color, it now led TV to be wide.

Film and Video Frames

The most advanced digital movie camera at the turn of the century, the *24p* or HDW-F900 invented by Sony in collaboration with Panavision, could shoot 2-Mp frames. As its name indicates, the 24p ran at 24 fps—to match film and to avoid the awkward conversion from 29.97 fps—and used progressive scanning to produce a more film-like frame. (A later model is discussed in the next chapter.) But a newly printed frame of 35mm movie film, at the standard Academy-aperture size, has over *12.5 Mp* per frame—because it has the equivalent of *3,072 lines and 4,096 pixels*.

A frame whose horizontal lines have roughly 4,000 pixels is a "4K" image, where K is 1,000 pixel lines of resolution. The HDTV 1080p standard—with its 1,080 lines, each 1,920 pixels wide—gave a 2K image (1.92K is close enough), the same resolution shot by the first 24p camera. *High-definition digital video* (HDDV), shot on a high-resolution digital camera such as Sony's 24p—or something less expensive—is informally called "high-def."

When watching a movie or a video, one deals not just with hard specifications but with *perceived resolution*, a focused image created by the brain from frames that, because the subjects were moving when photographed, are often blurred, much as the brain supplies motion to a series of stills. Most film prints have a literal resolution of 4K, in pixel terms, and a perceived resolution of 6K; a badly beat-up print might be 3K. The most advanced digital projection system contemplated in 2004 was 4K, with full sampling

of R, G, and B values. 4K was a big step up from the established 1K and 2K systems; in tests it delivered a perceived resolution comparable to film. Nevertheless, there is a big difference between a pixel and a grain of silver. Film is exposed at the molecular level, and there are millions of particles on a square inch of film, far more "dots" than there are in any video frame. Nor do molecules line up the way pixels do. The grain pattern—the shadows of the silver particles—is different in every frame, giving texture and a living quality to the movie-film image. A little galaxy of grain can define and color an area of film summarized as a pixel.

To show a video as a movie, one needs to rely on perceived resolution because there is always going to be much less information displayed, whether by a TV or by a digital projector. To be perceived as "filmlike," an image needs to be seen at a resolution of 4K pixel lines or higher. To look good on a TV, it needs much less.

Beyond the question of resolution and the fact that film can show many more colors than video are the issues of range and cropping. Video and film have different sensitivities; they differ markedly in their treatment of bright and dark areas, and some things that can be shot on film, like an extremely bright, unmoving light, could burn out a video camera or at least yield a poor image. (For a DV example, see the oil fire in *The Fast Runner*.) On the other hand, the only way Michael Mann felt he could capture the dark look of a city at night for his 2004 movie, *Collateral*, was to shoot most of the picture with a 24p on high-definition digital video. Film can show more levels of brightness and contrast than can video, both in color and in black and white, and it can be exposed over a greater range; this usually gives the film image greater richness and detail.

Although video can show many colors, they are not film colors. Film colors are created chemically, TV colors electronically. Film colors are thrown on a screen as the projector's white light shines through the dyes on the film; TV colors emanate from the screen as glowing dots, which gives them an inevitable and uncinematic phosphorescence.

When blown up to the size of a movie screen, the video image is relatively murky and subject to pixelation. Most people watch video on screens that are much smaller than those in theatres, so that a close-up does not have the impact—the sudden bigness—it would have in a theatre, and an extreme long shot loses so much detail that it becomes unreadable. Keeping this in mind, many filmmakers have been shooting more close-ups than long shots, the way TV is shot.

Another way the video image is smaller is in terms of how much of the original is displayed. To stabilize the image electronically and to remove the possibility of an irregular outline, a TV tube usually "eats" the perimeter of any image. A viewer loses the whole rim of a 1.33:1 image and the left and right edges of a letterboxed image. This cropping can be overcome in advance by *windowboxing* the entire image—giving it a black perimeter on all four sides—or letterboxing at a width less than that of the display, but this is rarely done, perhaps because consumers prefer their screens to be as full as possible. The inner part of the cropped 1.33:1 image, the 95 percent or so of the frame that is displayed by a normal CRT and many other display systems, is called the *TV safe area*, and that rectangle is drawn or etched on the viewfinders of most studio cameras so that when the movies are shot in the first place, crucial actions and titles are kept within the purview of the tube.

When wide-screen films are copied for full-frame network broadcasting—or, scandalously, for release in 16mm—most of them are *panned and scanned* with an optical printer or its digital equivalent. In other words, only a 1.33:1 area of the image is recorded, and this image area is moved around to keep the "essential" action within the frame, sometimes by panning and sometimes by introducing cuts so that the action area can leap from one part of the frame to another. A CinemaScope film that is not letterboxed and also suffers the usual loss of perimeter is cropped so drastically that half the image is lost.

Fortunately, because most videos carry a film's original soundtrack, a movie *can* sound the same at home as it did in the theatre, if one has the right equipment.

While some of the differences between movies on film and movies on video depend on commercial practices and some on technical compromises, both of which are subject to change, the essential differences are significant. Whether one approaches the differences in terms of chemical and electronic colors, or how much data is in each frame, or how sampling and compression can affect a frame, or in terms of one's own responses, the fact is that movies on film and movies on video just don't look the same, and ultimately they provide different experiences.

Nevertheless, by the end of the 20th century, consumers had accepted videos as movies—or, to put it another way, they considered video close enough to film to serve as an adequate substitute. Most of the people who missed a movie in the theatre and then saw it on video felt they had seen the movie.

Theatres responded to the boom in home video by raising their prices, converting to surround sound and then digital sound, building multiplexes with larger auditoriums and screens, installing better seats, and hoping for pictures people would want to see right away and on a big screen, like the three annually released parts of *The Lord of the Rings*. It was good to have the extended director's cut, with all its supplements, on the 4-DVD set of *The Two Towers*, but a lover of film still had to see and hear that movie in a theatre to experience the real thing. To some extent, the viewer of a video was simultaneously watching the tube and imagining how the movie would look in a theatre—or remembering how it had looked and drawing on the power of the original. It was best to have both the home copy and the full-scale experience—if that was possible. But when a movie left the theatres, it stayed out of circulation as in earlier times and was hard to find on film. And that was when the video became available.

Changes on the Set

Film producers and studios responded to the Video Era in many ways. In the first place, they defined the "TV safe area." They set up optical printers to pan and scan movies for TV. They made money from licensing old and new movies for video—especially the old ones, which had stopped making money.

Very early on, the factories and labs noticed that consumers were buying and processing much less small-gauge movie film. Home movies were being shot on video. Portable VHS and Betamax cameras became available in 1982, and smaller units such as Kodak's integrated camera and recorder (*camcorder*) in 1984. When their prices went down—and with the introduction of DV in 1995 and the extremely convenient miniDV shortly afterward—the home-movie business dropped film in favor of videotape, which didn't need to be processed and offered effortlessly synchronized sound. As the small-gauge market shrank, a number of film labs closed down, and the manufacturers made fewer kinds of film; 8mm black-and-white filmstock was the first to go.

Film producers began making movies for TV, often on the lots of movie studios. The arts of film and TV had affected each other in the 1950s, making possible movies and teleplays that were well-written, efficiently directed, and powerfully acted. In the 1980s the greatest indication of their mutual influence was the *music video*, which built on the montage aesthetic as well as the tradition of the *Soundies* and other music shorts (films of singers, played in special jukeboxes and in theatres) while lending its own style to film-makers like Oliver Stone, whose *Natural Born Killers* intercut different film stocks and video at top speed.

Film producers and distributors began to pay more attention to the question of video rights, and soon a film's showings on cable and its video release were as important as its showings in theatres. Video director's cuts flourished.

On the set, one of the most important new devices was the *video tap* in a 35mm movie camera, which allowed what was filmed to be displayed on a monitor. The director often watched the video instead of the set, to see how the action worked within the frame. The greatest boon to rehearsal was the video camera, which allowed actors and directors to work with a scene and evaluate it before shooting.

With the rise of HDDV and HDTV, many 21st-century filmmakers began shooting in the 16×9 aspect ratio, where previously the flat format of choice would have been American or European widescreen (1.85:1 or 1.66:1). They used 16×9 because they expected their films to show up on HDTVs and because many of the new cameras and computers were set up to deal most easily with that format.

With the rise of digital video, many movies were shot on video and transferred to film for theatrical exhibition. Shooting film was expensive. Video was cheap and erasable, and a video camera could easily shoot for 45 straight minutes—a great aid to documentary filmmakers who were waiting for the right moment to happen—while film cameras almost never shot more than 20 minutes. For these reasons, most early-21st-century documentaries were shot on digital video.

The analog video in *The Blair Witch Project* (Daniel Myrick and Eduardo Sánchez, 1999) looked like video, which was part of the movie's aesthetic: to mix 16mm and video footage, keeping track of which character was behind each camera and why. One of the first DV movies that looked as though it truly had been shot on film was a Dogme95 production, *The King is Alive* (Kristian Levring, 2000). Agnès Varda made her first use of miniDV part of the subject of *The Gleaners and I* (2000); as in her work shot on film, the image was as sharp as the technology allowed. In 1999, four DV cameras shot four simultaneous feature-length takes for Mike Figgis's *Time Code* (2000), all of which were shown at once on the split screen, with characters moving from one screen to another as they walked, for example, from a car to an office. That movie could not have been made without video.

Together with the computer, video opened the doors to a new generation of independent filmmakers, because shooting on digital video reduced costs and often looked all right when the results were "filmed out" or put on film. That was the case with the first widely circulated Inuit movie, the legend of *Atanarjuat the Fast Runner* (or *The Fast Runner*, Zacharias Kunuk, 2001). On the other hand, Ingmar Bergman held up the theatrical release of his last movie, *Saraband* (2003), for over a year because he had shot it on DV as a TV movie and was dissatisfied with the visual quality of the attempts made to transfer it to film.

Nonlinear Editing

In the 1980s, some editors began to edit movies by working with video copies of shots instead of bits of film. By the late 1990s, those shots were not video clips but digital video files, and nearly all movies were edited on a computer, even though some continued to boast in their tail credits that they were "Edited on Film." In 1995, about half of Hollywood's movies were edited on film; after a 1996 movie edited on computer won the Oscar for Best Film Editing—Anthony Minghella's *The English Patient*, edited by Walter Murch—the number of computer-edited movies increased. In *nonlinear editing*, which was to a film splicer what the first word processor was to a typewriter, shots that had been transferred to video could be pulled in any order and assembled and rearranged easily, rather than be committed to the spliced, linear sequence of a workprint. Many of the first nonlinear editing machines worked with video files that had been transferred to laserdiscs or hard drives. In *digital nonlinear editing*, each shot was digitized—unless it was shot on digital video in the first place—and stored on a hard drive or archived until the editor was ready to work with it. The *online* (or *on-line*) editor called up the shots in the desired order to see how they played, and by punching in a few frame numbers or moving a mouse (instructing the computer which part of the shot to display) could trim a shot to the desired length. The editor could also make the shot end with a fade, move it to a different scene, and so on. Then the negative was cut to match the *Edit Decision List* (EDL), a computer printout of all the shots and cuts, where previously the negative would have been cut to match the workprint.

Copies and Originals

From the point of view of the film production and distribution companies, the worst thing about video was the ease with which movies could be pirated—and the worst thing about digital video was that it allowed copies to be made that were indistinguishable from the digital original. It was not unusual for a movie to be circulated in unauthorized videos even before it first appeared in theatres, and it was easy for even an authorized video to be illegally copied; both of these practices constituted grand theft. To discourage piracy, distributors put copyguards on videos, and some studios even put flashing dots in the image area of 35mm prints (so that a copy would reveal from which print it had been made), a practice first widely objected to by the audiences of Peter Weir's *Master and Commander: The Far Side of the World* (2003).

From the point of view of 16mm film distributors, the worst thing about video was

that many people were renting video copies rather than movies. This was deplorable in the case of film professors, whose tight budgets sometimes mandated the showing of videos instead of films in film classes. The fewer prints were rented, the more distributors had to charge for them; the less a particular print was rented, the less incentive the distributor had to strike a new copy of that movie when the old print deteriorated. Thus many films began to go out of 16mm distribution, as distributors began to go out of business. With the closing of most revival houses, the distribution of old films in 35mm suffered equal casualties. As much as professors enjoy the ability to stop a video on a frame, it is literally essential that students also be exposed to the actual movie—what might these days be called the film version of the film—uncut, uncropped, and projected at the correct speed. After that, it is valuable, convenient, and cost-effective to use a video for further study, particularly since that protects the celluloid print from excessive handling. Home video has wonderfully improved our access to copies of films, but the films themselves are becoming ever harder to locate.

Finally, from the point of view of film purists, who were delighted at all the uncut and restored prints released on video, there were two problems with the new technology. First, it threatened to replace film. Second, it could be abused to create censored or revised versions that would circulate along with—or in some markets, instead of—the originals. The first matter has not been settled, but even if the digital cinema realizes all its goals, individuals and schools will still be able to collect and project 16mm and 35mm films. Of the second problem there was evidence right away, as classic films began to be colorized for release on video and showings on TV.

Colorization

Colorization was the practice of electronically adding color to videos of black-and-white movies. (Later, the technology was used to help make movies rather than change old ones.) In most cases the black-and-white versions of colorized movies became unavailable on video.

The first films to be colorized, in 1984, were shown in 35mm as well as released on video: two Laurel and Hardy shorts and the features *Topper*

Fig. 18-1

These stills from It's A Wonderful Life *give a sense of the eloquent range of visual tones in this black-and-white film, which was not shot in color and needs no color added to it. Fig. 18-1: James Stewart and Donna Reed; Fig. 18-2: the dark world of Potterville.*

Fig. 18-2

(1937) and *Of Mice and Men* (1939). The colors were not film dyes but the hues of color TV, assigned by computer to specific areas of each frame (blue to Cary Grant's jacket, brown to his hat). Nor did the colors have any necessary relationship to the original colors of whatever was photographed: In the computer-colored version of *Suddenly* (1954), Frank Sinatra's famous blue eyes were brown. The colorizer established a palette of video colors and assigned them in a pattern that was almost always aesthetically bland.

Movies were colorized to make them better TV programs, in line with the assumptions that a color TV was wasted if it wasn't showing a program in color, and that black-and-white films *lacked color* rather than *had* their own unique scale of tones. Many colorizers argued that black-and-white films would have been made in color if the money or technology had been available. But as Eisenstein recognized, color film and black-and-white film raise extremely different aesthetic problems and opportunities. John Huston could have made *The Maltese Falcon* in color, but he chose not to. When Ted Turner (whose purchase of the MGM/UA film library also netted him the pre-1950 Warner Bros. films controlled by UA, among them *The Maltese Falcon* and *Casablanca*) had the film colorized over his objections, Huston said the result was like a roast that had been covered with teaspoon after teaspoon of sweet syrup.

Electronic Cinema

One of the most creative applications of video was the "electronic cinema" championed by Coppola and used extensively in *One from the heart* (1982). Inspired by the ease with which TV studios could create and revise complex effects electronically, Coppola decided to use the video camera, a computer, and a video-effects generator as a painter might use a sketchbook and as a writer might assemble a first draft.

On a single screen he combined a background (a sketch or photo rather than a fully constructed set), the actors, and any materials to be superimposed or matted in. The soundtrack could be tentatively assembled just as the picture was, adding music and effects to the dialogue to see how the whole thing played. Or he could string together photos and sketches of the backgrounds he intended to use, from first scene to last. A cross between a rough draft of the film and an extensively illustrated script, the video composite let Coppola see just how much of the set would actually show up on camera and have to be constructed, how the actors and dialogue worked in this visual context, how the scene looked with and without camera movements or lab effects, and which visual elements yielded the most effective composites. It also let him present to co-workers and possible backers an electronic sketch of his vision of the film.

Coppola has further ambitions for electronic cinema, including the possible satellite transmission of high-definition images for playback in theatres. Whether this leads to a cinema without film (once considered a contradiction in terms) remains to be seen, but electronic cinema—transcending its roots in TV effects and using more computers, building on its ability to try out compositions by combining visual and musical elements on the fly, experimenting with high-definition video, letting the director work on different parts of the project at once, considering satellites and the Internet as distribution portals, and fitting in naturally with the concept of non-linear editing—has become a model for the digital cinema. Just as Lucas's desire for a better editing system led to the first nonlinear editing machine (part of his push for digital work in every aspect of production), Coppola's demand for an all-embracing system that would allow him to be more creative and productive provided part of the impetus that brought the programmers, the hardware designers, the sound editors and cinematographers, the distributors and communications experts—in short, the film people, the TV people, the computer people, and the phone people—together to invent a newly integrated way of filmmaking.

For Further Viewing

FILMS

Miscellany: The Age of Video
Point of Order (1964, Emile de Antonio)
Numéro deux (1975, Jean-Luc Godard and
   Anne-Marie Miéville)
One from the heart or *One From The Heart*
   (1982, Francis Ford Coppola)
Family Viewing (1987, Atom Egoyan)

The Celebration (1998, Thomas Vinterberg)
The Idiots (1998, Lars von Trier)
The Blair Witch Project (1999, Daniel Myrick and Eduardo Sánchez)
The King is Alive (2000, Kristian Levring)
The Gleaners and I (2000, Agnès Varda)
Time Code (2000, Mike Figgis)
Atanarjuat the Fast Runner or *The Fast Runner* (2001, Zacharias Kunuk)
Russian Ark (2002, Alexander Sokurov)
Open Water (2003, Chris Kentis)

DVDs

The Blair Witch Project (1999, **Daniel Myrick** and **Eduardo Sánchez**). Artisan Entertainment. Includes a commentary by the directors; the TV documentary, *Curse of the Blair Witch*; a map and dossier in the DVD-ROM section; and deleted scenes ("newly discovered footage").
Brazil (see Chap. 17 list).
The Celebration (see Chap. 14 list).
Family Viewing (see Chap. 16 list).
The Fast Runner (2001, **Zacharias Kunuk**). Columbia TriStar. A good example of the shot-on-video look; the film transfer shown in theatres looked much the same.

The Gleaners and I (2000, **Agnès Varda**). Zeitgeist Video. Includes the sequel.
One from the heart (1982, **Francis Ford Coppola**). Fantoma / American Zoetrope. Special Edition. Includes a remastered, high-definition transfer of the film, with a commentary by Coppola; a documentary on **electronic cinema**; a making-of documentary; videotaped rehearsals; a documentary on composer **Tom Waits**; deleted and alternate scenes; a look at Zoetrope Studios; and Coppola on the digital future.
Open Water (2003, **Chris Kentis**). Lion's Gate. A good example of the low-budget, independent, mainstream feature shot on digital video and released on film.
Russian Ark (see Chap. 16 list).
Time Code (2000, **Mike Figgis**). Columbia TriStar. This excellent disc includes the complete first version as well as the release version of the movie—takes 1 and 15—with commentaries by Figgis; the ability to hear the sound from *any* quarter of the split-screen image; Figgis's video production diary; and, in the DVD-ROM section, the "shooting score."

19

Digital Cinema: 1999–

The digital cinema is a comprehensive approach to producing and distributing movies without using film. Movies are shot on digital video or generated entirely by a computer. What is altered and edited is a digital copy of the footage, and the filmmakers can work on different parts of the movie in whatever creative order suits them. The final product is a computer file that can be digitally projected or transferred to film. This is not a far-fetched vision. Already, effects work consisting partly or entirely of computer-generated imagery (CGI) and digitally modified frames has made most optical special-effects technology obsolete, so that digital effects (DFX) dominate post-production. Film prints carry both analog and digital soundtracks, but the analog track is there only in case of a breakdown. If the digital cinema is ever completely realized, film prints and analog tracks will become as rare as silent movies did, and the projection of movies stored as huge digital files will become the norm.

Although the first feature film generated entirely on a computer was Pixar's *Toy Story* (John A. Lasseter, 1995), it is that movie's sequel, *Toy Story 2* (Lasseter, with co-directors Lee Unkrich and Ash Brannon, 1999), that marks the beginning of the digital cinema, because *Toy Story 2* was the first film to be entirely generated, edited, mastered, *and exhibited* in digital form, even though it was also released in 35mm. It was also in 1999 that the long-take DV breakthrough *Time Code* (Figgis, 2000) was shot; that the digital intermediate process was perfected for *O Brother, Where Art Thou?* (the Coens, 2000); that *The Blair Witch Project* (1999) made good use of its video

sequences and exploited the Internet as a publicity vehicle; and that Lucas's *Star Wars Episode I—The Phantom Menace* (1999)—which was not a completely digital project like *Toy Story* or *Star Wars Episode II—Attack of the Clones* (Lucas, 2002)—was projected both digitally and in 35mm. For these reasons and more (discussed later), but especially because *Toy Story 2* was the first movie to fit the entire package, it appears correct to give 1999 as the year that the digital cinema arrived. This is not a simple or final decision, however. After all, *The Jazz Singer* was not a fully realized talkie, but it was the film that gave the most momentum to the transition to sound, and the picture comparable to that is the first *Toy Story*, because it made so many people aware that a feature could be made entirely on a computer. That would make 1995 the key year, as it may in fact be. If one prefers to date the period from the first *live-action* mainstream feature produced without shooting a foot of film and still exhibited both digitally and in 35mm, that would be 2002 and *Clones*—but the computer film began with animation, most CGI is a variant of animation, and the fact that the *Toy Story* movies were created entirely on a computer gives them an apt separation from the world of photography from which the analog cinema grew.

Doing without Film

Film is heavy. Tapes and discs are light. Film costs a lot to ship in those big boxes and cans, but a hard drive or a set of high-definition discs containing a digital copy of a movie is extremely

460

Fig. 19-1
Toy Story 2. *Woody shows Buzz Lightyear (left) an episode of his old TV show, "Woody's Roundup," and is entranced by his video image.*

portable, and streaming a movie to a theatre via satellite or a broadband connection is weightless and practically free. On a Hollywood set, 35mm film costs about 100 times more than digital videotape; the makers of *Clones* spent $16,000 on the 220 hours of high-def digital tape they used to shoot the picture, rather than the $1.8 million they would have spent on buying and developing 220 hours of film. A great advantage that digital video, or any video, has over film is that it is instantly available for playback, requiring no trip to the lab.

A copy of a film has more contrast and less detail than the original, and copying is an essential part of working with film—but a digital copy is the same as the original. With each *generation* of copying (the negative is the first generation, a copy of it is the second, a copy of that copy is the third, and so on), the analog image becomes more "dupey" and the optical sound-track more harsh. The same thing happens with tapes, which build up surface noise with each generation until there is more noise than signal, or at least a conspicuous loss of fidelity. More than three generations can easily separate the camera negative from the release print even if no effects work is involved. Furthermore, the act of copying film, for example when making a positive release print from an intermediate negative (IN), can damage the film slightly—or grievously if it is scratched or picks up dust while being handled or run through a printer. Showing a film in a projector almost always damages it, and a new print needs to be made after a few hundred showings—but making that print slightly wears down the IN, so that eventually a new printing negative has to be struck from the positive copy of the edited camera negative.

If a film is scratched, many frames can be ruined, but the film will still run through a projector;

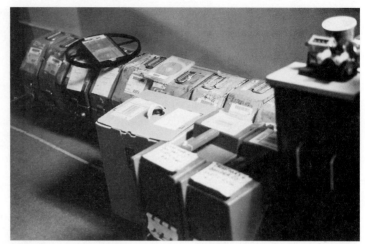

Heavy 35mm films in their sturdy shipping cans and cases. Usually there are two cans, each with two or three 2,000-foot reels, per feature. The envelope near the left contains a digital soundtrack on a CD-ROM, which is being shipped with one of the prints. Photo by Victor Jendras.

Fig. 19-2

if an optical disc is scratched or a hard drive is dropped, a new copy will have to be made, because a damaged disc or drive will not play reliably, if at all. Still, making that new digital copy costs less than making a new film print, and the former will look more like its original than the latter will. On the other hand, the film print will have a film image. In other words, a digital copy is famous for being identical to the original, but a digital original is not the same as a film original: scan lines, fewer colors, sharper edges, no grain, more depth of field, and so on. The digital print also has the disadvantage of needing to be played back on the software and equipment that created it, at least long enough to be transferred to some future medium, and both software and computers have a history of vanishing—or becoming useless or impossible to fix—once they go off the market.

Film isn't easy or cheap to copy, modify, or send, but a digital file certainly is. The convenience of digital work comes from a change of medium, which cannot help but bring a change in quality. A change in quality is not necessarily bad; the point is to be aware of the change. For example, electronic color is not worse than photochemical color, but it doesn't look the same. Analog does not have the characteristics of digital, which makes analog both inconvenient and irreplaceable. What "replaces" it will be standing in its place, but will not be its equal.

Digital has already become absolutely central to post-production work, its role in preproduction

is constantly growing, and enthusiasts see no reason that the entire moviemaking process should not become digital from first to last. Indeed, one of the primary arguments in favor of the total digital cinema is that the image is already being transferred from film to digital media for editing, effects work, and so on, then transferred back to film; all this costs money, and there is no loss of information in digital-to-digital copying, so why not skip the converting and transferring and just work the whole time with digital files? The argument is strong if taking film out of the cameras and projectors does not impoverish the image. But if digital movies are to approach film in visual quality, compression will have to be avoided or drastically improved. It is good not to lose any information when copying, but it is not so good to start out with less information. One reason *Russian Ark* (Alexander Sokurov, 2002) looked so fine when it was transferred to film is that it was shot without compression. The high-quality digital sound in IMAX theatres is uncompressed.

A major argument in favor of computerized filmmaking is that a digital image can be manipulated completely and seamlessly. This makes possible extraordinary special effects that look as real as anything else in the picture; subtle color corrections that can be applied to an entire movie; and changes in what was originally photographed, even to the extent of changing a camera angle or the lighting. It also makes possible *convincingly* combined images whose subjects were never in physical or temporal proximity, so that a living actor can touch a dead president (*Forrest Gump*, 1994). A digital image can be generated without any exposure to the world, like an animated film, or it can be modified so completely that it appears autonomous, entirely unconnected from any act of recording physical reality—presenting, in fact, an imitation of photography. Digital effects can look as if they were *photographed live*. In comparison, all earlier effects showed their seams. Painting, digital animation, digital composites, and CGI are found throughout the 21st-century "live" feature. Thus digital cinema has allowed a basic link between photography and physical reality to change: It is no longer self-evident that a live-action shot presents any live action.

This is not a question of fiction and acting; it is a matter of the presumed connection between image and reality. Even if special effects have long made it possible to show the impossible, those effects shots and other opticals were spread throughout films that were, primarily, photographed live action—and the effects weren't always as visually convincing as normally photographed scenes in the rest of the movie. (Of course, a masterpiece like the 1933 *King Kong* could make any images work together.) Now that the effects are a seamless part of the image and everything appears equally real, in some movies the whole frame has begun to resemble an effect and to be accepted, paradoxically, as *un*real or, at best, not necessarily real. Watching Fred Astaire dance or Jackie Chan slide down a building, one applauds what the actor did in the presence of the camera; when Spider-Man swings through the city (*Spider-Man 2*, Sam Raimi, 2004), one applauds the effects. For the willing suspension of disbelief to take hold, one has to believe the effects shots and the rest of the movie's world are equally real—to believe, for example, that in *Spider-Man* (Raimi, 2002) and its sequel both the actor and the graphic are the character—but many people are pulled out of that suspension when they notice how well an effect has been achieved, how cool and accomplished it is. The widely known fact that any image in a contemporary movie may have been digitally modified has led to a change in the ways some people respond to movies: as anything-goes, purely

artificial structures. This is a step in the direction of painting and music and away from photography—a medium that implies the subject was present to be photographed, and thus that what one is watching somehow did happen or is happening, no matter how outrageous or made up the action is.

One problem with film is that it keeps running out. Using DV, as in *Time Code*, or a hard drive, as in *Russian Ark*, or more recent technology, a digital moviemaker can shoot a feature in a single take, in real time, as Hitchcock could not. In this sense, the digital cinema is a step toward the long take of stage drama—or of the surveillance camera—opening up new possibilities in filmmaking. Working in real time, after all, enhances the possibilities of realism, and reality itself is comparable to an infinite long take, even if many aspects of consciousness and our lived experience correspond to the instantaneous changes of editing.

The digital cinema was made practical by advances in computer technology. Just as computer monitors made TV viewers want higher video resolution, creating the push to DV and HDTV, the computer revolution made workers in many fields want to share in the speed and convenience of the digital world, to which many of them were introduced by the Internet. When personal computers offered more memory, faster microprocessors, and greater storage capacity, and when correspondents began to use e-mail more than the postal service and researchers to use the Web more than the library—all of which happened in the mid-1990s—consumers and programmers found more uses for computers. By the end of the 20th century, people were able to load, play at full speed, alter, and save huge digital video files on home and office computers, instead of watching tiny computer videos and their boxy pixels jerk along. They could store their work on recordable DVDs and portable hard drives. They could transfer their old home movies to video, make new DV movies, and digitally edit both picture and sound. Later, they could do all that in HD. Filmmakers found that they could send each other digital files over the Internet and work on them together, modifying them with no loss of information; they found that workers spread across the globe could watch and evaluate a clip together in real time; they became interested in the way a project could evolve in digital space; and they saw the advantages of digital editing. They realized that digital was clearly the technology of the future and, in fact, the present, and they took up Coppola's dream of an electronic cinema—now seen entirely in the digital terms advanced most prominently by Lucas—hoping someday to be able to sit down at a computer and compose a whole movie.

But there is still more to the digital cinema than integrating production and distribution with an electronic network, more even than digitizing images so they can be manipulated on a computer, or getting rid of film. Digital cinema is a new paradigm, a *nonlinear* system that allows the movie to be produced in practically any order and that allows all the filmmakers to work on the digital files—the shots, the sound rolls, the composites, the music—at the same time. This model has already begun to replace the linear system of moviemaking, in which—to take just one representative example—the film has to be shot and then edited one reel at a time before the sound-effects editor can start to build a sound reel. This nonlinearity is possible only if the filmmakers use computers.

Beginnings

The first computer film artist was John Whitney. He started by designing and using mechanical drawing machines that created abstract patterns on cels that could then be conventionally photographed with an animation camera. Saul Bass shot the graphics for the opening credits of *Vertigo* on Whitney's "animation machine" in 1957, and Whitney shot *Catalog* on it in 1961; he considered *Catalog* a "sample reel" of computer-graphic effects, not a film. Whitney then invented coordinated mechanical systems that would draw on film with moving light and then advance to the next frame, eliminating the need to photograph the drawings; these abstract images were then systematically varied and combined by an analog computer according to principles Whitney was investigating that opened up a visual harmony, a mathematics and music of form moving in time. The computer varied and processed the images, then displayed them one frame at a time on a cathode-ray tube. A 35mm camera photographed the displayed images, which were in black and white; then Whitney used filters and an optical printer to color and combine the images onto a conventionally reproducible color negative. His experiments, funded by IBM from 1966 until his death in 1995 and executed on their huge digital mainframe computers, opened the door to the slit-scan techniques used in *2001* and to his own abstract shorts and demonstration films, including *Permutations* (1968), *Experiments in Motion Graphics* (1968), *Matrix* (1971), and *Arabesque* (1975), as well as his brother James's *Lapis* (1966).

Once Douglas Engelbart had invented the computer mouse and hypertext in 1968, computers were on the verge of new ways to navigate the world of data and instructions. The invention of the *graphical user interface* (GUI), which replaced typing a command with clicking on a picture linked to a command, is important to mention here because it made it possible for computers to display and manipulate visual files. The GUI was developed at Xerox's Palo Alto Research Center (Xerox PARC) and demonstrated in 1974 on the Xerox Alto, a computer that was not put on the market. The GUI made its definitive public appearance in 1984 as part of Apple Computer's Macintosh. By the mid-1990s, nearly every computer had a graphical interface. Beyond any issue of convenience—vital because it allowed untrained people to use computers—the GUI made visual data as important as text to the next generation of filmmakers and filmgoers, who learned to use computers in childhood.

In the 1990s, people realized they had entered a digital age. Virtually every aspect of public and private life had been touched by computers. All one's preferences were in a database somewhere, and anything from a cellular phone to a fuel injector was being run by a chip. Everyone—not just everyone on a project—was connected to everybody else and to vast resources of information. Not all of that information was true or complete, but it was certainly easy to find. E-mail had become a primary means of communication. Beginning in the mid-1980s, the film industry had shifted many operations to networked desktop computers, as did so many companies between then and the turn of the century. Every "business" aspect of the film business was computerized, from the executive's calendar to the accountant's spreadsheet. These and other changes, like the storyboard's being animated, were not evident on the screen. If audiences noticed that computers had come to filmmaking, it was thanks to decades of increasingly sophisticated special effects.

The first feature film to use a motion-control camera was *Star Wars* (1977). As its name suggests, the motion of the camera was controlled by a computer so that the camera could move exactly the same way—usually in relation to models and miniature sets—over and over again. With each *pass* (of film through the camera; the same term is used when film runs through a printer) the same footage was re-exposed, but some element or aspect of the visual field changed. In a *Star Wars* battle, for instance, each ship was shot separately, and so was the field of stars. If the camera appeared to swoop around an asteroid and after a ship, it had to move precisely the same way when the model ship was being shot as when the model asteroid was being shot—and in the other passes when the star background was being shot, or the ship was not illuminated but silhouetted against a bluescreen (also "blue screen"), or a foreground object exploded. This precise repetition, ensured by the computer, allowed perfect composite images to be created in the camera; it also made it much easier to create the elements for such conventional composites as traveling mattes, which were put together on an optical printer. By 2000, the technology was obsolete.

The motion-control camera was used most effectively in Cronenberg's *Dead Ringers* (1988), where it followed Jeremy Irons as he played one brother, then his twin, in the same frame, while panning between them or tracking with them through an apartment.

The 20-second "Genesis" sequence in Nicholas Meyer's *Star Trek II: The Wrath of Khan* (1982), in which a lifeless planet undergoes a sweeping, fiery transformation into a lush, green, brand-new world, was CGI from start to finish, the first of its kind. Created entirely within the computer, this historically crucial sequence pointed the way to the purely digital cinema. It was the work of a team headed by Ed Catmull at the computer-graphics division of Lucasfilm. In 1986, Catmull approached Steve Jobs with an idea for generating whole movies on computers. Jobs bought the CG division from Lucas in 1986; then he and Catmull co-founded Pixar Animation Studios. The most important animation company since Disney, Pixar released its first features through Disney.

Another founding member of Pixar, John A. Lasseter, directed the company's first film, a short called *Luxo Jr.* (1986), which introduced their hopping lamp and was nominated for an Oscar. As previously mentioned, Lasseter directed *Toy Story* in 1995, the first feature

Shooting Star Trek—The Motion Picture *with a motion-control camera.*

Fig. 19-3

generated entirely on computers, and *Toy Story 2* in 1999, the first digitally generated and mastered film to be digitally projected. These "3-D animations" looked like a cross between drawings and photographed puppets or models; their rich shadows and textures were the result of Pixar's ever-more-sophisticated software. The next Pixar features—*a bug's life* (Lasseter and Andrew Stanton, 1998), *Monsters, Inc.* (Peter Docter, 2001), *Finding Nemo* (Stanton, 2003), and *The Incredibles* (Brad Bird, 2004)—were so intricately planned that some frames took hours for even a computer to generate. One frame from *Finding Nemo* that showed complex underwater light on a coral reef took a 2,000-processor network 10 hours on Pixar's "RenderMan" software. Using a competing process, DreamWorks entered the field of digital animation with *Antz* (Eric Darnell and Tim Johnson, 1998) and had great success with *Shrek* (Andrew Adamson and Vicky Jenson, 2001).

The first computerized editing machine was Lucas's EditDroid, developed between 1984 and 1986; it worked with shots that had been transferred to laserdisc and was a nonlinear editor. The first feature cut on it was *The Patriot* (Frank Harris, 1986) in 1985; another was *The Doors*

(Oliver Stone, 1991), which was also one of the first films with a digital soundtrack (CDS, discussed below). The Avid Film Composer, which became the industry standard for editing film and sound as well as for creating effects formerly made only on an optical printer, was invented in the early 1990s. Film that had been transferred to video was fed into the Avid, which was a dedicated Macintosh computer (later, a program that could run on other computers) with two monitors and an array of hard drives. A digital nonlinear editor, the Avid digitized the video and kept the shots—that is, the picture and sound files—directly accessible in any order and ready to be modified. While it was mostly used for editing films, the Avid naturally could also edit projects that originated on analog or digital video. In the early 2000s, Avid introduced the Nitris, an editor that digitized images at a 10-bit depth, creating high-quality HD video files with resolutions as high as 2K and 4K. *The English Patient* (1996) was not the first movie whose picture and sound were edited on Avid, but it was the first to win an Oscar for film editing—and another, equally influential, for sound editing. By the end of the century, most films were edited on Avid or one of its rivals.

Fig. 19-4
Finding Nemo. *Dory (left), Marlin, and a swirl of Moonfish.*

The digital soundtrack was introduced by IMAX in 1988. The first mainstream digital soundtrack was developed by CDS (Cinema Digital Sound) and premiered on 70mm prints of *Dick Tracy* (Warren Beatty, 1990). The CDS track was not widely adopted because the industry was waiting for Dolby Labs to come up with a digital track that had an analog safety net.

Dolby Laboratories Inc., founded in 1965 by engineer Ray Dolby, first became known for its system of reducing system noise when re-recording tape: *Dolby Noise Reduction* (NR) selectively compressed and expanded the signal to suppress the frequencies where tape hiss and surface noise were recorded, increasing the signal-to-noise ratio and making possible several generations of clean copying and a better audio

A tri-format 35mm anamorphic print of **Lake Placid** *(Steve Miner, 1999) in projection position, shown here at twice its actual size. The squeezed image will be widened and inverted by the projection lens. Note the three digital soundtracks and the analog track.*

Fig. 19-5

master. Dolby decoders soon became part of most home stereo systems—at first because recording and playing back with Dolby NR increased the fidelity of audiocassettes, whose thin tape was only ⅛-inch wide and ran four times slower than the 7½ inches per second (ips) at which reel-to-reel tape begins to record music well; cassettes needed all the help they could get.

Dolby Labs introduced the revolutionary *Stereo Variable Area* (SVA) soundtrack in 1975, which allowed optical 35mm prints to carry four channels of stereo surround sound on two tracks. *Star Wars* used Dolby NR throughout production, from the first recording to the final mix, and it had a Dolby SVA soundtrack; from then on, Dolby was the recognized leader in film sound.

In 1986, Dolby improved the four-channel analog track with "spectral recording," increasing its ability to record and play back very soft and very loud sounds accurately, and *Dolby SR* became the standard optical surround soundtrack. The six-channel *Dolby Digital* optical track was invented in 1991 and first used on Tim

Burton's *Batman Returns* (1992); at that time it was called Dolby SR•D; prints also carried a Dolby SR soundtrack in case the digital system broke down or the theatre had conventional projection.

Soon there were two more digital systems, six-channel *Digital Theater Systems* (DTS) and eight-channel *Sony Dynamic Digital Sound* (SDDS). Most film prints now carry at least one of the three leading digital soundtracks and one analog track. A *tri-format print*, common at the turn of the century and shown in Fig. 19-5, was compatible with Dolby Digital, DTS, and SDDS. Dolby Digital and SDDS soundtracks were on the print. The sound in DTS was on a CD-ROM, and what was on the print was a synchronizing code. DTS was *double system* sound, with two machines linked as the old Warner Bros. projector and record player were, but by more reliable means. Magnetic striping, used from the 1950s to the 1990s, especially on 70mm prints, was costly, and there was the remote risk of accidentally erasing part of the track. Like any optical track,

A detail of part of the soundtrack area of one frame from the same print. The distance from the left side of the film to the image area is 5/16 of an inch. Starting near the outer edge of the film and looking from left to right: The field of dots running vertically to the left of the sprocket holes is half of the SDDS track, which is light purple. The square patterns between the sprocket holes are the Dolby Digital track, which is in black and white; there is a tiny Dolby logo, resembling two Ds facing away from each other, in the center of each block. The two wavy lines—white against a black background—are the stereo analog track, Dolby SR. The line of blips is the DTS control code, also white against black. Then the image area begins. In Fig. 19-5, the rest of the frame is visible: There is no soundtrack between the right sprocket holes, and the rest of the SDDS track runs along the right edge.

Fig. 19-6

a digital soundtrack was far less expensive than a mag track and did not have to be recorded in real time; it was also of better quality than any earlier optical format, and it could be printed wherever it would fit. Dolby Digital was printed between the sprocket holes on one side of the print. The analog track ran alongside the DTS track, which was a code that controlled the CD, and both of them fit between the sprocket holes and the image area (the "frame" itself). SDDS was printed as a stream of microscopic dots on the left and right sides of the film, between the outside edges and the rows of sprocket holes. The first DTS film was Spielberg's *Jurassic Park* in 1993. SDDS premiered with John McTiernan's *Last Action Hero*, also in 1993.

From the late 1980s through the 1990s, digital special effects rapidly became more common.

Still, audiences were surprised to find that hundreds of the people shown in long shot in *Titanic* (James Cameron, 1997) were made in a computer. The DFX in *Titanic* were state of the art but not unique; nevertheless, they were the ones that made many viewers recognize that the new effects in movies were specifically digital. Others realized that fact when Lucas publicized the digital aspects of his revision of the *Star Wars* trilogy in the same year, 1997, but it had been clear as early as 1991, when Cameron's *Terminator 2: Judgment Day* foregrounded its extreme digital effects, or in the aptly named "Genesis" of 1982. The rise of CGI stretched from *Star Trek II* to *Toy Story 2*—and beyond to such milestones as *The Lord of the Rings: The Return of the King* (Peter Jackson, 2003), whose film footage was mixed with CGI and digitally modified in unprecedented

Fig. 19-7
The four simultaneous long takes of Time Code *as they appeared on the split screen.*

ways—or the previous year's *The Lord of the Rings: The Two Towers*, whose Gollum was the most expressive and technically advanced of digital characters, created by a computer and a digitally replaced live actor, Andy Serkis.

Starting in the late 1990s, many films were shot on DV and transferred to film. *Time Code*, for example, was shot on DV, late in 1999, because the longest that Figgis could shoot film continuously was just over 20 minutes, and he wanted to shoot a feature in one take. The four takes in *Time Code* lasted between 85 and 94½ minutes. The takes started and ended at different times, but the cameras were perfectly synchronized with each other (by a time code, or timecode) so that 85 minutes of the film showed four simultaneous views of a sequence of events as it unfolded in real time, in locations that were adjacent to or far from each other but that always were reached in a continuous manner, by following a driving or walking character. The four soundtracks varied in volume so that one scene could be concentrated on at a time.

Late in 2001, Alexander Sokurov shot *Russian Ark* in one 90-minute take in St. Petersburg's Hermitage Museum (the other 6 minutes of the movie are credits). Sokurov wanted a better image than DV could provide, and HD tape was limited to 52 minutes. Shooting in uncompressed HD at feature length required that the camera feed its data not to tape but to a hard drive, which was carried along by the camera crew; they were limited to four tries before they ran out of the experimental, unerasable drives, and they got it on the fourth take. The perfectly choreographed *plan-séquence* that constitutes the movie, a shot as continuous as one's presence in the world and in some dreams, shows what an unnamed character (whose thoughts and speech were recorded by Sokurov) is given to see—a bit like Dante, but there is a strong sense that he is dreaming, along with a hint that he may be seeing all this after death. The modern-day narrator is never on camera because the entire movie is a POV shot (subjective camera) showing what he sees; it is also a mindscreen because what he is looking at is the world of his own dream or vision and because he is telling about it. We look through the narrator's eyes as he walks, often accompanied by a diplomat sometimes called the Stranger (the Marquis de Custine, who visited Russia in 1839), through a museum whose rooms are filled with people who once danced or gathered there or in rooms like these—Russian history come alive, one artistic period at a time. History,

Fig. 19-8
Russian Ark. *The Stranger, Custine (Sergei Dreiden), admires the palatial museum of art and time.*

art, society, and the observer are linked in an un-broken flow of perception, moving as the narrator does from one time to another without any cutting. They are also linked by the museum, an ark loaded with what needs to be saved and that seems at the end to be moving through a mist. The lighting (candles and daylight, since there was no time to set up, hide, and break down lights) was as carefully planned as the movement within the building of hundreds of actors. When the image and sound had been slightly polished, *Russian Ark* was transferred to film; it looked much better than the 35mm version of *Clones*, also exhibited in 2002.

In 1998, computer technology was put to a new use, previously explored only in commercials: the digitizing of an entire film after it had been edited. The makers of *Pleasantville* (Gary Ross, 1998) transferred all of their color-film footage to video, selectively removed the color from it, and then transferred the results to film: a black-and-white image that sprouts color here and there as the characters, who live in the world of an old TV show, begin to discover the more passionate and unpredictable aspects of life. In 1999, Lucas digitized all of *The Phantom Menace* in order to mix live-action and CG footage seamlessly. But it was also in 1999 that the Coens' *O Brother, Where Art Thou?* (2000) was completely digitized to make it look more realistic.

O Brother was shot in the lush South but was supposed to have been set in the Dust Bowl, which meant that many greens would have to be changed to browns. These changes, among others, were made in 1999 on a *digital intermediate* (DI). The fact that the changes were made without distorting the skin tones of the actors was the most impressive aspect of the *electronic intermediate* process, as it was also called, and because the changes were made not in the service of effects but as a way of fixing and polishing a normal movie, the DI caught on and was used on most studio pictures after 2000.

In this process, the image went from the edited camera negative to a digital intermediate (which could be adjusted digitally for color, brightness, and effects), then back to negative film (an intermediate negative, or IN, that could be used to make prints) with no discernible loss of image quality.

Many of the visual penalties for copying film in post-production were removed by the DI, so

that a printing negative—once separated from the original by several generations—had practically the same quality as the camera negative. The result of the DI process was a new 35mm negative with perfectly integrated live action and effects as well as corrected exposure, as though the final picture had been captured by the original camera. This was the most important change in post-production since digital nonlinear editing, and like digital editing, it was nondestructive. No change in the DI affected the negative, any more than calling for a trial cut on the Avid required a splicer and glue.

If 1999 saw the release of *Blair Witch*, the shooting of *Time Code*, the DI work on *O Brother*, and the *dual release* (that is, in both 35mm and digital prints) of the first feature made and projected without film, *Toy Story 2*, it also saw the dual release of *The Phantom Menace*, the first live-action feature to be digitally projected—and digital projection itself. In the history of digital cinema it was, as previously argued, the definitive year—its closest competitor 1995, when the computer world picked up speed, the use of e-mail and the Web markedly increased, *The English Patient* was edited, and *Toy Story* came out.

Two competing digital projectors were invented in 1999 by Texas Instruments (Digital Light Processing—DLP—a *micromirror* projector) and by Hughes–JVC (a liquid-crystal display, or LCD projector). The DLP projector reflected light onto the screen with incredibly tiny mirrors on three chips (optical semiconductors called *digital micromirror devices*, with each DMD chip dedicated to R, G, or B). DLP started with a pure white source and used a prism to direct the light to the three DMDs, which reflected R, G, and B light—one mirror per color per pixel—back into a prism that mixed the red image, the green image, and the blue image into a single frame and directed it toward the screen. The one million mirrors on each chip tilted to reflect or block the light thousands of times per second, creating a deeper blue, for example, by flashing the blue mirrors for the pixels with that color more often per frame; sky blue, by flashing them less often. R, G, and B filters, comparable to the dyes that color the white light as it passes through the film in a conventional projector, let the micromirror projector largely avoid the problem of electronic color. LCD projectors shone white light through an electronic LCD panel. By the time that *Clones*, shot entirely on 2K HDDV, was digitally projected in 2002—after Lucas had spent a long time on the DI, tweaking the actors' performances by manipulating their faces and reconstructing frames—the highest-resolution projectors were also 2K. Micromirror projection was used for *Phantom Menace* and *Clones*, as well as *Toy Story 2* and *Finding Nemo*.

In 2003, the studio group charged with adopting standards for digital projection (Digital Cinema Initiatives, or the DCI) endorsed 2K but called for systems that could be upgraded when higher-resolution technology was perfected. A year later, Sony privately demonstrated a 4K projector with *full-bandwidth*, or 4:4:4, RGB data.

After Sony introduced the 24p in 1997 as the HDW-F900, several companies modified it. *Clones* used a Sony camera whose body had been adapted by Panavision, which had worked with Sony on the 24p from the start.

In 2004, Panavision released its own 24p, a second generation of the camera that could use the same lenses as 35mm movie cameras (those for the first 24p had been smaller) and match film's depth of field. It captured far more information on its larger frame. It could run at 24 fps or any speed from 1 to 50 fps. It was completely portable, requiring no cable to connect it to the dockable video recorder, and it was the right size and weight to be hand-held, used in a Steadicam, or set on a tripod. It shot 12.6 Mp frames at 4K—equivalent to the resolution of 35mm film. It recorded full-bandwidth color. Its format was designed to work with the DI process, creating a digital negative perfect for a 4K electronic intermediate. In an unintended but wonderful historical irony, Panavision called its "Super 35 Digital Cinematography Camera System" the Genesis. That invention brought digital camerawork into its maturity.

Production and Distribution

Even in a digitized industry, making a movie begins when someone gets an idea. After that, the usual step is writing a script, but in the digital cinema one might also begin with a computer sketch, a set of picture and sound files that expands and develops. As a digital file, whether it is written with an ordinary word processor or with special software, a script can be (but rarely is, yet) illustrated with digital pictures, sounds, and clips that clarify how the writer envisions the movie.

The first stage of production is called development, and the usual key collaborators are the producer and the writer. When the story and approach have been agreed upon, the producer hires the writer to do a full-length script—or buys the script if the writer approached the producer with a finished one. Finding a producer is an important part of development: getting the money. Lawyers get out their digital templates and prepare contracts. When a "First Final Screenplay" (called that because someone will always demand changes) has been judged satisfactory, the producer keeps the writer around for revisions and hires a director, usually trying to interest her or him by showing the script. Sometimes, of course, a director can bring his or her own idea or script to a producer.

Working with DV is so inexpensive, however, that an independent filmmaker can write, direct, shoot, edit, and mix a digital video before having to find a company to pay for the transfer to film, make the prints, and distribute them. The filmmaker might even be able to produce the movie (pay for it) if the *mise-en-scène* isn't lavish and the actors either are unknowns or agree to be paid after the movie has been released. Independent filmmakers used to have this kind of freedom when working with 16mm, but 16mm expenses have soared far above those of DV. At present, many independents are making features on high-def or standard DV and breaking into the business with pictures that are of sufficiently high visual quality to be shown in 35mm theatres but that cost as little as $500 or as much as $2 million to produce, while the average Hollywood feature costs over $60 million.

A digital filmmaker can take a project from the first idea to the final *digital video master* (which can be converted to analog and scanned onto film or used to make digital prints), playing all the key creative roles or working with others, without waiting years for a conventional producer to get behind a $50 million idea. Using the digital master, the filmmaker can also bypass a film release altogether and output his or her work in PAL, NTSC, SECAM, or HDTV and sell it to TV worldwide; or make a DVD and enter that market; or post it on the Internet for paid or free downloading. But in whatever order the nonlinear artist approaches filmmaking, the tasks conventionally done in development, and then in pre-production, production, and post-production (all four of which constitute the production phase, which ends with the approval of a sync-sound print), and finally in distribution do all have to be done eventually.

One of the biggest changes the computerization of the industry has brought to development is screenwriting software, both because it has affected how movies are written and because it presents the script in a format that can be read and analyzed by other programs. These other programs can "break down" the script to determine the production requirements for each scene, decide which scenes can be shot with the same actors and sets, schedule each day's shooting, and construct a budget—not a budget inflated by actors' and directors' salaries but a practical estimate of what it will cost to shoot the movie. Most of this happens in pre-production and production, well after the script has been approved, but it is also useful in development, when a tentative budget must be determined. If it has been well-researched, a screenwriting program can produce a document in the rigorous and useful format of a professional script.

Often those who read scripts for producers have learned film structure not from watching new and old movies but from reading screenwriting books. The books and seminars have taught them to look for a particular kind of story: "the hero's journey," for instance. The three-act structure has become evident in a great many scripts written since the 1980s, simplifying the narrative film in unfortunate ways. In reality, some films have one act, and some have more than three. Godard's remark that a movie should have a beginning, middle, and end, but not necessarily in that order, does not compute. Hollywood and most mainstream producers around the world have insisted on linear plots for the last three decades, burying the influence of the New Wave along with the Hollywood Renaissance and concentrating on heroes who discover their true natures and overcome the many obstacles placed in their paths by a writer, a committee of writers, or a program with an attitude.

The major stars may be signed during development, which is when agents do most of their work, but the majority of casting is done in pre-production, along with many other tasks. Casting agencies use computers to match actors with roles, location scouts use them to find places to shoot, and agents use them to keep track of their clients' accomplishments. It should be noted that casting can be changed even after production: Eddie Murphy played many roles in *The Nutty Professor* (Tom Shadyac, 1996) thanks to the digital modification of his image into different characters. Production software breaks down the script into blocks to be shot on certain days. Accounting software keeps track of expenses. Programmers examine the script and drawings to design computer games based on the film.

Drawings can be scanned into a computer or generated on one, then lined up in the order of the script, creating a story outline that resembles a comic strip and is called a *storyboard*. The physical drawings used to be pinned on walls or big boards. Making a storyboard has been a basic practice ever since Eisenstein sketched his shots. Using arrows and several drawings per shot, a storyboard can indicate every camera, prop, and character movement. In a computer, the comic strip can turn into a cartoon or *animatic* (a computer-animated storyboard, usually with 3-D models), with the intermediate actions between the drawings filled in. The sound—or trial sounds—can be synchronized with the animatic. The characters, props, and sets can be moved in relation to each other—a creative, experimental process that can help one discover the best action, camera angle, lighting, blocking, or choreography; determine whether certain props are needed or which costume designs look best; and make it possible to begin designing sets, models, miniatures, and effects to scale. Only what will be photographed needs to be built, occupied, driven, hung, or worn; the rest still needs to be designed but can be added electronically in post-production. A growing set of files lets a digital rough draft of the film develop as each of its elements is tried out or completed. A pre-production animatic can serve as the visual spine of a movie, much as a screenplay is its dramatic spine.

The majority of design work is still done in pre-production, most of it with the aid of computer graphics. Research is carried out during development and pre-production: to get period details correct, for example, or to make sure no real person with a character's name lives in the city where the story is set. Much design and background research is done in libraries and special collections, but the Internet is a great resource too, if the source is reliable. (See the note on Web sites at the end of this chapter.)

In the digital cinema, production is the period in which live action is photographed. In conventional terms, it is "principal photography," the period when the principal performers and major scenes are shot. A high-def digital camera, now called a *camera system*, or a 35mm film camera is used on the set. The camera system produces an electronic image, digitizes it, and records the digital negative. 35mm film is run through a telecine or another device that digitizes the image, as previously explained. The film can also be transferred to analog video and digitized in an editor.

The video tap built into the camera, which sends a picture that is watched while the scene is being shot, is recorded—in sync with the digital sound that is recorded on the set, such as dialogue. A reel-to-reel analog tape recorder, in sync with the camera, records sound as it always has—so there will be a better recording to digitize in a sound studio and because the film's analog track may require it—but the digital recording is useful as a guide to sync and even as a primary track. The shots, kept in sync with their sounds, are digitally logged using the edge numbers on the negative, which are put there by the manufacturer and are unique, or a time code on the digital video. The script supervisor, who keeps track of the details of each take as it is shot, now works on a laptop, and her or his notes are included in a database linked to the shots. Mechanical special effects, such as explosions and car crashes, and special-effects makeup, such as zombie wounds, are shot on the set. However, it is less dangerous and sometimes gives acceptable results to create the explosions or stunts on a computer and mix them with live-action footage during post-production. Makeup, too, is a production art, as is acting. It is during production that the director gets the performances he or she wants from the actors and consults with the cinematographer about lighting and composition. (The director's official job is simply to make the best use of the resources the producer has provided.) In post, the director should work with the film editor, the composer, the sound supervisor, and the digital-effects companies.

Digitizing a feature intended to be released on film or HDDV is usually done at the highest possible resolution—from 2K with 8-bit color to 4K with 10- or 12-bit color—with minimal compression, to create the materials for a good DI, master, or print. 1K is fine for conventional TV, for standard DV, and for *rushes* or *dailies* (digital videos of each day's shooting, which unlike the film prints formerly used are ready to be shown without any lab work; rushes got their name from having to be rushed through the lab). Unless one is using a digital camera system, production footage has to be digitized before editing. When the editing, effects, and DI are finished, and the sound has been mixed and the soundtracks made, the movie can be released on video or transferred to film, either by a laser in a film recorder or by a movie camera facing a high-resolution monitor. Avoiding those high film-to-digital-to-film transfer costs is an important reason the technologies of digital shooting and projection have been improved.

Even if effects work can be done at 2K, many effects are created at full resolution on a digitized frame to achieve top quality. As previously mentioned, a standard Academy 35mm frame, uncompressed, consumes 56 MB. (The format using the smallest amount of the frame takes up 44 MB.) This does not pose a problem in an effects house, partly because most effects shots are short and are worked on frame by frame, but it's too much for a desktop computer to display in real time and too big to edit. If a 1.33:1 color movie is digitized at theatrical resolution, it runs at 1.34 GB per second, uncompressed. No one is yet working on a feature on an 8,000-GB drive. The most advanced DVD yet envisioned has a theoretical limit of 50 GB, or about 37 seconds of uncompressed footage. A conventional dual-layer DVD could hold almost 7 seconds per side; 100 minutes would take 460 two-sided discs, with half of one disc left for extras. Thus a DVD release is heavily compressed, as discussed earlier, and DVDs meant to be loaded onto the drive of a digital projector are also compressed, sometimes to 10 or 15 discs per feature.

In post-production, the film is edited, the effects are generated, the DI is adjusted, the music is composed, and the sound effects are recorded. Then the *D–M–E* (dialogue, music, and effects) soundtrack is mixed on computerized equipment while the mixer watches the edited print, which consists of the image and dialogue; all these tracks are digitally encoded, logged, and if necessary, fixed. Sound mixing can be done in analog or digital, but the final result is at least one digital soundtrack, along with an analog track that has fewer channels and may have been converted from the digital sound master. The final stage of post-production is making a series of trial prints until a final version—which must receive the approval of the producer—is agreed on. Making multiple prints is part of distribution.

Dialogue is often replaced in post-production, with the actors delivering their lines right into a mike and trying to sync with their performances on screen; as dubbing, it goes back to the first sound films. The difference now is that the recordings may be sped up or slowed down by a computer to achieve sync or alter the delivery of a line. The music may be written earlier in a non-linear production, so that a film could be edited to match the music instead of the current practice, in which the composer watches the edited film and writes music for particular scenes and sequences.

It is the essence of digital special effects that any image from anywhere can be seamlessly added to the original photograph or computer graphic, just as any area of the original can be electronically removed; there are no bluescreen lines leaking out at the seams. A frame or shape can be constructed in the computer and then have a photographed image superimposed on or "stuck" to it—which is how, in Charles Russell's *The Mask* (1994), a character is smashed flat as a pancake by a fall, then peels himself off the sidewalk and pumps himself back to his original volume, because the image of the actor (Jim Carrey) has been deformed to the shape of the computer-modeled "pancake" and rides it through all its changes; this is also one way that the evil Terminator, the T-1000 (Robert Patrick), in *Terminator 2* bears the guise of a policeman–robot over its computer-modeled body (supposedly of liquid metal, so that it can be sliced and heal, or change into any shape). Another technique perfected in *Terminator 2*, called *morphing* (from "metamorphosis"), allows one image to change into another—not with a dissolve, for example from the T-1000 as a cop to the T-1000 as a housewife, but with a series of intermediate

The T-1000 (Robert Patrick) prepares to pull a pole out of its side—sideways—in **Terminator 2: Judgment Day.**

Fig. 19-9

steps created by the computer, each one a complete and focused image, that begin 100 percent cop/0 percent housewife, then go to 99 percent cop/1 percent housewife, through 50/50 (which in a dissolve would be the most unreadable, double-exposed part of the transition, whereas in morphing this stage is clear and credible) all the way to 100 percent housewife. Computers allowed the T-1000's body to close its gaping mercury wounds, to walk through the steel bars of a door in a hospital corridor, and to shine with the right metallic quality.

If Industrial Light & Magic (ILM) could send a herd of dinosaurs romping over a huge landscape and then through and around a group of running actors (not merely behind or in front of them, as with rear projection, but interacting with them in their space), thus giving *Jurassic Park* the credibility that makes it work so well as a fantasy, they could also use computers to allow cartoons and actors to interact in *Who Framed Roger Rabbit* and to allow Jim Carrey to behave like a cartoon in *The Mask*, in each case making the incredible vivid and the suspension of disbelief easier. There are many points in *The Mask* when Carrey behaves like a character in a Tex Avery cartoon—usually Wolfie. To create the shot (Fig. 19-11) in which his eyes bug out of his head and he wags his suddenly long tongue, a regular production shot was made of Carrey, in his green mask make-up, walking down a hallway with a mallet, then opening his mouth and imitating the cartoonish action. Then a CG model of the bugged-out face—a *wire frame* of polygons—was superimposed on the plate of Carrey (the original photographed image). The wire frame changed with every frame of the shot and could be played with until it assumed the desired shape and comic movement. Then a CG image of the mask, eyes, and tongue was *rendered* (created as a picture from all the numerical data, based on the lighting of the scene, the desired colors, and the digital properties of the model), and that animation was wrapped around—or became a high-resolution version of—the wire frame. Where untransformed parts of Carrey could be seen around the animated computer imagery, they were erased (like his real tongue) or allowed to remain (like his hands, holding the mallet). Then the computer put the graphic through its changes, frame after frame, until the electronic-effects shot was complete.

Finally, that shot was transferred to film, ready to be cut into the rest of the movie and looking as if it had been photographed along with everything else.

The most common optical effect is the composite (a *digital composite* is one created on a computer instead of an optical printer), which combines into one frame elements that were photographed or generated at different times—like the actors, the alien landscape, and the 3-D animated giant bugs in Verhoeven's *Starship Troopers* (1997) or the many elements combined in the digital composites shown here from *Mighty Joe Young* (1998, directed by Ron Underwood; a remake of Ernest B. Schoedsack's 1949 original) and from *The Phantom Menace*. In the shot from *Mighty Joe Young*, the final image of the huge gorilla (Joe) was CGI, digitally inserted frame by frame into a live-action scene. The CG Joe replicated and replaced a man who played Joe through most of the film and who had been photographed in front of a bluescreen in an animatronic gorilla suit (*animatronics* use electronics, cables, and valves to control movement, say on a gorilla's facial apparatus, remotely), crumpling a 40%-scale model car on a 40%-scale set of Hollywood Boulevard—so he'd look over 13 feet tall. A real car had been imploded on a full-sized set, watched by full-sized actors, and that became the film plate into which the CG Joe was placed, along with his CG shadow and parts of the small-scale set. In the course of making this picture, Kodak discovered flaws in their finest-grain film, artifacts that could be found only with a computer, and they created a new filmstock that would improve all future bluescreen and greenscreen work. (A greenscreen is used if a character is wearing blue, which would create a hole in the character, and for most video composites.) The pod race in *The Phantom Menace* (Fig. 19-14) was built from an animatic storyboard, and every element in this composite is CGI; there was no film original. In the climactic battle scene (Fig. 19-15) there were no extras, and the cost of outfitting an army was eliminated by creating multiple groups of warriors that were all based on one CG character and that were moving, by groups, in repeated patterns that were difficult to trace. Live warriors were digitally modified. Fig. 19-13 is a perfect digital composite; from the 1930s to the 1980s it would have been an optical composite made with traveling mattes on an optical printer.

Fig. 19-10

Fig. 19-11
The Mask: *the wire frame superimposed on the photographic plate, as seen on the computer monitor (Fig. 19-10), and the completed image as it appears in the movie (Fig. 19-11).*

Fig. 19-12
Mighty Joe Young (1998): To create the illusion that a 13½-foot gorilla is destroying a car because its alarm irritates him, first a car was imploded on a full-sized set, crumpling the middle and blowing its back end upward; this was photographed and became the film plate. Then the actor who played Joe (John Alexander in a suit designed by Rick Baker) pulled up the back of a 40%-scale lightweight dummy car (scaled down because the suited actor was 40% the size Joe was supposed to be) on a bluescreen set. Computer animators generated, with the aid of much new software—for example, to create and light the thousands of hairs that made up its fur—a CG Joe that matched Alexander's actions and digitally inserted it into the film plate, along with its CG shadow. This shot had to match other shots taken of Alexander against a bluescreen on a 40%-scale set.

Distribution is the phase in which prints are struck, trailers and ads appear, the movie is re-leased, and prints are sent to theatres. Film distri-bution is followed by distribution on video. In the very final stage of distribution, the film negative is stored under ideal conditions—in a salt mine, for instance—ready for a re-release or the striking of an archival print. A film negative will outlast a dig-ital print or master by a factor of ten or more. As mentioned earlier, storing a digital print, whether magnetically or on an optical disc, means that the file has to be readable in the future. It will have to be copied onto fresh media before the tape or drive or disc containing the file—which never deteriorates and is always the same as it was—degrades, and it will require working equivalents of the equipment and software that created it.

Every transfer will cost money, and it is unlikely that enough funds will always be available to save every movie; thus many will be lost. Even if a movie has been a digital project from the start, it is best to transfer it to 35mm film for archiving and storage—preferably on three black-and-white negatives, one for each primary color.

When a film is distributed in 35mm, hundreds of prints are made, and many of them have no busi-ness use after a few months of playing in theatres—because they have been scratched or because there is no more demand for them. Film prints are expen-sive to make and very heavy. Making prints and hauling them around the country account for at least half of a distributor's expenses, so most dis-tributors would prefer to release movies in a format suited for digital projection.

Fig. 19-13

Fig. 19-14

Fig. 19-15

Three digital composites from Star Wars: Episode I—The Phantom Menace. *In Fig. 19-13 the city is a model, the sky is a separately filmed shot, the landscape is a composite of several shots of hilly countryside that were digitally joined and then anamorphically squeezed for a look that was both otherworldly and Earthlike, and the activity on the ground and in the skies is computer generated. No element of Fig. 19-14 was photographed; the landscape (artifically blurred because fast-moving objects blur when shot with a movie camera), the racing pod, and the rest were all created in the computer. The landscape in Fig. 19-15 was created the same way as that in Fig. 19-13, but the shot has no models; thousands of CG warrior–extras (modified from the Jar Jar CG character) were digitally generated and composited frame by frame into a digitally modified landscape.*

A digital print can be sent to the theatre on a set of discs, on a portable hard drive, by satellite, or over a broadband Internet connection. It weighs from a couple of ounces to nothing. It usually is copied to the digital projector's hard drive so there will be no lag time between discs or, in the case of a satellite feed, no danger of a dropped connection. A digital print costs very little to make, and there is no problem if one wants to release a picture in a few theatres and then make more prints if there is a demand for them; in a film lab, it is more economical to make all the prints at once. Prints for which there is no further use can be erased or tossed out, or even donated to community centers and film schools for a tax break, as the old film prints should be.

Most theatre owners and projectionists do not see digital distribution and exhibition in such a positive light. A movie still arrives at the theatre, by whatever means, and still has to be loaded onto the projector. With film, the only inconvenience is splicing the shipped reels together into the single big reel that is loaded on the platter of a contemporary projector, then unsplicing them to return the movie to its shipping cans. But if a digital projector crashes or a pixel breaks—leaving a permanent dark spot on the screen—it requires a projectionist trained in digital repairs, a trip to the factory, or, in the worst case, a call to tech support. A second projector has to be on hand for the next show.

Conversion to digital projection would cost a theatre at least $150,000 in the early 2000s, not counting a backup projector, and it was really for the distributor's convenience. Theatres already had digital sound. What could they significantly gain by presenting a digital rather than a film image? Converting theatres would prove economical only if audiences demanded to see digital prints as they once demanded sound . . . and digital sound.

As long as the film image remains superior to the digitally projected one, such a shift in audience preference is unlikely. But with the new 4K Super 35 camera system and the forthcoming 4K projectors, the digital cinema will be working with full color data and as close as possible to film resolution, and its clean, scratch-free look might prove appealing. It is also possible, of course, that distributors will force theatres to convert and that audiences will be encouraged, by a media campaign, to prefer the products of a completely digital cinema.

The Look of the Future

In 1993 a company announced that it was perfecting the technology that would allow the image of Buster Keaton to star in a new comedy. In 2004 the image of Laurence Olivier was digitally made to perform a new role in Kerry Conran's *Sky Captain and the World of Tomorrow*. Olivier excepted, every actor in that movie performed entirely against a bluescreen and was composited with the digital effects that constituted the rest of the movie: Actors and effects were the whole package.

Now that anything can be constructed as a digital image, whether it is finally recorded on film or copied to a digital print, the narrative film and the animated film have come closer together. The cinema is at an interesting crossroads, where it can explore the realism of the long take as readily as it can cut itself off from photographic reality. Acknowledging the importance of video and animation, as well as the fact that many movies may no longer be printed on celluloid, some Film Studies programs have renamed themselves Moving-Image Studies.

With 4K shooting and projection, the digital cinema is finally a complete system. It stands ready to replace 35mm film. What will happen depends on whether cinematographers and audiences embrace the new technology. Doubtless, many movies will still be shot and released on film, but many will avoid film entirely. Dual distribution will continue until one medium wins out, which could take a decade. The question is not how great a role video and computers will play in the cinema of the future, but how great a role *film* will play.

For it is clear that digital video and the other technologies described here have transformed the film industry and its product. It is equally clear, looking back, that cinema was the crucial art of the 20th century. But if the age of digital information is taken as license to store films on computer media, send compressed information to an electronic cinema booth, and offer the audience only a good-looking video; if the preferred alternative becomes to watch movies on HDTV at home, whether broadcast or on disc, cable, satellite, or the Internet's version of a drive-in; and if film, which gave the silver screen its silver glow, becomes an obsolete medium for the presentation of movies—then the cinema as an

Fig. 19-16
Lawrence's goggles, snagged on a branch: the last shot in the sequence of Lawrence's fatal motorcycle accident and the first shot restored to **Lawrence of Arabia.**

art of projected films may end shortly after its first century. The dialectical conflict of film and TV will have ended with a synthesis.

It may come down to an issue of what people get used to seeing. The brightness, sharpness, contrast, range, and dyes of the film image used to be recognized, respected, and considered among the essential and definitive characteristics of a unique medium. The film frame is an analog storage system. If it turns out that film is "warm" and the digital image "cold" in the same way that analog sound is said to have a fuller, richer quality than digital sound, then the digital image may lose something that is essential to film—some incalculable part of its visual range—no matter how "filmlike" a frame or a color can be.

Digital cinema may be adopted simply because of its convenience. Reel-to-reel tape has better quality, is transported more evenly, has more surface area, and can run at a faster speed than a tape cassette, but the cassette made it obsolete as a consumer item.

The Lord of the Rings and *Citizen Kane* both look better in 35mm theatres than they do on the best TVs. One prediction that can be made with assurance is that full-sized theatres will continue to be patronized because of their big screens and auditorium-scale sound. Another is that independent production will expand and that most of those productions will be shot on digital video.

Certainly more women will write and direct features. This is a worldwide development led by such brilliant artists as Chantal Akerman and Agnès Varda in France, Samira Makhmalbaf in Iran, Julie Taymor in the U.S., and a growing number of others. The adoption of digital filmmaking is another expanding worldwide movement. Zhang Yimou fell in love with computer effects in *Hero* (2002), where he made, for example, a fighter run crashing through the rain—not a rainstorm, but the individual drops. In his next film, *House of Flying Daggers* (2004), whose digital effects are masterful, there is a wonderful moment when snow covers a fall landscape, as gorgeous as the most painterly CG effect—but what actually happened was that it started to snow, and they decided to keep shooting because they were out of time.

In Hollywood, there will be even fewer co-directed features—the Directors Guild now forbids them—and even more three-act scripts with twists and happy endings. Black-and-white films will continue to be financed only if they are shot in color, then have the color removed in a DI, so that the movie can still be released in color. Digital movies will be distributed not only in theatres and on high-def DVDs, but also to desktop computers. More movies will be released on pay-per-view cable, which is out to replace the corner video store. Common video and DV standards, disc formats, and user expectations will expand to high-def as HDTV replaces standard TV, but 2K will begin to look shabby compared to 4K. Home movies will still be shot on video and edited on home computers.

International co-production will continue to increase. It is simply working too well and creating too many great pictures to disappear.

The "Return of the Myths" is not over yet—and not just in Hollywood, if one considers pictures like New Zealand's *Whale Rider*. In 2003 and 2004, for example, the biggest hits included *The Return of the King*, the second Spider-Man film, the third Harry Potter film, and Mel Gibson's *The Passion of the Christ* (2003, released 2004), the highest-grossing independent film to date. There will be more "effects-driven $100 million digital extravaganzas," as the industry calls them, and more low-budget "talking heads" pictures, between which poles a narrative cinema of quality will find its way.

Speaking of predictions, Disney said it was through with 2-D animation as of 2004, and the trendy nature of some digital advances might have made it seem likely that all new animation, not just at Disney, would soon be 3-D. But any look at a masterpiece like *Spirited Away* or *The Triplets of Belleville* makes it clear that 2-D animation is by no means finished. Some things, however, really never will come again. There will be no more films by Ingmar Bergman, because he declared *Saraband* his last, and there will be no more films by Stan Brakhage, because he died—which was the only thing that could stop him. Both would insist that the cinema of the future include film.

One trend that shows strong signs of continuing is the interest in restoring classic movies. In this respect, the look of the future includes the look of the past.

Restoration is the art of taking an old, perhaps damaged film, many of whose shots may be missing or out of order, and undoing the damage, finding and assembling the best surviving prints and fragments—and doing a staggering amount of research—in order to strike a new print that is as close as possible to the film as originally released. Ever since the enthusiastic reception of Kevin Brownlow's painstaking restoration of Abel Gance's *Napoleon* (produced and presented in 1981 by Robert A. Harris and

Francis Ford Coppola), the commercial value of the pictures gathering dust and turning to nitrate soup in their vaults has impressed itself on film companies both in America and abroad. Harris's own restoration of *Lawrence of Arabia*, which took three years and resulted in the best possible 70mm print of the film as David Lean had intended it to appear—a good 20 minutes longer than the abridged version that had been in circulation, including every shot that had been cut at the producer's orders shortly after the picture first opened—was one of the most significant film events of 1989. Indeed, Columbia's re-release of *Lawrence* received as much public attention as its purchase that same year by Sony, the former as important in the history of the art as the latter is in the history of the business. Spectacularly visual, elegantly paced, sweepingly historic, intellectually and emotionally profound, and with a perfectly clean soundtrack, the restored *Lawrence* hit a generation of film students right in the eyes—students who had seen films projected in 70mm (like *Alien*, blown up from 35mm) but nothing *shot* in 70mm—that is, nothing with the perfect detail of the 65mm camera negative. In a time of action–adventure teenpix and little adult pictures with two characters who come to appreciate each other, *Lawrence* appeared like the conscience of narrative film.

In 1987, Paramount began to inventory and preserve its film and television archives—200,000 cans of material. In 1990 it opened a building for the archive and announced a program of re-releases. By June 1990, both Warner Bros. and Columbia had announced their own film preservation campaigns, and eight filmmakers—Woody Allen, Francis Ford Coppola, Stanley Kubrick, George Lucas, Sydney Pollack, Robert Redford, Steven Spielberg, and the president of the board, Martin Scorsese—had formed The Film Foundation to raise at least $30 million for restorations to be carried out jointly by studios and archives. That same year, Disney completed a restoration of *Fantasia* for the film's 50th anniversary, the first time in decades that it had been seen full-frame.

Many restorations are now done on computer, not on film. From 1998 to 2002, *Metropolis* was restored at 2K; it was released on both film and DVD, and the film version looked as good as a perfect 16mm print or a fair 35mm print—except that it was longer, more coherent, more carefully motivated, and less silly. Some digital restorations result only in digital prints, however; that was the fate of *Singin' In The Rain* in 2002, whose projected image was full of jaggies and visible lines of resolution. DI technology is becoming more important in digital restoration, and the result can be a new negative—whether or not new prints are struck and shown—as well as a video release that pays for the restoration.

Computers can alter films in many ways, good and bad. Colorization, which evolved into a creative tool for a picture like *Pleasantville*, is a violation of the filmmakers' creative intentions when used on a previously released picture. It still is practiced and remains the opposite of restoration. In Joe Dante's *Gremlins 2—The New Batch* (1990), a cable station, modeled on one of Ted Turner's, announces a showing of *Casablanca*, "Now in color, with a happier ending."

In 1993, in the largest digital film-processing project yet attempted, all 120,000 frames of *Snow White* were cleaned in a computer, the dust removed and the scratches stitched together with excellent results.

The more films are restored to their original look and length, and the more new movies appear, the more the art and history of motion pictures will live and grow. We can only hope that many of those movies will be shot and printed on celluloid, because we want all the information every one of those frames can give us.

For Further Reading and Viewing

WEB SITES

Note: Some of this information is not yet in books but is available on the Web sites of the studios and certain other major companies. These are reliable, horse's-mouth sources.

Avid: http://avid.com/index_fl.asp
Buena Vista (Disney): http://www.disney.com
Dolby Laboratories: http://www.dolby.com
Metro–Goldwyn–Mayer: http://www.mgm.com
The Motion Picture Association of America (MPAA), with links to studios and to digital

cinema sources, a ratings database, etc.: http://www.mpaa.org
Panavision: http://panavision.com
Paramount: http://www.paramount.com
Pixar: http://www.pixar.com
Sony: http://www.sony.net
Twentieth Century Fox: http://www.fox.com
United Artists: http://unitedartists.com
Universal: http://www.universalstudios.com
Warner Bros.: http://www.warnerbros.com

The Internet Movie Database (IMDb) is the best place to start when looking up a person or a movie online, but it is not always accurate; unlike the others listed here, it is a secondary rather than a primary source: http://www.imdb.com

MAGAZINES AND TRADE PAPERS

Many more could have been listed, but these offer the most up-to-date, accurate, comprehensive information about the film industry, cinematography, and digital effects.

American Cinematographer. Published by the American Society of Cinematographers. Professional articles on film and digital production techniques—with an emphasis on the practice and aesthetics of conventional, special-effects, and digital cinematography— along with well-researched articles on historic movies and great cinematographers.

Cinefex. A state-of-the-art journal of special effects, usually covering 1–3 new movies per issue. Old issues are collectible and hard to find.

Daily Variety. Can be mailed outside the Los Angeles area; subscribers may search www.variety.com and receive electronic daily bulletins. The weekly version of *Variety* does not cover the film business as thoroughly as the daily one. Authoritative data on films, especially in the reviews; all showbiz obituaries; worldwide industry news—and the occasional non-story, printed to see whether it arouses interest in a project. Special issues on Women in Film, the Oscars, etc.

The Hollywood Reporter. An alternative to *Daily Variety*, preferred by many readers. Unless you're a studio, you don't need to get both every weekday.

FILMS

Pixar Animation Studios
Toy Story (1995, John A. Lasseter)
a bug's life (1998, John A. Lasseter and Andrew Stanton)
Toy Story 2 (1999, John A. Lasseter, Lee Unkrich, and Ash Brannon)
Monsters, Inc. (2001, Peter Docter)
Finding Nemo (2003, Andrew Stanton)
The Incredibles (2004, Brad Bird)

Miscellany: Digital Cinema
Catalog (1961, John Whitney)
Permutations and *Experiments in Motion Graphics* (1968, John Whitney)
Tron (1982, Steven Lisberger)
One from the heart or *One From The Heart* (1982, Francis Ford Coppola)
Star Trek II: The Wrath of Khan (1982, Nicholas Meyer)
Terminator 2: Judgment Day (1991, James Cameron)
Jurassic Park (1993, Steven Spielberg)
The English Patient (1996, Anthony Minghella)
Titanic (1997, James Cameron)
Star Wars: Episode I—The Phantom Menace (1999, George Lucas)
O Brother, Where Art Thou? (2000, Joel and Ethan Coen)
Waking Life (2001, Richard Linklater)
Shrek (2001, Andrew Adamson and Vicky Jenson)
Russian Ark (2002, Alexander Sokurov)
Star Wars: Episode II—Attack of the Clones (2002, George Lucas)
Spider-Man 2 (2004, Sam Raimi)
Ryan (2004, Chris Landreth). Canadian short
House of Flying Daggers (2004, Zhang Yimou)
The Polar Express (2004, Robert Zemeckis)

DVDs

Bit rates: See the Universal Legacy Collection (Chap. 11 list) and *Lawrence of Arabia* (Chap. 14 list).

Finding Nemo (2003, **Andrew Stanton**). Buena Vista Home Entertainment. Collector's Edition. Includes a making-of documentary, deleted scenes, and a way to turn your TV into a virtual aquarium.
Hero (see Chap. 14 list).
The Lord of the Rings (see Chap. 16 list).
Master and Commander: The Far Side of the World (2003, **Peter Weir**). Twentieth Century Fox. Widescreen Collector's Edition. Includes a making-of documentary emphasizing Weir's involvement from pre- to post-production, an interview with Weir, edited sequences that can be broken down into takes, a demonstration of microphone placement, a short on sound design, and clear demonstrations of **digital effects.**
Monsters, Inc. (2001, **Peter Docter**). Buena Vista Home Entertainment. Collector's Edition. Includes a **Pixar** short, *For the Birds*; information about the making of the film, laid out in a production-timeline menu; and more.
O Brother, Where Art Thou? (2000, **Joel and Ethan Coen**). Touchstone Video. Includes a documentary about the **digital intermediate** process, a music video, and a script-to-storyboard-to-scene comparison.
One from the heart (see Chap. 18 list).
Restored versions are **bold-faced** in all the lists: See *Metropolis* (Chap. 7), *The Passion of Joan of Arc* (Chap. 10), *Touch of Evil* (Chap. 11), *Lawrence of Arabia* (Chap. 14), etc.
Russian Ark (see Chap. 16 list).
Terminator 2: Judgment Day (1991, **James Cameron**). Artisan Entertainment. Ultimate Edition. Includes the release cut and the extended cut, storyboards, the script, and hours of making-of documentaries and shorts.
Time Code (see Chap. 18 list).
Toy Story: The Ultimate Toy Box (1995–99, **John A. Lasseter**). Disney/Pixar. Collector's Edition. Contains both of the movies and a third disc with excellent making-of documentaries and demonstrations.

Glossary

Academy aperture. Also **sound aperture.** The exact dimensions of the Sound-Era image area (also called the picture area or the frame) on 35mm movie film: .868 × .631 inch, with an aspect ratio of roughly 1.33:1. Also, the rectangular opening in the camera that admits light only to an area of that size on the film. In the Silent Era, a true **full frame** was 1.33:1 and measured .980 × .735 inch; that full frame, the whole 4 × 3 area bounded by the sprocket holes and the frame lines, is also called the **camera aperture, full aperture,** or **silent aperture,** and some lenses and formats still use that entire area when shooting. In 1931, the size of the picture area was reduced and slightly reshaped to make room for the soundtrack, creating the Academy aperture or sound aperture. A 1.33:1 flat image that uses the entire Academy frame can be called a full-frame image or a **full frame,** even though it is only ³⁄₄ the size of a true full frame or **full-aperture frame.** Note that through all these changes, the film remained 35mm wide with 4 sprocket holes on the left and right sides of each frame. *See* Academy ratio.

Academy ratio. The standard proportions of a 35mm image: four units wide by three units high (4 × 3), expressed as an aspect ratio of 1.33:1. In the Sound Era, when the Academy aperture was adopted, the actual aspect ratio of the frame became 1.375:1. However, the difference between 1.333:1 and 1.375:1 is widely ignored because it has a negligible effect on composition, and the Academy ratio is still referred to as 1.33:1. *See* Academy aperture *and* Aspect ratio.

Actualité. A nonfiction film that records a real event in an unbiased manner.

Alienation effect. *See* Brechtian cinema.

Analog. Information that is continuous, like a wave, and that indicates difference by having more or less of something, as the amplitude of a sound wave rises with an increase in volume; in an analog recording, the electrical waveform is analogous to the acoustical waveform, changing as it changes and continuing as it continues. *See* Digital.

Anamorphic. Any wide-screen process, lens, or format in which a wide field of view is **squeezed** (horizontally compressed) during shooting and **unsqueezed** (restoring normal width-to-height relationships) during projection. *See* Flat *and* Wide screen.

Anamorphic lens. A lens that compresses or widens the horizontal dimension of an image without affecting the vertical dimension. The camera lens squeezes a wide image to fit onto standard-sized film, then the projection lens spreads out the skinny image to fill a wide screen.

Animatics. Computer-animated storyboards; moving rough drafts of scenes—often 3-D graphics developed from photos, drawings, and models.

Animation. The process of making inanimate drawings or objects appear to come to life and move—usually by shooting sequential drawings, or an object in sequential positions, one frame at a time.

Animatronics. Moving puppets, robots, masks, etc. by electronically activating remotely controlled pumps and other implanted electromagnetic devices.

Anime. Japanese feature-length animated films.

Aperture. An opening through which light passes, especially in a lens or camera.

Art director. The person who designs a movie's sets and decor. *See* Production designer.

ASA. A measure of the photosensitivity of an emulsion, following specifications established by the American Standards Association; the higher the ASA, the faster the "speed" and the greater the sensitivity of the film.

Aspect ratio. The ratio of the width of the image (written first) to its height (a constant). A full 35mm frame is 1¹⁄₃ times as wide as it is high; its aspect ratio (1¹⁄₃ to 1, or 4 × 3) is written 1.33:1. Other common aspect ratios are 1.66:1 (35mm European widescreen, a flat format), 1.78:1 or 16 × 9 (HDDV and HDTV, the high-definition digital video and television aspect ratio also used for flat theatrical prints), 1.85:1 (35mm American widescreen, a flat format; called Super 1.85 when shot on Super 35mm film), 2.2:1 (70mm flat), 2.35:1 (late CinemaScope, early Panavision, and generic "scope"—35mm anamorphic), 2.4:1 (Panavision's 35mm anamorphic aspect ratio since the early 1970s, a shape that makes it easier to hide splices; also the aspect ratio of wide-screen Super 35mm, which is shot flat but squeezed during printing and projected anamorphically), 2.55:1 (CinemaScope's original aspect ratio), and 2.75:1 (70mm anamorphic). Today, most movies are 1.66:1 (European flat), 1.78:1 (HDDV flat), 1.85:1 (American flat), or 2.4:1 (scope), though some are still 1.33:1 (full-frame flat). Aspect ratios of video formats are sometimes expressed as the number of horizontal pixels, written first, by the number of vertical pixels (i.e., the number of pixels in a horizontal line by the number of horizontal lines). *See* Academy aperture, Academy ratio, Anamorphic, Flat, Pixel, Wide screen, *and* Widescreen.

Auteur.   A filmmaker—usually a director, but sometimes a producer or writer—with a distinctive style and coherent thematic vision that are developed throughout a body of work. French for "author"; thus, the primary creator of a movie, who guides the collaborative filmmaking project so that it expresses his or her creative intentions. Strictly, a director with a distinctive style and vision who also writes and edits the films.

Barney.   A padded bag placed over the camera to soundproof it. *See* Blimp.

Base.   The flexible component or vehicle of film stock, made of a cellulose compound and coated with a photographic emulsion.

Benshi.   In Japan, the live narrator of a film.

Beta movement.   *See* Phi phenomenon.

Bildungsroman.   A novel about the formative experiences of a central character; e.g., Joyce's *A Portrait of the Artist as a Young Man*.

Bi-pack.   Also **bipack.** A double load of film. *See* Printer.

Bit.   A minimal unit of digital information, or the memory needed to store it, in the form of a zero or a one. *See* Byte.

Bit rate.   The speed, usually given in megabits/second, at which the bits in digitized samples can be sent over a connection; the amount of information available per second to define a frame, reproduce a sound, etc.

Blacklist.   A list that prohibits the hiring of specific individuals and/or a particular class of people, such as left-wing screenwriters. Also the agreement to enforce such a list.

Blimp.   A rigid cover placed over the camera to soundproof it; a **blimped camera** is one with internal soundproofing. *See* Barney.

Block booking.   The practice of forcing an exhibitor to rent a group of films rather than to bid on individual titles.

Blockbuster.   A major box-office hit, conventionally defined as one that grosses $100 million or more during its first domestic release.

Blocking.   Planning and rehearsing the positions and movements of the actors and of the camera within a shot or scene.

Bluescreen.   Also **blue screen.** A bright blue background against which action or models may be shot; when filtered and printed, the blue area may be rendered opaque or transparent, permitting the generation of traveling mattes and composites. If the foreground subject is blue or wearing blue, this **color difference process** won't produce usable results, so a contrasting **greenscreen** or **redscreen** is used instead. TV effects use greenscreen.

Boom.   (1) The arm of a crane, which supports the camera platform and moves it through the air. (2) The lightweight pole from which a microphone is suspended above the actors (whose movements it accompanies) and outside the frame.

Boom shot.   Also **crane shot.** A shot taken from a crane.

Bourgeois.   Middle-class.

Bourgeois cinema.   Films, and the industry behind them, that encourage audiences to identify with fictional characters and situations, to forget their troubles, and to feel satisfied with fictional resolutions. Escapist fictions that make political analysis appear irrelevant and unnecessary. *See* Brechtian cinema.

Box-office grosses.   *See* Gross.

B picture.   (1) A film meant to appear at the bottom of a double bill. (2) A relatively inexpensive film, usually a genre picture without big stars.

Brechtian cinema.   Films, and certain devices within them, that encourage audiences to remain critically distant from the fiction, to analyze the dramatized situation in political terms, and to keep in mind the theatrical or cinematic nature of the spectacle; the opposite of bourgeois cinema. Inspired by the "epic theatre" of German playwright Bertolt Brecht (1898–1956) in which a variety of reflexive and stylized devices engage the audience's critical awareness. Brecht's *Verfremdungseffekt* or "estrangement effect," often called the **alienation effect,** removes or estranges the spectator from the illusion of reality in the spectacle and from the temptation to empathize with its characters and get lost in the illusion; from this distance, the spectator can study and judge the characters as well as the political and ethical implications of their problems and of the measures taken to solve them.

Breen Code. *See* Production Code.

Byte. Eight adjacent bits that are processed as a unit.

Camera aperture. *See* Academy aperture.

Cameraman. Also **cameraperson.** (1) The person in charge of lighting and shooting a movie. Also known as **cinematographer, DP, director of photography.** (2) Loosely, the camera operator.

CARA. The Motion Picture Association of America's Classification and Rating Administration, the board that awards a film its **MPAA rating** (G, PG, R, etc.), determining how old one must be—implicitly, how mature one ought to be—to see it.

Celluloid. Transparent material chemically derived from cellulose; cut into strips to be used as film base or into sheets (**cels**) on which to paint individual elements of composite drawings.

CCD. Charge-coupled device. A chip that registers the amounts of red, green, and blue light falling on it as voltage levels, capturing the frame as an electronic signal and converting that analog signal to digital information. The photocells on a CCD—sometimes called **photosites**—are usually square, are arranged in adjacent horizontal lines, and may be covered with microlenses and/or filters. Each site records R, G, or B information for a particular pixel. Some cameras have one CCD; others have three (one each for R, G, and B); still others use **CMOS** (complementary metal oxide semiconductor) chips. A photosensitive chip is often called a **sensor.**

CFF. *See* Critical flicker frequency.

CGI. Computer-generated imagery.

Changeover. The instantaneous switch from one projector to another, as the reel on the first projector ends and the next reel begins. **Changeover marks,** usually little circles in the upper right corner of the frame, appear near and at the end of the reel (before the tail leader) to cue the projectionist in a two-projector system.

Channel. The sound meant to be played through a particular speaker; e.g., the left, center, right, and surround channels of a Dolby Stereo analog soundtrack.

Chiaroscuro. The artistic arrangement of light and dark elements in a shot or in any pictorial composition.

Chip. (1) A wafer of silicon or another semiconductor material. (2) An integrated circuit on such a wafer, together with its connecting pins or wires. (3) A microprocessor. *See* CCD.

Cinéaste. (1) A knowledgeable film enthusiast. (2) Literally, a film producer, writer, or camerman.

Cinema. (1) The art of motion pictures; "the movies" in general. (2) A movie theatre. (3) The films of a country or group.

CinemaScope. The 35mm anamorphic process introduced by 20th Century–Fox in 1953; eventually replaced by Panavision. *See* Aspect ratio.

Cinématographe. The Lumière brothers' 35mm camera, which could also be used as a projector and a printer.

Cinematographer. Also **director of photography** and **DP;** sometimes **cameraman.** A motion picture photographer; the head of the camera crew.

Cinéma vérité. French for "film truth"; *kinó-pravda* in Russian. An unscripted documentary in which the catalyzing presence of the camera, with which the subjects interact, is acknowledged. In most cases the crew is small, sometimes only one person to run the camera and one to record the sound, and the equipment is lightweight.

Cineplex. Trade name of the first multiplex cinema.

Cinerama. Triptych format (three cameras, three projectors) employing a high, wide, deeply curved screen, yielding a panorama or a three-panel image that extended nearly to the limits of peripheral vision; a fourth projector played the eight-track stereo sound. Original aspect ratio about 2.75:1 but 2.1:1 when viewed from the center. Introduced 1952; changed from a multi-film system to a large-negative anamorphic system in the early 1960s.

Close shot. Also **CS.** (1) Unlike the far shot, a shot in which the camera is near the subject—or, thanks to a long lens, appears to be near the subject. (2) A shot whose field of view is slightly broader than that of the close-up; in terms of the human figure, the head and upper chest might fill the frame.

Close-up. Also **closeup, CU.** A shot whose field of view is very narrow; in terms of the human figure, a face or hand might fill the frame.

Color difference process. *See* Bluescreen.

Completion date. (1) The year a film is finished and ready to be released; usually the year it is copyrighted. (2) The day the final trial print is approved. *See* Release date.

Composite. *See* Digital composite, Optical composite, *and* Sound composite.

Composition. The arrangement of the elements of an image in relation to the boundaries of the frame and to each other.

Composition in depth. The composition of a visual field in relation to the axis that runs from the camera to infinity; in most cases, significant elements are distributed from the foreground to the background of the image. *See* Deep focus.

Conglomerate. A huge corporation made up of many diverse companies. A **media conglomerate** might include a film studio, a TV network, a cable or satellite system, a video chain, a music company, and a publishing house.

Constructive editing. Also **linkage editing.** A variety of montage in which many brief, distinctly individual shots (which are considered complementary and related rather than in polar conflict) accumulate into a dynamic whole; formulated by Vsevolod Pudovkin.

Contact printer. *See* Optical printer *and* Printer.

Continuity. (1) The narrative structure of a film, laid out in sequence; the plot as a string of scenes. (2) A list and description (including dialogue) of all the shots in the final version of a film, prepared by the editor; the film as a series of shots. Also known as **cutting continuity.** (3) The matching of details that allows shots taken at different times to appear to be recording a single, continuous event; the impression that conditions established in one shot continue to exist in later or related shots. (4) A list of the details—such as the length of a cigarette, the condition of a tablecloth, or the number of buttons left unbuttoned on a shirt—that have to be matched from shot to shot, either within a scene or from one scene to another. (Once the boot has been eaten in *The Gold Rush*, continuity demands that from then on, scene after scene, the tramp must have only one boot, and the correct foot must be wrapped the same way.)

Continuity editing. Also *découpage.* Editing to create the impression that events flow seamlessly from shot to shot; the opposite of montage (in which cuts are called to the audience's attention and discontinuity is heightened).

Continuous signal. A signal that is perceived as uninterrupted; e.g., a flickering light that appears to be shining continuously or a rapid series of beats that is heard as a single sound. Also a signal that actually is uninterrupted. *See* Critical flicker frequency.

Contrapuntal sound. Sound that is synchronized to clash with what is shown; a soundtrack that works against the image track or in counterpoint with it. Audio-visual montage.

Co-production. A film produced by two or more business entities (studios, partnerships, producers, etc.) that may be in different countries.

Core. A plastic hub on which film is wound.

Crane. A vehicle equipped with an arm (or boom); at the end of the arm is a camera platform that can be lifted and moved through the air. *See* Boom shot.

Cranking back. Rewinding the film a short distance in the camera, usually so it can be re-exposed; invented by R. W. Paul.

Creative geography. Also the **artificial landscape.** Creating through montage an impression of spatial contiguity that does not otherwise exist. Formulated by Lev Kuleshov.

Credits. Also **titles.** A list including the name of the film, its distributor, copyright and other notices, and the names and contributions of those who worked on it, found at or near the film's start (**head credits** or **opening titles**) and/or at its end (**tail credits** or **end titles**). *See* Intertitle *and* Title.

Critical flicker frequency. Also **CFF.** The slowest rate (48 alternations of light and dark per second) at which the human eye perceives a flickering light as an uninterrupted light—i.e., as a continuous signal. The point at and above which **flicker fusion** (perceiving "on-and-off" light as if it were always "on") occurs. *See* Continuous signal *and* Flicker.

Cross-cutting. Also **parallel montage.** Cutting back and forth between ongoing actions—usually between scenes that are presented as occurring in different locations at the same time and that are dramatically or thematically related. *See* Intercutting.

CRT. Cathode-ray tube. An ordinary TV picture tube.

Cult film. A movie, usually but not necessarily weird, with an insatiably devoted following.

Cut. (1) An instantaneous transition from one shot to another. (2) To splice one shot to another; also the splice itself. (3) The way a particular version of a film has been edited, as in the *director's cut.* (4) The instruction to stop shooting or to end a shot. (5) Abridged.

Cutaway. A cut away from a shot—or setup, figure, or action—to which the editor will soon return; the return is a **cutback.** A cut to a shot whose function is to provide a break from, offer information about, or evade a flawed portion of the primary shot, or to intervene between two similar shots so that their joining will not create a jump cut.

Cycle. A group of similar films made at a particular time, usually fueled by audience and industry support for movies with a certain tone, approach, or subject matter; a flurry of films in a particular genre, released continuously until audience interest dries up and the cycle ends.

Dailies. Also **rushes.** Film or digital copies of each day's shooting.

Day-for-night. Shooting in the daytime while using filters or underexposing to create the impression of night.

Deconstruction. The critical process of dismantling the logical, ideological, or fictional structures that support and are reflected in a text; analyzing the ways a work comprises contradictions and defers rather than delivers meaning. Formulated by Jacques Derrida.

Découpage. *See* Continuity editing.

Deep focus. A visual field that is in sharp focus from foreground to background (extreme depth of field) and whose foreground and background planes appear to be widely separated (impression of a deep visual field, usually created by a wide-angle lens); often used to accentuate composition in depth.

Density. Degree of opacity of processed film.

Depth of field. A measure of the range of focus in an image; specifically, the range before and behind the plane of focus within which objects remain acceptably sharp. (A lens might be focused at an object 8 feet away but still keep objects that are from 5 to 11 feet away in focus; at a setting yielding a greater depth of field, that same lens might be focused at 8 feet and keep objects in focus from 4 feet to infinity.) Thus, the distance between the nearest and farthest objects that are in focus, measured along the axis from the camera to infinity.

DFX. Digital special effects. Effects achieved on a computer.

Dialectical montage. Also **intellectual montage.** A variety of editing in which shots "collide" or significantly conflict with each other, ideally generating a synthesis (which may be a metaphor or a concept) in the mind of the viewer; formulated by Sergei Eisenstein.

Dialectics. The theory and practice of systems that develop through conflict between opposites. The **thesis,** or first term, gives rise to its opposite or opponent, the **antithesis,** and out of their conflict emerges a **synthesis** that becomes the first term in a new dialectical cycle.

Diffusion. The dispersion, unfocusing, or scattering of light, creating "soft" rather than "hard" effects.

Digital. Information that is discrete, like a flipped switch, and that signifies in yes/no, on/off, present/absent terms rather than varying an uninterrupted signal; usually in the form of electronically stored data, binary numbers, intermittent electronic pulses, or linguistic units. *See* Analog.

Digital cinema. Nonlinear production, using digital video and computers, of motion pictures that are shot, edited, and distributed without using film.

Digital composite. Any image created by combining two or more digital images or image elements on a computer.

Digital editing. *See* Nonlinear editing.

Digital print. A computer file that may be stored on digital videotape, a hard drive, etc.

Digital intermediate. Also **DI; an electronic intermediate** or **EI.** (1) A high-resolution digital copy of the edited film negative, which may be digitally modified in any way. After all the changes have been made—without adding any photographic generations—the revised DI is scanned onto celluloid in a film recorder, creating a new negative (if used for printing, an internegative or **IN**). (2) Loosely, a digital copy of the camera negative, edited or not, that is modified before being put back on film or copied to a digital printing element.

Digital soundtrack. *See* Dolby Digital, DTS, *and* SDDS.

Digital video. *See* DV.

Director. The person who guides the actors in performance, determines the staging of the action, supervises all aspects of shooting, and works with the producer, writer, and designer before production and with the film and sound editors after production to ensure the consistency and excellence of the movie as well as the best possible use of the personnel, materials, and resources provided by the producer.

Director's cut. The film as the director would like to see it released; the final version presented to the producer or studio, usually with the contractual understanding that it may be altered without the director's approval.

Dissolve. Also **lap dissolve.** A superimposed fade-out and fade-in; a transitional device in which one image vanishes evenly and gradually while another gradually appears.

Documentary. A nonfiction film that organizes and presents factual materials to make a point.

Dolby Digital. A digital surround soundtrack from Dolby Laboratories (six channels in a 5.1 configuration: left, center, right, left surround, right surround, and bass effects); the optical soundtrack is printed block by block in the spaces between one line of sprockets of the 35mm film print.

Dolby noise reduction. Also **Dolby NR.** A process for reducing system noise, particularly tape hiss, by compressing the signal during recording and expanding or decoding it during playback.

Dolby Stereo. (1) Also **Dolby SVA** (Stereo Variable Area), replaced in 1986 by **Dolby SR** (Spectral Recording). A Dolby NR-encoded, optical, variable area analog soundtrack that carries four channels (left, center, right, and surround) on two tracks; found on most 35mm prints; first major use, *Star Wars* (1977). (2) A magnetic soundtrack, each of whose six or more channels has been Dolby NR—encoded and is carried on its own track; most often found on 70mm prints; now rare. *See* Dolby Digital.

Dolly. A camera platform with rubber wheels that allow it to move (be pushed) freely over a floor, unlike the earlier steel wheels that had to run on steel rails (tracks). *See* Track shot.

DP. Director of Photography. *See* Cinematographer.

DTS. Digital Theater Systems and its six-channel, double-system (the sound is on a CD-ROM controlled by a synchronizing code on the print) digital surround sound format.

Dubbing. (1) Replacing one performer's voice with that of another (as in *Singin' In The Rain*). (2) Replacing all the performers' dialogue with dialogue spoken in another language, usually by other performers. (3) Re-recording with the same performer, especially when an actor replaces his or her dialogue as recorded during shooting with a new performance, under ideal sound conditions, of the same dialogue. Also known as **looping.** *See* Loop. (4) Copying or transferring a recording.

Dupe. A print copied from another print.

DV. Digital video. (1) Digital videotape. (2) A program, movie, or audiovisual signal recorded on digital videotape, a hard drive, or another digital medium. (3) The technology of recording a motion picture on digital media. (4) Standard digital video as opposed to a high-definition format. *See* HDDV.

DVD. A Digital Versatile Disc or Digital Video Disc. There is no standard name, so a DVD is a DVD.

Dutch tilt shot. *See* Tilt.

Editing. The art of selecting, trimming, and assembling in order the shots (film editing) and/or the tracks (sound editing) that make up the finished motion picture.

Electronic cinema. (1) The use of video and computers to storyboard, sketch, render, combine, and alter images from, for, or as a film. Invented by Francis Coppola. (2) Distribution and projection without film—originally using HD analog video, currently using HD digital video. The digital print is sent to the projection booth via satellite or broadband, or shipped to it on optical discs or a portable hard drive, and shown with a digital projector.

Electronic intermediate process. *See* Digital intermediate.

Emulsion. The light-sensitive component of film stock. *See* Base.

Establishing shot. (1) A long shot, early in a movie or scene, that shows where the action takes place. (2) Any shot that introduces a location.

Exposure. (1) The amount of light that is allowed to reach the film. Overexposure indicates too much light, underexposure too little. (2) The act of allowing light to reach film; the instant in which this happens.

Expressionism. (1) The artistic movement that held that the look and style of the visible, external universe could take its shape, color, and texture from the artist's intuition of its essential inner being or from human emotions and sensations. (2) The art of rendering inner states as aspects of the outer world. (3) Emotionally intense creative distortion.

Exterior. (1) An outdoor shooting location. (2) A scene that is set outdoors. *See* Interior.

Extreme close-up. Also **ECU, tight close-up.** A shot with a very narrow field of view; the camera appears to be extremely close to the subject. In terms of the human figure, an eye or mouth might fill the frame.

Extreme long shot. Also **ELS.** A shot with a very broad field of view; the camera appears to be

extremely far from the subject. An adult might be less than one tenth the height of the frame.

Fade. (1) A transitional effect in which the image gradually and evenly disappears into darkness (a **fade-out** or **fade to black**) or appears from darkness (a **fade-in**). (2) A dissolve to any monochromatic field (**fade to red, fade to white,** etc.). (3) To effect a fade; to fade out (rarely used alone to mean "to fade in").

Far shot. Unlike the close shot, a shot in which the camera is or appears to be distant from the subject.

Fast film. Film whose emulsion has a high "speed," making it extremely reactive to light and useful in low-light conditions.

Fast motion. Also **undercranking.** The effect of speeded-up movement, achieved by exposing fewer than the normal number of frames per second (i.e., shooting at a rate lower than the projection rate).

Faux raccord. A jump cut with a false impression of continuity; often a match of action over a change of scene. Perfected by Maya Deren.

Feature. (1) A movie whose running time is an hour or more. (2) A theatrical, narrative film that usually lasts over 85 minutes.

Film. (1) The flexible medium, consisting of a perforated base coated with an emulsion, on which images are photographically imprinted. (2) Perforated film base coated with magnetic oxide; sound is transferred from magnetic tape to **magnetic film,** which is the same gauge as the film run through the camera and can easily be kept in frame-by-frame sync with the picture and with other tracks. Also known as **fullcoat, mag film, mag, mag stock.** (3) A movie. (4) Like **cinema,** a general term for the art of motion pictures. (5) To shoot a motion picture.

Film d'Art. Early silent French "art" films consisting of filmed stage productions.

Film noir. An American genre of the 1940s and 1950s (named by French critics who noticed the resemblance between these "black" or "dark" films and the series of dark mystery novels—many of them by American pulp writers—published as the *Série noire*) characterized by sudden violence, tough romantic intensity, deceptive surfaces and emblematic reflections, unsentimental melodrama, narrative complexity, low-key lighting, and themes of entrapment and corruption, honor and duplicity, desire and revenge, compulsion and madness, betrayal and disenchantment, irony and doom.

Film plane. In the camera, the line formed by the upright frame that is held in the gate, ready to be exposed. The location of the film and its distance from the back of the lens, indicated by a line etched on the camera body.

Film recorder. A device that uses a laser to scan onto film, one line at a time, an image that has been digitally generated or modified.

Film stock. Also **filmstock, raw stock, stock.** Unexposed film.

Final cut. (1) The right given to some directors to have the director's cut released without any changes. (2) The final version of a film, after which it will not be re-edited.

Flashback. A cut to an earlier event, usually followed by a return to the present.

Flash forward. A cut to a future event, usually followed by a return to the present.

Flat. (1) Not anamorphic; a spherical-lens format. (2) Not 3-D; a two-dimensional format. (3) Not glossy; a dull, matte, or nonreflective surface.

Flicker. The rapid alternation of light and dark caused by the opening and closing of the projector's shutter. Noticeable below 48 fps. Dealt with by using a two- or three-bladed shutter to show each frame several times. *See* Critical flicker frequency.

Flicker fusion. *See* Critical flicker frequency.

Focal length. The distance in millimeters from the film plane to the optical center of the lens when the lens is focused at infinity. In 35mm Academy-ratio cinematography, a "normal" lens has a focal length of 50mm, a short or wide-angle lens has a focal length shorter than that (e.g., 28mm), and a long or telephoto lens has a long focal length (e.g., 200mm). *See* Zoom lens.

Formalism. Whether practiced by an artist or a critic, the emphasis on the form, structure, and strategies of a work of art, rather than on its subject or the circumstances under which it came to be created.

Format. The physical and optical characteristics of a negative or print, such as whether it is flat or anamorphic, the gauge of the film, the aspect ratio of the image, and the number of perforations per frame; also the placement and other characteristics of the soundtrack (single or double system, analog or digital, 4-track or 6-track, etc.).

Fps. Frames per second; the rate of exposing and/or projecting frames. Most sound films run at 24 fps; silent films ran at speeds that varied from 16 fps to 24 fps, with 16 fps common for most films before 1920. On today's projectors, "silent speed" is 18 fps, since most films in the mid-1920s ran at 18–22 fps. To simplify matters, the convention is to define silent speed as 16 fps. *See* Sound speed.

Frame. (1) An individual photograph or picture area on a strip of film. *See* Academy aperture. (2) The perimeter or boundary line of the picture area. (3) In the narrative film, a story or narrative situation within which another story or sequence is bracketed or presented. (4) A one-frame length of film.

Frame enlargement. A printed enlargement of an individual frame from a movie.

Freeze frame. Also **freeze-frame.** A sudden cessation of movement created by the continual reprinting of the same frame.

Full aperture. Also **camera aperture** and **silent aperture.** A format in which the camera exposes the entire picture area, including the area usually reserved for the soundtrack. *See* Academy aperture.

Full frame. *See* Academy aperture.

Full shot. Also **FS.** A medium long shot that offers a relatively complete view of the set and shows the human figure from head to foot.

FX. Effects. *See* DFX *and* Special effects.

Gate. In a camera, printer, or projector, the apparatus through which film passes as it is exposed to light.

Gauge. The width of a strip of film in millimeters.

Gendai-geki. In Japan, a film set in the present or recent past; the film of modern life.

Genre. (1) A subcategory of the narrative film, defined by the choice and treatment of subject—mystery, musical, western, and so forth. A group of films, or a narrative approach, that deals with a specific avenue of human experience in a characteristic manner (or a variation of it), structuring the story and its presentation in relation to a recurring set of terms, themes, values, figures, and images. (2) A particular variety or type of motion picture. Within the nonfiction film, for example, *cinéma vérité* and the newsreel are distinct genres.

Greenscreen. *See* Bluescreen.

Gross. The amount of money earned by a film before any expenses are deducted. The **domestic box-office gross** is the amount spent on tickets to a particular movie in the country where it was produced. After deductions by the exhibitor and distributor, the amount returned to the filmmaker or production company is the **producer's gross.** *See* Net.

GUI. Graphical user interface.

Hays Office. Colloquial name for Hollywood's bureau of self-censorship, the Motion Picture Producers and Distributors of America, as administered by its first president (1922–45), Will Hays. *See* MPAA *and* Production Code.

HD. High definition.

HDDV. High-definition digital video, abbreviated **high-def.** Current standards range from approximately 1–4K resolution and approximately 1–12 Mp per frame.

HDTV. High-definition digital television. Common formats are 720p (1280 × 720, progressive), 1080i (1920 × 1080, interlaced), and 1080p (1920 × 1080, progressive).

Head. The beginning of a reel of film or tape.

High-angle shot. A shot in which the camera looks downward toward the subject.

High-key lighting. A lighting plan in which the set is brightly lit and there is a low contrast ratio (in other words, the dark areas of the image are not much darker than the bright areas).

Hollywood montage. *See* Montage.

Hommage. A shot, a scene, or an element within either that is reminiscent of and pays tribute to the work of an earlier filmmaker.

Horizontal lines of resolution. *See* Line.

House. A theatre.

I. *See* Interlaced scanning.

Ideology. A set of interlocking assumptions, values, and expectations held by a person, group, or culture.

Imbibition printing. *See* Technicolor.

IN. Intermediate negative; also **interneg.** A printing element, made from an IP, that is used instead of the camera negative, to protect it. Used to make positive prints and positive intermediates (interpositives). The digital equivalent, an electronic IN, can be used to make a revised final negative. *See* Digital intermediate *and* IP.

Independent. (1) Also **Indie.** Always capitalized; other senses of the word are lower case. A film production company not affiliated with the Motion Picture Patents Company. (2) A filmmaker who works without studio support or interference and who may distribute the film personally or license it to a company that specializes in alternative, nonstudio products. (3) A producer or small company that makes a film autonomously but that may have a financing and distribution deal with a studio.

Insert. A shot, usually of an unmoving object, that is cut into a scene or a sequence; the principal actors, if they or any part of them should appear, are represented by doubles.

Intercutting. (1) Inserting one or more shots into another series of shots or into a master shot. (2) Interweaving shots from separate scenes, not necessarily in a cross-cutting pattern but usually to imply relatedness. *See* Cross-cutting.

Interior. (1) An indoor set. (2) A scene that takes place indoors. *See* Exterior.

Interlaced scanning, abbreviated **i** or **I.** Drawing a video image as two successive fields, one containing the even-numbered scan lines and one the odd lines. The brain combines or interweaves the lines of the two fields into one picture. *See* Progressive scanning.

Intermittent. Any movement, signal, etc. that starts and stops, starts and stops . . . usually at regular intervals.

Intertitle. Any title or title card, whether or not it is superimposed on another image, that appears anywhere between the head credits (or opening titles)

and the tail credits (end titles) of a movie. *See* Credits, Subtitle, *and* Title.

IP. Interpositive; a positive intermediate. Made from the camera negative or from an IN, and used to make a final negative or another IN. *See* Digital intermediate and IN.

Iris. (1) A circular mask. *See* Mask. (2) A transitional device in which the image appears as an expanding circle (an **iris in**) or disappears as a contracting circle (an **iris out**).

Iris shot. A shot whose picture area appears within a circle, whether or not the circle changes size.

Jaggies. *See* Pixelation.

Jidai-geki. In Japan, a costume drama or period piece set in the feudal past.

Jump cut. (1) A cut between two shots that are so similar that the subject appears to jump from one position to another. (2) A disjunctive, disorienting cut; a sudden transition that may be illogical, mismatched, or impatient with normal continuity and that—unlike the match cut—calls attention to itself. *See Faux raccord.*

K. 1,000 pixel lines of resolution, also called lines of horizontal resolution; the lines run vertically. A frame each of whose horizontal or scan lines has roughly 4,000 pixels is a **4K** image, regardless of how many horizontal lines it has (i.e., regardless of the height of the frame).

Kammerspielfilm. In German silent cinema, an intimate "chamber drama," relatively free of intertitles and usually concerned with the close psychological observation of a small number of characters who must deal with the problems of everyday life in realistic but evocatively lit settings; inspired by the *Kammerspiele* of Max Reinhardt (a theatre so small that the audience could see the actors' subtle gestures; also, the plays performed there); formulated by Lupu Pick in reaction against Expressionism.

KB. A kilobyte. *See* MB.

Kinetograph. Edison's first motion picture camera.

Kinetoscope. Edison's electronically operated peephole viewer, often powered by batteries.

Leader. (1) Opaque film spliced to the beginning (**head leader**) and end (**tail leader**) of a reel; used to thread film in a projector and protect it when stored on a reel. (2) Also **Academy leader.** The **countdown** head leader that permits the projectionist to adjust focus and framing as well as to load the projector for a proper changeover (by stopping right after the "3"). (3) Film base cut into a workprint or printing element, the same length as the missing or complementary footage it replaces.

Leitmotif. (1) A recurring musical theme that is associated with a recurring narrative element or theme; perfected by Richard Wagner. (2) A thematically significant narrative element that recurs and develops in the course of a movie.

Level. Degree of volume, intensity, contrast, brightness, pitch, color, etc.; amount of power.

Line. (1) A **scan line**, also called a **line of vertical resolution** or simply a **line;** a horizontal row of pixels. (2) A **pixel line,** also called a **line of horizontal resolution** and a **pixel line of resolution;** a vertical column created by pixels whose positions on their scan lines place them directly above and below each other. (3) The dividing line of a budget; **above-the-line** personnel include the director and stars; **below-the-line** personnel include the crew. (4) An imaginary line running across a set. The camera and action stay to one side of this line in order to maintain screen direction; **crossing the line** reverses screen direction.

Lip sync. Perfect synchronization between picture and sound, so tight that an actor's lip movements and recorded dialogue absolutely match.

Live sound. Tracks recorded during shooting.

Location. A shooting site that is not on a studio lot; often a place where the film's fictional events are set or actual events occurred.

Long lens. A lens with a long focal length and a narrow field of view, which flattens depth relationships and appears to bring the subject closer; a very long lens is called a **telephoto lens.** *See* Focal length.

Long shot. Also **LS, far shot.** A shot that gives a wide, expansive view of the visual field; the camera appears to be far from the subject. In terms of the human figure, a person might be less than half the height of the frame.

Long take. A shot that lasts longer than a minute.

Loop. (1) In the threading path of a camera, printer, or projector, a short length of film that is left slack. (2) A strip of film, tape, or magnetic film whose beginning is joined to its end. (3) To postsynchronize dialogue, specifically by **looping** (listening repeatedly to the live sound, and recording the new reading, on a loop of magnetic film loaded in a dubber that is synchronized with a projector). *See* Dubbing.

Low-angle shot. A shot in which the camera looks upward toward the subject.

Low-key lighting. A lighting plan in which the set is dimly lit, with rich shadows and occasional highlights, and there is a high contrast ratio (in other words, the dark areas of the image are much darker than the bright areas).

Mag. Short for **magnetic.** Magnetic tape or film.

Magnetic film. *See* Film.

Magnetic soundtrack. One or more stripes of magnetized iron-oxide particles bearing the final soundtrack, either on magnetic film that is played by a machine synchronized with the projector or bonded onto the release print (running alongside the frames) and played by the projector.

Mag track. A recording on magnetic film.

Majors. Hollywood's biggest studios, especially during the Studio Era. Originally Fox, MGM, Paramount, RKO, and Warner Bros.; later joined by Columbia and Universal.

Mask. A sheet of metal (a **matte plate**) or cardboard (a **matte card**), painted flat (**matte**) black— or a strip of exposed film (a **fixed matte**) that is transparent in some areas and opaque everywhere else—that admits light only to specific areas of the frame. Used to reshape the frame or in connection with the making of optical composites. *See* Matte.

Master shot. A long take, usually a full or long shot, that covers all the major action of a scene and into which closer or more specific views are intercut.

Match cut. A cut over which an action appears to continue seamlessly. *See* Jump cut.

Matrix. *See* Technicolor.

Matte. (1) Any surface or coating that is "flat" (nonreflective) rather than shiny; most photographic and lighting equipment and accessories are matte black. (2) A mask that admits light freely to certain areas of the frame and completely blocks it from reaching other areas. In most cases, a **mask** is a rigid physical object or camera accessory, and a **matte** is a selectively opaque shot or shot element. *See* Mask *and* Traveling matte.

Matte box. A black, accordion-like device mounted in front of the camera lens (and often fitted with a sunshade or **lens hood**), capable of holding matte cards and filters.

Mb. A megabit, consisting of 2^{20} bits.

MB. A megabyte, consisting of 2^{20} or 1,048,576 bytes. 1,024 **KB** (a kilobyte is 2^{10} or 1,024 bytes).

Medium long shot. Also **MLS.** A shot whose field of view is narrower than that of a long shot but broader than that of a medium shot. *See* Full shot.

Medium shot. Also **midshot, MS.** (1) A shot whose field of view is midway between those of the close shot and the far shot. (2) More precisely, a shot whose field of view is midway between those of the close-up and the full shot. In terms of the human figure, a view from head to thigh might fill the frame.

Melodrama. A popular narrative form that is characterized by intense emotion and draws strong, vivid distinctions between good and evil.

Mindscreen. The field of the mind's eye.

Miniature. A small, model set.

Mise-en-scène. The atmosphere, setting, decor, and texture of a shot. The way a scene has been designed and staged for the camera.

Mix. (1) To balance, combine, and re-record separate tracks, creating an intermediate or final composite soundtrack. (2) A mixing session. (3) The composite soundtrack. (4) A dissolve.

Monopack. Also **integral tripack.** A compound emulsion used in color photography; the three layers of the negative are sensitive to cyan, magenta, and yellow, respectively.

Montage. (1) The dynamic editing of picture and/or sound. (2) The intensive, significant, and often abrupt juxtaposition of shots. *See* Constructive editing, Continuity editing, *and* Dialectical montage. (3) Rapid cutting. (4) A series of overlapping images; in the sound film, usually accompanied by music and used as a transitional device; also known as **Hollywood montage.**

MOS. Minus optical sound; i.e., shot silent. Said to have originated with silent-trained German directors in Hollywood, who preferred to shoot "mit-out sound."

Motion Picture Patents Company. Edison's patent-sharing trust, comprising the nine leading film companies of 1908 (Edison, Biograph, Vitagraph, Essanay, Lubin, Selig, Kalem, Méliès, and Pathé) as well as inventor Thomas Armat and distributor George Kleine. The combine was incorporated and activated in 1908; Méliès was included in 1909, the same year that Eastman agreed to sell perforated raw stock only to members of the MPPC. Disbanded 1917.

Motion Picture Production Code. *See* Production Code.

Movie. (1) A motion picture. (2) A feature-length narrative film.

Movietone. The sound-on-film (**optical sound**) process introduced by Fox; virtually identical to Phonofilm. *See* Phonofilm, Photophone, *and* Vitaphone.

Mp. A megapixel; one million pixels.

MPAA. The Motion Picture Association of America, formerly the **MPPDA** (Motion Picture Producers and Distributors of America). The major studios' trade association.

MPAA rating. *See* CARA.

MPPDA. *See* Hays Office *and* MPAA.

Multiplex cinema. A theatre with many separate auditoriums. *See* Cineplex.

Mutoscope. Biograph's peephole viewer; each frame was printed on paper and mounted on a card, and the cards flipped by as the viewer turned a crank.

Narration. (1) The act of telling or relating, whether or not the account is fictive, the presenter (**narrator**) is personalized, the act is deliberate, or words are employed. (2) Also **narrative.** A text or discourse; the words and/or images delivered by a narrator—who may be a character (*Citizen Kane*), the writer (*The Last Laugh*), a persona (*Annie Hall*), the filmmaker (*2 or 3 Things I Know About Her*), or an impersonal voice (*Jules and Jim*). (3) In sound film, a voice-over commentary; in silent film, the intertitles attributed to a narrator (usually impersonal; sometimes a character).

Narrative. (1) The adjective for **narration.** (2) That which is narrated, whether true or false; the story (or series of events and perceptions) and the discourse in which it is presented.

Narrative film. (1) A movie whose story is primarily or entirely fictitious. (2) Any movie that tells a developing story; this general sense includes many non-fiction, avant-garde, and animated films.

Naturalism. A deterministic realism that accounts for behavior through the close observation of hereditary, instinctive, psychological, social, economic, and political forces, rejecting theistic explanations along with sentimentality.

Negative. (1) Film stock that turns black where it has been exposed to light. (2) The camera original; the negative film run through the camera. (3) The completed movie; the edited and perfected final negative, from which release prints may be struck directly or from which a printing element can be made. (So that the negative isn't worn out making prints, it can be copied to an IP, which is copied to an IN, from which the prints are struck until it wears out and another IN is made from the IP.)

Negative cost. The cost of producing a movie, exclusive of making and distributing multiple prints. All the expenses, from optioning the first script to paying the last bill from the lab, incurred in making one copy of the film—i.e., the final negative, from which the final approved print was struck.

Negative pick-up. Also **pickup.** A deal whereby a studio buys (or belatedly co-produces) and distributes an independently produced film.

Neorealism. Particularly in Italy after World War II, a "new realism" characterized by location shooting, scripted dialogue that sounds improvised, the use of nonprofessional actors in the majority of roles, an emphasis on the everyday struggles of common people and the unvarnished look of nonstudio reality, the rejection of bourgeois fantasy as well as of Expressionism, and the determination to present the characters in relation to their real social environments and political and economic conditions.

Net. The amount of money earned by a film after all expenses are deducted. *See* Gross.

New Wave. (1) In France in 1959–60, the sudden appearance, on many fronts, of a host of brilliant films by directors who had not previously made features or whose earlier work had gone unnoticed. Also **la nouvelle vague.** (2) Any sudden appearance of many exciting new filmmakers in a country whose films have been undistinguished—and may have done little or no international business—for a long time.

Nickelodeon. The first permanent movie theatre in America, which was converted from a store, opened in 1905; it was called a nickelodeon because admission to the theatre (*odeon* in Greek) cost a nickel.

Nitrate film. Film whose base is made of cellulose nitrate; explosive, and obsolete since 1951, but often visually superior to safety-base film.

Nonlinear editing. Assembling randomly accessible electronic copies of shots into temporary or final sequence, whether they are stored as video clips or—in the case of **digital nonlinear editing**—as digital files.

Normal lens. A lens whose focal length is neither long nor short and that reproduces perspective much as it is seen by the human eye. *See* Focal length.

NTSC. The conventional TV system used in the U.S., Japan, and many other countries. It shows 30 fps as 60 interlaced fields. The standard calls for 525 lines, of which 480 are displayed.

Offscreen. Also **OS.** Outside of camera range.

Online. Also **on-line.** Connected to a network.

Optical composite. Any image created by combining elements from two or more separately photographed images, or combining two or more complete images, usually on an optical printer. The term can also apply to a digital visual composite made on a computer.

Optical printer. A film copier in which the original and the printing stock are not in physical contact during the instant of exposure (in a contact printer, they are); instead, one or more optical systems intervene, allowing part or all of the original image to be rephotographed with or without modifications. An image might be cropped, flipped, repeated, superimposed on another, distorted, filtered, used in a special-effects composite, and so forth. The optical printer itself might be thought of as a camera facing a projector. *See* Printer *and* Special effects.

Optical soundtrack. A continuous black-and-white, **sound-on-film** image area running down one edge of the film (adjacent to the frames), containing the movie's final soundtrack and designed to allow varying amounts of light to pass through it to a photocell.

Orthochromatic film. Early black-and-white film stock, sensitive to blue and green (and, much less so, to yellow) but not to red or orange; replaced **monochromatic film,** which was sensitive only to blue. *See* Panchromatic film.

Overcranking. *See* Slow motion.

P. *See* Progressive scanning.

PAL. The conventional TV system used in China, most of Europe, and many other countries. It shows 25 fps as 50 interlaced fields. The standard calls for 625 lines, of which 576 are displayed.

Pan. (1) To pivot the camera horizontally, turning it from side to side. (2) Also **panning shot** and

panoramic shot. A shot within which the camera pivots on a vertical axis, turning in a horizontal plane.

Pan and scan. To copy a wide image to 1.33:1—usually for TV broadcasting, flat film prints, or full-screen video—by using an optical printer to move around a 4×3 frame (whose contents will be copied to the print, while the rest will be discarded) within the image, sometimes by panning and sometimes by cutting.

Panavision. The 35mm anamorphic format that replaced CinemaScope; also the company that developed a new line of cameras and lenses. The aspect ratio was 2.35:1 until the early 1970s, when it was changed to 2.4:1.

Panchromatic film. Black-and-white film stock, in use since 1926, that is sensitive to the entire spectrum. Because its speed, or photosensitivity, was less than that of the orthochromatic film it replaced, it required wider lens-aperture settings and yielded inferior depth of field.

Paper print. A positive copy of a film, made on sheets of paper and sent to the Library of Congress (until 1907, when copyright law was revised to allow the registration and protection of materials not printed on paper) to establish copyright on each of the photographs that constituted the movie.

Parallel montage. Cross-cutting between two or more separate actions (different enough to "collide" when juxtaposed) to imply that they are dramatically or thematically related.

Patent Company. *See* Motion Picture Patents Company.

PCA. *See* Production Code.

Perf. Perforation. Informal term for a sprocket hole.

Perforated stock. Film or mag stock that has sprocket holes along one or both edges.

Persistence of vision. Retinal retention of a bright image that is followed by darkness.

Phi phenomenon. Also **phi effect.** The process of combining perceived fragments into a mental whole, as when preconsciously deducing and hallucinating movement from a series of stills, believing that one sees a continuous action rather than a series of consecutive but frozen phases of motion. In the first experiments, the subjects saw a light move from position A to position B when, in fact, the unmoving light at A had flashed, followed by the unmoving light at B. What they saw is called **beta movement** if the light appears to traverse the whole distance from A to B (as a figure in a movie might appear to move from position A in frame 1 to position B in frame 2); seeing beta movement, or any apparent movement of "the" light, depends on the distance between the lights and the interval between the flashes. The subjects saw beta movement involuntarily, which suggests that the phi phenomenon has "hard-wired" neural aspects as well as preconscious ones. Discovered by Max Wertheimer.

Phonofilm. The sound-on-film process invented by Lee de Forest. *See* Movietone.

Photocell. Also **photoelectric cell.** A device that converts light into electrical impulses—for example, when responding to light that has passed through an optical soundtrack.

Photophone. The sound-on-film process developed by RCA; it used a variable area optical soundtrack (as most contemporary systems do) rather than a variable density track. *See* Movietone, Phonofilm, *and* Vitaphone.

Photosensitivity. The degree to which an emulsion reacts to light.

Pickup. *See* Negative pick-up.

Picture. (1) A movie. (2) The image track of a movie, as distinct from the soundtrack. The moving image in a projected scene. (3) The image area of a frame, surrounded by the frame-line, soundtrack, and sprocket-hole areas.

Pixel. Picture element. (1) The basic unit of an electronic image; the smallest block in a video display or frame. Usually square and displaying a single mixed color, but sometimes made of a tightly clustered triangle of red-value, green-value, and blue-value dots. The term is used whether the video frame is analog or digital. Pixels are laid out in tightly adjacent rows, creating a rectangle composed of tiny squares. The area, aspect ratio, and resolution of a frame can be calculated using the number of pixels in each scan line or horizontal row (the horizontal dimension) and the number of such rows (the vertical dimension, equal to the number of pixels from the top to the bottom of the image). Common frame and display sizes, in pixels, include 640×480 (.6K; .3 Mp; 1.33:1) and 1920×1080 (2K; 2 Mp; 1.78:1). (2) Loosely, the smallest discernible component of a film image. In pixels, a 35mm Academy frame is 4096×3072 (4K; 12.6 Mp; 1.33:1). *See* Aspect ratio, K, Line, *and* Mp.

Pixelation. Enlarging a video image so much that the individual pixels can be seen as little blocks; e.g., a diagonal line develops **jaggies** (jagged lines of blocky pixels where a line or curve should be smooth) and looks like a staircase or the blade of a hand saw.

Pixel lines of resolution. *See* K *and* Line.

Pixillation. The art of animating a person or an object that is capable of moving under its own power—and may well move between exposures. *See* Stop-motion animation.

Plan-séquence. *See* Sequence shot.

Plastic material. Visually expressive objects and images; formulated by Vsevolod Pudovkin.

Positive. An image or print whose color or black-and-white values correspond to those in the subject; created either by shooting **reversal** film (which yields a direct positive image) or by making a negative of a negative.

Post-production. The phase of filmmaking during which picture and sound are augmented and edited into final form, after the conclusion of principal photography.

Post-synchronization. (1) The process of recording, after the picture has been shot, a track that is to accompany a particular MOS (silent) shot—or to be substituted for a track recorded during production—and of synchronizing this and other wild tracks with the picture. *See* Dubbing *and* Wild track. (2) The process of creating and synchronizing a soundtrack for a film shot silent or in a foreign language.

POV shot. Point-of-view shot, also known as **subjective camera.** A shot in which the camera adopts the vantage point of a character's physical eye or literal gaze, showing what the character sees.

Pre-production. The practical planning phase of filmmaking, including all the work (location scouting, set construction, costume design, etc.) that must be done before shooting can get under way.

Primary color. *See* RGB.

Principal photography. The process of shooting the principal performers and every dialogued scene in the script; the core activity of the production phase of filmmaking.

Print. (1) A positive, projectable copy of a film. (2) Any printed copy of a film, whether positive or negative, intermediate or final. (3) To duplicate a frame, a shot, a reel, or a complete movie, with or without making alterations.

Printer. A film-copying machine that directs light through processed film (the original) onto raw stock (which, when processed, becomes the print). A **contact printer** is used for relatively simple duplication, such as making a release print from a final negative, a workprint from a camera negative, or a brighter copy of a shot that is too dark. A **bi-pack printer,** or a contact printer adapted for the purpose, exposes two or more sandwiched filmstrips at once to the blank film. An **optical printer** is used to create optical special effects. A **film recorder** "prints" a digital image on film.

Problem picture. An issue-oriented feature film, particularly one that calls attention to a contemporary, real-world topic of concern.

Processor. *See* CCD *and* Chip.

Producer. (1) The person who selects and hires the creative team to write and shoot a film, pays all the costs of filmmaking, owns the finished product, and arranges for the film's distribution. (2) The business entity that collectively performs the functions of an individual producer. (3) The studio or production-company executive who authorizes and directly or indirectly supervises the making of a film.

Production. (1) A filmmaking project. (2) The activity of making a film. (3) The shooting phase of filmmaking, particularly that involving the principal actors (which is called **principal photography**). It is prepared for in pre-production (scheduling, production design, etc.) and followed by post-production (editing, mixing, etc.).

Production Code. Also **The Motion Picture Production Code of 1930.** A moralistic list of what could and could not be shown or endorsed in a Hollywood film. A producer's self-censorship guide, considered preferable to censorship by groups outside the film industry, the Code was drawn up in 1930, approved by the Hays Office, and officially adopted by producers and distributors that same year. It was first enforced in 1934, when Joseph Breen was appointed to run the Production Code Administration.

Production designer. An art director responsible for designing the complete look of a film, coordinating and integrating its sets, dressings, props, costumes, and color schemes.

Production still. (1) A photograph, shot with a still camera, that is taken on the set, often approximating a scene in the film or illustrating some aspect of the making of the film. (2) The photographs included in a film's press kit, including production and publicity stills.

Program picture. A run-of-the-mill feature; a film made to fill basic programming needs, because theatres had to show *something.*

Progressive scanning, abbreviated **p** or **P.** Drawing a complete video image as a single field in a single pass. In most systems, each frame is shown twice to avoid flicker (two identical fields per frame, where interlaced scanning has two different fields per frame). *See* Interlaced scanning.

Prop. Also **property.** A physical object handled by an actor or displayed as part of a set; the term excludes set dressings and costumes.

Property. (1) An owned work. (2) A concept, script, or pre-existing work (a **literary property**) that is being considered for production. (3) A film currently in production. (4) A prop.

Rating. *See* CARA.

Raw. Unexposed and unprocessed.

Reaction shot. A cutaway or reverse shot that shows how one or more characters react to an off-screen action, usually one that has been shown in the preceding shot.

Realism. A representational style that attempts to present a state of affairs without distortion.

Rear projection. Also **back projection.** The projection of stills or footage onto a translucent screen, from behind that screen, to provide a background for the live action that is performed between the screen and the camera.

Reel. (1) 1,000 feet of 35mm film—in practice, between 900 and 990 feet—wound on a reel or core; in 16mm, a full reel is 400 feet of film. At silent speed, a full reel is approximately 12–17 minutes long; at sound speed, approximately 11 minutes long. (2) Up to 2,000 feet of 35mm film, wound on the metal projection reels in use today. In practice, 15–20 minutes at sound speed. Also **double reel.** (3) A metal or plastic spool on which film or tape is wound; unlike a core, a reel has outside rims or flanges.

Reflexivity. (1) Self-referentiality, displayed by a work or by its creator. (2) Also **self-consciousness.** The implication that a work of art is aware of itself as a work of art, either as an artifice in a particular creative tradition or as an autonomous and self-directing structure.

Release date. The date—loosely, the year—a film is first shown to a public audience, not on a sneak-preview basis but as an official opening. *See* Completion date.

Release negative. The final negative of the release version, from which IPs and release prints are struck.

Release print. An original positive print (not a dupe of such a print) that is officially put into distribution and designed to be projected.

Release version. The approved, final cut; the text or version of a movie that is approved for release and distribution.

Resolution. The degree of fine detail within an image; the extent to which a fuzzy circle, glob, or polygon can be seen as the sharp circle it's supposed to be; the extent to which the smallest components of a picture cohere into an image. Related to the number of dots per inch in a photograph and to the number of pixels in an electronic image at a certain display size. Resolution increases as the size of the smallest picture elements decreases and their number increases. All these definitions assume that the image is perfectly focused, so that each picture component is as sharp as it can be.

Restoration. Ideally, returning a film to the condition it was in when it was new and complete.

Reversal. *See* Positive.

Reverse-angle shot. Also **reverse shot.** (1) A shot that reverses the field of view over a cut, as if the camera had turned 180° to the rear. (2) One in a series of alternating, complementary views (a **shot/reverse-shot** pattern) whose angles are usually separated by 120–160°; often used for conversations.

Reverse motion. Backwards action, achieved by printing or projecting a shot from last frame to first.

RGB. Red, green, and blue. (1) The **additive** or **light primaries,** as distinct from the subtractive, pigment, or dye primaries. Full-strength red, green, and blue lights add to white light. **Subtractive** or **colorant primaries** (yellow, cyan, and magenta, or **YCM,** used in color negative film), equally mixed, subtract all their color values from white and produce black, as do RGB dyes. Magenta paint, for example, reflects magenta and absorbs all other colors. Film is a subtractive color system, removing its colors from the projector's white light; TV is an additive color system. (2) The level, shade, brightness, etc. of the red component of a color image is its **R** or **red value;** RGB is shorthand for those three values, which mix to produce the color of a pixel.

Rushes. *See* Dailies.

Safety-base film. Camera or printing stock that has a slow-burning base made primarily of cellulose triacetate (originally, cellulose acetate), in contrast to the explosive base of nitrate film, which it replaced.

Sampling. The process of regularly dipping into an analog flow, or anything that can be represented as a waveform, to measure its position, voltage, shade, or other value at that instant; done thousands of times per second. Each discrete sample is converted to digital form at a specified level of complexity (**digitized**); the number of bits per sample (and per second) directly affects the color accuracy and resolution of a digitized frame—or, in music, the richness and complexity of a digitized sound.

Scan. (1) To draw an image by moving a laser or other tight beam (originally, the beam in a cathode-ray tube) across a surface in a series of horizontal lines. *See* Film recorder *and* Line. (2) To capture an image, including the image of a document, with a scanner.

Scan lines. *See* Line.

Scenario. A film script or screenplay.

Scene. (1) A dramatic action or interaction that takes place in a single location. (2) A complete unit of action that is capable of being covered in a single shot, regardless of how many shots are actually used to cover it. (3) The shot(s) in which a scene is presented.

Schüfftan process. A production special effect that allows actors, artwork, partial full-scale sets, and miniature sets to be photographed together; developed by Eugen Schüfftan.

Scope. Anamorphic; derived from "CinemaScope."

Score. (1) The original music composed for a film. (2) The music arranged for a film.

Screen direction. (1) In the interests of spatial continuity and logic, the practice of keeping track of the directions in which people or objects are facing or moving. (2) The trajectory of movement (or direction of a gaze, orientation of an object, etc.) within, across, and in relation to the borders of the frame

(e.g., toward screen right); its orientation to real or hypothetical three-dimensional space (e.g., toward the east window); and the continuity of that space as it is created by the continuity of trajectory from shot to shot (e.g., to indicate in a cross-cut sequence that X and Y, who are never seen in the same shot, are running in the same direction up opposite sides of the street, X runs up the west side of the street and toward screen right, and Y runs up the east side of the street and toward screen left).

Screen left. The left side of the screen, as seen by the audience.

Screen right. The right side of the screen, as seen by the audience.

Screenwriter. The author or co-author of a screenplay; the artist who first determines the structure, characters, themes, events, and dialogue of a film as well as many of its crucial images.

SDDS. Sony Dynamic Digital Sound, an eight-channel digital surround soundtrack that is printed, as a stream of microscopic dots, on the outer edges of the 35mm filmstrip.

Segue. A sound dissolve; pronounced *seg-way*.

Self-consciousness. *See* Reflexivity.

Semiotics. Also **semiology.** The study of signs and signifying systems.

Sensor. *See* CCD.

Sequel. A film whose action follows or predates (as a **prequel**) that of a previously released film, whose essential narrative and thematic elements it sets out to vary, extend, and repeat. Unlike the films in a series, the original and its sequels are meant to be shown in numerical order (or release order, if the films aren't numbered).

Sequence. (1) Any group of consecutive shots and/or scenes. (2) A series of interrelated shots that is not restricted to covering an action in a single location and that has its own beginning, middle, and end (subtly limited structure) and distinct project (function, style, or concern) within the whole of the film; e.g., the dream sequence that opens *Wild Strawberries* or the Odessa Steps sequence in *Battleship Potemkin*. (3) A series of interrelated scenes with a consistent dramatic project, constituting a significant unit of the structured narrative; e.g., the Bernstein sequence in *Citizen Kane* or the chain-gang sequence in *Sullivan's Travels*.

Sequence shot. Also *plan-séquence*. A scene that is covered in a single long take whose camera movements are, in most cases, intricately blocked.

Serial. A film made of chapters that are shown at regular intervals—in most cases, weekly.

Series. (1) A set of films that feature the same main characters and generally may be shown in any order. (2) Loosely, a set of sequels.

Set. (1) A decorated sound stage. (2) An artificially constructed setting, whether interior or exterior. (3) Any site where a movie is shot.

Set dressing. (1) Furniture, fixtures, and objects attached to the walls or floor of an interior set. (2) Integral parts of an exterior set. *See* Prop.

Setup. The position (location and angle) of the camera, fitted with a particular lens, at the start of a take; any number of shots may be taken from the same setup.

70mm. Film that is 70 millimeters wide; most often used for release prints of films that have been shot on 65mm negative stock or of 35mm anamorphic and Super 35mm flat films that have been blown up.

SFX. Sound effects.

Shomin-geki. In Japan, the drama or comedy about ordinary, modern-day people, usually from the lower-middle class; a subgenre of the *gendai-geki*.

Short lens. A lens with a short focal length and a broad field of view, which exaggerates depth relationships in the visual field; a very short lens is called a **wide-angle lens**. *See* Focal length.

Shot. (1) A continuously exposed series of frames, beginning and ending with a cut or other transitional device. (2) A take. (3) In animation and special effects, a series of individual or composite frames that gives the impression of having been continuously exposed.

Shot/reverse-shot. *See* Reverse-angle shot.

Shutter. A device that, when open, allows light to reach and expose the film in a camera or printer—or shine through the film and the lens in a projector—and that, when shut, keeps out light and allows the next frame to be advanced into position.

Silent speed. Approximately 16–20 fps, but conventionally defined as 16 fps. *See* Fps.

16mm. Film that is 16 millimeters wide; the smallest professional gauge and a low-budget format.

Slow film. Film whose emulsion has a low "speed," requiring bright lighting.

Slow motion. Also **overcranking.** The effect of slowed-down movement, achieved by exposing more than the normal number of frames per second (i.e., shooting at a rate greater than the projection rate).

Socialist Realism. The Stalinist insistence that art serve the interests of the state and be clear to anyone; to be arty was to be elitist and confusing, and to deviate from the Party line was to fail to communicate plain reality.

Sound composite. Any recording created by mixing other recordings, whether analog or digital.

Sound speed. 24 fps, although some formats have been designed for higher rates (multi-film Cinerama ran at 26 fps, early Todd-AO at 30 fps). Movies compatible with PAL run at 25 fps. *See* Fps.

Sound stage. Also **soundstage.** A large, windowless, soundproof building in which sound films are shot on artificially lit sets.

Soundtrack. Also **sound track.** (1) The final sound composite; all the sounds heard in a film. (2) The optical, digital, or magnetic track(s) in which that composite is stored; usually an integral part of the release print. *See* Channel.

Special effects. (1) Physical effects that can be staged for the camera and shot in real time (e.g., a tree crashing through a window). Also known as **production effects.** (2) Production effects that entail the use of machines (e.g., an electronically detonated explosion). Also **mechanicals, mechanical special effects, special mechanical effects.** (3) Photographic illusions created through nonroutine shooting or printing techniques, usually during post-production (e.g., a traveling matte in which a bicyclist crosses the face of the moon). Also **opticals, optical special effects, special optical effects, special effects cinematography, SPFX.** (4) Visual effects achieved on a computer; also **digital effects, DFX.**

Speed. (1) The rate at which frames are exposed or projected. (2) The degree to which an emulsion reacts to light and the rapidity with which it does so; the "faster"—more photosensitive—an emulsion is, the less light is required for adequate exposure and the grainier an image is likely to be. (3) A measure of the light-gathering ability of a lens.

SPFX. Special effects, especially those achieved on an optical printer. *See* Special effects.

Spherical lens. A lens that preserves the normal horizontal and vertical relationships found in the subject. *See* Anamorphic lens *and* Flat.

Splice. The physical bond that joins one piece of film to another; also, to make such a bond, usually with glue or tape.

Split reel. (1) A film that is half a reel or less in length (where a full reel is 1,000 feet of 35mm film). (2) A reel, one of whose sides may be unscrewed to allow the insertion or removal of film that has been tightly wound on a core.

Split screen. Also **split-screen.** Any frame containing two or more separate and distinct frames or images.

Sprocket. Also **sprocket wheel.** The toothed wheel that engages and advances film in a camera, printer, or projector.

Sprocket holes. Also **perforations, perfs.** The regularly spaced holes—into which the pins of claw mechanisms and the teeth of sprocket wheels precisely fit—that run along one or both edges of motion picture film and one edge of mag film.

Squeeze. (1) The degree to which an image is horizontally compressed. (2) To make an image less wide, especially when photographing a wide field on normal film. *See* Anamorphic.

Steadicam. A camera mount, worn by the operator, that allows the camera to remain level even when the operator moves, ensuring extremely smooth hand-held traveling shots.

Still. A single photograph, taken by a conventional still camera rather than a movie camera.

Stock. *See* Film stock.

Stock footage. Miscellaneous shots and scenes kept in a studio's film archive for repeated use; sufficiently famous (major news events) or anonymous (planes in flight) to be cut into a movie without the expense of new shooting.

Stop-action photography. Also **stop-motion photography.** Stopping the camera, making a change or letting a change take place in the action area, and then restarting the camera, creating what appears to be a continuous shot within which everything suddenly shifts position or something is instantly changed into something else.

Stop-motion animation. Frame-by-frame shooting of a model (e.g., King Kong), a cutout, or any object incapable of moving under its own power. *See* Pixillation.

Studio. A large production company with its own lot; ideally, equipped with everything necessary to plan, shoot, edit, mix, and release motion pictures.

Studio system. The control of all aspects of film production, distribution, and (when legal) exhibition by a small number of big studios. Also the division of labor within the studio, with one department for writing, another for costumes, etc., and the practice of keeping all employees—including directors and stars—answerable to the studio executives' plans for their careers, decisions about which films should be made, and concepts of the studio's "house" style and entertainment mission.

Subjective camera. (1) A shot or setup that shows what a character sees; a **POV** (point-of-view) shot. (2) Loosely, a shot, scene, or sequence that shows what a character remembers, relates, dreams, hallucinates, or imagines; a mindscreen.

Subjective sound. A track that presents what a character hears, does not hear (e.g., if deaf), or imagines hearing.

Subtitle. A line of words printed near the bottom of the screen; in most cases a condensed translation of foreign-language dialogue. Considered intertitles only when part of the original movie.

Superimposition. Multiple exposure; printing or shooting one image over another.

Super 35mm. Film that is 35mm wide and that is shot full aperture—using the entire available picture area, including the area normally reserved for the analog soundtrack. Wide frames are achieved by masking. **Super 1.85,** or American widescreen shot on Super 35, is 1.85:1 and projected flat through a conventional masking aperture plate. Even 2.4:1 is shot flat, but the frames are squeezed on the print for anamorphic projection. *See* Academy aperture *and* Aspect ratio.

Surrealism. An avant-garde movement that sought to pursue within artistic structures the juxtapositions, transitions, and bizarre logic characteristic of dreams and the unconscious.

Surround. In theatrical stereo, a channel played through speakers on the side and rear walls of the auditorium. In **split-surround** (used in *Apocalypse Now* and later in Dolby Digital), there are two distinct surround channels, permitting sounds to be placed in the left rear or right rear of the sound field, or a sound source to appear to move diagonally above the audience.

SVA. *See* Dolby Stereo.

Swish pan. A panning movement so rapid that the image is reduced to streaks.

Sync. Synchronization, especially between picture and sound. *See* Lip sync.

Tail. The end of a reel of film or tape.

Take. (1) An unedited shot, beginning when the camera starts exposing film and ending when the camera stops. (2) An attempt to photograph a shot; the attempts that prove satisfactory are printed.

Technicolor. **Imbibition printing,** also called the **dye transfer process,** and the company that perfected it. The process of applying dyes directly onto the print (rather than putting the dyes through the film developing process) by means of a **matrix,** which is a celluloid strip bearing various thicknesses of hardened gelatin that is capable of absorbing and shedding dyes. In three-strip Technicolor, each of the three matrices is a black-and-white record of the red, green, or blue in the image (in negative, the cyan, magenta, or yellow, respectively).

Telecine. An apparatus that converts a film image to a video signal and then digitizes it; it can also synchronize frame rates between film and video.

Telephoto lens. (1) A lens with a very long focal length and a very narrow field of view; it has a high factor of magnification (as if telescopic) and flattens depth relationships. (2) Loosely, any long lens. *See* Focal length *and* Wide-angle lens.

35mm. Film that is 35 millimeters wide; the standard professional film gauge.

Tilt. (1) To pivot the camera upward or downward. (2) A shot within which the camera pivots on a horizontal axis, moving in a vertical plane; a tilting movement. Also known as **tilt shot, tilting shot.** (3) A shot in which the camera is tilted to the side, so that the top and bottom of the frame are not parallel to the lateral horizontal axis of the set. Also known as **Dutch angle, Dutch tilt shot, off-angle shot.**

Time code. Also **timecode.** Time information, recorded on film or tape; used for synchronization and for locating particular scenes or frames. Originally developed for synchronizing videotape and film, it can also synchronize multiple devices. (1) A windowed display of the elapsed time the picture has been running, in hours, minutes, seconds, and frames. (2) A crystal-generated pulse that is invariable and for which a start time, shared by two or more devices, can be established; from then on, all the devices run on the same time and in perfect sync, driven by or referenced to the time code. Any irregular film and tape they might produce can be sped up or slowed down in reference to the time code.

Timing. Correcting overexposure, underexposure, and color values when making a print.

Tinting. The process of evenly and monochromatically coloring an originally black-and-white shot, either by dyeing the film or by printing on colored stock. In a tinted shot of a face, the whites of the eyes are colored. *See* Toning.

Title. (1) A shot consisting primarily or entirely of words; it may appear on its own, as did most of the narrative and dialogue intertitles in silent film, or be superimposed over another shot. The term includes head and tail credits, intertitles, title cards, scrolling titles (titles that "crawl" up the screen), and subtitles. (2) The name of a work.

Title card. A stable, full-frame title; also the card (which may or may not be decorated) on which the words are drawn or printed, and the shot of the card. Includes virtually all head and tail credits and narrative and dialogue titles in silent film and the majority of superimposed or stand-alone titles today, but excludes crawls and subtitles.

Titles. (1) The sequence of title cards that includes the name of the film. (2) The opening or closing credits. (3) The intertitles, considered as a group.

Toning. The process of chemically converting a black-and-white image to a monochromatic color image; the darker the image (i.e., the greater the concentration of exposed silver crystals), the deeper the color. In a toned shot of a face, the whites of the eyes are white. *See* Tinting.

Track. (1) An individual recording. *See* Channel, Dolby Stereo, Mix, *and* Soundtrack. (2) One of the steel rails on which the steel wheels of a camera platform could smoothly ride; also one of the boards, laid over uneven terrain, on which the rubber wheels of a dolly may ride. (3) To move the camera forward, backward, to the side, diagonally, or along a curve, usually with perfect smoothness. The term excludes pivoting (pans and tilts), crane, and aerial movements as well as apparent camera move-

ments (zooms in the camera or an optical printer). *See* Dolly, Track shot, *and* Traveling shot.

Track shot. Also **tracking shot, trucking shot.** (1) A shot taken from a camera platform whose steel wheels ride on steel rails (**tracks**); characterized by smooth movement along straight lines and relatively gentle curves. (2) Any shot in which the camera moves (**tracks**) forward, backward, to the side, diagonally, along a curve, or across the ground; the term excludes shots taken from a crane or plane—as well as pans, tilts, and zooms. *See* Traveling shot. (3) A track shot taken from a dolly; often characterized by complex movements that would be almost impossible to lay out in steel and by the absence of rails on the floor. Also known as **dolly shot.**

Traveling matte. Also **travelling matte.** (1) A matte that can vary the contours of its opaque area(s) from frame to frame; a film of a moving silhouette. (2) An optical composite that seamlessly, and without see-through ("phantom") effects, integrates elements from different shots into one image; isolated through special photographic and printing techniques, the elements are combined in an optical printer. (3) A video or digital composite, created by electronic matting techniques, of moving elements from separate sources.

Traveling shot. Any track shot, dolly shot, crane shot, following shot, hand-held shot, or aerial shot in which the camera moves from one place to another. The term excludes pans and tilts (in which the camera only pivots) and zoom shots (in which the lens is adjusted and the camera stays put).

Tri-format prints. Also **triformat prints.** Release prints that include Dolby Digital, DTS, and SDDS digital soundtracks.

Trust. A group of companies in the same field, formed to reduce competition and control prices. Illegal.

TV safe area. The part of a film image that is sure to be displayed on a properly working television. Vital actions and credits are kept inside it. A rectangle sometimes etched on the camera's viewfinder (as are the Academy frame and a rectangle corresponding to the film's theatrical aspect ratio).

24p. A digital video camera that can expose 24 progressive frames per second at 2K or 4K. The first model was Sony's HDW-F900.

Two-shot. A shot of two people.

Uncut. Unabridged.

Undercranking. *See* Fast motion.

Underscoring. Music that accompanies a shot, scene, or sequence but is not being played by any character or object (radio, record, etc.) in the movie; nondiegetic music.

Variable area track. An optical soundtrack whose amplitude or contour varies but whose density (a measure of opacity) remains constant.

Variable density track. An optical soundtrack whose dimensions remain constant but whose degree of opacity (**density**) varies.

VCR. *See* Videocassette recorder.

Vertical integration. An economic structure in which every aspect of production and distribution is controlled from the top.

Vertical lines of resolution. *See* Line.

Video. (1) Closed-circuit television. (2) The art and technology of television. (3) A work made to be televised or shown on a monitor. (4) A videotape, laserdisc, or DVD copy of a movie or of a video work. (5) An electronic image or work that can be electronically displayed or transferred to film.

Videocassette recorder. Also **VCR.** A videotape deck that electronically records and plays back audiovisual information that may be displayed on a television; the videotape is wound on cores in a case, so that the tape itself need not be handled.

Visual masking. The phenomenon whereby the brain stops processing a frame that is followed by an instant of visual noise (a period of no information or random information; in some experiments, a white card worked best and black did not work at all), clearing the mental slate for the next frame and defeating any image-confusing effects that might be caused by persistence of vision.

Vitaphone. The **sound-on-disc** process first used by Warner Bros.; eventually made obsolete by the sound-on-film process. *See* Movietone, Optical soundtrack, Phonofilm, *and* Photophone.

Vitascope. Edison's first projector, invented by Thomas Armat and C. Francis Jenkins and incorporating the Latham loop. *See* Loop.

Voice-over. Also **voice-over narration, V-O.** A commentative dialogue track (sometimes presented as an interior monologue) that is not being delivered aloud by any onscreen or offscreen indigenous source; instead it is laid "over" the indigenous sounds of the scene.

Wide-angle lens. (1) A lens with a very short focal length and a very broad field of view; it deepens or exaggerates depth relationships in the visual field and produces distorted, bowed images of objects that are very near the camera. (2) Loosely, any short lens. *See* Focal length *and* Telephoto lens.

Wide screen. Any film format, whether flat or anamorphic, that has an aspect ratio greater than 1.4:1. The adjective is **wide-screen**.

Widescreen. A 35mm flat format whose aspect ratio is 1.85:1 in America, 1.78:1 in HDTV and most HDDV, and 1.66:1 in Europe. The adjective is **widescreen**.

Wild track. Also **wild recording, wild sound.** A recording made without camera synchronization.

Wipe. A transitional effect in which one image appears to push another off the screen (the moving boundary between the images is the **wipe line**) or in which parts of one shot are removed while parts of the next shot appear in their place.

Workprint. Also **work print.** A working copy of the film, edited on film into rough final form; also the positive print of the camera footage, which is cut and recut by the editor. The final, approved workprint is used as a guide when mixing the sound and cutting the negative. Made nearly obsolete by digital and video editing machines.

Writer. *See* Screenwriter.

Zoom. To adjust the focal length of a zoom lens while the camera is running; also a shot taken while the zoom is being adjusted. As the focal length is shortened (a **zoom out** or **backward zoom**), the lens behaves more like a wide-angle lens, exaggerating depth relationships, decreasing magnification, and widening the field of view so that the camera appears to move away from the subject; as the focal length is increased (a **zoom in** or **forward zoom**), the lens behaves more like a telephoto lens, flattening depth relationships, increasing magnification, and narrowing the field of view so that the camera appears to move closer to the subject.

Zoom lens. A lens with a variable (rather than a fixed) focal length, which allows the camera operator or assistant to widen or narrow the field of view without moving the camera or stopping to change lenses.

Acknowledgments

Film Stills

The author and publisher wish to thank the following for making available photographic stills:

from *Scorpio Rising;* courtesy of Kenneth Anger.

from *Wavelength;* courtesy of Anthology Film Archives.

A Kinetoscope Parlor and *Fred Ott's Sneeze;* reprinted courtesy of Arno Press, Inc., 1970.

from the films *Diary of a Country Priest, 8½, Closely Watched Trains, Viridiana, Pather Panchali, Throne of Blood,* and *The Bicycle Thief;* courtesy of Audio-Brandon Films.

from *La strada;* courtesy of Avco-Embassy Films.

from the films *Mothlight* and *existence is song;* courtesy of Stan Brakhage.

from *Faces;* courtesy of Ray Carney and the Estate of John Cassavetes. Frame enlargement from *Faces* reproduced by permission; copyright © Faces International Films. Photography by Al Ruban.

from *Terminator 2: Judgment Day;* courtesy of Carolco Films.

from *The White Balloon* by Jafar Panahi, 1995, Iran. Reproduced by permission of Celluloid Dreams, Agent for Jafar Panahi.

from *Women on the Verge of a Nervous Breakdown;* courtesy of Cinevista, Inc.

from *Blood Simple* and *The Killer;* courtesy of Circle Releasing Corporation.

from the films *Lawrence of Arabia,* copyright © 1962, and *On the Waterfront;* both courtesy of Columbia Pictures Industries, Inc. All rights reserved.

from *Halloween;* courtesy of Compass International Pictures.

from the films *Breathless, Vivre sa vie, The Children of Paradise,* and *A nous la liberté;* courtesy of Contemporary Films/McGraw-Hill.

from *La Cienaga;* Courtesy Cowboy Pictures.

from *Blue Velvet;* courtesy of DEG Communications.

from the films *New York Stories, The Skeleton Dance, Steamboat Willie,* and *Who Framed Roger Rabbit;* courtesy of The Walt Disney Company. Used by permission, copyright © The Walt Disney Company.

from *Mighty Joe Young;* courtesy of Disney Enterprises, Inc.

from *The Fall of the House of Usher;* courtesy of the George Eastman House.

from *The Book of All the Dead,* Canada. Reproduced by permission of Bruce Elder.

from *Once Upon a Time in America;* copyright © 1984 Embassy International Pictures.

from *A Trip to the Moon, The General, The Pawn Shop, One A.M., The Last Laugh,* and *Easy Street;* courtesy of Em Gee Film Library.

from *Hiroshima Mon Amour,* 1959, France, Argos Films S. A. R. L. Reproduced by permission of Gades Films International Ltd.

from *France/Tour/Détour/Deux/Enfants;* courtesy of Jean-Luc Godard.

from *Stranger Than Paradise;* courtesy of the Samuel Goldwyn Company. © 1984 Cinesthesia Productions Inc.

from *Chunhyang,* Courtesy Korean Film Commissioner Hong-Joon Kim.

from *Iphigenia;* courtesy of Andrew Horton.

from *Down By Law;* courtesy of Island Pictures Inc. © 1986, Black Snake, Inc. All rights reserved.

from the films *The 39 Steps, The Rules of the Game, Jules and Jim, The 400 Blows, L'avventura, Citizen Kane, Ugetsu, Wild Strawberries, The Seventh Seal, The Blue Angel,* and *Grand Illusion;* courtesy of Janus Films.

from *Grass;* "Protest by the Hollywood Ten," courtesy of Paul Jarrico.

from *Salt of the Earth;* courtesy of Paul Jarrico.

from *The Jazz Singer* © 1927 Turner Entertainment Co. An AOL/Time Warner Company. All rights reserved. Courtesy of the Al Jolson Estate.

from *Interrogation,* 1982. Courtesy of Circle Releasing. Reproduced by permission of Kino International.

From *Ménilmontant,* 1925, France. Courtesy of Circle Releasing. Reproduced by permission of Kino International.

From *Sop'yonje,* 1993, Korea. Reproduced with permission of the Korean Cultural Center, Los Angeles.

from *The Passion of Joan of Arc;* courtesy of La Societé Nouvelle des Establishment Gaumont.

from *Lola Montès;* courtesy of Les Films de la Pléiade.

from *Speedy;* courtesy of The Harold Lloyd Trust.

from *Raiders of the Lost Ark;* courtesy of Lucasfilm Ltd. TM & Lucasfilm Ltd. (LFL) 1981. All rights reserved.

from the films *Star Wars; Star Wars: Epidosde I-The Phantom Menace;* Courtesy of Lucasfilm Ltd.

from *Eraserhead;* courtesy of David Lynch.

from the films *Black Narcissus, Blonde Venus, Brazil, The Breakfast Club, Do The Right Thing, Foolish Wives, Frankenstein* (1931), *The Last Temptation of Christ, The Mummy* (1932), *The Scarlet Empress, They Live, Trouble in Paradise, Videodrome,* and *Zoot Suit;* copyright © by Universal Pictures, a Division of Universal City Studios, Inc. All courtesy of MCA Publishing Rights, a Division of MCA Inc. Still from *The Last Temptation of Christ* courtesy of Martin Scorsese.

from the Universal releases: *In the Name of the Father, The Birds,* copyright © 1963, and *Vertigo,* copyright © 1958; copyright © Universal City Studios, Inc.; courtesy of MCA Publishing Rights, a Division of MCA, Inc.

from *Ladybird, Ladybird,* © 1994 Channel Four Television Corporation. All rights reserved. Reproduced by permission.

from the MGM releases: *Greed,* copyright © 1925 Metro-Goldwyn Pictures Corporation, copyright renewed 1952 by Loew's Inc. Courtesy of MGM/UA Communications Co.

from *The Road Warrior;* copyright © 1982 Kennedy Miller Entertainment Pty., Ltd.

from the Miramax releases: *Farewell My Concubine, Like Water for Chocolate,* and *The Piano;* courtesy of Miramax Films.

from *Jackie Brown,* 1997, copyright © Miramax Films. Reproduced by permission of Miramax Films and Quentin Tarantino.

from *sex, lies, and videotape;* courtesy of Miramax Films. Film by Outlaw Productions, 1989. Photo by Miramax Films.

from *Vanishing Fiancée* (a.k.a. *The Green Room*), © 1978, Les Productions Artistes Associes S.A., France. All rights reserved. Reproduced by permission of Ms. Madeline Morgenstern for the Estate of François Truffaut, Dominique Le Rigoleur, KIPA, and MGM.

from the films *Isn't Life Wonderful, The Joyless Street, The Love of Jeanne Ney, Sunrise, The Mummy, Fury, Ivan the Terrible, Andrei Rublev, Repentance, J'accuse, La Roue, I Walked with a Zombie, The Curse of the Cat People, Frankenstein, It's A Wonderful Life, Sullivan's Travels, The Magnificent Ambersons, The Lady from Shanghai, Singin' In The Rain, Workers Leaving the Lumière Factory, Feeding Baby, Boat Leaving the Port, Rescued by Rover, Queen Elizabeth, The Joyous Microbes, The Lonely Villa, The New York Hat, The Birth of a Nation, Intolerance, Broken Blossoms, Way Down East, The Surf Girl, High and Dizzy, The Thief of Bagdad, Nanook of the North, Long Pants, The Cabinet of Dr. Caligari, The First Vitaphone Program, Shaw Talks for Movietone, Applause, The Bank Dick, Shadows of Forgotten Ancestors,* and *Yellow Earth;* and for the stills of Persistence of Vision Toys, Muybridge's Leaping Horse, the Kinetoscope, the Black Maria, George Eastman and Thomas Edison, the Mutoscope, a Nickleodeon, D. W. Griffith, Theda Bara, William S. Hart, Tom Mix, Moguls and Morals, 3-D, and Cinerama; courtesy of the Museum of Modern Art/Film Stills Archive.

from *Salaam Bombay!;* courtesy of Mirabai Films. Used by permission of Mira Nair. Photo by Mitch Epstein.

from *The Mask* (computer image) and *The Mask* (completed frame); copyright © 1994 New Line Productions, Inc. All rights reserved. Photos appear courtesy of New Line Productions, Inc.

from *Gabbeh* (1997 in US, 1996 in Iran), Iran. Reproduced by permission of New Yorker Films.

from *Sans Soleil,* 1982, Switzerland. Reproduced by permission of New Yorker Films.

from the films *Vidas secas, Alice in the Cities, Stroszek, The American Friend, Effi Briest, Ali: Fear Eats the Soul, Aguirre, the Wrath of God, L'Atalante,* and *Shoah;* courtesy of New Yorker Films.

from *Carmen* (by Carlos Saura); courtesy of Orcine-Omnifilms. *Carmen* produced by Emiliano Piedra-Madrid.

from *The Conformist;* courtesy of Paramount Pictures.

from *Days of Heaven;* courtesy of Paramount Pictures Corporation. Copyright © 1978 by Paramount Pictures Corporation. All rights reserved. Photo by Edie Baskin.

from *Star Trek—The Motion Picture,* copyright © 1979 by Paramount Pictures. All rights reserved. Reproduced by permission of and courtesy of Paramount Pictures.

from *The Cook, The Thief, His Wife and Her Lover,* A Miramax Films release, 1990. Reproduced by permission of Photofest.

from *Moon Streams;* Courtesy of Mary Beth Reed.

from *Red Desert;* courtesy of Rizzoli Editore Corporation.

from *The Informer;* courtesy of RKO Radio Pictures, a Division of RKO General, Inc.

from *The Gold Rush;* copyright © Roy Export Company Establishment.

from the films *Battleship Potemkin, Mother, October, Arsenal,* and *The End of St. Petersburg;* courtesy of R. & S. Madell, Russian Film Library.

from *Clepsydra* by Phil Solomon, © 1992. All rights reserved. Reproduced by permission of Phil Solomon.

from the films *The Love Light* and *This Modern Age;* and for stills of Lillian Gish, Joan Crawford, Gloria Swanson, Clara Bow, Greta Garbo, and Mae West; courtesy of Special Collections, the Joseph Regenstein Library of the University of Chicago.

from *Citizen Kane* © 1941 RKO Pictures, Inc. All rights reserved.

from *The Magnificent Ambersons* © 1942 RKO Pictures, Inc. All rights reserved.

from *Swing Time* © 1936 RKO Pictures, Inc. All rights reserved.

from *I Walked with a Zombie* © 1943 RKO Pictures, Inc. All rights reserved.

from *The Curse of the Cat People* © 1944 © 1935 RKO Pictures, Inc. All rights reserved.

from *Metropolis;* courtesy of Standard Film Service.

from *Faithless;* Courtesy of Joakim Strömholm.

from *To Sleep With Anger;* copyright © SVS, Inc. All rights reserved.

from *Mr. Hulot's Holiday* and *Playtime;* courtesy of Jacques Tati.

504   ACKNOWLEDGMENTS

from *Gone With the Wind* ©1939 Turner Entertainment Co. An AOL/Time Warner Company. All rights reserved.

from *Strangers on a Train* © 1949 Turner Entertainment Co. An AOL/Time Warner Company. All rights reserved.

from *It's Always Fair Weather* © 1955 Turner Entertainment Co. An AOL/Time Warner Company. All rights reserved.

from *Singin' in the Rain* © 1952 Turner Entertainment Co. An AOL/Time Warner Company. All rights reserved.

from *An American in Paris* © 1951 Turner Entertainment Co. An AOL/Time Warner Company. All rights reserved.

from *2001: A Space Odyssey* © 1968 Turner Entertainment Co. An AOL/Time Warner Company. All rights reserved.

from *The Maltese Falcon* © 1941 Turner Entertainment Co. An AOL/Time Warner Company. All rights reserved.

from *The Treasure of the Sierra Madre* © 1948 Turner Entertainment Co. An AOL/Time Warner Company. All rights reserved.

from the Warner Bros. releases: *Bonnie and Clyde* © 1967 Warner Bros.-Seven Arts and Tatira-Hillar Productions; *Day for Night* © 1973 les Films du Carrosse S.A.; *Full Metal Jacket*, copyright © 1987 Warner Bros., Inc.; *McCabe and Mrs. Miller* © 1971 Warner Bros., Inc.; *Mean Streets*, copyright © 1973 Warner Bros., Inc.; *A Star is Born* © 1954 Warner Bros., Inc.; *The Wild Bunch* © Warner Bros.-Seven Arts, Inc.

from *New York Stories: Life Lessons;* courtesy of Touchstone Pictures and Martin Scorsese. © Touchstone Pictures.

from *Nosferatu* and *Destiny;* courtesy of Transit Films.

from *The Last Wave;* copyright © 1977 Turner/United Artists.

from *Stagecoach;* courtesy of TV Cinema Sales Corporation.

from *Alien,* © 1979; courtesy of Twentieth Century–Fox Film Corporation. All rights reserved.

from *Edward Scissorhands, Lacombe Lucien*, and *Walkabout;* courtesy of Twentieth Century–Fox.

from *Kiss of Death* © 1948 Twentieth Century–Fox Film Corporation. All rights reserved. Reproduced by permission.

from the films *Lucía, Xala, Memories of Underdevelopment*, and *The Last Supper;* courtesy of Unifilm.

from the films *Annie Hall; Carrie,* © 1976; *Gold Diggers of 1935; Heaven's Gate,* © 1980; *The Jazz Singer; The Manchurian Candidate,* © 1962 M. C. Productions; *Persona; Red River;* and *Raging Bull,* courtesy of Martin Scorsese, © 1980. All courtesy of United Artists Corporation. All rights reserved.

from *The Mummy's Ghost;* copyright © 1944 by Universal City Studios, Inc. Reproduced by permission of and courtesy of Universal Studios Publishing Rights, A Division of Universal Studios Licensing, Inc. All rights reserved.

from the films *The Kiss, The Magic Lantern, Life of an American Fireman, The Great Train Robbery, The Adventures of Dollie, A Corner in Wheat, The Musketeers of Pig Alley, Barney Oldfield's Race for a Life, Making A Living, Kid Auto Races, Fatima, Sherlock Jr., Berlin: Symphony of a Great City, M, Strike, The Man with a Movie Camera, Storm Over Asia, Return to Reason, Un Chien andalou, Zéro de conduite, Blackmail, Pickup on South Street, Viaggio in Italia, The Battle of Algiers, H₂0,* and *Open City;* courtesy of the University of Chicago Film Archive & Study Center.

from the films *Once Upon a Time in America,* © 1984 Embassy International Pictures; *Rebel Without a Cause,* copyright © 1955; *The Road Warrior,* © 1982 Kennedy Miller Entertainment Pty. Ltd. All courtesy of Warner Bros., Inc. All rights reserved.

from *Gun Crazy* © 1949 Pioneer Pictures Corporation. Reproduced by permission of Warner Bros.

from *Finding Nemo;* Walt Disney Pictures/Photofest.

from *The Lord of the Rings* (Gollum), courtesy of Photofest.

from *Toy Story 2;* Disney/Pixar/Photofest.

from *Way Down East, The Greatest Question;* courtesy the Museum of Modern Art/Film Stills Archive.

from *Whaler Rider;* Newmarket Films/Photofest.

from *Duck Soup;* Paramount Pictures/Photofest.

from *Russian Ark, Amélie, Stan Laurel and Oliver Hardy, Body and Soul;* Photofest.

from *Time Code;* Red Mullet Productions/The Kobal Collection/Marks, Elliot.

from *Lake Placid;* © 1999 Twentieth Century–Fox. All rights reserved.

from *Sop'yonje;* reproduced with permission of the Korean Cultural Center, Los Angeles.

Non-Film Stills

The Capitol Theatre ("Bank Nite"), opening of *The Tigress,* Grauman's Chinese Theatre, Haggar's Royal Electric Bioscope, Interior of the Roxy, from the ceiling to the orchestra, The Carthay Circle Theatre, The Carthay Circle Theatre: one of the many snack bars, The Carthay Circle Theatre: the mezzanine, The Carthay Circle Theatre: the painted asbestos curtain at the front of the circular auditorium; Courtesy of the Academy of Motion Picture Arts and Sciences.

Cans of film; Photo by Victor Jendras © Used by permission.

Lobby card for the Lone Defender; Courtesy of Robert Harris.

Douglas Fairbanks's name and prints in cement; Roy Rogers' imprints of his gun and horse along with his hands and boots; Mary Pickford's name and prints in cement; Courtesy of Bruce F. Kawin.

Mary Pickford and Douglas Fairbanks; The Mary Pickford Foundation.

Lobby card for *The Blot;* courtesy of the Museum of Modern Art/Film Stills Archive

Stage Show; Courtesy of the Academy of Motion Picture Arts and Sciences

Index

Note: Page numbers in italics indicate illustrations.